PACIFIC
DESTINY

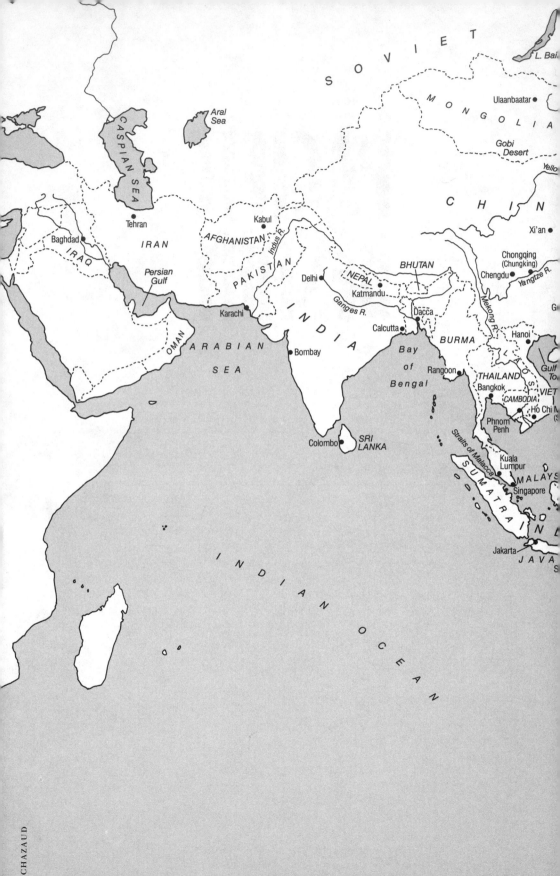

CHAZAUD

ROBERT ELEGANT

PACIFIC DESTINY

Inside Asia Today

CROWN PUBLISHERS, INC.
NEW YORK

for

Joseph Fromm

but just as much for

Yoshiko and Satoshi Ushioda

Published by Crown Publishers, Inc., 201 East 50th Street, New York, New York 10022

CROWN is a trademark of Crown Publishers, Inc.

Manufactured in the United States of America

Library of Congress Cataloging-in-Publication Data
Elegant, Robert
   Pacific destiny: inside Asia today/by Robert Elegant.
      p.   cm.
   1. Asia—History—1945-   I. Title.
DS35.2.E44   1989   89-9947
950.4'2—dc20   CIP
ISBN 0-517-57234-6

10 9 8 7 6 5 4 3 2 1

First Edition

Contents

Acknowledgments

I have been assisted with generosity and goodwill by so many during the decades when this book was in gestation that my problem is not to recall those who have contributed to its birth but to limit the list.

At the head of any list, however, must come James O'Shea Wade. He not only edited the manuscript skillfully, sensitively, and compassionately, but was responsible for its existence. The concept was his, and he chose me to put it into execution. I owe a debt of gratitude almost as great to my literary agent, Ed Victor, who was never too busy to put aside one of his megadeals to offer much prized encouragement and wise counsel.

Finally, like Abou ben Adam, at the head of the list must stand Landrum Bolling, who sent me to Asia in the first place, and who later helped underwrite the first stages of the specific research for this book through the Lilly Foundation and the American Enterprise Institute.

Would that I had time and space to categorize the contributions of those whose names follow—or to list everyone else who contributed. Let it stand, however, that the following gave particular service.

Australia

Dr. Kevin & Marianne Bleasel
Peter Coleman
Kenneth Gott
Donald Horne
Richard Krygier
Robert Santa Maria
Frank Mount
Sir Nicholas Parkinson
Denis & Peggy Warner
W. Ted Wright

China

Ambassador Hannspeter Hellbeck
Pitman B. Potter
Consul-General Mark Pratt
Stephen Schlaikjer
Daniel Southerland

Consul-General Herbert S. Thomas, III
Shelley Warner
Antonio Zamorra

Hong Kong

David Bell
Sir Jack & Lady Cater
Francis & Monica Cheung
Raymond Chow
Cecil E. Coleman
Eric Hotung
Wendy Hughes
Father Lazlo Ladany S.J.
Ambassador Burton Levin
Michael A.G. Matthews
Ian Rae
Brian Tisdale
Eddie Tseng

Indonesia

T.K. Adhyatman
Ide Anak Agung gde Agung
Marshall Berg
Ambassador Frans van Dongen
Daisy Hadmoko
Consul-General Barbara Harvey
Ambassador John Holdrige
Leonard Milson

Japan

Atsuo Ishida
Kinji Kawamura
Yoshihisa Komori
Bernard Krisher
Toru Nagatsuka
Masaru Nakamura
Ryoji Onodera
Yoshiko and Satoshi Ushioda

Korea

Professor Mija Kim-Rhee
Ambassador James R. Lilley
Toh Sang Moon
Assistant Minister Ku Chang Rim
Ambassador Richard L. Walker
Y.K. Yang

Philippines

Miguel Cerqueda
Mark Fineman
Ambassador Nicholas Platt
Maximo Soliven

Singapore

Siegfried Beil
Dennis Bloodworth
Monique Clug

Simon and Yoke Ling Elegant
James Fu

Taiwan

David Dean
Syd Goldsmith
Hope N.F. Phillips
Diane Ying
Yu Wei

Thailand

Nick B. Williams, Jr.

United Kingdom

Dr. Jonathan Mirsky
Carmen Navarro-Pedrosa
Maggie Phillips
Stephen & Margot Southon
Ray Whitney M.P.
Maynard Frank Wolfe

United States of America

Caroline Ahmanson
David Aikman
Arnaud de Borchgrave
Robert A. Burton
Ambassador Charles Cross
Joseph Fromm
Frank Gibney
Robert W. Gibson
Willard & Marybelle Hanna
Robert P. Martin
Jane von Mehren
Douglas Pike
Roy Rowan
Professor Stanley Spector
Katie Towson
Charles Wolf, Jr.

I

Making the West Obsolete?

EAST ASIA, WITH JAPAN IN THE LEAD, IS THE NEW AND THE MOST DYNAMIC CENTER OF WORLD POWER. AFTER CENTURIES OF BACK-WARDNESS AND SUBJUGATION, ASIANS HAVE ASSERTED THEMSELVES IN REALMS WHERE AMERICANS AND EUROPEAN HAD BEEN SU-PREME: TECHNOLOGICAL INNOVATION, INDUSTRIAL PRODUCTION, AND MASS MARKETING. THEIR PROWESS IS A MORTAL CHALLENGE TO WHICH THE WEST, WITH THE UNITED STATES IN THE LEAD, HAS RESPONDED FALTERINGLY.

At half past eight on a stifling evening in mid-July, a pearly fog swaddles the Tsushima Straits. No wind stirs, and a lumpy moon casts a yellow trail across the glassy sea. The Pukwan Ferry, a substantial vessel of 5,000 tons, plods across the 120 miles that separate Pusan in Korea from Shimonoseki in Japan, her foghorn gruffly lamenting the tens of thousands whose bones calcine the shallow bottom. For more than two thousand years fighting men have died in these straits: Japanese and Korean, Chinese and Mongol, Russian and American.

In the Spartan dining cabin, passengers drink endless cups of barley tea, and the round-faced purser observes: "We're about twelve miles west of the islands. On a clear night you can see both islands: Upper and Lower Tsushima, like two war horses."

By midnight the fog has lifted, and the big ferry is just halfway between Korea and Japan. The moon is outshone by the incandescent rim cast around the horizon by the arc lights strung on a flotilla of small vessels to lure fish. The Pukwan Ferry is steaming through an amphi-theater of white light broken from time to time by faint red-and-green trails that signal the passage of other ships.

When Moira and I return to the dining cabin for a last cup of smoky barley tea, two of our fellow passengers look up inquiringly. They are a German forklift engineer from Hamburg and a Chinese-Canadian

1

salesman from Vancouver. Both are puzzled when I tell them we are passing the point where the Battle of the Tsushima Straits was fought in 1905 between the Japanese Empire and the Russian Empire. They are not particularly interested when I recall the American troops who in 1950 sailed across the same waters to Inchon on the west coast of Korea, to stage an amphibious counterattack on the Communist invaders from the north. They are, it seems, only concerned with repeating their previous happy travels in expensive Japan. The engineer expects to be passed again from household to household of elderly Germanophiles, starting with a professor emeritus of Old Gothic and ending with the Berlin-born widow of a Japanese diplomat. The salesman does not discuss his strategy, which, I suspect, involves shinnying along the spiderweb of overseas Chinese communities that crisscrosses Japan.

Neither has heard of the Battle of the Tsushima Straits—nor of the Russo-Japanese War (1904–05), which that battle ended. They *have* heard of the Korean War (1950–53), which, I realize, ended before either was born. Proud of his learning, the engineer recalls that the Korean War was fought between the Japanese and the Chinese.

Moira nods infinitesimally, and we go to our cabin. Even if the Pukwan Ferry were not getting into Shimonoseki very early that morning, an hour past midnight is no time to begin a discussion of the electrifying rise of modern Asia and its profound influence throughout the world.

Afterward, I was a little sorry about my silence. I shall not pretend that casual encounter cemented my intention of writing a book about the present astonishing state of the great continent where I have spent most of my adult life. I was already committed to portraying the flood tide of talent and energy that has in only four decades set a new high-water mark in industrial production, technological application, and scientific accomplishment—and thus created a new center of world power. The encounter on the Pukwan Ferry did, however, confirm the need for such an attempt to penetrate the complacent, perhaps dangerous, disregard of Asia in the West.

For someone who has devoted most of his life to Asia, I got into it rather casually. When I began my senior year at the University of Pennsylvania in 1945, I no longer had any wish to follow a pre-medical course. Instead, I wanted to make my living as a newspaperman, preferably as a glamorous foreign correspondent.

Some knowledge of an exotic language and culture would obviously be an advantage. Leafing through the university's course catalogue, I found that Arabic was taught at eight in the morning and Chinese at a civilized four in the afternoon. I chose Chinese.

Only six years later did I finally see Asia, which was then very far away in time and space—and, above all, psychologically. In those days there were no cheap fares on jumbo jets. There were no jets at all, and the only reasonably economical way to cross the Pacific Ocean was by freighter. The world was much bigger then, although not quite as complicated as it is today.

After getting my degree, I enlisted in the U.S. Army, which taught me some Japanese. Discharged in 1948, I took intensive Chinese at Yale and a master's degree in Chinese and Japanese languages, history, and culture at Columbia. I had amassed the course credits for a Ph.D., but I was by that time weary of formal education. Instead of writing a doctoral dissertation, I entered Columbia's School of Journalism.

I hoped that course would get me a job, and it did. In September 1951, I became the Far Eastern correspondent of the Overseas News Agency. That title helped make up for having to pay all my expenses, including fares, out of a salary of $60 a week. And there was glory by association. Theodore H. White, already famous, was ONA's Chief European correspondent.

I worked as a full-time foreign correspondent until 1976. Except for five years in Europe, I spent that quarter of a century in Asia, covering the Korean War and the Viet Nam War, as well as the Emergency in Malaya and sundry smaller disturbances. But war reporting was secondary to learning and writing about the sweep of the world's most densely populated region—from Japan and China to Australia and India.

Asia gave its greatest gift to me at the British Officer's Club in Tokyo in 1953. There I met Moira Clarissa Brady, an auburn-haired Australian who was a junior executive with Pan American Airways. We were married in New Delhi in 1956 and spent our honeymoon traveling in Asia from Nepal and Ceylon to Singapore, Thailand, and Viet Nam.

I had just been hired by *Newsweek*, having already reported at one time or another for the International News Service, the Columbia Broadcasting System, and the North American Newspaper Alliance. I was to remain with *Newsweek* until 1965, when I joined the *Los Angeles Times*, serving first as Hong Kong bureau chief and later as foreign affairs columnist.

Before leaving daily journalism in 1976, I had written six nonfiction books on Asia and three novels, all, naturally, set in Asia. I had also acquired a reasonably good knowledge of the region, as well as an awareness of how much more there was to learn. I knew, too, that it was impossible to comprehend present-day events in Asia without some idea of their origins. We Westerners simply do not have the same basic acquaintance with Asian civilization that we do with European culture. For the moment, however, it is enough to go back to 1945.

*   *   *

On September 2 of 1945, the Japanese Empire formally surrendered to the Allied Powers on the foredeck of the battleship USS *Missouri* in Tokyo harbor. That ceremony marked the end of a campaign, not the end of a war.

On that same day a new campaign began. Japan has won it by attaining economic predominance—not just in Asia, but throughout the world. In 1945 the USS *Missouri* was already obsolete, an immense gray relic of the era before naval supremacy passed to the warplane and the aircraft carrier. Asia could now be making the West obsolete, reducing us to consumers and followers.

The two billion human beings living in East Asia are 40 percent of the world's population. They produce close to half of the world's manufactured goods. The United States, a Pacific power, already exchanges with Asia goods worth $308 billion a year, about 70 percent of its total U.S. trade. The most coveted franchise in civil aviation in the late 1980s was the Seattle-Tokyo route. Travel to the Pacific and Asia, increasing at 12 percent annually, will be one-third of worldwide air traffic by 1992. Volume will have doubled in two decades.

Asia's big expansion is just starting, but the United States is already substantially in debt to Asia. Japan alone sells at least $55 billion more worth of goods to the U.S. each year than it buys from the U.S. Those hi-fi systems, television sets, cars, cameras, and tons of construction steel add up. Korea, which only recently entered the competition, has an overall trade surplus of $9 billion with the U.S. and Taiwan a surplus of $11 billion. Even little Hong Kong, with no more than 7 million people, sells goods worth $9.9 billion to the U.S., but buys only $3.4 billion worth from the U.S.

Without Asian goods the American standard of living would fall sharply. Without Asian tolerance and loans, the United States could go bankrupt, insofar as nations ever go bankrupt. If the U.S. stopped buying Asia's goods, the interdependent world economy would tilt, and many countries would slide into depression.

Japan is on a worldwide buying spree, with its overvalued yen. The Japanese already own a quarter of the commercial property in downtown Los Angeles and nearly half the high-rises. In Australia they are gobbling up hotels, universities, office buildings, mines, high-rise parking garages, shopping complexes, and even retirement villages for its elderly citizens. The return on those investments, including corporations' profits, are already flooding home. The embarrassment of Japan's fabulous riches thus increases. But what are the hard-pressed Japanese to do?

The world's nine biggest banks, three largest trading companies, and Nomura Securities, the biggest trader in stocks, bonds, and other financial instruments, are all Japanese. The students have taken over their teachers: Sony owns CBS Records, and Bridgestone owns Firestone. With its surplus of devalued dollars, Taiwan is now acquiring land, real estate, and companies abroad. Being transformed from a debtor to a creditor in a few years, Korea has begun to follow the same course.

The West *must* trade with the resurgent nations of Asia. The United States above all *must* greatly increase its sales to Asia.

Yet Americans have never put much effort into developing markets abroad, largely because of the extraordinary size of their home market. The entire world market is only two and a half times the U.S. market. The U.S., with 240 million people, consumes 40 percent as much as the rest of the world, with a population of 5 billion people— almost half of whom live in East Asia.

The U.S. Government and the governments of the leading Asian nations have for years been in conflict over the tariff and non-tariff barriers that restrict the entry of American goods to their home markets. The fiercest fights concern the entry of American *agricultural* products. Aside from some specialized items like aircraft, the country that led the second industrial revolution, which was mass production, cannot keep pace with the leaders of the third industrial revolution, which is electronics. Moreover, the leaders of the third industrial revolution now produce far more efficiently than the inventors of the goods of the first and second industrial revolutions: steel, ships, locomotives, and, of course, automobiles.

The U.S. consumer is understandably addicted to Asian products, which are cheaper, more attractive, more efficient—and are backed by better service. Unable to compete effectively in their home market, American manufacturers manifestly cannot compete in their rivals' home markets.

I fear they could not compete effectively even if *all* barriers were removed, which will not happen. Yet they must learn to hold their own if the West is to retain its freedom of action.

General knowledge of the nature of Asia and the challenge of Asia is essential to meet the challenge of Asia. This book is, therefore, not written for specialists, all of whom know more than I about their specialties. This book is for the men and women who must strive to restore the competitiveness of the West, the United States above all, with the young giants of Asia. To regain superiority is, I believe, impossible.

I shall try to describe East Asia and its people as I have seen them during almost four decades. I want to convey an idea of what those people are like, how they behave—and also why they are as they are and why they behave as they do. In short, I hope to portray the fundamental character on which their success is based.

I shall write as if I were talking over a drink after dinner—in a living room, not a seminar room. I shall keep figures to a minimum. They cannot possibly be right up to date or perfectly accurate; it takes too long to assemble statistics, and different sources give different figures. Statistics can, at best, be indicators of tendencies and a basis for comparison, but no more.

Our encounter with the carefree travelers in the Tsushima Straits reminded me that I had never before crossed the straits by ship, although in the early 1950s I had often flown over them. I was then reporting the war between the United Nations Forces (the troops of eighteen nations commanded by an American general) and the Communist Chinese and the North Koreans, backed by the Soviets. Early in this century, Japan's defeat of the Imperial Russian Fleet in the straits had set Asia on its twentieth-century course by proving that Asians could compete with Europeans—and win. Forty-five years later, the United Nations' landing at Inchon had checked the aggressive expansion of Marxist-Leninist totalitarianism, which would have stifled Asian initiative if it had won.

This time Moira and I were crossing by ship because we wanted to see one of the world's great choke-points. The key strategic positions called choke-points occur where the land draws close together, forcing ships to sail through narrow channels. Command of a major choke-point confers control of the sea lanes for thousands of miles around, even in the age of jumbo airliners. Those points still dominate commercial and naval strategy because automobiles, grain, and timber must go by sea—as must mechanized divisions. Such narrow passages have for millennia imposed the great patterns of settlement, alliance, and trade that shape earthly power.

Two choke-points dominate Asia: the Straits of Malacca and the Tsushima Straits. Bounded by the Malay Peninsula and Sumatra, the Straits of Malacca are the primary sea lane from the Far East to the Middle East and Europe. They have been a channel for alien conquest since Indian fleets sailed through to Java a thousand years ago. After 1500, Portuguese, Dutch, and English adventurers came to the port of Malacca to colonize Southeast Asia—followed by Saint Francis Xavier, the Apostle to the East.

The Tsushima Straits have been a locus of battles between assertively independent Asian forces, as well; for northern Asia has generally been more energetic and more aggressive than southern Asia. But in the sixteenth century the Portuguese moved into Japan through the port of Nagasaki, which lies on the straits.

Tsushima bars—or gives access—to the sheltered waterways between continental Asia and the island chain that lies as close as an armadillo's shell: Kyushu and the Ryukyus with Okinawa; Taiwan and the Philippines; and eastward, New Guinea, Borneo, and the Indonesian archipelago.

In the Tsushima Straits in the thirteenth century, the Mongol Hordes sailing to Japan were sunk by the *kamikaze,* the "divine wind," which gave its name to Japanese suicide pilots in World War II. Off Pusan in the sixteenth century, Admiral Yi Sun-sin's ironclad "tortoise ships" destroyed the invasion fleet of Toyotomi Hideyoshi, whose passing led to the era of the Tokugawa Shoguns. In the late nineteenth century, Japanese squadrons steamed westward through the Straits to break the corruption-crippled squadrons of the decadent Manchu Dynasty—and thus hastened the collapse of imperial rule in China.

The most decisive battle in the Tsushima Straits was fought on May 27–28, 1905. Having already shattered the Imperial Russian Far East Fleet at Port Arthur in Manchuria by a surprise attack before war was declared, the Imperial Japanese Navy awaited the arrival of the Tsar's Baltic Fleet. Having steamed around the Cape of Good Hope because Britain had closed the Suez Canal to them, the Russian ships were battered and their crews exhausted. Formidable on paper, the Baltic Fleet was obsolescent beside the spanking new Japanese warships.

Admiral Heihachiro Togo streamed the broad Z signal flag that commanded every man to give all for the emperor—and his warships fell on the weary Russians. In the course of two days' fighting, the Japanese sank or captured the entire Baltic Fleet, except for the few ships that limped toward Port Arthur. Captured Russian warships and shiploads of wounded Russian seamen put in to Shimonoseki. The enemy was sorely humiliated in full view of the Japanese people—and the world.

Admiral Togo's total victory at sea set the seal on the Japanese superiority already demonstrated in land battles. No longer need the Japanese feel inferior before the military prowess, the scientific learning, the industrial power, and the commercial acumen of the Europeans. They had proved themselves at least the equals of the foreigners—and, perhaps, their superiors.

Yet the Japanese continued to strive frantically to surpass the Europeans, who had been their teachers in every endeavor from railways and constitutions to education, gunnery, toy making, and astronomy. Nor have they relaxed their competitive frenzy to this day.

Despite the glorious victories crowned by Tsushima, self-doubts lingered. The Japanese felt a settled sense of inferiority to China, the civilization that had given them their writing, their aesthetics, and their classical literature, as well as such commonplace artifacts and practices as chopsticks, kimonos, and profound bowing. The victories of 1894 over the Chinese Empire had not erased that sense of inferiority. No more did the splendid victory of Tsushima in 1905.

Japan's leaders were nagged by the fear that their victories had been won on the cheap. The Chinese warships they had defeated in 1894 were badly designed, ineptly manned, incompetently commanded, poorly maintained, and virtually disarmed. Universal Chinese corruption had ensured that the three or four shells available in each turret were loaded with sand or lacked detonators. Although in 1905 the Tsar's Baltic Fleet was unquestionably Western, it was made up of old ships with worn-out crews.

Not the Tsar, but inertia ruled the vast Russian Empire. Once committed to war, it could not agree to end the war, despite major defeats. Tokyo therefore turned to President Theodore Roosevelt, who instinctively preferred plucky little Japan to big despotic Russia. By cajoling and threatening, Roosevelt brought the belligerents to the conference table, where he cajoled even more winningly and threatened even more fiercely. The treaty signed at Portsmouth, New Hampshire, in 1905 recognized Japan's victory and granted Japan major concessions.

Portsmouth certified Japan's emergence as a major power—and deepened the psychological dependence on the United States that has been as consistent a feature of Japan's modern history as the compulsion to excell. The treaty also convinced Japan that war could provide what it required: glory for its underemployed warrior class, resources for its growing industry, markets for its goods, space for its expanding population, and balm for the perpetual itch of its perceived inferiority. Japan was set on a warlike course.

On Sunday, December 7, 1941, that course led to the Imperial Navy's attack on the U.S. Pacific Fleet at Pearl Harbor before war was declared. Its economic aspirations blocked and its craving for American approbation frustrated, Japan turned on its mentor. The aircraft carrier *Akagi* hoisted the Z pennant as the warplanes took off to savage the American fleet. Reverently preserved, the same pennant Admiral Togo had flown in the Straits of Tsushima thirty-six years earlier enjoined every aviator to do his utmost for the emperor.

Togo's great victory and the present era, which it initiated, display parallels inherent in the geopolitical shape of Asia. The last coaling stop of the Tsar's Baltic Fleet had been Cam Ranh Bay in Viet Nam. Thirty-six years later, the Japanese used Cam Ranh Bay as a springboard for their conquest of the Dutch East Indies, the American Philippines, and British Malaya.

That broad assault shaped present-day Asia. The Japanese inspired Asia's peoples to revolt against their colonial rulers and claim their independence. The Japanese promised to create a Greater East Asia

Co-Prosperity Sphere to ensure that all the peoples of Asia benefited equally from the new order. They knew they were initiating an entirely new era—win, lose, or draw.

Above all, the Japanese fostered self-aware nationalism by training young men to drive out European and American colonial overlords. In Kuala Lumpur I met an overseas Chinese engineer who had been one of that elite. He was sent to a special school as the protégé of two Japanese lieutenants who spoke to the governor-general as equals and who flew back to Tokyo as they wished, returning with gifts of cigarettes from the Imperial Palace. So important was the program to train native leaders!

Both Sukarno, later president of Indonesia, and Ngo Dinh Diem, later president of Viet Nam, were given special instruction. So was Subchandra Bose, who was destined to rule India; he failed, but in failing encouraged his countrymen to throw the British out. The Japanese rallied anticolonialists in Burma and the Philippines, failing in Malaya because they had alienated the vital overseas Chinese by attacking their motherland. In China the new Communist era was born of Japan's war.

In Jakarta, then Foreign Minister Mochtar Kusumaatmadjah told me with deep feeling how the Battle of the Tsushima Straits had awakened "true Asian nationalism." Describing the war in the Pacific as "the Great Asian War," he added: "An entire generation remembers the Japanese with gratitude. . . . It was the end of the white man when we saw them as prisoners of war. . . ."

The Japanese assault drove the white man out of Asia and inflamed Asian nationalism. After the war in the Pacific, a common patriotism moved the people of the vast archipelago of Indonesia. Nationalistic ardor rose in French Indo-China and in the American Philippines. Battered by Japanese aggression, the Nationalist government of Chiang Kai-shek fell to the onslaughts of the Communists. The new era thus began![1]

When it became clear that the war was lost, Japan's leaders had activated their plans for the peace. They surrendered militarily, but neither politically nor economically. The long-range goal toward which they strove was finally to be attained in the 1980s.

---

[1] In spelling Chinese place names, I have used traditional spellings or traditional and new spellings interchangeably—Peking or Beijing, Canton or Gwangzhou, depending on the context—but only the traditional spellings for Chungking, Nanking, and Suchow. I have used only the new spellings, however, for Xi'an (not Sian) and Chengdu (not Chengtu) because the traditional spellings are not familiar. For personal names I have used common forms—Chiang Kai-shek, Sun Yat-sen, Mao Tse-tung, and Chou En-lai; note that for names of persons active primarily after Beijing officially changed the rules for romanization of the Chinese language, I have employed the new forms—Deng Xiaoping, Zhao Ziyang.

Thirty-six years passed between Tsushima and Pearl Harbor. Forty-five years passed between Pearl Harbor and the year 1987, when Japan clearly emerged as the preponderant economic force in the world. That was eighty-three years in all, no more than the span of a long-lived person. In Yanagawa, shortly after disembarking from the Pukwan Ferry, I actually met the son of the man who was Admiral Togo's chief-of-staff at the Battle of the Tsushima Straits—who at eighty is a living link between present-day Japan and the decisive battle that shaped it. Now commercially and industrially dominant, the Japanese, in pursuing their own interests, have assisted the peoples of Asia toward the promised well-being of the Greater East Asia Co-Prosperity Sphere. They have created by peaceful means the economic empire for which they once fought.

The Japanese are today reviled by nations that possess neither their vision nor their vigor. They merit respect, wary respect, not denunciation.

When we crossed the Tsushima Straits, Moira and I had completed half the travel necessary for this book. Although we had, over the decades, lived in Hong Kong, Japan, Singapore, and India, we had to rediscover modern Asia. We were to travel seventy-five thousand miles, making three sorties from our home near London and many side trips by airplane, train, bus, car, street-car, subway, horse-drawn carriage, and ship. We were to ride in stately seven-passenger limousines and in the bicycle-driven three-wheelers that had been universal only a decade earlier. Nowadays there are more limousines in Asia and very few three-wheelers.

We were to trudge through hundreds of streets, avenues, bazaars, alleys, compounds, and lanes. We were to be drenched by the monsoon in Bali and whipped by typhoons in Japan. We were to be trapped in crowds in Xi'an, to be thwarted by bureaucrats in Seoul, and to blanch at the wild new drivers on the narrow roads of Malaysia.

We were, further, to cross China in jolting trains and to sail down the fogbound Yangtze River on a battered steamer even its officers complained was dangerously overcrowded. We were to be mired on a mountain in Australia and to lay over repeatedly in the torrid old airport of Bangkok. We were to fly in the splendid comfort of the 747s of Cathay Pacific Airways and Philippine Airlines, and we were to be crammed into antiquated DC-3s. At the end of two years, we were tired—and exhilarated by what we had found.

When I began as a foreign correspondent, Asia was a very difficult beat. Transportation was slow and uncomfortable. Communication was cumbersome, whether within Asia or with the rest of the world. Wars, riots, and revolutions interested editors and readers. So did maharajahs, ceremonial elephants with mascaraed eyelashes, the saxophone playing of Prince Norodom Sihanouk of Cambodia, and the sexual athletics of Bao Dai, the last Emperor of Viet Nam. However, the complexities of an evolving Asia commanded little attention in the Western media.

Contrast the present day, when cocktail party conversation dwells on new Japanese schools around the corner, Taiwan's assault on the personal computer market, and Korea's sales of second automobiles to American families. I have, during the past three years, been asked many more informed or alarmed questions about Asia than I had during the three preceding decades.

Newly aware, although perhaps still not fully aware, how critical Asia is to their own future, Westerners are now keenly interested in events they would once have ignored. The press and television consequently run ten to twenty times more about the newly discovered region than they did a decade ago. Much more appears to be happening, perhaps in part because of the region's new dynamism. Between May 1989, when this manuscript was completed, and August, when it went to the printer, major events cascaded over Asia.

> • In China the aged autocrats still in control of the Communist party and the People's Liberation Army slaughtered several hundred students who were demonstrating for democratic reforms. Terrified by the success of the students' appeal to intellectuals, workers, and even bureaucrats, the old guard condemned that nationwide wave of support as *fan'goming dongluan*, "counterrevolutionary upheaval." Careless of the effect on world public opinion, the authoritarian clique ordered its troops to fire on the students massed in Tienanmen Square, under the lenses of foreign television crews. The campaign of repression that followed significantly set back the economic development to which even the old guard was pledged. It severely strained China's relations with the West and cast into grave doubt the largely beneficent role China had been playing in the affairs of the region.

> • In Japan, after an era had closed with the death of Emperor Hirohito, the dominant Liberal Democratic party was shaken by scandals too outrageous for even its tolerant electorate to disregard. Three elections in succession showed a sharp drop in support for the LDP, which had ruled without a break for more than three decades. Many votes were transferred to the Socialist party, led by a woman—in male-dominated Japan. Trade concessions to the United States and domestic tax reforms also shook the government's popularity. Although Japan was hardly on the verge of

liberal multiparty democracy, the previous automatic hegemony of the LDP was in doubt.

• In Korea, a contentious people who had recently won a good measure of democracy was demanding greater popular power and a greater share of the wealth produced by the most dynamic economy in the world. After decades of submission to authoritarian rule, workers were unruly, indeed violent. Waves of strikes imperiled the future of a productive machine long fueled by low wages and long hours. Prices were rising, as was unemployment, and foreign buyers were casting about for alternate suppliers elsewhere.

Despite those upheavals, East Asia is still the most productive region in the world, and the fastest growing. The globe's center of gravity is shifting—and a Pacific Trading Region to rival the European Common Market is becoming a strong likelihood.

The United States would be a very important part of any such association, for the United States is a Pacific power. The weight of U.S. population is already shifting toward the dynamic western states, where most Asian immigrants live. American universities are besieged by Asian applicants, whose excellent transcripts mock policies designed to keep them out. Asians now make up more than 25 percent of the student body at the University of California at Berkeley—by and large the top 25 percent. Everywhere their numbers are in excess of their proportion in the population: 22 percent at the Massachusetts Institute of Technology and 14 percent at Harvard.

Asian students come to advance themselves, not to play. Most therefore study the sciences or business, where the big opportunities lie. Perhaps the next generation will pursue the humanities, producing a cultural flowering like the one that followed mass immigration from Eastern Europe a century ago. Perhaps their secret is greater talent, but it is certainly harder work.

America's face is turning toward Asia—and the Port of New York is declining. Shipping to Europe, South America, and Africa is not sufficient to maintain New York's standing as the busiest port in the United States. Los Angeles is the fastest growing port in the U.S. today.

If Japan should, somehow, disappear, the United States would lose one of its biggest markets—and its biggest supplier. If the United States should, somehow, curtail its voracious consumption, all Asia would suffer severely.

Even the great strategic balance is shifting. *Above all*, the great strategic balance is shifting, and Asia could soon equal Europe in weight. That statement evokes instinctive resistance. I am inclined to doubt it even as I set it down, for it defies the conventional wisdom that has guided American policy for at least half a century.

Yet Europe and America were drawing apart while Asia and America drew closer. In 1986 only Britain assisted the American attack on Colonel Momar Gadaffi's Libya as a breeding ground of terrorism. In 1989 the European Community was being drawn farther from America by the inspired wooing of Soviet President Mikhail Gorbachev.

In Asia it was otherwise, particularly after the massacre in Tienanmen Square. For some time after the North Vietnamese took South Viet Nam in 1975, the United States had appeared to be receding from Asia. Nonetheless, the United States during those years formally recognized the People's Republic of China; began a painful redefinition of its vexed relationship with Japan; retained its bases in the Philippines, where popular indignation had toppled Asia's most corrupt regime; and reaffirmed its commitment to the defense of the Republic of Korea, which had also moved away from dictatorship. True, the United States no longer provided the bulk of the manufactured goods Asians used; Asians were making their own. But the United States was still the only power that could provide the security and stability Asians needed as badly as goods. It was a reasonable trade-off: American protection in exchange for Asian goods, which the U.S., rolling down the endless slope to national bankruptcy, could no longer buy for cash.

Although its motives were in good part altruistic, America was becoming a roving gun for hire. Americans might shrink from recognizing that role, but they were mercenaries and arms salesmen paid in high-tech trinkets.

The greatest concentration of American naval power since the Viet Nam War was sent to the Persian Gulf in 1987—in part to keep the Soviets out and to assure the flow of oil to Western Europe. Above all, the warships served the Asian countries, Japan foremost among them, which draw more than half their oil from the Gulf.

The Asian connection was not stressed. No one wanted to tell emotional Americans that their sons' lives were at risk to make sure that they themselves received an unbroken supply of electronic gadgets, inexpensive automobiles, and trendy clothing from the Asian factories that deprive Americans of jobs. But the Japanese let the cat out of the bag. Tokyo refused to send Japanese warships, but offered $20 million for an electronic navigation system. Already paying $1.5 billion a year for the American troops stationed on its islands, Japan was buying protection.

The Soviet Union has reaffirmed its intention of enlarging its influence in Asia. Even though Moscow is apparently altering its expansionist ways, the Japanese greatly prefer two superpowers in their backyard to one.

In July 1986 Mikhail Gorbachev, speaking in the Siberian naval and air base of Vladivostok, offered closer relations to Asia—on his terms. The hopeful read his speech as heralding a new, benign Soviet policy; the pessimists read it as the continuation of Soviet ambition, but under a more attractive cloak. Two years later, at Krasnoyarsk, also in Siberia, Gorbachev reaffirmed that the Soviet Union was, as much as the United States, a great Pacific power.

He could hardly expect immediate results from his proposals for economic cooperation with Japan and South Korea. Japan's long memory resented the Soviets' detention of hundreds of thousands of Japanese prisoners long after World War II—and the Soviets' continued occupation of the Kurile Islands. Indeed, several previous Japanese attempts to cooperate with the Soviets in developing Siberia had failed. South Korea was more interested in China, and its reservoir of manpower for foreign ventures was running low.

During the two years between Vladivostok and Krasnoyarsk, Mikhail Gorbachev had, however, acted decisively. Continuing his penetration of the South Pacific, he was refurbishing the Soviet image in the North Pacific. He had placated a suspicious China by meeting her three chief conditions for normal relations with Moscow: (1) the Soviets' client state, the Democratic Republic of Viet Nam, was withdrawing its occupation troops from Cambodia; (2) Soviet forces in Afghanistan were beginning the total retreat that was to end in confusion in February 1989; and (3) almost 250,000 Soviet troops were scheduled to be withdrawn from China's northern and western borders, although many divisions would remain.

The meeting between Gorbachev and China's paramount leader Deng Xiaoping in mid-May 1989 was clouded by that knowledge. The first Sino-Soviet summit in decades was also clouded by student-and-worker demonstrations demanding greater democracy. That "counter-revolutionary upheaval" not only forced alterations in Gorbachev's schedule, but raised doubts as to the durability of the Chinese leadership. Besides, China remained suspicious of Soviet intentions while agreeing to improve trade and political relations. Remembering thousands of years of conflict with the barbarians on their northern and western borders, the Chinese would stake little on one man's ability to transform the Soviet Union into a peaceable state with an efficient economy.

The Chinese had themselves started struggling out of the intellectual straitjacket of Marxism-Leninism in 1979. They had begun to alter the economic—and, albeit most reluctantly, the political—structure of a totalitarian state years before Mikhail Gorbachev came to power. They knew how arduous that task was and how much suffering it could inflict.

The suppression of the "counter-revolutionary upheaval" of the early summer of 1989 was unique because it was substantially conducted in view of the foreign press. But China had suffered even greater catastrophes since the Communists came to power in 1949.

The incident in Tienanmen Square on June 4 and its aftermath proved that China was far from attaining political stability. Isolated by power and age from reality, the old guard somehow believed that the program of economic expansion could continue unmarred despite the odium China now bore.

In that continuing endeavor, Moscow could contribute little to the productive and commercial transformation they called "modernization." Only the West, Japan, and possibly Korea could provide technological and industrial support for that immense effort. Requiring American assistance in modernization, China also needed the United States to maintain the balance of power in Asia. She feared not only Soviet encirclement, but the revival of Japanese military power.

Almost all Asian nations were in accord with the Chinese and Japanese desire to keep American power in Asia—above all, to prevent a vacuum others would fill. Those nations also wanted a counterweight to China's potential military power and to the possible renewal of Japanese militarism. Another possible counterweight, Australia, the southernmost country in the region, was thinly populated, inadequately industrialized, and no longer as concerned with its Asian neighbors as it had once been.

Some Asians were pessimistic. Prime Minister Lee Kuan Yew of Singapore, the elder statesman of non-Communist Asia, told me in a resigned tone: "I can live with a militarized Japan—just as long as it doesn't go nuclear." He warned that a stable and progressive China was essential to the region's well-being—and he stressed the need for a continuing American presence.

Asian attitudes regarding American economic performance are less cheering. Between 1985 and 1989, the U.S. dollar fell dramatically, in good part because America's imports from abroad were exceeding America's exports by $10 billion a month.

Given to simple solutions, the Reagan Administration had believed that shearing the dollar of half its value against foreign currencies would solve most of America's economic problems—and that the trade imbalance would automatically vanish. The depreciated dollar was supposed to make American products cheaper abroad—to sell better. Imports were supposed to fall because it took more dollars to pay for the same goods. Presto, no more trade deficit.

Unfortunately, it hasn't worked that way.

American exports have not increased sufficiently, in part because other nations erect barriers, tarriff and non-tariff. Rather appallingly, the world no longer thinks very highly of American goods, aside from agricultural products and airplanes. Perhaps a little lower in volume, perhaps a little higher, imported goods actually cost *more,* now that it takes twice as many cheap dollars to pay for the same amount of foreign goods.

Today the building blocks of the industrial world are not just steel or bricks, but the memory chips used in computers and the other micro-electronic devices that govern our lives. In 1989 the most advanced was the one-megabyte DRAM (dynamic random access memory) chip, which stores and allows instant access to one million pieces of infor-mation. Total world production of those mega-chips in 1988 was 173 million, worth $2.66 billion. West Germany produced 3 percent and the United States 8.1 percent. Japan produced 86.6 percent. South Korea produced 2.3 percent, having attained that share in a single year.

The Koreans were eager to take the potentially profitable risks Amer-ican companies avoided. Both Japanese and Koreans were also working on five-megabyte DRAMs.

Dominance in hyper-fast super-computers, the machines that design the future, was also passing out of American hands—in good part because of the lack of American-made super-chips and in part because American manufacturers like Cray, which originated the super-computer, are now dependent on Japanese components. That decline was, above all, a function of loss of nerve and loss of capability. American firms were not organized to compete against either collective—Japan Inc. or Korea Inc. That was the Americans' fault, not their competitors'.

In mid-1989, however, a consortium of American companies that included Hewlett-Packard and International Business Machines was formed to produce four-megabyte DRAMs. The initiative was encour-aging. American companies were not only taking necessary risks, but were uniting to do so. Yet, even if, after several years, the initiative succeeds completely, the U.S. would be making no more than 10 percent of the world's super-chips. Instinctively competitive, American corporations find it hard to work in cartels; the Japanese are *encouraged* to form cartels in the national interest. All Japan instinctively strives as one toward goals designated by the "national consensus," which is directed by a few hundred men.

The United States may soon have no more valuables to exchange for the Asian gadgetry it is either too lazy or too musclebound to make for itself—and far too self-indulgent to do without. Wataru Hiraizumi, a former cabinet minister in Japan who possesses great wealth and a cutting intelligence, characterized the American predicament—and a Japanese reaction: "Uncle Sam is already broke, but we're supporting him. We Japanese are paying for American self-indulgence with our hard work. . . . We buy your Treasury notes and your bonds, although they're virtually valueless. Then you use our money to buy more goods from us—and from *our* protégés in Asia: Taiwan and Korea. Uncle Sam won't work to feed his habit."

Clearly, dependence upon the United States for security does not necessarily inspire respect for the United States. Neither does gratitude.

The U.S. helped to rebuild much of Asia, as well as much of Europe, after World War II. The Japanese benefited immensely from American assistance and American counsel during the Allied Occupation that shaped present-day Japan. "Support activities" for the Korean War, such as rebuilding equipment and staffing bases, got the Japanese economy rolling again. Vast American purchases of civilian and military goods for Viet Nam gave Japan the momentum for take-off. The climb to the stratosphere was fueled by the American consumer. Yet, Japanese now ask: "What has the U.S. done for us lately?"

Japanese are neither the only nor the most vehement critics of America. At Chiang Kai-shek Airport in Taiwan I overheard a portly diplomat with a Shanghai accent lecturing his family and subordinates. Democracy was decaying in America, he declared, because there was no respect for elders.

A clash of cultures? Undoubtedly. Trivial? Definitely not. Respect for elders is fundamental to the successful Confucian cultures of East Asia: Japan, Taiwan, Korea, Hong Kong, and Singapore.

Many Asians no longer emulate American accomplishments. Instead, they look down on American failures.

The Taiwanese magnate Wang Yung-ching, who is particularly well disposed toward Americans, runs the biggest plastics corporation in the world, including fifteen factories in the U.S. "Why did Mr. Wang succeed when American plastics factories were closing?" his senior aide asks rhetorically. "We went in when we learned that the Americans were buying large-diameter plastic piping from Canada at very high prices. Smaller diameters they made themselves, but the bigger pipes were too much trouble. They were too lazy and too rich to bother."

Jack Kim, a razor-tongued editor, saw the United States come back from the brink of defeat to limited victory in Korea. Nonetheless, after a drink or two, he talks about the "decline and fall . . . and fall . . . and fall of the United States. . . .

"More and more, others look on the U.S. as a kind of *very* fat sow. All it does is eat and eat and eat."

Some of this criticism is unfair. But a wry confirmation comes from a senior American ambassador.

"I've seen the U.S. in Asia since the 1940s," he confides. "Mine was

the lucky generation in the foreign service. We knew we really could
change the world. The United States really had the power then."

He pauses, pulls his earlobe, and says slowly, almost diffidently: "We
achieved some remarkable results then. But I've come to the conclusion
that the best thing we've done . . . the greatest thing . . . is to encourage Asian productivity. Just by consuming we've done more than we
have any other way."

A more balanced overview was given to me by Chen Li-an, then
chairman of Taiwan's National Science Council, who was subsequently
appointed minister of economic affairs. He took a B.S. in electrical
engineering at the Massachusetts Institute of Technology and a Ph.D.
in mathematics at New York University, and he worked in the United
States for fourteen years.

"In America the technical people have no place in corporate strategy," he says. "They're just serfs. In Europe and Japan, the best
engineers are assigned to products. But in the U.S. they do research.
The Japanese and even the Europeans can provide customers with an
advisory engineer who really knows the product. The Americans often
cannot."

Ascribing American problems to Wall Street's domination, he explains: "Japan approaches industry with a long-term strategy. That is
impossible in America. Management always has its eye on the quarterly
reports of earnings and on mergers and acquisitions, rather than on
production. In Japan and Germany, banks provide basic finance by
buying shares—and they're not as eager for quick bucks. In Japan, half
of the company directors have engineering backgrounds. In the U.S.,
a third are lawyers, a third accountants, and a third managers.

"Say we purchase American equipment. Then departments or companies split or merge, and we can't get delivery. If we order a general-
purpose computer, it can take six to eight months from the U.S. The
Japanese deliver in three days."

Many Asians now feel superior to the West—and not only in the
material realm. *Asiaweek*, published in Hong Kong, recently remarked
regarding film censorship: "Yet, most Asians do not advocate adopting
the lax standards of the West. . . . While Western psychologists and
social historians debate the decline of values and its cause, in Asia
religion and the family still hold sway."

That smug puritanical view is a reaction against the West's pop
culture. Yet that pop culture holds sway over the youth of Asia—and is
the largest U.S. export "product."

Anti-Asian feeling is rising in the U.S., above all anti-Japanese feeling.
It is easier to blame others than ourselves. It is much easier to rail
against the new "Yellow Peril" than to analyze the rise of Asia. It is far

easier to demonstrate against unfair Asian practices than to go beyond prejudice and pride to see our own shortcomings.

Yet, fruitful cooperation is still possible. Much goodwill still underlies Asian criticism. Almost every nation from Korea and China to Indonesia and Australia is strongly attached to the United States. Historical and cultural affinities are sustained by common economic and security interests.

Despite a certain falling back, the United States occupies a stronger position in Asia, particularly the Confucian Far East, than it does in Europe. In Asia it is still powerful, influential, and respected.

I have over the decades in Asia seen few graffiti demanding YANKEES GO HOME! Americans may have blundered between arrogant assertiveness, which belittles Asians, and quixotic self-deprecation, which belittles themselves, but such slogans have never become the municipal decoration they are elsewhere.

American prestige is still high in Asia. So, too, are expectations of America.

2

Taiwan: Past and Present

TAIWAN IS CHINA IN MICROCOSM; THE ULTRAMODERN FACE OF
CHINA—AND CHINA IS THE HUB OF ASIA. CONFUCIANISM DEVEL-
OPED IN CHINA AS A CREED, A CODE OF MORALITY, A WAY OF LIFE,
AND A PRACTICAL POLITICAL DOCTRINE. CONFUCIANISM RESTORED
IS THE FOUNDATION OF THE GREAT ASIAN RENAISSANCE.

Through the fog, the thunder, and the lightning of the collapse of
the old world order, it is clear that Japan has more cash than any
other country. The United States, still theoretically the richest,
has more debts. But how many know that the second-largest
hoard of cash in the world belongs to the Republic of China?
Claiming to be the legitimate government of the vast mainland of
China, that state actually rules some twenty million inhabitants of the
14,000-square-mile island of Taiwan, 100 miles off the coast of Asia. And
that pygmy is the second among the cash-rich countries of the world.

Preposterous, yet true.

Foreign-exchange holdings are the equivalent of an individual's saving account. At the beginning of 1989, the foreign-exchange holdings of
Japan were $97 billion; of Taiwan, $75 billion. Since the balance of
nuclear terror makes unlikely all but localized armed conflicts, economic power is now paramount—and Taiwan stands in the vanguard of
economic powers.

That reality underlines the importance of the new Asia to the future
of mankind. But it is all so recent—and so topsy-turvy—that it requires
a major intellectual effort to think of little Taiwan as a major power,
much less as a superpower. Only in 1951, Taiwan was an impoverished
and demoralized pauper state that could not even make its own rifles,
much less the arcane electronic devices it now pours forth. After fifty

years of Japanese occupation and five years of reoccupation by Generalissimo Chiang Kai-shek's Chinese Nationalist regime, the island was an economic wasteland. Further, it was riven by dissension between native Taiwanese and the carpetbaggers from the mainland. Although Chinese by blood, the long-settled families complained that they had been "liberated from the Japanese dogs by the Chinese pigs." Oppression by generals from the mainland and looting by their troops had in 1947 ignited a Taiwanese revolt, which was ruthlessly suppressed.

The people were tense with fear of invasion, even though the Chinese Communists were heavily engaged in the Korean War. It appeared that they would not challenge American power on another front and invite direct retaliation against the People's Republic itself, by mounting an invasion of Taiwan. Yet no one could be sure. And the broken Nationalist armies had abandoned most of their guns in their retreat from the mainland.

Taipei, the capital, was dusty, grimy, and stench-ridden, and its atmosphere medieval. Military police prodded deserters, wearing manacles and leg-irons, across the broken cobblestones. And civilians glanced away in fear. Presumed Communist spies were ritually executed by firing squads. And the resentful Taiwanese longed for the good old days under the Japanese, who had ruled from 1895 to 1945.

Generals and officials, bankers, clerks, and industrialists—all were bewildered by the abrupt alteration in their lives. The Nationalist generals were mourning the loss of honor by their flight from the mainland. Some were salving their hurt by counting the gold bars they had salvaged, even when they could not salvage their big guns. A generation that had fought a long war for a nation as big as a continent had been relegated to a small island. That was the price of having lost the last campaign—the civil war against the Communists.

The ponderous red-brick edifices built by the Japanese to accommodate their colonial government—and to intimidate the subject populace—loomed over ramshackle hovels and over walled compounds enclosing dilapidated single-story houses. The open-fronted shops offered few goods beyond bamboo pails, iron dishpans, and coarse blue coolie clothing. Foodstalls lined the narrow streets, their patrons perched on minuscule stools beside drains flowing with sewage. On a red-letter day in 1951, the first skyscraper was completed—and was immediately occupied by the American economic aid mission. It was five stories high.

Aside from the army's battered jeeps and staff cars, the chief transportation was the trishaw. Passengers jounced on a high wooden seat set above the two rear wheels; a sweating coolie clung to the handlebars that steered the forward wheel and pedaled desperately. Unsurpris-

ingly, the highway from Taipei to the south turned into a rutted dirt road
even before it crossed the city line.

Throughout the island only one production enterprise prospered.
Slogans newly painted in giant blue ideograms on a white background
simultaneously mourned and exhorted, FAN KANG TA LU!—"Reconquer
the Mainland!"

A *less* likely prospect for economic and industrial stardom would be
hard to imagine. Aside from strips of fertile land, the island possessed
in abundance only water and mountains. But development of hydro-
electric power awaited adequate investment. In 1951, Taiwan had
fewer than eight million inhabitants, almost two million of them mainlanders. In 1981 the population was almost twenty million, and the
differences between mainlanders and Taiwanese were fading. In 1951,
Taiwan's total exports had been worth $58 million. In 1988 total exports
were $60.6 *billion*, just half the Gross National Product. The excess of
exports over imports was $10.9 billion—of which $10.4 billion was the
surplus in trade with the United States. In 1951 each individual's
nominal share of the GNP was $48. In 1988 it was $6,045, very comfortably ahead of inflation.

The people of Taiwan are today moving from satisfaction to repletion
and, perhaps, satiation with the extraordinary variety of goods available
in the specialty shops, supermarkets, and department stores that jostle
each other in their cities. The glare of multicolored neon signs and the
din of loudspeakers make every night a festival of consumerism. Plums
from California compete with rambutan from Indonesia and $100 shirts
from Switzerland with gold lamé skirts from Japan. But most goods,
manufactured or agricultural, are produced in Taiwan itself.

Bored with the glittering restaurants that offer twenty varieties of
regional Chinese cuisine, teenage youths and girls flock to French cafés
to eat "authentic Parisian food" and dance to suave combos.

Stores displaying pre-faded blue jeans and tight dresses with Lurex
panels are packed with shoppers from sixteen to twenty-six. Cameras,
binoculars, and computers draw acquisitive appraisal along with multicolored shoes, high boots with spangles, and silk scarves. Department
stores are thronged with young buyers of chinaware, foodstuffs, and
appliances ranging from refrigerators and dishwashers to air condition-
ers.

The young have money in their pockets, as they never had before.
The young are escaping from parental restraints, as they never have
before, spending as if good times will never end—and 56 percent of
Taiwan's people are under twenty-five.

The big restaurants are awash with tourists, mostly Japanese. The
atmosphere is hectic and close. The décor is tawdry: worn carpets
blotched with stains, frayed curtains not quite meeting, and faded

vermilion pillars entwined with tarnished gilt dragons. The hostesses wear long satin skirts split to their hips. AIDS does not frighten away the farmers, clerks, and laborers in sharp suits who come for a fling, as their fathers or grandfathers came, but in the uniform of the Imperial Japanese Armed Forces.

The massage parlors that were once fronts for brothels are now passé. Now luxurious "barbershops" cater to such needs. A three-story neon sign proclaims: FAR EAST BEST TONSORIAL PARLOR—SPECIAL TREATMENTS. Plush reception rooms are glimpsed through filmy curtains on the shop windows. Sometimes a token barber chair is on display.

Amid the colored lights that glisten on the rain-wet Nanking road, a woman in her early twenties twirls a pert tartan umbrella. She wears scarlet boots, a black miniskirt that just covers her buttocks, and a green silk blouse open to her navel. Her hair gleams jet black, every strand lacquered into place. Haughty disdain on her smooth olive features, she stands voluptuously impatient.

A lass waiting for her lover? A call girl waiting for her next appointment? I do not know. I only know that such sights were never seen in outwardly puritanical Taipei four decades ago.

On broad boulevards, narrow side streets, and dark alleys, yellow taxis squeak around portly silver buses. Hordes of automobiles and motorcycles make walking a trial and parking virtually impossible. A five-lane highway leads to the south, where political slogans are now hardly ever seen. No one is much concerned about reconquering the relatively impoverished mainland. A little blasé, the people of Taiwan are too busy producing and enjoying the fruits of their dynamic economy.

The complex process that made Taiwan an economic colossus can be expressed in a single formula: *American aid and American purchases + Chinese talent + the Confucian work ethic = a miracle.* The two native factors are at least twice as important as the American factor. Yet the miracle would not have occurred without the Americans, who, further, guaranteed Taiwan's survival as an independent entity.

In addition to the pursuit of wealth by industrial production, Taiwan is dedicated to the preservation of traditional Chinese culture, which has been battered in the rival People's Republic of China. Those divergent purposes are manifest in two complexes about five miles apart: the World Trade Center and the National Palace Museum.

In 1989 the Trade Center was the largest in Asia, perhaps the largest in the world. It includes an immense display hall with a floor area of twenty-five acres; an office building thirty-four stories high; and a hotel with 1,022 rooms.

The Palace Museum is equally grand, showing fifteen thousand exhibits at a time. That is no more than 2.1 percent of the 700,000 treasures stored in massive, low buildings built like traditional imperial palaces.

The Trade Center is, however, totally apart from Chinese tradition. The seven-story display hall with striated pink-and-rose outer walls under a great glass-and-steel roof owes its inspiration to the blunt pyramids of the Mayas and the stepped ziggurats of Babylon. Galleries sweeping around an enormous atrium display tens of thousands of products ranging from bulldozers and steel girders to cosmetics and sun glasses.

A heated toilet seat that sprays, dries, and perfumes the pertinent parts is described in a slick brochure for the "tepid medical shower, toilet, and bidet combination," that asks: "Why do the Japanese enjoy longest life in the world?" It answers: "This is simply because they pay special attention to personal hygienics and popularly use shower toilet equipment with warm water cleaning device."

Importers, mostly American, are lured by highly publicized names: Gucci, Ralph Lauren, Valentino, and Lacoste among them. Taiwan manufactures goods for those designers, but does not object if an independent affixes his own label.

The Palace Museum is the antithesis of that splashy display. A cavern within a green hillside overlooking smoky Taipei hoards the supreme masterpieces of more than three millennia: paintings, jade, calligraphy, sculpture, bronzes, and ceramics, as well as lesser arts like enamel and lacquer.

Fourteen thousand crates were prudently packed up in Peking before the Japanese attack in 1937. They were carried across China by steamship and junk, by freightcar and truck, by man-drawn cart and on the backs of coolies, before being unpacked on Taiwan. Those treasures had been accumulated by successive imperial dynasties since A.D. 960 when the first Sung emperor ascended the Dragon Throne.

Among the masterworks of the world's longest-lived culture is a greatly beloved painting called *Pai Ma, "A Hundred Horses,"* which is signed Liang Shih-ning. That is not the artist's original name. The Italian Jesuit Guiseppe Castiglione took that Chinese name at the court of the Kang Hsi Emperor of the Ching Dynasty in the seventeenth century. He was a mandarin there, a member of the elite civil service that administered the Great Empire. He is today still foremost among the thousands of artists in China who have painted horses over thousands of years.

Except for periods of uncharacteristic seclusion, like that under the Ming Dynasty (1368–1644), the Chinese have been receptive to outside influences, always ready to adapt foreign talent and foreign ideas for Chinese use.

The Manchu emperors of the Ching Dynasty (1644–1911) happily employed dozens of foreign Jesuits. But the Jesuits did not succeed in teaching the Chinese to make and use the West's new bronze artillery. The Chinese had not only invented black gunpowder centuries earlier, but had used both cannon and rockets against the Mongol invaders in the thirteenth century. Yet they could not master the technologically superior cannon of seventeenth-century Europe, the atom bomb of that time.

The Manchu emperors could not employ the high-tech European weapons, despite the occasional brilliance of their generals and the great skill of their artisans. Although China was the best-ordered, richest, and most cultivated nation on earth, Chinese officers could not use artillery effectively because artillery, even their own artillery, made them supremely uneasy. Their image of themselves, their fundamental self-esteem, was menaced by the big bronze guns.

Knowing themselves to be the inheritors of the world's oldest and highest civilization, the Chinese could not admit that other peoples might be their equals, much less their superiors. If the foreign bronze cannon were accepted as decisive weapons, they would have demolished China's assertion of supremacy. Since the Chinese of the seventeenth and eighteenth centuries could not thus acknowledge Europe's technological superiority, they were psychologically incapable of employing European cannon—even if their lives depended on it.

The conflict between what they knew they should do and what they could actually bring themselves to do was to bedevil China's rulers for the next three centuries. That conflict still inhibits material progress in the Communist-ruled mainland. In June 1989 that conflict became violent. The student demonstrators and the intellectuals who supported them stood for the fundamental political, social, and cultural changes that alone could make possible industrial progress in the Western manner. The aged autocrats who ordered their slaughter were defending the traditional approach, for they still believed China could use Western technology without altering her authoritarian character.

Yen Jyaqi, who was, until June 1989, director of the Institute of Social Sciences on the Communist-ruled mainland, was forced to flee to save his life. He had earlier expressed China's fundamental dilemma forthrightly, declaring, "We must rid ourselves of the conviction that we are superior to all other nations and cultures. As long as we continue to believe that we are the center of the world, we will not be able to learn from the experience of foreign nations—and our progress will be very slow."

Most Chinese have preferred to believe they could utilize the West's mechanical devices, which are, after all, little more than ingenious toys, without altering their own essential habits of mind. A great viceroy of the Ching Dynasty declared succinctly: "Western learning," which meant technology, was useful for base practical purposes, but "Chinese learning," which meant morals, philosophy, and government, would forever shape cultural and spiritual life. The viceroy could not imagine that mastering Western techniques, that is, science and industry, would require reshaping the very foundations of Chinese life.

As Yen Jyaqi of the Institute of Social Sciences has pointed out, the People's Republic has not yet broken with the conservative view of China as *the* uniquely superior civilization among virtual barbarians. The guns in Tienanmen Square proved his point, modern weapons massacring modern men and women to preserve the past.

Modernizers and conservatives have contended ever since Matteo Ricci, the first Jesuit missionary-scientist, came to the Imperial Court. The stark alternatives were irreconcilable: retain Chinese culture and do without Western machines, or adopt Western ways and virtually jettison the Chinese heritage, an entire way of life.

The conflict for the power between the conservative Nationalist Generalissimo Chiang Kai-shek and the radical Communist Chairman Mao Tse-tung, from 1921 to 1949, epitomized that intellectual conflict. Chiang Kai-shek was profoundly attached to the teachings of the great Sage Confucius, who died some 2,500 years ago. Mao Tse-tung was determined to scrap Confucian teachings. Yet not the mainland, but Taiwan has, like no Chinese regime before it, adopted Western ideas with great flair and employed Western techniques with great skill.

Looking down on the pale pink modernity of the World Trade Center from the traditional upswept emerald-tiled eaves of the Palace Museum, it is clear that the Chinese of Taiwan have mastered high technology and mass production as their ancestors could not. They appear to have resolved the centuries-old dilemma: How to adopt foreign technology without surrendering Chinese moral, spiritual, and intellectual values—and thus becoming un-Chinese.

Yet the social tensions are great. I fear Taiwan has sidestepped the fundamental conflict, not resolved it. No one can remain traditionally Chinese in thought and behavior while living at the hyper-rapid pace imposed by today's technology.

Taiwan's example has, however, served the Republic of Korea, Singapore, and Hong Kong well. All Confucian by heritage, they have retained or modified many Confucian practices. Japan's growth from seclusion to worldwide primacy in little more than a century also sprang from Confucian roots.

Born more than five hundred years before Jesus Christ, Confucius has had an effect as profound as Christ's. For a time it appeared that the doctrines of Karl Marx would sweep Confucianism away. But Confucianism, adapted brilliantly to the late twentieth century, as it had adapted to previous eras, has largely edged Marxism off the stage in Asia.

Confucianism is at once a state ideology, a way of life, a religion, a moral code, a manual for rulers, and a handbook for officials. Like Karl Marx, Confucius was a failure in practical terms. Like Marx's, the doctrines of Confucius have been greatly altered by disciples. Yet present-day Confucianism possesses a moral core fashioned by the great sage himself. Hundreds of millions still behave as he directed men and women to behave two and a half millennia ago. Essentially, Confucius taught that human beings would live in harmony and prosperity if they followed a few simple rules. Above all, he taught, mankind was divided between inferiors, whose task was obedience, and superiors, whose task was to provide for the common welfare, largely by setting a sterling example. Paradise could be realized on this earth rather than in a problematical hereafter.

The advantages of a society so ordered are obvious for a modern industrial—or even postindustrial—nation. The doctrine ensures order. Those at the top *must* look after those at the bottom, and they in turn *must* toil cheerfully.

Industrious harmony does not, however, arise spontaneously. Practical Confucianism therefore provides substantial rewards for good behavior and severe punishments for bad behavior. The founders thus created a political, social, and economic entity that endured in China until 1911, little changed in essentials.

Unlike his contemporary Socrates, no portrait of Confucius has survived. All we can see of the man himself is a stereotyped portrait of a long-robed, middle-aged Chinese with a broad face, a high forehead, a benevolent smile, and a wispy beard. He may even have looked like that, but we do not know. His name was Kung Chiu-ni, but later generations called him Kung Fu-tze, which means Kung "the master." The early Jesuits Latinized Kung Fu-tze to Confucius.

He was born in 551 B.C. into a poor but learned family in the feudal state of Lu, one of a number of independent kingdoms that lay in the coastal area now known as Shandong Province, near Korea and Japan. His father was a middle-rank official, the keeper of the state forests. His beloved mother was wise, gentle, and devoted.

That is almost all we know of Confucius the man today. Although he inspired succeeding generations to keep detailed records of the lives of kings and commoners, there is no contemporary record of his life.

Confucius became a teacher, rather than a practicing statesman.

Supported, like Socrates, by his students, Confucius, unlike Socrates, was not condemned. He was honored—as long as he kept his fingers out of practical politics. Like Socrates, he pronounced on every aspect of the condition of mankind. Unlike Socrates, he was not blessed with a disciple like Plato to record his discourses at length. His disciples jotted down pertinent points, as if taking notes for an end-of-course examination. Their notes were collected later and called *Kung-tze Lün Yü*, (*The Analects of Confucius*).

That work instructs on such matters as the proper way to receive old friends (with joy) to the correct way to serve food (cut into small bits so that diners can use hygienic chopsticks, rather than knives). The Analects' primary emphasis was, however, on politics being the art by which human beings could live together with as little friction as is humanly possible.

One of my favorite homilies tells of Confucius coming upon a woman who was weeping over the clawed body of her husband. Her son, too, she said, had been slain by the vicious tiger of the nearby forest.

"Why," the sage asked, "do you not go elsewhere?"

"Here there is no oppressive government!" the woman answered.

The moral is left to the reader to draw. However, Confucius manifestly considered oppressive government the worst evil that can befall men and women.

A visitor once boasted to Confucius that discipline in his state was so perfect "that a son will even denounce his father for stealing a sheep." The sage replied, "With us, the relationship between father and son is more important than [the value of] a sheep. Here the son would not denounce his father."

The moral is more complex. For Confucius, the reciprocal obligations of protection and obedience between father and son were the model for *all* human relationships—and for the government of mankind. If one were to inform on the other, the foundation of the social structure would crack.

The Confucian state was modeled on the sacred familial relationship, and the emperor was hallowed as the father of all the people. In Chinese everyone is *dajya*, literally "big family," and nation is *gwojya*, literally "country-family."

Confucius replied to the disciple who asked about the gods: "The superior man behaves as if the gods existed so as to present a good example to the common people. . . . Do not worry about whether the gods exist or not!"

Confucian peoples are to this day fundamentally agnostic—except in times of trouble, when they have been Buddhist or Taoist—and are now increasingly Christian. But the successive Confucian dynasties made religious ritual an integral part of government. Every spring the emperor offered sacrifices at the Temple of Heaven and plowed a symbolic furrow to ensure good crops. So did the lesser emperors and kings of Viet Nam, Korea, and Japan.

Those states sometimes made formal obeisance to the emperor of China. They followed Sino-Confucian customs and ethical standards, which have been preeminent in East Asia for two millennia.

The great edifice of the Confucian state rested on the assured hierarchy of superiors and inferiors: ruler and subject, father and son, husband and wife, older and younger. Rigidity was tempered by tolerance. The sage taught that the highest responsibility of the prince was the welfare of the people.

Life within that edifice was directed by men in whom Plato might have recognized his ideal philosopher-kings. Members of that small group were called *gwan*, which means "official," but are known in the West as mandarins, from the Portuguese *mandar*, "to command." Although some greedy and cruel men slipped into office, most mandarins were upright and dedicated. Confucianism meant rule by men rather than by law. It was, however, above all, a meritocracy.

Even poor boys could win admission to the mandarinate by passing the entrance examinations. They could rise by the merit of their work and by passing two further examinations, the equivalent of the modern master's and doctoral degrees. They could even become prime minister if they attained high marks—and pleased the emperor. The examinations and the civil service became a model not only for East Asia, but for the West as well. Indeed, most Western nations patterned their administrative services on the Chinese example. Like the Chinese, the Germans put civilian officials as well as military officers into uniform. The nine grades of mandarins wore large insignia of rank on their chests: birds for civil officials, beasts of prey for military officers. In China, however, unlike Germany, the civilians always ranked before the military.

Despite corruption and favoritism, promotion was normally decided neither by birth nor by wealth, but by merit. The emphasis upon talent and achievement today nurtures both ambitious managers and diligent workers. Obedience to superiors and consideration for inferiors knit the social fabric tightly.

Neo-Confucian behavior has produced the world's most dynamic nations: not only Taiwan, Korea, and, of course, Japan, but also the city-states of Singapore and Hong Kong. Except for Japan and Korea, they are also predominantly Chinese by race. The small overseas Chinese minority has also led the economic development of Southeast Asian nations, largely because of the Confucian work ethic.

*   *   *

Rural Taiwan, still Confucian, has not yet been totally transformed into an industrial hinterland poisoned by noxious fumes and clangorous machinery. There is still space, and there is still a little leisure. On Sunday mornings, farmers bring their finest teas and prize flowers to market under the overpass that crosses Jenai Road near the Howard Plaza Hotel in Taipei. Three and a half dollars buys a pound of the best ooloong, big leaves of a quality rarely exported to the West. You can also buy orchids: cattleyas with big mauve blossoms and great sprays of symbidium. You can buy bird-of-paradise plants with brilliant blue-and-orange flowers, gold-tasseled arum lilies, miniature palms, and crimson hibiscus.

Whether you buy or not, you are welcome to sip tea and to discuss the ancient secrets of horticulture. The country people still have time to chat and gossip. All the time Moira and I lived in Hong Kong, Taiwan was our closest refuge. When we needed a respite from the Crown Colony's urban intensity, we would go to Sun Moon Lake and to the mountain peaks called Ali Shan in central Taiwan.

The aboriginal people lived in their own villages around Sun Moon Lake. The *gao shandzu*, the "people of the high hills," were no longer as fierce as they had been at the beginning of the century, when even the conquering Japanese feared them. But they had not yet been reduced to costumed extras in a staged pageant. Their feather head-dresses, bamboo pipes, and big curved knives were not theatrical props, but parts of their normal life around the great lake that on calm evenings mirrors the moon and the stars.

Much has been sacrificed to progress, but much remains. Wispy clouds still drift before the nine-tiered Tzu En Pagoda and veil the golden roofs of the temples of Peace and War beside Sun Moon Lake. Seen from the vantage of 2,500 feet, the island below is intensely green and exuberantly fertile.

This, too, is Taiwan, the eternal Asia. Community with nature and the continuity of humanity are both enshrined in a small Confucian temple with black walls and red doors half hidden among the dark green pines.

At my first visit in 1951, Taiwan was an embarrassment to the United States—a disreputable hanger-on that domestic political pressures prevented successive American administrations from casting off. As late as 1972, I saw Taiwan on the brink of despair. Later President Chiang Ching-kuo, then prime minister for his aged father, President Chiang Kai-shek, was aghast at America's moves toward transferring diplomatic recognition from Taiwan to the Communist regime on the mainland. But he told me, with bitter realism, "We can put up with almost anything and survive. As long as America doesn't try to strangle us economically, we will survive!"

Chiang Ching-kuo had, some two decades earlier, stage-managed anti-American riots that culminated in the burning of the U.S. Embassy in Taipei. They protested being forced to withdraw Nationalist troops from several small islands to avoid close confrontation with the Communists. Despite such recurring antagonism, both the government and the people of Taiwan today cherish the special relationship with the U.S. The Nationalists remain partially dependent on the U.S. for their military security. Besides, unofficial diplomatic relations also endure, although they are studiously *non*official. The American Institute in Taiwan has replaced the United States Embassy and the Chinese Nationalist Embassy in Washington has become the office in the United States of America of the Coordination Council for North American Affairs. Both the institute and office are headed by senior diplomats who have formally retired from government service, in order to maintain the ostensibly nonofficial bond between their countries.

Confucian constancy and gratitude would ensure the United States a special place in the hearts of Taiwan, even if mutual interest did not still bind the two states. Many of Taiwan's leaders are American-educated. Diane Ying, one of the island's most prominent journalists, herself American-trained, actually deplores the large number of Ph.D.s from American universities in both government and private enterprise. "They're out of touch with the ordinary people," she says.

The Confucian injunction to honor one's teachers all one's life strengthens the bonds between Taiwan and the United States. About 26,000 students from Taiwan are normally pursuing graduate studies in the U.S. It has lately been remarked with satisfaction that more than 25 percent are now returning home, for in the old days, few did. Industry and academia on Taiwan are also recruiting Chinese-Americans with scientific and managerial skills to serve the land of their ancestors.

American influence is pervasive. Taiwan's Little League baseball teams, regular winners in Asian competitions, have often beaten American champions in play-offs. A proud Chinese father explained, "The American kids think it's a game!"

Between 1949 and 1965, American grants, commodities, subsidized loans, and technical advice worth $1.5 billion laid the foundation for Taiwan's present economic structure. The Joint Chinese-American Commission on Rural Reconstruction took on *the* fundamental problem: modernizing the island's backward agriculture. American technology, channeled through the Joint Commission, altered everything from prenatal care and primary education to fertilizers, pesticides, and plows—and made Taiwan a better place to live.

The most radical—and beneficial—alteration was land reform. The moving spirit was the American agronomist Wolf Ladejinsky, a stocky, amiable, complex man who spoke with a Russian accent and had overseen land reform in both Korea and Japan. Distribution of land to new owners revitalized the rice crop in the paddy fields; the farms that produced vegetables, hogs, and chickens; and the groves that yielded bananas and pineapples.

Having resisted land reform on the mainland, the Nationalist authorities gladly cooperated on Taiwan. Dr. Sun Yat-sen, the founding father of the Republic of China, had promised, "The tillers shall own their land!" Besides, the mainlanders were not giving away their own land, but the land of Taiwanese.

In return, landowners got shares in government-owned industries like the Taiwan Cement Corporation, which had little value. Later, when industry prospered, the Taiwanese got rich—and assertive. Virtually monopolizing political and military power, the mainlanders had generally left commerce, industry, and agriculture to the old families. Becoming rich, the Taiwanese reached out for the levers of political power. Even before the death of President Chiang Ching-kuo, in January 1988, the Nationalist regime had begun to liberalize its structure—largely to meet Taiwanese demands for a much greater role in the government. After the June 4 massacre in Tienanmen Square, Taipei could boast even more convincingly that it was truly the only "Free China." The effective dictatorship of the mainlanders of the Nationalist party had passed with the elections of 1989, which were for the first time contested by legal opposition parties.

The evolution toward limited democracy would occur because the American shield had, since 1950, kept the Communist People's Liberation Army from following up its victory on the mainland by attacking Taiwan. For decades American destroyers had patrolled the Taiwan Straits, and American fighter squadrons had blocked air raids. The Nationalists can today defend their island alone—*because* American matériel and American counsel made their armed forces highly effective.

Only American support sustained the island I first saw in 1951, which was so different from present-day Taiwan it might have existed in another era. Yet the fate of Taiwan is today still intertwined with the continuing prosperity of the U.S.

Since there were no hotels, most nonofficial visitors then stayed at the rather archly named Friends of China Club. The concrete building had once housed a Japanese officers' club and later the Chinese Officers' Moral Endeavor Association. Generalissimo Chiang Kai-shek, a Methodist convert, attempted through the Moral Endeavor Association to keep from lewd diversions—like social dancing—the officer corps he could not keep from major corruption. A block away, "special restaurants" catered to appetites not satisfied by food and drink, as ornate "barber shops" did in the 1980s.

The exodus from the mainland had brought to Taipei the culinary talent that had served a great nation of gourmets. The restaurants were, however, small and cramped. I was introduced to Sichuan cuisine in a shack called the Yü Yüan. When a train passed on the track two yards away, the spindly stools trembled, the pots rattled, and the walls shook. But the clear oxtail soup was the best I ever tasted—or hope to taste.

I was in my early twenties, and I was a real foreign correspondent. I was also something of a pet of the experienced correspondents and local officials because I could speak and read Chinese. Although it was too hot for trench coats, I reveled in the glamour of foreign reporting when I boarded an overnight train with American-educated Major Herbie King. We were going south to see the commander of the ground forces of the Republic of China. The dimly lit Japanese Pullman car was drab, and the narrow bunks were child-length. Since Taiwan was at war, the train was blacked out and the station platforms were dark. The 220 miles from Taipei to Kaohsiung, now forty minutes in a Boeing 727, took more than fourteen hours.

Our train lumbered into Kaohsiung at 10:00 on a late-summer's morning in 1951. Now the chief industrial complex of an industrial nation, Kaohsiung was then still deeply scarred from American bombing in World War II. Shabby, lethargic, and dispirited, it appeared to have abandoned all hope.

An ancient Chevrolet staff car took us to Pingtung, the headquarters of General Sun Li-jen. He received me cordially. I was writing an article for *The Reporter* on the Nationalist military forces, and even a very junior American reporter was important. The Nationalists' survival depended on America.

Besides, General Sun genuinely liked Americans, perhaps more than he liked most of his brother officers. A graduate of the Virginia Military Institute, he had been a protégé of General Joseph W. Stilwell, the American chief-of-staff of the Nationalist armed forces during the war. He was also a favorite of American correspondents. That popularity did not endear him to Generalissimo Chiang Kai-shek.

After the war the Generalissimo promoted only generals who were personally devoted to him. Professional competence did not count. After the retreat to Taiwan, the American connection still handicapped General Sun Li-jen. Blaming his defeat on American intervention, or, alternately, on lack of American intervention, the Generalissimo set his face against the general who was so close to the Americans.

But the Generalissimo soon realized that American goodwill was his only hope of surviving in Taiwan, much less reconquering the mainland. To please the Americans, he appointed General Sun commander of the ground forces. Sun was not restored to the Generalissimo's favor; he was swallowed with a shudder like a particularly nasty medicine.

Although they had lost China by their ineffectiveness and their corruption, the Nationalists, epitomized by the Generalissimo, still appeared to many vociferous Americans to be the white hope of anti-communism in Asia. President Harry S. Truman had been reducing the level of American representation on Taiwan and had been maneuvering toward diplomatic recognition of the Communists. Whatever their faults, they did rule the Chinese mainland. Attacked for being "soft on communism," Truman was forced to reverse that policy.

When the Communists committed the "Chinese People's Volunteers" to battle against American troops in Korea, the president's options were foreclosed. Having sent those troops into action against the Communists, he was forced to send an ambassador to Taiwan. He also ordered the U.S. Navy to patrol the Taiwan Straits—to prevent either Nationalists or Communists from invading the other's territory.

Harry Truman staged a big show in Taiwan, largely to placate Taiwan's American friends, who were called the China lobby. Starring the U.S. Military Advisory and Assistance Group, Truman's show was virtually Chinese in its emphasis on appearance over substance. As long as it appeared that Washington was staunchly supporting the Nationalists and effectively retraining their armed forces, the reality was of secondary importance.

General Sun Li-jen felt a pressing need to make the strongest possible case for his troops and himself to the American public. The general was heavy-boned, in gray-green fatigues with four silver stars on the collar. His tanned features were blunt, bold, and open. I have since that time seen the same expression on the faces of other generals. William Westmoreland, who commanded in Viet Nam, had that trusting, direct look—as if life and politics were essentially simple matters that had been maliciously complicated by civilians.

Sun Li-jen noted that the army he commanded had been routed and humiliated. His first task, he said, was to restore the confidence of the bone-thin, ragged regulars who had retreated to Taiwan rather than surrender to the Communists. They were bewildered and depressed—in a word, demoralized. His troops, the general said, had to be re-equipped and retrained if they were to become effective fighters. But first they had to unlearn the bad lessons of the past.

"I'm like an artist who's been given a canvas spoiled by someone else's daubs," he explained. "Before I try to paint my masterpiece, I've got to scrape the canvas clean."

His troops nonetheless put on a brave show for an audience of senior officers of the U.S. Military Advisory and Assistance Group and a lone reporter. Shouting hoarse war cries, the infantrymen charged. Explosions mimicking artillery fire threw up fountains of earth, and firecrackers popped like small arms.

Possessing no radios and few field telephones, the officers conveyed their orders as had their ancestors in battle against the Mongols seven hundred years before. Bugles blared, whistles shrilled, and colored flags gyrated.

A lean lieutenant semaphoring scarlet signal flags was a stick figure against the faded blue-velvet sky. Around him rolled gray smoke streaked with black. Grinning soldiers were firing Browning automatic rifles into the traditional horseshoe-shaped graves on the hillside.

The live rounds shattered the tombstones. Already indignant at the soldiers' scarring their fields with explosives, the Taiwanese farmers were infuriated by the desecration of their ancestors' graves. A Nationalist major explained half apologetically that the infantry had to hold its maneuvers *somewhere*.

"These troops need to start with basic training," an American colonel later confided. "Elementary squad tactics afterward. The officers obviously never heard of a flanking movement. All they know is the frontal attack, which is sure to get them all killed."

During the next four years, General Sun Li-jen was to work at his masterpiece with much success. He created a new and effective army, even enlisting Taiwanese, whom most mainlanders distrusted. He also intrigued ineptly against the Generalissimo.

He went to the Americans, who were also fed up with the Generalissimo's authoritarianism and ineptness. With American support, he promised, he would mount a *coup d'etat*; establish a progressive and efficient regime; train a crack army; and be ready to retake the mainland.

General Sun had chosen the wrong confidants. True, the Americans would have preferred a more progressive regime. But they did *not* want the Nationalists to invade the mainland—and provoke a wider conflict in which the Soviet Union would come to the aid of the Chinese Communists. Besides, backing a *coup* against the Generalissimo would have aroused the wrath of the China Lobby.

Sun Li-jen's offer inevitably leaked—and he was arrested. He finally reappeared in public in 1988, after more than three decades of house arrest. The American connection had not served him well.

3

Taiwan: Present and Future

TAIWAN, WHICH MEANS TABLE BAY, IS THE JAPANESE AND CHINESE
NAME FOR THE BEAUTIFUL ISLAND. FORMOSA, PORTUGUESE FOR
BEAUTIFUL, THE NAME LONG USED BY THE WEST, IS TODAY
FORGOTTEN—AND THE ISLAND IS ONLY BEAUTIFUL IN PLACES. THE
CITIES HAVE BEEN SCARRED BY THE ENVIRONMENTAL DAMAGE
ATTENDANT UPON ECONOMIC DEVELOPMENT. THE CHINESE CARE
EVERYTHING FOR MATERIAL WEALTH, BUT LITTLE FOR NATURE,
WHICH BELONGS TO NO ONE.

During twenty-one centuries of Confucian rule, generals repeatedly seized the Dragon Throne and founded new dynasties. After the Revolution of 1911 destroyed the Confucian Empire, the nation-continent suffered so grievously from the depredations of generals that even today the word *warlord* immediately evokes China. Generalissimo Chiang Kai-shek and Chairman Mao Tse-tung, who contended for supreme power for two decades, were both men on horseback. China's history has been more often carved with the sword than drawn with the writing brush.

Yet nowhere else, except, perhaps, ancient Israel, has the written word been paid greater reverence. Moreover, generals are despised by the Confucian ethos, which still prevails. Beneath the scholar-official in the rigid social hierarchy stood in succession farmers, artisans, merchants, and, finally, soldiers. Every Chinese knows the old folk saying, "Good iron is not used for nails, and good men do not become soldiers!"

Dominant during protracted periods of disorder, the generals are no longer as important in the Republic of China on Taiwan. The formal abolition of martial law in 1987, which was a good deal *more* than a sop to progressive opinion at home and abroad, accelerated their decline. In Taiwan, as elsewhere, the computer has sapped the power of the gun.

Besides, the external threat is no longer immediate. The balance of political and military power is too delicate for either the Republic of

China on Taiwan or the People's Republic of China on the mainland to start a conflict. Few on Taiwan today expect a Communist attack or still hope to retake the mainland.

The soldiers are suffering from their own success. The 400,000 regulars now under arms are far more effective than were the ragged millions of 1949—and most of their weapons, including warplanes, are manufactured on the island. Although American power has guaranteed Taiwan's survival as a distinct political entity, the prowess of Taiwan's own soldiers, sailors, and airmen has been a major deterrent to an attack. If the U.S. were removed from the equation, the Communist People's Liberation Army could probably take Taiwan. But at what cost?

The infantrymen one sees around Pingtung today bear little resemblance to their forerunners in 1951. Yesterday's men were lean, almost emaciated, their skin was gray, and their cheekbones protruded beneath their dull eyes. They were ill-armed, ill-trained, ill-treated, and illiterate—in sum, traditional Chinese soldiers. Today's men are cocky, muscular, and educated; their weapons and equipment are ultramodern. Singapore, which can afford the best, sends its infantry to Pingtung to train with Nationalist units. I found it hard to tell the two apart.

Nor were the soldiers as conspicuous around Pingtung as they had been thirty-odd years ago. They had stood out then because they were so numerous and because the jade-green valleys were sparsely settled. Villages of huts with thatched or gray-tiled roofs were few. Rice, the staple—almost the sole—crop, was spread to dry on the little used few roads.

Big gaudy tourist buses now lope along the high roads, shouldering aside taxis or private cars and sniffing the trucks' black exhausts. Heavy-headed, short-stalked "miracle rice" has replaced the slender stalks. Broad-leafed banana plants and spiky pineapple bushes have displaced many of the silvery flooded paddy fields. The four-lane coastal highway runs between broad seawater ponds, where miniature paddlewheelers throw up great plumes of spray.

Those miniboats aerate the water, which is seeded with hundreds of thousands of prawns and eels. Aquaculture began with the modest aim of providing cheap protein for the island's tables from the fast-breeding tulapia fish. Few water-farmers now raise fish, which are slow developers. Prawns and eels grow quickly, and the demand is virtually unlimited—from Japan above all, but also from prosperous Taiwan itself. Taiwan produces almost $1 billion worth of prawns and eels a year, and exports about $850 million worth, mostly to Japan.

The extreme south was once poor for a subtropical island with fertile soil, abundant fisheries, and a basic infrastructure built by the Japanese, who ruled Taiwan for fifty years. Today, brick-and-tile towns that were once thatch-and-wood villages flash by our car's windows, one every five minutes. Big restaurants cater to residents as well as to tourists.

Many Confucian and Buddhist temples have risen in the past decade, glittering vermilion, gold, green, and silver. Only the wealthy can build temples, thus acquiring merit and winning remission of their sins. There are obviously a lot of wealthy people around.

On the landward side stand three rows of steel pylons strung with high-tension cables and two rows of wooden electricity/telephone poles. On the seaward side, two further rows of wooden poles supplement the microwave dish antennas that carry much of the island's communications. The harshly practical Chinese are not abashed by those unlovely artifacts of economic progress.

Not so long ago, bits of string and holed pots were treasured against need. Today, automobile graveyards line the highway, and discarded refrigerators and washing machines testify silently to the carelessness bred by prosperity.

The epitome of modern taste is Caesar's Palace, the resort hotel at the island's southern tip. The building is well designed, the service is excellent, and the cuisine is standard Cantonese, which means it is better than that served in 95 percent of the better restaurants of the world. Its newly rich guests are high-spirited, loud, and numerous. The enormous swimming pool, shaped like a gigantic amoeba, is so jammed one can hardly stand, much less swim. Most swimmers are under fifteen; none looks over twenty-five.

Youth and elders are just as avid at work in nearby Kaohsiung, Taiwan's chief port. Kaohsiung means "high heroism." The port may have been heroic when it was the springboard for the Japanese invasion of Southeast Asia. But, thinking of Kaohsiung only a few years ago, I recall palm fronds rustling comfortably in the gentle breeze—and not much else. Although Taiwan's sparse industrial plants, such as the government-owned Aluminum Corporation, were concentrated in Kaohsiung, it was primarily a sluggish harbor for small-scale fishing and leisurely shipping.

I came back to discover the third-largest container port in the world. Walking to avoid the traffic jams, I assessed the scope: more than two thousand factories operating and more being built to produce more plastics and paints, ships and steel, machine tools, fertilizer, chemicals, and petroleum. Already outdated, the official figure of two thousand did not include additional thousands of small plants that made parts for motorcycles, tractors, pumps, flashlights, radios, and hundreds of other light industrial products. Nor did it include hundreds of small plants processing foodstuffs or brewing oyster sauce, shrimp paste, soya sauce, chili oil, and other condiments.

Thirty-two flights a day now connect Kaohsiung and Taipei, where there had formerly been only the night train and the day train. Everyone over fourteen in Kaohsiung appeared to have been inspired to frenzies of diligence, perhaps under a spell. The inspiration was the spell—the vision of getting rich by hard work.

Cupidity—or, put more gently, material aspiration—is hardly a Chinese monopoly. Most peoples yearn to be rich. But few pursue riches as zealously as the Chinese—and few are as candid about that yearning as are the Chinese. They bow before three statuettes representing the primary goals of life, with embodied wealth foremost. They burn incense to the god of wealth, and they express admiration of plumpness, which bespeaks prosperity, with the compliment, *"Ni fa fu la!"* "You've put on riches!" On the Lunar New Year, their chief holiday, they exchange the greeting, *"Fa tsai!"* "Get rich!"

Those traits have been vital to the making of modern Taiwan. Most Chinese are born entrepreneurs. They are obsessed with wealth, and they love a gamble, a risk that is potentially profitable. Such men and women build great industrial and commercial enterprises. The discipline imposed by neo-Confucianism ensures that those enterprises thrive.

Add great adaptability, compulsive industry, and extraordinary ingenuity—and you have the open secret of Taiwan's success, which the regime on the mainland hopes to emulate. Only recently, Chinese were considered mechanical nincompoops. But the Communists supplied Silkworm missiles to Iran, and the Nationalists built many of the big tankers plying the Persian Gulf that were Silkworm's targets. The eager American consumer who makes the vast American market also made the Taiwan miracle. Furthermore, the American and Japanese companies' search for cheap labor led them to transfer production to Taiwan. The economy expanded very rapidly in a hospitable environment. First came the Confucian virtues: diligence, obedience, responsibility, orderliness, and education. Second came the Chinese lust for wealth and passion for gambling.

Moreover, a government once justly excoriated as repressive and backward had altered greatly. During the decade before his death in 1988, President Chiang Ching-kuo had become much more realistic. The relationship between the ruling Nationalist Party and the nominal government of China, the national and the provincial governments of Taiwan, is complex. But Chiang Ching-kuo was the ultimate authority—and the chief innovator. The administration that came to power after his death is equally firm in its public anticommunism—and was even more flexible in expanding contacts with the mainland until the June 4 massacre.

Many critical decisions are, however, still taken by refraining from bold decision. Instead, developments are quietly, often privately,

nudged in the desired direction. The government is structurally cen-
tralist and authoritarian. In the Confucian manner, departments,
boards, commissions, and bureaus abound, but Confucian reluctance to
interfere closely prevails in the economic realm.

The administration once decided to reduce punitive duties on imported wine and liquor—largely to please the Americans, who were
complaining loudly. No decree was sent down to the Taiwan Tobacco
and Wine Monopoly Bureau, which bitterly opposed liberalization.
Instead, journalists and academicians began writing about the abhorrent, but unavoidable, need to placate the Americans. After six months,
the Monopoly Bureau was outflanked. Yielding gracefully to public
opinion, which it had created, the government did what it had always
planned—and cut the duties.

Liquor duties were actually handled a little more forcefully than most
economic issues. When the Nationalists ruled the mainland, the Japanese invasion and the Communist revolt made it impossible for them
to leave well enough alone. They would have preferred to intervene
sparingly and thus permit the native ability and the native cupidity of
the Chinese people to ensure progress. That is the traditional Chinese
way, antedating even Confucianism. The old folk religion, Taoism, calls
it *wu wei*, "creative inaction." The Nationalist regime has been authoritarian. It has also been a laissez-faire dictatorship, wary of any action
that might hamper economic expansion.

Confucianism enjoined a man to cultivate his own virtue, rather than
worry about his neighbor's.[1] His perfect behavior would then inspire
others, including his neighbor, to virtue. Thus would arise a state that
was perfect because it was inhabited by perfect men practicing perfect
virtue, scrupulous honesty, and total obedience to their ruler.

Confucianism also enjoined every man to look after his own family
above all else. That practical injunction naturally overrode the abstract
duty to the state. Alliances made up of cousins to the tenth degree
provided mutual assistance and mutual defense against outsiders.
When a man became prime minister or a junior magistrate, his remote
relations *expected* to get government jobs and government contracts. If
he did not provide for them lavishly at the expense of the state, he would
be shamed.

Thus sanctified as a moral obligation, nepotism has always been
widespread—even more today, when there are so many more jobs to
hand out to the boys and even the girls. Although even the long-
underpaid bureaucracy now gets adequate wages, small-scale squeeze
is, as ever, endemic, but does little harm to the body politic. Although

---

[1] Women were enjoined to be modest and obedient, being deemed incapable of aspiring
higher.

somewhat reduced, large-scale corruption lingers, as it has lingered and expanded in even more prosperous Japan because the takings are so enormous. Official corruption is, however, no longer a *major* social ill.

Only Prime Minister Lee Kwan Yew of Singapore has purged a successful Confucian society of corruption—and that antiseptic cleanliness may not long survive his passing. The recruiting of airline stewardesses demonstrates the great difference between Singapore and Taiwan.

Singapore Airlines has earned a reputation for excellent service. Service on China Air Lines of Taiwan is at best lackadaisical.

"Above all, Singapore hires girls who *need* the jobs," explained an airline executive in Taipei. "Need is the first qualification, so they'll really buckle down. Next come intelligence, charm, and languages. For China Air Lines the first qualification is *not* needing the job. The daughters of the well-to-do want the travel and the glamour. They get their jobs through their families' pull, regardless of qualifications. Since nobody can fire them, the young ladies don't exactly break their necks."

The public domain is a happy hunting ground, and the environment also falls into the public domain. Since it belongs to everyone, it belongs to no one—and is, therefore, fair prey. Chinese who are intensely sensitive to the shading of a black-ink painting or the nuances of classical couplet are utterly insensitive to their surroundings. They simply do not see garbage mountains, or streams choked with debris that bubble with filthy effluent.

Taipei's air is so polluted it is officially classified as harmful to health one day in five. Rice fields are contaminated with cadmium, with imperishable plastic wastes, and with toxic effluvia. Along with Shanghai, Taiwan has the world's highest incidence of hepatitis, particularly hepatitis B. And the government is finally talking about cleaning up the rivers of northern Taiwan.

Blessed by neither climate nor terrain, Taipei is a very ugly city. Choking smog lies heavy in the bowl of hills that cups the city; the streams are slimy with refuse; and the roads are littered.

Residential neighborhoods are tormented by discos, by "barbershops" disguised as brothels, by abattoirs, and by sidewalk automobile repair shops. There are no zoning laws.

The torrent of motor vehicles is not just undisciplined, but chaotic. The innumerable bicycles that formerly made driving or walking perilous have largely been driven out by motor scooters and motorbikes, which are even more dangerous. Walking in downtown Taipei requires constant vigilance—and a wary eye on the cracked and buckling sidewalks. Driving means constantly dodging motorbikes while maneuvering through crooked lanes between cars parked helter-skelter.

Streets clogged by selfish parking appeared a nuisance that could be abated by firm measures employed elsewhere: wheel-clamping, towing, and punitive fines. I did not see them a symptom of a deep social malaise.

My impression was corrected by a man who has been a designer, a builder, and a captain of the powerful vessel that is Taiwan's economy. Between puffs on his steel-jacketed pipe, Minister of State Chao Yaotung declared that the moral and legal crisis Taiwan faced was epitomized by the chaotic parking.

"We suffer from much law breaking," he said. "I don't mean just the criminal side, but the economic side. For example, all high-rise buildings in Taipei must be built with big basements for parking. Those basements are then turned into supermarkets, discos, dance halls, and restaurants. That's why we have a terrible parking and traffic problem. It's also the reason those establishments evade taxes. They're illegal already, so . . ."

Mr. Chao, who was born in Shanghai in 1916, had a highly successful career, within government as well as outside. Still, he insists that he knows nothing about politics, only industry. Now chairman of the Council for Economic Planning and Development, he had for three years been minister of economic affairs.

He acquired his forthrightness, indeed bluntness, in America. In 1944 he took a master's degree in mechanical engineering at the Massachusetts Institute of Technology, having worked as a machine fitter in New Jersey and New York. Both his sons have also taken advanced degrees in the U.S., which Mr. Chao regards highly. He is also highly critical of the U.S., maintaining that Taiwan now possesses what America has lost.

"Foremen were very efficient and very powerful in America in those wartime days," he recalls. "Now there's no comparison. There is no spirit of hard work in the American factories I've seen recently—and the foreman's power has decreased sharply. With no discipline, how can anyone expect good production?"

That assessment is, further, based on his experience as a textile engineer, as an executive of private corporations, and as chairman of the highly successful government-owned China Steel Corporation. So is his guardedly optimistic assessment of Taiwan's future.

"We import almost all our energy, and we face strong pressure to cut our exports to the U.S.," he says. "But we'll be all right. We've got going for us lots of intelligent manpower that is still reasonably, not yet excessively, paid. Also a high standard of education, about the same as Japan. Higher than Korea, Singapore, and Hong Kong."

Chao Yao-tung's mouth and eyes are humorous, but his nose juts like the prow of a ship. Compactly built and muscular, though past seventy, he looks like a tough, self-made man. He actually came from a well-to-do family on the mainland.

I went directly from Chao Yao-tung's office to the Formosa Plastics Corporation Building, which is owned by a self-made Taiwanese. In his outer office hangs a scroll reading, JU YI, which means, "May you attain your heart's desire." In his assistant's office twin scrolls sum up the tough-tender official philosophy of the biggest corporation in Taiwan: "No quarter in battle! Magnanimous in victory!"

The man behind those sentiments, at once aggressive and chivalrous, is Chairman Wang Yung-ching. Tall and slender in a silky gray suit, Mr. Wang, who was born in 1917, looks like an aristocrat, even to his long, tapering fingers and his courtly manner.

But no Taiwanese was considered an aristocrat by the Japanese or by the mainlanders who took over the island after the war. Besides, he started with neither financial nor social advantages. His father was a small tea grower; his formal education ended with elementary schooling under the Japanese; and his first job was as an apprentice in a rice mill.

Wang Yung-ching is, by a modest estimate, personally worth more than $2 billion. The basis of his glory is PVC, humble polyvinyl chloride, which is hardly a new invention. He is the world's largest manufacturer of a product that has caused difficulties for both Du Pont and B.F. Goodrich, which is now the world's *second* largest manufacturer. All his creations, the Formosa Plastic Corporation and its subsidiaries, have an operating revenue comfortably in excess of $4 billion a year. (Their net income was more than $380 million, a profit of 9.4 percent on turnover—and a very comfortable 37.5-percent return on capital.)

Among the Taiwan corporations ranked by the glossy business monthly *Tien Hsia,* three of the first seven were Wang Yung-ching's. His Nan Ya Plastics was outranked only by the quasi-governmental Chinese Petroleum Corporation and the Taiwan Tobacco and Wine Monopoly Bureau.

Yet, only one other private corporation beside his three ranked among the top seven. Taiwan's great strength—and potential weakness—is the distribution of production among thousands of small and medium-sized companies. That configuration makes for flexible response to new demands. It also makes for vulnerability. Still, a colossus like Formosa Plastics is virtually invulnerable to passing trends.

"How do you do it?" foreigners regularly ask Mr. Wang. "What is your secret?"

He gladly shares part of his secret: workers put in 48-hour-weeks, executives 70-hour weeks, and the chairman a hundred-hour week. Those freehand figures allow him nine hours a day for sleep, meals, entertaining, and natural functions, as well as his regular jogging and swimming. His point is, of course, that Wang Yung-ching and his employees work a good deal harder than anyone else in the world, except some Japanese and some Koreans.

Like his own appearance, the classical Chinese quotations on the scrolls in his office are misleading. He spoke Taiwanese at home as a child, and his brief education was in Japanese, not Chinese.

In 1945 he heard Mandarin spoken for the first time. Today, despite a strong accent, he speaks with ease the language of the mainlanders, which is based upon the language of the mandarins who once ruled the Chinese empire.

I apologize for asking again a question he must have answered innumerable times: "Did you envision what was going to happen when you got into plastics? Did you have any idea where you'd end up?" A grin breaks his concentration, and he says, *"Mei-yu. Wo pu tso meng."* ("No, I didn't. I don't dream ahead.") After a moment, he adds, "I take one step at a time."

That simple statement from a simple, although most uncommon, man may sum up Taiwan's miracle. Like Wang Yung-ching, Taiwan took things as they came. Like him, Taiwan has been ambitious, diligent, disciplined—and very lucky. His account of his life—modest in the best Confucian manner—portrays a practical man who proceeded step by step—and is a little surprised by his immense success.

I continue looking for the hidden motor that drives one man to amass a vast fortune and to preside in a self-interestedly enlightened manner over more than forty thousand employees in Taiwan and America. His relations with his two sons and his eight daughters, as well as the three wives he married in succession, appear to be conventionally patriarchal in the traditional Chinese manner. I, therefore, concentrate on his own extraordinary career.

Apprenticed to a rice miller on leaving elementary school at the age of fourteen in 1930, he stayed in rice after the war. But business became difficult, he says, because of the "very unfortunate historical incident that occurred in 1947." That is a diplomatic description of the near revolt and the slaughter that followed a minor clash between Taiwanese civilians and mainland troops. In 1948 Wang Yung-ching went into the lumber business, which he found no more satisfactory. When dealing in rice, he had had great problems with the corrupt and inefficient bureaucracy. Afterward, he could not get enough timber.

"Most of my stock was imported," he recalls. "Even plywood we couldn't make, but had to import. So I began looking around for a substitute."

By 1955 Wang Yung-ching knew he had to get out of the lumber business. He had failed to make a go of either rice or timber, and he was thirty-eight years old. As he relives his life, his expression is calm, although his words are spirited. But his left knee jiggles up and down in the characteristic Chinese gesture that reveals and relieves tension. Recalling his commercial beginnings, he becomes vivacious.

He turned to plastic, he says, because it was cheap, low-risk, and virtually unknown in Taiwan. The American aid mission had introduced PVC, but no one knew quite what to do with it. He saw an opportunity. There was not enough lumber for the needs of new construction. Aluminum, steel, and tiles were also in short supply. Perhaps plastics could fill the need. Although he denies any grand vision, the outlines are emerging.

A grand vision is apparent in the thirteen-story Formosa Plastics Building, where half an acre on the ground floor is devoted to a permanent exhibition of plastic products. The chief exhibit is a house within a house: a full-scale reproduction entirely made of plastic, down to the skirting and the plumbing, not to mention bedspreads, curtains, and wallpaper. The dining-room table and chairs look like real wood, only a bit too shiny.

Mr. Wang found his substitute construction material three decades ago—and persuaded not just Taiwan, but the world to use it. Yet, he says, caution is his guiding principle. Having stimulated the Taiwan market with low prices and crusading education on plastic's versatility, he still concentrates on the Taiwan market. Only 20 percent of the output of the world's biggest plastic maker is exported directly. Taiwan's manufacturers use 80 percent of the output of the world's biggest plastic producer to make finished products, almost all for export.

Wang Yung-ching eschews the yachts, the multiple homes, the king's ransom in jewelry, and the other gewgaws that advertise the success of men who have made only hundreds of millions, not billions like himself. One self-indulgence on a grand scale, however, is his pushing ahead with a petroleum-cracking plant against the opposition of Taiwan's few environmentalists. The China Petroleum Corporation has annoyed him greatly by its high price for his basic raw material.

His days are, however, austere, particularly for a billionaire. He rises at 4:30 A.M. for Chinese calisthenics, jogging, and swimming. He gets to his office at nine, which is rather late for Taiwan, and his day closes at seven in the evening. He never vacations, but calls his frequent business trips to the U.S. his recreation. Yet a blizzard of telexes, faxes, and telephone calls keeps him on top of events in Taiwan.

By this time, I have gained some understanding of Wang Yung-ching, as well as the internal motor that drives him. Basically he is an old-fashioned Chinese businessman guided by Confucian principles. The family comes first: his brother, younger by four years, is president of the Formosa Plastics Corporation; his sons and his sons-in-law are the senior executives. There is no room for females at the top, not even daughters, and there is no room for a son or a son-in-law who has not proved himself on the production line. After that Confucian trial by hard work, promotion is very quick for the family.

"Everyone in the world must work," Wang Yung-ching asserts. "Otherwise, he has no right to be fed—or to live!"

Confucianism virtually invented paternalism, enjoining rulers to educate subordinates so that they might enjoy greater opportunity and work more efficiently. Mr. Wang's privately established Ming-chi Institute of Technology offers industrial management and industrial design; mechanical, chemical, and electrical engineering; and nursing. His major medical centers in Taipei and Kaohsiung treat his employees, operate research laboratories, and provide graduate medical training.

A highly practical Confucianist, Wang Yung-ching insists that every department of his schools and hospitals, like every component of his industrial empire, must pay its own way or, at least, keep strictly within its budget. Otherwise, he leaves the medical facilities alone. A decent restraint is also Confucian.

Intrigued by the oddity of a foreigner who can speak his languages, Mr. Wang presses me to join him at lunch. For the moment, however, he must excuse himself to deal with urgent business. He is off to confront the environmentalists again. Or, I wonder, to reason with them?

His assistant will not speculate.

But I can foresee the outcome of the encounter. Wang Yung-ching and the demonstrators will arrive at an amiable compromise. It will appear mutually satisfactory, but will really work in his favor.

Capable Taiwanese were virtually forced to make money after World War II, rather like the Jews in Europe some centuries earlier. Excluded from the professions, Jews went into money handling, which Christians avoided because lending at interest was considered sinful. Excluded from political and military careers, Taiwanese went into commerce and industry, which most mainlanders disdained.

But, as restrictions loosened, Taiwanese have advanced in politics and the military services, gradually at first, but rapidly after 1986. Moving into the higher echelons of the Nationalist Party and the government, Taiwanese have taken positions previously monopolized by mainlanders. Change came most dramatically at the very top. After President Chiang Ching-kuo died on January 8, 1988, his successor was Lee Teng-hui, a Taiwanese.

Skeptics said that appointment was like the sugar lumps smeared with opium with which lazy nursemaids soothed babies, a sop to lull the Taiwanese, who are 85 percent of the island's population. The skeptics contended that mainlanders' control of the executive organs of the

Nationalist Party would keep President Lee from acting decisively, even though three-quarters of the membership of the party was Taiwanese. A number of Taiwanese had risen to senior military rank, the skeptics noted, but none had attained high command.

Nevertheless, the Taiwanese are grasping more levers of political and military power. Moreover, President Lee Teng-hui has decisively reformed the leadership of the Nationalist Party. He dropped from the party's Central Executive Committee Chiang Wego, the former president's half-brother, ending the dynasty founded by their father.

Liberalization will, however, proceed on Taiwan. Youthful Minister Without Portfolio Wei Yung, chairman of the prime minister's Research, Development, and Evaluation Commission, is himself a mainlander, and, almost inevitably, an American Ph.D. He pointed out to me that the Nationalist party "must encourage liberalization if it is to remain in power." By the same reasoning, entrepreneurs must be given even more freedom if Taiwan is to continue to prosper.

That rationale may be selfish. But it is eminently enlightened self-interest.

Sometimes disconcerting, but usually refreshing is the way graduates of American universities talk about America. Most feel affection, but they also feel free to criticize bluntly. Chen Li-an, Ph.D. from New York University and minister of economic affairs, gets down to cases regarding the differences between Japanese and American practices.

"Americans overengineer," he says. "We can get switches from America for six dollars and from Japan for one dollar. The American switch will last forty years. The Japanese switch lasts ten years—all that's necessary. We purchase American equipment. Then departments reorganize . . . companies merge or split—and we can't get delivery. Getting a general-purpose computer from the U.S. takes six to eight months. The Japanese deliver in three days."

Respecting the Japanese, he also fears them, for he adds: "The Japanese teach our people to write specifications for new equipment only Japan can fill. Those who defend the Japanese say: 'We must work with them like a family.' The Japanese send teams of engineers, and they help with financing. Thus they know every detail of your technology and your finances. Thus they increase *their* family."

One counterstrategy can greatly benefit America, as well as Asia.

"We're trying to tap American resources, which are still enormous [particularly in basic research]," he says. "We target American companies that are not big enough to look for international opportunities on their own, middle-sized companies with sales between $100 and $200 million. And we show them the great opportunities here, so that we can work together."

American-educated men and women make Taiwan function—and
talk as candidly. Two in their middle forties are particularly interesting.

The successful man or woman on Taiwan is now preeminently neither
mainlander nor islander psychologically—and probably did graduate
studies in the United States. Two immediately come to mind, both in
their middle forties. Steven Hsieh is deputy director general of the
Science Based Industrial Park at Hsinchu south of Taipei. Diane Ying
is publisher and editor of the business monthly *Tien Hsia* (*Common
Wealth*). Dr. Hsieh comes of a Taiwanese family, while Miss Ying was
born in the ancient imperial capital of Xi'an on the mainland.

After thirteen years in America, Steven Hsieh gave up a professorship
to return to Taiwan "to serve China, my country." That decision to
return to Taiwan was much easier for Steven Hsieh than for his
mainland-born wife, whose family now lives in the U.S. Nor has Mrs.
Hsieh found much satisfaction in her work as a senior accountant for
McDonald's. His highly gratifying work is encouraging development of
industry that is based on advanced technology: super-chips, super-fast
computers, molecular biology, and genetic engineering.

"The most important thing that happened to me was also a key event
on Taiwan—land reform," he recalls emotionally. "My folks were tenant farmers. Without land reform, I'd never have gone anywhere. They
got their own land and they had a little spare money to help me. Also
they didn't need my labor on the land so badly. They weren't right up
against it."

After her father's death, Diane Ying and her mother were brought to
Taiwan by her uncle, a Nationalist Air Force officer who was fleeing the
Communists' advance. Her roots are on the mainland, but she is now
concerned above all with the reality of Taiwan.

She is the island's most successful journalist, her eminence recognized in 1987 by a Magsaysay Award, the all-Asian equivalent of a Nobel
Prize. The glossy monthly *Tien Hsia* (*Common Wealth*) is largely her
own creation, although, as she acknowledges with a grin, "It owes a lot
to both *Time* and *Fortune*."

She explains: "We don't get professors to write up their opinions on
complex issues in a complex way. Unlike most magazines here, we are
not hifalutin. Instead, we go for thorough reporting and clear, sprightly
writing. Those were major innovations in Chinese journalism when we
started in 1981."

I had assumed that Diane Ying would be the epitome of the glossy,
hard-edged businesswoman to the last lacquered hair. But she is neither
tough nor lacquered. In the slacks and pastel shirts she picks off the
racks of bargain shops, she is bouncy, plump, attractive, and enthusiastic.

After taking a master's in journalism at Iowa University, she was for two years a reporter for the *Philadelphia Inquirer*. Characteristically, her opinions are incisive—as is her candor.

IS THE U.S. BACKWARD? asks a cover line on *Tien Hsia*. It certainly is, answers the well-documented article inside. Elsewhere, Diane Ying warns Americans that the Japanese are taking over Taiwan's automobile industry, greatly assisted by Taiwan's dismantling its barriers to imports in response to American demands.

"We on Taiwan have devoted the past thirty years to economic development." She turns to a related issue. "Naturally, culture has suffered. We have culture in the museum, but there's no place in our lives for music, painting, and poetry. We're too busy making money."

Strange words, perhaps, from the editor and publisher of a business magazine. But Diane Ying's interests are wide. I suspect that she has not always been fascinated by the making of goods and money. When, with two friends and $7,500, she started *Tien Hsia* in 1981, she chose to concentrate on business reporting because economic development was *the* story on Taiwan. A good businesswoman as well as a good journalist, she chose the product with the greatest appeal.

Diane Ying is, however, deeply concerned with the fundamental currents of her society. She is, above all, concerned about girls and boys, about teenagers, and about men and women under twenty-five, who together make up 56 percent of Taiwan's population.

"All the old traditions are changing so fast," she says. "Education, hard work, saving money, all the virtues we were taught, don't count as much anymore. Instead, it's fun and spending. Like French and Italian restaurants with candlelight, red wine, and music. Young people are making a lot of money, and they're spending it all. . . . Remember, Chinese are all individualists—and they like to enjoy themselves."

Her plump features intent, she refines her meaning: "We're detached from our roots. And we don't have the artists and writers to focus our eyes on our own society. . . . All the old ways are being destroyed. Yes, I know it's happening everywhere. But it took more than two hundred years in the States. In Taiwan we've gone from basic agriculture to sophisticated industrialization in thirty years. No wonder . . ."

Her fears for the future turn naturally to the Japanese, and she says: "They're spreading their nets wide—over all Asia. The big Japanese trading companies control the import and export of most Taiwanese goods. They know better than the government does what's happening on the island. It's the Greater East Asia Co-Prosperity Sphere all over again. The Japanese don't only want to be number one, which they are already. They want to be number two and three also."

Diverting her from the prospect that terrifies so many Asians, I ask how the new prosperity affects the common people of Taiwan, those who are neither the gilded youth of the cities nor the American-educated elite.

"Taiwan's society is chaotic," she answers. "Some people are smoking marijuana and worse. They never did before. You know Chinese are so afraid of drugs because of the opium wars by which the West forced narcotics on the Chinese. There's also motorcycle drag racing on the roads. All illegal and many accidents.

"But it's the gambling that's worst. Chinese just love to gamble. The latest craze is called Everybody's Happy. Farmers and factory workers get together and bet heavily with bookies on the government's Patriotic Lottery. This leads to tragedies—broken families and crime. Bookies can't pay off, so they run away. Then gangs send hit men to get them. So we have murders, too."

She sums up, her words oddly at variance with her habitual smile, "It's worse here than in Japan or even Korea. The Japanese may be turning away from their emperor, but he's still there. The Koreans take it out in political strife. But we Chinese like to enjoy ourselves. Koreans and Japanese are naturally competitive. We Chinese are not. So, when the social fabric frays . . ."

When I suggest that Taiwan's woes are benign by comparison with those of many Western countries, Diane Ying agrees. The Philadelphia she knew in the late 1960s was more troubled than is Taipei today. Beside London or New York, Taipei's youth problem hardly appears grave.

Nonetheless, Taiwan is facing the gradual breakdown of a social order whose stability and security have depended upon the Confucian virtues. Filial piety was *the* foundation of society. Children unreservedly obeyed their parents in their late teens and twenties, even into their thirties and forties. But young people now have so much money of their own, and parents are bewildered by the new society growing up around them. Parental wisdom is questioned, and parental authority evaporates.

Virtue and consequent success thus consume themselves. Confucian tenets nurture the rapid growth of industry, which bestows much money on young people, making them independent. That independence then breaks down the common morality and the mutual responsibilities upon which Confucianism depends. The children of Confucian prosperity devour Confucianism values.

"We got rich, and that was good," Diane Ying says. "But we got rich too fast!"

Michael Hsiao put a scholarly gloss on Diane Ying's journalistic observations in his minuscule office at the Academia Sinica. It is Taiwan's equivalent of not only the Princeton Institute of Advanced Studies and the International Institute of Strategic Studies, but the Rand Corporation and the Smithsonian Institution. Like those intellectual communities, the Academia Sinica has many scholars, but no students.

Michael Hsiao, like Steven Hsieh, is a Taiwanese success story. His parents were tenant farmers who found a better life in the city after 1945, and he has an American Ph.D. in sociology. Before he turned forty he was a professor at Taiwan University, a research fellow of the Academia Sinica, and an activist vice-president of the National Consumers' Association. He is, above all, a perceptive professional observer of the changing society of his native island.

"I was born in 1948," he says. "Mine was the last generation to experience poverty at first hand. Mine was also the first generation to grow up amid prosperity and stability.

"Next was the 1960s generation—and they've had everything. We're only a few years older, but when we talk about defining our goals and suffering to attain goals, they can't quite comprehend what we mean. . . . They have much more freedom than we had, especially freedom of choice. Yet they're very hardheaded about reaching their very practical goals. We were naïve and idealistic, but they are pragmatic and materialistic. They really know how to get ahead."

Michael Hsiao muses aloud on the character of his elite students at Taiwan University, the island's premier institution of learning. His long face lights up with the joy of discovery behind his heavy glasses. Himself looking more like a student than a professor, he is finding new thoughts and shaping new concepts as he speaks.

"The new generation doesn't have much that is Confucian about it," he says. "Students are far more calculating. We were happy to work on a teacher's research project, because we were learning. The new lot feel they're working for the teacher's benefit, not that they're learning. . . . Anyway, they think they know it all already. They're interested in pleasure and in practical results, not in learning. That's why problems are building up with drugs and teenage sex . . . with heroin and very young pregnancies."

"In a Confucian society?" Moira asks.

"There is much conflict with parents." Michael Hsiao's tone is dispassionate. "Parents today want to be liberal—not authoritarian like their own parents. Today's parents confuse love with license. They can't balance necessary discipline with love for their children."

"And where is Taiwan going?" Moira asks. "Young people especially?"

"It seems to me this generation wants to be so Americanized it's going to destroy the basis of our prosperity," he replies slowly. "In the 1970s, people really worked, even for meager incomes. Now they won't. I don't blame them, but we're all becoming very self-indulgent. . . . A

major modification of behavior patterns is occurring very rapidly. . . .
You know, the trouble with Taiwan is we don't know where to put the
limits. We all want to be free and liberal. And we don't know where to
stop—or how."

Michael Hsiao is still young enough to see issues in black and white,
even though he is getting old enough to look askance at the younger
generation. I believe the issues are a little more complicated.

As Diane Ying pointed out, the Chinese lack the brute determination
to excel that motivates both the Japanese and the Koreans. As a group
the Chinese are not compulsive, but hedonistic. Having been unchallenged superiors for centuries, they are not driven to prove themselves.
Instead of working even harder when successful, they usually turn to
self-indulgence and amusement.

Yet Taiwan is the most impressive of Asia's miracles. Starting under
enormous handicaps, it developed so rapidly it has served as a model
for others, including South Korea. Because of the character of its
people, Taiwan is also the most fragile of those miracles.

4

South Korea: The Nation, Really Half a Nation, Once Voted *Least* Likely to Succeed

THE KOREANS CANNOT STOP, NOT EVEN TO CATCH THEIR BREATH. REACHING ONE TOWERING GOAL, THEY IMMEDIATELY BEGIN CLIMBING TOWARD THE NEXT. EVEN MORE CONFUCIAN THAN TAI-WAN, KOREA IS A NATION OF COMPULSIVE ACHIEVERS. KOREANS ARE COMPULSIVE BECAUSE THEY WERE DEEPLY HUMILIATED DURING THE MANY CENTURIES WHEN THEY WERE TRAMPLED ALTERNATELY BY CHINA AND BY JAPAN. THEY THEMSELVES JOKE: "THE JAPANESE ARE GOOD WORKERS . . . ONLY A LITTLE LAZY." BUT THEIR ADDICTION TO CIVIL VIOLENCE COULD IMPERIL THE WORLD'S FASTEST-GROWING ECONOMY.

Tear gas and euphoria filled the streets of Seoul on Monday, June 29, 1987. Although the caustic gas fumes were beginning to blow away, mass exhilaration was rising to a new crescendo. For the first time in many weeks, university students were *not* rioting in the capital of the Republic of Korea. Shuffling wearily in padded gray jumpsuits and hard black masks, like robots from the twenty-first century, the exhausted riot police had withdrawn to their barracks.

That Monday afternoon the people believed that they were entering an era of perfect democracy after the repression of the past quarter-century. Starkly dramatic because so matter-of-fact, the country's most powerful general had just pledged on television to dissolve the military regime and hold free elections.

Such a total concession had been totally unexpected—and frenzied rejoicing swirled through the city. By the solar calendar, it was a very hot midsummer day. By the political calendar, it was the first glorious day of a long-awaited springtime. Everyone knew that a splendid new era was opening, and even pessimists hailed "Korea, Year One." The world was new again, everyone was young, and hope gleamed brighter than fresh-minted silver coins. For the people of the nation that occupies the southern half of the Korean Peninsula, it was the Fourth of July, Bastille Day, and Runnymede all in one—and all for the first time. Yet Seoul had almost despaired only the day before, and pessimists had talked of civil war. One day the city had been battered by the violent riots that finally forced the generals to yield; the next day it rang with universal rejoicing.

Such immense swings of emotion are not unusual for Koreans. An intense and passionate people, they seem to live at one or the other extreme: either great suffering or great good fortune; either gray depression approaching despair or Roman-candle joy soaring to exaltation.

Now one of the most buoyant peoples on earth, only a generation ago the Koreans were among the most depressed. In the mid-1950s, shortly after civil war had scourged them both, the Republic of Korea, which was actually South Korea, and the Republic of China, which was actually Taiwan, were manifestly the two countries of Asia *least* likely to succeed.

South Korea looked even less promising than the star-crossed Nationalist regime on Taiwan. Despite friction between mainlanders and Taiwanese, internal discord did not threaten the existence of the Republic of China. But internal discord did threaten to tear the Republic of Korea apart. And, like Taiwan, South Korea lived under an acute external threat.

The forces of the Communist-ruled Democratic People's Republic of (North) Korea, having been driven back by American intervention after they invaded the South in 1950, were massed north of the Demilitarized Zone that divides the country roughly along the thirty-eighth parallel of longitude. The North only refrained from attacking again, it appeared, because the United States was totally committed to the defense of the South.

Three decades have passed, and the Koreans are prosperous and relatively secure—and as turbulent as ever. Shortly after the euphoria of June 29, students and strikers were again battling the riot police. Through the democratic elections of December 1987 and the triumphant Olympic Games of September 1988, civil disorder persisted. Even now, violent strikes occur almost daily, and demonstrators regularly hurl Molotov cocktails at the police to demand reunification with the North—as if the government could create a single nation by a single act.

Yet South Korea's prospects for the future are brilliant, even better than Taiwan's. The South can, by and large, defend itself alone today. Its military forces are far more effective than they were during the war; and it manufactures most of its own sophisticated weaponry. Besides, the American commitment to the defense of the South, although less vigorous, has endured.

Public demonstrations will undoubtedly continue—and will often be violent. The students, always the militant vanguard of a modern Confucian society, will riot to demand reunification and internal reform. They will not necessarily riot to destroy the government as they did in the spring of 1987, when they were supported by the new middle class and the discontented working class. Popular discontent now arises not from privation, but from the desire for betterment: a bigger share of the economic pie and greater individual liberty.

Fair shares could be given to all with no great strain. The great conglomerates that have long dominated the economy are, under heavy pressure, already paying their employees somewhat more. After spectacular growth on sweat-shop wages, the wealth available for sharing is growing rapidly. The Republic of Korea has had the fastest-growing economy in the world.

Foreign-exchange holdings tell the tale, as they do for Taiwan. Korea was some $45 billion in debt in mid-1987 because its growth had been financed by widespread borrowing. At the beginning of 1989, its foreign-exchange reserves were $15 billion, coincidentally the same as the growing annual surplus of exports over imports. The entire foreign debt has not yet been liquidated, primarily because it was more advantageous to pay it off gradually.

Even more revealing than foreign-exchange reserves, however, was per capita income. Each individual's theoretical share of the national income is calculated by dividing total population into GNP, all the goods and services produced in any one year. In 1986 the per capita income of the Republic of Korea was roughly $2,500. In 1987, a year of upheavals, it rose to nearly $3,000. In 1988 it was about $3,700. Short of a catastrophe, it was by 1990 to exceed $4,500. In 1961, when the generals took over, South Korea's per capita income was $87.

In the late summer of 1989, strikes and riots stemming from social discontent were perhaps a passing squall, perhaps harbingers of disaster, threatening the Korean miracle. Paul H. Kreisberg, one of the most gifted and reliable observers of Asia, reported that the country's growth rate had dropped from 12 percent in 1988 to 7 percent and that President Roh Tae Woo had privately warned that South Korea was on the way to becoming an "Asian Argentina." Kreisberg ascribed that sudden decline to stagflation, to the glaringly inequitable distribution of the wealth, and to rising corruption. His grave warning demanded grave consideration. Still, the Koreans had come through much worse storms in the recent past.

At 3:31 P.M. on Monday, June 29, 1987, glassware tinkled and crockery rattled as Korean Airlines Flight 66 from Taipei landed at Kimpo International Airport, outside Seoul. Moira and I craned to peer through the window. It was her first visit to Korea. It was my first return after fifteen years to the country where, from 1951 to 1953, I had spent the most exciting—and most terrifying—moments of my young life as a war correspondent.

Kimpo in 1987 looked like any other modern airport: a vast, shifting kaleidoscope of bright, gumdrop-colored buses, vans, and airplanes. Utilitarian and featureless despite the big sign reading WELCOME TO KOREA, it recalled a hundred other jet-age ports of entry. Having expected nothing else, I was still a little let down.

I had, of course, not expected to see the packed earth airfield, dusty in summer and ice-rimed in winter, where the bucket-seated DC-4 Skymasters the U.S. Air Force called C-54s had jolted on runways of linked metal plates to discharge passengers in crumpled field-green. We war correspondents had returned to this airfield after conscientiously misspent five-day leaves in Tokyo. I had certainly not expected to see again the shabby wooden terminal where we had waited for the brass: in the beginning generals, but later, as policy disagreements between South Koreans and Americans intensified, diplomats and politicians. Combining the dignity of all three callings, Dwight David Eisenhower, president-elect and General of the Army, had, as promised in his campaign for the presidency, duly appeared in Kimpo in December 1952, in a round fur hat and a parka with a wolverine-trimmed hood.

In June 1987 that hectic past had not *entirely* vanished. Seeking its berth, the 747 lumbered around the periphery of the airfield. Instead of sandbagged revetments and barbed wire, a high cement-block wall enclosed the field. Between the rolls of barbed wire on the wall stood glass-enclosed sentry boxes.

A sentry waved at the 747, enjoying the slight break in the monotony of his watch for an invisible enemy. The silhouette of a twentieth-century infantryman was achingly familiar against the fierce afternoon sun, although his rifle and his field uniform were better than those of his predecessors, thirty-odd years before. The long barrels of antiaircraft guns snuggled under camouflage netting, and somewhere out of sight the surface-to-air missiles awaited the radar's command.

Everything had changed except the essentials: armed threat and armed response. South Korea clearly still considered itself at war thirty-four years after the signing of the armistice. A cabal of generals had for twenty-five years justified its heavy-handed rule as essential to mobilizing the nation against the Communist menace. That justification seemed thin to me. Yet the Army of the Democratic People's Republic of Korea was not massed north of the border solely for defensive purposes—no more than it had been in June of 1950. Since appearances had altered, but not the underlying reality, it appeared that South Korea would remain a repressive front-line state.

A wiry, nervous bureaucrat called Byung Goog Yug had been sent to meet Moira and me by the unfortunately named Ministry of Culture and Information. If the terminal had been on fire, Mr. Yug might have shortened the ritual of welcome by a few minutes. Driven by greater urgency, he virtually omitted the normal courtesies to speak directly from his own emotion.

"We are all celebrating," he declared. "This is a day of general celebration. . . . All Korean citizens are very happy today!"

Then, a little calmer, he reported the astounding denouement of the crisis that had wracked Korea for more than a month. Students demonstrating to demand popular election of a new president had won widespread support, and most Koreans had expected the army to take over from the battered riot police. The last time the army had intervened was in 1980, and more than a hundred people were massacred. But the army had not intervened this time. Instead, the general had suddenly granted the students' demands—and had spontaneously promised other liberal reforms, even true freedom of the press.

The enthusiasm of a middle-aged, middle-rank bureaucrat like Byung Goog Yug showed how widespread resentment was against military rule. The fervor of a twenty-four-year-old university senior who had cautiously stood on the sidelines of the demonstrations was even more revealing. Jung Hyung-min, who was to be our interpreter for the next two weeks, was like an earnest puppy just given the biggest, meatiest bone ever seen.

As we crossed one of the sixteen bridges spanning the Han River, which, during the war, had been spanned only by a wobbly pontoon bridge, Hyung-min pointed to a sixty-three-story skyscraper. It was, he told us proudly, the second-highest building in Asia. But his tourist-guide patter dried up, and he beamed behind his glasses and burst out, "Koreans have already made an economic miracle. Now we'll make a political miracle! We'll create *real* democracy here in Korea, where it's never existed before!"

The initial miracle had occurred earlier that day. General Roh Tae Woo, designated by President Chun Doo Hwan (general, Army of the Republic of Korea, ret.) as his successor, had met with the executive committee of the administration's Democratic Justice party to outline his strategy for dealing with disorder. When the television cameramen began to pull the plugs of their cables in order to leave the politicians alone, General Roh Tae Woo had motioned them to stay. His every word and gesture were recorded on film and tape, as was the astonishment of the executive committee when he told them he did not propose to fight.

The next presidential election, he said, would be decided not by the packed legislature as in the past, but by a popular vote that would

choose among rival candidates. And the election, although scheduled
for the following spring, would take place before the end of 1987.
Moreover, Kim Dae Ying, a leading opposition politician and presidential candidate, was to be released immediately from house arrest. It
would be a national catastrophe, Roh Tae Woo warned, if the Olympic
Games scheduled for Seoul in September 1988 were withdrawn in fear
of civil disorder. To avert that catastrophe, he had promised wide
reforms that went far beyond the students' demands.

For the rest of that day, the general behaved like the presidential
candidate he had just become. Continuous television programs not only
broadcast his speech over and over again, but showed his hectic activity.
He visited a hospital; he paid his respects at a shrine for the war dead;
he flew to Pusan, the country's second city; he attended a formal
political dinner at a *kisaeng* house, [1] and he called at the Blue House to
see President Chun Doo Hwan, who looked glum.

The details of their talk were not revealed. But almost everything else
was. Roh Tae Woo, the lawgiver, dominated that extraordinary day. It
was like watching the descent of Moses from Mount Sinai with the
tablets of the law relayed in full color and stereophonic sound—before
he saw the golden calf. Aside from commercial breaks, General Roh Tae
Woo was constantly visible, repeatedly uttering the same words and
repeatedly performing the same candidate's rituals.

The American Forces Korea Network, however, restricted its coverage to its scheduled newscasts and to Cable News Network, which,
rather eerily, showed Seoul what America was seeing happen in Seoul.
A considerate guest, eager not to offend the host by directly depicting
internal affairs, AFKN nailed the banner of normalcy to its mast: it
broadcast a drama about the Mafia, which was comfortingly familiar
down to the last killing and the last cliché, preceded by a young woman
called Roberta Baskin interviewing that perennial crusader Ralph
Nader on the iniquities of the cosmetic industry.

Korean television was, by that time in the evening, getting its second
wind—and was soliciting the world's reaction to that day's events in
Seoul before the world was quite sure what was happening. Interviews
with American and British foreign correspondents in Seoul were followed by interviews with editors in Hong Kong and Tokyo. Electronic
incest gave way briefly to other imperatives: soccer for the insatiable
fans of the world's most popular sport; and a relentlessly didactic
program in which the principles of electromagnetism were expressed
first in complex mathematical formulas and then demonstrated by

---

[1] The Korean equivalent of the Japanese men-only geisha party. Entertainment and alcohol
are the main purposes. Sexual activity, if it occurs, is a private arrangement between guests
and *kisaeng*.

simple moving models. The world's reaction was sought even more avidly the next day. Between more interviews with foreigners flashed the headlines of newspapers from Florence, Paris, and Frankfurt to London, New York, and Tokyo.

That characteristic concern with outsiders' opinions demonstrates that Koreans' self-confidence still requires external buttressing. South Korea has been truly independent, albeit only half a nation, for some forty years—after centuries of subjugation to China and Japan. And backward North Korea still lies under a deadening Stalinist dictatorship.

Equally characteristic was the compulsive self-improvement of the television lesson in electromagnetism. Intense effort achieved Korea's miracle, intense effort and obsessive stress on education. Since more than 98 percent of the adult population is truly literate, Koreans can use old skills productively and learn new skills readily. Education could not pause, not even on the glorious twenty-ninth of June, when a new era opened.

The election campaign that began the following day ended in mid-December with a victory for Roh Tae Woo. He won 36 percent of the vote, a remarkable share for the man looked upon as the heir of the discredited military regime. His two chief opponents, each a major political figure, won not quite 54 percent of the vote between them. That was obviously enough to have elected either one handily, although each lagged about ten percentage points behind Roh.

But neither opposition candidate would defer to the other. They could, perhaps, have struck an Israeli-style compromise, taking turns at holding the office, but structural problems would have made such a deal difficult (Korea holds a direct presidential election, rather than an indirect prime-ministerial election through a parliament). The Koreans demonstrated clearly that they were even more intransigent than Israelis.

It was not a wholly clean election. No Korean election has ever been wholly clean. But it was not blatantly rigged. The defeated opposition made charges of widespread intimidation and ballot-box stuffing. Some of the charges were undoubtedly true.

Still, the impartial American observers invited to inspect the process found no gross irregularities—as they would if there had been any. Major intimidation could not be concealed. Besides, the opposition was eager to parade its grievances. The charge that Roh Tae Woo had stolen the election could, at the very least, not be proved.

A separate election under similar conditions actually gave a clear majority in the National Assembly to the opposition, which enabled them to unite and then attack the administration. That voluble, intel-

ligent opposition boded well for Korea's progress, although true democracy in the Anglo-Saxon sense was not likely to appear in this decade
or the next. Yet Roh Tae Woo, who stood for stability and prosperity as
well as political reform, clearly commanded great public support. Having continued their demonstrations throughout the campaign, student
leaders were deeply disappointed on the presidential election night.
They tried to whip up a mass protest, but the demonstration was so
feeble the riot police ignored it. Middle- and working-class support had
deserted the students.

The race toward economic and educational goals resumed the next
day, if it had ever paused. Koreans do not like pausing. They have had
to run very fast to keep up—and very much faster to pull ahead.
Opportunities have been great, but so has competition.

No more than Taiwan could Korea have emerged from the chrysalis
of poverty into the full-winged glory of an NIC, a Newly Industrialized
Country, without the apparently insatiable American consumer. If
Americans had not bought incessantly, Korea's endeavors would have
been in vain. Yet, given an opportunity, they seized it as few nations in
Asia—or elsewhere—have. Others lack the Korean qualities of dili-
gence, ingenuity, foresight, and self-discipline—in sum, the paramount
Confucian virtues.

The rise of the Republic of Korea further required great patience and
deep humility. Those qualities are not inborn in Koreans, who are
inherently proud, rash, and contentious. But self-restraint was essential
to survival under both alien and native tyrants.

I saw that virtue displayed when I went to the Business Center of the
Shilla Hotel to send a telex reporting our arrival. Even on the day a new
era began, business was continuing normally—and it was normal to
conduct business at ten in the evening.

A blond woman of about thirty was seated with a Western man and
two Korean men on easy chairs at the far end of the room. In a
penetrating accent that was unmistakably American, she said, "No, you
don't *have* to. . . . You don't *have* to put everything through the test.
Not *every* one. *Only* those you hope to sell to us!"

One of the Koreans spoke softly, too softly for me to hear.

The American man replied, in a tone heavy with mock concern, "I
want to be sure, Mr. Park. It's important to me. Do you understand?
Are we communicating?"

Such language, bullying and patronizing, may be normal in American
business dealing. It is humiliating to sensitive Koreans. There may well
be a reckoning some day.

Among my many homecomings in Asia, Korea was for me the most
moving. I had been there only twice since the end of the war in 1953:

once in 1968 to cover the expected release of the crew of the U.S. Navy spy ship *Pueblo* by North Korea, and again in 1972 to take part in an academic conference on the press.

I clearly remembered Seoul as it had been on October 12, 1953, when I left after covering almost two years of war and three months of armistice. No more than a dozen large buildings were still standing, and none was intact. Seoul was then no longer a true city, no longer a focal point of human life, a center of commerce and culture.

Alone in the transparent nose of a B-26 bomber, I watched the runway of Kimpo Air Base fall away beneath me. It was like flying on a magic carpet. Riding in front of the engines' noise, I was alone in the silent sky, behind a film of Plexiglas.

I was sick of Korea on that long-ago Columbus Day. I had not been out of the country since July 27, 1953, when an armistice was signed between the Communist forces (China and North Korea with support from the Soviet Union) and the United Nations Forces (the U.S. and South Korea, with substantial reinforcement from sixteen other countries).

How long ago it really was became clear when I looked at the faded list of the military units that preserved the Republic of Korea from aggression. The United Nations Forces, Korea, were the last grand parade of the old world, united by a new peril five years after having triumphed together over German Nazis, Italian Fascists, and Japanese militarists.

The French fought in Korea, and as usual fought very well, as did the Belgians and the Dutch. From Asia came Filipino and Thai units. The Greeks sent eight DC-3 transports, which they rapidly lost—not to enemy action, but to "operational accidents," which meant pilot error. The Greeks' hereditary enemies, the Turks, were magnificent soldiers, if occasionally irritating allies.

Nearly fifty thousand men of the British Commonwealth came to Korea, including an Indian field hospital. The medics were noncombatants, for India was nonaligned. But India was then also a member of the British Commonwealth, and the United Nations had sanctioned the enterprise.

Those nations went to war because of American resolution—and a technicality. The Soviet Union was boycotting the Security Council in June and July 1950 to protest against the United Nations' failure to replace the Chinese Nationalists with the Chinese Communists. Relieved of a Soviet veto, the United States pushed through resolutions authorizing a joint response, under the blue-and-white United Nations flag, to the North Korean invasion.

The North's initial victories drove the UN forces into a cramped perimeter around Pusan in the extreme southeast, but the invaders were thrown back in September by a daring landing far behind their lines, at Inchon on the west coast, near Seoul. That was the finest moment of the UN Commander-in-Chief, General of the Army Douglas MacArthur. When his troops reached the border with Manchuria, regular troops calling themselves the Chinese People's Volunteers entered the conflict—and transformed it into a positional struggle like the trench warfare of World War I. Two years of negotiations finally produced an armistice that left the two sides just about where they had been when the fighting began.

The commitment to Korea was the first all-out United Nations response to aggression. The first, the biggest, and, we can now realistically hope, the last conflict between the massed conventional forces of the East and the West was, quite appropriately, fought in Korea.

For centuries, Korea had been the high road between China on the Asian mainland and Japan—and, therefore, a battlefield for others' wars as well as its own. The Koreans excelled in many endeavors, even in the art of war. But they were too small in numbers to fend off any but the Japanese—and them not always. The Koreans perfected many techniques, whether improved bows for archers or finer glazes for pottery. But they were overwhelmed culturally and militarily by the sheer weight of their neighbors on the Asian continent. If it were not China invading and subjugating them, it was Mongols or Manchus.

Ground between their powerful neighbors, the Koreans became touchy, proud, hard-drinking, and argumentative. They also became great tellers of tales; that is, they learned to evade or temper oppression by deceit. Under harsh Japanese occupation during the first half of the twentieth century, they also learned to hold authority in contempt—and not only alien authority. They became accustomed to defying authority and to employing public violence in political disputes.

On the other side of the globe, another people, insular, rather than peninsular, developed similar traits under similar pressures. Almost inevitably, the Koreans became known to the West as the Irish of the East.

The Koreans were fortunate in having not one, but two enemies who could often be played against each other. They were also more fortunate than the Irish in living in a less gentle environment, in enduring a particularly harsh climate. They had to develop the habit of hard work to survive, and the Korean language, unlike Irish, was never overwhelmed by a neighbor's language.

National languages are trails that reveal their speakers' past and character. Transmitted across Central Asia, from Turkish origins, the Korean language reveals a people drawn close together by the pressure of having larger neighbors. In grammatical structure, Korean is very much like Japanese: suffixes are piled upon suffixes attached to basic roots to convey changes of meaning, rather like Latin run amok. Like Japanese, Korean borrowed both the Chinese writing called ideograms[2] and many Chinese words. The Korean pronunciation of those borrowed words is closer to Chinese than is the Japanese pronunciation. Moreover, *all* Korean names are of Chinese origin, whereas almost all Japanese names are native.

Nonetheless, the Korean language is unique—and in one respect uniquely superior. The native writing system owes nothing to outsiders. *Hangul,* which means "Korean letters," was invented by a committee of scholars commissioned by King Sejang the Great in 1443 to develop a phonetic script for the common people. It is ingenious and compact. Twenty-four fundamental letterlike shapes come together in different combinations to form square blocks. Each block is a distinct syllable and, often, a separate word. In part because of the simplicity of *hangul,* adult literacy is today virtually universal.

Although the Great King wished to free the common people from the burden of learning Chinese ideograms, he did not wish to replace those ideograms entirely in literary works or in official documents. Today, however, Korea is discarding the ideograms that link it to the other great cultures of the Far East.

That trend is deplored as chauvinism by conservatives, who warn that it will cut off the next generation from the literature and the history of their past. It is deplored by internationalists because it will isolate Korea culturally from its neighbors. The utilitarian North has totally abandoned Chinese ideograms, and the general who established the military regime in the South wanted to do the same. That revulsion is in part a reaction to the recent past, when educated Koreans spoke Korean for domestic purposes, but Japanese for public purposes.

Korean had become a second-class language in its own country. During two years there, I learned no more than a half-dozen words, although I usually pick up a smattering of a language quickly. But I had no need to learn Korean. Everyone with whom I dealt spoke English, Chinese, or Japanese. Until the present generation, Koreans had not in the twentieth century used their own language for administration, they used Japanese; for education they used Japanese and Chinese; and for high culture they used classical Chinese.

During the past hundred years Korea has lived through four major wars: Sino-Japanese, Russo-Japanese, World War II, and UN-Communist. Forty years of Japanese hegemony were followed in 1945 by division

---

[2] Ideograms are so called because each one, by and large, represents an idea rather than a sound. Similarly, the numeral 1 always has the same meaning, whether it is pronounced *ein* in German, *une* in French, *eck* in Hindi or, for that matter, *yee* or *yat* in different Chinese dialects.

into a Soviet Zone in the north and an American Zone in the south, which became, respectively, the Democratic People's Republic of Korea and the Republic of Korea.

The Soviets armed the North heavily; the United States hardly armed the South at all because its first president, Syngman Rhee, Ph.D., Princeton University, frightened his American sponsors with bellicose talk. Afraid that he would attempt to reunify the country by force, the Americans left his meager armed forces virtually devoid of artillery, tanks, and warplanes. Worse, official American statements led the Communists to believe that the U.S. would not defend the ROK. Vulnerability invited attack—and on June 25, 1950, tank columns of the North Korean People's Army lanced into the virtually defenseless South.

In 1952 I wrote an article on Korea for *The Reporter*—my impressions of a very poor farming country broken on the rack of war. The article conveyed the commonplace sights, sounds, and smells of daily life. Over all hung the stenches of Korea at war: sour rice, urine, excrement, rotting meat, gangrenous wounds, and the sharp tang of DDT, the miracle insecticide that was then still effective against disease-bearing lice, although not for long. The counterpoint was the pungent odor of *kimchi*, garlic-laden cabbage preserved in brine against the long winters when no vegetables grow. Syngman Rhee was the only Korean I met in those days who did not exhale *kimchi* like a fire-breathing dragon. In the spring, the sullen, musty smell of old, earth-stained snow and ice, which is rather like very dirty, very damp socks, was supplanted by the primeval fragrance of fresh-turned earth.

In the spring the forsythia flung its golden tendrils over old gray stone walls. But the flowers had no scent, not even the faint fragrance one catches elsewhere. None of Korea's sparse flowers had any marked fragrance, certainly not the scarlet poppies that bloomed in the rocky valleys under the muzzles of the big guns.

The earth, the Koreans said, was tired after millennia of intensive cultivation, too exhausted to produce more than undersized flowers with spindly stalks. The earth itself seemed ancient beyond imagining. I could envision the great dragons of Far Eastern folklore stalking across the bare, boulder-strewn ridges. The people of Korea lived against the backdrop of the jagged ravines that cut through the barren mountains to make meager valleys.

The women held together with incessant effort whatever remained of normal life amid danger and dislocation. Most were spectacularly unattractive by Western standards—not only because they were very dirty, but because they were wrung by labor and deprivation. They had no choice but to be dirty, although most rather pathetically tried to wash their coarse clothing and their thick bodies in half-frozen, silt-laden streams. They wore canoe-shaped shoes of black or white rubber, with no difference between left and right; bell-shaped skirts of blanket cloth that exposed their bare, chapped red ankles; and bolerolike bodices tied with bows, which left their nipples free for nursing children up to two or three years old.

Some women carried heavy burdens strapped to their backs on the *chige*, the wooden rack we called an A-frame because of its shape. The A-frame was, however, normally a masculine prerogative. Tortoiselike under the carapaces of their burdens of artillery shells or gasoline drums, older men clambered up the hills to the trenches where the young soldiers waited. Behind the lines, I saw graybeards toting enormous loads of rice or firewood, almost hidden under sacking and branches.

Rather mysteriously, I occasionally came upon groups of young male civilians, aflame with alcohol, roistering down the roads in the early afternoon. Yet, all the young men had presumably been inducted into the armed forces. Most visitors saw only women, children, and old men in the thatch-roofed villages with their crumbling adobe walls, their muddy paths, and the strips of dried octopus hanging from their spindly eaves. Having been fought over three or four times within a single year, no village was untouched. Most were half-destroyed, and many were totally destroyed. No stick or stone stood more than four feet high, other than a few tenacious chimneys.

The villagers hardly glanced up when outsiders appeared. Their small eyes, slitted defensively, were almost invisible in their wind-burned red cheeks. They seemed sullen. They were actually so depleted physically and emotionally by the unending battle to survive that they could not rise to curiosity about their alien visitors. Anyway, by the second year of the war, most Koreans had already seen too many foreign soldiers.

I remember few sunny days; somehow, the atmosphere is always bleak in memory, and the people are dour and drab.

Koreans are not given to bright colors. Even their automobiles are gray or black. They prefer subdued shades, except for their traditional formal costumes, when women wear brilliant blues, violets, and reds, or a farmer comes to town for the day in the traditional white cloth jacket and white cloth trousers tied at the ankle.

I remember ghostly gray figures flitting through the rain under gray paper umbrellas between projecting roofs of cracked gray tiles. Even the light is subdued, except when I see again the waxen dead, borne down twisting red earth trails under a gloating noon sun, on litters improvised from dark green rubberized ponchos strung on rifles.

The press billets in the old Naija Apartments in Seoul were our refuge. Correspondents' lives centered on the two three-story blocks with antique iron fire escapes straggling down raw cement walls. The wire services, the networks, the larger newspapers, and Time-Life had their own suites. Hardly luxurious, those suites were not even comfortable when six men worked, slept, and entertained in two rooms, each room measuring about ten by fifteen feet. But they were home— and each possessed a cramped Japanese toilet cubicle and a minuscule washbasin.

In the bitter Korean winter, the headquarters company of the First Marine Division slept on canvas cots inside two down-filled sleeping bags with two blankets on top and two blankets underneath. Often the marines woke to find the shaving water frozen in the basin on the kerosene heater that had burned all night. But correspondents were warmed by central heating when in Seoul.

One winter morning, however, I woke and stared in amazement. Twelve slender columns of strawberry ice rose surrealistically at the foot of my cot, each crowned by a cork. A case of red wine had frozen during the night when the central heating failed.

The big freeze lasted for a week before the furnace was repaired. We tried typing in thick gloves and found it impossible. The charcoal fumes of the hibachis regularly poisoned the unwary, who had to be carried out to the subarctic fire escapes to recover.

Even for pampered correspondents, Korea was a harsh and hostile environment. The press billets were, by Western standards, a glorified slum. Vastly overcrowded, the plumbing inadequate, they were noisy and dirty. But they were unimaginably luxurious to most Koreans, as well as to generals and cabinet ministers.

When I left in 1953, the Naija Apartments were one of no more than a dozen public buildings still substantially intact. Also standing were the shattered Capitol, with its great dome; the presidential residence, called the Blue House; City Hall; the Bando Hotel; and an old royal palace that had been taken over by the American Embassy.

So scarce was accommodation that I once tracked down the acting prime minister sleeping in a room above a bakery. I had to talk with him, but I didn't like leaving my jeep unattended at four in the morning. Jeeps were constantly being stolen. Parking was no problem. The entire city was one vast parking space. Leveled by war, it was virtually without cars. Civilians were prohibited from returning because the battered capital could house no more than fifty thousand.

Deserted then, Seoul now accommodates a population of almost 11 million in an area of about 240 square miles. If it were not for the elevated roadways that snake through the downtown areas, the dense traffic would lock into immobility. Those roadways sweep close to second-story windows to reveal one root of Korea's prosperity. In hundreds of sweatshops pale women and men toil over sewing machines, producing the cheap, attractive clothing that was the first major export.

The heyday of those sweatshops is already passing. Korea is being pursued by Indonesia in textile production, normally the first breakthrough for an emerging nation. Besides, the pale women and men are protesting their long hours and their low pay, which is, nonetheless, several times the pay in Indonesia.

At night the main streets of Seoul are speckled with yellow light. Because the national taste is subdued, there are few colored lights or signs. The streets are, however, astir with pedestrians, mostly in their teens. Koreans are young: 60 percent of the population of 43 million is under forty. Many of the pedestrians are students attending night classes. So many well-qualified applicants besiege secondary schools and universities that all cannot be accommodated in the daytime. Besides, many teenagers work during the day, for compulsive diligence begins young. They pile into taxis for even a few blocks, since fares are low to keep the overcrowded city moving.

Yet public transportation is excellent. Seoul's subway is spectacular even in Asia, where both Hong Kong's and Tokyo's subways are attractive and efficient. Neither can challenge the grandeur of Seoul's, which displays replicas of ancient Korean art and an ever-changing exhibition of contemporary Korean art. Big public buses, all Korean-built, display efficiency almost brutal in its simplicity. Most municipal buses elsewhere have two rows of double seats with a narrow aisle between them. In Seoul, single seats extend along the sides, and the aisle is so wide the interior of the bus appears cavernous. Obviously, many more can ride standing than sitting.

That efficiency reached its apogee in the Seoul Olympic Organizing Committee, known by the unlovely acronym SLOOC. Moira and I saw the site just 440 days before the opening of the Olympic Games on September 17, 1988. We knew the exact figure because big illuminated signs throughout Seoul counted the days to the opening ceremony that would mark the Republic of Korea's attainment of maturity in the community of nations.

Koreans' fervid anticipation of the Olympics was already so high that it ensured political reform. General Roh Tae Woo had declared on June 29, 1987, that demonstrations must be halted at any cost and democracy instituted, lest the nation suffer the ultimate humiliation of losing the games. An editor I know synthesized national opinion when he said, "After being kicked around for centuries, my country is finally winning recognition as an equal, free nation in the world through the Olympics."

Korea was to win much more than recognition as an equal, free nation. It was to be hailed as a model of efficiency, intelligence, and tact

for its splendid hospitality to the Olympics. Even the few minor incidents burnished Korea's luster because they were so handily settled. All
the world now knows how brilliantly Seoul mounted and managed the
Olympics. The painstaking preparations were virtually complete 440
days before the grand opening.

For most nations, that would have seemed plenty of time. Some have
still been building when the Olympic flame was borne into the stadium.
But SLOOC had, a year and a half before the opening, already completed and tested every facility from the corps of interpreters to the new
roads and the ample new accommodations for visitors. Only the roof of
one secondary arena required a few finishing touches.

SLOOC had also solved the problem of financing those temporary
accommodations. It simply made them permanent. Each apartment
designed to house several athletes had already been sold to the family
that would move in after the games. The Tourism Board was equally
confident that five thousand additional hotel rooms would be filled
regularly once the games had put Korea on the map.

Korean confidence was based on meticulous efficiency and obsessive
hard work throughout the country. Every morning at six, a task force
of fifteen young men and three young women in crisp white sweatshirts
and shorts swept over the extensive terraces and the hillside surrounding the Hotel Shilla's swimming pool. Joking, gossiping, and laughing,
they polished tiles and chromium, swabbed down decks and counters,
wiped dew from tables and chairs. They even manicured each blade of
grass individually.

Not only places frequented by foreigners were immaculate. Provin-
cial trains and buses were spotless, and their windows sparkled. Even
Pusan, a port city that I remembered as a good deal dirtier than
Calcutta, was trying hard to clean up its act—with success.

Luck was also on Korea's side. Our interpreter and informant on
turbulent youth, Jung Hyung-min, insisted that miracles were occurring every day. Almost all Asians believe luck decides human fate—and
all of them avidly woo good luck. Perhaps that faith softens the logical
rigor of the Confucian tradition, or perhaps they are simply more candid
about their superstition.

In the spanking new Olympic Tower, the elevators were numbered
1, 2, 3, 5. Elsewhere, indicators read: 1, 2, 3, F, 5. (F stands for "four"
in English, the country's second language.) The number four is pronounced roughly *shee* in Korean, which is very much like the word for
death. To be absolutely sure, some buildings omit both the fourth and
the thirteenth floors—another kind of Westernization.

Like the Chinese, the Koreans seem to become more superstitious
as they prosper. But the Koreans are *not* Chinese of any kind, despite
close cultural ties. Emphatically themselves, they have already altered

markedly on their epic journey to modernity. Dr. Nam Duk Woo, a former prime minister and one of the chief makers of modern Korea, agreed emphatically with my observation that "economic growth has transformed the character of the people."

Certainly I found it hard to connect the smiling, vigorous, healthy, ambitious, and boundingly optimistic Koreans of today with the dour, close-faced, scowling people I had known during the war. Those Koreans were aggressively pessimistic—and sour enough to turn milk.

I have always admired the Koreans for their proud endurance of great suffering. But most outsiders found them bad-tempered and brutal. I once saw a division commander enforce the speed limit by shooting an offending driver.

George Suh, my oldest surviving Korean friend, recalled that his wife, a Korean educated in Japan, protested against coming back to Seoul after their long residence in Tokyo.

"I really love Korea," she said. "But the thought of going to the market in Seoul! Everyone is unbearably rude—and so unhappy. I hate that great Korean stone face!"

She no longer sees that great stone face. All has not changed, as continuing civil strife demonstrates. But Koreans are obviously far happier today.

Human beings do not live by bread alone, but they can pursue spiritual, aesthetic, or scientific goals far better when they have enough to eat. Amid relative plenty, Koreans today seek nonmaterial goals. Buddhism is enjoying a revival, as is Christianity, which claims the devotion of 20 percent of the people.

Prosperity has not, however, dulled the edge of material competition. I like to check on elevator operators, security guards, receptionists, and salespeople, all of whom spend much time waiting. The broad Korean faces with the split-pea eyes are usually bent over textbooks, studying. English is the most popular subject, followed closely by mathematics, for which Koreans share the general East Asian flair.

Conversely, full-time university students sally early into the business world. Jung Hyung-min, our interpreter, proffered a visiting card identifying him as the president of the Student Interpreters Association of the Hankuk [Korea] University of Foreign Studies.

Intense ambition has made the school system so competitive that until recently the authorities banned outside coaching. No professional tutoring was permitted. Some parents were afraid to help their own children, for proficiency markedly above the norm aroused suspicion. The purpose was, however, *not* to make all students equal in attainment. The purpose was twofold: to keep capable students who could not afford tutoring from suffering; and second, to keep the fight for honors from getting *too* nasty.

Student competition, like business competition, is often ugly. When a nearsighted twelve-year-old forgot her glasses, none of her classmates, not even her closest friend, would read the blackboard for her. Her father suggested that she keep an extra pair in her desk at school. She replied sadly, "Daddy, that wouldn't do any good. They'd just hide them or break them!"

Not exclusively Korean, such compulsive competition *is* characteristically Korean. It has led to extraordinary accomplishments.

In 1985 South Korea's exports of automobiles to the United States were precisely zero. In 1987 three-quarters of Korean automobile exports went to the United States. A quarter—more than 200,000—were sold elsewhere, and the domestic market absorbed some 300,000 vehicles. In 1987 Korean exports of automobiles to the United States were 650,000, and in 1989 more than 800,000. It would have been a million had it not been for the crash of 1987 and the slight contraction of U.S. imports produced by the falling dollar.

From zero to almost a million in five years is, as they say, some going. The Koreans did it by spotting an unexploited market and concentrating on that opening. In this case it was subcompacts, at a cost of $6,000 to $7,000 for a second or third car.

As in Taiwan, sales abroad fueled the extraordinary rise of the Korean economy—again, primarily sales to the United States. South Korea's total exports were $56 billion in 1988, one-third of the GNP—and 40 percent of those exports went to the United States. American purchases of Korean goods rose sharply, despite the Administration's halfhearted attempts to cut back foreign purchases. In 1988 the U.S. bought $8.5 billion more in goods from Korea than it sold to Korea.

American labor and American management charge that Korea enjoys unfair advantages. Its wage rates seem ridiculously low, indeed exploitive, to Americans and Europeans. In 1986 the average factory hand worked a minimum of fifty-five hours a week, but usually more, at an average hourly wage of $1.50 to $1.60.

That level was low, but just two decades earlier, South Korea had been largely rural—with an annual cash income of no more than thirty dollars a head. Average family income in 1987 was between $550 and $650, and it was fairly evenly distributed. No one was deprived, not even the farmers. The *Saemaul Undung*, the "New Community Movement," revitalized the countryside, and government intervention maintained the price of farm products.

"Competition also minimizes inequity in pay," a foreign economist pointed out to me. "Labor-intensive industries have absorbed the entire available labor force. . . . Because industries vie for the good workers, wages have kept pace with the per capita growth of the GNP.

So economic discontent has not been very high—unlike political discontent."

Nonetheless, in mid-1989 workers were striking for a bigger share of the constantly expanding wealth of the nation, inflamed by a 38 percent rise in corporate profits that was not reflected in their wages. The growth of the South Korean economy in the 1980s was almost explosive. Successive annual rates of growth are even more impressive than they at first appear, for each starts where the last leaves off. It was like enormous acrobats standing on each other's shoulders—with each successive giant markedly taller than the one who supports him.

Just $76.3 billion in 1984, the GNP increased by 9.7 percent in 1985 to reach $83.7 billion—and by 14 percent in 1986 to reach $95.1 billion. Growing 12.1 percent in one year, it was more than $120 billion in 1988.

That is *very* fast growth. During the four years from January 1, 1985, to January 1, 1989, South Korea's total output grew by more than half its original size, actually by 63.6 percent. More simply, for every hi-fi set or delivery van produced in 1985, two will be produced in 1990.

5

South Korea: The Secret of Success

ANY NATION PREPARED TO WORK INHUMAN HOURS FOR A PITTANCE CAN DO IT. ANY NATION WITH A HUNGRY, INTELLIGENT, WELL-EDUCATED POPULACE AND CONSISTENT AMERICAN BACKING CAN DO IT. ANY NATION WITH A STRONG AUTHORITARIAN TRADITION AND A RUTHLESS STREAK CAN DO IT THE KOREAN WAY.

NEO-CONFUCIANISM PROVIDED THE BASIC ELEMENTS: FAMILY-CLAN SOLIDARITY, SACRIFICE OF INDIVIDUALITY, SUBMISSION TO DISCIPLINE, AND ADMINISTRATION BY A MERITOCRACY. ALSO CORRUPTION.

How does a country blessed with few resources except a clever, literate, diligent, and emotional people become a major economic power in the late twentieth century? How did South Korea in just twenty-five years reach a stage of development that took Japan almost a century?

Japan was a modern industrial country with a strong infrastructure and a skilled work force at the beginning of the War in the Pacific in 1941. At the time of the Communist invasion in 1950, South Korea was a labor-intensive, moderately fertile agricultural country with little sense of nationhood. What industry and mining functioned in the Korean Peninsula was concentrated in the North, which was ruled by the Communists.

The South Koreans' chief advantages were their ignorance and their poverty. Since they did not know it was impossible to do everything at once, in a whirlwind rush, they did it. Besides, they were not hampered by an inefficient industrial plant. Starting with nothing, they built a highly efficient productive machine.

Nor have Korean merchandisers been hampered by previous experience that would have kept them from innovating. They have, however, been hampered by their dependence on the American market and on American agents, jobbers, and wholesalers. Now learning to sell direct, they are developing new markets. The range of merchandise is displayed in a telephone book, *Korea Yellow Pages*, published in English every January.

The ten-page index lists some 850 different goods and services on offer to foreign visitors. A few products taken at random: abrasives, agar-agar, and artificial flowers; badminton sets, balloons, and barbecues; gelatin, ginseng, and glow starters; industrial plants, insecticides, and integrated circuits; parachutes, sheepskin, and shoes; velveteens, wallets, yachts, yeast, and zippers.

To entice the professional buyers for foreign firms, more than twenty trade fairs and exhibitions are held every year, such as KISS '89, the Korea International Safety and Security Exhibition, 1989. To entice bargain-hunting tourists, Korea's *Yellow Pages* provides a guide to Itaewon, Seoul's spectacular shopping district, which is, by a whisker, the Far East's leading bazaar—no small distinction in a region of avid traders.

Most tourists react like conditioned dogs to that abundance. Located conveniently near the headquarters of the U.S. Eighth Army, Itaewon is several dozen city blocks of large and small stores centered on the giant Hamilton Department Store and the UN Shopping Center. Everything is offered. I believe I saw a show-window sign that said FIANCÉES ARRANGED. But it may have been "finances." The gaudy bars, cocktail lounges, and nightclubs draw the GIs—and the stores draw the tourists.

American shoppers are, however, neither as numerous nor as open-handed as Japanese, who are interested chiefly in high-priced goods. Japanese Customs grants each an exemption of 300,000 yen (about $2,400), and many use it all. Besides, duty is only 20 percent on a sable coat that goes for $17,500, against three times as much in Tokyo. It's not real money, but play money. Not yen, only dollars.

How does a backward country like Korea make an economic miracle? I asked earlier. I then described what the Koreans had achieved. But I did not say *how* they had done it.

The one-word answer is *authoritarianism*. Other factors have been essential: the Confucian heritage, the technocrats, entrepreneurship, resentment of poverty and inferiority, and the compulsion to self-improvement. But authoritarian direction made them pull to-gether.

All these horses were harnessed to the chariot of progress by the dictatorship that began in 1961. Heavy-handed and paternalistic, the military regime was also harsh and repressive. Given the Korean propensity for civil disorder, someone apparently had to take the reins in hand and whip the team into a gallop.

In Korea, it was the generals. Run by generals or not, every successful Asian state has been authoritarian. Japan, the most successful, is neither wholly authoritarian nor wholly democratic, despite the trappings of parliamentary rule. Taiwan and Singapore have long justified one-party rule by the Communist threat, external and internal.

Despite some liberalization, no Asian country is moving toward Western-style liberal democracy. Western criteria should be applied to Asia with great caution. Their histories and cultures have bent Asians in many directions—all different from the West's. The "Oriental mind" does not exist, for there are a dozen Oriental minds, all different.

As the Viet Nam debacle demonstrated, it is not only arrogant and foolish to attempt to impose Western—specifically Anglo-Saxon—institutions on Asians. It is impossible. Regardless of Western distress, which I share, most Asian nations will remain largely authoritarian.

"The government's Economic Planning Board has been the center of Korea's development," an acute counselor of embassy from an Asian country explained to me in Seoul. "The EPB is unique, though it is often compared to MITI [the Ministry of International Trade and Industry], which guides the Japanese economy. The EPB closely directs aspects of life MITI has never touched. MITI has had no need to intrude to the same extent. Japan Incorporated has from the beginning functioned much more smoothly than South Korea with its many factions. The EPB is unique—and it has been uniquely successful."

The Economic Planning Board—indeed, the economic miracle itself—was one man's creation. General Park Chung Hee seized power by a military coup d'etat in 1961, when Korea was in its habitual turmoil. Students and workers demonstrating against fixed elections and police brutality had just forced crafty President Syngman Rhee to give up power at the age of eighty-five. In 1963 Park Chung Hee became president in an election so blatantly manipulated by the army as to make Syngman Rhee's enthusiastic ballot-box stuffing appear amateurish. Park was reelected by large majorities in 1967 and 1971. On October 26, 1979, he was assassinated by the director of the Korean Central Intelligence Agency.

No statue of Park stands in Seoul today, although he shaped present-day Korea, and the generals who ruled until 1988 were his disciples. His murder has never been fully explained, no more than has his wife's earlier murder by an assassin who was shooting at him. Yet Park Chung Hee has as much right to be called the father of the nation as has Syngman Rhee, who fought for decades for independence from Japan— and then misruled the independent state.

Since I knew Park Chung Hee only fleetingly, I must depend on others for an understanding of the granite-faced general-turned-nation-builder. His vision was narrow, but he saw every minute detail very clearly, says Dr. Nam Duk Woo, who was prime minister for two years after Park's assassination. That, Dr. Nam observes, was a difficult job, nowhere as enjoyable as his preceding five years as minister for economic planning for President Park.

At the beginning, Dr. Nam recalls, the president told him flatly: "We can't eat democracy. We have *only* two priorities: first, national defense; second, economic development."

Dr. Nam adds, "President Park always guarded against the temptation to accommodate political expediency with economic measures." The phraseology is convoluted, but the meaning is unmistakable: Park Chung Hee would do anything, including murder, to ensure that his economic plans succeeded. All Koreans agree on his ruthlessness. Even his political foes agree on his genius and his immense accomplishments.

George Suh is a critic of Park Chung Hee. George and I worked together as war correspondents until 1953, but I did not see him again until 1968, when he called my hotel room in Seoul. He refused to come up for a drink, insisting that we meet in the crowded bar, where we almost had to shout to be heard.

"This is fine," George said. "Now we can talk."

When I looked astonished, he added, "No bug could work here. In your room, they would hear every word perfectly. Now let me tell you what a bunch of bastards are running my country."

After he had talked for an hour about intimidation, repression, and murder, I asked, "And what are you doing now? You never told me."

"Oh, didn't I? I'm a member of the National Assembly."

"The opposition, of course," I said.

"No," he replied, "the government party. I was President Park's campaign manager last year."

That excellent judge of talent and fisher of capable men, the dictator Park Chung Hee had appointed George to the National Assembly. Appalled by the military dictatorship, George finally broke with Park by speaking against sending Korean troops to Viet Nam. George is that unstable and self-destructive mixture, a courageous and impatient idealist. The rapid success of Park's economic measures had reconciled George to the regime's excesses—until he could take no more.

Today George acknowledges Park Chung Hee's great accomplishments—and recoils from his crimes. He cannot, besides, forgive two misdemeanors: the matter of the tiles and the matter of the *hangul*.

Park Chung Hee was pragmatic, but his taste was garish. He ordered all the new houses he built for the people to be roofed with colored tiles. Bright reds, oranges, blues, and greens replaced the gray roof tiles hallowed by the centuries. George, who is essentially an artist, complains that Park destroyed part of his life by sweeping away that remnant of the past.

The Japanese had hidden away the Kwang Hwa Mon, the Gate of Brilliant Civilization, which was a premier symbol of Korean nationalism. Park Chung Hee ordered the old gate-tower placed at the head of Seoul's main avenue, King Sejong Boulevard, before the restored Capitol. He also ordered that the name be inscribed under the sweeping eaves in *hangul,* rather than the original Chinese ideograms. George Suh feels that was populist desecration.

Yet Chinese ideograms are now vanishing rapidly, except from the hewn stone and brass plaques on the scores of buildings that accommodate the great conglomerates. Those edifices are to modern Korea what the palaces of princes and the mansions of mandarins were to old Korea. The gigantic corporations that dominate the economy were virtually Park Chung Hee's personal creation. Eminently practical, he based Korea's reconstruction upon a dozen or so big entrepreneurs. He thus promoted rapid growth and buttressed his power with aggressive businessmen who owed their wealth directly to him.

They were almost all new men, as the Romans used the term. They neither came from established families nor had much education. Dynamic and ambitious, they made their own destiny—with a leg-up from the president.

Chung Ju Yung, the founder of Hyundai,[1] the biggest conglomerate, was born in North Korea and once worked as a motor mechanic for the American forces. Today he presides over thirty-two companies whose scope extends from building ships and automobiles to writing insurance and making domestic appliances. Hyundai's total assets in 1988 were more than $1 billion, and sales were more than $8 billion.

Such conglomerates can take far bigger risks than smaller firms. Present-day Korea is itself the result of an enormous gamble that paid off spectacularly. Park Chung Hee built it on a tripod. The first leg is the conglomerates; the other legs are the technocrats, to whom I shall return, and the educated, energetic labor force. The Korean miracle started by transmuting the blood and the sweat of the workers into salable products.

Korean wages are today still well below world levels, but then so are domestic Korean prices. Workers have been fairly rewarded—by their *original* standards. But they have hardly been pampered. Moreover, wages, never generous, still lag well behind productivity—and Korea leads the world in industrial accidents.

Five industrial fatalities and 390 injuries *every day* are five times the rate in Taiwan or Japan, and fifteen times the rate in the West. Given a twelve-hour day in clangorous, ill-ventilated, and badly lit factories,

---

[1] *Hyundai* means "modern." The second conglomerate with nearly $7 billion in sales is Daewoo, which means "universe."

with few safety devices, serious accidents are inevitable. Oddly, perhaps, increasingly sophisticated equipment is raising the incidence of accidents. Afire with Korean impatience, both management and labor fall on new machinery before they understand its hazards.

Workers have always grumbled, for they too are contentious, independent Koreans. But they have unquestionably been suppressed, largely on the pretext of the Communist threat. I was assured that the two armored cars I saw at the vast Pohang Iron and Steel plant were for use against any invasion from North Korea. But Pohang is several hundred miles from the Demilitarized Zone.

Park Chung Hee and his successors would not let workers strike. The generals believed labor would work more efficiently and, assuredly, more docilely when stringently controlled by law and by the police. Park would not allow his great enterprise to be disrupted by slowdowns or strikes, for he was, in all things, rigorously practical. He knew precisely what goals he sought, and he chose the most direct means to attain them, regardless of the human cost.

Yet he was also a great man. He was a Japanese-trained infantry officer, who had become a civilian intelligence specialist. When in 1953 I met him briefly, he was back in uniform, as deputy commander of ROK II Corps. But he did not depend upon the military.

"His personal staff were not soldiers, but civilians," former Prime Minister Nam Duk Woo observed. "He always participated personally in the regular monthly assessment meetings of the Economic Planning Board. Any junior official who impressed him would be moved up. His personal staff was made up of very talented civilians, many of them trained abroad."

Park Chung Hee himself created the class of technocrats who are the third leg of the tripod. Specialists in administration, finance, or engineering, they spurned employment with private industry. Conditioned by centuries of reverence for learning and for official service, those eminently modern men responded enthusiastically to Park Chung Hee's summons. Directing the economic revolution for the government, they are the modern Korean equivalent of mandarins, Confucian scholar-officials.

Through the centuries, extremely intelligent men had, in the Confucian manner, been given the opportunity to rise, whether their families were rich or poor, although it was better to be rich. Furthermore, the genetically homogeneous Koreans, even more than the heterogeneous Chinese and Japanese, consider themselves one big family in the Confucian manner. They therefore regard each other as equals. Every man is as good as any other. Most women are too, for Korean women have enjoyed greater freedom than their Chinese or Japanese cousins.

That egalitarian heritage has also made Koreans very contentious. Since any man's opinion is as good as any other's, why should someone not assert his opinion by force when necessary?

The Confucian tradition of equality of opportunity, joined with that inherent egalitarianism, enabled resurgent Korea to make use of talent wherever it appeared. Moreover, the American occupation at the end of World War II offered an opportunity to the most talented men and women to be educated in the United States. Dr. Nam Duk Woo was among the hundreds who studied at American universities between 1945 and 1950. After the Korean War, Syngman Rhee, himself an American Ph.D., continued to send the best Korean students to the U.S. The military regime actually enlarged their number.

"Note Seoul's determination to reach out over Japan and link its future with the U.S., which at that time seemed to offer answers for modernization," former American Ambassador Richard L. Walker advises. "The result: today at the minister, vice-minister, and assistant-minister level, as well as their counterparts in business, commerce, banking, industry, and the military, there are proportionally *more* advanced degrees from first-class American institutions of higher learning than in any other country in the world—including the U.S."

International loans and grants, primarily from the United States, had by 1961 totaled $5 billion, which is still not a teenager's allowance and was a lot more money thirty years ago. Yet Korea was a shambles economically, as well as politically, when Park Chung Hee took over. Quite daringly, his master plan was based on exports—at a time when Korea could not produce enough goods to satisfy even part of its own needs. In order to create an exporting industry, he needed extensive loans from private bankers, because government-to-government loans were limited and cumbersome. Somehow he got those loans—on increasingly better terms as industry and exports grew.

The infrastructure was practically nonexistent in 1961. Roads were few and bad. The two chief cities, Seoul in the northwest and Pusan in the southeast, were linked only by a capricious railway. Park Chung Hee built the Seoul-Pusan Expressway, which had been Syngman Rhee's pet project.

In return for Rhee's not sabotaging the armistice, the U.S. had promised several hundred million dollars for that great arterial highway. His obsession with the expressway had appeared to Americans a further sign of the old man's megalomania. Although it was not built (it fell victim to the corruption and inefficiency that fouled Rhee's last years in office), he was absolutely right about its decisive utility.

The entire industrial-commercial structure Park Chung Hee built was strong enough and flexible enough to survive the repeated oil and dollar shocks of the 1970s[2]—and to expand. An even greater apparent danger actually stimulated heavy industry, thus buttressing both prosperity and self-confidence: from 1976 to 1980, U.S. President Jimmy Carter repeatedly threatened to pull out the 40,000-odd American troops who were South Korea's chief safeguard against another invasion. Carter believed his threats would compel the dictatorship to relax its suppression of human rights.

Even above the economy, President Park Chung Hee's chief priority was security—and effective defense depended not only on American troops, but also on American war matériel. Park behaved like a man obsessed. He built factories and dockyards to make tanks, artillery, and naval vessels; he built steel plants to provide the raw material. He ordered Korean industry to produce all the multifarious hardware and the complex electronic devices essential to modern warfare. He excluded only warplanes since their entirely new technology required vast capital investment.

"The economy overheated as a result of Park's new stress on weapons and the diversion of resources," Jin-hyun Kim, the editorial director of the newspaper *Tong-A Ilbo*, explained to me over lunch. "And inflation returned—strongly. But Jimmy Carter only succeeded in making the human rights situation in Korea far worse. Repression and economic inequity were, once again, justified by defense needs."

Park Chung Hee would not loosen control. He knew what was best—and that was that. Neither did his last successor, President Chun Doo Hwan, permit liberalization. But Chun's chosen successor, General Roh Tae Woo, realized he had to make radical concessions if he were to win the presidency by election—as he did.

The flexible, intelligent Roh Tae Woo ruled with panache. No dour autocrat, but a modern politician, he has wooed the voters—and played tennis with Australian Prime Minister Bob Hawke's wife as his partner and his wife as Hawke's partner. In 1989, Roh also evaded the referendum on his performance he had promised to hold after two years in office. Autocracy dies hard in Korea.

The spirit of the old military government was epitomized by a scroll I saw in a shop window a few doors from the iron gates of the offices of the ruling Democratic Justice Party. The black Chinese ideograms read, LOYALTY, SUBMISSION, AND DIGNIFIED RESPECT. THE PATIENCE TO ENDURE AND AVOID DISHARMONY IN LOVING GOODWILL. THAT IS THE WAY OF THE GOOD MAN. The scroll was signed, CHUN DOO HWAN, PRESIDENT.

*   *   *

[2] And to weather the shocks of the 1980s. In October 1987, when the stock markets of the world were quaking with each new low, the Korean stock market was edging ahead a few points a day. Foreigners were virtually excluded from participation.

Assistant Minister Jin Nyum of the Economic Planning Board is the quintessential technocrat. Outwardly a suave civil servant, he can be very tough. He routinely overrules even cabinet ministers, who must submit their departmental budgets for his approval. He is backed by his boss, the minister for economic planning, who is also the first deputy prime minister. Foreign-educated technocrats like him will run the Korean economy for some time to come, regardless of who occupies the Blue House.

Jin Nyum is among the most brilliant of Korea's technocrats. Born in 1940 in Chonju in the isolated southwest, he attained ministerial rank at forty-two, still a stripling in a neo-Confucian nation that venerates age. He had been meticulously groomed for responsibility, having already spent two years studying economic theory at George Washington University in St. Louis and three years as economic counselor of the Embassy of the Republic of Korea in London.

Jin Nyum's office is on the fourth floor of the Kwachon Center, recently built south of Seoul to relieve the pressure on the capital. The center's modern towers of pale brown stone dwarf the mock-thatch roofs of the self-consciously ethnic buildings of its neighbor, the National History Project. All pale wood and bright fabrics, the assistant minister's office is spacious. A vice-minister's office is twice as large, and a full minister's three times.

When he slips off the jacket of his electric-blue suit, Jin Nyum looks like a graduate student, rather than a middle-aged official who controls billions of dollars. He is slight and no taller than five foot five; his clever, swarthy features are unlined; and his black hair is untouched by gray. The office is warm despite air conditioning, but the traditional drink of welcome, bitter ginseng tea, is cooling.[3] The assistant minister talks animatedly, emphasizing his points with his hands and leaning across the low wooden coffee table in his enthusiasm.

He does not worry about his dignity. Yet he would not take his jacket off if he were receiving a Korean whose rank was equal to his own or higher. But Jin Nyum learned during his studies in the U.S. that foreigners, particularly Americans, are charmed by informality.

The visitor is an outsider, apart from Korean society, and he will be gone in a few days. Perhaps paradoxically, the assistant minister can, therefore, speak quite candidly. Yet the visitor seems to have no idea where to draw the line. Some of his questions regarding the minister's personal and official life are intrusive, almost embarrassing. The minister can either be evasive or candid—and he is not accustomed to

---

[3] Ginseng is a medicinal root shaped rather like a man. Korea has been known for two thousand years for the quality of its ginseng, which was formerly one of its chief exports. Ginseng is a general tonic that Asians consider an aphrodisiac. Laboratory tests in hypercautious Switzerland have confirmed its beneficial effects.

evading direct questions. In fact, he is unaccustomed to direct questions from outsiders. So he answers candidly.

Jin Nyum's career began just as Park Chung Hee began to quick-march the country into the modern world. He had attended a provincial middle school, which had been under Communist control for a few months during the war, before winning admission to the economics department of Seoul National University. That was decisive. Seoul National is *the* premier university of Korea, where—as in France and Japan, but not necessarily the United States and Great Britain—one's university determines one's fate.

Since Seoul National led to an official career, Jin Nyum took the higher civil-service examination upon his graduation in 1962, when he was twenty-one. Besides, there was little industry, and private enterprise was not attractive. He is today content with the modest comfort his family enjoys on his salary of somewhat more than a thousand dollars a month. The respect paid his high rank in the neo-Confucian technocracy makes up for the greater sums he might have made in industry.

He is, at any rate, hardly deprived. He lives in a comfortable apartment in fashionable southern Seoul and drives a Daewoo Royal SQ, which cost 6 million *won*, about $7,500. The Royal SQ is the automobile the government and corporations provide for distinguished visitors who are not quite of the first rank. Best of all, his two sons are attending the right school—and the right schools lead to the right universities.

The family lives better because his wife, Nijung, who studied at the University of Indiana, now teaches musicology at a college in Seoul. The Jins would manage if she did not, but working wives are the hand-maidens of progress in Korea, as elsewhere.

When I call on him, the assistant minister is preoccupied with the Sixth Economic and Development Plan, which, like a detailed road map, shows the exact route to precisely defined goals. With obvious pride of coauthorship, he produces a 252-page book entitled *The Process of Creating the Sixth Plan*.

Like the framed slogans on the wall, the book of the plan is written largely in Chinese ideogram by the new mandarins. The common people are all literate in *hangul*, the phonetic script, but their rulers continue to use ideograms. *The Process of Creating the Sixth Plan* is, therefore, beyond the comprehension of most Koreans. Ironically, it is intended for wide distribution.

"I'd like it to be on the list of nonfiction best-sellers," jokes Jin Nyum, who recruited journalists and novelists to advise on the style, as well as academics, doctors, lawyers, and scientists, and, of course, other bureaucrats to advise on the content. His boss, the first deputy prime minister, had told him, "Make it a story everyone can read."

The assistant minister explains: "We wanted to build a popular

consensus on the future economic and social course of Korea. . . . So
we formed forty-three subcommittees to draft working documents,
each with two co-chairmen, one from the government, the other a
private citizen. The drafts were then released to arouse discussion. . . .
We got a very big response. The minimum wage was discussed on TV,
in newspapers, and at seminars. We also got many letters, so public
interest is obviously high. . . . Also, of course, our social structure is
changing very fast."

Social development is the chief goal of the Sixth Plan, for the major
economic goals have already been attained. Among the paternalistic
regime's formal priorities are "popular demands for fair shares and equal
treatment"; better health care; "restructuring agriculture" and rural
life; reforming education "to fit socioeconomic demands," which means
more technology and less humanities; encouraging small and middle-
sized enterprises; and women's rights.

Everything is minutely detailed from the top. Assistant Minister Jin
Nyum, whose entire career has been devoted to planning, likes it that
way. He expresses grave reservations about the trend toward less
central direction.

But former Prime Minister Nam Duk Woo insists: "What we need is
indicative planning, rather than *command* planning. Our economy is
now too complicated to control from the center. We've got to indicate
the general direction—and not try to dictate every detail. We must give
the economy its head."

For centuries the center of Korean life, Seoul is today a super-
metropolis where some 11 million people live, a quarter of the country's
population. Yet no more than most New Yorkers are most residents of
Seoul natives. Even those born in Seoul speak of their grandparents'
villages as their true homes. They yearn toward their ancestral roots
among the rice fields.

Moira and I succumbed happily to our own yearning for the rice
fields, where lives the soul of Asia. Our destination was Kwangju, the
old capital of the remote southwest, which is today famous for its
cuisine, its prickly local pride, and the massacre of 1980. The journey
was, however, a revelation of the new Korea.

The Kwangju train [my notes read] waited red-and-silver at its
platform like an ocean liner in its slip. Car is Korean-
manufactured. Good air conditioning. Reclining chairs with foot-
rests are only minutely narrower than first-class airline seats.
Announcements interspersed between music; free newspapers
and barley tea distributed by attractive young women. All this for
11,400 *won*, a little more than fourteen dollars. Korean Railways

should send technical advisory missions to Amtrak and British Rail. From Seoul to the now-industrial suburb of Yongdongpo, once a long way, takes a few minutes. On that stretch of, say, ten miles, I see more substantial buildings than I had seen in the entire country during two years of war.

Banks of flowers stand on the station platforms, and lots between factories are either vegetable plots or recreation grounds. They're clearly not for show to outsiders, but for the people. But construction is rapidly swallowing those strips.

Even in the countryside, the impression of unremitting activity is intense. It was a shock to see an old man sitting on a bridge, just sitting. Signs on factory buildings: Slazenger, 3M, Steel Foundry, Concrete Plant.

The rural landscape was once depressing: bare, rocky fields and shattered villages. Today there are no draught animals, but small tractors are everywhere. Boy Scouts with yellow shirts and red hats march behind a big banner against the backdrop of the dark rice terraces that climb the peaks like a gigantic staircase.

Korea is like the setting for a model railway: neat little wooden bus shelters, poplars lining the roads, long concrete aqueducts, and neat irrigation canals.

Not only the people, but the land itself has been transformed. Korea is now as tidy as Switzerland: little boxy houses with bright colored roofs. Actually, Switzerland is a little untidy by comparison. And green trees clothe every hill, the hillsides that were once totally bare. Nurseries with thousands of seedlings march past the train window. There's been an intensive reforestation program for years. Children are encouraged to plant trees—and not only on May 1, which is, typically, not Labor Day, but Arbor Day. Does Arbor Day still exist anywhere else?

Kwangju was the second stop on an extensive tour of South Korea I made in 1951 to learn what war had done to the civilian population. Traveling alone by ramshackle bus, I had been grateful for the hospitality of Jim Markey of the United States Information Service. He had observed wryly, "I don't mind the guerrillas so much. Kind of got used to them. But I'm having a hell of a time convincing the auditors they should pay for the third roof in two months. Have you ever seen what machine-gun bullets do to a tile roof?"

Although I had not expected to find it in 1987, the USIS building was still there, as was its gray tile roof. But it was no longer imposing. Its two stories were dwarfed by surrounding buildings ten to fifteen stories high.

Driving through the suburbs to the Seijong Institute of Education, I saw housing developments and factories where paddy fields had surrounded the city in 1951. In Seoul, they were talking about assuring that agricultural progress would keep pace with industrial progress. They were also talking about paying special attention to industrial development in the southwest, which has long been disaffected.

Kwangju's antipathy toward Seoul sprang not just from provincial chauvinism writ large, but from age-old disputes over the legitimacy of long-vanished dynasties. Hatred sprang from the demonstration in 1980 when the army killed more than a hundred students demanding direct popular election of the president.

Despite the bitterness aroused by that massacre, I felt the centuries-old resentment of Seoul must have dissipated somewhat. Kwangju was, after all, incomparably better off materially than it had ever been. President Ko Jai-kee of the Seijong Institute briskly refuted that belief even before I expressed it.

Now in his seventies, Professor Ko has been a firebrand all his life. As a newspaper reporter he got into trouble with the Japanese administration in Manchuria in the early 1930s—and later in Korea. He could not stop agitating when the Republic of Korea was created in 1947, so Syngman Rhee put him in jail.

Ko Jai-kee looks and acts the part of the intransigent patriot. He is thin and intense; his mustache is startlingly white against his dark face. He is also impassioned and vehement.

Pulling on a cigarette and slipping back and forth between Korean and Japanese, he declares: "Of course we still hate Seoul. They've given us a few sops. But ever since urbanization and modernization began, they've been neglecting us down here. Nobody likes Seoul, and we don't hesitate to speak out. . . . I don't care what happens in any election. No government will be legitimate until it has brought to trial those responsible for the 1980 massacre. Only after a full investigation and full recompense to the families of the victims can we have real democracy in Korea."

The old firebrand knows exactly what he is saying. Further investigation of the Kwangju incident would not merely stir ill will, but could create a major crisis, perhaps bringing down the wrath of the army and the security agencies on the government. Ultimately, of course, then-President Chun Doo Hwan was responsible. The army was obeying his orders, although, perhaps, interpreting them freely. The current president, Roh Tae Woo, was, at the very least, involved, for he was effectively Chun Doo Hwan's chief of staff at the time.

His government finally approached that problem very gingerly in 1989. President Roh knows a whitewash could be worse than no investigation at all. Even government officials in Kwangju side with

Professor Ko, agreeing emphatically that the region suffers discrimination.

"This is a low-wage area," Ko Jai-kee asserts. "We are exploited. The big steel plant in the bay? I'm glad they're building it. But it won't provide many jobs for *our* people. Between bringing in outsider experts and automation, there aren't many jobs left. . . . It's the conglomerates, the giant corporations. The whole country is dominated by the conglomerates—and they are the creatures of Seoul."

"What about the new emphasis," I ask, "on small and middle-sized enterprises?"

He snorts incredulously and says, "So they told you about fair distribution of the wealth? Don't you believe it. All substantial businessmen are former generals or former bureaucrats. Those few who weren't are very closely connected to the generals and the bureaucrats. . . . They pour money into *other* parts of the country. It reminds me of the way the Japanese ran Manchuria. Big parts of this country are exploited just the way the Japanese exploited Manchuria."

Professor Ko's views are not extreme—for a Kwangju man. Yet Korea is still so regionalized that candidates in the last presidential election got the bulk of their votes from their home areas. The rural population has not enjoyed the same benefits as the urban population—and farm income is only two-thirds of urban income.

Professor Ko talked further about cronyism, that is, the military-bureaucratic-oligarchical triad. Charges of corruption are prevalent in Korea, as they are everywhere in Asia. Sensitive to Western—and native—concern about that blemish of Confucian societies, I asked dozens of Koreans and foreigners about official graft and its effects. All agreed that it existed, and many felt it was a significant problem. But few considered corruption so widespread as to impede progress.

Jin-hyun Kim, the editorial director of *Tong-A Ilbo*, pointed out: "Corruption and pollution of the environment are linked problems. Both are endemic. Yet we have the second-biggest nuclear power industry in the world, second only to France.[4] And there's been no significant protest. Koreans feel it's necessary. So there's no need for bribery to get permission.

"Of course, money does change hands. Sometimes big sums. If generals or politicians need money from their friends, they're sure to get it. But it's Confucian corruption, and so far it actually facilitates economic movement—and, thus, progress. Remember, the man who gets the most respect is the *great man* who looks after his family—all the way to distant cousins. He is respected because Confucius said the family came first."

---

[4] The U.S. built seven of those nuclear power plants, France built two, and Canada one.

It became plain that corruption was widespread, although, as my informants had judged, not yet crippling. In 1988 the brother of former President Chun Doo Hwan was indicted for large-scale graft after a student campaign for his arrest. Humiliatingly dressed in coarse white prison clothing, he was tried in open court and found guilty.

The former president himself was the next criminal arraigned by public opinion. But he was not formally indicted. President Roh Tae Woo did not want his former patron tried. He was moved not only by personal loyalty, but by the knowledge that a public trial would damage him, too.

Chun Doo Hwan and his wife Soonja, who was implicated, retired to rural exile after promising to repay "$3.3 million in personal wealth and $20 million in surplus political funds." The retired director of the National Security Planning Agency, formerly the Korean Central Intelligence Agency, was, however, indicted for corruptly diverting funds to himself and to the research institute Chun Doo Hwan had established as his personal power base.

The opposition, which controlled the National Assembly, was not satisfied. A special committee pressed for a full investigation. Although it did not charge President Roh Tae Woo with complicity, the opposition wanted the entire Democratic Justice Party investigated. The future was full of the promise of further confrontations.

Professor Ko Jai-kee has a keen nose not only for corruption. He points out the future crises incubating in the fact that 55 percent of the electorate is between the ages of twenty and twenty-nine. Youth is now aware of its power. The militant students who destroyed the military dictatorship are the vanguard of a generation that does not hold its elders' beliefs. Complex moral and political issues divide that generation from the older generation and from the administration. The fundamental issue is the precise threat posed by the People's Democratic Republic of (North) Korea—and the South's proper response.

The military-political-industrial triad created by President Park Chung Hee was protected by security agencies like the KCIA, whose actions were shockingly brutal even in a harsh nation. Their violent intrusion upon individual freedom was justified by the need for constant vigilance against Communist infiltrators. Institutionalized repression was justified by the contention that only a disciplined society could resist the Communist menace.

That fundamental conviction sprang from the horrors of the Korean War. Exactly how long ago the war appears to those in their twenties I realized rather uncomfortably when our interpreter picked up a remark I'd made and asked, between awe and skepticism, "You mean you really *knew* Syngman Rhee?" I felt for a moment as if I had fraudulently claimed personal acquaintance with George Washington or Napoleon.

The Communist menace is self-evident to the generation that grew up during the Korean War and, of course, to its elders. But the severity of the menace, even its existence, is by no means obvious to the generation born during or after the war, the twenty-to-twenty-nine-year-olds who are now the majority of voters. The Communist menace appears to many hardly more than a pretext for repression. Secret police brutality they have experienced, but danger from the North is unheard and unseen.

Communism exists, but it does not appear to be a serious problem. Students and workers wave banners and chant slogans in the classic agitprop way, but they prefer Molotov cocktails, volleys of stones, and massed charges against the riot police, in the classic Korean way. Clandestine circulation of Communist propaganda is minimal, and public circulation of Communist documents, historical or otherwise, is virtually prohibited, even for study. The security agencies rather foolishly try to make the youth anti-Communist by denying them knowledge of communism. Yet they do not face an upsurge of orthodox Marxism-Leninism or New Left fervor—not yet at least.

The recurrence of violent demonstrations after the euphoric twenty-ninth of June had other roots. First, the students knew they could get away with more. Unlike the Kwangju massacre, the army was not called in before June 29, and the riot police were relatively gentle. Besides, the faculty in universities were relieved of personal responsibility for individual students' actions. Professors had previously been compelled to plead with students and their parents not to demonstrate—with remarkable success in the neo-Confucian society.

In large part, Korean students continue to demonstrate because they are still righteously indignant at the ills in their society and at the wrongs they believe the U.S. has done them—and, above all, because they have the leisure to vent their youthful enthusiasm. After struggling through the obstacle course of lower and middle education, they can relax when admitted to university, for they are no longer held to strict account. Naturally, Korean students relaxing are different from other students relaxing; outsiders might think they were working very hard indeed. Still, they can, for the first time, raise their eyes from their books and look critically at the world around them.

Politically, Korean students are as romantic as students anywhere—and even less conversant with political realities. They are nostalgic for village life, and they glorify the Tong Hak Rebellion of 1894, which failed ignominiously. Their heroes, Mao Tse-tung, Fidel Castro, and Che Guevara, inspire them to violence.

No organizing cadres have been identified, except a group of "professional students" in their late twenties and their thirties who attend no classes. Those alienated men and women, who "always have plenty of money," as one student told me, woo the young students—and they are highly visible in storm centers like the Catholic Myongdong Cathedral in Seoul. No one could tell me how large that cadre was or whence it drew its funds and its inspiration. Since a massive failure of intelligence is unlikely, major North Korean influence can probably be ruled out.

Yet the intelligentsia yearn for unification. The most popular literary school has for a decade fed that yearning. "Chirisan literature" is called after the mountain range near Kwangju that was once the most remote corner of South Korea's most remote region. Now traversed by the Olympic Expressway to the east coast, Chirisan is developing rapidly, but its mythic power is undiluted.

In Chirisan in 1948, the illegal Communist party led an armed rising against the onerous regime of Syngman Rhee. In Chirisan in 1952, I accompanied a ROK army division withdrawn from the front line to attack a large Communist guerrilla force. In Chirisan in 1987, our bus paused at a spacious pavilion that offered hot food, newspapers, potent Korean *sake* drunk cold—and a peddler in a white hatchback offering "a genuine mink coat," which our ingenuous interpreter Jung Hyung-min bought for his beloved mother for $100.

In the days of strict censorship, Chirisan novels attacked the military regime obliquely. Then, as now, they celebrated social justice and, above all, reunification. The authors owed much of their inspiration to a few revisionist American historians. That inspiration is not remarkable; American examples, conventional or unconventional, are the predominant external influence in South Korea. The revisionists' argument was irresistible to many Korean authors. Those historians contend that Korean society—and individual Koreans—are maimed psychologically because the country is divided in two.

The American academics, being American, naturally blame the United States. As they see it, America's sins are threefold: having divided the country in the first place, as if the Soviets had wanted unity on any terms; maintaining the division by defending the South against the North, which was either provoked to attack or was actually invaded itself; and, finally, perpetuating the division by blocking the South's normal wish to unite with the North.

That simple thesis appeals greatly to university students. It explains everything, including the normal pangs of adolescence, in one sweeping proposition: *If only Korea were reunited, all would be well in a perfect country.*

President Roh Tae Woo could, therefore, not allow himself to appear to be blocking reunification—or a rapprochement with the North. The

Democratic People's Republic, for its part, realized how desperately it was isolated after the South's triumphant Olympics. Moreover, the North's two patrons, the People's Republic of China and the Soviet Union, were looking with favor on the economic advantages of dealing with the high-achieving South. Pressure thus increased on both North and South to enter into real communication.

The two halves of Korea had been talking for decades in the Armistice Truce Commission at Panmunjom in the Demilitarized Zone. But they had not really been hearing each other. In 1989, they were talking and, at least, listening. Official visits had begun cautiously. More dramatic was the brief return to his birthplace in the North of Chung Ju Yung, chairman of Hyundai, the biggest conglomerate of all. Mr. Chung had earlier been denounced by the North as "the Satan of capitalism." He went back to discuss economic cooperation—specifically tourism, manufacturing, and land reclamation. Yet Seoul in 1989 arrested an individualistic Protestant minister who visited the North after being denied permission, and arraigned a businessman as a Communist agent.

Suspicion and fear are still so strong that movement toward rapprochement would be glacially slow. Nonetheless, there was movement after the ice years.

Commercial need was already forcing radical change in Seoul's foreign policy. Korea needed an alternative and/or a supplement to the American market, which might not indefinitely remain so avid. Since the other miracle economies of East Asia were hard to crack, Seoul was looking to Beijing, to Eastern Europe, and even to Moscow.

Having put a foot into the doorway of the People's Republic of China, South Korea had been invited into the parlor. The Chinese had been deeply impressed by the smooth-running Asian Games in Seoul in 1986, and had, even before the Olympics, asked the South Koreans to assist them in preparing for the 1990 Asian Games in Beijing. The Koreans have responded with their usual efficiency, and the prospects for Seoul-Beijing cooperation have grown.

Loath to depend on any single country for its economic expansion, China sees the Republic of Korea as an adjunct and, perhaps in time, a substitute for both the United States and Japan. The Americans are, after all, not Asian, and lately they have not looked particularly efficient. The Japanese, China's hereditary enemy, have already taken a greedy lion's share of China's trade. Investment, joint ventures, and technical association with South Korea could prove not only more effective but more congenial. Sino-Korean trade was, in early 1989, already $3 billion a year.

Except for East Germany, every country of Eastern Europe maintains official commercial relations with South Korea. Pioneering Hungary established full diplomatic relations early in 1989. The Soviet

Union, too, was looking to Korea for cheaper and better consumer goods than it could produce itself. Moscow was also thinking of machine tools, oceangoing ships, and Soviet-Korean joint ventures to develop the great natural resources of backward Siberia.

Prosperity has altered the character of the Korean people, as former Prime Minister Nam Duk Woo and George Suh's wife observed. Can the challenge of a new horizon that reaches as far as Beijing, Moscow, and Budapest alter the 20 to 30 percent of students who are the vanguard of agitation? Some, but, I fear, not many.

Still, most of Korea's 1.25 million university students do not long for wider horizons or embrace idealistic causes. They are the devoted sons and daughters of the economic miracle; their imaginations and their idealism are kindled by their excellent prospects of self-betterment through bettering the nation. Undoubtedly inspired by patriotism, they are also inflamed by lust for material wealth.

Korea is becoming assertive. Korea is tired of being patronized by the U.S.—and is striking out alone. But Korea remains dependent on the U.S.

Americans in Seoul repeat an apocryphal tale that reveals Korean ambivalence—and American condescension. A Korean executive is reported to have told the American ambassador: "You must ensure that Korea is ruled democratically. . . . It's your responsibility. And you must do so without interfering in our internal affairs."

Korea's dramatic rise and immense potential have made Americans a little less inclined to behave toward Koreans as if they were clever, but rambunctious children. Their new self-confidence has made Koreans less inclined to submit to such treatment. That psychological confrontation is heightened by disputes over trade barriers.

The U.S. charges that Korea's protectionist measures are the most inequitable in the non-Communist world. The Koreans reply that they must still protect their domestic industry and their vulnerable farmers, who, not coincidentally, have a lot of votes. Koreans also note that American firms selling, say, machine tools do not offer the same strict quality control and delivery dates as do the Japanese—and, moreover, do not provide the same comprehensive after-sale service. Americans ask what those arguments have to do with Korea's removing one bottle in every case of California wine for "testing"—and imposing exorbitant duties on the remaining eleven bottles. Koreans ask why an economic superpower like the U.S. should be so bothered about the small Korean market—very small indeed for wine.

Tension between Washington and Seoul was higher in the late summer of 1989 than it had been since 1953. That was when right-wing dictator Syngman Rhee was bullied and bribed into tolerating a truce settlement he considered disastrous because it perpetuated the division of Korea—which left-wing revisionists lament today.

Sneaking contempt for Americans is particularly strong in Itaewon, the shopper's paradise, near the headquarters of the U.S. Eighth Army. Tradesmen and hoteliers are always contemptuous of their patrons, even if they do not mulct them. Increasing familiarity—and increasingly familiar behavior on both sides—has, naturally, bred mutual contempt between some Korean and American business associates. Jay Tunney, who recently opened a Hobson's Ice Cream outlet in Seoul, blames tensions equally on ill-advised American pressure and on Korean bureaucracy and favoritism. But business will be done, since the businessmen need each other.

Ill feeling is most acute among students and young intellectuals, who have been taught that the U.S. is responsible not only for the division of their country, but its crass materialism. Unlike their elders, students feel grateful neither for the preservation of the Republic of Korea nor for bourgeois abundance.

The Olympics dramatically displayed that tension—and aggravated it. The Olympics also exaggerated the tension. So many correspondents and so many television cameras were in town that their coverage overwhelmed reality. The Olympics, which were the high point of South Korea's modern existence, were also the low point of U.S.-Korean relations.

The Olympics were actually a brilliant backdrop against which long-standing ill feeling showed up dramatically. Americans and Koreans have been rubbing along together since the occupation began in 1945. Naturally, they sometimes rub on each other's nerves.

The American Olympic team affronted the Koreans gravely the moment it entered the arena for the opening ceremony. Every other team marched in good order, participating solemnly in the Republic of Korea's great rite of maturity. The Americans joked and waved, danced impromptu jigs, held up funny signs, and shouted wisecracks.

For Americans, that behavior was the sign of an open society—not robotic discipline, but free goodwill. The Koreans were disgusted. They felt those antics showed America up as an undignified, rowdy society—and displayed American contempt for Koreans.

American behavior did not improve during the games, and Korean tolerance diminished. Militant students proved they were adults in an adult country by demonstrating against the American presence in Korea. The world saw on its television screens a quarrel between allies that looked like a clash between enemies.

Koreans thoroughly dislike the Japanese, who subjected them to forty years of harsh colonial exploitation. Yet Japan is now their biggest trading partner and by far their largest investor. Although only a minority are Christian, Koreans, too, find it easier to forgive someone who has done them an injury than someone who has done them a service. Many are very angry at the Americans, who preserved their nation's existence, educated their leaders, and helped rebuild their economy.

Respect for the U.S. has fallen. As a Korean lawyer points out, the United States no longer looks as strong as it did in the 1950s and the 1960s. Some Koreans are disturbed by the morality of the American intervention in Viet Nam. Many more Koreans, he says, are appalled because their own powerful protector was unable to enforce its will in Southeast Asia. As admiration waned, resentment surfaced.

Americans have also been too candid in Korea, the lawyer added. American newspaper reports, magazine articles, television, and films depict an America riven by crime and immorality. The Armed Forces Network, Korea, convinces television viewers that sexual license and repudiation of the work ethic, as well as drug addiction and crime, are now the norm in the U.S. Left-wing or right-wing, Koreans respect self-discipline, dignity, and diligence—virtues apparently in eclipse in the U.S.

A problem exists, but no crisis—yet. Koreans are, however, reexamining their relationship with their chief ally.

"We are a complex and dynamic society." Choi Chang Yoon, vice-minister for culture and information, gave me a sophisticated assessment. "That is why we have student disturbances. The American reaction has been excessive: too many statements, hearings, declarations, resolutions, and threats. That reaction is resented not only by the students. It is very provocative to a sensitive people. . . . Korea is now out of the vortex and thinking about itself. We are thinking about our pride and the U.S.-Korean relationship—and there is much resentment."

When I asked about the contempt for Americans I had sensed, he replied, "Relationships change. It was always very much top dog and underdog. Now we should be at least middle dog. . . . Yes, there is some contempt—and definitely less respect."

6

Japan: The Mold of the Past

THE FRAGILE GILT AND LACQUER JUGGERNAUT WITH TURBO EN-
GINES AND ELECTRONIC STEERING IS ALMOST AS HARD ON ITS
PASSENGERS AS ON THE MULTITUDE OF OUTSIDERS CRUSHED UNDER
ITS WHEELS.

In his mid-forties, Dr. Takanori Fukushima has the energy of a
hyperactive child. He is the product of a culture that venerates age,
and his given name, Takanori, means "filial virtue." Yet he candidly
delights in being told that he looks more like a twenty-eight-year-old
intern than a leading international neurosurgeon. His normal attire in
the Mitsui Memorial Hospital is a green T-shirt, an operating cap
cocked over his left eye, and rumpled white slacks.

When, every month or so, he flies to Europe, America, or Australia
to do the star turn at a professional conference, his street clothes are
even more assertively youthful. He turned up among the staidly
dressed delegates to the 1987 Asian-Australian Congress of Neurological Surgery in Brisbane wearing a cream suit, a pastel-striped shirt, a
wide floral tie, and loafers with heels built up to give him the additional
height he does not need among his countrymen. As always, he brought
along a collection of videotapes, clippings, and microscope slides regarding his most spectacular operations. He also brought along sheaves
of photographs of his patients, before and after—and another sheaf of
photographs of himself.

Dr. Fukushima dismisses the thought of settling abroad, where his
talents, his energy, and his ebullient personality could earn him ten
times his present income. "I am a Japanese always!" he says. The
devoted son of a country that considers modesty a cardinal virtue, he

is an irrepressible self-promoter. Occasionally he reminds himself, "I must be humble and talk less." But his fervid devotion to neurosurgery immediately leads to another statement that is braggadocio even by more tolerant Western standards—and gaudily extravagant by austere Japanese standards. Withal, he is engaging. His singlemindedness and his boasting are touchingly childlike.

He acknowledges that he wants to win even higher esteem abroad. But, above all, he wants the esteem of his countrymen, who render profound respect only to those over sixty. Yet he persists in making himself appear much younger than he is—and, therefore, a little light-minded in his countrymen's eyes.

Takanori Fukushima's behavior is odd, but by no means un-Japanese. He stems from a Japanese tradition that, though minor, is tenacious. A few brilliant eccentrics have written their names large in the annals of a state where most men and women conform to survive.

Such courageous nonconformists brought knowledge of the outside world to a society that was, either by intent or circumstances, normally sealed tight. In the fifth and sixth centuries they introduced Buddhism, which profoundly altered Japanese life. In the eighteenth century they introduced *Rangaku*, "Dutch learning," the Western science that totally altered Japan. Some nonconformists paid with their lives for defying the prohibition on traveling abroad or pursuing Dutch learning.

Takanori Fukushima has never been in danger of execution. Aside from the stress any maverick suffers among his tautly disciplined people, the chief penalty is social isolation. But his ninety-hour work week leaves him no time for recreation. Like so many Japanese wives, his devoted second wife lives without complaint in her own female world—but is always available to run errands for her husband or to chauffeur his big Nissan sportscar.

He is an assistant professor of neurosurgery at Tokyo University, although his professional eminence and his brilliance at both public relations and fund-raising would win him higher academic rank abroad. But Tokyo University, Japan's oldest and most influential, does not bestow appointments lightly; age is as much a prerequisite for a full professorship as is learning.

Dr. Fukushima has not merely survived, but prospered because he is so good at what he does. The pragmatic element in the Japanese character tolerates his eccentricities because Japan needs his skills.

Takanori Fukushima follows his individualistic course in a conventional setting, the Mitsui Memorial Hospital. As chief of neurosurgery, he presides over ten subordinate surgeons. The private hospital was endowed by Mitsui, one of the three *zaibatsu*, the giant conglomerates that have dominated Japan's economic life for a century and a half. It stands big and square, white and characterless, in the Yoyogi District in the northeast quarter of Tokyo.

The first impression, the chief impression, and the lasting impression an outsider forms of Mitsui Memorial is crowding: crammed corridors and overflowing wards. That is not remarkable, for the overall impression of Japan itself is masses of human beings. With a total population of more than 123 million, which means 830 persons to every square mile, the chain of islands has the densest concentration of humanity among the developed nations, except for Hong Kong.

As in most hospitals, most patients at Mitsui Memorial and their solicitous visitors are middle-aged. Besides, Japan's population is aging. More than half its people are over thirty-five—for the expectation of life is over eighty for women and almost seventy-five for men.

Broad bands of different colors run across floors, along walls, and upon ceilings to guide visitors to their destinations. The red band leads to neurosurgery. Dr. Fukushima appears after ten minutes. His features are small and neat, the nose straight and narrow, almost aquiline, and the unlined forehead high.

He is constantly in motion, exuding energy. But he appears to be weighing every word when he tells a tale he has already told a hundred times. Like a great orator, he sounds newly inspired on every repetition.

"Asians get excited very easily," he confides. "It's simple mass psychology. . . ." When he realizes that his visitors are not new to Asia, he segues smoothly into Japanese medicine: "The younger generation must stand respectfully behind the chair . . . always self-effacing. Young doctors do research—and the professor claims all the credit."

That is good solid stuff, but hardly new. But Takanori Fukushima will not be rushed.

"The Japanese standard of living is very low compared to Australia or the U.S.," he observes. "And the Japanese people now know about that. . . . A physician's life is nowhere as comfortable in Tokyo as in New York or Sydney—not if he wants to practice good medicine. . . . Health care is also very bad. Too many doctors want only to make a lot of money, and at least half are incompetent. So they practice insurance medicine, getting paid separately for every patient and every procedure. And they make lots of money.

"But who has the boats, the swimming pools, and the two cars that are standard for a family in Australia? Very few Japanese! Yes, there is lots of money around. But not space or leisure. Certainly not big houses. So even office girls spend their salaries on clothes and travel."

"As they do everywhere," Moira observes, sotto voce.

Not drawn in, Dr. Fukushima adds, "Japan has the most commercial medical system in the world. Plus very low-grade medicine."

His generalizations are obviously well informed. They are also highly individual.

I ask, "And what about yourself?"

He practices good medicine, Dr. Fukushima says, because he is not primarily interested in the financial rewards. His salary from Mitsui Memorial is about $40,000 a year, and he earns a few thousand more from Tokyo University, which is known to pay a visiting professor all of five dollars a lecture.

Duly recording that ludicrous figure, but unable to swallow it completely, I ask what the university pays a full-time full professor of medicine. He replies, "No more than $3,600 a month."

He has made his point: monetary rewards for hospital physicians and surgeons are low in prospering Japan. Of course, his standard is the incomes of such professionals in the United States and Australia, not the relative austerity of Britain and continental Europe.

"Why," I ask, "do you put up with it?"

"Because I want to practice good medicine, and I couldn't under the insurance regulations," he replies. "Still, they could replace me here in a minute."

"Replace *you*?" I echo, bemused by his apparent descent from absolute self-confidence.

"I am the best." His tone is again normal. "But there are many others. The university could easily replace me. So could the hospital."

Before meeting him, I knew that Takanori Fukushima was the best in the world in his special fields. I should have believed neither his account of his achievements nor his assessment of his abilities if I had not been told by an eminent non-Japanese neurosurgeon that he was truly extraordinary.

His complaints of poverty should, however, be heavily discounted. He performs more than one thousand operations every year, a good number in outside hospitals. Three hundred is a substantial number for an average neurosurgeon. He is also a regular consultant at fifteen outside hospitals. All his outside patients pay him directly, although he notes, "The hospital decides how much. A Japanese surgeon can't discuss his fee."

He has, further, invented specialized instruments for neurosurgical procedures. The royalties paid by manufacturers are not immense, but neither are they meager. He also enjoys hidden income: a trip abroad every month or two, to speak to a medical conference.

"That's the best part," he confesses. "I'm crazy about neurosurgery.

It's 95 percent of my life, almost everything! So I like talking about it very much."

He opens a thick photo album. "Look here. My guests come from all over the world to learn my techniques. . . . To relieve tics and facial pain, I do the best work in the world."

Each Monday at Mitsui Memorial he sees eighty to ninety outpatients. Since all the raw data is collected for him beforehand, he need give no more than five minutes to each. The same backup enables him to perform five to seven operations every day.

"Sometimes I may have to devote as much as an hour or two to a single operation," he says. "But my assistants always open the head so I don't have to wait."

Despite that macabre phraseology, the junior surgeons do not remove the top of the cranium like a skullcap to present a throbbing gray mass to the scalpel. Dr. Fukushima is particularly proud of his "keyhole operations"; he works through a one-centimeter opening, where other neurosurgeons may require four centimeters. Aware of the skepticism his claims awaken, he declares, "Many think Fukushima is a liar when he says he even works through an opening of half a centimeter. But I show them. Professors from America and Europe come to see me. Everybody knows my name."

I wonder briefly whether Takanori Fukushima learned such un-Japanese self-celebration during his studies at the Mayo Clinic in the U.S. or during his residency in Germany. I conclude that he is his own man, not to say his own creation. And his dedication is absolute. His first wife left him because he was obsessive, and he rarely sees his three children. His present wife has no illusions about his priorities.

"I have no hobby, and I go home to my wife only once or twice a week," he says. "I have no summer holidays, no Saturday, no Sunday, no Christmas. I sleep only a few hours a night. . . . A twitch in the eye or paralysis, who can cure them? Only two professions: the neurosurgeon and God!"

Amid such eloquent self-appreciation, I am shocked by his next words: "Some procedures others still do better. I must learn and catch up. I *must* be Number One!"

As much as his assertive self-approbation, that confession reveals the essential Takanori Fukushima. He runs furiously because he is terrified of being outdone. Although extraordinarily gifted, he scales the peaks chiefly because he fears others will outdo him. Characteristically Japanese, he is obsessed by the need to excel.

Characteristically Japanese, but *not* typically Japanese, Dr. Fukushima is an innovator and a pioneer. Most of his compatriots are tautly disciplined by external forces. They perform well, often magnificently, because they are whipped on by their tightly organized society. Most are, however, followers rather than leaders, the moist clay rather than the potter's hands. The people are also Japan's only abundant natural resource aside from its rainfall.

Utilizing the human resource brilliantly, a few hundred inspired leaders transformed Japan from a semifeudal despotism into the most powerful economic force in history in a period of 120 years, which spanned their disastrous defeat in World War II. Without brilliant pioneers like Takanori Fukushima, however, Japan might today be a Third World nation. With luck, it might just be reaching self-sufficiency.

Instead, Japan dominates the international economy as no other modern nation has done, except the United States in the fifteen years immediately after World War II. The U.S. was dominant because all the other powers, including Japan, were exhausted; the U.S. was dominant because of its vast industrial resources, which had expanded mightily in building the mightiest war machine ever seen. Having catastrophically failed to dominate by military might, Japan was prostrate in 1945. Yet thirty-five years after it began to clamber back in 1955, Japan is predominant.

The palace of the emperor dominates Tokyo as Buckingham Palace has never dominated London, a metropolis almost as enormous. The emperor of Japan, who has not totally lost his divinity, is central to the life of his nation as even the queen of England is not to hers. He is also richer than the sovereign often described as the richest woman in the world. Extending over 284 acres in the center of the most valuable real estate in the world, the grounds of his residence are worth $288 billion—not counting the buildings.

After the death of Emperor Hirohito at the age of eighty-seven in January 1989, his son Akihito came to the throne. Educated in part by an American tutor, the new emperor is married to a commoner, who was educated at the Sacred Heart Convent, although she is not a Catholic. The couple sent their eldest son, Naruhito, to Oxford and to Harvard to study amid foreign commoners, and the new empress fought to appoint two ladies-in-waiting who were Catholics. Change has come to the Imperial Palace. Akihito is a modern man with modern sympathies. He is also *Tenno*, the Heavenly Emperor, and the center of the devotions, or *Shinto*, the "way of the gods," which is the national creed. From his palaces at the hub of Tokyo, the new emperor looks out on the material symbols of his country's dominance. Sleek skyscrapers rising high above the medieval-looking gray stone walls of the Imperial City house the world's largest financial institution, Nomura Securities; nine of the world's ten largest banks; the world's largest airline; the world's second- and third-largest construction companies; trading companies that control commerce between other nations ten thousand miles away; conglomerates that own tens of billions of dollars' worth of real estate everywhere from Queensland to London and from Los Angeles to Rio de Janeiro; the center that calls the tune for the world's music business, software as well as hardware;[1] and hunter-killer enterprises that are despoiling the seas of whales, dolphins, prawns, tuna, and, worst of all, the plankton on which all marine life ultimately depends.

The collective entity called Japan is not as benign as Dr. Takanori Fukushima. His obsessive behavior helps thousands of patients, hurting only himself and, perhaps, less-gifted neurosurgeons. There are lots of patients to go around. But Japan's compulsion to excel is sometimes destructive. Not always, but often enough to inspire profound fear.

The font of that ruthlessness is desperation. Having been desperately poor for centuries, Japan is desperately afraid of becoming poor again. Japan is terrified that it will, somehow, fail and be despised again if it does not run even faster *after* having attained its goal.

A century ago the country that is now by far the world's largest exporter was shocked to discover that its exports per head were less than .76 percent those of France.[2] Its *only* staple exports were tea leaves and skeins of raw silk. Today, with the world's largest exports and holdings abroad worth about $250 billion, growing by at least $50 billion a year, Japan should feel at least minimally secure today. But Japan does not feel secure—and perhaps never will.

Since emerging from self-enforced seclusion in the mid-nineteenth century, Japan has been a *ronin* among nations, just as Dr. Takanori Fukushima is a *ronin* among surgeons. The term *ronin*, which means literally "wave man,"[3] was applied in semifeudal times to masterless samurai.[4] A hereditary warrior who had lost his overlord—whether by his own misdeeds, the treachery of enemies, or circumstances—had no place in the hierarchical society. Therefore he had no means of support except brigandry or, if he were lucky, service as a mercenary.

[1] Sony bought CBS Records in November 1987 for $2 billion, roughly Y270 billion, about half what it would have cost in yen two years earlier before the Japanese currency soared toward the stratosphere. In mid-1989 Sony bought Columbia films.

[2] As pointed out by Haru Matsukata Reischauer in her charming book on her eminent ancestors, *Samurai and Silk* (Boston: Harvard University Press, 1986).

[3] In the original Chinese, the term means "vagabond" or "ruffian." *Lang*, pronounced *ro* in Japanese, means not only "wave," but also "profligate, reckless, dissolute," or "licentious." Nowadays, *ronin* also describes students who fail their university entrance examinations. They, too, are cut off from their peers.

[4] *All* fighting men were called samurai, but the common people were not allowed to bear arms in war or peace. Samurai were not knights in the European sense; nor were they officers or nobleman. The hereditary professional soldiers were yeoman.

Living as best he could, the *ronin* was governed only by his own rules. His behavior, often lawless, was justified in his own eyes not only by the necessity to survive, but by a code of honor that defied the law. The *ronin* tradition has little in common with the Robin Hood legend, for the men tossed on the wild waves of fate were neither merry nor philanthropic. Sad and self-obsessed, they sought death in battle. Most of those not so fortunate as to die in battle finally found honorable release in suicide.

Such masterless men are the heroes of Japan's favorite tale, *The Forty-seven Ronin*, which has for centuries also been Japan's most popular play. The leitmotif is loyalty, revenge, and suicide, themes not unknown in Western dramas. In Japan, however, self-destruction is exalted as it is nowhere else.

The Japanese act is usually called *hara-kiri* by outsiders, who like the assonance. It literally means "stomach-cutting," but the Japanese prefer the term *seppuku*, which means "abdomen-slitting." The privilege was restricted to samurai, and the ritual was fixed: first, bathing, putting on clean clothing, and making farewells; next, kneeling and plunging a short sword into one's abdomen, just below the breastbone; then, drawing the blade down and across; finally, the coup de grace administered by one's second, usually one's closest friend, a single sword-stroke that takes off the head.

Although that ritual is rarely practiced nowadays, many Japanese are obsessed with suicide. Unlike the novelist and right-wing agitator Yukio Mishima, who dispatched himself in traditional fashion with a short sword, most suicides choose other means. Most are, nonetheless, painful and dramatic. Some star-crossed lovers climb the sacred mountain Fuji-san to hurl themselves into its crater. Driven by indignities even greater than those they have been trained to endure without complaint, some barren wives take caustic soda, which agonizingly burns out their alimentary tracts. Some students who fail examinations place their heads under pile-drivers. Their inspiration is, however, always the abdomen-slitting of the samurai.

Other peoples naturally wonder somewhat warily about a people who cherish a cult of ceremonial self-destruction amid great agony. "What kind of people are these," I have often been asked by Westerners, "whose ways are so completely different?" Or, alternately, "The more I see of the Japanese, the less I understand them." Finally, the bald declaration: "They're so strange, I wonder if they're really people like you and me."

Stringently racist themselves, the Japanese provoke racism. Contemplating mass suicide attacks by desperately outnumbered Japanese infantrymen and the extremely small number who let themselves be taken prisoner, their enemies came to believe that Japanese were fundamentally unlike themselves. Even today, in peacetime, ruthless Japanese competition often leads to the same conclusion.

It is, therefore, worth restating the obvious: *Of course, they are human beings rather like you and me. But they are by no means just like you and me. They have been shaped by their own particular culture, which is not at all like our Judeo-Christian culture with its Greco-Roman influence. Japanese culture was formed by the pressures of life in cramped, marginally fertile islands and by the presence next door of the overbearing Chinese civilization. Moreover, the character of the Japanese people has not changed remarkably during the 120-odd years since they reluctantly came out of the self-imposed isolation the world would no longer permit them to maintain.*

The Forty-seven Ronin, I believe, reveals that essential character. Early in the eighteenth century, it relates, a *daimyo,* a "feudal nobleman," was executed for wounding a corrupt official who had mortally insulted him. Forty-seven samurai, reduced to *ronin* by their lord's death, swore to avenge him by killing the official.

Their first task was to disarm the official's natural suspicion by feigning to fall into debauchery. Their leader not only allowed himself to be spat upon as he lay in the gutter, but divorced his wife for pleading with him to reform.

Nothing mattered except revenge. Any means was justified—and noble—if it led toward that end, even murder, which violated the law of the state.

Winning entry to the official's mansion by deception, the forty-seven *ronin,* whose ranks included aged fathers and adolescent sons, slew his guards in a terrible fight. Ransacking the mansion, they found the evil official's hiding place—and cut off his head.

Rejoicing, they made their way to the shrine near Yedo, which is present-day Tokyo, where their lord was buried. They were hailed by householders on their route and the abbot of the shrine welcomed them cordially. After washing their enemy's head, they laid it on the grave of their lord. Their mission completed, they all committed *seppuku.*

By our standards, the *ronin* behaved deceitfully, indeed treacherously. They compulsively pursued a single purpose, benefiting no one—not the state, nor any of their lord's family, nor themselves. They sacrificed their good names and the welfare of their families. They flouted the law—and cravenly evaded punishment through suicide.

Yet they were honored while they lived. In the centuries since their death, their memories have been hallowed and their deeds have been extolled. Implacable vindictiveness is apparently still laudable.

Even then prohibited by authority, the vendetta was thus sanctified in eighteenth-century Japan. Only with great difficulty had *junshi,* self-immolation on the death of one's lord, been suppressed in the seventeenth century, although human sacrifice, voluntary or involuntary, was largely abandoned in China by the second century B.C. In Japan, the sacred vendetta, often culminating in *seppuku*, flourished into the 1930s, justifying political assassination.

The principle was the same. Twisting Confucian doctrine to its own purposes, the doctrine of *bushido*, "the way of the warrior," had been promulgated about 1665. *Bushido* justified a parasitic class of hereditary warriors at the apex of the social pyramid and exalted loyalty to one's lord above *all* other virtues. The vengeful forty-seven *ronin* were ever loyal to their deceased lord, and twentieth-century political assassins believed they served the emperor against his enemies, as well.

Although it violated the law and flouted conventional morality, *any* action was justifiable, indeed noble, if it stemmed from devotion to one's lord. The forty-seven *ronin* have subsequently inspired obedience to the death and defiance of authority; transcendant conformism that submerges the individual in the mass for the glory of another individual; and even sacrificing one's family, the *worst* Confucian sin, for one's sworn comrades and one's lord.

Dr. Takanori Fukushima embodies those contradictory and essentially medieval qualities. He has already sacrificed his family to his calling, and he may be sacrificing himself as well. He smokes heavily, takes no exercise, gets little rest, never relaxes, and eats poorly. Quite remarkably, he suffers no physical consequences—at least, as he acknowledges, "Not yet!" He *must*, however, surpass all others at all costs. Like the *ronin*, he is obsessively singleminded.

The single trait that defines the Japanese is, I believe, their singlemindedness. Short of poleaxing, they cannot be turned aside once set on a course. In frenetic action, sometimes even self-destructive action, they find surcease from the pain inflicted by the contradictions within society and within themselves. Their motto is today, as it has been for centuries: "Do not look aside, but only at the goal!"

Like enraged bulls, Japanese charging with their heads down are very dangerous—primarily to others, but also to themselves. Since they do not want to see, they cannot see where they are going. And they cannot stop themselves.

The goal is all. Even formal crime is not reprehensible, but noble if it brings the goal closer.

Most Japanese are, moreover, deeply involved with their own problems. It is exceedingly difficult—if not impossible—for them to put themselves in the place of others. Empathy is not a word often used in Japan. Like their disregard of moral absolutes and their exaltation of violence, their difficulty in imagining, much less feeling, the pain of others makes them formidable in action. Scruples about the effect of their actions on others do not impede progress toward their own goal.

A few *ronin* like Dr. Takanori Fukushima are pioneers, but most Japanese seek a *collective* goal. They can prove their individual worth to others—and, thus, to themselves—only by submerging their individuality in common success.

Thus, success, prevailing over others, becomes the chief—if not the only—value. To collective success the Japanese sacrifice the environment, physical well-being, reputation, principle, even their families, and their own lives.

Naturally, they will employ almost any means. Striving to dominate, Japan in this century employed first military and then economic means. Singleminded in pursuit of their goal, the Japanese have been extraordinarily supple, readily abandoning old means and adopting new means. They recall the character in a brilliant comic novel by Peter de Vries of whom another character observed: "Way down deep, she's shallow."

At their apparently solid core, the Japanese are hollow. Lack of abstract principles is their greatest strength and their worst weakness; they are almost infinitely adaptable, but no immutable values sustain them. They can bend deep without cracking. "The supple bamboo bows before the wind," declares the folk saying, "but does not break." The hollow bamboo has soft pith, but hard joints—and is firmly rooted.

In the past, Japanese loyalty was rooted in the *daimyo*, their hereditary lords; in the village headman; and in comrades in work or battle. Their loyalty is now rooted in entities like small firms or subdivisions of big corporations. Blood-and-bone loyalty is not given to abstractions, not even to such potent symbols as: *kokutai*, the "national essence"; *Shinto*, the "way of the gods"; *bushido*, the "way of the warrior"; and *Tenno Heika*, "the heavenly emperor."

All four concepts were in good part contrived to unite a loosely affiliated people. *Kokutai*, which attempts to provide the guiding principle the Japanese lack, is not precisely defined, but is widely revered. Shinto is a made-up religion composed of elements of animism, Confucianism, and nationalism. *Bushido* was, as I have noted, promulgated in the seventeenth century, in part to bolster the Tokugawa Shoguns, who ruled in the name of the emperor. The emperor has reigned for some 1,500 years, but has not ruled for more than nine hundred years. In 1868 he was "restored" to power so that the country could be unified and modernized in his name.

All four institutions evoke loyalty that can be profound in crises. Today everyday loyalty is given to the community by its residents and to the company by its employees, not to such abstractions.

The character of the Japanese has been discussed in scores of books by Westerners, as well as Japanese. The people of the island empire have fascinated foreigners almost as much as they have fascinated themselves. And they have produced almost as abundant explanations of their own psyches as they have produced merchandise for others. Those explanations range from spiritualism to statistics and from mysticism to electrocephalic measurement. Clearly, the knotty enigma of the essential Japanese character cannot be laid open by a single Gordian stroke.

I have been in and out of Japan regularly since 1951, but I have never spent more than two or three months there at a time. Moira, who lived there for two years, has a better perspective. Her comments, which I have incorporated, are at once sympathetic and realistic.

To Dr. Takeo Doi, a leading psychiatrist who has studied in the United States as well as Japan, the Japanese character is the quality he calls *amae*. That word is written with the Chinese ideogram that means "sweet" and, by extension, "pleasant" or "compliant." Much discussed since it was introduced to the West by Frank Gibney twenty-five years ago, Dr. Doi's thesis remains a key to Japan.

He ascribes to *amae* the dependence he sees as fundamental to the Japanese character. He does not mean dependence in a Western sense. No more is "dependence" a direct translation of *amae*, which, in this context, means, as close as I can come to it in English, to be ingratiating or endearing.

Doi contends that Japanese are by Western standards inordinately dependent upon the approbation of their fellows and, even more, their superiors. Their psychological security derives from the good opinion of their own microcosm of society, and they require constant reassurance. They, therefore, behave so as to win approbation. Incapable of defying either the obligations imposed by their superiors or the expectations of their fellows, most Japanese therefore act collectively.

Dr. Doi observes that *amae* is the feeling a devout Roman Catholic has for the Virgin Mary; it is loving and dependent ingratiation (even puppies, indeed puppies in particular, *amaeru*, to use the verb); and there is, in any case, no English equivalent.

With what does all that very Japanese and very studied ambiguity leave us? It leaves us with a tough and ruthless, goal-driven and success-oriented personality that is also fragile, vulnerable, and totally dependent upon the good opinion of others. The individual Japanese and the collective Japanese are two entirely different entities, and they behave quite differently. Charming in personal relationships, they are ruthless in commerce.

The demands of survival shaped that divergent character. Japan is a very poor country, which possesses in abundance only rain, mountains, and seacoasts. It lacks not only mineral resources, but fertile land enough to support a large population. Over the centuries, most Japanese therefore lived in small communities that scraped from the soil or wrung from the sea a meager existence. In those cramped circumstances, all men and women had to behave with great circumspection to avoid giving offense to each other.

Naturally, the strong and ruthless took the greater share of sparse food and goods. The circumspection required of inferiors therefore became self-restraint so stringent that the West was to regard it as pathological, indeed virtually inhuman. The alternative was immediate decapitation by any hereditary warrior who felt himself offended; samurai were empowered thus to maintain summary discipline among the lower orders. The samurai were in turn subject to equally Draconian discipline by their superiors. Women's subservience was unquestioned. Men practiced good manners and rendered strict obedience—lest the sword intervene.

That intensely inhibited society was also deprived. Although it was not quite poverty, existence was hardly bare comfort. Japanese life therefore made much of little.

Not vulgar abundance, but tidbits exquisitely presented was the ideal for cuisine. Not gaudy display, but subdued elegance was the model for clothing, houses, and conveyances. Not camaraderie and affability were the norm of social behavior, but *enryo*. Meaning approximately "reserve," *enryo* is written with Chinese ideograms that mean literally "distant concern."

Austerity was exalted. Works of art were valued above all for their restraint; a simple earthenware cup of exquisite shape was a supreme achievement. The sacred *katana,* the long curved samurai sword, is superior to any Western blade, but the hilt and scabbard were subdued. Exuberant display of jewels and gold like that on Toledo blades were anathema.

Certain safety valves for tension were, however, sanctioned: the gorgeous armor and robes of the rulers and the license granted subjects at *matsuri*, the "temple festivals," when all the bearers of the palanquins of the gods were *expected* to be very drunk.

The word *shibui,* which came into vogue two decades ago in the West, somewhat proximately describes Japan's straitened aesthetic vision. When an enthusiastic American editor pressed my former classmate at Columbia, Charles Terry, for a word that would characterize the constrained culture, he came up with *shibui*—and the editor made it popular. *Shibui* means "astringent and spare, detached and refined," perhaps most accurately in modern parlance: "cool."

Language is the single most powerful influence on an individual's development because most other influences work *through* language.

The character of a people is also determined as much by the character of its language as by its climate, its resources, and its machines.

Idiosyncratic and ingrown, the Japanese language has shaped the minds and the emotions of the Japanese people. A grammatical structure that differs radically from the classical Western models, Greek and Latin, as it does from Chinese, does not handicap a non-Western, non-Chinese people. But the Japanese *are* handicapped by their language's propensity for diffuseness and imprecision. They do not understand each other precisely unless they take pains to be lucid. Even more burdensome—and distorting—is a system of writing by far the most complex in regular use anywhere.

The spoken and the written forms of all languages differ markedly. Speech is loose, spontaneous—and vanishes instantly. Made to last, writing is inherently more formal. Since writing limits the range of both sound and meaning in order to communicate clearly, it cannot reproduce the almost infinite variety of speech. Written Japanese is, however, *extraordinarily* remote from spoken Japanese; that luxuriant tongue is badly clothed in garments designed for the Chinese language, which has an entirely different shape.

Japanese and Chinese use the same ideograms, which were invented by the Chinese. Otherwise they are at least as far apart as, say, Turkish and English. Like Turkish, Japanese is agglutinative. It changes meaning by adding suffixes—sometimes a half-dozen, one on the tail of another—to the root, which contains the word's basic meaning.[5] Like English, Chinese is analytic. Both rely primarily on the logic of word order to convey meaning and use few suffixes.

Those ideograms, which the Japanese call *kanji,* "Chinese letters," are the most intricate extant form of writing. Some four millennia ago, they began as pictures. A circle around a dot represented the sun, and a sickle-shape represented the new moon. *Kanji* later became stylized. The sun is now a rectangle crossed by a bar, and the moon is an elongated horseshoe crossed by two bars. Some ideograms became fanciful. One, which means "black," is a bird without an eye—that is, a jet-black crow whose jet-black eye cannot be seen. Sounds, too, are now represented. A stylized symbol meaning "leather" combines with a symbol pronounced *ahn* to mean "saddle," which is *ahn* in spoken Chinese. The Japanese use exactly the same ideogram for "saddle," but they sometimes pronounce it *ahn,* as the Chinese do, and sometimes *kura,* as it was in original spoken Japanese.

---

[5] Take the root *aru,* at once verb and adjective (which parts of speech are indistinguishable in Japanese), meaning "to have." *Arimasu* is the polite form. *Arimasen* is negative polite. *Arimasen-deshita* is past negative polite, while *aranakkata* is past negative rough colloquial. *Aru-hasu-desu* means "I (you, he, she, it, or they) should like to have." Incidentally, *de-aru,* meaning "to be," takes the same full set of affixes, of which I have here given only examples.

Japanese also uses symbols called *kana*, which stand for sounds. Combining like Latin letters to make words or parts of words, *kana* are used for postpositions, that is, prepositions placed *after*, instead of before words. *Kana* are also used for the complex suffixes that give the tenses of verbs, making them positive or negative, respectful or brusque.

The nearly surrealistic complexity of simply learning to read and write makes the Japanese very good at memorization. Discerning patterns amid complexity, the Japanese are also adroit at the intellectual somersaults demanded by modern science and technology. However, learning Japanese draws heavily on intellectual capital—and Japanese do not learn foreign languages well.

The spoken language, too, presents unique difficulties. It can be brutally direct or so allusive that exact meaning vanishes. Such vagueness limits conflict in a very crowded society by avoiding offense; it also conceals thoughts. Swear words are, moreover, few. The worst direct insult is *bakka*, normally translated as "stupid." Yet, using the simple root of a verb shorn of respectful suffixes can be a fearful insult.

Overcoming inherent imprecision is a formidable task. The military invented a new form called *heigo*, literally, "troop language," which is brusque, relatively precise, and used for orders. Employing angular *katakana*, rather than scriptlike *hiragana*, to write foreign words also makes Japanese more flexible and more precise. Bread is *pan* from Portuguese. Beer is *biiru*, not to be confused with *biru*, meaning a building.

My favorite recent usages are both from journalist Yoshihisa Komori. *Masikomi* stands for "the media of mass communication." Beside a string of six ideograms, *katakana* give the meaning. They read *daburu sutandado*, "double standard," a term now more widely understood than its complex expression in ideograms.

Typewriting Japanese is actually slower than handwriting because of the multiplicity of symbols: 112 *kana* and a *bare* minimum of 1,300 *kanji*. A century or so ago, each was assigned a code number for use in telegrams. Today, facsimile can send even handwritten *kana* and *kanji*, although word processors still cannot quite type Japanese as fast as it can be handwritten.

Technological advances do not, however, alter its circuitousness. Honorifics expressing respect and subordination generally come not at the end of verbs, but at the beginning of nouns. The simple word for tea, *cha*, is, for example, never used without the prefix *oh*, meaning "honored" or "exalted." One asks for *ohcha*, not *cha*.

Women use honorifics and self-deprecating expressions so profusely that their speech is almost a separate dialect. Because my Japanese deteriorates between visits, I find some women impossible to understand on the telephone. The worst are young receptionists and secretaries, who are hyper-respectful. But men are quite intelligible, since they normally convey the same information with much less politeness. Yet I met a male municipal official whose sentences were so clotted with honorifics and self-deprecation that another Japanese observed, "He's so polite two-thirds of what he says is meaningless."

Courtesy also requires many more words than are necessary and rarely allows a simple, direct statement. Hiroshi Kida is a modern and hard-headed savant who is considering the future of education. Yet a major technical article from his brush bristles with superfluous verbiage—superfluous, that is, from a Western point of view. To Japanese it is unthinkable that most of his sentences should *not* end with formulas like ". . . this sort of such-called thing is the matter of which I unassumingly speak."

Poor in swear words, Japanese is fabulously rich in self-demeaning apologies like *Shitsurei itashimashita!*—"I have violated the canon of propriety!"; *Gommen nasai!*—"I crave pardon!"; *Ki no doku sama desu!*—"My spirit is poisoned!"

Sumimasen is most used. Appropriately, both its origin and its root meaning are unclear. It may originally have meant "I have not stopped" or, alternatively, "I am not residing." Now it means "I am so terribly sorry, and I so deeply regret." Expressing such regret can be a symbolic form of *seppuku*, ritual suicide, depending on the gravity of the offense. Hardly suicide if I have spilled soup on you, but virtually suicide if I have damaged your reputation.

A formal apology was unquestionably equivalent to *seppuku*, which is not in vogue in the new, presumably democratic Japan, when the minister for trade and industry made a contrite pilgrimage to Washington, D.C., in 1987. He humbly conveyed the sincere regret of all Japan for the Toshiba Corporation's having sold equipment that enabled the Soviet Union to build more menacing nuclear submarines. That apology was grueling for the minister. Afterward, the Japanese people could, quite sincerely, not understand why the American people were not placated by his profound self-abasement.

Japan and the Japanese are different—not only from the West, but from their neighbors in East Asia. Those neighbors instinctively regard Japan as Western, not because it is Western, but because it is *not* Asian.

Japan is the only country of the region that is mature, complex, and intricate—not only industrially and commercially, but intellectually and socially. Contemporary Japanese painting, literature, scholarship, and even fashion are fully equal to that produced elsewhere—if such "equality" can be measured quantitatively, as the Japanese believe it can. They are striving to overtake and surpass all others in those endeavors in which they are not yet equal, whether, say, music or sports. The spirit of Dr. Takanori Fukushima moves an entire people.

Although rich in traditional forms, most of them Chinese-inspired, Japan's culture appears highly Westernized to other Asians. The Japanese adopted Western models in order to assert their equality—and potential superiority—even in Western fields. They buy Western paintings for tens of millions of dollars in order to prove first, that they can afford to do so; and, second, that they truly possess the sensitivity to appreciate those works. Why else would they pay so much money for them?

A new, highly materialistic culture is, thus, growing out of the old austere culture. *Shibui*, "cool," hardly fits a materialistic society that splurges on Pierre Cardin clothes and Dom Perignon champagne. Nor can *shibui* describe the mentality of the golden youth who are called *shin jinrui*, "the new human race," to emphasize their divergence from their parents.

The older generation are socioneurotics in conformists' clothing. Nine out of ten of their automobiles are white, the color of mourning. Most women's modern—that is, Western—clothing is mousy, but traditional kimono and their broad obi belts are gorgeously pastel. The females of the *shin jinrui* are, however, soignée by any standard—and their men are bandbox-dapper. Alternately, both sexes are trendily layered or disheveled.

Yet those devotées of manic late-twentieth-century consumerism spring directly from the culture of scarcity. Somehow, the ascetic ideal coexists with the gumdrop-colored plastic artifacts poured out by modern industry—and it coexists not merely peacefully, but robustly. It is not just mutual tolerance. The two opposites do not merely live side by side, but somehow feed each other.

Why else are an intensely visual people like the Japanese *not* appalled by the terrible incongruities they see everywhere? Navy-blue *noren*, the traditional scalloped or split half-curtains bearing understated white ideograms, hang above a café's sliding glass doors that are defaced with credit-card decals. The public telephone within comes in four plastic hues: fire-engine red, aniline blue, margarine yellow, and shocking pink.

Such insensitivity is helpful to survival in cities blighted by industrial ugliness. Selective blindness is fostered by the dictates of good manners. One does not see what should not be seen, such as the other sex naked in the old communal baths. Selective blindness is trained by the theatrical convention of the *kuroko*, literally "the black one," the invisible stage attendant who casually shifts scenery in the midst of dramatic action.

Past and present coexist incongruously for the Tachibana family, once the *daimyo*, hereditary feudal lords, of Yanagawa on Kyushu, the big southern island. Their ancestral home is now a resort hotel called Ohana, a complex of old and new buildings. A clan museum now occupies the Edwardian mansion that was once the Tachibanas' private residence. Moira and I stopped there because the Tachibanas' daughter and son-in-law are our old friends.

Kazuo Tachibana, the head of the house, was eighty that year. His irises were clouded by a pale gray film, and the whites were delicately bloodshot. A convivial drinker, he was setting off for a convivial lunch when we met him, wearing the blue-and-gold wheel of the Rotary Club in the buttonhole of his dove-gray suit.

His wife, Aiko, two years younger, was the *real* Tachibana. Plump, jolly, and a little overly made up, she was everyone's favorite great-aunt in a fitted black dress and four strands of pearls. Handling the big gray Nissan with racy insouciance, she drove her husband off to his Rotary lunch.

Aside from the snack bar and the coffee shop, both American in décor, the muted colors in the public rooms were traditionally Japanese. The gray stone façade of the oldest building was green with moss; the wooden side walls had weathered to a gleaming, almost iridescent, pale gray. Once a country shooting box on the salt marshes where the wild duck still flock, that building was now the central structure of a big hotel in a big town.

Except in the mountains, the Japanese countryside has almost vanished. On Kyushu, which is somewhat less heavily settled than Honshu, the main island, the chief railway line passes a village, a town, or a city every five minutes. On Honshu, it is every two minutes.

A middle-aged maidservant in pastel kimono and mittenlike white socklets showed us to a Western-style room. The Japanese suite next door was austerely beautiful with its tatami-mat floors, its sliding doors of painted paper on delicate wooden frames, and its sparse furniture: only a knee-high table and a recess where a scroll painting hung above a vase holding five flowers, two sprays of fern, and seven twigs. Tatami rooms require expensive labor, including regular meal service, but vacuum cleaners and other appliances have made foreign-style rooms cheaper to look after. Even senior Japanese executives visiting the enchanted old capital of Kyoto choose foreign-style hotels. The old-fashioned inns, called *ryokan*, are too expensive.

A twelve-volume guest book invited our comments. A ballpoint might be all right for jotting notes. But this formal record required a traditional writing brush, which would formerly have required a labor-intensive clutter of ink stick, water pot, and ink stone. Instead, the Ohana provided a high-tech writing brush, essentially a Pentel pen with soft bristles.

Beneath our second-floor window, long, narrow boats poled by squat boatmen in traditional short coats and conical straw hats carried parasol-bearing tourists between the green banks of the Willow River. They had come in groups, all employees of one company or all members of one association, and few had brought husbands or wives. Their posture was tense, for the Japanese take their obligatory pleasures with eager embarrassment, and they were attentive to the loudspeakers prescribing the correct reaction to each sight they saw.

Disembarking from their placid adventure, tourists stopped at a minuscule shop where a portly craftsman was making lanterns. Each the skin of a single *fugu*, a "blowfish," the puffed-up lanterns were menacing with their clenched, malign features and their spiky, gray surface. A demicult of death centers on the *fugu*, whose gall and ovaries contain tetrodotoxin, which brings almost instantaneous death by paralyzing the respiratory tract.

The Japanese passion for *sashimi*, "raw fish," which Moira and I share, finds macabre expression in the eating shops that specialize in *fugu*. Since a slip of the knife can bring death, iron lungs used to stand in the corner. Nowadays, state-licensed slicers are certified safe, but the fillip of danger still titillates the daredevil gourmets.

Later, hundreds of tourists invaded the Ohana to sit under red-and-white umbrellas and eat sukiyaki cooked on braziers fueled by bulbous gray gas cylinders. Afterward, they danced in groups, applauding each other uproariously. We fell asleep to the doleful lyrics in Japanese of "Ghost Riders in the Sky."

The next evening, gray-and-black clouds reared in immense terraces over the Willow River, and the television warned of the coming of *taifu*, a typhoon. The umbrellas were furled; the chairs were put away; the tables were tied down; and the windows were bolted. The throngs took refuge in the coffee shop, the snack bar, and the big restaurant. Signally favored, we were led to the Bamboo Room, whose only furniture was a broad coffee table. Sitting on tatami, we were served by the middle-aged maidservant with local delicacies: *sashimi*, raw slices of the fish caught that afternoon in the bay; *agemaki*, a local shellfish; and *unagi no seiromushi*, the celebrated eel steamed in the manner of Yanagawa. With dinner we drank the local rice wine, which the maidservant assured us was far more delicious and far less toxic than any other sake in all Japan.

Pride in local food, drink, and customs is universal. Each region, town, and village developed in substantial isolation from its neighbors in the days when all but a few walked everywhere. Strong loyalty is still given to each district's *lares et penates*, the native spirits of the rivers, the trees, the stones, and the mountains.

The economic colossus called Japan is made up of thousands of virtually contiguous but decidedly independent communities, which only a hundred years ago spoke mutually unintelligible dialects. When Japan entered the modern world, its rulers had to create a moral, political, and linguistic consensus. Although that great work was done well, regional differences linger pleasantly.

The shoes lined up before the sliding doors of the neighboring tatami room belonged to seven men and two women. The local sake cheered them; their voices rose; and snatches of song drifted through the paper partitions. It is not mannerly but rude to remain unaffected by drink when gathered with equals and superiors for diversion. One must let go of habitual inhibitions.

The boss is in theory bound to forget criticism directed at him amid revelry. A subordinate may in theory say whatever he wants, thus venting his resentments. Tolerance of truths spoken in drink is certainly broader in Japan than in the West. But the wise, I suspect, do not test the limits of the boss's toleration.

Kazuo Tachibana joined us between the eel and the clear soup with the slivers of white radish and the minute clams in burnished shells. He wanted to drink rather than eat. As he drank, he told us about himself with none of the contrived jollity of the plebeians next door. The sake only enhanced the easy dignity of the old aristocrat.

Yet, he recalled, he came of samurai, not *daimyo* stock. By birth he was a yeoman rather than a hereditary nobleman. He had been adopted by the Tachibana family when he married their eldest daughter in order to carry on the name as well as the line. For all purposes other than blood itself he *was* a Tachibana.

Behind us, the sliding partitions of paper and wood rattled in their tracks, and the storm outside wailed through the sliding glass doors. No Japanese-style house can shut out the cries of nature, and the typhoon was growing in fury.

"Come!" Kazuo Tachibana directed. "You must see my visitors. My family have been visiting for six days. Now it's time for them to go."

In the glare of the floodlights the rain streamed horizontally across the terrace like the black streaks of a downpour in a Hiroshige print. A palm frond with knife edges hurtled across the path. What foolish travelers, I wondered, were setting out in the teeth of a typhoon?

"There they are," my host shouted over the wailing wind. "In the boat."

The only boat I could see was a dumpy craft of woven straw no more than four feet long. The masts were bundles of long grasses.

"There they are," Kazuo Tachibana repeated. "The ghosts of our ancestors, ready to go back after their visit."

Bemused, I remembered the festival called Bon Matsuri, when the spirits of the ancestors come back to earth. The patriarch introduced his granddaughter, who was going to Australia to live with our friends, her aunt and uncle, and study English. The boat tugged at its line, which was held by a gardener wearing only a loincloth and standing knee-deep in the lake.

The flames started amidships, leaping up the masts and down the sides. Firecrackers popped, just audible above the wind. On the shore, Roman candles spewed balls of red, gold, and silver fire into the typhoon. In three minutes, the flames had consumed the ghost ship, and the charred remnant of the hull floated upside down on the lake.

Kazuo Tachibana smiled and shouted into my ear. The wind was battering my eardrums, and I could not make out a word. But I knew he was happy. His adopted ancestors had just completed another round trip from the abode of the spirits—exactly as they had in the time of the Emperor Meiji and for many centuries before that.

When a squadron of square-rigged sailing ships of the United States Navy dropped anchor in Edo Bay on February 2, 1854, a millennium of Japanese history came to an abrupt end. The protracted feudal era closed on the day Japan was forced to open its doors to the foreign commerce and the foreign ideas it had so long shunned.

Korea was called the Hermit Kingdom. Yet that description was at least equally appropriate to the peculiar monarchy where the powerless emperor in Kyoto in the west was ignored by the hereditary regent in Edo in the east—and both turned their backs on outsiders.

By February 1854, Japan could no longer ignore outsiders whose military power was so greatly superior to its own. The regent's armies were made up of hereditary samurai, who were led by their *daimyo* and armed with swords, halberds, and spears, supplemented by some old firearms. The brave samurai would fight fiercely in single combat, but were untrained in modern tactics. The armies of the past, resplendent in their brightly colored armor, could not face disciplined foreign fighting men in drab modern uniforms.

The American warships did not open the gunports in their sides. There was no need. Commodore Matthew Perry had shown the muzzles of his cannon on a brief visit the preceding year—to very good effect. He could now carry out his instructions to breach Japan's self-imposed seclusion—and to open the country to American diplomats and American merchants.

He was, however, not simply to compel reclusive Japan to deal with the rest of the world. He was to set in motion a train of events that were to alter Japan's every visible aspect and were to end with the world's most dynamic and most potent economic power.

Commodore Perry was, in February 1854, confident of a more cordial reception than he had been given in July 1853. After delivering a letter from President Franklin Pierce that suggested closer relations, he had then withdrawn to Hong Kong to give the feeble regent time to reflect on his vulnerability to modern naval power.

Possessing neither a navy nor an army of nineteenth-century caliber, the hereditary regent, whom his countrymen called Shogun, was virtually defenseless. Having studied Western treatises on gunnery, his advisers knew that naval bombardment could destroy Edo, which was built largely of wood and paper. A blockade could also cut off the staple foodstuffs that came by ship from Osaka.

Commodore Perry came at the right time. Japan was ready for radical change—after three centuries of resisting change—and foreign visits. Internal tensions were finally making thoughtful Japanese look outward. Since the intellectual climate was hospitable to Perry's message, the fear he inspired was complemented by deep respect. For many, he was as much the emissary of enlightenment as the commander of a hostile military force.

"We cannot sleep at night," a poet wrote, "for terror and *admiration* of the black ships!"

That reaction to the "black ships" forced the Shogun to give in—as did the new intelligentsia's conviction that change was essential. On March 31, 1854, at Kanagawa near present-day Yokohama, Japan signed its first modern treaty. It granted American merchant shipping access to two ports, and it provided for the establishment of consular relations.

Britain, Russia, and Holland signed similar treaties during the next eighteen months. But none had practical effect until Townsend Harris arrived in 1856 to set up shop as the consul-general of the United States of America. Harris had great difficulty gaining admission to the country to which he was accredited. But he was an accomplished politician from New York City. Although he commanded no warships, he effectively deployed threats of warships. Bullying and cajoling, alternately imperious and ingratiating, he played on the native feeling that Japan must learn from the West, or perish. A second treaty, signed on July 29, 1858, on an American frigate anchored in Edo Bay, truly opened Japan to foreign commerce and to foreign residents.[6]

Matthew Perry and Townsend Harris created a special relationship between Japan and America that still endures. Through major disputes, mutual threats, strained relations, and, ultimately, war, the Japanese have regarded the United States with particular warmth—or with

---

[6] It included discriminatory terms pioneered in foreign dealing with China: (a) extraterritorial rights, i.e., foreigners would be tried for criminal offenses under their own laws by their own consuls, rather than by the Japanese authorities; and (b) tariffs fixed by treaty, rather than by the Japanese authorities. Based on the then-justified view that the Japanese authorities were too capricious to entrust with foreign lives or foreign property, those privileges later bred much friction.

particular loathing. The United States is today, as it has been since the beginning, the most important foreign power in the eyes of both Japanese leaders and the Japanese people.

Most Japanese are eager for American approbation, despite the gratified contempt many Japanese now express at America's recent failures at home and abroad. That ambivalence was vehemently expressed by Wataru Hiraizumi, who is chairman of the Foreign Affairs Committee of the ruling Liberal Democratic party and a very complex personality among a complex people.

After pointing out with disdain that "five years of mismanagement destroyed the wonderful American economy," he added, "Many Japanese still cannot believe the U.S. is in such bad shape. Unlike the Europeans, who never accepted American supremacy, we did."

"The two countries," he observed, "after World War II virtually become one nation with identical interests. . . . Americans and Japanese feel at home with each other wherever they may meet, particularly in Europe."

Ignoring my raised eyebrows, he asked in a plaintive tone somewhere between that of a hurt child and a rejected lover, "Why are you neglecting us to pay so much attention to China? China can never be as important to you as Japan!"

America's very special relationship with Japan is a major question today, *the* major foreign-affairs question for Japan. For Americans, Japan is also a major foreign-affairs question. The two probably need each other more than any two other nations in the world. That is why "Japan bashing" in America is only matched in fervor by "American bashing" in Japan.

In the late nineteenth century, sweeping consequences flowered from the first major encounter between America and Japan. After ruling from Edo for more than two and a half centuries, the Shogun was overthrown. A new state structure was created, and Edo was renamed Tokyo, Eastern Capital.

The emperor moved from Kyoto, which means "capital city," where his predecessors had for some 1,400 years reigned but rarely ruled. One emperor is reputed to have hawked his calligraphy outside the palace gates to survive. Until Commodore Perry's appearance, the true rulers of Japan had been hereditary shoguns. They had maintained the useful fiction that they acted for the emperor.

The Japanese are good at useful fictions. The new Imperial Government created by a small number of intelligent patriots in 1868, just a decade after Townsend Harris's treaty, utilized a number of brilliant fictions. At best, tenuously linked to real experience, those fictions were closely linked to real myths. The patriots invented the past, borrowed the present from abroad, and dreamed the future. Someday, they knew,

Japan would be dominant. In the meantime, Japan would learn from the West.

The young Emperor Meiji[7] was moved into a foreign-style palace and was dressed in bemedaled Western-style uniforms for public appearances, although he wore the comfortable *yukata* at home. He was tendered respect akin to worship, for he was the direct descendant of the sun goddess, Amaterasu Omikami, who had given the Japanese islands to her family to rule in perpetuity. The creed called Shinto, the "way of the gods," was refurbished and was officially declared superior to the Buddhism that had for centuries expressed the spirituality of Japan. The emperor, a divinity of that new Shinto, stood at the apex of both the state-religion and the state-administration.

The practical and the modern were spiced with the traditional to beguile the pragmatic, yet mystical Japanese people. The installation of the Emperor Meiji was hailed as "restoration" of the monarchy, and the essence of Japan was called the spirit of Yamato, a legendary golden age. In that respect it was the shogunate all over again: an emperor in whose name others ruled. Yet the emperor was visible, and policies were outward reaching.

Among many comprehensive reforms, the Emporer Meiji promulgated a Rescript (decree) creating a new educational system. Built by foreign specialists after the American and German models, the new system was to instill universal literacy. A literate working class was essential for industrialization, and literate conscripts were essential for a modern army. Those plebeian draftees were soon to defeat in battle the *daimyo* and samurai who rose in revolt against the destruction of the old order and their privileges.

Railroads and steel mills, a constitution and law courts, a navy and a police force—all were modeled on Western originals and initially operated by Western experts. On the principle that clothes make the man—and, of course, the woman—the new administrative class togged itself out in foreign finery. When the emperor promulgated the Constitution in 1889, he rose from a Western-style throne under a canopy that could have graced Versailles, pulled down his gold-encrusted field marshal's tunic, and spoke to an audience of men in choker-collared tunics and women in low-cut dresses with bustles.

The externals were all-important. What, after all, was the power of the West except externals—cannon, ships, rifles, locomotives, telegraph wires, machine shops, and, above all, armies and navies? When Japan mastered those externals, Japan would, at the very least, be equal

---

[7] Meiji is a reign name, rather than a personal name. It means "brilliant rule" or "enlightened government." The emperor known to the West as Hirohito, which is a personal name, was known in Japan as Showa, which means "bright peace."

to the West. In reality, Japan would be superior, for the essential character of the Japanese people was immutable—and was unquestionably superior to the character of any other people.

The Japanese are as good at reworked myths as they are at useful fictions. *Bushido*, the "way of the warrior," was, like Shinto, the "way of the gods," created by reverse grafting. A rather feeble old slip was grafted onto the stock of the new purpose—and the hybrid was diligently nurtured. *Bushido* was a brilliant combination of myth and modernity, old swords and revolvers, clan loyalties and torpedo boats. It invoked the spirit of the death-defying, often suicidal, samurai to inspire the peasant conscripts of the new Imperial Armed Forces.

The favored slogan of the time was *Fukoku! Kyohei!*: "Rich nation! Strong soldiers!"

The same spirit suffused foreign policy. Described by sympathizers as militant, the Meiji regime's actions were described by outsiders as aggressive. Regardless of nuance, they were blatantly expansionist.

Military adventures abroad, the expansionists argued, would focus the national spirit. A common purpose abroad was also necessary to unify a nation that had recently been a congeries of antagonistic feudal fiefs. Moreover, samurai dissatisfaction with radical changes at home could be deflected against outsiders.

In 1873, only five years after the Meiji Restoration, the expansionists were tempted by Korea's weakness. Intervention offered a low-risk way to further undermine the tottering Manchu Dynasty by shattering its claim to rule the Korean Peninsula. At the last moment caution prevented an invasion of Korea.

The next year, however, a punitive expedition was sent to Taiwan, which was a province of Imperial China, to teach its aborigines not to attack fishermen from the Ryukyu Islands, which lie between Japan and Taiwan. That expedition eroded China's rule of Taiwan and displayed Japan's paternal concern for the Ryukyus, which were then an independent kingdom with its capital in Okinawa. In 1879, just eleven years after the Meiji Restoration, Japan took the Ryukyus.

In 1894, just forty years since Commodore Perry's visit and twenty-six years since the Meiji Restoration, Japan went to war with China over Korea. The Japanese Imperial Armed Forces won sharp victories, and the peace settlement gave Taiwan to Japan.

The great victory over China, the ancient mentor and enemy, inspired Japan to challenge Russia. The Imperial Navy opened hostilities by striking without warning at Port Arthur; the Imperial Army rolled up a string of victories in Korea and Siberia; and Admiral Togo smashed the Tsar's Baltic Fleet in the Tsushima Straits. Those triumphs gave Japan control of Korea, the prize it had sought above all.

Victory over a European power enlivened the new spirit and strengthened the new power that was to dominate Asia. During the next forty years, Japan was to extend its sway over much of China by intrigue, sabotage, threat, incursions, and, finally, open war. All-out invasion of China led to a bitter quarrel with the United States. That quarrel did not concern only China. It primarily concerned the great natural resources of Asia, which the U.S. would not leave to Japan; the motivation on both sides was economic self-interest.

The Imperial Japanese Navy opened hostilities with the United States by attacking Pearl Harbor without warning on December 7, 1941. At its greatest expanse in 1942, Japan's military empire reached south through the Dutch East Indies almost to Australia, west through Burma to the border of India, and east across the island chains of the Pacific Ocean almost to Hawaii.

In 1945, ninety-one years after Commodore Matthew Perry's treaty and eighty-seven years after Consul-General Townsend Harris's treaty, the United States, allied with Britain, Holland, and China, finally brought down the Japanese Empire. Seventy-seven years after the Meiji Restoration, Japan's aggressive expansion was finally checked.

So, at least, it appeared to the Americans, who occupied Japan and ensured a well-ordered society by retaining the emperor, presumably shorn of his divinity. The victors wrote into Japan's new democratic constitution renunciation of war as an instrument of national policy. Thus they made certain that Japan would not again attempt to dominate Asia and the world. Not, at least, by force of arms.

7

Japan: Yesterday and Today

FACELESS AUTOMATA IN BUNNY SUITS LIVING IN RABBIT HUTCHES
CRAMMED WITH ELECTRONIC GADGETS AND SUPER-APPLIANCES?

One man above all is responsible for the romantic image of quaint old Japan inhabited by a people of the most refined sensibility. Among the images he painted were cherry blossoms and white-painted geishas with cherry lips; the austere tea ceremony and frail paper lanterns; exquisitely understated gardens and gorgeously muted brocades. Lafcadio Hearn, the son of an Irish military surgeon and a susceptible Greek lady, came to Japan in 1891 at the age of forty-one and never left. Sensitive, sympathetic, and an inspiring writer, he moved his foreign readers to sentimental transports over his adopted land. And the Japanese honor him above all others among the large band of foreigners who have written about their country.

Yet he went far beyond mere romantic tales in a charming style, for he was an acute observer who disdained dissimulation. He was a highly realistic writer from his earliest days in Japan, when he lived in the provincial city of Kumamoto on Kyushu, the southernmost island of the archipelago and lived by teaching English. Not restricting himself to the beautiful and the good, he also depicted the ugly and threatening aspects of his beloved Japan.

"A Glimpse of Tendencies," published in 1896, dealt forthrightly with clashes between Japanese and foreigners. Hearn foresaw that the Japanese would come out on top. But even he did not foresee quite how decisively.

His essay described the self-governing foreign settlements that had been established in several seaports after Townsend Harris's treaty of 1858 won extraterritoriality for Westerners, that is, the right to live under their own laws in Japan. The solid order of the settlements, Hearn wrote, contrasted with the "interminable narrow maze of Japanese streets . . . [where] the dogs bark at you and the children stare. . . ." The names the children shouted at foreigners, he noted primly, are "not intended as a compliment."

The children's hostility mirrored the resentment of their elders, who felt that they were constantly cheated by the foreign merchants, who controlled both imports and exports. Yet the young men of Japan, Hearn wrote, were prepared to "suffer in the service" of foreign employers who "were usually harsh, and sometimes brutal."

How else, he asked, could the new generation learn all that had to be "learned to save the country from passing under foreign rule?" But, he predicted: "Some day Japan would have a mercantile marine of her own, and foreign banking agencies, and be well able to rid herself of these haughty foreigners; in the meanwhile [the Japanese feel] they [the foreigners] should be endured as teachers."

Educated young men worked for foreigners only "to fit themselves for the same sort of work in Japanese business houses, stores, and hotels. The average Japanese would prefer to work fifteen hours a day for . . . his own countrymen than eight hours a day for foreigners paying higher wages." The Japanese, he reported, had already learned to combine against foreigners, but only after exercising patience "of that kind which endures so long as to be mistaken for oblivion [unawareness] of injuries."

Soon the positions of natives and foreigners began to change. The Japanese ended the monopoly of foreign commerce that had enabled the outsiders to buy Japanese products cheap and sell foreign products dear. Retail trade passed first into Japanese hands. When native shops offered daily necessities at significantly lower prices, even foreigners bought from them. Soon, Japanese provided not only staples like bread, meat, fish, and salt but also services, whether curing illness or shoeing horses.

When the foreigners had become dependent upon the Japanese, prices rose steeply. Charged much more than the natives, the foreigners grew angry—and the barriers between the Japanese and themselves rose higher.

Still, the foreigners were not greatly alarmed. They were confident that they would always control wholesale and export trade. The few Japanese, initially no more than a dozen, who settled abroad to sell Japanese goods were, foreigners reassured each other, bound to fail. How could they trade abroad when they could not master foreign languages?

In their isolation, foreign residents of Japan disregarded the dislike that, upon occasion, rose to hatred. Few recognized that, as Lafcadio Hearn pointed out, "the existence of foreign settlements in Japan, under consular jurisdiction [i.e., extraterritorial rights], was itself a constant exasperation of national pride. . . ." The foreigners also disregarded their own growing "knowledge of the national desire to control the whole of Japanese commerce, and the periodical manifestation of hostility to foreigners. . . ."

Insulated from reality by their innate conviction of superiority, the Westerners hardly noted the rise of the Japanese.

"It signified little," Hearn wrote, "that Nippon Yusen Kaisha had become, during the [Sino-Japanese] war [of 1894], one of the largest steamship companies in the world; that Japan was trading directly with China and India; that Japanese agencies were being established in the great manufacturing centers abroad; that Japanese merchants were sending their sons to Europe and America for a sound commercial education."

Only in July 1895 did the complacent foreigners begin to recognize their predicament. After a foreign firm won a major lawsuit against a Japanese competitor, a mass boycott forced it to give up the advantage it had gained. "The law could do nothing" against that expression of popular will. The great change had begun. Hearn foresaw the time when the Japanese, having "learned through defeat," would control all exports and imports of their country." He concluded: "It would be the next great step toward the realization of the national desire—*Japan only for the Japanese*. Even though the country should be opened to foreign settlement, foreign investments would always be at the mercy of the Japanese combinations."

Lafcadio Hearn was extraordinarily prescient. Writing just twenty-seven years after the Meiji Restoration, he delineated Japan's future commercial behavior. And what else was to be half as important? Nothing short of war, in which Japan was also triumphant. In 1895 Japan had just won its war against the Chinese Empire. A decade later, it was to win its war against the Russian Empire.

Lafcadio Hearn was to write just as penetratingly about the Russo-Japanese War. He was to foreshadow Japan's conquest of Asia by force of arms when he recounted the ecstatic reaction of rickshaw-pullers and housewives to their emperor's victories over the Tsar. Toddlers' toy battleships and toy rifles portended the great battles that were to be fought later in the twentieth century. Those war toys were a tool, albeit a small one, in the forging of an entire nation into a weapon for military conquest.

Lafcadio Hearn's contemporaries were not impressed by his foresight. They preferred cherry blossoms, geishas, and paper lanterns to his penetrating vision. But he understood the essential Japanese character—their purpose, and their determination. He therefore knew the direction Japan *must* take—and he depicted the ruthlessness, the energy, and the intelligence that would make Japan virtually irresistible.

Outsiders, whether Western or Asian, have been loath to give the Japanese full credit for their achievements or their talents. Even today, when no one can deny Japanese achievements, there is a widespread tendency to ascribe those achievements to sharp practice. Because they have, generally, been neither charming nor prepossessing abroad, the Japanese have been consistently undervalued. In the 1930s, both Chinese and Americans derided Japan's military capability.

Although China was repeatedly defeated by the "inferior" Japanese, its cultural arrogance was undiminished. The Chinese *knew* that their civilization was far superior to Japan's, which they considered no more than an inferior copy of their own. Given better weapons, the Chinese knew they could handily defeat the Imperial Japanese Armed Forces.

America's racial arrogance dismissed the Japanese as too craven to stand up to American fighting men—and too clumsy to manufacture first-class weapons. Many Americans really believed that Japanese were bad aviators because they were nearsighted. The Japanese, who are equally susceptible to racist nonsense, believed that Westerners were bad aviators because they could not see around their big noses. It was all so reassuring. After the war, Americans preferred to believe that Japan had won its victories unfairly—by stealth, deceit, and treachery, rather than by courage and proficiency.

American self-esteem could not acknowledge that the Japanese were, man for man, better soldiers than Americans because they were eager to die for the emperor. Nor could Americans acknowledge that the small dark men from the small, poor island country had outmaneuvered and outfought the United States and its allies before finally being overwhelmed by its massively superior American industrial capacity. They could not admit that Japan had been defeated by neither American generalship nor American courage, which were, at least, matched by the Japanese.

America actually won by machining metal, that is, by making tanks, guns, warships, and planes—and by moving them at high speeds in the air, on the sea, and beneath the sea. But who wanted to believe that World War II had been won not on the playing fields of West Point and Annapolis, but in the steel mills of Pittsburgh and the factories of Detroit?

Nor could Americans concede that the conflict in the Pacific was not morally equivalent to the crusade against evil in Europe. Economic self-interest had brought them into the war, as much as their devotion to justice and their indignation at Japanese aggression. The attack on Pearl Harbor followed an American ultimatum demanding that the Japanese disgorge all their gains in China and Southeast Asia. The choice before Tokyo was either war or surrendering the raw materials and the markets of Asia. The war in the Pacific was perhaps necessary, but it was not an immaculate crusade.

That truth was abhorrent. Besides, reports of atrocities had made the Japanese appear not merely inhuman, but subhuman. The Imperial Japanese Armed Forces did sack Nanking like well-organized barbarians. Looting, raping, and killing with drunken precision,[1] they slaughtered more than a hundred thousand human beings, a greater number than were to die when American atomic bombs fell on Hiroshima and Nagasaki. The Imperial Forces did mistreat prisoners of war cruelly, and their brutality and greed did alienate many Asians who should have been their allies. Obsessively courteous at home, the Japanese were vicious, rapacious, and cruel abroad.

Totally subservient to their superiors, Japanese soldiers were casually brutal to their subordinates. Slapped by the corporal, the private first-class beat the private second-class, who turned on the private third-class, who bayoneted the civilian. The Korean private, the lowest form of military life, revenged his indignities on the prisoner of war, who had forfeited his humanity by allowing himself to be captured. Equally horrifying to Americans, who valued individual life above all else, the Japanese committed suicide in battalions, rather than surrender.

Some scholars and psychological warfare specialists penetrated beyond surface stereotypes. But, even after the war, few foreigners bothered to examine the complex character bred by the complex Japanese society. Did it really matter that unremitting tension had made Japanese either subservient or domineering? Some foreigners knew that Shinto, the contrived state religion, exalted honorable suicide as the noblest human action. Most did *not* know that centuries of institutionalized insecurity had made the Japanese as hard outside as they were so often squishy inside.

In the early 1950s, Americans warily accepted Japan as another bulwark against communism, but felt little warmth toward their new ally. Revulsion against Japanese inhumanity lingered. So did the feeling

---

[1] None of my observations on American attitudes and motives is intended to exculpate the Japanese, whose motives were, at best, equally selfish. Only one Japanese came forward to express sorrow for his participation in the rape of Nanking—and that fifty years later. In the meantime, Japanese textbooks obfuscated the crime, and as the repentant former Private Shiro Azuma said, "They [his fellow veterans] hate me for speaking out."

that the Japanese really were inferior—as they had demonstrated by their folly in attacking the invincible United States.

When I first landed in Japan in 1951, the men and women of the Allied Occupation Forces felt patronizing fondness for the people whose labors made their own lives so comfortable. The small group that knew a little of the language and something of the culture and history regarded its involuntary hosts with respect and even affection. I was part of that group, and I shared that attitude. Yet few, including myself, regarded the conquered Japanese highly.

In the 1960s, most airliners over Asia carried a few sleeping Japanese cocooned, head and all, in blankets. I could rarely emulate that admirable practice. I was usually tempted by the food and wine provided because my employers, like theirs, paid first-class fares to make long journeys less tiring—and to make less tired employees more efficient. Besides, I felt, the Japanese needed the advantage. They *had* to try harder.

The Japanese were very good at adapting—even improving upon— the breakthroughs made by others. Only a few years earlier they had still been regarded as no more than a nation of copyists. They were now on the verge of being regarded as a nation of brilliant adaptors. But it appeared unlikely that they would ever be hailed as a nation of innovators.

On my latest visit, Japan impressed me just this side of awe. Yet a trace of condescension still clouded my thinking. In 1987, I chuckled at the claim that introduced an eight-page advertising section in *Scientific American*. Beside the ideogram *ryo*, meaning "excellent," stood the assertion: "Applying the tools of innovation . . . has been a trademark of Japan for centuries . . . a tradition."

Not quite! Innovation is hardly a tradition in a country that, before the nineteenth century, invariably got its best new ideas, whether abstract or practical, from China and Korea, or occasionally farther afield, like Buddhism from India by way of China. In the late nineteenth and the twentieth centuries, the source was Europe and America. Not even today, I told myself, is Japan truly innovative.

The text initially sustained my prejudice by acknowledging: "technical innovation in Japan must be regarded in context. The benefits of a consensual approach to business planning do not apply as well to individualistic undertakings like invention . . . four decades of economic growth have been made possible more by the 'salaryman' and by bureaucratic planning than by the entrepreneur. Japanese value their similarities more than their differences. . . ."

I liked that candor, even though it disregarded modern *ronin* like Dr. Takanori Fukushima. The tune then changed slightly:

"Top corporate officers [the advertisement said] mandate new ventures and research. . . . Staff for the new enterprises are drawn largely from the organization. . . . Thus, benefit is drawn from the collective consensus approach . . . applied to high-risk, venture-capitalistic undertakings. There is certainly no shortage of either Japanese talent or brainpower, as performance of Japanese who study and/or work in Western university and corporate environments can attest."

That touch of braggadocio enlivened a passage evidently written by a committee. Present Japanese mastery of the constipated jargon of international business makes me long for the days when a sign in the window of a dressmaker's shop in Yokohama read, LADIES CAN HAVE FITS INSIDE. Such attempts at idiomatic English were, at least, individual. The Japanese are very good at jargon, particularly in their own language. Prose written by a committee is "consensual," and no individual sticks out.

Making the intuitive breakthrough that opens an entirely new field like the binary computer is, therefore, not really the Japanese forte. *Applying* such a breakthrough to production and marketing is, however, their greatest strength. They are foremost in the world in exploiting others' breakthroughs, largely because of their backup. Technological and financial encouragement for developing and marketing new products is provided by a virtual consortium of governmental, academic, and commercial institutions acting in concert to advance the interests of Japan Inc.

The advertisement cited *practical* achievements on the frontiers of present-day technology. Those achievements included the 265K DRAM, a dynamic random-access memory chip for computers that has 265,000 bits for storage of information. The standard number of storage bits had been sixty-four thousand.

The 265K chip was developed by the Nippon Electric Company in 1980. Three years later, NEC developed a one-megabyte DRAM and in 1986 went into production.[2] In 1988, as I noted in the first chapter, Japan produced 86.6 percent of the world supply of that new super-chip, which can hold a million bits of information. In 1989 Japan increased its production by 57.3 percent to produce 390 million super-chips, more than had been produced throughout the world the previous year. Electronics move very fast—and so do the Japanese.

Such practical achievements are transforming the realm of computers—and ensuring that Japan continues to rule that realm. Moreover, fundamental Japanese research is throwing off discoveries that are not immediately applicable.

The government-run Electro-Technical Institute is developing a successor to the bullet train, which now provides the world's fastest railway transportation, except, perhaps, for France's *train de grande*

---

[2] NEC, which was founded in 1889, did a total business of $22 billion in 1988.

vitesse. The new train will utilize electromagnetic levitation to minimize the drag of friction. Tangentially, the Institute has developed the splendidly named SQUID, or superconductive quantum interference device, which measures minute magnetic fields like those generated by the brain. The neurological, psychological, and physiological insights gained through SQUID may not contribute directly to Japanese commercial products. Yet they may, and other discoveries certainly will.[3]

A spectacularly ambitious research project could bestow an unparalleled advantage for half a decade. That is a monstrously long time in electronics, in which a decisive advantage normally lasts no more than a few months.

Somewhat obscurely called TRON, for the real-time system nucleus, it will open an entirely new era for computers, indeed for all human communications. TRON will not only provide instantaneous—that is, real-time—performance, but will speak directly to cameras, optical recording discs, telephones, video recorders, and home appliances, as well as, of course, other computers.

The TRON enterprise displays the "consensus collective approach" at its most productive. The Department of Information Science at Tokyo University is in the vanguard, joined by Mitsubishi Electric, Hitachi, NEC, and Fujitsu. The potential is vast: an entirely new infrastructure for the so-called information society. Since TRON could not fulfill that potential if it were not compatible with other systems, the Japanese have invited participation by AT&T, Data General, and Texas Instruments.

Such invitations are rare. Few countries welcome foreign competition, but aggrieved foreigners complain that the Japanese fight them off with unique tenacity—and unique viciousness. The bitter resentment Lafcadio Hearn identified as the spur to commercial expansion has not greatly abated in our era, although Japan is dominant.

The exact nature of competition among the big Japanese companies themselves is, however, very difficult for an outsider to fathom. Nor did I find any Japanese authority who could give me a precise description. Yet, firms like Sony and Matsushita compete wholeheartedly to develop and market their electronic products, as do Honda and Suzuki in motorcycles. Even divisions of conglomerates compete against each other. Moreover, the parent companies, the descendants of the

---

[3] A single issue of *The Asian Wall Street Journal Weekly* lists the following among new and useful Japanese products: a paper-thin battery; antiskid chains made of rubber; a robotic device for teaching languages; an Intelligent Circuit Exchange System, which boosts the efficiency of international digital circuits by 40 percent; and an electric wristwatch powered by a minute integral automatic generator.

zaibatsu,[4] like Mitsui, Mitsubishi, and Sumitomo, also compete hotly, even in their ventures abroad.

Yet something happens when competition abroad or even at home gets too fierce, that is, when it works against the national interest. A decision-making process by "collective consensus," as the advertisement put it, is then orchestrated by the paternalistic government through its corps of advisers and consultants in academia, think tanks, industry, finance, and commerce.

Normally, action is initiated by the Ministry of International Trade and Industry. Nothing so crass as a direct order is normally issued. But the competitors are given to understand that they might well abate the zeal with which they have been belaboring each other.

In the Japanese view, it would be foolish for the government *not* to intervene. Only results matter. The Japanese are not fettered by the dogmas of either free enterprise or socialism. Nor do they mind fostering cartels—as long as the cartels work to the national advantage.

Rarely arbitrary or dictatorial, the process is upon occasion peremptory. The "collective consensus approach" ensures that little coercion is needed, as it does within individual corporations. No Japanese who has risen by ability, diligence, and prudence will imperil his reputation, his future, and perhaps even his self-esteem by dissenting from the general conclusion.

He will not dissent even if he believes the decision is bad for the collective enterprise, for open disagreement would be even more harmful. A Japanese executive can derive from such self-abnegation the same conviction of virtue that a Western executive may derive from personally hazardous disagreement with the majority for the welfare of the corporation.

Exceptions, of course, exist—and some Japanese companies are dictatorships run by despots. In some, too, fierce infighting occurs. Normally, however, decisions are taken by the technique called *memawashi*, drawn from transplanting. A tree is prepared for moving by the protracted and gentle process of first freeing its roots and accustoming them to new soil. Ideally, the same nonadversarial process shapes the major decisions of corporations—and government. Since all levels have taken part in the decision, it does not come as an unpleasant surprise to anyone, and since the lower ranks have a major share in their making, policies are carried out with enthusiasm.

The limits of competition are sharply defined—and the government

[4] *Zaibatsu*, literally "financial clique," are the great conglomerates that arose in the nineteenth century as the most efficient means of making rapid economic progress. In theory broken up by the Allied occupation, they are today more powerful than ever.

militantly supports Japanese enterprises abroad. By guaranteeing private loans to finance a bridge over the Bosporus, it ensured that a Japanese consortium would win the contract over French and British competition. The government indemnifies Japanese companies abroad against loss and condones restrictions on foreign construction companies' bidding in Japan. Neither at home nor abroad is there to be ruinous competition between Japanese.

CHYARENJI the top line reads, and beneath it, TOPPU KUWARITEI. That cryptic message is actually meant to be English. Although distorted by the inflexible Japanese phonetic writing, it means: CHALLENGE . . . TOP QUALITY.

The green, red, and white plastic badge bearing that exhortation now sits on the pedestal of my word processor, for whatever good it may do. The logotype in the corner reads NEC for Nippon Electric Company. Except when bundled up in pastel or white bunny suits in dust-free production rooms, every employee of NEC Kyushu has that badge pinned to the pale blue Eisenhower jackets worn by all the men or the white tunics with navy blue pinstripes worn by all the women.

NEC's division on Kyushu, the southernmost island of Japan proper, appears obsessed with quality control. NEC Kyushu also makes 9 percent of the world's output of integrated-circuit chips, which are the building blocks of the information age. NEC is overall the world's largest producer of chips. In 1988 its output, worth $4.5 billion, was 16 percent of world production. Overall, Japan produced 66 percent of all chips, against the 29 percent produced by the U.S.

More than a third of the three thousand employees of NEC Kyushu's main plant do nothing except look for flaws. Stray hairs, humidity, or even motes of dust can spoil the minute silicon chips that carry such heavy burdens of information. Nonetheless, NEC undoubtedly devotes greater effort to quality control than may be absolutely necessary, certainly more than successful chip producers elsewhere in Asia.

That virtual obsession with quality control is not unusual among Japanese manufacturers, whether they make automobiles or cameras, gaskets, gauges, or wrapping paper. Their prewar reputation for turning out shoddy goods at bargain prices still embarrasses them; foreign skepticism regarding quality hampered the postwar recovery. The campaign for quality is, therefore, more like a crusade than an industrial process. Although the president of NEC Kyushu would not commit hara-kiri to apologize for a run of defective chips, he might well commit professional suicide—by resigning.

He might have no choice. Tolerance of defects in either products or personnel is scant. That is the other side—the rough side—of silk-smooth policies like lifetime employment and decision-making by consensus. The president of NEC Kyushu could be *ordered* to commit professional suicide if he did not quickly end a run of defective chips.

Such rigor is a major reason for Japan's spectacular success. The *challenge* to overcome a reputation for shoddy goods has been met triumphantly. Customers everywhere now depend absolutely on Japanese *quality*. Even foreign businessmen who are galled—emotionally as well as financially—by Japan's unique success acknowledge that Japanese products as diverse as steel and textiles are, beyond challenge, the best in the world.

Curiously, Japan's obsession with quality and efficiency owe much to American models. The six-and-a-half-year-long occupation under General Douglas MacArthur changed Japanese society—at least on the surface—where it could readily be altered. The presumably conservative supreme commander and his liberal administrative officers also guided and directed the reconstruction of Japanese industry. Japan was fortunate in having to start all over again because so much of its industrial plant had been destroyed by bombing. Japan was doubly fortunate in being guided by engineers who had just taken part in the biggest expansion of productive machinery ever executed—the lightning buildup of American industry to produce the weapons that defeated Germany and Japan.

"MacArthur's experts remade Japanese practices," an Asian executive explained. "Japanese management today is American management as it used to be. Plus the special Japanese qualities, of course. But still what America would be if it hadn't slipped so badly."

Responsibility for production worth more than $1.5 billion a year does not bow the shoulders of Masaru Nakamura, who was appointed president of NEC Kyushu in 1984, when he was forty-eight years old. He is relaxed on a Saturday evening when he chats about the past of the Kumamoto region over the gleaming steel slab on which a chef is deftly preparing *teppan yaki*—broiled steak, crayfish, and vegetables. What's more, he rather irritatingly looks ten to fifteen years younger. That apparent blessing did not help his career.

Saturday is the only evening he can relax and look forward to a free tomorrow. On Sunday he has nothing to do except take his wife shopping, although an emergency could call him back to his office. The main plant works four shifts, twenty-four hours a day, seven days a week—not only to utilize expensive equipment to the fullest, but to avoid the cost of resuming production after a stop. His own work week is at least fifty-five hours—and often longer. He takes no regular vacation; indeed, he regularly takes *no* vacation.

As he remarks, "When Dr. [Koji] Kobayashi [chairman of NEC] said he would take a vacation this summer, the senior executives were very happy. Then he said, 'Yes, I shall take three days off!' " Vacations are for junior employees. Senior executives must strive incessantly to increase NEC's lead over domestic and foreign competition, although in 1989 the company was producing 16 percent of the world's silicon chips, more than any single competitor, and chips accounted for no more than 20 percent of sales.

Masaru Nakamura is, however, shocked when I tell him that the Pohang Steel Company of Korea boasts that its production workers are given neither holidays nor vacation from a work week that always exceeds fifty hours. The young women who are the majority of the work force at NEC Kyushu's main plant outside Kumamoto are entitled to two to four weeks of vacation—and they work just thirty-five hours a week. Not only that, Masaru Nakamura volunteers with a grin, but they don't sing the company song anymore. Indeed, he adds with insouciance that does not quite compel belief, he can hardly remember the words himself.

At the plant his uniform blue jacket identifies him with the young work force, but he concedes that a great divide separates executives and labor. Like feudal samurai, the executives of NEC are a different caste that carries much greater burdens and responsibilities.

The young women of eighteen to twenty-five earn a minimum of Y135,000 a month on the production line. With regular bonuses of four and a half months' pay, that amounts to Y2,350,000 a year, between $18,000 and $19,000. Since their living expenses and taxes do not exceed Y15,000 ($115) a month, that recompense is generous. The days of cheap Japanese labor are long past. In a tight labor market, high pay is necessary to attract good employees.

Most of the young women are saving for the dowries they will bring to their bridegrooms when they leave. NEC can afford to underwrite that traditional practice—and also compete very successfully in the hypermodern international market. Eyes glinting behind his rimless glasses, Masaru Nakamura points out with mock innocence, "Remember, Japan went to automation when the United States went to cheap Asian labor."

He does not dwell on the results of those epochal decisions made more than a decade ago. There is no need to point out that Japan is a highly productive exporter and the United States is a voracious importer. He is not malicious, although his habitual humor is occasionally edged.

Besides, he prefers to talk about Kyushu. Before the Meiji Restoration, the southern island was more exposed to foreign influence than anywhere else in Japan. Closer to Korea and China, it was relatively isolated from the Shogun's government at Edo on Honshu, the main island. Regional patriotism led Kyushu to resist central authority with arms after the Emperor Meiji was enthroned in Edo, renamed Tokyo.

Since centralization meant modernization, Kyushu has remained a little backward, still slightly feudal.

Today the governor of Kumamoto Prefecture is a Hosokawa, a descendant of the *daimyo* who ruled under the Shogunate. Governor Hosokawa is vigorous, glamorous, and virtually undefeatable. When another candidate filed for the gubernatorial election, a crowd bundled him out of the registrar's office. A naïve foreigner protested that using force was not democratic, and a son of Kumamoto replied, "What difference does it make? He couldn't have won anyway."

Despite such semifeudal tenure, Governor Hosokawa is forward-looking. In 1987 he instituted a policy of openness. Any citizen can now see any government document simply by applying at the prefectural hall. Few do, but the principle has been established. Such official candor is truly extraordinary for Japan, where the *bakufu*, the "government behind the curtain," ruled in secrecy for centuries—and the limits that good manners impose on frankness are narrow.

Governor Hosokawa has also sponsored a center of scientific research, education, and practical application. Like the Science-Based Industrial Park at Hsinchu in Taiwan, Kumamoto's Technopolis is an attempt to channel the rich currents of high-tech to a backwater that might otherwise stagnate.

In 1987 it was just getting started. The associated private Far East Universe University had, however, already erected its satellite dishes. In addition to training a few students, it was selling extremely accurate and detailed weather forecasts to the fishing industry. The Independent Research Institute was a well-equipped building without occupants. But the science museum was in full operation, informing the general public and attracting youngsters to technology. Optical readers and computers donated by their makers were tomorrow's models, as were the big discs that could store an entire library's contents, words and pictures, and display them instantaneously.

A cunning robot is most visitors' favorite. Its metal arm draws a credible pencil portrait of anyone who stands in its line of vision. That late-twentieth-century miracle can, however, only be approached in stocking feet. Good manners require shoes to be removed before entering any dwelling, even a robot's.

In overachieving Japan, Kumamoto is still an old shoe, a comfortably provincial city. Because of his job Masaru Nakamura is now one of Kumamoto's leading citizens. A son of Tokyo and a graduate of the University of Hokkaido, the snowy northernmost island, he is delighted by his temporary home on subtropical Kyushu.

He is largely free of traditional inhibitions on displaying emotion that are still widely prevalent among the Japanese. His compact body moves with the rhythm of his sentences, and his small, neat hands gesticulate.

His half-smile is genuinely humorous. Unlike the habitual smiles of so
many of his countrymen, it is neither apologetic nor evasive.

He jokes with the vivacious young woman who is serving us. The
manager of Kumamoto's best restaurant, although no more than
twenty-five, is not visibly impressed by his eminence.

She is not obsequious, but direct and candid. Hers is, perhaps,
professional vivacity. Nonetheless, the excruciatingly shy young
woman who was the ideal of femininity in the storied past—or even
twenty years ago—is slowly vanishing. The new generation has new
manners. Just as Korean dourness is being transformed by prosperity,
Japanese reserve is being melted around the edges by super-prosperity.

Masaru Nakamura's manner toward her is playful but not amorous,
avuncular but not predatory. Perhaps Moira's presence inhibits him.
Yet the new super-executives seem to have little time—and, perhaps,
not quite enough money—for the elaborate womanizing traditional
among politicians and the old upper classes. Our host is, however,
traditional enough to have left his wife at home. Quite traditionally, he
neither apologizes for nor explains her absence. In fact, he doesn't
mention it.

"Kyushu has always had more foreign visitors than any other part of
Japan," he points out. "From the Philippines, China, and even Indonesia. That's why the people are so good-looking, why the prettiest girls
in Japan come from Kumamoto. It's the mixed blood. Now the chef,
doesn't he look like a Mexican? That olive skin, those big eyes, and the
hairline mustache?"

I was astonished. Most of his countrymen are instinctive racists. Yet
Masaru Nakamura just hymned the advantages of mixed blood—and
had acknowledged that many Japanese came of mixed blood.

The cult of a pure Japanese race was only in part a creation of the
myth-makers of the Meiji Restoration. Feeling inferior to their Chinese
neighbors, the Japanese had for centuries cherished the myth of racial
purity that made them superior. They still do so. In an unguarded
moment, Yosuhiro Nakasone, who was ironically the most forward-
looking prime minister in half a century, let slip his conviction that the
Japanese bestrode the economic peaks because of the hereditary talent
conferred by their racial purity. They were, he observed, far more
capable than a mixed nation like America because their genes had not
been adulterated by inferior strains.

All this nonsense is earnestly believed, although the pure race in
question is really a mixed stew of Mongoloid, Malay, Melanesian, and
Polynesian elements. That admixture helps account for the extraordinary capability of the Japanese. Yet, Japan today admits almost no
outsiders to permanent residence. It also discriminates severely against

Koreans and Chinese, its only substantial minorities. They are not normally citizens even if born in Japan.

Nonetheless, Masaru Nakamura happily talks about hybrid vigor. Evidently he does not need the myth of racial superiority to bolster his self-esteem. He was trained as a scientist; he has lived abroad; and he is an indisputable success. The cold realism that successful Japanese bring to their work can, therefore, be allowed to inform his view of his society.

Rank has its privileges, just as rank has its responsibilities. Since a Japanese corporation is like a tautly disciplined volunteer army, those responsibilities are stringent. One might, therefore, expect privileges to be particularly marked. On the whole, they are not.

The great magnates, who work just as hard as anyone else, perhaps harder, live luxuriously. Otherwise the difference between the basic lifestyles of management and labor is not as great as it is in the rest of the industrialized world—or the Soviet Union. Egalitarianism is a legacy of wartime, when all were deprived.

Masaru Nakamura and his wife of just four years live in an apartment of about one thousand square feet, not the mansion set in several acres that his Western equivalent would occupy. Still, a thousand square feet for two is spacious by Japanese standards. Almost twenty years younger than he, she is enjoying her new affluence. Her dresses and fur coats overflow the apartment's limited storage room. In spare Japan, clothes are normally folded on shelves or in chests; hanging takes too much space. Separate bedrooms are rare; bedding is folded away in the daytime and laid on the tatami-mat floor at night.

Lack of living space makes many Japanese feel constrained amid their bounding prosperity. Most know how much more room families enjoy elsewhere. Some painters and writers, who can keep in touch electronically, have moved to snowy Hokkaido, where there is so much more space inside and outside their homes.

I have heard of no senior executive's throwing up his position to run off to Hokkaido or Tahiti. What would he do there? Having been rigorously trained from childhood to be a Japanese executive, he can be nothing else.

Lower-level workers are also highly specialized Japanese. Wanting more space, they make do with holidays in remote places made cheap by the rise of the yen. Few taxi drivers have *not* been to Guam, and few teenagers of professional families have *not* been to Hawaii. In the summer of 1989, Rome, London, and Paris swarmed with Japanese tourists, most no longer middle class, but farmers, laborers, clerks, and salesgirls.

Australia is, however, most favored. It is remarkably cheap and, lying due south, it entails no jet lag. Entire hotel complexes, communities in themselves, have grown up in Queensland.

Japanese executives living in Sydney confide happily that in this age of AIDS they are no longer forced to take visiting worthies to raunchy King's Cross, which offers the Southern Hemisphere's most imaginative sexual diversions with the possible exception of Rio de Janeiro.

Normal Japanese egalitarianism does not operate in the matter of AIDS. Only the less affluent males still crowd the charter flights to Taipei, Bangkok, and Manila to partake of local sexual specialities. The same disregard of danger in a noble cause that animated kamikaze pilots to die may inspire such bravery. But Bernard Krisher, the editor who has been a resident of Tokyo for decades, points out: "Most Japanese are not conscious that the AIDS scourge could hit them. There are very few cases in Japan. To most Japanese it's something happening elsewhere."

Whatever their purpose, yen-bearing Japanese are welcome guests. From Peking to Paris and from Stockholm to Buenos Aires, Japanese tourists and businessmen are greeted with enthusiasm, fawned upon, and waved farewell with sincere regret.

"It's better than being in a conquering army," one young executive candidly remarked of his reception in Hong Kong. "Everything you want—very, very cheap. And you don't have to carry a gun."

From such neo-imperial glories, Japanese return to homes that are, to say the least, rather small. An apartment of four hundred to six hundred square feet for a family of four is a little above average size in metropolitan areas. Many apartments are even more cramped. A concatenation of tax policy, tradition, and export orientation has created a nation of reasonably well-to-do, extremely industrious, and highly skilled men and women tucked away in virtual filing cabinets.

The latest high-definition, glowing color, stereophonic, flat-screen television set and the latest super-automatic, practically-does-your-thinking-for-you video recorder are not quite as much fun when they don't need the remote controls because you can hardly get farther away than arm's reach. A Lilliputian washing machine with a Lilliputian dryer stacked on top is promoted as ideal for the working girl who needs to wash out a few things. Super-compact dishwashers sit on minuscule draining boards, and gas stoves are doll-size. Other gadgets fold up or come apart for easier storage in apartments that make a sailing-boat cabin seem spacious.

The Japanese have miniaturized many products, but not because they themselves are small or because they prefer dainty objects. Before the economic miracle began, street scenes were dominated by old-fashioned bicycles and dray horses, both enormous. The Japanese actually like big things. They use little things because space is the scarcest and therefore the most precious thing in all the world for them.

Frustrated by such constriction, the Japanese detest descriptions like *Faceless automata living in rabbit hutches crammed with electronic gadgets and super-appliances.*

They particularly resent being called faceless, presumably so lacking in character that one individual is indistinguishable from any other. Yet they acknowledge a high degree of conformity.

They are not automata, they say, although they do work harder than anyone else—at least until the Koreans entered the game. Nor do they live in rabbit hutches, they protest, even if their homes do provide far less space than dwellings anywhere else. Yet they candidly envy the Koreans' bigger homes. Possession of electronic gadgets and super-appliances they cannot deny, although those automatic devices do not automatically bring happiness.

Masaru Nakamura of NEC is hardly a typical Japanese executive, although he's representative. He is casually humorous and he is tolerant. He likes provincial Kumamoto and thinks wistfully about going abroad again, rather than to NEC headquarters in Tokyo.

Nonetheless, he hopes his next move will be to Tokyo, where careers are made. He, too, has been brought up to put his career above all else except the welfare of the corporation.

His advanced attitudes, which the nation is now supposed to emulate, derive from his residence abroad. His own education was conventional. Born in 1936, he was not yet ten when the empire surrendered. A bright student, he advanced rapidly through elementary and secondary schools to take his undergraduate degree in physics at Hokkaido University. As an engineer, he did not suffer because he had not attended one of the elite universities. Besides, he spent three years at the Tokyo Institute of Technology, the equivalent of MIT or Caltech.

After working for three years in the state-run Machine Laboratory in Tokyo, Nakamura joined NEC as a specialist in semiconductors, that is, chips and circuits. Since then, he has been a production man. In 1978 he was appointed president of NEC Ireland, which, like NEC Kyushu, is almost entirely a manufacturer. After three years in Ireland, he spent two years in Scotland, again in manufacturing. It was then a natural transition to Kyushu, NEC's biggest complex of factories.

Engineers are prized in Japan. Yet, only yesterday, Masaru Nakamura's lack of marketing experience might have hampered his further rise. But today, NEC, like all major corporations, is looking outside Japan for cheaper labor to produce goods that are not priced in expensive yen. Moreover, the consensus-makers have decreed that industry must assume a posture indicative of greater international cooperation.

His experience abroad should therefore outweigh his nuts-and-bolts background. Anyway, the big corporations take talent where they can find it—and they almost invariably find it inside the corporation.

Immense itself, NEC is a subsidiary of Sumitomo, one of the three vast conglomerates descended directly from the *zaibatsu*, the "financial clique" of the Meiji era. Sumitomo's interests are so wide that it would be easier to list the fields in which they are *not* involved. But this is not a catalogue.

Sumitomo is old. Sumitomo is also right up to date, enlightened in ways that would chill an American corporation. Every six months, two hundred employees of the Sumitomo Trust and Banking Corporation chosen by lottery are given Y250,000 ($2,000) for entertaining outsiders with whom they have *no* business connections. The extended contacts are, somehow, expected to benefit Sumitomo by fostering new ideas. Sumitomo is definitely not thinking about the general advantages to society from such intellectual cross-fertilization.

"Maybe the people our young employees get to know will be top officials of other companies later," a spokesman explains with hard-headed wishful thinking. "Maybe some great new product will emerge."

When Moira and I went to the Sumitomo Bank in Kumamoto to change a traveler's check, we were bemused by its paternal concern. But Sumitomo's paternalism has its limits.

Wishing to draw cash against a Visa card, we visited a Sumitomo branch in Tokyo. After a half hour of filling out forms, internal tele-phoning, and intense discussion, we were turned down.

"Honorable sir, your honorable card," said the cashier courteously, "is no good here."

More concerned about being further embarrassed by an invalid credit card than I was about the embarrassment of such un-Japanese insistence, I pressed him.

"Yes," he finally conceded, "Sumitomo's advertising does say it's an *international* card. It *is* international. Japanese abroad can get cash on a Sumitomo Visa card. But how can we give you cash on a Visa card that is not Sumitomo's?"

The bank's paternalism clearly did not embrace non-Japanese.

The new production line at the big NEC plant just outside Kumamoto is pure Walt Disney—animated, colorful, and super-clean. "Downdraft ventilation" that blows from grilled ceilings to grilled floors removes dust, which is as harmful to silicon chips as bacteria are to flesh and blood. With their body oils, loose hair, and constant exhalations, human beings are even more dangerous. Everyone who enters the production area is, therefore, "showered" with forced air after donning a bunny suit.

Lacking only artificial ears to justify its nickname, the bunny suit covers everything except the hands and a strip across the eyes. Hands are bare only because NEC has not yet found a glove that allows precise work; so everyone scrubs as thoroughly as a surgeon. The baggy legs that make the bunny suit look like an unfashionable ski suit are sealed with Velcro strips to the rubber-soled slippers. The tight hood not only covers the hair, but comes down low on the forehead. Mesh over the mouth and ears allows the wearer to speak and hear—just.

Inside it *is* the twenty-first century, where computers control sophisticated machinery making integrated chips for new computers. Human beings are, however, still necessary to program the computers, to oversee their operation, and to assure uniform quality in their product. Somebody has to finger the keyboards, check the glowing screens, and monitor the digital readouts. Computers do not reason independently or spontaneously. Machines do not purposefully create other machines.

Still, the needs of computers rule this sterile realm. The background is white, chrome, and glass, like a bloodless operating theater. The human attendants are disciplined and categorized. The bunny suits are color-coded: white for staff, baby blue for visitors, and pale green for outside maintenance men. Soothing the regimented Japanese psyche, the hoods worn with the staff's white suits are separately color-coded: yellow for engineers, pink for team leaders, white for general staff, blue for quality control, and green for inside maintenance. Nonetheless, the shrouded, faceless figures are inhuman.

The visitor feels the fluttering of incipient claustrophobia. Almost hermetically sealed within the bunny suits, individuals are isolated, voices are faint, and expressions are invisible in the eerie half-silence.

This temple of silicon is, however, not wholly proof against humanity. A melody played on a tinny electronic xylophone tinkles through the funereal hush. The tune, raucous and cheery, is Stephen Foster's "Camptown Races." I look for the loudspeakers, but see none. Yet the melody swells, catchy and banal.

It is coming from a rubber-tired vehicle the size of a steamer trunk laid on its side. The little red buggy halts, and the music stops. It turns with a series of high-pitched grunts, moves off, and resumes playing "Camptown Races." The words sound inside my head: "Camptown ladies sing dis song, doo dah, doo dah . . . Camptown racetrack five miles long, oh, doo dah day . . ."

Those cheeky little vehicles, which stridently warn of their approach, are the closest thing to artificial intelligence in the plant. Programmed for different tasks, they dart about delivering and collecting steel canisters to spare the feet of the human workers. When their batteries begin to run down, they return to their base to recharge themselves, still tinkling *their* company song.

Moderately sophisticated, the little messengers are, of course, robots, the metal-and-plastic workers Japan employs in greater numbers than any other country. No need for them to take breaks as do human workers, ostensibly for a cigarette or a soft drink, but, above all, to escape the dehumanizing atmosphere. Taking off our bunny suits, Moira and I look at each other, appalled.

Later, when we are alone, she says, "You were thinking that it was sad that the most human thing was the robots, weren't you?" I was.

By that time we have entered another building. Slightly less artificial, it is one of the new dormitories that house the young women who make up a little more than half the work force of 3,100. We are back in the world of human beings.

The scrupulous cleanliness is as much Japanese as it is high-tech. So is the self-discipline imposed by the accommodations. Two young women share each tatami-mat sleeping room, which measures about thirty-five square feet. One is normally working while the other sleeps. The only furniture is a small chest a foot high with a mirror perched on top—a vanity table judging by the open lipsticks lying on it. It is also a dresser, holding those garments not folded with the bedding in the closet with the sliding door. A common living room a shade larger serves each pair of sleeping rooms.

But women spend much of their free time in public rooms that are commodious and well-appointed, if bare and cold to a Western eye. A snack bar with a vending machine is furnished with metal-and-plastic tables and chairs. Telephones, television sets, hair dryers, refrigerators, and washing machines are all available; notices promote lectures, movies, and discotheques; leaflets offer at a discount NEC products like home computers. Despite their rural origins, the young women of NEC are all thoroughly modern misses.

The vestal virgins of the temple of high-tech also maintain Japanese tradition. In big tatami rooms they study two essential feminine skills: *ikebana* and *cha no yu*. *Ikebana* is the unique Japanese art of arranging flowers with delicacy and economy. *Cha no yu*, the tea ceremony, is a complex ritual performed with simple implements. It honors guests; produces an astringent, pea-green beverage; and bestows inner serenity by imposing formal discipline on every gesture.

In those egg-crate dormitories, hundreds of young women voluntarily live under restrictions that would appall their sisters in the West. Yet they are clearly not greatly discontented or they would not flock to NEC. Anyway, Japanese women are still trained to be subservient and acquiescent; even in the normally rebellious late teens, they *expect* their lives to be circumscribed.

Yet a woman now heads the Socialist Party, which humiliated the male-centered Liberal Democratic Party in a series of elections in 1989. Some women have attained high positions in business or academia, and in journalism and television they are by no means restricted to women's subjects. Such high fliers are always the exception—and nowhere more so than in Japan.

There is no Japanese equivalent of the class of competent but hardly extraordinary female professionals in the United States. In big firms almost all women either are working out their dowries on the production line or they are office ornaments who are expected to pour tea and giggle prettily until they, too, marry. Once married, they are required to devote themselves entirely to the home and the children.

Much is changing as a new generation of women demands not only rights but such privileges as family vacations. No longer does a husband invariably vacation with his workmates, perhaps on a sex tour to Southeast Asia, while the wife cozily stays home with the children. Yet the *sarariman* (salaryman), who is the prime mover of modern Japan, works a fifty-hour week—and plays in company with his colleagues another ten hours or so. Obviously, he is rarely at home. The salaryman's wife cannot go out to work, even if someone will give her a job, because she must wait for his brief visits.

Super-prosperity has nonetheless made its impression. Few Japanese women now live in desperation, cowering before harsh and violent husbands. Far fewer enter the half-world of the bars, the nightclubs, and the geisha houses than did a few decades ago. Parents need no longer sell their daughters, and daughters no longer see demiprostitution as their only hope. They can earn their dowries—and a useful reputation for diligence—by working for corporations like NEC, rather than in houses of assignation. So much has changed that Sosuke Uno fell from the premiership in the summer of 1989 largely because of the public complaints of his geisha mistress.

The tradition of the acceptable demimonde is, however, still even stronger in Japan than elsewhere. Art and literature draw upon the twilight life called *karyukai*, "the flower and willow world." The Japanese male still frequents that realm, which was depicted in the prints called *ukiyo-e*, "pictures of the floating world." His wife is part of neither his business life nor the complex social life that derives from his business associations. When he drinks with colleagues or customers, he *expects* to meet compliant and charming women. Throwing off the twin burdens of responsibility and maturity, he plays childish games with them. He may or may not sleep with those women. Chances are, though, that he will—at least occasionally.

In Kumamoto, Filipinas have largely replaced Japanese women in the *mizu shobai*, "the water business." Those illegal immigrants are driven to prostitution by their country's miserable poverty amid the prosperity of East Asia. Some stroll the glassed-over main street called Shimo-dori, exhibiting themselves in the bright lights. Others work in the topless bars with the color photographs posted outside.

Taxis with bright, flashing lights deposit raucous loads of middle-aged men who are boisterous with drink. Traffic is so heavy taxis take ten minutes to go one city block. The crowds thicken on wide Asahi-dori and clot in the narrow alleys, where the moonlight hardly penetrates. The little six-patron bars, the minute coffee shops, and the miniature teahouses of the side streets, withdrawn behind dim door lamps scrawled with half-intelligible ideograms, are mysterious and alluring.

Watchful men with closed faces and tattooed hands take up stations on streetcorners. They are the *yakuza*, the "foot soldiers" of the organized gangs who rule the floating world.

For a moment, medieval Japan is restored. Neither super-prosperity nor high-tech has altered the essential nature of a society of feudal *daimyo*, hard-handed samurai, and white-powdered geisha.

8

Japan: Today, Tomorrow, and Tomorrow

THIS WORLD, JAPANESE BUDDHISM TEACHES, IS *ALL* ILLUSION. THE MULTITRILLIONAIRE NATION *KNOWS* THAT RICHES ARE UNREAL. IT FEARS HARD TIMES WILL SOON RETURN.

The Japanese dearly love their newspapers, which enjoy the world's largest circulations: the big three sell 14 million, 13 million, and 7 million copies a day. Since even Japanese technology has not yet produced a self-delivering newspaper and Japanese boys don't like getting up at four in the morning, distributors are importing newsboys from Taiwan. The lure is three-year contracts at $1,600 a month plus housing and free classes in Japanese, the language of the future, for the likely lads, who may be as old as thirty.

Despite enticing foreigners for such "unsocial work," Japan accepts almost no permanent immigrants. Most Japanese believe foreigners are inferior and foreign countries are dirty and dangerous. Yet they are now told that it is their patriotic duty to travel abroad—and help reduce their country's bloated foreign-exchange reserves.

A pesticide manufacturer has offered reassurance to his fearful countrymen and his even more fearful countrywomen. A quick puff of his pocket-sized spray called Handy Bactericide protects against AIDS, cholera, and innumerable other foreign scourges by disinfecting toilet seats, telephones, escalator rails—and notoriously filthy foreign currency.

The Japanese can be arrogant and insensitive, but they are, above all, apprehensive. Most are not convinced in their hearts that these golden days of unexampled prosperity and unchallenged superiority will last.

Most fear that the future will confront them with challenges even greater than those they have vanquished during the last four decades.

Suppressed guilt intensifies their fear. Their instinct tells them they don't deserve their affluence—and nemesis will surely follow. Are the Japanese, I wonder, the only people who feel in their hearts that they have it *too* good?

A 747 jumbo jet is much faster and far more comfortable than a single-engine Cessna—and thousands of times more expensive to buy and operate. Those who can afford it, as the Japanese manifestly can, naturally prefer the 747 for the long run.

Biggest and most costly is, however, not always best. If it should lose power on all four massive engines, the 747 will plummet. In the old aviator's wry characterization, "It has all the gliding qualities of a brick." The Cessna can, however, glide sweetly to earth, its light weight borne smoothly downward on its broad wings. Besides, a jet must maintain minimum cruising speed—or stall and fall.

Chronically apprehensive, many Japanese fear that their luxurious 747 could run out of the fuel provided by foreign markets and foreign raw materials. Japan must not only maintain its momentum, but must constantly increase its speed. Modern economies cannot reach a comfortable cruising speed and soar along happily. They must go faster and faster, lest they crash.

Japan's prosperity has been created by Japanese talent and Japanese diligence, but Japan's super-prosperity depends upon foreigners continuing to buy Japanese goods. Yet foreigners are not merely unreliable, they are cantankerous and treacherous. Foreigners are now pressing the Japanese to be idle and spendthrift hedonists. Foreigners further declare their determination to buy fewer Japanese goods.

Under that threat, a prudent person *must* look to the future—above all by laying up provender for the stormy season ahead. Accustomed to being poor, the Japanese still feel in their hearts that they are poor people who are enjoying momentary good fortune. They therefore behave like poor people. They drive very hard bargains; they compete ferociously; they work incessantly; they employ tactics their competitors consider at best sharp trading or actual dishonesty; and they relentlessly pinch pennies.

The new generation, it is often pointed out, is different from the old generation, having grown up amid prosperity with bright expectations. An enormous difference divides Japanese over sixty, who vividly remember the war and the occupation, from those below forty, who were born either as the miracle burgeoned or afterward. Those in their twenties or thirties are not only the most hedonistic, but the most nationalistic and assertive, since they remember neither war nor defeat and foreign occupation. Yet in 1989, the new generation, like its elders, was worrying aloud about the approaching—if not imminent—end of the miracle. Prosperity is making Japan more fragile—and more vulnerable to outsiders' whims.

Nonetheless, the younger generation *is* different in its vision and its expectation. Rather than hide prosperity behind a subdued pastel kimono and a humble demeanor, it defies fate with colorful clothes and a swagger. The elaborately simple mansions of the noble and wealthy used to be concealed behind blank gray walls; the skyscrapers that are today's mansions thrust assertively into the clouds.

Ostentation is the natural manner of the successful new generation. The New Otani Hotel, an affiliate of the Sheraton chain, which stands in the fashionable Akasaka section of Tokyo, is a vast temple of the new self-confidence, which is often indistinguishable from arrogance.

Its neighbor, across a ravine spanned by a plastic-and-brass replica of a wood-and-brass bridge of the feudal era, is one of the most arrogant buildings in the world. The Akasaka Prince Hotel epitomizes the new aesthetics: spare Japanese utilitarianism joined with brutal Western utilitarianism in a sleek, high-tech envelope. It is a forbidding ice palace. The exterior is as frigid as an iceberg. The interior shines balefully in myriad shades of white, as welcoming as a chasm in a glacier.

Within its acres of landscaped gardens, teahouses, traditional restaurants, and health centers, the New Otani is by contrast warm and hospitable. It is even cozy, as cozy as is possible for an edifice with 2,100 guest rooms and six floors of shops within two separate skyscrapers.

The miles of public corridors, once dominated by foreign visitors, are now the promenade of hundreds of ostentatiously prosperous Japanese. The women's hair is beautifully coiffed, often dyed a fashionable dark auburn. Their clothing is Paris-London-New York trendy—the antithesis of the traditional restrained Japanese costume. The men wear elaborately styled hair, gold cufflinks and gold wristwatches; their tasseled loafers, like their briefcases, are likely to be crocodile. Supremely self-assured, they come to be seen—and to buy. Art galleries unblushingly ask the yen equivalent of five thousand dollars for a small print by a virtually unknown artist. Crystal, silverware, and leather goods in specialty shops are avidly bought at comparable prices. Louis Vuitton, which becomes *Rui Buiton* on Japanese tongues, sells luggage so expensive even rich Japanese buy abroad. The Louis Vuitton shop in Hong Kong makes eager Japanese patrons queue for admission.

A steamer trunk in the *Rui Buiton* show window at the New Otani carries a price tag of Y1.47 million, which is $10,000 to $12,000, depending on the fluctuating rate of exchange. I ask the salesgirl how many she has sold in the past year, and she replies: "Just one . . . to a man who was going on a cruise on the *QE II*. But he was *very* rich!"

Since prosperity can*not* last, it is imperative to get hold of every last possible yen, not to speak of every infinitesimal sen, *right now*. Other results of that psychology are the high tariffs and the spiderweb of "administrative regulations" that deny entry to so many foreign products. Those barriers supplement the Japanese consumer's conviction that Japanese goods are invariably better than foreign goods, as they so often are in reality.

Despite that conviction, a few wealthy consumers crave the distinction of foreign luxury goods. That great status symbol, Scotch whiskey, whose entry is relatively unhampered by barriers, sells very well at relatively low prices. But only a few thousand foreign automobiles are sold each year. Chief among them are German Mercedes and BMWs, with British Jaguars and Minis next, and also a few Cadillacs, Thunderbirds, and Mustangs. *New* American automobiles do not interest the people who have made Detroit notable for antiquated design, obsolescent production, and nineteenth-century salesmanship.

Although some administrative restrictions have been relaxed, they remain formidable. Take the Jaguar Sovereign sedan followed through the obstacle course. Rear side-reflectors were changed to red from the amber that is the standard elsewhere in the world, and the vehicle identification number was repeatedly scrutinized. Automobiles with a minute variation in the length of the downstroke in the letter *K* have been held up for weeks. After payment of the additional taxes, the automobile, which sells in Britain for roughly $50,000, was cleared to sell for Y9.5 million, $75,000. A comparable Japanese-made car retails for about Y3.5 million or $24,500 in Japan—and for $24,057 in Britain, the price cut to increase Japan's market share.

Jaguar sold not quite five hundred vehicles to Japan in 1987, and realistically hopes only to increase sales to 3,000 in the early 1990s. Jaguar may attain that modest goal—if the Japanese do not panic and reimpose the even more finicky restrictions they have grudgingly lifted.

The European Common Market, which includes Germany and Britain, also imposes high tariffs on automobiles. The Japanese simply cut prices to compensate and move into the European Community. Originally, Japanese firms put up new factories; now their collective strategy is shifting to taking over or buying into established firms, as Honda recently did with Peeble British Rover. Britain is a favorite site, largely because it speaks the international language, English. Moreover, Britain woos Japanese investment, which it seems to prefer to American investment, despite popular anti-Japanese feeling.

Under intense diplomatic pressure from the United States, South Korea and Taiwan are taking down some of their barriers. Both contend that cutting tariffs and removing obstacles will increase Japanese penetration of their markets. As an American economist said in Taiwan,

"Even if there were *no* barriers, I don't think Detroit has the savvy—or the interest—to grab a share of the market here. It's all going Japan's way."

Many Japanese qualities compel admiration, though not necessarily affection. But Japanese tactics inspire fear. Japan's predominance is also based upon foresight, and a ruthless appreciation of Japan's needs, as well as American sloth. Encouraged by the American Occupation authorities, Japan began protecting its internal market for its domestic producers before there was much to protect. The export-driven strategy for reconstruction required drastic limitations on imports, particularly consumer goods.

In 1959, when recovery was just getting up steam, a traveler could bring in several cases of foreign wines and liquors duty free. The market was minuscule, since most Japanese do not drink foreign liquor. Automobile tires were different. Coming from Hong Kong by ship, I brought a set of Morris Minor tires for a friend. Although that size tire was not made in Japan, the duty was 100 percent.

Bridgestone, which started as a maker of *zori*, thonged straw slippers, built up its sales at home and abroad behind such protective walls. The first time I encountered Bridgestone tires was in 1966, when I was traveling widely by car in Indonesia. Three new Bridgestones in succession suffered frightening blowouts before we found a non-Bridgestone retread. Today it's the other way round in Indonesia. Bridgestone is esteemed for its reliability above Goodyear and Firestone; anyway, Bridgestone bought Firestone outright in 1988. Also praised for their quality are Japanese automobiles, earth-moving equipment, and, of course, electronic equipment.

Some tariffs on American agricultural products have been reduced. Native cattlemen, who produce a small quantity of very high-quality beef, have been extravagantly protected. Producer subsidies and import barriers, as well as export incentives, can come to 75 percent of the farmers' income in Japan—against 9 percent for cattlemen in the U.S. Not remarkably, steak costs at least $50 a pound—often more.

Wataru Hiraizumi, the chairman of the Foreign Affairs Committee of the Diet, Japan's legislature, reacted strongly when I remarked that the price of oranges seemed inordinate, almost extortionate, even in purely Japanese terms.

"We must," he said hotly, "protect our *satsuma nikan* producers."

Japan's *satsuma nikan* tangerine crop is a rather small part of a big market. But the agricultural lobby, which represents cattlemen and tangerine producers among others, contributes tens of billions to the coffers of the Liberal Democratic Party, which, it appeared until recently, would rule Japan forever. Even the slight reduction in protective tariffs cost the LDP dearly at the polls.

Politicians and political parties spend immense sums. Diet members pay out as much as $1 million a year for "legislative assistants" who are really ward heelers, and about $250,000 a month for gifts and parties for constituents. But their salaries and allowances are no more than $100,000 a year. They get the cash not only through large contributions, but from massive corruption, which seems inseparable from Confucian societies. A single fund-raising party contributed $14.7 million for Noburu Takeshita shortly before he became prime minister late in 1988.

He resigned in disgrace in mid-1989 over the latest—and worst—scandal. It concerned massive personal bribes from Recruit Electronics, a scandal that involved dozens of LDP leaders and blackened the party's reputation.

Such corruption encourages fraud against the almost defenseless Japanese consumer—and very high prices. Japan Inc. has consistently promoted the interests of producers and exporters, not the interests of consumers. Consequently, the consumer has carried the weight of the miracle, paying significantly more for Japanese good than do purchasers abroad.

Yet only the United States, among the ten leading industrial nations, is *less* dependent on foreign trade. Japan's exports fell from 13.2 percent of the GNP in 1985 to 10.7 percent the next year and 9.7 percent in 1987. However, total imports fell from 9.8 percent of the GNP to 6.3 percent from 1985 to 1987. Since the GNP was soaring, those reductions in comparative terms meant no reductions, but some increases, in absolute terms.

Japan, Inc., exploits the domestic market to support its exports. Networks of thousands of middlemen dominate an internal distribution system of Byzantine complexity and medieval inefficiency. Prices rise as each middleman takes his cut, many for moving the merchandise only a few miles, some not even touching the goods.

Several years ago I followed the progress of apples grown in Aomori, three hours by fast train from Tokyo, through the hands of more than a dozen middlemen to the final purchasers in Tokyo's Marunouchi district. Starting at twenty-five cents, each apple cost the consumer four dollars.

The price of rice, the staple of the Japanese diet, is more than twice the world standard. Imported rice is greatly overpriced to maintain the market for expensively produced—and highly prized—home-grown rice. Japan depends on foreign suppliers for most of its raw materials, including foodstuffs. But Japanese-grown rice is mystically entwined with the national spirit.

The government is naturally reluctant to change the basic patterns of commerce and agriculture, which have been very good for the Liberal Democratic Party. Middlemen and rice farmers do *not* vote for the

Communists or even the Socialists. Great change was, however, presaged in the reforms proposed by Prime Minister Yasuhiro Nakasone shortly before he left office in compliance with the LDP's regulations in 1988. Those reforms, which are slowly coming into effect, deal with sales taxes, land taxes, and internal investment. Touching both farmers and consumers, they have exacerbated the LDP's electoral discomfort. Yet they offer a clear blueprint for a new Japan—or, at least, a Japan substantially altered. Above all, greater resources will now be devoted to internal development.

The essential Japan hardly changes. The sociologist Chie Nakane, who was the first woman to hold a full professorship at Tokyo University, pointed out: "Once you have such conservative roots [as Japan does], you can do very radical things and still be sure that it won't affect the basic foundation. Thus, we can easily accept innovations like computers and automation without resistance."

Once fixed, Japanese policies acquire a momentum of their own. Extremely large sums will be spent on housing, roads, sewers, and recreational amenities—the unglamorous infrastructure that shapes the people's life.

The hundreds of billions—indeed, trillions—of dollars needed are not a problem. But the land needed is. Although Japan possesses just enough land, it cannot bring the "faceless automata" out of their "rabbit hutches" and also maintain rice farms in cities. Land taxes that encourage agricultural use have made building sites fantastically expensive. Their reform will make Japan more residential and less agricultural—and, perhaps, reduce the price of rice a little. The opposition Socialist Party, however idealistic, is also led by practical politicians; the Socialists support a virtual guarantee of continued high prices to woo farmers.

The fortunate Japanese may, nevertheless, see most retail prices fall—and not primarily because of the rise of the yen. The high price of imported goods has hardly altered, and the volume of exports has actually increased. Other pressure should, however, bring prices down in a nation with virtually no inflation—primarily the pressure of commercial and technological change.

The supermarkets that are supplanting small shops *must* compete with each other. If "Computers and Communications," NEC's proud slogan, means anything in commerce, it means radical changes in retail outlets. Orders recorded by salesmen on handheld computers, which then feed the data down telephone lines to master computers, will be shipped by robot directly from the manufacturer—or from a single wholesaler. Such automation must in time break down the layers of exploitive middlemen.

*   *   *

The first person Moira and I talked to in Tokyo on our most recent visit was indignant at the Japanese consumer's oxlike patience. Miss Taki Katoh, as they call her, spoke with forthrightness and humor still highly unusual among her repressed countrywomen.

"Every time I come back from a trip abroad, I'm shocked at prices here," she said. "Foreign goods are six times what you pay abroad, despite the rise of the yen. The Japanese know it, but do something about it? Never!"

Taki Katoh is not an obsessive shopper, but an activist in life, who was at the moment considering the plight of the Japanese consumer. She was later to comment pithily on education, women, and the massive insensitivity of the elite.

She was the first of the wise men and women we were to see in an enormously stimulating and enormously demanding fortnight in Tokyo, which I find the most vital city in the world. Having known the Japanese for more than thirty-five years, I had never before been so deeply impressed. I was impressed almost as much by their pleasure in sharp discussion as I was by their outstanding ability. The immense self-confidence born of immense national success inspired them to speak candidly, as Japanese have so rarely spoken in the past.

The wise men ranged from professional savants like Naohiro Ayama, a former vice-minister of foreign affairs who is now director of the grandiloquently named Institute for Human Studies founded by Dentsu, which is the world's largest, but by no means most effective advertising agency; to professional diplomats like Ryuichi Onodera, deputy director general of the Policy Planning and Analysis Bureau of the Foreign Office; to a professional gadfly like Hideaki Kase, a right-wing author and lecturer who specializes in military security, advises Japan's conservative premiers, and lectures from time to time at the Staff College of the Chinese People's Liberation Army; to Wataru Hiraizumi, the mercurial former minister of technology and subsequently of economic planning, to whom I have already alluded.

I was profoundly impressed by their competence and their intense concentration on the problems of Japan and the world. They were the most notable group I have ever met in so short a period, although I have spoken professionally with many of the presumed movers and shakers of the world, not least on my journeys for this book. Aware that they were a handpicked group, I nonetheless came away convinced that the Japanese were far more impressive, indeed admirable, than I had ever imagined.

I also came away feeling that the Japanese are, in general, not much liked by outsiders because they do not much like themselves. They have altered with success, as much, perhaps, as Japanese can alter. They are, like the Koreans, still driven; unlike the Koreans, they have not mellowed with success. Japanese society breeds high achievers, but not many individuals are at peace with themselves. Japanese are tense and insensitive, largely because they are self-obsessed.

In public places Japanese still walk into strangers, whether foreigners or compatriots; it seems they do not really see strangers. Watching the crowds in the lobby of a public building in Tokyo, you will see many more collisions and near collisions than even in New York and Paris. Yet the Japanese are not rude, but elaborately polite to those they already know or meet in a structured social or business context. They are also enormously helpful to strangers—once they have been made aware of a stranger's existence and needs, as we learned again when we traveled by train with heavy luggage.

Taki Katoh is not wholly at peace with herself. Yet the different parts of her being work in harmony. She is very engaging and almost compulsively forthright.

We were calling her Taki five minutes after entering her cramped office in the glossy district called Harajuku, for we had discovered a dozen friends in common. She is very American about her work, albeit in a very Japanese way. As Mrs. Masayuki Kurokawa, she is also the doting mother of a son called Sho, who was born in 1987, when she was forty-two.

Taki is determined to make Sho self-reliant, just as her own mother made her self-reliant. Most Japanese children, she says, are undisciplined, self-indulgent, and far too dependent—initially on their mothers, subsequently on their superiors, and always on their peers.

Taki scoffs at the conventional Western impression that Japanese children are allowed to run wild until girls are five and boys seven—but are strictly disciplined thereafter. Not only children and teenagers, she maintains, but her own contemporaries, the first postwar generation, are spoiled, conformist, timorous, and self-indulgent.

Her assessments *are* sweeping, but her tone is moderate, rather chiding and maternal. She is not vehement, just spirited. But she is clearly a maverick, a female *ronin*. Having worked as a reporter, an interpreter, and a factotum for foreign correspondents, she is now a successful impresario who brings foreign pop stars to Japan. She is also highly visible on television and highly voluble on radio.

Her second husband, whom she married when she was in her late thirties, is an architect. Clashes of temperaments and interests roiled her relations with the singer and theatrical promoter she married when she was twenty-four. But that marriage endured until she discovered— to his astonishment and her own surprise—that she was deeply wounded by his casual liaisons. A good Japanese wife is not supposed to care, but she did. Yet they were divorced only after years of agonizing on her part.

Her accent and her command of American idiom testify to her peripatetic education in White Plains, New York; Washington, D.C.; Portland; and Palo Alto, as well as Tokyo. She came to the United States through the Moral Re-Armament movement, and she came to Moral Re-Armament through her mother, whose attitudes shaped her daughter's life even as she strove to make Taki utterly self-reliant.

To understand either one of those ladies, you must speak with both. A week after seeing Taki, I called on her mother. Perhaps I should say I was *received*. Although direct and unpretentious, she is undoubtedly a *grande dame*.

Baroness Shidzue Ishimoto had in 1920 herself left Japan, Baron Ishimoto, and two young sons to study English and secretarial skills in the United States. The Russian Revolution of 1917, she says, inspired her to work for social change, and she reveled in her friendship with American radicals.

An American exerted the greatest single influence on her life. Margaret Sanger, the pioneer of birth control, convinced the young Japanese aristocrat that "the way to save unhappy families of the slums [in Japan, as everywhere] was by knowledge of birth control."

When I talked with Shidzue Katoh, she was, at ninety, not merely lucid, but penetrating. Still militant in her cause, she was shortly to receive the United Nations Population Award for her work as president of the Family Planning Federation of Japan and vice-president of the Japanese Organization for International Cooperation in Family Planning. Bowing for once to her age, she did not go to New York for the award, but sent Taki—and a videotape of her acceptance speech.

During a lifetime dedicated to social and political change, she has spilled out her energy and talent unstintingly. That lavishness has obviously done her nothing but good. Nor was she marked when she was jailed in the 1930s by the militarists, who wanted large families to provide soldiers and war workers. Instead, she was renewed.

Taki does not reproach her mother for neglecting her. She says, instead, that she became independent because her mother was usually too busy looking after the world to look after her. A stream of little notes conveyed maternal concern, and, Taki says, "I knew I was loved."

Her mother was elected to the Diet in 1946, just thirteen months after Taki's birth. Shidzue's second husband, Taki's father, was a founder of the Japanese Socialist party. She herself took to the fray ardently when finally allowed to direct participation in politics. Japanese women were at last given the vote in 1946, and thirty-nine were elected to the first postwar Diet, which nowadays usually has ten to twelve female members, perhaps a few more.

The gently nurtured lady had, however, begun her career of political activism in 1917. Wearing a kimono, she spoke at miners' meetings, exhorting them to demand their rights. Her husband, a senior executive of the Mitsui Mining Company, was one of very few Japanese aristocrats who was concerned with the mistreatment of workers.

Shidzue Katoh tells her tale with deft restraint that makes it more moving. Her daughter Taki is rarely less than dramatic. The theater is, after all, her world.

Taki's hair is cut short around her long, mobile face to emphasize her big, expressive eyes. With her dark purple linen suit she wears long jet earrings and wristsful of baroque bracelets—"lots of good, expensive costume jewelry," as Moira observes. Accustomed to discussing her life, her loves, and her likes, she speaks with evident enjoyment. The total effect is not so much Japanese as Italian, only more vivacious.

Taki's mother is now more judicious, with occasional flashes of her fiery youth. She is still passionately committed to her causes, but the years have bestowed serenity as well as wisdom. She remains the devout believer she has been all her adult life.

"My mother is a devoted Christian," says Taki. "Myself, I believe in God, but not in Christ."

Shidzue Katoh talks to me about Buddha, not Christ, while a striking, centuries-old portrait of the Buddha gazes calmly down the long living room of her fourth-floor apartment in the Meguro district. A major element in Japanese civilization, Buddhism has always been particularly attractive to women. Despite exceptions like the warrior abbots of the Nichiren sect, it has striven for peace and harmony. The affinity between the ancient religion and the nonagenarian lady is highly personal.

"When Buddha was born, his mother was forty-eight," she says with a subdued twinkle. "And Taki was born in 1945, when I was forty-eight. . . . My two sons were much older, grown men, in 1945. I knew I must bring up this girl as fast as possible. I didn't know how long I could look after her. . . . When I entered the Diet, I had nice women to look after her. But, in principle, she had to walk by herself. I swore I wouldn't boss her."

Shidzue Katoh pauses in reflection, her thoughts going back more than four decades. That seems a quarter of eternity to me, but, I suspect, only the day before yesterday to one who was already fifteen when the Emperor Meiji died in 1912. Her eyes soften behind her gray-tinted glasses, and her slender hand seeks the white-bead necklace in the Vee neck of her beige shirt. She fluffs her immaculately coiffed hair; a pensive expression possesses her long, aristocratic face; and she seems for an instant almost as young as her daughter.

The two are remarkably alike. Taki has, however, acquired a hard, professional edge in journalism and show business. Shidzue has preserved the gentle manner of an earlier time despite her lifelong immersion in social agitation, journalism, and practical politics. Yet she is still vigorous. It no longer seems strange that she should, at ninety, have a grandson less than a year old.

Shidzue's vigor has not always won her admirers. A photograph in a book called *Red Bear or Yellow Dragon*, published in 1924, shows the then Baroness Ishimoto demure and old-fashioned, except for her bobbed hair, in a formal dark kimono with small white circles bearing the family crest.

"No movement was too new or too outré for her to take up," the author, Marguerite E. Harrison, wrote. "When Mrs. Sanger came to Japan with the . . . idea of curbing Japanese militarism by instituting birth control, Baroness Ishimoto was the first to take it up. . . . journalism was considered rather vulgar for a woman, and Baroness Ishimoto shocked her conservative friends by writing frequent articles for the daily papers. She was a suffragist, and interested theoretically in all movements for improving the condition of women, but yet I had the impression that she was playing with all these things. . . ."

That was a feminine view. Now, I have always been charmed by Japanese women, who are virtually a different—and superior—race from their men. I have the impression that Shidzue Katoh has always been deadly serious about "all those things" and still is. Since Moira could not come with me, I cannot offer a modern feminine assessment of the lady once known as the Red Baroness.

One of Japan's most lucid social commentators, Keiko Higuchi, who is also a woman, wrote a passage so graphic I must quote it: "The impact on the family of the period of high economic growth that began about 1955 is immeasurable. One of the greatest changes was the beginning of the mass movement of both goods and people. Every town and village accumulated mountains of durable consumer goods, which transformed the people's life style. The mass movement of people resulted in the division of Japan into two distinct categories: overpopulated cities and underpopulated countryside. It also entailed a rise in the number of salaried workers and their families, drawing the working population away from the traditional mode of life in which families either farmed or ran their own businesses."

From a nation of poor farmers and hard-pressed artisans, as well as a few workers in factories, Japan became a nation of prosperous entrepreneurs and well-paid factory workers, as well as a few farmers on the land. Rapid changes on the surface of Japanese society have transformed women's role in society.

Full-time wives and mothers are a minority now, when women make up 40 percent of the regular work force. The average Japanese woman's life expectancy is now 82.5 years, the world's highest. She will thus live forty-seven years after her youngest child starts school. Her prewar equivalent lived only fifteen years after that happy event gave her partial freedom. Today's woman will live for 7.9 years after her husband's death; in 1930 she would have lived only 4.9 years longer. Clearly the number of years spent as wife and mother has decreased, and free time for other pursuits has greatly increased. Yet the social myth defining ideal female behavior, more powerful than the reality, holds that a woman's *sole* role is to be a good wife and mother.

Still, as in so much else, Japan has taken considerably less time about making radical changes in women's circumstances. Transitions that required sixty to a hundred years in the West have taken place in Japan in a decade or two.

In 1950, 36.7 percent of female junior-high-school graduates went on to senior high school, compared to only 13 percent in 1930. In 1985, 94.9 percent of female junior-high-school graduates went on to senior high school, while 92.8 percent of male graduates did. However, 40.6 percent of men, but only 34.5 percent of women went to university or junior college from senior high school.

Women have clearly not pulled ahead of men in general education, although they are very close. Nonetheless, several times as many women are now receiving far better education to a much higher level than they did before the war. Such qualifications make them more useful to employers—and more discontented with the stringent limits on their opportunities.

Marrying later, today's women bear fewer children, two against five in 1930, and they do so in much shorter time, 3.8 years as opposed to 12.5 years. More than half the working women of Japan are over thirty-five, and the great majority are already married. Women are obviously far more widely available for employment, to which they bring far greater skills and continuity than in the past. Yet they are only marginally more advanced.

Women make up 13 percent of all professional and technical workers, but they are concentrated in teaching and pharmacy. Although medicine is also considered suitable for females, they are no more than 10 percent of doctors. Women occupy less than 1 percent of managerial positions, except in elementary schools, where they are 56 percent of the staff and 2.9 percent of the principals.

Women are still believed to desert their employers for marriage and/or child rearing. The facts are otherwise, but that hardly matters. Old prejudices and folk beliefs are too powerful. Brilliant leadership can bring a people from feudalism in the nineteenth century to world predominance in the twentieth century. But no one can yet convince that people that spirits do not inhabit rocks, trees, and mountains—or that women are not by nature inferior to men.

The original Japanese practice was totally different from Confucianism, which treated females as born menials, who were bound to obey their fathers, then their husbands, and, when widowed, their sons. Japanese animism, as amended by Shintoism, enshrined the goddess Amaterasu-Omikami as the creator of the Japanese isles and the progenitor of the Japanese race, and several reigning empresses exercised great power before the imperial family was reduced to a symbol. The hereditary Fujiwara regents thereafter maintained their sway by marrying their daughters to the emperors.

The court of the powerless emperors in tenth-century Kyoto produced two of Japan's greatest authors: Lady Murasaki Shikibu, who wrote that inimitable novel *The Tale of Genji*, and Lady Sei Shonagon, who wrote a pungent account of men and politics. Those works molded the Japanese language, as well as fundamental Japanese concepts of society, which was shaped and civilized by the ladies of the court.

That cultivated society crumbled with the *Heian Jidai*, the "period of peace and tranquility," in the mid-twelfth century. The violent and divisive feudalism that took its place required that women play no other roles than wife and mother. For the last seven hundred years, Japanese society has been intensely male-centered, largely because the warrior was so long its central figure.

Their training still makes Japanese women diffident today, and practical difficulties stand in the way of their attaining regular promotion and equitable pay. A Japanese supervisor is expected to get drunk with his subordinates from time to time, relaxing within the embrace of the company. Moreover, important visitors are entertained at geisha parties, where they get just as drunk. Not *too* often, since the cost can nowadays run to $2,000 a head, but from time to time every senior Japanese manager must give a geisha party.

A female manager would find it exceedingly difficult, if not impossible, to get drunk with the boys. She would find it impossible to invite male colleagues to a geisha party, which always involves sexual enticement, although lightly veiled and often unfulfilled. Aside from the impropriety of a respectable woman drinking with men, much less getting drunk in public, the geishas would not put up with it.

Companies can, therefore, go just so far in treating a woman as an honorary man. So companies don't try very hard. Women are usually glorified tea girls or flower arrangers and fill traditional female jobs: secretaries, receptionists, and bank tellers. They are supervisors or managers only when other women are to be supervised or managed. Women have a long way to go against powerful social prejudice.

That is the conventional assessment. Herself a career woman of formidable success, Taki Katoh does not accept it. Perhaps all right as far as it goes, she feels, it is not the whole truth or even the most important part of the truth. She believes the women of Japan are largely to blame for their own predicament.

"Of course it's a man's society," she says. "You know why? Women don't grow after a certain age, but men have to grow. . . . Women are spoiled. Most of the young ones only work because that's the fashion. Then they concentrate on their kids—as *toys*. Do you know, after the kids get bigger, only half of Japanese women work?"

I am nonplussed. Taki has just set on its head the long-cherished belief that Japanese men have arranged their world to their own satisfaction, regardless of their women's wishes and that discrimination prevents women's advancement, although most *want* to work and get ahead. Moreover, the fact that slightly more than half of Japanese women above thirty-five are regularly employed normally gives rise to congratulation. Yet Taki maintains that almost half do *not* want a career. They are too frivolous, she implies with the acid scorn of an intelligent woman assessing her sisters.

"They'd rather spend their time flirting with door-to-door salesmen and plumbers." She is in full flight. "And mooning over soap operas until they can't tell the difference from reality. . . . Then they complain that they're neglected: 'My husband doesn't think of me. . . . My kids don't think of me.' More and more I've heard that story in the last three to five years. Everybody's middle-class now. We have money, and we have time. But it's not an interesting life for them—and they're bored."

Taki's mother, Shidzue, considers the issue from another perspective. Women's lot, she notes, is far better than it was in her youth.

"I had an uncle who lived with us, my mother's brother," she recollects. "He told me the story of Jeanne d'Arc, and I was so impressed that a *woman* could dedicate her life to her nation." She calls to her maid for iced coffee and resumes, "In those days, how miserable we were. Women had *no* rights under Japanese law. We were not treated as people, as individuals."

No more than Taki, however, is Shidzue Katoh given to illusions about her sisters.

"I am now trying," she says, "to create a strong movement among middle-aged housewives who have a profound knowledge of life. They have the time and the money, which wives normally control. But they have no eyes opened to public affairs—only to their husbands and their children. I often speak to groups and say, 'Open your minds to public affairs. . . . You have a duty to do something for your nation.' "

Although she is, at ninety, no longer as tireless as she was at seventy or eighty, Shidzue Katoh is working on a newsletter to arouse those women to their potential. Through the Organization for International Cooperation on Family Planning, she is also working to help the underdeveloped countries of Asia and Africa.

"We're supported by a grant from the Foreign Office," she says. "We're showing them how to dig wells so they can get good water. We also provide medicines and pesticides. If people are healthy, they don't need to have so many babies. They know the few they have will live."

Taki and Shidzue Katoh's horizons are not bounded by female issues. They are, for one thing, both intensely concerned about the mass media. With popular journals that reach every home,[1] and almost as many television sets per head as the United States, Japan is profoundly influenced by the media. Like the United States, Japan is moving headlong toward a society in which the media almost inadvertently exercise the dominant influence. Neither lady is happy with that prospect.

"There is no leadership in the Japanese media," observes Shidzue, the social activist. "Everyone is lukewarm and afraid. Yet we need leadership *from* the media."

Taki, the individual activist, feels the media are already telling their audience too much about what is going on—and thus making matters worse.

"Newspapers are always calling attention to the boredom and frustration from which women suffer," she points out. "Worse are TV and the magazines, especially the cartoon magazines. Phone-ins make it even worse. So do astrologers and fortune-tellers, who are always giving advice about sex problems. . . . One result is that women are much freer about sex than they ever were. They have so many opportunities. Even university students work in bars and nightclubs as 'hostesses.' " The quotation marks around the word are audible. "That always ends in sleeping with strangers for money. Some are only too happy to pose as amateur models for the twenty or more magazines that specialize in nudes."

Gesturing broadly to encompass the middle-class affluence of the Harajuku district, she adds: "Even in this area girls are approached on the street and asked to agree to be photographed naked. You get Y20,000 [about $150] and you're famous. Then you appear in porno movies and you're really famous. . . . No wonder mothers are afraid to tell their daughters about sex. They're embarrassed. The girls think they know so much. . . . They just laugh at their mothers."

Extramural tuition is readily available through *manga*, literally "ca-

---

[1] Total newspaper circulation of more than 75 million a day means more than one copy for every two Japanese, infants and children included. In addition, a good deal more than four billion magazines are sold each year.

sual pictures." The story line in *manga* is not important—as long as every other page provides soft pornography shading into hard pornography. The erections and the labia are not always hidden under flimsy sheets or diaphanous silk. Nor are the inventive postures, mass rapes, and unusual partners. In a café in the Harajuku district that offers coffee at five dollars a cup, no refills, which is reasonable for Tokyo, are great piles of *manga*, which are free. The store is no more than ten-by-fifteen, with a very low ceiling, mock-rustic benches, an electric kettle, and a microwave. The *manga*, or comic books, are the favorite reading of both adolescents and adults in a nation with effective 100-percent literacy. They are the largest-selling publications in a nation of enormous circulations. One of the leading *manga* sells more than twenty million each week, and the others not much less. They offer competently drawn tales of mystery, horror, the supernatural, war, crime, and heroism.

The *manga* are the heirs of a lusty and lurid tradition. For centuries, brightly colored and minutely detailed anatomical drawings circulated widely. Those quintessential Japanese prints were highly commercial. Cherished for their own inherent titillation, they also lured patrons to discreetly shuttered brothels that proclaimed their wares with names like *Raku! Raku!*, "easy joy."

The Japanese have long been preoccupied with innovative variations on the sexual act. Helpful devices of great ingenuity were widely available for centuries before sex shops became normal features of the urban landscape elsewhere. With their characteristic flair, the Japanese greatly refined and improved the erotic literature and pictures derived originally from Chinese models.

The youth of this new gilded age are even more fascinated by such fantasies than were their parents. Affluence has made them more childlike and more avid, Shidzue and Taki assert. Both believe that super-prosperity has made children, youth, and young adults cling to their parents more closely, rather than make them less dependent, as elsewhere. Mothers, both say, must assume too much responsibility, largely because salarymen fathers are hardly ever at home—not like the days when families worked together at farming, crafts, or shopkeeping. Listening to them—and to others—I am half-convinced that Japan, once the land of fierce samurai and dauntless kamikaze pilots, is becoming a nation of wimps.

Pathological dependence persists into adult life. Men in their twenties or thirties who occupy positions of great responsibility often behave like children. Sometimes they behave like lost children and sometimes like vicious children.

Taki talks as if the worst examples were invariably alumni of Tokyo University, which she detests. Called Tokyo *Imperial* University before the surrender, that university guides the collective called Japan Inc. It has been *the* premier institution of learning and advancement since the Meiji Restoration, the foster mother of ministers and chairmen of the board. Taki, however, cites two alumni as typical.

First: A brilliant economist who was appointed director of a major tax office at twenty-five brought his mother along on his first day. She exhorted his subordinates: "I do hope you'll like my son and work hard for him." Second: A respected doctor carried on fifteen love affairs—and killed his nurse, who was the sixteenth. Taki feels that his excessive dependence upon his mother made him unstable. Finally, she believes, he had to revenge himself upon his mother—and on his foster mother, Tokyo University.

The view of the Japanese—men in particular—as mother-dominated weaklings seems to me farfetched. But I found that specialists, patently more detached, make much the same judgment. Keiko Higuchi, quoted earlier, is a serious journalist. She reflected on dependence in an article distributed by the quasi-official Foreign Press Center, which is not in the business of running Japan down.

"In the past, parents had some authority," she wrote. "It was not the authority of personal character, however, but an authority bestowed by the fact that the very role of parent was held in respect and that the laws of the land saw that it stayed so. . . . Ironically, the poverty . . . and hardship . . . made the parents' task easier. Unlike today, when many parents and children are *incapable of becoming independent of each other*, children had to become independent earlier; otherwise the whole family would suffer. Most mothers . . . worked very hard on the land and did not have the leisure to fuss over their children. From an early age children learned to be independent and to pull their share of the load."

I am still not convinced. I suspect that the three distinguished ladies are overstating their case, perhaps looking back to a mythical golden age when Japanese were more individualistic. Yet, if they are exaggerating such pathological dependence, it is only by a hair.

Dependence is, of course, *amae*, the fundamental Japanese trait noted by the psychiatrist Dr. Takeo Doi—himself, not remarkably, a graduate of Tokyo University. It means vying for approval, that is, conforming to the wishes of others to win their approbation. The Japanese are, of course, super-conformists. They are also keen competitors—as the struggle for elite education demonstrates.

Beginning at eighteen months with competition for admission to the better pre-nursery schools, children are relentlessly pointed toward five or six great universities, among which Tokyo University stands highest. Successful careers are virtually guaranteed if they gain admission to those universities after running the gauntlet of successively more selective pre-nursery schools, nursery schools, kindergartens, primary schools, junior, and finally senior high schools. They have endured ruthless rivalry, relentless cramming, parental tears, and successive *shiken jigoku*, "the hell of [entrance] examinations." Many falter and fail. Some commit suicide, the traditional escape from failure that transforms dishonor into honor. Those who succeed prove that they have already been molded. They know they must compete, but they also know they must conform.

Pressure is relaxed when students enter the right university. They are neither pressed hard nor, except on the most severe provocation, ever expelled. If you are admitted, you graduate—and enter the paradise of an assured position with certain promotion and your rise limited only by your own ability.

You have thus returned to the familiar, nerve-twanging tension of normal Japanese life. You must trim your behavior to the winds of prevailing opinion among your colleagues. You must tactfully prove yourself better than they are, but not set yourself apart from them. The rare maverick I have called a *ronin* may perform remarkable feats and provide the stimulus indispensable to achievement. He is *not* promoted to chairman of the board—or even seventeenth vice-president.

Such behavior is, of course, a manifestation of *amae*, which was discussed in chapter 6. The concept was first called to outsiders' attention in *The Fragile Superpower*, by Frank Gibney, who has written most perceptively about the Japanese character, as has Robert Christopher in two important books.

Stiff demeanor and the blank expression so often presented to strangers are also functions of *amae*. Society demands uniform behavior. That means the individual—and the group—must know exactly how to behave under any set of circumstances, even before encountering those circumstances. Spontaneity is, therefore, bred out of the conventional Japanese. They are, further, loath to reveal any feeling that might set them off from their fellows. By subordinating the individual will to the common good, they ensure that the collective organism operates effectively for the good of all the individuals—whether the collective is a corporation, a research institute, a laboratory, or Japan Inc.

Such subordination is hateful to Westerners, who value the individual and the individual will above all else. Subordination not only comforts but strengthens Japanese, individually as well as collectively. Because their vision transcends the individual, Japan is therefore far more powerful than the sum of the individuals who make it up.

In times of crisis a single will prevails, as it did in 1941 when Japan chose to fight the Americans, the British, and the Dutch, as well as the Chinese. It did again in 1945 when the emperor instructed the cabinet to surrender. Such explicit direction by the emperor is infrequent, since the consensus stems implicitly from him. The emperor himself later explained that he could, constitutionally, only intervene to bring peace because the cabinet was divided.

Japan's consensus is not formed by free interchange of ideas. A *directed* consensus, it is formed by a very small group of the elite. Catastrophe can follow—as it did in 1941. The power of the directed consensus over the organism is almost illimitable. It is, therefore, virtually impossible to halt Japan or turn it aside once it is committed to a strategic course—except by collision. Only after a disaster like the surrender can the consensus be altered and the nation be set on a new course.

Hardly a perfect democracy in the Western sense, neither is Japan authoritarian in the Western sense. No general or politician imposes his will on the people by coercion, for coercion is unnecessary. Both the feudal and the Confucian traditions induce spontaneous acceptance of authority, indeed veneration of authority. *Consensual* authority therefore functions far more efficiently than could *coercive* authority.

Since little coercion is necessary, dissidents are allowed much leeway. Particular tolerance is given to students, who are the anointed of the Confucian order. They may demonstrate, riot, and destroy—as long as they do not strike directly at the foundations of society. So may the striking workers who mount such dramatic confrontations between unions and management. Afterward, both groups of course conform to the collective will.

The strains imposed on the individual by a demanding society have been intensified by Japan's triumph in the competition for material superfluity. No Japanese can suddenly cast off the austere values of his ancestors and revel unreservedly in the abundance they despised. Many Japanese are trying strenuously to turn themselves into jolly consumers, as the consensus now directs. Most are finding the strain severe. Materialism is really *not* the Japanese vice.

Each society adopts the vices that suit it best. The West uses drugs like heroin and cocaine to escape from activity and responsibility. The West wants to slow down. In Japan, they favor amphetamines, which make life move faster. For some Japanese the present frantic pace is still too slow.

When I first came to Japan in 1951, I was goggle-eyed at the *pachinko* craze. The sound of the word describes the game: a kind of pinball played on vertical boards with balls slightly larger than BBs. Nearly forty years later, hundreds of thousands still sit twitching before the same game. Yet the challenge is slight, and the rewards are meager. Pachinko is hectic activity for its own sake.

Conditioned to constant activity, the Japanese are so habituated to disaster that they domesticate it with pet names. When B-29 Superfortresses unloaded hundreds of thousands of bombs on Japan's fragile cities, their victims called them *B-san*, "Mr. B.," as if greeting a favorite guest. The firestorms that followed those raids were only a little more severe than the conflagrations that had in the past periodically consumed Japanese cities. Edo, as Tokyo was called before the Meiji era, was accustomed to conflagrations. They were called *Edo no hana*, "the flowers of Edo," in the same spirit that greeted the Superfortresses as *B-san*.

Nature herself continually threatens the vulnerable islands. Earthquakes are endemic, and not all volcanoes are dead. Typhoons sweep across the plains and the mountains tossing locomotives around like toys and hurling tidal waves at the shores.

Anomalies flourish in the rich soil of success:

- Heavy industries like steel, mining, and shipbuilding are beset by competition from Taiwan, Korea—and even Indonesia. Plans to substitute high-tech and service industries leave the people fearful. They do not believe that nonmaterial products can ever replace good solid hardware.

- Individual foreigners are generally treated with courtesy, but the Japanese feel little affection for the foreigners they brush against in big cities or resorts at home or abroad. Still, they may now realize that foreigners are *not* a species of vicious animal.

- Seeing few Jews, most Japanese do not know Jews when they see them. Yet outspoken anti-Semitism has taken the place of anti-foreignism, which is now bad form in this age of "opening and internationalization." Many Japanese books have revealed Jewish vices and Jewish plots to take over the world.

- Intellectuals are particularly susceptible to delusions, for Japanese teachers, artists, writers, and journalists embrace the prejudices of the extreme left. Environmental concerns are, however, virtually nonexistent. Few Japanese champion the whales and dolphins their fishermen slaughter or care for cows, cats, and dogs. The Japanese Society for the Prevention of Cruelty to Animals is still run primarily by foreigners, who founded it.

- Callousness toward human as well as animal suffering is inherent after centuries when compassion was a dangerous luxury. In their hearts, the Japanese still consider themselves menaced and vulnerable.

I almost missed Michio Nagai, which would have been a pity. A former minister of education, he is senior adviser to the rector of the United Nations University in Tokyo and the Japanese voice at the International

Institute of Advanced Studies. I called Mr. Nagai to apologize and break
our appointment because I could never make it through the afternoon
traffic. Wary of prickly Japanese self-regard I was surprised when he
suggested that we talk on the telephone instead. He is, I found, not
primarily worried about the problems of Tokyo, the world's largest
metropolis.

"No one has written about the sheer size of Tokyo—and what it
means," he says. "This is the biggest concentration of power in the
world. There are now thirty million people in the metropolitan area—
and population will grow by at least three million in the next decade.
Tokyo already takes in three counties—and the area will be enlarged.
All because of the Japanese obsession with growth. *We want to be the
biggest, as well as the best.*

"Tokyo also has the strongest government in the world. It operates
on two levels: the highly centralized national government and the
metropolitan government. That power is sustained by an immense
amount of money, the biggest concentration of wealth in the world.

"Yet the shadow of Japan's great economic success lies over the
metropolis. I'm afraid it's analogous to places like São Paulo and Calcutta, which growth finally choked."

This, I reflect, is remarkable—a Japanese thinker so dispassionate he
can compare Tokyo and Calcutta, one the pride and the other the shame
of modern Asia. I need hardly say a word, for he continues without
prompting.

"Human beings are alienated by such gigantism. The space of a
normal home in Tokyo is one-twentieth the space of a normal home in
Los Angeles. Japanese money is coming back to Tokyo from investments abroad—and driving up land values. Land now costs so much that
ordinary people suffer much deprivation. Above all, they are deprived
of a normal, comfortable home life. They are making money and losing
a decent life. That is an unacceptable trade-off.

"Yes, the per-capita income is higher than it is in, say, London. But
the purchasing power of the yen is so low at home that housing and
necessities become barely attainable. An example: The price of land in
Los Angeles is one twenty-third the price in Tokyo—and Los Angeles
is not cheap. That means incomes have to be 2,300 percent higher here
than they are in Los Angeles. And, of course, they're not."

Here, I realize, is the authentic voice of prosperous Japan lamenting
the troubles that come with prosperity. Michio Nagai is giving his
audience of one an overview of the acute predicament in which his
country finds itself.

"That difference in land values," he sums up, "results in the export
of even more yen to Los Angeles. The big interests get more for their
money. Ordinary people, even ordinary millionaires, just can't partic-

ipate in the boom in Tokyo. You need billions and billions. One *tsubo* [thirty-five square feet] costs Y20 million [$5,000 a square foot] in a near-central district like Akasaka and Y30 million [$7,500 a square foot] in Marunouchi, in the heart of Tokyo."

In one endeavor, Japan is emphatically *not* number one. Conventional crime is not a serious problem, certainly not in comparison to the West. Lately the United States has averaged for every million persons 8.6 homicides, 37.5 rapes, 225.1 robberies, and 48,562.6 larcenies. The figures for Japan are homicides, 1.4; rapes, 1.4; robberies, 1.6; and larcenies, 1,130.

The closed-circuit surveillance camera, as much a fixture in American and European shops as ceiling lights, is unusual in Japan, even in Tokyo, which seems to require *less* policing than in the past. Normally one sees far fewer policemen in Tokyo than in any Western city, and the street patrolman, called *Omawari-san*, "Mr. Esteemed Go-Around," appears virtually extinct.

Japan has no more than thirty thousand lawyers in a population of more than 123 million. The U.S. has approximately 700 thousand in a population of 240 million. That disparity is not really due to the low crime rate, for most lawyers anywhere are not concerned with crime, but with property. Besides, many Japanese lawyers do not practice, but work for corporations, often in nonlegal capacities.

Japan is biased against lawyers—who did not exist in Confucian or feudal society—and does not need many. Instead, it has a homogeneous population and a strong moral consensus. Quarrelsomeness that elsewhere finds expression in litigation is largely controlled by social pressure. The *yakuza*, "organized gangs," are so interknit with normal society that they are practically its obverse, rather than an aberration. The national consensus controls even gangsters.

As my taxi approaches the Yamato Building, I realize that I have come to Japan at a moment of ripeness. Despite the passion for gigantism, Tokyo is, by and large, cleaner, more orderly, and more manageable than it has ever been in the past.

Even taxi drivers have been mellowed by prosperity. They no longer drive like kamikaze pilots, and most now even know streets and addresses—as very few did in the past. The tangle of Tokyo makes the maze of London appear geometrically regular. Most remarkably, all the drivers are courteous.

Besides, all wear ties, which are obviously important to their own self-respect. Japanese are generally not overly concerned about the status of their jobs. They are concerned with dressing appropriately and with doing the job well, whether they are waiters, taxi drivers, or professors of astrophysics. Whatever one's work, competence and diligence win approbation. The Italians call it *bella figura*, and the Japanese call it *memboku*.

Entering the modest Yamato Building, I reflect. I do not particularly want to talk with cabinet ministers or chairmen of the board, even if they have time for me. They come and go. I want to see the men and women who make things work, like Hiroshi Kida, former vice-minister of education. Now director of the Japan Society for the Promotion of Science, he was once director of the National (i.e., government-sponsored) Institute for the Study of Education.

The title doesn't really matter. Hiroshi Kida is simply *the* man responsible for the future of education. Since education is *the* single most important element in the making of present-day and future Japan, I want to know how it worked—and how it will work.

Certain aspects are already clear to me. Obviously the educational system must have been extraordinarily flexible; only constant adaption could have coped with all the changes in society since the Meiji Restoration in 1868. Educators must clearly have favored students of outstanding ability; only stringent cultivation could have produced the brilliant leaders of industry, commerce, finance, technology, and the civil service.

A spare, gray man with a warm laugh and beautiful manners, Hiroshi Kida takes no joy in telling me that I am totally mistaken in those assumptions. The educational system, he says, has changed little during the past hundred years. It has, moreover, never sought to create a special class of the outstandingly able by cultivating the gifted.

In 1872, four years after the Emperor Meiji was "restored" to power, a comprehensive statute established a modern educational system on European and American models. The number of both students and institutions of learning doubled in a decade. That system endured to create a well-educated populace for a modern state.

The Allied Occupation is often hailed as a democratic revolution in Japanese education. Hiroshi Kida disagrees.

The most virulently nationalistic and militaristic courses, he agrees, were excised, particularly *shushin* ("ethics"), which was political indoctrination and compulsory study of Shinto. Japan also adopted the American practice of dividing primary and secondary education into six years of elementary school, three years of junior high school, and three years of senior high school. But the content and the purposes of Japanese education hardly changed at all, Hiroshi Kida says. And textbooks evaded Japanese responsibility for aggression against China and Southeast Asia, ignoring atrocities like the rape of Nanking.

Later, the compulsory pledge to the red-sun flag and the compulsory singing of the national anthem *"Kimi ga Yo"* ("Your Imperial Era") were restored. Nationalism is now primary, and war guilt is unknown. In any event, the response to the war was shame, not guilt. Japanese felt shame at having failed the nation and the emperor by being defeated, not guilt for their deeds.

Hiroshi Kida is just as unorthodox in his assessment of elitism in education. By and large, he says, teachers have *not* sought to cultivate the best students. Concentrating on neither the gifted nor the handicapped, they strive to bring the entire class up to the same reasonably high—but not stratospheric—level of attainment.

All the students must, however, prove that they can do good work. But "streaming" students within a school according to their ability is not the Japanese way. It would not do for those relegated to the lower streams to be humiliated or for those elevated to the higher streams to become arrogant. Instead, highly selective admission policies operate from pre-nursery schools to the elite universities. Thus, the collective entity, rather than the outstanding individual, is exalted.

Mr. Kida, however, believes the present system must be revamped to meet the needs of the new Japan, starting at the top. Universities must be more hospitable to foreign staff and to foreign students, both now discouraged. They must also be enlarged, particularly their research function—or Japan will fall behind progress elsewhere.

"If it ain't broke, don't fix it!" Americans now say. That is a strange motto for a nation that became great by restlessly tinkering with existing machinery—and making it better. The disciplined Japanese now say: "Find out what could cause a breakdown or a drop in efficiency—and fix it before it does. While we're at it, let's see how we can improve it."

Hiroshi Kida notes three chief requirements to improve education:

1. The challenges of the future will be complex and sophisticated. Educators must not be complacent; they cannot be satisfied with the present system because of its past success in molding the generation that made the economic miracle.
2. Business and industry now demand that students study more "international subjects" so that they can negotiate and/or work more effectively with foreigners; beginning when they are very young, children must be taught to think "individually, internationally, and creatively," so that they can cope with foreign ways and foreign technology.
3. Parents must demand that schools teach "better morals" in order to stem the increase in juvenile delinquency produced by the increased number of working mothers; the greater influence of television, as opposed to reading; and the tendency to disregard parental authority.

Although those trends are minor, almost infinitesimal, compared with the problems of the West, they are troubling. Disturbed by new difficulties at home and abroad, the Japanese have been reinventing themselves since 1985. Malleable because their core is hollow, they have, of course, reinvented themselves several times since the Meiji Restoration, their most spectacular reinvention. Yet their fundamental nature has altered little, if at all.

The response to the pressures created by Japan's new position in the world has been a policy of "opening to the outside world and internationalization at home." It is, however, irritating to be told to become more like outsiders and to invite outsiders to share the fruits of Japanese diligence and genius. Such irritation was expressed at length earlier in this account by Wataru Hiraizumi, the former cabinet minister who is influential in the Liberal Democratic Party.

Public irritation has turned on the Liberal Democrats, who have ruled from 1955 to 1989. Having in summer 1989 lost their majority in the Diet's upper house, which can delay but not initiate legislation, they were facing an election in which they could conceivably lose their majority in the lower house—and thus be forced to relinquish power after thirty-four years. No individual opposition party, but a coalition of opposition parties might then succeed them.

In the lead was the Japan Socialist Party under that formidable lady, Takako Doi, who could become prime minister. She had proved herself a skillful professional politician by exploiting women's dissatisfaction— and by pledging to restore the high tariffs on agricultural products such as oranges and beef that the LDP had lowered a little in deference to American demands. Should she come to power, she could unsettle the essential relationship with the U.S. by pressing her party's antinuclear policy; by cutting American troop strength in Japan; and by reducing defense expenditures.

The coalition of interests that was the Liberal Democratic Party, however, remained resilient, despite its scandals and its maladroitness. The vote for the opposition parties, moreover, appeared to be primarily a protest against the LDP's corruption, laxness, and self-satisfaction— not necessarily an endorsement of the opposition's programs. Shocked by that vote, the LDP was examining the multifarious faults developed by three and a half decades of virtually unchallenged power. It was extremely corrupt, but it was still the best-organized and most effective political machine in the country.

The essential Japan could survive an LDP defeat, even a JSP victory. The product of centuries of evolution, Japan Inc. will not dissolve in a day—or a decade. The features most important to the outside world will endure.

The Japanese are superior, not only by their own standards, but by the standards of the West. They know it, and they don't mind showing it. Good manners may enjoin a certain modesty even on manifest superiors. But they are likely to become assertive in word and deed.

The Japanese have reason to be proud. In less than a century and a half, they have moved from inferiority to even the moribund Manchu and tsarist empires to predominance in the world economy.

They are, not unnaturally, determined to enjoy the fruits of their superiority and their success. Their chief priority is now to rebuild Japan to make it more comfortable and even more efficient. In response to foreign pressure, they are urging their people to buy more foreign goods, not to work as hard, to play more, and to travel abroad. Foreigners believe such changes will make Japan less of a threat. The Japanese keep their own counsel and appear to go along. But they will work almost as hard, and they will strive to preserve—and enlarge—their predominance.

Combined with the extraordinarily high value of the yen, those measures are intended to reduce Japan's enormous trade surplus and thus spread the wealth among other countries. The campaign to induce Japanese to buy more foreign goods is, however, carefully tuned to make sure they do not buy too much. In 1990, the Japanese were buying one-third as many imports as Americans. Most come from fellow East Asians, notably Korea and Taiwan, not from the United States.

An assertive Japan, exercising great power, is no longer a vision. A reality today, it will loom even larger tomorrow.

That reality is manifest in the title chosen for Emperor Akihito's reign, the words that will appear in every date on every document as long as he lives. His father Hirohito's reign title was Showa, meaning "Brilliant Harmony." His grandfather's was Taisho, meaning "Great Brilliance." His reign title is Heisei, which means "Peace Achieved"—or, alternately, "Domination Established." The first version is better public relations, but the second is equally correct.[2]

Domination in our era is no longer simply a matter of master and subordinate. Although economically dominant, Japan must look to the United States and to its neighbors in Asia. Without their markets, their labor, and their raw materials, Japan must also look to the European community, where it is building factories and acquiring corporations. But Japan's hegemony depends primarily on America.

The inevitable conflicts between the two during the next decade will not *all* be about trade. They will also be about sharing technology, about

---

[2] *Heisei* is classical Chinese, which the Japanese use as we do Latin. *Hei* means "flat," or "level," and, thus, peace. *Hei* further means to pacify, a ruler's crushing resistance and imposing his sway. *Sei* means "to achieve, to accomplish, to establish."

defense, and about foreign policy. No longer content to be solely an economic animal, Japan is asserting itself abroad, through diplomacy and aid. Allotting more than $11 billion for foreign aid in the year 1989 and planning total expenditures of $38 billion, Japan is the world's largest donor. Japanese interests will naturally be served by that aid. Japan fears protectionism, and the U.S. fears bankruptcy. Joseph Fromm, the eminent consultant on foreign policy, points out: "The U.S.-Japan struggle over trade policy goes to the heart of our relationship with Asia and, even more, to the heart of American and Japanese culture and psychology. We must both do what comes unnaturally: for us, contraction in our living standard; for them, expansion of their domestic economy and really joining the outside world."

Japan will do what outsiders want—up to a point. Above all, Japan will do what it wants. While spending much more at home, it will maintain, and probably expand, its share of world trade. Most politicians, as well as most mandarins of the civil service and private industry, sincerely want to decrease the trade imbalance—a little.

Some mandarins are, however, remarkably far-seeing and objective. Taroichi Yoshida, who is senior adviser to the Industrial Bank of Japan, a decisive force in the economy, spoke to me in a must unbankerly way.

"The West has long mistaken Japan for another developed Western country," he points out. "It therefore expects the same internal market mechanism to work the same way. But Japan is different—and Japanese rules are different. Most Japanese feel they are playing fair, even when the West accuses them of sharp dealing. . . .

"Japanese stubbornness and tenacity are inherent. That psychology made the attack on Pearl Harbor unavoidable, even though Admiral Yamamoto, the commander-in-chief of the Imperial Navy, didn't want war with America."

Taroichi Yoshida believes that Japan must change much more fundamentally than is presently envisioned. He stresses, "If we are to survive, we must move beyond automatic competition and the market mechanism. Joined by the United States, we must give up our belief in the possibility—and the desirability—of infinite expansion of economies and unending elevation of living standards.

"The motto has been 'Expansion and Prosperity.' It must now change to 'Harmony and Fairness.' It is foolish and destructive to keep expecting fast growth.

"The new generation is realizing that—in Japan and throughout the world. It seeks not goods first, but a better quality of life. . . . Even before that, one simple change can come about here. In the U.S., executives are expected to work very hard, for very long hours. In Japan, *everyone* is expected to work like an executive. That, at least, can change."

That comparison may be changing—albeit very slowly. I have, however, seen few signs that the yuppies of Japan or the West are recanting their materialism. In the full flush of their acquisitiveness, they must learn, as Taroichi Yoshida has learned: *Survival requires getting along with a greatly enlarged human race in a world of shrinking natural resources.*

The Japanese are unlikely to attain empathy with the rest of the human race for some time. Nor will they soon feel the concern for the environment and for other species of animals that is rising in the West. Even without the sanctum of the book of Genesis, the Japanese, like the Chinese, have long believed the world and its creatures were there for them to exploit. Look at China's cynical utilization—and slow extermination—of the giant panda for diplomatic and commercial advantage. Look at Japan's slaughter of dolphins caught in small-mesh tuna nets, and insistence on killing several hundred whales each year for "scientific purposes."

Japan's insatiable appetite for timber is, further, destroying the tropical rain forests at the rate of two billion dollars' worth a year. With Southeast Asian timber reserves running low, Japanese buyers are moving on to the gravely threatened Amazon Basin, to Africa, and to Canada.

"I have high hopes for the twenty-first century." Taroichi Yoshida sounds as if that were a long way off, which it is not. "There is much dissatisfaction with the way things are in Japan. There is even a retro-boom. Youth is nostalgic for the Meiji era, when Westernization and industrialization were just beginning. We call that feeling *kokoro no yutakasa,* 'a fullness of the heart.' "

It would be rude to say that such fullness of the heart is largely sentimentality and eminently exploitable for commercial purposes. Besides, he has an instinctive feeling for his own people.

"So the new era must come," he says. "After the *pax Britannica* came the *pax Americana.* New stability and prosperity for the entire world must also have an element of *pax Japonica.* First, we Japanese must have more to do with Asia. We are not really part of Asia now, except for our aggressive and predatory commercial role. We cannot live with that . . . with fear and resentment. We must sacrifice and pay out. We cannot always expect to benefit from our role, but must be prepared to pay the tax."

His views are not unique, and they are not widespread. Such views are expressed by mature men and women who possess the experience, the funds, and the leisure to think beyond day-to-day problems. Diplomats in Tokyo underscore Japan's need for a broader understanding of its place in the world. Above all, they feel Japan will in time be compelled to realize that relentless pursuit of self-interest can injure itself.

"Japan cannot remain a solely economic power," notes a senior European ambassador. "Great power comes from investments abroad, which are expanding by the minute. But so do responsibilities and difficulties.

"Big investment abroad makes Japan vulnerable to events abroad. I expect some nasty incidents, perhaps major clashes with other countries, perhaps terrorist incidents. Immense power also breeds anti-Japanese feeling. Most people are not very attractive abroad—and Japanese are certainly no exception! With all this, nerve ends get exposed.

"Besides, Japan is not really Asian. It has no affinities with anyone in Asia—and it is very much disliked. Japan is unique, and it is isolated, except for its super-special relationship with the United States. . . . But, whether the Japanese like it or not, they are acquiring the problems of a world leader!"

9

Singapore: A Lion in the Southern Seas

SINGAPURA IS SANSKRIT FOR THE CITY OF THE LION; "THE SOUTHERN SEAS" IS COLLOQUIAL CHINESE FOR SOUTHEAST ASIA. ROUGHLY SHAPED IN THE NINETEENTH CENTURY OF SIMPLE EXPORT-QUALITY PORCELAIN, THE LION, NOW POLISHED TO A HIGH LUSTER, HAS AN ELECTRONIC ROAR—AND A LASER-SHARP EYE FOR THE DOLLAR.

W hen I first saw Jamaica," said Lee Kuan Yew, "I thought to myself: If only I had been given an island this size, what could I have done with it!"

The prime minister of the Republic of Singapore, the *only* prime minister Singapore has ever had, is not normally introspective. He was, however, discussing with an old acquaintance the growth of his city-state and his own career, the two being virtually indistinguishable.

"Your letter said you wanted to know my philosophy of government," he had begun. "I'm not sure I have any definite philosophy."

Lee Kuan Yew thus candidly defined the relentless pragmatism that has transformed the old Crown Colony, which was lethargic even in its vices, into a highly productive, consumerist republic that is both energetic and puritanical. Unburdened by ideology, he has moved agilely from quasi-Socialist populism to brusque, capitalist-oriented authoritarianism such as the old colonial government would never have dared attempt.

If a policy worked for Singapore, if it moved the island-state toward the prime minister's highly practical goals, it was a good policy. If it did not, it was summarily abandoned. And that was that.

The great seaport on the island that hangs like an emerald pendant from the mainland of Asia was founded by Sir Stamford Raffles in 1819.

A servant of the British East India Company, Raffles had been instructed to develop trade with the old port of Malacca on the Malay Peninsula and with the great island of Sumatra, opposite Malacca. Since sailing ships were providentially slow in bringing further instructions, he used his own judgment.

Malacca, he felt, was played out. Singapore, at the southern mouth of the Straits of Malacca, commanded the sea lanes from Europe to the Far East—and was, therefore, the port of the future. Raffles accordingly bought the island from its sultan, who was delighted with a small payment. Inhabited by a few thousand Malays and a few score Chinese, it was of no importance in the politics and trade of Asia.

Raffles's settlement duly became the gateway to East Asia. To its harbor soon came large numbers of merchant ships and also men-of-war, for it became Britain's chief base in the Orient. Because such commerce required a larger and more energetic population, the British brought in Chinese and Indians, whom they ruled with British detachment and rough British justice. At the beginning of the war in the Pacific, Singapore was the chief Western stronghold in Asia. It was the apparently impregnable home base for Britain's forces in China, and a secure stepping stone to Australia and the South Pacific. British rulers and Chinese subjects lived in mutual sufferance, though not mutual admiration. Both were making money, and that endeavor fostered prodigies of tolerance.

Japanese invaders destroyed that pleasant and profitable manner of life. Singapore proved vulnerable, not impregnable. British forces proved ineffective—and not terribly valorous. The Chinese fought well—not for their British rulers, but for their homes and for China, their homeland, which had earlier been invaded by the Japanese. When the British returned after victory in the Pacific, the Chinese no longer believed in British rule in Singapore. Neither did the Labour Party government in London.

The stage was set for the slow rundown of colonial rule. Lee Kuan Yew, who entered as a supporting player, was to become the superstar of that drama.

More than two and a half million people now live on the small island that is clenched north, east, and west by Moslem Malaysia, while the narrow waters to the south are speckled with the islets of Moslem Indonesia. Lee Kuan Yew transmuted the many races of that beleaguered territory into a city-state—if not quite in his own image, after his design. Customs and language, bricks, mortar, and tarmacadam, all mirror his taste. The personality of Lee Kuan Yew and the philosophy he cannot define dominate both affairs of state and daily life.

Singapore lived in slothful ease before he came to power. It is today always in motion, a kaleidoscope that constantly throws off new, brilliant images.

Behind their immaculate sidewalks and grass strips, the uniform apartment blocks of the Housing and Development Board now house 86 percent of the population. Skyscrapers palisade the harbor, and the colored lights of assertively hygienic foodstalls glow on the manicured palm trees. Raffles, one of the world's most romantic hotels, lolls white and low behind its circular carriage drive, refurbished by a decision that almost came too late.

The relentless efficiency of the relentlessly honest civil service is visible in the city-state's compulsive cleanliness. Savage fines prevent littering, and construction workers hose every last grain of sand or cement off the tires of their dump trucks before using public roads. Equally apparent is the incessant pressure applied by the government through its instruments, including the controlled press, to ensure the crushing electoral victories of Lee Kuan Yew's People's Action Party.

The kaleidoscope reveals ingenuity and impositions, benevolence, and enigmas: Change Alley, a narrow lane hedged with moneychangers and hawkers, has been supplanted by skyscrapers that house international banks. But moneychangers still operate on almost every corner—painstakingly honest moneychangers.

Only recently, couples were encouraged by severe penalties to produce no more than two children. They are now encouraged by singing commercials and also by large tax rebates to produce three or four. That campaign is directed at the "educated"—the intelligent, studious, and industrious Chinese who would otherwise be overwhelmed by the indolent, unlettered, and fecund Malays.

Bells and lights on their roofs reveal where taxis and vans are exceeding the speed limit. Yet pedal trishaws still carry passengers throughout the downtown business district.

The English language is paramount. But an ordinance requires every ethnic Chinese taxi driver to speak the official language of China, Mandarin, presumably to end the babble of Hokken, Hakka, and Cantonese that once divided the Chinese community.

Lee Kuan Yew found Singapore sloppy, dirty, poor, and relaxed—with a number of cuisines, but none to inspire great enthusiasm. He will leave Singapore efficient, antiseptic, well off, and tense—with a greater variety of cuisines, most excellent.

Cuisine is crucial to the overseas Chinese, who are the great majority of his constituents. If the food is good, they will put up with a great deal. If the food is not good, even paradise will not content them. In Singapore today, the food is very good and very abundant.

Lee Kuan Yew found Singapore a scattering of divergent communities. The Chinese middle class lived in bungalows with red-tiled roofs and in two-story shop-houses. A few hundred colonial mansions, largely built of wood, housed rich Chinese and Europeans. The poor Chinese lived in cramped, damp-blotched tenements on narrow, clamorous streets. In scattered *kampongs* (villages) amid the remnants of the jungle, the Malays lived in thatched huts set high on stilts to deter cobras. In the downtown business district, only two structures, the Bank of China and the Asia Building, were more than ten stories high. Breasting the filth-and-debris-silted Singapore River, the sailing junks tied up near the rusting Anderson Bridge with cargoes of rice, rubber, and alligator skins.

Lee Kuan Yew will leave a Singapore with peaked red-roofed bungalows and high-rise housing—and flat-roofed shop-houses replaced by vast shopping centers. A few dozen wooden colonial mansions still stand amid the new concrete villas of the newly rich and the geometrically regular housing developments of the new upper-middle class. Although few *kampongs* remain, vestiges of jungle have been preserved among the orchid plantations in the north of the island and the golf courses of the nature preserve in the center.

Beige and pink hotels resemble the aggressive opulence of Beverly Hills. Downtown, skyscrapers cluster around the seventy-story Overseas Union Bank, touted as the tallest building in Asia. Beneath those towers, the squeaky clean Singapore River flows, albeit still sluggishly, under a silver-painted Anderson Bridge—and there are no more sailing junks.

The prime minister halted the demolition of congested Chinatown and other relics of the past when he realized that he was also demolishing his few tourist attractions. But it was too late to leave more than artificial flies in synthetic amber.

He found a Singapore that possessed no moral consensus. The Islam of the Malays and the Anglicanism of the British coexisted uneasily with the pragmatism of the dollar-hungry Chinese. He will leave Singapore with a slapdash moral consensus: general agreement that it is good to be well off. But few Malays share the Chinese passion for hard work, and many Indians prefer to talk, always brilliantly.

Lee Kuan Yew will also leave a society he describes as "accidental" in origin, lacking internal cohesion. As a substitute for a unifying doctrine, his own pragmatic philosophy may not be enough.

His basic principle he states succinctly: "Let everyone live his own life as he wishes—as long as he doesn't cramp or confine the life of others."

Men and women of goodwill disagree in their assessment of Lee Kuan Yew's consistency. To protect the realm he created he has meted out sharp treatment. His model is Confucian society, which he says is, above all, tolerant.

I wonder just how much the prime minister knows about Confucianism when he says its *chief* characteristic is tolerance. His pressure for achievement, academic and practical, is truly Confucian, as are his requirement that his people obey their superiors implicitly and his disregard for abstractions. The sternly paternalistic Singapore of Lee Kuan Yew smacks of old-fashioned Confucianism. He is now institutionalizing Confucianism.

"There is a systematic campaign to establish a 'national ideology' based on 'core values,' " points out a practiced observer. "There is much talk of 'Asian values,' but the essence is 'Confucian ethics.' The main thing is to avoid 'degenerate Western morality.' They go on as if they had invented the family, filial piety, and submission of the individual to society.

"All the speechifying, press correspondence, and feedback will ultimately lead to a definitive document that will be generally honored and taught. It maintains that the Confucian individual puts society first, which is poppycock. It refuses to see that the family orientation, which breeds corruption, can be a bigger menace to society than individualism."

Practicing the journalist's trade, I have visited many prime ministers around the broad arc from Europe to Asia. Except in the wartime laxity of Seoul, none threw fewer safeguards around himself than does Lee Kuan Yew.

Once the gate in the iron railings is opened by two policemen, no guards challenge my car's progress. Two Gurkha soldiers do stroll on the wooden veranda, wickedly curved knives a foot long at their sides, and short-barreled .38 revolvers in their black leather holsters. I see no other security.

The waiting room is open to the breeze in the old Singapore way. The air-conditioned reception room, where hang big colored lithographs of Singapore birds, is a sealed box with cane chairs set against the walls as if for a school dance. It is all a little stiff.

The prime minister, too, is a little stiff. He wears a fawn sports shirt under a beige polyester leisure suit—and a remote expression. He looks old, although he once looked too young for his age, not to speak of his responsibilities and his power. He is balding; his remaining hair and eyebrows are white. Yet beneath the pouched eyes and puffy cheeks the vigor and the vision are intact—only a little blurred.

Early in the hour and five minutes he has allotted me, Lee Kuan Yew speaks wistfully of what he could have done with a bigger island. Jamaica is immense by comparison with Singapore: 4,682 square miles against 243.

Unwontedly humble, he observes: "If we had to start all over again in 1954, to get to the same advanced stage of development, I'm not sure we could get here. Fortunately, the coin flipped heads on several occasions."

Singapore is virtually unique as a trading nation. Its exports in 1987 were worth $27.4 billion, against less than $1 billion in 1954. Exports actually exceeded Gross Domestic Product, and total trade was three times the internal production of goods and services. As the port for peninsular Malaysia and a major oil-processing center for the entire region, Singapore today transships raw material—as it always has. It also processes much raw material—as it did not in the past.

The prime minister sums up the problems of a minuscule city-state: "The foundation is not broad enough. We have to create our stability by dynamism, like a gyroscope spinning to stay upright. We have to run as fast as we can to stay in the same place."

In 1987, at the age of sixty-three, Lee Kuan Yew should be serene and confident. He has built true and strong, and he is respected as beyond question the second-wisest statesman in Asia, perhaps the world.

Lee Kuan Yew is also the most interesting statesman in Asia—and the most successful. Among those who lead fights for independence, only Lee Kuan Yew afterward ruled wisely—and shaped the new state to his will. Others failed the transition from revolutionary to ruler: Mao Tse-tung in China, Pandit Jawaharlal Nehru in India, Ho Chi Minh in Viet Nam, and Sukarno in Indonesia. Those great men left disorder— economic, political, and administrative—compounded by corruption. Lee Kuan Yew created a briskly efficient industrial mini-power that is virtually free of corruption.

After the first decade or so, however, Singapore did not offer him problems that truly tested his talents. Arrogant but never smug, he has remained dissatisfied.

Yet he is curiously apprehensive about the future of Singapore. The elder statesman of Asia still fears Malay intransigence and Islamic fundamentalism, Indonesian ambitions, Soviet expansionism, China's assertiveness, and Japan's ruthlessness. He is further concerned that Singaporeans could lose the sense of common nationhood he has instilled in its diverse races and could recede from the industriousness that has brought prosperity.

He is, nonetheless, buttressed by his conviction of absolute superiority. He has always found subordinates who are not only capable, but will put up with his imperious moods. He has followed his own vision— and they have followed him.

Still, he is human enough to enjoy showing off. In Moscow in 1962, I came upon Lee Kuan Yew dining with a group of Russians and obviously bored. His People's Action Party was facing *the* critical election that would determine whether he retained the office of prime minister, which he had won in 1959. Urged by Marvin Kalb of NBC, I asked in Mandarin if we could talk with him. He agreed, delighted to display his command of a language that he, like I, had learned through hard study.

He then calmly, almost dispassionately, predicted the outcome of the forthcoming election—and was right within two percentage points. He exuded confidence, not the edgy assertiveness of a politician shouting as he passes the polling station, but calm certainty. He *knew* he would win—and remake Singapore.

Then, as ever, Lee Kuan Yew's humor and joviality were measured. Essentially cold, he saw nothing remotely laughable about himself or his mission, which preoccupy him.

No humor, indeed no lightness, enlivened my most recent meeting with Lee Kuan Yew. Moira and I were just beginning our voyages to rediscover Asia, and I wanted to talk with Lee Kuan Yew first. His insight is formidable, and his judgments are sharp.

We have known each other since 1954, but have not been terribly fond of each other. Moreover, I have written critically about him. Although I hope we feel mutual respect, I can only be sure that I respect him.

The prime minister is gracious in his own brusque way. I sometimes wonder what it is like living inside Lee Kuan Yew, a man of enormous gifts who is not gifted in what the world calls human relations. Detachment from others can be a strength, but also a weakness for a politician—or for any human being. However, his temperament is not my immediate concern.

In the spring of 1987, my son Simon has been the Singapore correspondent of the AP–Dow Jones News Service for half a year. He naturally wants to meet the prime minister, but when I propose that he accompany me the initial reaction is not encouraging. I persist, pointing out in good Confucian fashion that Simon has a duty to his father as well as to his profession—and would no more report remarks the prime minister prefers to keep confidential than I would.

My pieties may have helped. Simon is invited as a concession. The prime minister is angry at the American press. He is furious at Dow Jones, which owns not only the news service, but the *Asian Wall Street Journal* and the *Far Eastern Economic Review*, whose criticism Lee Kuan Yew deeply resents. He has virtually expelled the correspondents of both publications and has curtailed the circulation of both in Singapore because they have refused to print his rebuttals in full every time.

The prime minister's feud with Dow Jones does not appear vital to us, but rather another of those slightly embarrassing, slightly childish conflicts that regularly arise between martinet governments and disrespectful foreign correspondents. Lee Kuan Yew, however, fixes Si-

mon with a weary yet piercing eye—and reads him a five-minute lecture
on the iniquities of the press, particularly Dow Jones. Quite evidently,
the conflict is vital to him.

Lee Kuan Yew is also annoyed at the United States because he fears
it is receding from Asia. The Americans, he says flatly, saved Asia by
their military actions and must remain because their strength is still
badly needed. Somehow, the trivial matter of American correspondents
in Singapore has become entangled with that major issue. The First
Amendment to the U.S. Constitution, he points out, guarantees great
privileges to the press, but *only* in America; the British tradition, from
which derive most of the laws and practices of Singapore, is less
indulgent. Under Lee Kuan Yew today the issue is not what Singapore's
newspapers, magazines, radio, and television can*not* say; it is what they
must say.

No British government could get away with the stringent control he
exercises over the press. As in the past, he turns his back on the British
tradition and British practices whenever he finds them irksome or
inconvenient. The Privy Council would rule unconstitutional the way
he runs Singapore just as firmly as would the United States Supreme
Court.

Yet Lee Kuan Yew is complex, a man of conflicting traits. Although
he could dissemble coolly when he was using the Communist underground to carry him to power, he is by nature hotheaded. He has
naturally become imperious through decades of unchallengeable
power; few have dared contradict him—and none consistently.

He is also hypersensitive, almost pathologically so. Most politicians
would have shrugged off the mild criticism that embroiled him for years
in a public quarrel with Dow Jones. Even if he had won the battle and
the editors had given in to his demands, he would still have lost stature
in the world's eyes. But he could not pull back.

One of the prime minister's closest associates was later to offer a
plausible rationale of that behavior. Sinnathamby Rajaratnam, a Tamil
from Sri Lanka who was born in 1915, had been Lee Kuan Yew's
spokesman and adviser over the years, as well as his foreign minister and
first deputy prime minister. I have also known him since 1954 but have
felt closer to him than to Lee. He was a good newspaperman before he
gave himself to politics, and he is much warmer than Lee, which is no
great feat. Dark and white-haired, his nose aquiline, Rajaratnam looks
like an amiable Pharaoh.

The prime minister's predicament, he is to say, is the same as that in
which George Orwell found himself as a young colonial officer in
Burma. Orwell was begged to kill a rogue elephant that villagers said
was damaging their crops and threatening their lives. He found that the

elephant was not a rogue, but he had to shoot it nonetheless. If he had not, he would have lost his authority.

The analogy is tempting. It would be more convincing if similar imbroglios had not occurred time after time.

The prime minister could not control his ire against *The Eastern Star*, a daily published in Kuala Lumpur, the capital of Malaysia. The *Star* had declared that his government was not as spotlessly clean as he maintained, but was marred by corruption. Indignant at that slur, Lee filed a suit for libel, incidentally entertaining the lawyers by raising some questions regarding the limits to criticism of a public figure. Accustomed to using the law as a blunt instrument to beat his enemies, he may have overlooked the fact that this time it was not *his* law.

We met in 1954, the year Lee Kuan Yew became a public champion of the anticolonial movement. After the war in Korea ended in 1953, I had come to Singapore. I was to live there for two years while studying the overseas Chinese on a grant from the Ford Foundation.

Lee Kuan Yew had returned to Singapore in 1950 from Britain, where he had studied law at the University of Cambridge. He had also married his Singapore sweetheart, who was herself a lawyer; sat at the feet of Social Democratic thinkers like Harold Laski of the London School of Economics; rejected Marxism as self-contradictory; and concluded that the British must be driven out of Singapore and Malaya if they would not go voluntarily. He was thirty-one years old in 1954, and he was called Harry by his friends, not Kuan Yew.

His great-grandfather had come to Singapore as an illiterate coolie to reenact the classic success story of the overseas Chinese: from carrying-poles to carriages in one generation. The Lees were Hakka, which means "guest families." Hakkas had come to South China a thousand years earlier, but had lived apart, following their own customs and speaking their own distinctive language. In Southeast Asia, they still kept their distance.

Harry Lee was himself a little apart from his own people, the overseas Chinese who were almost 80 percent of the population of the Crown Colony of Singapore. Most of them came from Fukien Province, especially the great seaport of Amoy. They called themselves Hokkien in their own harsh dialect, and they dominated the commerce of Singapore. Harry Lee could get along in the Hakka language, but his Hokkien was rudimentary, for the Lee children had not been encouraged to play in the streets. He was, moreover, as illiterate in Chinese as his great-grandfather, just able to write his own name in ideograms. He spoke the English of a well-educated man, but not a word of Mandarin.

In the new emotional climate of Singapore, those twin deficiencies were grave. Mandarin, the officials' tongue, had decades earlier been declared the common spoken language of China. All educated Chinese spoke it, and the new Communist rulers of China were substituting it for local dialects. Mandarin was also the language of the China-oriented schools of Singapore. More numerous than English-language schools, they ardently promoted Chinese culture and instilled pride in being Chinese. Half the youth of Singapore were indoctrinated with cultural and racial arrogance. Because the Communists ruled China, pro-Chinese sentiment became Marxist sentiment and anticolonial fervor.

The Communist underground turned Chinese-language schools into training camps for militant Marxists. The Chinese-educated were angry. They were second-class citizens in a land they believed to be their own, whatever the claim of the indigenous Malays, who were no more than 15 percent of Singapore's population. Unlike Lee Kuan Yew, one of the small English-educated elite, the Chinese-educated had no regard for British culture. They despised all things Western as degenerate. Recalling Japanese victories, they scorned Britain for its weakness and hated the British for their arrogance.

Long the underclass of a colonial society, the Chinese-educated now knew themselves to be the heirs of the world's oldest civilization. They also knew their mission: to create a *Chinese* Singapore, a *Communist* Singapore.

It was not that simple for Lee Kuan Yew in 1954—and it was never to be that simple. Although he shared their resentment of the British, his feelings were not virulent. He still called himself Harry—and he stood between two increasingly antagonistic worlds.

Early in 1954, Harry Lee let it be known that he wanted to be called Kuan Yew. He reverted to his Chinese name to make his anticolonial position unmistakable. He also began to study Mandarin, pasting lists of ideograms to his shaving mirror. He appeared to be abandoning the English-educated elite for the intense world of the Mandarin-speaking militants who were either the willing tools of the outlawed Communist movement or its secret members.

That was how he wanted it to look. If he was to use the underground movement for his own ends, he had to look and sound like one of its stalwarts.

Nonetheless, his first major public appearance in his new role required him to wear the stylized white wig of an English barrister with its sausage curls and little pigtails. As a junior counsel, he assisted the chief counsel, the eminent British barrister D. N. Pritt, who candidly declared: "I'm not a Communist. I'm what is called a fellow traveler."

The brief trial at which the two appeared was just what the new movement and Lee Kuan Yew needed—public victory over the colonial government. Lee had not recruited the protagonists or manufactured the issue. But both perfectly suited the plans he was perfecting as a labor lawyer.

Lee already had strong ties with those among the English-educated who refused to be the pets of the colonial establishment. Those rebels included not only Chinese, but Indians, Eurasians, and even a few Malays. From that group Lee drew the men he planted in union offices. Others, although in their thirties, were still students at the University of Malaya in Singapore, having returned to the campus from jail. They had been detained as suspected members of the underground Anti-British League or its parent organization, the Chinese-dominated Communist Party of Malaya, which had risen in armed rebellion in 1948.

Having feigned repentance to secure their release, they might have been expected to lie low. Instead, they formed a Socialist Club; unlike communism, socialism was not outlawed. The Socialist Club's journal, *Fajar (Progress)*, in May 1954 published an article headlined "Aggression in Asia." It denounced the Southeast Asia Treaty Organization as a mechanism for renewed Western imperialism, and it called Malaysia a police state because of the harsh tactics the government used against the Communist uprising.

The authorities reacted with blind fury that would have embarrassed a rhinoceros—and with mammoth stupidity. They charged the editorial board with sedition, that is, incitement to overthrow the government.

Lee Kuan Yew had found his opportunity. Lithe beside stout D. N. Pritt, he argued dramatically in court. His accent pure Cambridge and his tone mellifluous, he appealed to British justice, administered though it was by a colonial court his clients despised. Naturally, his picture was on the front page of every newspaper in Singapore.

The presiding judge agreed with the defense lawyers that there was no case to answer. When counsel and clients celebrated, Lee wore a shirt that gaped open over his belly. Having displayed his professional aplomb, he was promoting his new proletarian image.

Yet he was still a man apart in November 1954, when he spoke at the founding meeting of the People's Action Party, which was later to carry him to power. He wore the cotton shirt and wash trousers that were the uniform of the new radical movement, but he spoke in English. At that inaugural meeting, no more than 60 percent of the assembly was Chinese—and most of those Chinese spoke English.

The passage of half a year worked a radical change. When the People's Action Party convened its first annual conference in June 1955, Secretary General Lee Kuan Yew appeared isolated, almost pitiable. It was a Chinese-speaking meeting—and he could not yet speak in Mandarin.

Frightened by vicious rioting spearheaded by the students of the Chinese-language high schools, London was rapidly divesting itself of responsibility for Singapore. A local politician named David Marshall held the equivocal title of chief minister, *not* prime minister, and exercised limited authority. His was clearly an interim regime, but Lee Kuan Yew did not appear a likely successor. Lee, it seemed, would be swamped by the rising tide of Chinese nationalism on which the Chinese-educated were riding toward power.

At the PAP's annual conference in Victoria Hall, whose broad stage was also used for concerts, Lee Kuan Yew stood alone. Physically as well as psychologically, he was distanced from both the ordinary members of the PAP in the hall and the officers on the stage.

Lim Ching Siong, the labor activist, student leader, and secret member of the Malayan Communist party, dominated the meeting. He dispensed the revolutionary rhetoric the crowd wanted—in Mandarin. Only 5 percent of the assembly was *not* Chinese, and those Chinese who could speak English, as Lim Ching Siong could not, were not doing so. Long Mandarin dialogues between Lim and his admirers on the floor frustrated the few non-Chinese present, but their protests were ignored. The man who then rose was obviously not Lee Kuan Yew, but Harry Lee. Speaking in English, he spoke across an abyss.

When I left that hectic meeting, I felt that the decision had been made for Singapore. The PAP had become a Chinese party, and Chinese-educated Marxists would assuredly rule the city-state, probably sooner rather than later. Lee Kuan Yew could be useful as an English-speaking agent, but he would remain a subordinate. No matter how hard he studied Mandarin, he would always be an outsider. Had he not made submission to the colonial overlords by learning their language, which the Chinese-educated called "dog farts"?

That was half the truth, the obvious half. But Lee Kuan Yew and his English-speaking followers had made a secret deal with the Chinese-speaking radicals, a deal both sides naturally looked forward to betraying.

The PAP was to be Lee's. The radicals were to withdraw from the executive committee, which would consist entirely of English-speaking moderates. The radicals would concentrate on the expanding labor movement, considered the true vehicle to revolutionary power. Lee was thus to be the go-between and front man for the radicals, and the PAP was to appear a moderate party. Confident that they could manipulate the new "clean" executive committee, the radicals did not stand for office.

Manipulating the labor movement, the radicals imperiled themselves. In late 1956, after fresh Communist-directed rioting, Chief Minister David Marshall interned Lim Ching Siong, who had become a PAP member of the new National Assembly along with others who had earlier been interned by the British. Lee Kuan Yew was left free, although he had declaimed in the red-and-gold chamber that he would "prefer communism to colonialism."

He was so patently a spent force that I wrote in a book called *The Dragon's Seed* two years later: "The PAP was still a legal party, though only poor, trapped Harry Lee remained at liberty among its leaders."

I prefer not to dwell on how often I have been wrong during four decades of reporting. But I have rarely been so spectacularly wrong as I was about Lee Kuan Yew. Small consolation that I was right about the force he was to use to seize power. In the same paragraph I also wrote: "The executive leadership [of the PAP] was in jail and the organization uprooted, but a generation was committed to the Communists."

Lee Kuan Yew, however, brilliantly manipulated the Communists, using their racism and their fervor, as well as their joy in hard work, hardship, and sacrifice, and also their genius for organization. He is, I believe, the only democratic politician ever to use the Communists and then discard them—as they have others. During protracted Machiavellian maneuvering, he lost interest in working democracy, which he judged "not suitable" for Singapore. Later, he again interned the militants who had been confined by the British and by David Marshall, among them men D.N. Pritt and he had cleared of charges of sedition in the *Fajar* case.

Dennis Bloodworth has comprehensively recounted Lee Kuan Yew's adroit strategy against the Communists in his book *The Tiger and the Trojan Horse*. Despite the clumsy title, it reads like a first-class thriller—with its intrigue, double-dealing, and violence. It is a *true* thriller. Bloodworth went through the files of the Special [political] Branch of the Singapore Police, and Lee Kuan Yew told him about clandestine meetings with the chief delegate of the Communist parties of Malaya and China. The candid account shows how closely Lee was allied with the Communists during the days when he derided as alarmists those who pointed to the Communist peril.

That protracted deception, which showed Lee Kuan Yew the true face of Communist subversion, accounts in part for his present repression. Strong measures, be believed, were necessary to stave off Communist subversion. If asked why freedom must still be curtailed, when China has gone out of the business of exporting revolution, Lee and his associates reply, "Threats remain. You must not judge us by Western standards. You cannot expect an Asian government to adopt its tenets from the West. We act as is necessary."

The threat was originally China. In February 1989 the Republic of Singapore and the equally nervous Republic of Indonesia began moving toward formal diplomatic relations with the Communist People's Republic of China. Singapore had previously recognized neither the

People's Republic nor the Nationalist Republic of China on Taiwan. Yet Lee Kuan Yew was, as always, pragmatic. Although he had exchanged ambassadors with neither, the Communists maintained a trade mission in Singapore and the Nationalists an information office. The Communists also sent him cheap labor under the guise of "trainees," and the Nationalists helped train his troops.

After capturing the revolution from the mainland-oriented Communists, the prime minister purged the China orientation of so many Singaporeans of its political content. He has, somehow, created a new Singaporean consciousness that is distant from China, although based on Chinese culture. Turmoil and suffering in China obviously assisted that delicate process.

I earlier asked young men and women the deliberately naïve question: "What are you?" Index finger touching the nose, each invariably replied in Mandarin: *"Waw shr Junggwawren."* "I'm Chinese." Today the same question draws the answer, *"Waw shr Singjyapawren."* "I'm Singaporean."

That answer is still delivered in "South Seas Mandarin," the slurred dialect of the overseas Chinese. Curiously, that language is no longer known in Singapore as *guanhua*, Mandarin, the "officials' tongue," or *putunghua*, the "common tongue," or any of the other terms used in China. It is called *huayü*, which means literally "China language," a new coinage—and it is *the* speech of Singapore.

Although all Chinese are expected to be proficient in *huayü*, English is the working language of Singapore, the common tongue of educated Malays and Indians, as well as educated Chinese. But Malay is officially the first language of Singapore. Conveniently, Malay is known to almost all; it is not difficult, not offensive to any, and not inextricably identified with the potential enemy, Moslem Malaysia.

The clash of original languages and cultures, which could have been a constant irritation, has thus been finessed. But Lee cultivates fear of a hostile world to encourage his people to submerge their differences. His success in so doing almost transcends logical explanation. His personal mystique, it appears, has wrought the miracle, just as it miraculously leached *huayü*, which is undeniably the Chinese language, of Chinese chauvinism.

The judgment around the courthouse is that Lee Kuan Yew's wife, Lee Kwa Geok Choo, is a better practical lawyer. He is, moreover, a practical politician, not an intellectual. His pleasures are not cerebral, and he is not concerned with ideas for their own sake.

However, he responds to concrete problems with imaginative solutions. His intelligence is of a high order, if intelligence is the ability to adapt rapidly to new circumstances. His mind is very quick, but has little depth. A dedicated pragmatist, he is an absolute Confucian ruler by temperament.

Despite his great achievements, his ambition longs for new challenges. Others disappoint him by failing to come up to his expectations. He disappoints himself by failing to live up to his own expectations.

Winning solid majorities of the popular vote, he worries that they are not greater—and has, therefore, stacked both elections and the media. Although his rivals can hardly find a platform from which to oppose him, he persecutes those few who dare, methodically altering the law to suppress them.

Lee Kuan Yew wept in public in 1984, when the PAP won *only* 62 percent of the popular vote. Despite a 12-percent swing to the opposition, Singapore's artfully gerrymandered electoral districts gave the opposition only two seats in a parliament of seventy-nine. Nonetheless, he warned that the city-state stood in dire peril. Singapore would disintegrate if the People's Action Party ever lost power—and that he would not permit.

The prime minister declared that the one-man, one-vote system had thrown up "freak results." He then revamped the system, ostensibly to ensure a fair racial balance in Parliament. In "group constituencies," three candidates of the same party must now run together—and one must be of a "minority race"—Malay, Indian, or Eurasian. The opposition is usually hard-pressed to find one candidate, much less a mixed trio. The PAP monopoly of power has thus been preserved.

The prime minister is arbitrary, as well as hypersensitive, perhaps because he has never been tested to the utmost. The stage is too small and the demands of the drama too narrow, for he is a veritable giant. He has never found employment that would engage all his talents, despite talk of his becoming Secretary General of the United Nations. The offer was never made—it might not have been accepted had it been, for Lee Kuan Yew could not subordinate himself to the pressures of a hundred and fifty governments. Nor has he been offered prestige-laden assignments within the British Commonwealth, such as the intermediary's role two Australian prime ministers played: Robert Menzies during the Suez crisis in 1956, and John Fraser toward South Africa. Lee Kuan Yew has for thirty years remained no more—and no less—than supreme ruler of Singapore and a highly respected spokesman for the Southeast Asian region.

That static career has nothing to do with racism, for both the UN and the Commonwealth are assertively nonracist. It has far more to do with his personality. He is abrasive, intolerant, impatient, and contemptuous of those who displease him.

It may also be due to his politics. He has been the most outspoken foe in Asia of both Soviet and Chinese expansionism. Other politicians would speak favorably of the American presence in Viet Nam—in private. Only Lee Kuan Yew had the courage to do so in public.

Above all, I believe, Lee Kuan Yew frightens people with his intensity and his singlemindedness. He would have made a titanic wartime prime minister. When he was at war with the Communists he appeared happier than he does now. He has, in any event, conducted his peacetime prime ministership as if he were at war.

The greatest enemy of Lee Kuan Yew's Singapore may be none of the forces he fears—not Islamic fundamentalism, Japanese ambition, China's glacial southward movement, or his other bugbears. The greatest enemy may well be boredom.

The material paradise Lee has created is exceedingly monotonous. Most differentiation has been glossed over, and it is differences that give zest to life. When they are not overachieving, many Singaporeans are bored stiff. Men and women in their twenties and thirties yearn aloud for the excitement and variety of the life their parents led in crowded *kampongs* and tenements.

When I ask the prime minister about such vocal dissatisfaction, he replies, "They're just romanticizing the past. There was no sanitation and no running water, hot or cold, for many not even electricity. . . . And what was there to do? The people could grow tapioca, make children, and drink."

Many residents of the Housing and Development Board's vast developments praise their safety for children, the convenience of their shopping centers, and the refreshment of their swimming pools. Lee Kuan Yew cannot be faulted when he justifies his often intrusive role not only by Singapore's stability, but by the great material benefits he has brought to Singapore.

Yet Singapore is no welfare state. The individual gets no guarantee of anything except the opportunity to advance by his own endeavors.

"The function of government is to provide opportunity," says Sinnathamby Rajaratnam, the PAP's theoretician. "And that is the *only* responsibility of government."

Educating the people to utilize their opportunities is implicitly part of that responsibility. But even the school system is slowly being privatized, and all principals are being given greater autonomy. Nonetheless, all will assuredly foster only the approved ideology with its "Asian values and Confucian ethics."

"The people get used to the idea of buying what they need," explains Rajaratnam, who was once a passionate advocate of socialism.

Repudiation of the welfare state extends even to government health programs. "If they don't pay for it," Rajaratnam tells me, "they can't get the best service. Eventually, every citizen will have his medicare in his savings."

Yet Lee Kuan Yew, ever the dedicated pragmatist, minutely controls the economy when necessary. The Central Provident Fund has forced individuals to save for their retirement—and to provide a pool of dollars for investment. Every working Singaporean must deposit 22 to 25 percent of his wages in an escrow account held by the government, which allows withdrawals on stringent terms. In 1985, when the economy grew sluggish, the employer's matching contribution was reduced from 25 to 12 percent of the salary. In order to put more money in circulation, it was later raised to 16 percent.

Rajaratnam notes: "It could go back to 25 percent. We can't have a Hong Kong–style free-for-all here."

Control is selective. To promote economic growth, the government has from the beginning encouraged competition—on the government's terms. A free-enterprise economy was directed in an authoritarian manner, much as are the guided economies of South Korea and Japan. Today the government is selling off some of the quasi-public enterprises created with the Central Provident Fund. Efficiency is Singapore's Holy Grail, and nowadays efficiency requires privatization.

Sinnathamby Rajaratnam shares the perception that has moved authoritarian regimes in Korea and Taiwan to relax their control over the economy. He, too, believes that, as the economy grows and everything gets so much more complicated, centralized direction becomes much less effective.

"It's easy to govern in the beginning when you start low and a 10-percent gain means prosperity," he observes. "But affluence creates its own problems. Other Southeast Asians are easily satisfied, unlike the Chinese. So we have the politics of envy. . . . When there are race riots in neighboring countries, anti-Chinese or anti-Japanese race riots, they always burn motorcars because cars are a symbol of affluence."

Settled by Chinese imported as laborers, Singapore now imports Filipinas as housemaids and chambermaids, Thais and Indonesians as construction workers, and Malaysians to collect its garbage. Unemployment among citizens is 2 to 3 percent, effectively full employment. The few unemployed also have a big cushion—a family cushion, not a governmental cushion.

"Singaporeans would rather get jobs as hotel receptionists," Rajaratnam says. "When they're unemployed, they've got savings. So they can afford to wait till the right job comes along. If they don't having savings, their sisters, fathers, and brothers will."

Confucianism is clearly much more than rhetoric, for the family is central. Yet the extended family is being weakened by apartment living

and by the modern economy, which gives children financial independence early. There, too, diversity is slowly expiring, and life is becoming more limited. Boredom therefore threatens. Diversion is badly
needed, even if it requires the direct intervention of the prime minister,
as does so much.

Almost by chance, a massive street party turned Orchard Road, the
city's main artery, into the world's longest dance hall in late August
1988. Having already broken up a party for the twenty-third anniversary
of independence on August 9, the police were not inclined to allow an
even bigger party.

But Lee Kuan Yew understood youth's need "to let off a bit of steam
. . . to find something to do beyond the beaches and the shopping
centers," as one father watching the madness observed. There was, the
prime minister declared, no harm in a big party. "We've got to find new
ways of expressing ourselves," he said. "And this is not only harmless,
but may well do us good."

A quarter of a million danced in the streets amid a bedlam of discos
and bands. But Singapore remained Singapore. Lee Kuan Yew undoubtedly approved when a denim-clad disc jockey, swung high in a
cherry-picker festooned with Coca-Cola advertisements, led the throng
in singing the refrain of the song "Count on Me, Singapore": "We're
going to show the world what Singapore can do. . . . We can
achieve. . . . We can achieve."

Neo-Confucianism is promoted more assiduously in Singapore than
anywhere else in Asia. Obedience to authority is *the* cardinal virtue, and
the next is hard work for national betterment. The individual's responsibility to the state is constantly stressed, as is the necessity to
subordinate personal goals to the needs of society. Because the prime
minister fears that Singapore will become a "fake Western society," he
lauds the strength of the family in Asia—in contrast to the disintegration
of the family in the West. Unlike its Confucian cousins Taiwan and
Korea, Singapore is become *more* authoritarian.

Dissidents look over their shoulders when they recall their time in
prison. Francis Seow, a former solicitor general, is now in exile. When
he rallied candidates to run against the People's Action Party, he was
arrested under the all-purpose Internal Security Act. Yet, despite some
brutality, such preventive detention is not generally harsh. Francis
Seow was released to run in the general election, which he narrowly
lost. After flying to New York for medical treatment, he was tried in
absentia for tax evasion. When he was fined $10,000, he was automat-
ically disqualified from taking the nonvoting seat in Parliament the PAP
had created as a consolation prize for some defeated opposition candidates.

Speaking as a declared opponent of the regime, he says, "The time is coming when absolute totalitarianism is going to take over. You are witnessing a steady erosion of what little freedom we have got left."

Mr. Seow was referring to the dismantling of legal safeguards for the rights of the individual. Another opponent of the prime minister was convicted of fraud, disbarred, and expelled from Parliament. Sitting in London, the Privy Council, which is the highest judicial body of the British Commonwealth, described those actions as "grievous injustice." Inspired by other Privy Council rulings, the Singapore Appeals Court later released four alleged Marxist conspirators. They were rearrested under the Internal Security Act as they walked out the prison gates.

The prime minister declared that the Privy Council should no longer have jurisdiction because it was ignorant of Singaporean affairs. He does not like listening to those who disagree with him.

State-run campaigns like those that repeatedly disrupted China under Chairman Mao Tse-tung impose puritanical uniformity. No longer are male arrivals with long hair given haircuts at the airport. Nor are they any longer denied entry. But long-haired males are still served last in government offices. During the "toilets of shame" campaign, officials of the Ministry of the Environment, disguised as public-toilet attendants, pounced on culprits who failed to flush after using. Photographs of the offenders being led away by the police were published in the *Straits Times* to shame them.

The two-child campaign was a very serious matter. Additional children were to be denied education—a powerful threat in an achievement-driven Chinese community. Parents were cowed, not only regarding birth control. The managing director of the local branch of an American company confided plaintively, "I'd like to run for the opposition. But I know my sons wouldn't get into the right schools. How can I do that to them?"

In 1986, however, the two-child policy was turned around. A grim-faced Lee Kuan Yew warned on television that Singaporeans were not even reproducing themselves. Fewer young workers might soon have to support a large number of the retired. Suddenly the slogan was "Have three children—more if you can afford it."

A sister campaign sprang from Lee's discovery of eugenics and the heredity principle. The quality of Singapore's people was declining, he lamented, because educated women married late, and, in any event, educated men preferred less-educated wives. Women with degrees were, therefore, exhorted to marry earlier. The Ministry of Communications and Information set up a Social Development Unit to encourage men and women with good examination grades to meet—purpose: matrimony. Television ads showed an old lady sitting alone in her rocking chair, sipping tea disconsolately. A voice-over expressed her regret for having "been too aggressive." Her "success-oriented exterior," she said, had driven away potential husbands.

The prime minister's sudden passion for creating a super-race was served, as are all his passions, by a government bureaucracy and a People's Action Party apparatus that have become almost indistinguishable. Civil servants, the judiciary, and government agencies are all beholden to—or subsumed in—the PAP. Even the National Trades Union Congress, which is not *officially* an organ of the state or the party, threatens to expel anyone who supports the opposition.

Potential opposition candidates are intimidated by arrest and imprisonment. They are, the PAP says dismissively, usually taxi drivers. That calling is a last refuge of individualism in homogenized Singapore. But the National Trades Union Conference sends out agents provocateurs to draw drivers into political discussions. Those caught criticizing the government are given "detriment points" on their employment records. If they get too many demerits, they are fired.

The Housing and Development Board can, in theory, enforce good behavior. Yet residents' committees modeled on the "street committees" of totalitarian China are largely ignored. However, American and British sociologists regularly make studies to determine why the HDB projects are orderly and clean, even happy—unlike the crime-terrorized, stinking high-rise tenements of New York and London. I believe the reason is the neo-Confucian moral consensus instilled by example and, to a certain extent, by fear in a largely Chinese populace. Dispersing Malays and Indians among those Chinese has, moreover, ended the ghetto isolation and alleviated the fear sprung of ignorance that once fomented race riots.

Whatever outsiders' and Singaporeans' criticism of the regime, Singapore is, for the great majority, a very pleasant place to live. Life may be dull and unadventurous, but it is secure and orderly. Food is abundant and varied, as are consumer goods. The streets are spotless, and the crowds are well behaved. Crime is not a serious problem, families are not disintegrating, and addicted young people do not loll on the sidewalks.

The golden haze of legend that once enveloped Singapore, the City of the Lion, has dissipated. But the exotic and mysterious Singapore ridden by Oriental vice and crime always existed more in the minds of romantic Westerners than in reality. The crooked alleys radiating from the typhoon drains were not the haunts of desperate men and loose women, but the homes of poor families striving to make an honest living.

Nowadays the streets are straight, and the broad boulevards flow with traffic that is heavy, but always orderly. A smooth three-lane express-way swoops north to the narrow straits that divide the island from peninsular Malaysia. Other expressways swing along the coast, where green parks with enormous seafood restaurants overlook the beaches. One expressway darts straight to the new airport in formerly remote Changi, where once stood only a grim prison and stalls serving delectable crabs and shrimp.

Changi Airport is itself a new art form compared to hackneyed, look-alike airports elsewhere. High-roofed like a modern cathedral, it was the first airport to sell duty-free liquor *on arrival*. Spacious, quiet, and competently run, it does not induce tension, but soothes. That remarkable efficiency, which mirrors the remarkable efficiency of Singapore, was presaged in mid-April 1981. The driver taking Moira and me to Paya Lebar Airport told us cheerfully that next time we would be using Changi, which was opening in June. Aside from finishing touches, he added, only five miles of expressway needed to be built. Astonished, we said that work could never be finished in time.

"This is Singapore," the driver said. "It will be finished."

It was. Such efficiency is even manifest in the bureaucracy—of all places. Individuals' identity cards, passports, and driving licenses all bear the same number. Such foresight and competence would make totalitarianism easy to impose. But Singapore is no more likely to become truly totalitarian than it is to become truly democratic.

Above all, Singapore is convenient, comfortable, and orderly. The precisely spaced orchid stalls under the equidistant palm trees on Bukit Timah Road attract shoppers leaving the big Cold Storage Supermarket, which stocks seven foreign beers as well as Singapore's own Anchor and Tiger and six flavors of Perrier. By American or European standards, prices are very low. The parking lot opposite Fitzpatrick's Supermarket, where strictly licensed foodstalls set up at night, is an asphalt patch amid the glass-and-steel high-rises that have transformed once bucolic Orchard Road.

But the smells are sweeter, or at least more pungent, than in most big cities. Here and there a green vista opens suddenly. Lee Kuan Yew wonders if he has left enough grassy parks and squares in his rush to prosperity and modernity. Though perhaps not enough, he has left many.

Throngs of pedestrians are free and easy, calling loudly to each other, chattering and laughing. I sense no constraint, no repression, and no fear. They are totally unlike the subdued, almost furtive, unsmiling pedestrians I have seen in Peking, Moscow, and Bucharest. Graceful in crisp cotton dresses, women walk happily at midnight amid crowds of young men in starched white shirts and cotton trousers. They are inhibited neither by traditional Oriental prudishness nor by modern fear of violence.

The movie theaters spill their audiences onto neon-brilliant side-walks. The crowds climb the slender bridges that cross the light-streaked avenues or wait for the big red-and-white buses that arrive precisely on schedule. Multistory shopping centers compete for cus-tomers, offering at very low prices the usual enticements: hi-fis and cameras, binoculars and silks, custom-made clothing and jewelry, lug-gage, curios, and furs. Singapore does not enchant the visitor with its old and exotic charms, although a section of old Chinatown, a Hindu temple, and a few mosques still stand. Nor does it enchant Singapore-ans, but they are a matter-of-fact lot.

The average Singaporean is mundane and prosaic. Not for him or her the flights of imagination that make great art and sometimes great fortunes. Besides, the comfortable uniformity fostered by the mother-knows-best government does not inspire creativity.

Yet that lack has not visibly impaired the working of the economy. Ingenuity there is in plenty, chiefly among the protégés of the prime minister. And ingenuity has created a dynamic—if not too sturdy—economic machine.

Singapore's prosperity is based primarily upon two enterprises, elec-tronics and oil, as well as its vast entrepôt trade. Second to Hong Kong, which it has never been able to overtake, Singapore is also the regional center of financial services ranging from insurance and letters of credit to complex loans, foreign-exchange trading, and stock flotations—all at minimum cost. As Hong Kong approaches ingestion by the People's Republic of China in June 1997, some of its abundant talent and capital are flowing to Singapore. But by no means all. For the time being, the city-state depends largely on services and light industry, with virtually no indigenous entrepreneurial base for manufacturing.

When the price of oil falls, Singapore suffers badly. Profit from the big refineries declines—and there is an exodus of the foreign oilmen, mostly Americans, who work the Indonesian rigs, but prefer to keep their offices and their families in super-clean Singapore.

Japan is investing in Singapore because it is efficient and strategically placed. But the Japanese are, as everywhere, reluctant to transfer the advanced technology Singapore wants—and has now secured from European and American investors like Phillips and Rollei, who are themselves hard-pressed by the Japanese. The prime minister loathes depending on the Japanese, who, he knows from wartime experience, are uncomfortable bedfellows. He worries about the departure of American commerce and investment, as well as American military power.

As he says, Singapore's base is too narrow. Hampered by that lack of breadth, Singapore also lacks flexibility. Hong Kong and Taiwan, where small manufacturers predominate, can readily switch product lines or retrench against recession. With its bigger enterprises and its massively foreign investment base, Singapore cannot move as fast. A big fall in the demand for computers would badly hurt the city-state whose biggest nonpetroleum export is more than half the world's disc-drives, worth about $2.5 billion.

Yet Singapore Ltd., the public and private sectors responding in concert to the prime minister's baton, can respond very effectively to challenges—from the top down. It did so in 1985, when the government created a recession and retarded growth by allowing wages to rise too fast. Costs were cut across the board, and money was released by reducing contributions to the Central Provident Fund.

Within a year, growth had resumed at 8 to 9 percent. But in the year 1989, the government was forced to throttle back. Growth was simply too fast to sustain. Again, the Provident Fund and other levers were adroitly adjusted. Money was withdrawn from circulation by higher contributions, but was available for large-scale investment under government direction.

The key is the man who began this account and now closes it. Although outsiders may look askance at him, Lee Kuan Yew is, to most Singaporeans, a figure out of legend, their only leader and their only mentor.

By and large, Lee Kuan Yew rules with his people's consent, for the PAP generates fervent loyalty. He is an Oliver Cromwell without a Bible, a prophet without a creed. He sincerely wants a tolerant government that interferes with individuals only to the extent necessary to prevent their interfering with others' well-being and property. Although his ideas of tolerance and noninterference differ markedly from most Westerners', he is not an extremist among Asian autocrats. He is only more efficient—and much more honest.

The social covenant between the government and the overseas Chinese, who feel isolated and vulnerable in the Southern Seas, is straightforward. Above all, they want security for life and property. They want government stability and an environment in which they can work hard with the expectation of good returns. They want to educate their children to do even better than they have done. In the absence of heavy-handed, universal repression, they will continue to vote for the regime that provides those essentials.

However, the younger generation, unlike its parents, does not respond viscerally to the dangers to which the prime minister constantly points. Youth takes stability, security, and economic opportunity for granted and yearns for other things—even if it is not quite sure what.

Lee Kuan Yew is not, to that new generation, the legendary hero he is to its parents. The small intelligentsia dislikes him, and he irritates executives and professionals. Nonetheless, the People's Action Party is probably secure for a decade—unless a catastrophe intervenes.

Even the apostolic succession is in place. Unlike some despots, Lee Kuan Yew has not shrunk from selecting a successor. Like many despots, he has chosen his son. But Lee Hsien Loong, whose name means "the Dragon Apparent," will only be thirty-eight years old in 1990.

The prime minister evidently plans to retire to the office of president, whose powers he has greatly enlarged. He plans initially to be succeeded by Deputy Prime Minister Goh Chok Tong, who has been his understudy for years. If the master plan works, as the prime minister's plans generally do, Goh will in turn be succeeded by Brigadier General Lee Hsien Loong.

The heir presumptive had attained that rank by his retirement from the armed forces after just thirteen years' service, six of them spent as a student at Harvard and Cambridge. Lee Kuan Yew's passion for eugenics, the selection of the brightest and best by their birthlines, convinces him that his own son is his natural successor. Who else but Lee Hsien Loong has inherited the unique talents of Lee Kuan Yew?

Wags speak of the "Holy Trinity": the Father, the Son, and the Holy Goh. As that formula implies, Lee Kuan Yew will exercise decisive influence as long as he is capable, regardless of the title he bears. His own father, Singaporeans pointed out with some alarm, was still robust in 1989, although well past eighty. Until Lee Kuan Yew dies, Singapore will follow the course he has mapped—spiritless, passionless, but content.

10

Malaysia: Backing into the Future

THE LANDSCAPE SEEMS AS GENTLE AS THE NATIVE MALAYS. BUT
ROCKY OUTCROPS THRUST THROUGH THE JADE-GREEN VEGETATION,
AND THE MALAYS SOMETIMES RUN AMOK, SLAUGHTERING THEIR
NEIGHBORS. THE CENTRAL REALITY OF MALAYSIA IS RACIAL CON-
FLICT: THE LANGUID MALAYS, TWO THIRDS OF THE POPULATION,
AGAINST THE ENERGETIC CHINESE, WHO ARE ONE THIRD. SINCE
THE EARLY 1800S THAT CONFLICT HAS DOMINATED THE LAND,
ALTHOUGH IT WAS FORMERLY RESTRAINED BY THE BRITISH. AND
THE FUTURE?

In 1955, when Moira and I first crossed the half-mile-long causeway
from British-ruled Singapore to British-ruled Malay, we were
waved through the roadblock. The police were not interested in
casual travelers who were obviously not Chinese.

They were looking for Chinese terrorists, for guns, and for explosives,
even for excessive amounts of food. The guerrilla rising the British
called the Emergency, which had racked Malaya since 1948, was slowly
being quashed by such vigilance and by aggressive patrolling of the
jungle. Above all, the overseas Chinese sympathizers of the Communist
Chinese insurgents had been forcibly resettled behind barbed-wire in
New Villages so that they could not supply the insurgents with arms and
food. But the war was not yet over.

Although the war was later won, in 1987 Moira and I were halted at
the end of the causeway while our passports and our car were minutely
examined by Malay officials. We were entering another country. During the intervening thirty-two years, Singapore had become a state in
the independent nation called Malaysia, but had been expelled after
two years. The Malay governing class could not tolerate so many more
Chinese citizens competing hotly for political power.

In 1987 we were not shaken down for bribes, largely because we were
carrying only personal articles. A month later, a German businessman
moving from Singapore to Malaysia had all his household goods strewn

across the asphalt. After twenty minutes' haggling, customs officers agreed on just how big a bribe they would take to let him go on. Held at bay by British rule for more than a century, widespread corruption, the curse of Asia, had come to Malaysia.

Somewhat curiously, in a continent in flux, the works of men had not altered as much between 1955 and 1987 as had public morality. Aside from a few enlarged towns, the virtually unaltered high road to Malacca passed through rural communities that were themselves little altered. Some had obviously begun as the New Villages that had confined their Chinese inhabitants behind fences to keep them from contact with the "Communist terrorists" in the surrounding jungle. By such measures the British had won their war—and had, in 1957, left behind them an independent non-Communist nation called Malaya, which was later to be enlarged and called Malaysia.

We were driving to Malacca, the old city 150 miles from Singapore, which had become the first European foothold east of India when the Portuguese seized it in 1511. We had also driven to Malacca in 1955, but this time the journey took longer. Not because the road was worse, for a few stretches had been improved, but because there were so many more vehicles on the road.

Justified fear of terrorists had kept traffic to a trickle three decades earlier. Yet the main road north from Singapore through Johore to Malacca had been well graded, and the shoulders were cleared so that there was little cover for ambushes. Those few who used the road after dark needed a special pass and, usually, an armed escort. Travelers by day saw that great stretches along Malaya's main north-south artery had been abandoned. A quarter of Johore's population, more than 200,000 men, women, and children, had been herded into New Villages. Almost all were Chinese, for the uprising called the Emergency was a continuation of earlier conflicts between Chinese and Malays.

The jungle could provide shelter for tens of thousands of Chinese guerrillas, but it could not provide sustenance. Segregated in guarded New Villages, Chinese civilians could not supply the Communist Liberation Army with food, clothing, weapons, funds, and recruits.

The five-hour drive along the west coast to Malacca through ferocious tropical cloudbursts in 1987 renewed our acquaintance with peninsular Malaysia, which used to be Malaya. The island states of Borneo, which joined the peninsula and Singapore in 1963 to form Malaysia, are more like the bewitching and tormenting South Seas of Joseph Conrad and Somerset Maugham. Always a little dull, peninsular Malaysia does not inspire but is languidly pleasant. In the north the tin mines have left their dun slag heaps on the land.

The ever-smiling face of the southern part of the peninsula was little changed from 1955. The red-clay soil threw pink dust over every living being from oxen to humans and over every object from game old automobiles to small pastel-painted wooden houses. We rejoiced on entering the new two-lane highway out of Johore. After twenty miles, it reverted to the same single-lane road we used to drive at high speeds to baffle the terrorists presumably lurking in the shrubbery. The road was slightly smoother, despite a hundredfold increase in use. But wildly erratic drivers, high on the new power of the wheel, made our later journey far more dangerous. The terrorists had been too busy to bother with young correspondents in decrepit yellow sports cars.

A utilitarian concrete bridge had supplanted the old wooden-scow ferry near the town of Muar, which had thrust up a dozen new buildings, some ten stories high. But the people and the houses and the cattle, even the automobiles, were hardly changed. All were still miniatures. We felt as if we were driving through a new Lilliput when we saw the tiny black goats tripping on their tiny pointed hooves like ballerinas.

The smells of the land were the same: frying garlic, hot dust, pungent woodsmoke, coconut milk, and chilis. From time to time we were overwhelmed by the virtually indescribable—and to some virtually unbearable—aroma of durian. Stuck behind a truckload of that spiky green coconut-sized fruit, we were assailed by the mixed odors of sautéed onions, open drains, hot chocolate sauce, rotten eggs, and Limburger cheese. Thatched stalls beside the road still sold less assertive tropical fruit: thumb-sized bananas that tasted of strawberries; spiky red rambutan, like sweeter litchis; and shiny green starfruit, whose five-pointed pale yellow slices puckered the lips. Street vendors still crushed sugar cane between big gear-wheels, and let the juice run into tall glasses filled with chopped ice and a splash of brilliant vegetable dye.

The shop signs were in bright Chinese ideograms, as were restaurants' menus. Most Malays are too poor to patronize restaurants, and very few could raise the funds to set up their own shops or restaurants. Besides, the Malays are not inclined to the daily drudgery of commerce.

In a nation devoted to the pleasures of the table, even their food sets the races apart. The Chinese will eat anything, just as long as it tastes good. Faithful to Moslem dietary laws, Malays eat no pork and only the flesh of sheep, cattle, and fowl that have been ritually slaughtered. Hindus from India and Ceylon do not eat beef because of religious prohibition—and avoid pork by preference.

Caste divisions keep many Indians from sharing meals with any outsider—or with most fellow Hindus. Yet those obstacles are crumbling in Malaysia, which is removed from the stark orthodoxies of India. Less than 8 percent of a population of 17 million, the Indians have usually moved easily among the larger racial groups. The clients of Indian lawyers and accountants are not limited to the stick-thin Indian laborers on road gangs and slight Indian tappers moving through the sun-striped aisles between rows of rubber trees.

Devoted to ideas and to words, the Indians are highly politicized and generally inclined to the democratic left. Their ancestors were brought to Malaya to perform the hard physical labor that Chinese coolies escaped as soon as they could. The Indians are today clerks, small shopkeepers, teachers, and laborers, with an elite of bureaucrats, lawyers, accountants, and doctors.

Most Indian politicians have made their names as spokesmen for the underprivileged, usually the underprivileged of the Chinese and Indian communities. The conservative Malay establishment is no more sympathetic to the rabble-rousing Indians than it is to the money-grubbing Chinese.

The racial compound the British assembled in their search for profits is inherently explosive. Nonetheless, the diverse peoples of Malaysia have lived together in peace most of the time, passing amicably together through the maze of divergent cultures, religions, customs, and prejudices.

For a century, British law enforced a truce on the conflict behind the façade of peaceful coexistence by the races. The heritage of British law has generally kept the peace since independence—despite some gory clashes between Malays and Chinese. But the Malay politicians are now discarding the institutions they call the "unnecessary baggage of the British past."

All citizens are Malaysians, regardless of race, as they used to be Malayans. *Malay* refers only to one race, who are all Moslems. And all Malaysians smile. Malaysia is a happy country. It was pleasant, indolent, and amicable even during the horrors of the Emergency. So it has remained, smiling amid the strain of economic development that is hardly frenzied.

On the edge of the inhabited strips, everywhere lies the jungle, painted with a hundred different hues—all green. Walking on the jungle's floor, soft with fallen leaves, is like strolling through a neglected aquarium thick with algae. The dappled light falls green and moist and dim through trees festooned with boa constrictor vines.

That green cast was virtually unbroken in 1955. For a hundred miles one would see no more than half a dozen flowers. In villages, as in the jungle, the only bright color was the occasional flame tree burning scarlet against the green backdrop.

In 1987 a passion for gardening appeared to have seized Malaysians. For the first time they possessed both the leisure and the money for that innocent pastime. Between Singapore and Malacca we saw five garden centers, those glassy temples of bourgeois virtue. We also saw dozens of meticulously cultivated gardens with neat rows of roses and clipped hedges beneath trailing wisteria and bougainvillea.

When we drove to Malacca on the country's first election day in 1955, Malays were bicycling and walking to the polling stations in a holiday spirit. Men wore bright sarongs over their trousers, as does the Malaysian Army in dress uniform. Women wore ankle-length sarongs with filmy, hip-length blouses. Boys and girls wore many different costumes in many different colors, usually shorts or knee-length skirts. In 1987 Malay schoolboys and schoolgirls walking slowly homeward were attired like miniature mullahs and Fatimas.

The enveloping *hijab* was not imposed upon the girls. They did not look like perambulating black tents, as do devout women in the Middle East. Their magnolia-petal faces were not covered. Nor were their slender cinnamon hands. But all wore the same pointedly modest costume: long white skirts that trailed the ground under white tunics that feel below their knees. Their heads were covered with long white scarves, the tails looped over their shoulders, ready to hide their faces.

All the boys wore black *songkoks*, a brimless felt hat like an inverted flowerpot. In Malaysia the *songkok* is a symbol of orthodoxy, like the fez, which was banned in Turkey as an obstacle to modernization. The boys also wore long white tunics over their long white trousers—staid garments that were obviously uncomfortable.

Those impractical school uniforms are meant to confuse the Malay people. Schoolchildren and their elders believe that such puritanical trappings are quintessentially Malay, when they actually are Middle Eastern. The Malays, even the most devout Malays, are by nature sunny offspring of the generous tropics, not dour children of the meager deserts.

Puritanical fundamentalism is winning. The issue is no longer between democracy and theocracy. Instead, discussion centers on just how far Malaysia will go toward dominance of *syariah*, Islamic religious law, over civil law. No Malay politician can now stand foursquare for a secular, pluralist state. Whatever his convictions, he must dissemble to placate the fundamentalists, who thus exercise veto power over the moderate majority.

So far, that yearning toward the imagined past has not strongly affected economic growth, whatever it is doing to social progress. Growth averaged a low 3.9 percent between 1983 and 1987, but the rate in 1988 was 7.4 percent, which is good. Yet that growth has not spectacularly transformed the nation as it has others in Asia. Moreover, most economic activity is still largely directed by Chinese. Many Malays are therefore turning to religion to define their cultural identity and to enhance their self-esteem.

Islam can be stark and demanding, as the Ayatollah Khomeini so persistently demonstrated. Extreme Islam does not merely sanction, but encourages killing for the faith. In Indonesia and the Philippines, as well as Malaysia, Islam has at times inflamed the mercurial Malay temperament—and men have run amok, slaughtering their presumed enemies.

Islam can also be tolerant. All human beings are divided into believers, who are cherished, and infidels, who are enemies. Race has nothing to do with it. I once knew a man named Ma; he was a Chinese who spoke excellent Mandarin. Born a Moslem in heavily Islamic Xinjiang in China's northwest, he was a religious officer in the bureaucracy of Johore. Mr. Ma was, to the people of that Malay state, indisputably a brother Moslem, while a Christian from Manado in Indonesia, indisputably Malay by race, was an infidel.

Despite that antiracist ethos, the outside world is making racists of Malays. They used to adopt Chinese babies because they liked children, felt sorry for orphans, and those babies, brands from the burning, would grow up Moslem. Many Malays are now becoming as prejudiced as their Chinese neighbors, who are inculcated with racial arrogance from infancy.

I once heard a striking expression of the Chinese attitude from a Chinese woman then popular as a sentimental novelist. At a reception celebrating the declaration of a White Area, that is, a terrorist-free zone, around Muar, she demanded of a senior Malay official: Do you think you are my equal? Do you really believe *any* Malay is my equal?"

Government is, however, a Malay monopoly. The Chinese control the modern economy, which would collapse if they left in large numbers; the Indians dominate the unions and the legal profession, which would wither if they left; but the Malays ruthlessly ensure that they continue to control the government and its coercive arms—the courts, the police, and the armed forces.

Prime Minister Lee Kuan Yew's fear of Islamic extremism no longer appears quite so farfetched. It is not wholly unlikely that a Malay government could someday turn on Singapore to divert its Moslem people from its economic failures. It might mount a long-term confrontation in the name of the faith, as Sukarno of Indonesia once proclaimed *konfrontasi* with Malaysia itself in the name of nationalism in order to retain power.

The new atmosphere in which such absurdities are no longer completely absurd is delineated in a booklet called *Islamic Revivalism in Malaysia*, by Zainah Anwar. She writes:

> Malaysia is no different from other Muslim countries . . . in the throes of Islamic revivalism. In . . . Kuala Lumpur, the capital, young women covered from head to toe in the loose flowing *hijab*

and young men wearing the *jubah* (ankle-length garment worn over regular clothes) with turbans and little beards are a common sight. Partying and merrymaking are no longer the popular social activities among the Muslim students on university campuses. Alcohol is no longer served at government receptions. Sparkling apple juice now fills champagne glasses as the prime minister toasts his foreign guests. The Islamic opposition party stridently calls for the *syariah* [Islamic law] to replace the British-based legal system of Malaysia and the *sunnah* [the Prophet Mohammed's God-inspired rules] to replace the man-made infidel constitution. . . .

For Islamic activists . . . [s]cience and technology are . . . to be subordinated to Islam . . . to guard against the infiltration of Western values.

To a Westerner, that may read like an attempt to catch up with the past, a retreat from the benefits as well as the distortions of progress. But even moderate Moslems are a little tired of Western moral laxity, a little disenchanted with the Western concept of progress, and a little fed up with Western claims of superiority. In Malaysia almost all Moslems are also disgusted with Chinese materialism—and indignant at Chinese wealth that has been gained, Malays believe, by exploiting the *bumiputera*, "the native sons and daughters of the soil."

Yet austere Middle Eastern Islam is ill-suited to an essentially tolerant people. The Malays, like their neighbors in Indonesia, had before the colonial period created a society that drew upon Islam, but did not make Islam its sole pillar. Other sources like native *adat*, or "community law," indigenous folklore, and Indian mythology also provided inspiration, diversion, and moral precepts.

Yet the Malays feel bereft. Sustained neither by economic triumphs nor by intense nationalism, their self-esteem is low. Surrounded by the success of others, they doubt their own capability. More Malays are therefore basing their self-esteem on their religion. As Zainah Anwar writes:

Islamic activists and organizations range from the moderate to the radical, from pro-government to anti-government. . . . The moderate ABIM (Muslim Youth Movement of Malaysia) while advocating the formation of an Islamic state, emphasizes the Islamization of the *ummah* [the community] first. The radical Islamic opposition party PAS (Partai Islam Se-Malaysia) demands the immediate establishment of an Islamic nation [centered on] the Quran . . . .

The government and its supporters are branded as *kafirs* (in-

fidels) who have no right to rule. In response to the pressures of
resurgent Islam, the government embarks on an Islamization
policy, a step-by-step process to inculcate Islamic values and
introduce Islamic versions of institutions like banking, insurance
and pawnbroking.

Perhaps in time the computers and the satellites that are integral to
modern finance can put on Islamic vestments. The same process subjects human beings to great strains. Norsiah, a twenty-two-year-old
student of economics at the University of Malaya, resented the discipline to which she has been subjected by her own spiritual side and by
emotional blackmail.

"Nobody in my hostel," she said, "had ever gone to discos. Most of
the girls were from the rural areas. . . . The hooded girls (as she kept
calling the *dakwah* [ultra-religiously inspired] girls [who wore head-
scarves that obscured their features]) kept telling me it was improper
for me to mix with boys and gave me articles about women in Islam,
their proper role, behavior and character."

After giving in to their demand that she wear concealing clothing and
behave demurely, she asked, "Must I cut out my friends? Can I go to
movies and concerts? . . . these people make Islam into such a 'no-no'
religion. . . . The *dakwah* movement's most distinctive characteristic
is that it always tells you . . . what not do. You can't watch TV. You
can't ride bicycles. It's unladylike. No fun fairs, no cultural shows, no
bands."

For Ishak Ali, a thirty-one-year-old engineer for Petronas, the government petroleum monopoly, the conflict was resolved. Holding a
degree in fuel and energy engineering from the Brighton Technical
College in England, he nonetheless believes, as Zainah Anwar reported, "in Ayatollah Khomeini's theory of the '*Velayat-e-Faqih*,' gov-
ernance by Islamic jurists who will exercise authority over the
executive, administrative and planning affairs of the country. He also
believes that a single *alim* [learned theologian] from among the *ulama*
[clergy] could emerge with near-infallible authority . . . [and] leadership of the [supra-national] Islamic nation. . . . He denies that this
would lead to a theocratic dictatorship."

If fundamentalists are working toward an intercontinental, authoritarian superstate that would unite all Moslems under the rule of a single
superhuman priest-dictator. Non-Moslems are entitled to be apprehensive. That vision raises the specter of a holy war waged to bring all
humanity under Moslem dispensation—in part through greatly expanded terrorism.

That will not happen. Nonetheless, the government of Malaysia fears
that vision could destroy it. It is, therefore, drawing the mantle of Islam

around its own essentially secular self. Yet the fundamentalists can deny the present state structure the Islamic sanction it now must possess to rule effectively.

Malaysia is riven by the confrontation between those who would preserve it and those who would totally remake it. Not only Lee Kuan Yew fears that Malaysia will become a menacing theocracy. The country's first prime minister, Tunku Abdul Rahman, has warned of the danger that the nation he founded will be transformed into an oppressive religious state.

Such fears seemed illusory when Moira and I completed our journey from Singapore to Malacca in the bright sunlight. Change itself seemed illusory, for that small territory of a half-million souls had hardly changed at all. Again we saw with delight the distinctive houses with their high peaked roofs reminiscent of Sumatra and their stone stoops recalling Holland. In that serene atmosphere the dangers that stalk Malaysia seemed phantoms of the imagination.

In Malacca, it appears, Malays and Chinese, Indians and Eurasians live beside each other without conflict. The population is almost evenly divided racially. One half are the Malays and the aboriginal people the government classifies together as *bumiputera*, "children of the soil"; the other half are Chinese and Indians.[1] Although a melting pot since the fourteenth century, even Malacca has not blended the cultures and races.

Lying at the juncture of the trade routes from Europe and the Middle East, Malacca was, in the sixteenth century, the last staging port for the Far East. The Portuguese therefore seized the city at the beginning of that century and found not only Malays but Chinese already well settled. The conquerors built churches and buried in one church the great Apostle to the East, Saint Francis Xavier. The Chinese community which adapted Malay clothing and cuisine to its own tastes, has survived intact as the Babas of Malacca, the oldest Chinese settlement in Southeast Asia. The Portuguese did not endure, but were driven out by the Dutch in the seventeenth century. The Dutch gave way in the nineteenth century to the British, who left voluntarily in 1957.

The Malays are not going anywhere. They are remaining, as they have since 1400, when Malacca was the capital of a Moslem empire founded by a Sumatran prince.

[1] The same division, roughly half and half, prevails in Johore. In the Federal Territory around Kuala Lumpur, Chinese are an absolute majority, and there are half as many Indians as Malays. Elsewhere on the peninsula, Malays are preponderant, as they are in Sabah and Sarawak on Borneo, although there they are diluted by aborigines. Chinese remain one-third. That is why the threat of 2 million Singapore Chinese joining some 5.5 million Chinese in a Malaysian population of 17 million so frightened Malay leaders.

The oldest buildings in Malaysia—Chinese, Hindu, and European, as well as Malay—are concentrated in the city. It almost appears that Malaya had no past until the settlement of Malacca; it certainly had little recorded history. Unlike some Asian governments, enlightened Malaysia is preserving, rather than deliberately destroying, the monuments of the colonial past.

The government of Malacca is as mixed as its people. The first governor after independence was Chinese, but the subsequent four have all been Malay. Few Chinese rise in the civil service to the heights where governors are selected. Yet the lower ranks are a good mixture of Chinese, Malays, and Indians. Everywhere outside Malacca, Malays predominate. As one keen observer wrote:

> Discrimination is strongest in the public sector. It is very difficult for a non-Malay to get into the huge civil service—and equally difficult to rise. Despite exceptions, notably in the Central Bank, the bloated civil service is the classic bureaucratic animal, static and self-preserving.
>
> When visiting ministries in Malaysia, one feels transported to Eastern Europe. Huge dilapidated buildings house thousands of men and women, almost all Malay. Many of the women are veiled to different degrees of *purdah* [seemly concealment of face and form]. The functionaries are either shuffling aimlessly in slippers over the cracked linoleum or, if at their desks, chatting in a desultory manner, eating *nasi lemak* ["rich rice" seethed in co-conut milk], or crocheting. Little work is evident—and almost every Malaysian has a favorite tale of gargantuan proportions regarding the bureaucracy.

In Malacca the horrors are muted, largely because of the racial mix. Chinese inspectors of police are rare elsewhere, but not there. A civic festival on the *medan*, the village green, reminded me of British days. The Public Works Department and the police actually behaved like public servants eager to tell the public about their work. Booths of old colonial firms like Frazier and Neave soft drinks and Harrison, Crossfield Plantations, now locally owned, reinforced that impression. Senior civil servants of all races sat side by side in their booths.

The private sector is different. At the teak-and-mahogany Malacca Village Hotel of the Beaufort chain, the races are about equally distributed in lower-level jobs. But department heads are 95 percent Chinese, 3 percent Malay, and 2 percent Vietnamese.

Although Malacca is relatively enlightened, Malaysian bureaucracy makes hotelkeeping a minor ordeal. Every brand of whiskey requires its individual license, as does every television set. A multitude of

licenses, each expiring at a different time, offers great scope for corruption. One form of payoff comes when ministers and other dignitaries
hold parties at hotels, naturally at sharply reduced rates. In the increasingly puritanical country, such dignitaries are ostentatiously tee-
total in public, like good Moslems. But many stagger out of such private
parties, and some are carried out.

The saddest man in Malacca was Tony Rodriguez, whose robust
baritone rose over the broad verandas of the Malaccan Village Hotel
every evening. He was, as his name indicates, a Portuguese Catholic,
husky and handsome, with aquiline features. He was also, as his name
does *not* indicate, so black that his complexion appeared blue. He was
a descendant not only of the Portuguese, but of the African slaves the
Portuguese brought with them. He was not well placed in an increasingly sectarian and racist society.

A black Catholic in a Moslem country living among Chinese who look
down on dark skins, Tony was very poor. Not gifted and scrappily
educated, he picked up a few dollars singing popular ballads learned
from tapes. Like most of the black Catholics, who are the poorest
community in Malacca, he was by day a fisherman. Their small skiffs and
small catches are now threatened by government-sponsored motorized
fishing vessels financed with foreign-aid funds—so that the black Catholic community is almost beyond hope.

Mass at St. Peter's, on the street called Gereja, which means
"church," displayed multiracial Malacca at its most diverse. A white-
haired Indian in a bush jacket, his black eyes solemn behind gold-
rimmed spectacles, passed the chrome collection basket. Big-eyed
Chinese schoolgirls with violet sashes over their bouffant party dresses
sang lustily. One altar boy was a Eurasian and the other was jet black.
A Portuguese woman in her thirties recited the responses loudly in
English.

St. Peter's was an English-speaking church. Malacca also had four
other Catholic churches: two that held services in Chinese, one in
Mandarin and the other in the dialect of Teocheo, near Swatow; a
church for speakers of Malayalam, a southern Indian language; and
another for Portuguese speakers.

Mass at St. Peter's also foreshadowed the gradual eclipse of freedom.
Christianity is being squeezed by a government responding with in-
tolerance to the threat of Islamic fundamentalism.

The priests are being driven out. Just one Portuguese priest remained, and he was under notice from the government to leave. All
foreign priests and Protestant missionaries are to be expelled. There are
few native clergy, and it is a criminal offense to introduce a non-
Christian under eighteen to Christianity.

*   *   *

Modern Malaysia was shaped in the crucible of May 13, 1969, an election day. The vote was a triumph for the smaller Chinese-oriented political parties that opposed the dominant United Malays National Organization and its virtual satellite, the Malayan Chinese Association. By midnight, triumph had been transformed into tragedy. The Malays had massacred several hundred Chinese in Kuala Lumpur and Penang, where they outnumber the other races.

According to the Malays, violence was provoked by the triumphant Chinese, who taunted Malays on their electoral defeat. According to the Chinese, they were holding quiet victory celebrations when the Malays attacked them without provocation. According to disinterested observers, both sides were at fault—and the largely Malay police stood by while their brothers slaughtered Chinese.

The illusion of a harmonious, multiracial nation was shattered. Race riots had occurred in the past, but hardly on such a scale. Tunku Abdul Rahman, the Malay prince who had been prime minister since independence in 1957, sincerely believed before the massacres that a new society had come into being. Although not purged of racial prejudice, that society had appeared beyond pogroms.

Yet the fiery antagonism between poor Malays and well-to-do Chinese had obviously not even been banked, and only strong measures could prevent the nation's disintegration. The Malay-dominated government concluded that Malays' justified resentment of Chinese wealth had been the spark that ignited the violence, and it adopted a long-range plan to cool that resentment. Chinese feelings were of no particular concern, for the Chinese had nowhere else to go. Anyway, the Chinese were too intelligent to start riots when they were a vulnerable minority, although they had rioted in Chinese-dominated Singapore.

The New Economic Policy promulgated in 1971 was designed to give the Malays a fair share of the wealth of their own country, so said its proponents. The NEP's intention was to distribute Malaysia's abundance more equitably—and placate the Malays—by transferring wealth from the Chinese to the Malays. Its goal was by 1990 to have placed 30 percent of all shareholdings in the hands of the Malays, who already owned almost all of the land. The first step was the creation of a vast, Malay-dominated civil service to administer the NEP and to run the private companies that were coming under government control through the NEP.

The statistical goals have generally been attained, but the social effects are not what were expected. The Malays had not been energetic when the British coddled them with special privileges. Further coddling made them even more lethargic. Besides, politicians could not resist the new honey pots: corporations that were, in effect, government-owned. Sloth and corruption thus increased, further handicapping the Malays in their competition with the Chinese.

Of course some Malays have benefited greatly from their privileges, actually competing against the compulsively industrious Chinese with some prospect of success. Since World War II, a small Malay professional and middle class has come into existence, although the easy life of government service still draws too many of the capable, as well as the incompetent. Nonetheless, the Malay community remains divided between the broad mass and the small elite, which is for the most part derived from the princely families and their retainers. Still, the intellectual and professional competence of hundreds, perhaps thousands, of individual Malays has risen markedly—and they have dared to enter the modern world.

Yet their special privileges confuse and corrupt many Malays, exacerbating the racial tension the New Economic Policy was presumably designed to alleviate. Racial quotas for admission to secondary and tertiary education, as prescribed by the constitution, make for a student body 60 percent *bumiputera*, "the sons and daughters of the soil." Although there are fewer places than there are qualified candidates, unqualified Malays are admitted long before qualified Chinese, Indians, or Eurasians. That is the law.

Malays with D's and C's on their secondary-school finals get in, but few Chinese make it without straight A's, particularly in law, medicine, and engineering. The resulting difference in academic performance is spectacular—and breeds further resentment. Malays resent being required to compete far out of their class; the Chinese resent being held back by classmates they feel should never have been admitted.

Reasonably bright Malay students are automatically sent abroad for higher education on government grants, while much brighter Chinese have to pay their own way.[2] Since the Chinese have the money, that may appear rough justice. Yet the indifferent Malay students who are left at home must compete with much brighter Chinese and Indians. Besides, many Chinese, who don't have that much money, deeply resent the favoritism shown the Malays. Many Chinese students who go abroad do not, therefore, return, but make new lives elsewhere. Thus is precious talent lost to Malaysia.

Malays also suffer when thrust into the modern competitive world. A largely rural people, they are accustomed to a simple environment

[2] Most Malaysian students have gone to the U.S. since Prime Minister Margaret Thatcher decreed that all foreign students in the U.K. must pay substantial tuition. Britain was formerly first, but the U.S., itself hardly cheap, now leads, followed by Australia and New Zealand. About 25,000 students from Malaysia are normally studying in institutions of higher learning in America, where they are the fifth-largest foreign contingent.

where fixed values are maintained by recognized authority. Going abroad as students, many are distressed by a complex alien environment where values are relative, authority is nebulous, and emotional security is precarious. Besides, they must compete with students of different nationalities who have *not* been eased through their earlier schooling.

Many Malay students abroad turn to religion, which is almost invariably fundamentalist when Moslems from three continents meet on a fourth. Some simply break down, unable to face a bewildering modern world.

Within Malaysia, young women lured from their rural *kampongs* to work in electronics or textile factories display similar symptoms. Deprived of the only reality they have ever known, those country girls cannot adjust to the soulless new reality of their new lives. The apparently placid Malays are actually high-strung.

Nowadays breakdowns do not often end with running amok and killing. Such outbreaks have become more a communal complaint than an individual complaint in the Malay countries. Indonesia and the Philippines, as well as Malaysia, have recently experienced mass slaughter for ideological or theological causes.

Kuala Lumpur, the capital of Malaysia, was unique in the 1970s because of the curious juxtaposition of government buildings reminiscent of Whitehall and religious buildings reminiscent of Cairo. It was a relaxed Southeast Asian city with Middle Eastern undertones. The railway station and the mosques were domed and minareted behind fringes of palm trees. The government buildings were verandaed and cupolaed. Most commercial buildings were gimcrack and squat.

Kuala Lumpur is now a jostling, noisy metropolis intent on its own rambling growth, and its modest skyline is jagged with new commercial high-rises. In the satellite communities devoted to light industry and homes that rim the old city, McDonald's and Kentucky Fried Chicken outlets outnumber mosques.

Nowadays they serve palm-leaf lunches at the Selangor Club, which was long the citadel of British good form and British snobbery. Membership is now more than 90 percent Asian, and the club provides South Indian food served on palm leaves to be eaten with the fingers. However, palm-leaf lunches must be taken outdoors in the muggy heat; they are not eaten in the big dining room with its chilly air conditioning.

Such quasi-British standards still govern the life of Malaysia—to a point. The police are smart in British-style uniforms with British insignia of rank. So are the army, the navy, and the air force, which late in 1988 ordered British tanks, guns, and airplanes worth about $2 billion. Judges wear British robes and wigs even as the prime minister undermines their British-style independence. Although the bureaucracy has become bloated to Middle Eastern proportions, it is based on British models, as are decrees, administrative regulations, traffic signs, hospitals, and newspapers.

In 1989 the British heritage was being purposefully hacked away by the prime minister, Dr. Mahathir Mohamad. Yet he had taken his British medical degree in Singapore in 1962 and, like most educated Malays then, joined the civil service. He broke away to go into private practice and politics in 1957, the year of independence. Dr. Mahathir is thus as much a symbol of Malay alienation as he is an instrument for the disruption of traditional values, Malay as well as British.

In 1988, wishing to balance any pro-Chinese bias in my thinking, I interviewed a retired Malay civil servant. I shall call him Ali, a good Moslem name, for his frankness deserves the anonymity he did not request. A distinguished Malaysian, he possesses a reputation for rectitude, which is not common nowadays. Although a man of generous sympathies, he rather tellingly speaks not a word of any Chinese dialect in a city with a Chinese majority (few Chinese in Malaysia do not speak adequate Malay). Devout and learned, Ali is no fundamentalist and certainly no fanatic. Yet, when talking of the fundamental precepts of Islam, he demonstrated why it would be hard to find two peoples as opposite as Chinese and Malays.

The four cardinal commandments of Islam, Ali pointed out, prohibit murder, fornication, gambling, and drink. The next sin is usury—that is, lending money at interest.

The Chinese do not, of course, exalt murder. But fornication is a major pastime of the overseas Chinese male; gambling is his favorite diversion; and he likes to cool the risks with brandy or beer. Besides, most overseas Chinese are in business, which depends upon lending and borrowing money at interest. Further, the favorite meat of Chinese is pork, which is forbidden to Malays.

After those wry observations, Ali discussed the Malay-dominated government—with true inside knowledge.

"People who come to power," he said, "want to stay in power—for the benefit of the people, they say. Then they do things out of the public eye . . . things that only come out later. Policies are rammed through before anyone knows what it's all about.

"Widespread irregularities began with the government's secret—and disastrous—intervention in the market for tin."

The bottom dropped out, and tin, long one of Malaysia's major exports, was for a time nearly valueless. But "the friends of the government" had already made their profits.

"The public was badly hurt," Ali said, "and the public will be hurt again and again as long as the government swims with sharks."

Despite legal prohibitions, quasi-governmental cooperatives borrow and lend at high interest rates, take excessive profits, and speculate in the stock market. Politicians make large secret profits on those transactions.

"Privatization has been the rage lately," Ali observed. "Without announcement the government will suddenly hive off companies it owns—then announce it's already been done. MAS [Malaysian Airline System, the lackluster national airline] was a joint stock company, all government owned. Telecoms was a government department. They weren't sold directly to the public, and Parliament was not informed. . . . Privatization proceeds in private—with no publicity or public knowledge. Privatization really means *privately* selling assets to *private* friends of politicians with *private* access to *private* information."

Ali sighed and voiced the plaint I have heard from India to Borneo: "The government used to be considered pure—like Britain. In the days of the British, corruption was limited. But now . . ."

The sharpest spur to corruption, he declared, is the electoral process. Politicians spend very large sums in their campaigns, and the party apparatus runs on large infusions of cash.

"The people see that politicians have access to such large amounts of money from unknown sources," Ali said. "Since the source can only be wholesale corruption, the people are encouraged to graft. Such cynicism is the worst environment for democratic government."

The extent of institutionalized corruption in Malaysia was revealed at the beginning of the 1980s. George Tan, a Malaysian Chinese financier operating in Hong Kong, went bankrupt for $1 billion, a vast sum then and not exactly coffee money even in the inflated early 1990s. He was subsequently brought to trial for wholesale fraud. Among his victims were American and Hong Kong banks that had been quite undisturbed by his privateering business methods. Tan, it was revealed, had been launched by large loans from the Bank Bumiputera of Malaysia, which was chartered to assist deserving Malays with small loans—definitely *not* to help Chinese businessmen with enormous loans.

"Immorality becomes endemic throughout society," Ali added. "The state is so powerful it actually promotes corruption."

I might have expected to hear such views from discontented Chinese or Indian intellectuals. But I was hearing them from a senior member of the Malay establishment who happens to be an honest man.

Corruption's twin evil, he said, was the negation of democracy by the concentration of power in a few hands. The government takes power to which it is not entitled, and the prime minister exercises that power dictatorially. In 1987 Dr. Mahathir interned for a time 106 of his enemies, who ranged from opposition party leaders to environmental activists and consumer advocates, under the Internal Security Act inherited from the British.

"The press," Ali said, "lives by sufferance only."

Amendments to the Printing Presses Act have given the government wide powers to regulate the press. Licenses are required for all publications, and renewals are treated as new applications.

"Dr. Mahathir padlocked two newspapers," Ali recalled. "One was the *Eastern Star*, which Lee Kuan Yew of Singapore sued for libel. There are no avenues for alternate views today. Most upset at the closing of the *Star* was Chairman of the Board Tunku Abdul Rahman."

The eighty-five-year-old founding prime minister, who enjoys the prestige of a George Washington, came out of retirement in late 1988 to speak against the administration. He called Dr. Mahathir's government a "growing dictatorship" and declared that he would fight the prime minister. That was just after Dr. Mahathir suspended six justices of the Supreme Court, eventually forcing three off the bench, including the lord president, the country's chief justice.

"There is no Koranic injunction toward open government," Ali conceded. "But there is a strong injunction against making a scandal out of what is not true. The governed should know about matters that will affect them. Rulers must be just and open."

Dire predictions come not only from liberal activists and concerned Moslems, but from a man who was until recently Dr. Mahathir's protégé. Datuk Musa Hitam, who in 1986 resigned as deputy prime minister of Malaysia, told the Hong Kong Foreign Correspondents' Club in late 1988: "[There exists] the serious trend . . . which I unhesitatingly describe as a threat to the Malaysian democratic way of life. . . . Dr. Mahathir [is recognized widely] as the man who is taking us along this path. . . . The problem with Dr. Mahathir is that he is crass, rough, and hard. This man pushes things down your throat. . . . Any project is now literally named by the prime minister as to who should get it [and the illegal gravy]. . . . He would create trouble so that there is an excuse to declare an emergency."

Despite Dr. Mahathir's shenanigans and growing corruption, Malaysia is still reasonably well off. If it lacks the enormous natural wealth of its neighbor Indonesia, corruption is at a much lower level than it is in Indonesia, and the average annual income is many times higher, roughly $2,000 against $300.

Oil is a relatively new but highly remunerative resource. Although production of 500,000 to 600,000 barrels a day is less than half Indonesia's 1.3 million, it is 8 percent of Malaysia's GNP. Other major products are natural rubber, although the market has shrunk; and tin, which is recovering from the disastrous fall in price partially engineered by Kuala Lumpur itself. Palm oil for use in foodstuffs is, however, becoming a casualty of health consciousness throughout the developed world. Although a vegetable product, palm oil is, unfortunately, rich in harmful saturated fats.

Attempts to reduce the country's dependence on raw materials have not been particularly successful. New products like textiles and chips do not rank as major exports, which remain agricultural or mineral. Yet in 1990 the recovery from the slump of the mid-1980s was continuing—with a growth rate of more than 7 percent. Beneath the roiled surface of political and racial tension lay a strong infrastructure and a functioning productive machine.

The British built an institutional structure that was, despite some flaws, solid and well designed, and much of that structure has endured. Moreover, the Chinese run a tight economy—when governmental interference does not handicap them, as it does more and more. No nation can, however, survive intact the strains to which Malaysia's economy, administration, legal system, and morale were subject in 1990.

The trouble with portraying a country warts and all is that the warts tend to dominate the picture. Most of Malaysia's troubles, it must nonetheless be said, may well lie ahead. The intensified racial strife that induced large-scale Chinese emigration could gut the economy. The bureaucracy and corruption, both expanding rapidly, could induce creeping paralysis in the body politic. Both justice and communications could come close to breaking down as the judiciary and the press are terrorized. Increasing authoritarianism could crush both civil liberties and initiative. Islamic fundamentalism could severely inhibit economic activity.

Nonetheless, Malaysia is well off today—and has a chance of remaining well off. A number of immediate and long-term factors are in play.

Most Chinese, as well as most Malays, want no more than to enjoy life as they do now. Neither people is moved by great aspirations or tormented by sublime dissatisfaction.

Blessedly untroubled by heroic purposes, Malaysia should get along well, as long as two conditions are met: as long as the new generation—37 percent of the population is under fifteen—eschews fanaticism; and as long as the balance of power in the region does not alter radically.

II

Indonesia: The Spice Islands

LURING MERCHANT-ADVENTURERS, THE FABLED INDIES CREATED THE ERA OF WESTERN IMPERIALISM. TODAY, INDONESIA, THE WORLD'S FIFTH MOST POPULOUS NATION, IS QUINTESSENTIAL TROPICAL ASIA. ITS MYRIAD ISLANDS ARE GORGEOUS IN THEIR DIVERSITY AND OPULENT IN THEIR NATURAL WEALTH. AFTER WINNING INDEPENDENCE FROM THE DUTCH, PRESIDENT SUKARNO ALMOST DESTROYED THE NATION HE HAD THUS CREATED. BLOODIED BY COMMUNIST AND RIGHT-WING RISINGS, HIS REIGN ENDED WITH NATIONWIDE MASSACRES.

NOW ENJOYING RELATIVE STABILITY AND PROSPERITY, INDONESIA IS PREY TO THE RAPACITY OF THE FAMILY AND HENCHMEN OF PRESIDENT SUHARTO, AN AUTHORITARIAN RULER WHO TOLERATES MASS CORRUPTION.

The state guest blinking in the glaring sunshine was a pale, squat creature of the north, as powerful and as dangerous as a polar bear. Nikita Sergeyevich Khrushchev, first secretary of the Communist Party of the Soviet Union, peered curiously at the throng on the *medan*, the vast parade ground of Surabaya. His gaze was returned by more than a million brown-skinned people of the south who had converged on the city. In the spring of 1960, East Java was the most densely populated place on earth.

Travelers came to a new village every two minutes. The green paddy fields were divided by the irrigation canals the Dutch had built in colonial times. But the long screw-gears that controlled the sluice gates were rusted, and the banks were overgrown. Lean dogs barked at strangers from the few dilapidated brick houses that stood among the palm-frond-thatched huts. On the sea, which glinted beyond the narrow beaches, *perahus*, great sailing boats, swooped across white-capped waves under wind-swollen sails.

Nikita Khrushchev was not interested in picturesque villages or in heart-stopping vistas—only in progress. He rubbed his potato nose and mopped sweat from his bald head with a colored bandanna. He discarded his sleazy tan jacket, but still sweltered in his baggy trousers and a rumpled white shirt.

At ten in the morning, the sun was a molten ball directly overhead.

Fat, flushed, and quietly furious, Khrushchev would have been comical were it not for the menace in his intelligent pale blue eyes.

Crisp in a tailored bush jacket with military insignia and medal ribbons, President Sukarno of the Republic of Indonesia was the model of a relaxed host. But his eyes moved avidly, almost hungrily, over the crowd.

He saw a multitude of slender, well-made men and women with smooth brown skins, shining black hair, and large brown eyes that were oval, but not slanted. Although accustomed to the heat, they nonetheless suffered under the sun's direct rays 350 miles south of the Equator. His people gazed in rapture at Sukarno. If not hemmed in by their neighbors, many would have fallen to their knees in homage. Fathers lifted infants over their heads so that they could someday say they had once seen the greatest man in all the history of the Indies. Their bursts of laughter and their glad shouts sounded carefree, even festive. But the people were edgy and irritable. Most were also ragged and hungry.

Their beloved Sukarno had, a decade earlier, made them a nation and given them pride. He was now reducing the best-endowed nation of Asia to poverty. In normal times they harvested two or three rice crops a year, and tropical fruit hung heavy on their trees. But their leader's extravagance and carelessness had pushed the people to the edge of starvation.

Nikita Khrushchev spoke first. His blunt words boomed through gigantic loudspeakers, first in sibilant Russian, then in crisp *bahasa Indonesia*, the common tongue of some thirteen thousand islands that speak more than a thousand languages and dialects. He was not really addressing the crowd, but Sukarno, the capricious demagogue who wanted Soviet money and Soviet guns.

At the pinnacle of his power, the Soviet first secretary scorned both orators' flourishes and politicians' evasions. He was direct, and he was harsh. Speaking to a chief of state whose guest he was, he said: *You must!* And he said: *You cannot!*

Yet he was eager to extend the influence of the Soviet Union in the Indies—and to counter the growing power of the Soviet Union's new enemy, the People's Republic of China. Abrasive frankness appeared a strange way to win friends, but Khrushchev knew his host badly needed funds and guns that only the Soviet Union was likely to provide. Anyway, he was interested in results, not atmospherics.

Indonesia was important to Khrushchev because of where it was, what it was, and what it possessed—as it still is important. The great archipelago is the southern fringe of Asia, only twelve miles from Singapore in the north and two hundred miles from Australia in the south. Another metaphor was favored in the days when Chairman Mao Tse-tung of China and Sukarno, President for Life of Indonesia, were

talking of "liberating" first Asia and then the entire world. Indonesia
was the anvil on which the hammer of China would crush all Southeast
Asia. Perhaps more to the point, it lies athwart the great trade routes
of the Orient.

Thirty years ago it was heavily peopled. Today the population is about
180 million, although the government claims to have brought the annual
rate of increase down from a catastrophic 2.3 percent to 1.9 percent. But
even that rate will mean a population of more than 210 million in the
year 2000. The nominally Moslem people were in 1960 a link to the
Middle East—and still are. Moreover, Indonesia was rich in oil and
natural gas—as it remains. Liquefied natural gas was, as it is still, sent
to Japan in ships crowned with several domes, like seagoing planetar-
iums. Crude oil and partially refined petroleum products are also
shipped to Japan and the rest of Asia. Extensive deposits of tin and gold;
rain forests for timber; remarkably fertile soil producing rice, fruit, and
sugar cane; millions of square miles of rich fishing grounds; and numerous plantations: in all a nation most bountifully endowed by
nature—as it obviously still is.

The problem then was the government. It still is, although it is much
less acute. Indonesia is a giant. But it is a drowsy giant that does not
appear eager to wake up.

Sukarno addressed the crowd in Surabaya that day in 1960 with the
singleminded ardor of a lover speaking to his new mistress. He spoke
of honor and glory and tradition. He flung his head back, and his teeth
flashed joyously. Yet he repeatedly glanced over his shoulder to see
whether his arrows were hitting the mark. Khrushchev, the northern
barbarian, had dared to read him a lecture before his own people. No
matter how much he wanted Soviet help, he could not let that humiliation pass unrevenged.

Sukarno was as unabashedly theatrical as an aging matinee idol. He
smiled warmly, and he smiled sardonically. His husky voice soared,
swooped—and occasionally rasped. Now he cooed throatily at his beloved people, an indulgent father with a million cherished infants. The
next moment his tone was harsh and his words stern. He joked and he
wheedled. He cajoled and he threatened. He stroked the people with
praise and he whipped them with invective, punishing them for Nikita
Khrushchev's effrontery.

His people responded ecstatically, their woes forgotten, as he had
known they would. Understanding a little, but getting the gist from a
running translation, I, too, was moved. Exactly why I could not say
then, nor can I say now. But I knew I was hearing one of the greatest
orators of any era, at the peak of his immense virtuosity.

The tiny stick-figure under the canopy was crowned with the black *songkok*, the tasselless fez he always wore to conceal his baldness. The people could not see the bloodshot eyes, their whites blotched brown. They could not see the coarse skin with enlarged pores, the cracked lips, or the tremors of his hands.

Dissipation had eroded Sukarno's health, and egotism had undermined his judgment. He could no longer distinguish his personal whim from the national interest. He was already a broken man at fifty-nine. But his people saw a demigod, a semidivine king from an old Javanese legend. They loved him all the more for the Balinese fecklessness inherited from his mother and for his public pursuit of other men's women.

Histrionics bored First Secretary Nikita Khrushchev, unless they were his own. He had been subdued, almost morose, as Sukarno led him on a tour of the cultural showplaces of Indonesia. Culture was even less interesting than other men's histrionics. He preferred machine tools to paintings, and factories to ruins.

After Surabaya, the traveling carnival and its attendant press corps went on to Bali, the enchanted island where all men and women are artists. One evening we all trooped up to Tampaksiring in the central hills, where Sukarno had built himself a love-nest with forty or fifty rooms. The torches lining the paths burned brilliant in the shy beams of a crescent moon, and fragrant jasmine grew in the shadows.

But the little ruler of all the Russias was bored. He yawned at the silversmiths with their tiny hammers, and he frowned at the weavers' hand looms. In exasperation he spat out a few sentences.

I asked Foreign Minister Andrei Gromyko what his boss had said. A flicker of embarrassment ruffled the great stone face, which was not yet perfectly petrified, and he replied, "The first secretary says Indonesia must get rid of all this handmade rubbish. Instead, it must have machinery. All that counts is production! Production!"

An inherent Philistine, as Sukarno was an inherent libertine, Khrushchev was getting his own back. Sukarno had bored him with culture, horrified him with lechery, and disgusted him with egotism. At the beginning of their tour, in Bandung, a pleasant town in the hills above Jakarta, Khrushchev had deeply offended his host by walking out of an interminable recital of classical Javanese dances.

Sukarno got his revenge when he stalked into the bar of the Savoy-Homan Hotel, followed by Andrei Gromyko. We correspondents had been told to remain just out of earshot. Sukarno lectured the Soviet foreign minister like a naughty schoolboy. The dictator's head thrust forward belligerently; his full lips spewed flecks of spittle; and his forefinger fixed Gromyko.

They left after ten minutes, the dictator grinning like a victorious prizefighter. Publicly humiliated by Khrushchev's departure from the dance recital, he had publicly humiliated Khrushchev's foreign minister.

At that level of childish, almost infantile, spitefulness were high politics conducted in the era of the President for Life. His people were suffering severely from his erratic, self-serving behavior. He terrorized even senior figures, so that they dared offer him only the most fulsome flattery. Those who spoke out, he refused to see or imprisoned. His chief, overriding concern was to glitter before the world as he had on the *medan* at Surabaya.

For the Indonesian people it had begun as a fair trade. They gave Sukarno power, glory, and adoration; he gave them inspiration, pride, and entertainment. That social contract enabled him to play the despot and, too often, the tyrant. But the contract broke down when he made the people suffer. Among the patriots who finally turned against his self-indulgence and irresponsibility were his closest companions in the war against the Dutch: Vice President Mohammed Hatta and Foreign Minister Adam Malik.

Sukarno had invented causes, crises, and spectacles so that he would shine even more dazzlingly amid their confusion. In 1955 the leaders of the Third World had assembled in Bandung for the First Afro-Asian Conference, perhaps his best inspiration. He had not been happy when Prime Minister Pandit Jawaharlal Nehru of India and Prime Minister Chou En-lai of China shone brighter than he. But he had cunningly used their light to enhance his own luster, becoming the embodiment of the Bandung spirit of Afro-Asian unity.

In 1957 he had survived an amateurish uprising. Alarmed by Sukarno's inclination to the left and by the chaos he was making of Indonesia, the U.S. Central Intelligence Agency armed troops led by generals who could no longer bear their master's profligacy. Doomed to failure because most generals sat on the fence, the rebellion was revealed as a CIA endeavor when a B-26 bomber piloted by an American civilian was shot down.

In revenge, the dictator humiliated the doughty new American ambassador, Howard Jones, who arrived in a U.S. Navy Catalina amphibian at Jakarta's Kemajoran Airport, which was closed to all civilian traffic by the crisis. I shall always remember Howard Jones trudging wearily across the tarmac, carrying his own briefcase. A rather dry teacher, Ambassador Jones had never expected to dance on the command of the president of Indonesia. But dance he did, because he felt it his duty.

Better attuned to Sukarno's foibles, Peking set aside its puritanical inhibitions—and provided a different woman every night when he visited China. The masterstroke was, however, printing a two-volume

catalogue of the art collection he cherished. Most of the color repro-
ductions were nudes painted in the mock-realistic, yet highly idealized
style the despot loved. He delighted in his notoriety as the sexy bad boy
among world statesmen. He had little competition, since even Jack
Kennedy did not publicize his equally extensive amours.

The despot got his hormones and his vitamins from an American
manufacturer until he fell out with the U.S., told the Americans to go
to hell with their aid, and turned to the Chinese for magic potions. He
got a cruiser, patrol boats, tanks, and MIG fighters out of the Russians.
He also got the Russians to build him a steel mill at Cilegon, in West
Java. Far from any source of ore or coal, not even on a railway line, the
plant was initially a disaster. But in the mid-1980s, when prices rose,
it exported the cheap steel it made with cheap labor.

Sukarno loved grandiose slogans, mysterious acronyms, and striking
monuments. He talked of "guided democracy"; he talked of NEFOs,
new emerging forces, which were good, and OLDEFOs, the established forces, which were bad; he talked of NASAKOM, *Nasionalisme*,
Agama, Komunisme, cooperation among Nationalists, the religious, and
the Communists in Indonesia; and he talked of TAVIP, *Tahun Vivere
Pericoloso*, "the Year of Living Dangerously." He erected enormous
statues of jagged bronze in the manner of Socialist realism. On Medan
Merdeka, or Independence Square, in the center of Jakarta, he put up
a marble pillar 440 feet high, topped by symbolic golden flames. It is
now known to Indonesians as Monument Nasional or MONAS and to
foreigners as Sukarno's last erection. Often, however, his antics were
not funny, but damaging.

Sukarno drove out the Dutch, who were the principal foreign businessmen, Indonesia's chief link to the outside world. Naturally, the
economy suffered. But the people delighted in the oratory and violence
that accompanied the expulsion—until their low living standard fell
even lower. He then took on the Americans and British, thus maintaining patriotic tension and staging circuses of retribution to divert his
people from their deprivation.

Fulminating against Western imperialism and Western aggression,
Sukarno made Indonesia an imperialist aggressor. He used threats and
force to "take back" territory he called Indonesian because of historical
associations and because the Dutch had brought it under their colonial
rule. He claimed Irian Jaya, which we know as Western New Guinea;
Timor Timur, East Timor, which had been Portuguese; and, further,
parts of Borneo, which is called Kalimantan in Indonesian. He thus
challenged British forces in the Borneo territories under British protection in a great *konfrontasi*, or confrontation, which he lost. He also
sent a handful of commandos to undermine Singapore. They were
promptly arrested by the police.

A nation that could neither rule itself nor feed itself was fighting for the right to maladminister other peoples. But Sukarno survived in office until 1965, when his uncanny luck ran out. He was deposed by his own generals—after he had plotted with the Communists to murder them. The despot's fall was followed by the mass slaughter of hundreds of thousands.

The final crisis of Sukarnoism arose from the running conflict between the army and the Communists that had begun a generation earlier. The despot aligned himself inextricably with the Communists, who planned a mass uprising to seize political power—and failed. The roots of Sukarnoism, however, go deep into the soil of the great arc of islands so long inhabited by so many varied peoples.

The Republic of Indonesia impresses with its size and its diversity. Its 13,667 islands extend in an immense sickle south and then north again across 3,200 miles, the distance from Oregon to Bermuda. In territorial extent Indonesia is the sixth-largest political entity in the world, and it is the fifth-largest producer in the Organization of Petroleum Exporting Countries. Its total exports of some $19 billion are three-quarters agricultural and mineral: timber and rubber; tin, bauxite, and nickel; as well as oil. Yet almost a fifth of those exports are now manufactured goods, chiefly textiles, steel, and plywood.

Its 180 million inhabitants, increasing by almost 3.5 million a year, make Indonesia the fifth most populous country in the world. Some 80 percent of those Indonesians are nominally Moslem. Their other creeds range from modern Christianity through Hindu-Buddhism to animism—that is, primitive worship of the spirits of the earth and the waters. Many Indonesians sacrifice animals to their gods, and some ritually collect the heads or eat the flesh of their enemies. Yet the civilizations of the archipelago are rich and sophisticated, growing from deep roots in the past. The peoples are extremely diverse in race, origins, and culture; they speak more than three hundred distinct languages and at least twice as many dialects.

The historical record is neither complete nor orderly, for much has been lost during periodic upheavals. Even the origins of the varied peoples are by no means clear. We know only that they came from many places, and that India was very early a major influence on them. Some of our earliest information comes from those compulsive keepers of historical records, the Chinese, who were briefly acknowledged as the overlords of the Indies.

A lacework of islands great and small, Indonesia has naturally been a seafaring and trading culture. From the sixth to the eighth centuries A.D., the kingdom called Srivajaya built the largest ships in the world, vessels of four- to six hundred tons that were not matched in Europe until the Middle Ages. The primary centers have been two great islands: Sumatra and Java, which cradle Malaysia and Borneo. With more than 60 percent of the populace and a complex society, Java has always been dominant. The Javanese shaped the Republic of Indonesia and now rule it.

Moreover, the Javanese and the people of the smaller island directly to the east, magical Bali, have created highly sophisticated religions, literature, art, and governments. Most of the people of those two islands are today farmers; their ancestral fields, which are called *sawah*, have for many centuries been the abode of powerful spirits that are today honored and feared by Moslems, Hindu-Buddhists, and Christians alike. The other islands, including underpopulated Sumatra, are inhabited chiefly by *ladang* cultivators who slash and burn the rain forests to make a clearing they cultivate for a few years—and then move to another virgin site. But that way of life is passing with the destruction of the rain forests.

Some Indonesians are now employed in modern industrial plants. Others are still roving hunters, fishermen, sea gypsies, and hereditary pirates. They chiefly inhabit the fan of smaller islands that opens out from Bali and extends north to Borneo, which is partially Indonesian-ruled. An even greater number live in the islands that extend east through the Celebes, called Sulawesi, and the Moluccas, called Maluku, to the Indonesian-ruled western half of the enormous island of New Guinea, otherwise Irian Jaya. Extraordinary cultural, racial, and linguistic diversity is found in those distant islands, which produce aluminum, oil, nickel, and copra, as well as exquisite handicrafts. The greatest concentration of Christians is found in the east because the Portuguese, who were the vanguards of the Europeans, first landed on those islands.

Long before the Europeans shattered the pattern, successive waves of migration, conquest, and colonization had swept over the archipelago and shaped its civilization. The proto-Malays came first and then the Malays, no one knows exactly whence, to subdue the aboriginal people. Thereafter, Indians established great empires and implanted both Hinduism and Buddhism, which were often embattled. Islam came between the fourteenth and the sixteenth centuries. Quite unusually, it extended its sway through peaceful traders, rather than through the men-at-arms who were in that era the chief missionaries of both Islam and Christianity.

The people became Moslems when their rulers were converted. But neither rulers nor people gave up their ancient beliefs and practices. Indonesia is today titularly a Moslem country. There are, naturally, many devout believers, but there are even more who are casual Moslems. Not dominated by its religion, Indonesia is emphatically a secular state.

Christianity came to the islands in 1509, when the Portuguese arrived in search of spices, treasure, and steppingstones to the Far East. They found all they sought, and they enjoyed all they had found for almost a century. But the Dutch began pushing them out in 1596. Competition became three-cornered when the British arrived in force in the eighteenth century. The Dutch, however, prevailed in the Indies by force of arms and by canny negotiations, such as exchanging Malacca for British holdings in Sumatra.

By might and by guile the Dutch established their sway from almost the northern tip of Sumatra to the Moluccas. They ran the Indies as a business concern: profits were all-important; the people were of little importance. Wherever they could, they ruled through native princes and potentates, normally not imposing Dutch ways except on the willing elite. But the diverse East Indies became even more diverse through rival European influences.

Today, unadulterated Islam is practiced almost exclusively in Sumatra, where live only a small portion of the people who make Indonesia, statistically at least, the world's most populous Moslem nation. Next door, Java is the home of more than 100 million. The creeds and the culture of the Javanese are rich and ornate, owing much to Indian influence, particularly in the drama. Almost all Javanese are nominally Moslem. But, aside from the few small Arab communities, most are also a little Hindu, a little Buddhist, and a dash animist. The world's greatest Buddhist monument stands at Borobodur, near the old capital of Jogjakarta in central Java. Built by a short-lived ninth-century kingdom, the towering shrine with its hundreds of stone Buddhas has been comprehensively restored by international effort. In 1960 Sukarno and Khrushchev prodded each other to climb it—but neither made it to the top.

Bali is unique in its harmonious blend of Hinduism and Buddhism. Historically and doctrinally, Balinese religion and culture are as strange as would be a functioning combination of Judaism with Catholicism, Anglicanism, and Greek Orthodoxy. In the fan of islands to the east of Bali dwell Christians and idolators, animists, pagans, cannibals, and headhunters, as well, of course, as Moslems.

Revolt against the Dutch was inevitable, not primarily because of harshness, but because they had trained an Indonesian elite to administer the country under their direction. Since Dutchmen could not be everywhere, they created a small cadre of educated Indonesian men— and thus created an Indonesian national consciousness. Students in

Dutch-run schools began to organize for freedom at the beginning of the twentieth century. A Pan-Islamic movement strengthened nationalism, as did a small Communist movement. When the Communist International came under the control of the victorious Bolsheviks in the Soviet Union, the clandestine Partai Komunis Indonesia was organized by delegates from Moscow.

Through the 1920s and 1930s, Nationalists and Communists cooperated against the Dutch. With the Japanese conquest, the Nationalists came into their own, although the Communists were forced to remain underground. By 1944 a paramilitary force of 200,000 had been organized with the blessing of the Japanese, who allowed the red-and-white flag of Indonesia to fly beside the Rising Sun.

That foresight was justified on August 9, 1945, the day the second atomic bomb was dropped on Japan. The Japanese commander-in-chief for Southeast Asia summoned Sukarno to Saigon to grant independence to the Indies. Led by Sukarno, the Nationalists proclaimed the Republic of Indonesia on August 17, 1945.

Joined by the Communists and Pan-Islamic groups, the Nationalists fought first against a British occupying force and later against the returning Dutch. Conferences and battles alternated until August 17, 1950, the fifth anniversary of the proclamation of independence, when the Dutch finally acknowledged that independence. One of the first nations to formally recognize the new republic was the United States, which had actively assisted its fight for independence.

The Indonesian Army had already won its first campaign against the Communists. In 1948, the Partai Komunis Indonesia had attempted to seize control of the independence movement through a coup d'etat following a mass rising. The Communist International had ordered that rising—and simultaneous risings all the way from Korea and the Philippines to Malaya, Burma, and India in the year of the Berlin Blockade. The Emergency was to last for years in Malaya, as was the Hukbalahap revolt in the Philippines. In Indonesia, as in Korea, the regular armed forces crushed the Communists in battle.

But the pattern of the future had been set. Bitter enmity was thenceforth to divide the military from the Communists—and Sukarno was to play the two forces against each other. He was for some time successful, largely because his personal prestige was the single most important factor in the power equation.

Even most anti-Communist generals remained loyal to Sukarno in 1957, when some disaffected generals revolted in Sumatra and the Celebes with the backing of the CIA. But even those loyal generals were aghast at his irresponsible tyranny and his collaboration with the Communists. At home and abroad, Sukarno allied himself with the extreme left. The Partai Komunis Indonesia was controlled by revolutionary

Maoist China, which became the despot's greatest foreign supporter.

Even the adoring public began to turn against the despot. Students, who might have been expected to be leftist, demonstrated against the Communists. Slogans scrawled on walls denounced Sukarno and his henchman, Foreign Minister Subandrio, as *Anjing Peking*: "Peking dogs." In response, the despot aligned his policies even more closely with the Communists at home and abroad.

By 1965 the Indonesian Army was ponderously preparing to take action. Eight years after the Sumatra revolt, the generals were still inhibited by residual allegiance to their president, like the German generals who waited too late to strike at Hitler. Sukarno was the demigod of Indonesian nationalism, greater to his countrymen than even George Washington and Abraham Lincoln to Americans.

The Communists struck first. On the night of September 30, 1965, assassination squads murdered six generals and thrust their bodies down a well. Sukarno, who condoned the plot, panicked when two senior generals survived, one by climbing over a back fence in his pajamas. The despot fled to Halim Air Base, where the Communist-controlled air force received him warmly.

The surviving army generals finally struck back. Their leader was not the thoughtful—and vacillating—chief of staff whom all revered, but a junior general called Suharto. The chief of staff was Sumatran, an outsider, while Suharto was, like Sukarno, a Javanese and therefore in the mainstream.

Halim Air Base offered no effective resistance to the army's attack except halfhearted passes by fighter bombers that then prudently fled. Sukarno and his air force generals were captured with ease.

An era ended in September 1965—in reality, but not yet in form. Sukarno remained president. All he had left, however, were the title and the trappings that had evidently become more important to him than the reality or the responsibility of power.

The Communists had planned to seize absolute power in Sukarno's name—and retain him as their figurehead. That strategy was delineated in the documents the victorious army took from the defeated conspirators. So, at least, the army said.

To attain legitimacy for their regime, the generals had to show that they had not struck first, but only in self-defense and, of course, in defense of the nation. Besides, they preferred to rule for a time in the name of the revered President for Life, whom, they declared, they had rescued from leftist captivity. The Communists were to pay a fearful price for their failure.

The motto of the Republic of Indonesia is *Bhinneka Tunggal Ika*, "Unity in Diversity." Sukarno believed in holding the variegated nation together with contrived internal tensions and imaginary external threats. In the end, he failed. His successor, Suharto, has a more humdrum approach: economic progress. He has been reasonably successful.

The motto implies local autonomy, but Jakarta strives to inculcate a commonsense nationhood. All citizens will in time speak the official common language, *bahasa Indonesia*, which was originally a traders' tongue. But almost all will also continue to speak their native tongues. Millions have been shifted from desperately overcrowded Java to Sumatra in the west or to the smaller islands in the east, but assimilation is mortally slow. That diversity has kept Islam from dominating.

In the 1950s a group called Darul Islam, "Soldiers of Islam," mounted an armed revolt against the new government. It was one of those wildly romantic, slightly sinister, and ultimately futile movements that Asia casts up from time to time—and it failed. Islamic political parties were active in the early Sukarno period, when elections were more open. One Islamic party was moderate doctrinally, but extreme politically, even to bully boys in black shirts. The other was extreme doctrinally, championing an Islamic theocracy. Neither gained significant power in the first general election in 1955. The people then voted heavily for Sukarno's Nationalists and substantially for the Communists, who promised them paradise on earth—now. The Islamic parties only promised them paradise in heaven—later. Only in fundamentalist Sumatra, linked by linguistic and emotional ties to nearby Malaya, did the Islamic parties do well.

Today an Islamic revival stirs the unemployed of the cities, who amount to 30 percent of the work force. Islamic fundamentalism is also in vogue in some of the outer islands. But such movements, like the remnants of the Moslem parties, are neutralized. The Suharto government has invented a complex mechanism that lets it run elections without stuffing ballot boxes, yet ensures that it will remain in power.

That ingeniously practical authoritarianism was still in the future when Sukarno's impractical authoritarianism crashed to earth. The army then made certain that Indonesia would not, for at least a generation, be troubled by another Communist bid for power. The cure was effective—and stark. The army wiped out all Communists, all Communist sympathizers, and all potential sympathizers. If a few thousands or even tens of thousands unconnected with the Partai Komunis Indonesia were also sacrificed to personal enmity or to chance, the army was not deeply concerned.

Early in 1966 I traveled slowly west to east through Java and then on to Bali. In that area, where two-thirds of the people lived, the greatest massacres had occurred. Almost invariably, I found, spontaneous anger against the godless Communists had been fanned by the military. The army had also provided leadership and transportation for the people's "spontaneous" attacks on the Communists and fellow travelers.

After a week, I was almost inured to eyewitnesses' tales of rivers choked with bodies or of villages where half the people had destroyed the other half. Goaded by the army, the people had run amok—not one man with a machete in a killing frenzy, but thousands marching with axes, clubs, and sharpened hoes. Some mobs killed everyone who could not prove that he was not a Communist. Women and children were slain beside their husbands and fathers to ensure that later generations would not seek vengeance against the killers.

No one knows how many perished in October and November 1965, although estimates range from 100,000 to 750,000. I arrived at a tentative figure of 200,000 to 250,000 at the end of my travels. I may have exaggerated the toll, but it is more likely that I understated it.

Indonesia had briefly become a rogue nation. Neither numerically nor morally was the outburst of fury as heinous as the Nazis' methodical extermination of millions, or Stalin's institutionalization of mass murder. For sheer horror it approached, but did not match, the systematic slaughter of more than a million Cambodians a decade later. But the orgy of killing scarred the nation deeply.

"Not all those killed were Communists," a Balinese nobleman told me. "But all were fouling our land and desecrating our religion. They had to die to purify Bali."

Bali, gentle Bali, was worst. At least fifty thousand died out of about 2.5 million. On the island of Lombok, just east of Bali, fifty thousand died of disease and starvation during the winter of 1965–66.

All this Sukarno had contrived. The broken man was to retain the title of President for Life until 1967, when it pleased Suharto to displace him. He was to live until 1970, a discredited leader who had betrayed his people. His legacy included four wives. Dewi, the youngest, a Japanese he had met in a Tokyo nightclub, was an ornament of café society. At the end, his country was on the verge of starvation. Burdened with great external debts, it was bleeding from internal strife. When the Sukarno era ended in 1965, an impoverished Indonesia was on the verge of dissolution.

CAFE VENEZIA
ITALIAN ICE CREAM AND STEAK
JAPANESE RESTAURANT

In 1987 I looked at that sign on a bamboo fence in a Jakarta square with incredulity. It brought home the extraordinary alteration Indonesia had undergone in a little more than the two decades. Although not a world economic leader like the neo-Confucian countries, it had made a rapid transition from near hopelessness to relative abundance.

The Cafe Venezia was an integral part of the new Indonesia. Its artless promise of international variety pointed the dramatic transformation Jakarta and, to a somewhat lesser extent, the countryside have undergone since I first saw both in 1955. In those days, Jakarta and Indonesia were the depths. Viet Nam and Cambodia, which have since fallen low, were far higher in sophistication and comfort—for inhabitants as well as visitors. Present-day Jakarta, despite its faults, is, by comparison with its condition a generation earlier, a quasi-miracle.

Unlike the tempura and sushi bars of the big international hotels, the Cafe Venezia was not staffed by highly paid Japanese chefs. Nor did the chief who prepared Italian dishes come from Florence, where *bistecca Fiorentina* was invented. Like all the chefs, he was an Indonesian who had learned to cook foreign dishes.

Candidly, the results were mixed. Still, I marveled that they did it at all, and I was wonderstruck that they did it competently. In 1955 there was only one foreign restaurant—and very few Chinese or Indonesian restaurants—in Jakarta, the depressed, filthy, and disease-ridden capital that had once been spick-and-span Dutch Batavia. Mario's catered to a small foreign clientele. Mario and his wife, Vicky, who had come to Jakarta as refugees, pieced out the meager Italian ingredients they could find with marginally satisfactory local substitutes. The Parmesan cheese was often cheddar, but rarely Kraft.

In 1987 I could not count the foreign restaurants of Jakarta—and they spilled over to Surabaya, Jogjakarta, and Denpasar. There were certainly many dozens, perhaps a hundred, offering, among other cuisines, Korean, French, Italian, Japanese, American, and Burmese. The seafood restaurant at the Inter-Continental Borobodur served a remarkable variety of imaginative dishes. Supervised by a young Dutchman, the Executive Club of the Jakarta Hilton offered sparkling crystal, gleaming damask, and suave service. Chinese restaurants had naturally proliferated as the small but highly enterprising overseas Chinese community prospered—and its prosperity extended outward to its Indonesian partners, suppliers, and neighbors.

The chain that served the highly seasoned food of Padang on the island of Sumatra at first glance appeared just another fast-food operation. Those dishes have been popular for decades: from curried squid and charcoaled giant shrimp with cumin, to eggs deviled with shrimp paste, and my own favorite, *daging rendang*, chunks of beef sautéed with shredded coconut. Yet it was remarkable that such native food was now available throughout Jakarta in conscientiously clean and hygienic surroundings. Most remarkable was the clientele from the brand-new middle class, drawn by the signboard with the chain's trademark: a dead ringer for the fat little maharajah who for years symbolized Air India.

In the past, the native middle class was minuscule and could not, in any event, afford restaurants. The overseas Chinese middle class, which was small but rich, preferred its own food, usually at home. Among the many attributes Indonesia did *not* possess was a confident native middle class to patronize restaurants—or to promote economic and cultural advances.

There was almost nothing between the two extremes. At the lower end, hawkers and street stalls served the poor for ten or twenty *rupiahs*, perhaps two or three American cents. The ostentatious *rijstaffel*, Dutch for "rice table," was usually served in private clubs to foreigners and to the very few wealthy Indonesians by dozens of gorgeously uniformed waiters, who bore dozens of lavish courses.

My memories of those early days are lit by joy at the natural or artistic beauty and spontaneous grace of an attractive people. Aside from those bright moments, I remember scarcity and squalor. Material well-being is not the beginning and the end of human aspiration. But it is certainly a beginning. In those days, Indonesia had not even approached that beginning.

Jakarta is today swollen with millions attracted from the countryside by the lure of better pay and modern goods. Most of the hundred fifty families arriving every day are disappointed. The urban bloat created by their migration will be unbearable in the year 2000, when the population of Jakarta, if unchecked, will reach 22 million.

Yet those migrants are better off than were their parents. The lower middle class, now rising, are the children of those who were poor under Sukarno. Today a few are professionals, but many are shopkeepers, artisans, stall owners, drivers, tailors, and repairmen. Remembering the past, they marvel at the changes in Jakarta. I, too, marvel when I remember the barren past.

On my most recent visit, I was struck by city streets with far fewer potholes than New York's—and by the superhighway to the airport. I was also struck by teams cutting the grass on the verges with gasoline-powered "weed whackers," rather than tiny *arit*, "hand sickles." Other worldly wonders were air conditioning, a functioning telephone network, supermarkets, far fewer beggars, and the absence of belligerent soldiers or suspicious policemen with submachine guns. I used to spend a lot of time in Jakarta afraid that an accidental burst of gunfire from some unfledged youth would abruptly end my career, which was dear to me at least.

In the 1950s there was *no* hotel except the dilapidated Trans-Aerea Hostel. It was used primarily by unfortunate KLM flight crews, until

KLM's landing rights were canceled during the anti-Dutch campaign. Before the war, the des Indes had been *the* hostelry of the Indies, like Raffles in Singapore, shimmering with the glamor of the exotic East.

The des Indes was, in the 1950s, crumbling, smelly—and permanently sold out. Embassies and companies had taken rooms as offices and living quarters, leaving no accommodations for transients. Only Time-Life, gloriously spendthrift, had a room on long lease. When all else failed, one could usually find a bed in a corner of that room or, at least, a corner without a bed.

Normally, friends in the diplomatic community rescued correspondents from such squalor. The obligations of friendship in those days required housing the homeless and feeding the hungry. It had long been thus for Indonesians, who fended off mutual suffering by mutual cooperation in a deprived and often dangerous environment.

Downtown Jakarta, once the center of colonial Batavia, was dominated by great drainage canals called *kali*, which were as wide as a two-lane highway. Homesick for their own waterlogged lowlands, the Dutch had built those canals through the middle of the city and lined them with hewn stones—to last, apparently, forever. Jakarta, too, is low-lying. Vast tropical cloudbursts would have washed away half the city if their flash floods had not been channelled into the *kali*, which boiled brown with mud and tossed logs or drowned dogs on their white wavelets.

Children sported in the green-scummed water while, a yard away, men and women defecated unselfconsciously into the depths. At landings built into the walls, women washed clothes, which miraculously did not emerge dirtier than before. Women also bathed infants in those sinks of infection or washed themselves modestly within the screens of their sarongs. Men, women, and children brushed their teeth conscientiously and slaked their thirst with the same water.

Those who survived such sanitation were obviously tough. Many were also misshapen and chronically diseased. The fortunate among them lived in shacks made of waste paper, rusty metal, and battered wooden boards from discarded packing cases. The less fortunate slept on the cracked pavements amid the red-black stains of betel-nut spittle and the rotting rinds of oranges, grapefruitlike pomelos, and spiky durians. Emaciated cats with evil leers carved on their faces by the scars of a hundred fights chased fat black rats through the heaped filth. A miasma compounded of a hundred foul stenches was pierced only by the sweet scent of burning cloves in fat, conical cigarettes called *kretek*.

A cloud of hopelessness also hung heavy, for the people despaired in the final years of Sukarno. The costumed mountebank was still cavorting onstage, but the audience was too hungry to respond to his spectacular showmanship. The outside world was kept outside. Sukarno was happy to be quit of the foreigners, particularly Westerners, who, he said, came only to exploit his people. "To hell with your aid," he told the United States. Aside from a few sycophants and the Communist powers, Indonesia was virtually cut off.

In the era of Sukarno, the only vehicles for hire on the streets were *becak*, the local version of the bicycle-driven three-wheeler that was once the universal transport of Asia. *Becak* have now been banished from central Jakarta. Many were dumped into the sea, depriving illiterate coolies of their livelihood—"in order to clean up the city for the rich," some Jakartans complained. Jakarta is now served by a horde of yellow, buglike, Australian-made Ford Laser taxis that are air-conditioned—and, almost miraculously, radio-dispatched. Surprisingly, the traffic jams on the much-enlarged road system are a whisker less horrifying than the traffic jams that occurred when there were far fewer roads and far fewer vehicles using them. Even the police are a shade less eager for bribes.

Of course, everything did not change immediately. Nor had everything changed even in 1990. The government still kept the domestic press on a rein, albeit a longer rein than Sukarno's—and still obstructed foreign correspondents. Visas were still denied from time to time. All Australian correspondents were banned because Suharto was offended by some Australian reports on Indonesian suppression of local resistance in formerly Portuguese East Timor, as well as by other Australian reports on the corruption over which he presided.

The reports on Timor were unfair and inaccurate; the reports on corruption were accurate. Yet other reporters had written at length about corruption and, although hardly lionized, had not been expelled. Obstruction of the press was, it seemed, an automatic but discriminating reflex.

The general election in the spring of 1987 had two major objectives, one of which was *not* to arrive at a democratic consensus. The first was to unite the country behind the government by mass endorsement of GOLKAR, Suharto's super-party that transcended political parties. The second was to demonstrate by a free election, in which several parties participated, that Indonesia was truly a democratic country.

Although anxious to thus impress outsiders, the government issued regulations restricting both domestic and foreign correspondents. Above all, they were not to travel without special permission. Yet no one tried to enforce those regulations. Moreover, ministers and officials were freely available, despite their electoral busyness.

It is now virtually impossible to control foreign correspondents once they've been allowed to enter Indonesia. Short of twenty-four-hour surveillance, the authorities cannot keep correspondents from traveling freely and filing freely. Roads are far better, and Garuda Air Lines flies even to remote islands. An efficient telephone system connects Indonesia to the outside world, while satellites in stationary orbit over the equator bounce internal communications over the arc of 3,200 miles. Unlike the inherent delays even in electrical communication in the Sukarno era, telex and facsimile transmissions to the outside world are now instantaneous. Since they can be dialed like a telephone call, covert censorship is impossible.

Tillman Durdin of the *New York Times* was one of the wisest correspondents who ever worked in Asia. His manner was gentle, but his soft voice could be cutting. I once heard him bring up short a young correspondent who argued that American policy had been highly effective in Asia considering the short time America had been involved there.

"The U.S. has been in Asia for a long time," Durdin said. "Centuries, in fact. The trouble with you newcomers is that you think history only begins the moment you step onto the stage."

The more I read on Asia, the more I appreciate that observation. Asians' political and economic decisions are, naturally, based on their own past, as seen through the prism of their own character. A foreign correspondent not acquainted with that past or that character is badly handicapped.

Shortly after leaving Indonesia in 1987, I read a dispatch from a major American news service. The alarmed correspondent reported that the Indonesian people were infuriated at President Suharto's autocratic rule and his family's wholesale theft. Corruption, the dispatch said, was almost as vast as that which had finally aroused the Filipino people to throw out President Ferdinand Marcos. Clearly, Indonesia was in a very bad way, the dispatch concluded. Major unrest and violence were not far off. The report was solid, and every fact was right. Yet the total effect and the conclusion were misleading.

Indonesians do not like Suharto's autocracy or his family's corruption. But they remember the horrors of the recent past, and they are extremely reluctant to force radical changes. Revolution is not on the agenda of a nation that in 1986 began to export rice for the first time since 1941. The harsh deprivation of the Sukarno era remains in the forefront of too many minds.

Fear of the carnage that followed Sukarno deters the people from mass civil disorder, although the passion of the Malay personality periodically erupts into violence. Indonesians are also a little chastened by the destruction and killing of the anti-Japanese riots of 1974 and the anti-overseas Chinese riots of 1984. Yet Jakarta continues to swell larger with the migration of the discontented and the ambitious from the countryside. New violence will undoubtedly break out at some time. It will not threaten the present government's existence unless present dissatisfaction becomes desperation.

"Rattling and jolting so loud we have to shout to hear each other," my notes read, "the crack BIMA, pride of the Indonesian railways, clatters, creaks, bumps, and rocks nauseatingly toward Solo [in Central Java, near Jogjakarta], where legions of small, stocky men in numbered yellow sweatshirts clamber aboard. Laden with baggage, those porters escort passengers to their places for tips of a few cents."

Despite marked improvement in most fields since the Sukarno era closed with massacres, railroad travel has deteriorated. For all of Indonesia's progress, its potential is still much greater than its achievements. Progress has generally come from leaving the people alone to get on with their own business, particularly the energetic overseas Chinese. That approach does not work for the state-owned railways, which offer no prospect of profits and little prospect of graft. Since nobody cares, time has worked devastation upon the railroads. My notes go on:

Depart 16:00 Saturday, arrive 10:00 Sunday. Elapsed time eighteen hours, overall speed 33 miles an hour. BIMA is the *best* train, not cheap for Indonesians. Yet *everything* is filth-coated, including the windows, which are *never* washed. "Fully air-conditioned," said the porter on the platform, to our delight. But the air conditioning is not working properly, if at all. The temperature outside is in the high eighties. Inside, it's a degree or two lower—sometimes.

Ancient three-tier bunks, since first class has vanished. Reading lights and locks have been removed and replaced with plastic patches. Floors are gritty, *kamar kecil* ["toilet"; literally "small room"] has running water—i.e., water running back and forth on the floor as the carriage sways, and a nauseating urine stench. In our compartment every surface is so grimy we shrink from touching anything. Many windows are cracked, and a number are smashed. Footplates between the trains are heavily rusted, eaten right through in places.

Pillows rent for 350 *rupiahs* each [about U.S. twenty cents]. Providentially, water is sold in bottles. We have foolishly failed to bring either food or drink, having been assured that the BIMA carried a dining car.

Night falls abruptly, and it is suddenly cold. Our plight is largely our own fault. We squeamishly rejected the blankets offered for rent—not, God knows, because of the cost, which was, to us at least, infinitesimal, but because they were impregnated with dirt.

Unable to sleep, I end up in the dining car and have a long conversation with a surgeon from a big provincial hospital outside Surabaya. Educated in Australia and Holland, he bemoans low medical standards in Indonesia. Although his salary is abysmal, he insists on paying for the unsweetened tea we drink out of cracked, grease-smeared glasses.

Leaving Jakarta, the train runs between dwellings, offering intimate views of family life. At first it's all squalor: cramped corrugated iron shanties and wash hanging everywhere. All grayish, for it's impossible to get anything completely clean in the polluted water and the perpetual smog of Jakarta. Most sleepers are crammed into tiny spaces in the back of food stalls or other stores.

The yellow banners of Suharto's GOLKAR are everywhere as polling days draw near—plus a few red or green banners of the two other parties. *All* parties except GOLKAR were lumped into one, and the lump was then divided into two to create a plausible opposition. Youths hired for 500 *rupiahs* (U.S. thirty cents) a day to wear T-shirts and headbands in party colors and beat tomtoms pass in open trucks, shouting and waving. An adult demonstrator costs 1,000 *rupiahs* (U.S. sixty cents), but adults are not much in demand. I am startled by the enthusiasm Indonesia's youth apparently feels for its denatured politics. I am not startled by the re-emergence of Sukarno, who is *the* great villain to the present government, as *the* great romantic hero for frustrated youth.

A small girl defecates into a stream. Cocks and chickens peck nearby. Only three dogs seen during entire trip, but many lean cats.

An old depression creeps over me. The suffering, filth, and poverty seem just like that which clouded the Sukarno era a generation ago—and I feel the same despair.

My despair begins to dissipate when I see flocks of schoolchildren in neatly ironed school uniforms. In the old days few went to school, and uniforms were too expensive for most of those who did. Many Chinese are mixed among those school groups, playing and joking with the Indonesian children, as they would not have in the old days.

Abruptly when the train enters the countryside the world becomes neat and orderly. The irrigation canals are well kept and flowing with bright water. They are good, solid nineteenth-century technology. A bamboo bucket on a long bamboo pole dips smoothly into a canal, pivots on its fulcrum, and pours the water into a field. That is ancient technology, millennia old.

Extraordinary beauty, too. As dusk falls over the paddy fields, the rice shoots glow softly, their pale green stalks reflected in the silvery water. White smoke drifts across the paddies into the fringe of trees, and the sun is a pale orange memory behind the clouds.

Urea fertilizer from a petrochemical plant in Palembang [in south Sumatra] arrives in new blue-and-yellow freight cars. Men and women in conical bamboo hats stoop to transplant rice shoots in the squishy mud of flooded fields. Others cut mature rice with tiny *arit* sickles, as have Javanese farmers for many centuries.

The past is still very much with them. But modernity is coming in. I see many bicycles, most gleaming bright; new buses; a number of cars, apparently private; and many tough little mini-vans, all called Colts after the Mitsubishi brand name. The Colt Revolution is opening up Indonesia, as other Colts won the American West. A fisherman in Madura no longer *has* to sell to the local Chinese middleman. He telephones, using another instrument new to his milieu, and finds that prices are higher that day in Surabaya. He then loads his catch into a Colt for sale in the city.

The roadbed under the rails is spectacularly rough, but many new motor roads are under construction. Road gangs use Kubota, not Caterpillar, earth-moving machinery, although both the American and the Japanese companies have assembly plants in Indonesia.

Crops are abundant: rice in all stages of development, for the growing season is continuous; sugar cane, tall and thin; papaya and mango trees with their bulky orange and green fruit.

The train draws into the cluttered suburbs of Surabaya, a shade less squalid than Jakarta's. We see an old sight now hardly ever seen in the capital: high on twenty-foot-long bamboo staffs hang small bamboo cages holding *perkutut*, "turtle doves." TV antennas jut rakishly against the pale blue sky—and a pirate satellite dish shines silver.

[In Surabaya in 1955 I stayed in the venerable Oranje Hotel.] The Oranje still exists, moderately refurbished. It's now called the Majahpahit, commemorating the great Hindu empire, rather than the ruling House of Orange of the Netherlands. Fair enough!

We stay at the Hyatt, which was not dreamed of three decades ago. As we enter the room, Cable News Network is on the television screen, courtesy of the United States Armed Forces Radio and Television Service. Also available, presumably by agreement: CBS and NBC, BBC and ITN. Under the door slides a copy of *USA Today*, printed in Singapore from a satellite transmission and flown to Surabaya.

All this is eerily American—in Surabaya, which once seemed

the end of the earth. When Bertolt Brecht wanted the ultimate in exoticism, he wrote a song called "Surabaya Jonny." Now American cultural influence—subliminal as well as overt—is strong in remote Surabaya.

My impressionistic review of the countryside was amplified by closer observation. I also heard the incisive views of the surgeon I met on the BIMA and of an exceedingly well-informed diplomat who had known Indonesia closely for more than a decade.

Indonesian medicine is as dolorous as the BIMA. Foreigners and informed Indonesians offer the same advice: "If you're ill, don't call the doctor. Call for a reservation to Singapore."

Some excellent Indonesian doctors practice in Jakarta, many of them trained abroad. But they cannot practice modern medicine because they lack the backup of sophisticated equipment and laboratories. Investment in medicine is low, in part because the powerful men who decide how much to invest can always go to Singapore.

The surgeon, who is from Melang, near Surabaya, was scathing. After nineteen years of training, mostly abroad, he discussed with near despair the acute shortages of doctors, nurses, and facilities. Java has about six thousand doctors, one for every 16,500 persons, and the outer islands have fewer. A professor of surgery, he was training new doctors, but not enough.

"We are also very short of nurses," he said. "Pay is low, but educational and professional requirements are high. Who wants to do hard work at uncongenial hours for a pittance? Few are so dedicated. And many nurses are paramedics in the countryside. That's hard to argue with when there are so few doctors. But it doesn't make for effective modern hospitals."

And the fundamental causes?

"Standards are low, very low," the surgeon said. "Especially in hospitals, which should be models. It's almost impossible to preserve simple cleanliness, not to speak of sterile conditions. And what equipment we have is constantly breaking down. Not only because it's old and overused. Indonesians just don't believe in maintenance."

The diplomat spoke good *bahasa Indonesia*, as well as working Javanese. He cited two apparently contradictory phenomena: the extraordinary resilience of Indonesian society, which is largely due to the strength of the old ways; and the rapid pace of change, very rapid indeed for a highly conservative society. Indonesia, particularly Java at its center, he concluded, can accommodate major changes without cracking because its foundations are so deep and so firm. But he could not predict how long major cracks could be avoided.

"In the old days, they used to harvest rice by hand," he remarked.

"In some places they still cut stalk by stalk with little *arit* sickles. Afterward there's dancing and singing and feasting, an old-fashioned harvest festival. But nowadays most farmers will sell half their crop to a Chinese merchant. He comes out from, say, Semarang with twenty men and power scythes. More and more nowadays they use power scythes. The rice is cut in an afternoon. There is no harvest festival—and five hundred people wonder what became of their livelihood."

The old sickles, perhaps symbolically, left green stubble in the fields, but the new power scythes leave the fields yellow. Fleeing the jaundiced fields and the new unemployment, farmers crowd into the cities, Jakarta above all.

"Life in the slums is often worse than it was twenty years ago," the diplomat said. "In Tanjong Priok [the port of Jakarta] the *kalis* have silted up and there's no water—not even contaminated water. . . . Yet, overall and countrywide, everything's much, much better. And stability? Well, few countries have had just two rulers in the past forty years. But Indonesia has: Sukarno and Suharto."

Pertamina, the government oil monopoly, was once thoroughly plucked. Among other self-indulgences, the management ran a private air service that had more aircraft than Garuda, the national airline. Controlling all of Indonesia's oil and natural gas production, Pertamina managed to get into debt for several billion dollars. That grand larceny began in the days of Sukarno, whom the people called *Bung*, which means "Brother."

In the days of Suharto, whom the people call *Pak*, which means "Papa," corruption is more sophisticated. I can, therefore, only say that the Surabaya Shipyard of the government-owned Indonesian Shipbuilding Industry appears well run and not excessively corrupt. I don't really *know*.

I was particularly taken by the motor-assisted sailing vessels ranging from nine hundred to two thousand tons it was building. Small cargo vessels driven by sails with small motors to help them along are an ingenious answer to Indonesia's inadequate interisland communications. The archipelago has the winds to move sailing ships—and the skills to man them. Lying at the approaches to the shipyard were scores of Buginese schooners of two hundred to nine hundred tons' burden, probably the biggest working fleet under sail left in the world.

Retired Admiral Sukono, the director of the shipyard, was a small, brisk man in his mid-sixties. Speaking English with a Dutch accent acquired during his training in the Netherlands, he was meticulously shipshape. Even his thinning hair was dyed jet black.

When he took Moira and me on a tour of his realm, we saw cutting machines made in West Germany and drill presses made in Japan working beside Belgian and Dutch machinery. We saw only a few machine tools from England and none from the U.S.

"Sonar for antisubmarine vessels comes from the United States," Admiral Sukono said. "But that's all. We invited General Motors and Caterpillar to bid to supply diesel engines for patrol craft. But they didn't. Perhaps they thought it was all too small."

The United States appeared generally to be losing interest in Indonesia, to which it has contributed $3.5 billion in grants, loans, and foodstuffs. In the city of Surabaya two big white buildings a block apart bore the big trademarks familiar throughout Asia and the entire world: Suzuki and Toyota. The showrooms and offices of each Japanese firm occupied an entire building. *No* signs advertised the presence of American firms, for there was virtually nothing to advertise.

The new supermarkets did reflect the American cultural influence that had struck me on arriving in Surabaya. But supermarkets are now an international phenomenon, not specifically American. The most obtrusive American products were toiletries like Gillette and Old Spice shaving cream, as well as some foodstuffs.

At the checkout I was startled at being handed a coupon good for *1 (satu) Ice Cream Horn dari Swensen's*, with a slogan in English: "In the rich tradition of old San Francisco." But Americans would have to sell a lot of ice cream to match even one Suzuki jeep—and Suzuki had taken over the jeep market.

Only two American businessmen were resident in the vast consular district of the Surabaya American Consulate-General, which stretches from East Java to the Moluccas and West Irian, almost two thousand miles away. But more than two hundred Japanese businessmen lived in that area, where Japan maintains two consulates-general, as well as a simple consulate in Bali. Japan had investments of more than $9 billion throughout the country, disposed to benefit Japan greatly, but Indonesia far less.

The next contender was already challenging. Korean consumer products were highly visible in Surabaya and Korean construction firms were adding to the din of hammers, cranes, and motors that made the busy city totally unlike the malnourished, ill-clothed, and despairing city I had seen in 1960.

The United States played a major role in Indonesia from the 1940s to the 1960s, but thereafter it declined, and sharply in the late 1980s. True, even Japan was cutting back, declaring bluntly that obstruction, corruption, and inefficiency made Indonesia unattractive for further investment. But Japan continued to sell its products aggressively, reinforcing their appeal with outright grants and subsidized loans. Japan also held on to the firms in which it had already invested. Most of them neither produced for export nor transferred up-to-date technology to the Indonesians, but all served Japan's interests.

By 1990 the only American firms that still had substantial investments in Indonesia were the oil companies, despite a sprinkling of assembly plants, banks, and construction firms. Each year the U.S. bought about $4 billion worth of Indonesian goods, chiefly oil and timber, but sold Indonesia only $1 billion worth of American goods, chiefly aircraft, cotton, machinery, computers, and telecommunications equipment.

American companies were actually withdrawing from Indonesia, as from so much of Asia. In the 1960s Weyerhauser, the great timber corporation, bought out a friend of mine who had pioneered logging in Borneo. In the early 1980s, Weyerhauser gave up its interests there. So did Georgia Pacific, which sold out to an overseas Chinese corporation run by an intimate of President Suharto.

Weyerhauser had shipped logs to South Korea to be transformed into plywood when the Korean economic miracle was just starting. When Indonesians went into plywood manufacturing, which is essentially low-tech, the necessary machinery came from Germany and, of course, Japan, but not from the United States.

Further devaluation of the dollar after 1985 did not materially enhance America's competitiveness. Not only high prices but institutionalized inflexibility continued to reduce America's share of the market sharply. Concentrating their vast domestic market, big U.S. corporations would not be bothered to modify their products to suit Indonesia's needs. Nor did Americans offer the "soft loans," that is, long-term money at low interest, the Japanese were eager to extend.

Back in Jakarta, I discussed those problems over tea in a café with an American executive.

"Buyers here want the best," he said. "Say, IBM and Wang computers. But they can't afford them. Then the Japanese, say NEC, come in with magical offers: loans at two and a half percent for twenty-five years. I call that questionable financial practice. But it buys a big share of the market. And that share stays bought!"

He waved at an Indonesian friend, signaled to the waiter, and resumed: "The only way Americans can compete is with soft loans backed by the Import-Export Bank or some such. But just try to get the synchronized cooperation Japanese firms get automatically. Congress authorizes loans one year and won't renew them the next. . . . But all the Japanese firms act like a single corporation. NEC can make a sacrifice here, actually lose money, because it will be recompensed elsewhere. An outfit like NEC could offer computers at $1.98 if it was in their long-term interest."

The executive asked the waiter for two Scotches, then added: "It's damned hard for an American to operate here. Not only are we debarred from giving 'presents' to our associates, we can't even condone the practice, wink at it, though *nobody* gets anywhere here without bribes. The Foreign Corrupt Practices Act hogties American companies. Their lawyers tell American executives, 'Be very careful of countries like Indonesia.' So a big American corporation considering, say, a $1-billion investment here has to ask, 'Can Indonesia provide the infrastructure? Can we get firm promises that we won't be asked for bribes?' . . . And, of course, all that's impossible to guarantee. . . ."

He sipped his Scotch and summed up vehemently: "Everybody bribes. The Japanese don't have to lie about it. Any successful American is also handing out bribes, but he's got to lie about it."

Commercial America having largely abdicated its position, official America followed suit. American aid did continue, albeit on a severely reduced scale. Of course, cutting back was not in itself a change for the worse. The United States was strapped for cash after pouring out aid to the world for decades. Moreover, Indonesia had actually suffered economic and social disruption because of misplaced aid from the Soviet Bloc and the World Bank.

The new focus of American aid was, however, likely to do neither the U.S. nor Indonesia much good. Shifting from capital transfers and building the infrastructure, it was addressing "basic human needs with particular emphasis on overcoming the problems of the rural poor." Yet the U.S. needed quick results to furbish its image. Besides, outside aid had over the years proved incapable of solving those fundamental problems.

The U.S. was, moreover, no longer involved, either commercially or officially, with the big projects that impress both the public and politicians. American influence was therefore declining when a robust American presence in Indonesia was badly needed by both countries. Bigger and more profitable involvement, essential for America's own well-being, could also foster the economic growth Indonesia needed. Yet the U.S. was looking negligible, apparently receding not only from Indonesia, but the entire region.

The new American image was modest to the point of self-effacement. The U.S. Information Service, whose purpose is to furbish that image, was no longer shouting about the United States. It was hardly whispering. USIS publications and services had been cut back sharply in 1987 to provide more money for the global television services that infatuated an administration that had learned about foreign affairs in Hollywood.

Although its courses in the English language and American culture were *the* foundation of American influence, even the American-Indonesian Institute was cut back. The Netherlands was reasserting its influence through courses in Dutch and through widespread cultural activities, but the Netherlands was too small to weigh much in the balance of power in Asia. The U.S. was obviously big enough—and should have been more active.

American potential was great. Beside the graduates of the American-Indonesian Institute, there were more tens of thousands of Indonesians who had studied at universities and advanced armed services schools in the United States. Those alumni and alumnae were a vast—and largely untapped—reservoir of influence. They had learned, among other things, that American culture was not only Kentucky Fried Chicken and Madonna. Yet the U.S. appeared to have lost interest in them as well as their country.

Mochtar Lubis, who was in his late sixties when I was last in Jakarta, has been my personal barometer for Indonesia for decades. He has invariably forecast the rise and fall of political and social power with great accuracy—not just by his acute intelligence, but by his own misadventures, primarily by his sojourns in jail.

Tall, handsome, and charming, Mochtar might have been type-cast for the role of a fiery yet wise journalist, novelist, and patriot. His relaxed manner belies the passion he feels for his country—the land, the trees, and the wildlife, as well as the people. Unable to report except accurately or to comment except honestly, he was bound to get into trouble with both the despot Sukarno and the autocrat Suharto.

Sukarno held him under house arrest for four years and kept him in prison for four and a half years, all without a trial. Confined in comfortable circumstances with other prominent enemies of the tyrant, he was only released on the tyrant's fall in 1965.

When we both spoke to the American Society of Newspaper Editors in San Francisco in 1971, Mochtar knew that Suharto would soon send him back to jail. He asked me to make as much fuss as possible when that happened.

I wrote several columns about his imprisonment—and also managed to arrange some television and radio coverage. After two and a half months he was released. A month later I received a letter posted in Holland. Mochtar wrote that he had been released because of the furor abroad. That, in essence, was the difference between the tyrant and the autocrat. Sukarno *never* stopped for red traffic lights; initially at least, Suharto did.

In 1990 Mochtar Lubis could write as he wished—within limits. He was chafing against certain restrictions, but he was not in imminent danger of being imprisoned again. And he was completing a series of novels telling the great saga of Indonesia's history.

Mochtar and his wife were also working to conserve Indonesia's resources, human as well as natural. The lack of opportunity for young people disturbed them deeply. In theory, primary education was free, but "contributions" were required. Some 6,000 *rupiah* ($3.75) plus extras each month was too high for most in a nation where the per capita income was hardly more than three hundred dollars—and 40 percent of the population was under fifteen years of age.

"The army and the bureaucracy have had no pay raise for two years," Mochtar said. "The people in the shacks are very unhappy. Logging operations in Borneo and Sumatra are looting our timber without replacing it—largely to benefit foreigners. The destruction of the forests brings erosion and floods. Even the tigers have disappeared. . . . And there's no end to corruption."

Another close friend was even more forthright—and even more alarmed. She said: "It can't go on indefinitely. Already we're getting a revival of Sukarno as a heroic figure—and God knows where that could lead. Furthermore, the Ministry of Technology seems to be going mad. Why else put up ethanol plants in the jungle? Why else expect to sell the world an Indonesian-built short-haul turbo-prop airliner based on an outmoded Spanish design? . . . And you know our legal system is completely corrupt. Plaintiffs and defendants submit their bids to the judge—and he naturally takes the highest. Even in criminal cases, even when foreign embassies are involved, justice is always for sale to the highest bidder."

Her husband, who is a history scholar, added, "I often have the feeling that we're living again in the last years of Sukarno. It may take five or ten years, but the situation will explode again."

Such dire predictions certainly spring in part from the febrile Malay-Javanese temperament. Despite such forebodings, Suharto, who was reelected in 1987 against a nearly invisible opposition, still looked un-challengeable. Like Sukarno before him, he ruled by the divine right that has for many centuries cloaked Javanese rulers. Islam teaches that no human being, not even Mohammed, can be divine, only Allah Himself. Nonetheless, the kings and sultans of Java were virtual demigods.

Like those predecessors, Suharto was expected to live in a state befitting a demigod. He was not personally extravagant, but his family made up for his restraint. His children's depredations rivaled those of Ferdinand and Imelda Marcos in the Philippines.

Corruption was not new in Indonesia in 1990, and it was not restricted to the upper levels. It was endemic, as it had been for centuries. Corruption was, however, more efficiently administered than it had ever been in the past. The Suharto family had institutionalized corruption, so that illicit gains were often indistinguishable from the profits of legitimate trade. They had no need to launder their money.

In 1987 Suharto's sons and their overseas Chinese partners clinched a spectacular deal. A communications satellite built for Indonesia had been damaged on launching and was subsequently recovered by the space shuttle *Columbia*. The syndicate bought the damaged satellite from the insurance company for $12 million. After spending about $3 million for repairs, they were to sell it to the government for $72 million. That is $57 million profit on an investment of $15 million—with no risk at all.

The president's sons were out to gain a virtual monopoly in all major industrial and commercial areas. It appeared that they wanted to control the economy totally, so that their power and their wealth would survive their father's passing unscathed.

The embassy of a friendly country simply does not publicly attack the family of the chief of state. Nonetheless, American foreign service officers drafted a report on the imperial ambitions and imperial malfeasance of Suharto's family—and gave it to the press. The embassy explained blandly that the information was essential to American businessmen operating in Indonesia—as it undoubtedly was.

That public indiscretion was also a shot across Suharto's bow. The embassy had evidently reached the same conclusion regarding Suharto in 1987 that Nikita Khrushchev reached regarding Sukarno in 1960. Only plain talk could possibly convince the autocrat that he was leading Indonesia into grave peril.

The embassy report was leaked shortly before the election of April 23, 1987. It had no discernible effect. A year and a half later, however, the Suharto administration reacted to the barrage of complaints against the family's monopolies in which the American report was no more than a single shell. P. T. Mega Eltra, a trading company with two Suharto sons on its board of directors, was to lose its monopoly on plastic imports. Thenceforth, the administration declared, P. T. Mega Eltra would be no more than an equal competitor with other firms.

Also welcome was some opening for competition in steel imports and in the wholesale trade. But few Indonesians believed Mega Eltra would thereafter be no more than another equal competitor. That firm had already established a commanding position through its monopoly, and the Suharto name would assure that Mega Eltra continued to take the lion's share of the trade.

Besides, it had a major stake in the new polypropene plant being built in Sumatra, in combination with Panca Holdings. Headed by Sudwikatmono, a foster brother of the president, Panca had two of Suharto's sons on its board of directors. That monopoly in plastics went back to 1985. Other Suharto family monopolies were of longer standing.

For years, the American Motion Picture Association refused to do business in Indonesia because of the exorbitant fees levied by the monopoly importers. More important, Pertamina, the state-owned petroleum monopoly, granted private companies with Suharto connections exclusive rights to market and refine its oil. Other virtual monopolies controlled universal necessities like cooking oil, sugar, pesticides, and pharmaceuticals.

The Bimantara Group, 54 percent owned by Bambang Trihatmodjo, Suharto's second son, controlled fifty-four companies. All benefited from their exalted connection. So did the HUMPUS Group, directed by Suharto's fifth child, Hutomo Mandala Putra, with interests ranging from avionics and electronics to toll roads. His sister, Siti Hardijani Hastuti, was a major contractor for new highway construction.

In Indonesia, as in Britain and France, state-owned companies were being privatized. That move, too, served the interests of Suharto's family, who were technically private entrepreneurs. The state sold, and they bought—cheap.

Even the all-powerful Suharto clan, however, needed the financial and commercial acumen of overseas Chinese to make their enterprises efficient. Without those Chinese, the Indonesian economy itself would not function; with those Chinese, the country has arrived at new prosperity. Mohammed Sadli, a former minister of mines who is a pure-blooded Indonesian, put it to me succinctly: "Overseas Chinese talent and energy has moved all of Southeast Asia into a new era. Here in Jakarta they brought Glodok, the former Chinese ghetto, to Kuningan, the most glamorous suburb. Just look at all those high-rises."

But an eminent overseas Chinese scholar cautioned: "Your experience on the night express to Surabaya is a good example. By and large, the new prosperity caters to the rich, who go by air; not to the poor, who go by train."

Nonetheless, taking the frightful Sukarno era as the benchmark, the entire nation is far better off today. Aside from the new urban dwellers, even the poor are better fed and better clothed. But the entire structure is fragile.

When the price of oil is stable, Indonesia retains it gains. When the price rises sharply, Indonesia resumes its economic expansion. Despite Pertamina's inefficiency and corruption, it earns more than $8 billion a year from oil and natural-gas exports.

But the price of oil is volatile. Jakarta must, therefore, depend upon roughly $2.5 billion in loans and grants provided each year by the Inter-Governmental Group on Indonesia, which was formed by a number of countries with the U.S. in 1967 to salvage the economy Sukarno had devastated. The country's external debt, public and private, is almost $50 billion. Indonesia may be the richest pensioner in the world.

                               *   *   *

President Suharto is an authoritarian Asian ruler who is a little weak on economics. He was, however, wise enough to take advice from a group of American-trained technocrats who are known as the Berkeley Mafia. With his backing, the Berkeley Mafia has conducted an effective salvage operation.

But Suharto's will is supreme: he fired his brilliant senior economic adviser because the adviser's wife complained of her husband's philandering. Although Suharto's standards of personal and familial honesty are not those professed by the liberal West, he feels paternal concern for his people as well as his clan. He is well balanced, unlike the megalomaniacal Sukarno, but many of his decisions are based on caprice or on astrology.

Sukarno's barbaric and useless monuments still stand, epitomized by MONAS, the Monument Nasional, which thrusts its golden flames into the sky above Jakarta. Jalan M. H. Thamrin, the city's main avenue, exhibits Suharto's monuments: shiny steel-and-glass, tile-and-concrete high-rises that accommodate hotels, embassies, department stores, and offices.

The difference between their monuments exemplifies the enormous difference between the two men who have been the Republic of Indonesia's only presidents in the four decades since it came into existence. Suharto is more efficient than Sukarno, although efficiency is relative in Indonesia. Far more important, he is a responsible human being. Nonetheless, Suharto is today, as Sukarno was in the past, an unreconstructed Javanese autocrat.

No more than most Westerners am I enamored of authoritarianism, Asian or otherwise. A liberal Christian Indonesian, however, set such Western distaste in an Asian context for me: "Who ever said," he asked softly, "that democracy was the eleventh commandment?"

12

Australia: The Lucky Country?

AUSTRALIA IS A BIG COUNTRY THAT THINKS SMALL.

AN AMERICAN ECONOMIST

AUSTRALIAN PREOCCUPATION WITH FIGHTING LAND BATTLES . . .
MAKE[S] IT IMPOSSIBLE TO PROJECT POWER INTO THE SOUTHWEST
PACIFIC. . . . THE INDONESIAN ARMY IS THE BIGGEST IN THE
REGION. JUST THINK OF FIGHTING IT!

FLAG OFFICER,
ROYAL AUSTRALIAN NAVY (RET.)

Moira, who was born in Australia, fled shortly after her twentieth birthday, largely, she says, because of Australian men. Her love for the country has drawn her back every other year or so since then, and her judgment of her countrymen has become less jaundiced. Australia itself has changed remarkably. Sydney and Melbourne have become cosmopolitan in their tastes and their customs—in part because of more convenient travel, but primarily because of the influx of New Australians from Europe and, later, from Asia.

Neither Australia nor its men had changed much when she and I made our first visit together in June 1959. We flew around the world in piston-engined aircraft, then known as "conventional" airliners. The Boeing 707 jet airliner came into general service later that year—and the world immediately became much smaller. Australia also became much closer to the rest of the world.

Since I was going anyway, I suggested to *Newsweek* a cover story on Australia, which was hardly known elsewhere. The editors had agreed. They would pay the substantial airfare, and I could take a breather from covering wars, threats of war, and calamities in China to write about an attractive country that was wholly un-Asian, although situated on the edge of Asia.

Australia appeared to be on the verge of pronounced change, I reported, but it was still very British. Sydney, the queen city, looked like a collection of English seaside towns set down on the shores of the South Pacific. Since the climate was so much better, the tight ranks of little houses with red-tiled roofs were decidedly more cheerful. Nonetheless, the city might have been transplanted from the British Isles into the subtropical sunshine, as, in a sense, it had been. Not skyscrapers with gleaming flanks, but six-story office buildings like those in London clustered around Pitt Street in the center of the downtown business district. The ferry piers on Circular Quay were covered by arched wooden roofs like those in Dublin.

The Returned Services League regularly marched to brass bands in Martin Place to commemorate the battles in which Australians had died for the British Empire. Afterward, the veterans retired to the pubs that stood on almost every corner to quaff pints of beer and josh each other as they would have in Britain. June was the dead of winter in the Antipodes, and both sexes wore drab, British-style clothing. Twelve thousand miles from London lay a very British city, which had been created as an overflow for Britain's criminals and a bridge for British trade with Asia.

So I reported. But my copy, most unusually, suffered a total change. After my report passed under the pencil of the foreign editor, himself a transplanted Welshman, *Newsweek* told its readers that Sydney looked very American.

The foreign editor was perfectly right. He only anticipated reality by a decade or two. Today, Sydney is, outwardly at least, a microcosm of America, from the skyscrapers that palisade the miniature Manhattan of Pitt Street and Martin Place to the Malibulike resorts of Palm Beach and Avalon.

I sometimes describe the so-called Eastern Suburbs as Carmel, California, with a slight Cockney accent. Moira points out with strained reasonableness that Double Bay, Darling Point, and their neighboring communities are populated in good part by immigrants who come from the continent of Europe. They are still called refos, short for refugees, by the older generation of Australians whose ancestors came, voluntarily or involuntarily, from the British Isles. The refos, Moira points out acerbically, speak with many accents, but Cockney is not one of them.

She still reacts strongly to the hackneyed—and by now hardly accurate—description of Australian speech as Cockney. She also reacts to those hearty amateur comedians, usually English, who mime leg irons and manacles to show Australians that they cannot conceal their convict ancestry. The woman can take herself out of Australia and live happily ever after abroad. But she cannot rid herself of Australian resentment of outsiders' slurs.

Moira has no convict ancestry of which she knows. But that is not the

point, as Australians demonstrated at the year-long party for the country's two-hundredth anniversary that began in January 1988. They
hailed the sailing ships that reenacted the passage of the convict-
carrying First Fleet from Portsmouth, and they acknowledged that they
had treated the aboriginal natives very badly.

Above all, they celebrated the birth of a unique nation and a unique
culture. Australians consider themselves a new breed, although they
are, like Americans, descended from a number of older breeds. No
longer British, they are certainly not American.

The basic texture of Australia is quite different from America, despite
the adoption of many American artifacts. Allowing for variations in
climate, places three thousand miles apart smell and feel much the
same, as widely separated places in America do not. Instinctive optimism pervades Australia, and even widespread "wingeing," the
Australia-coined word for bitching, is half-humorous. I usually feel
spritely and hopeful in Australia, as I do not always in the United States.
Problems, personal or general, still seem solvable.

Moreover, Australia remains more homogeneous. Where Americans
differ greatly, Australians are still reasonably alike. Many manage to be
both matter-of-fact and whimsical, rather like Peter Pan played by a
deadpan Buster Keaton. Most Australians are also ostentatiously down-
to-earth and aggressively unsnobbish. They don't call a spade a spade,
but a bloody shovel.

Yet Australia's painters, who have become internationally renowned
during the last thirty years, roam the shores of fantasy, a very pragmatic
and Australian fantasy. David Boyd portrays without sentimentality a
fountain of white cockatoos rising from a pond under the eyes of two
captivated children. Sir Sidney Nolan, who is perhaps the best-known
painter abroad, paints highly sophisticated primitives depicting folk
heroes like the outlaw Ned Kelly and the doomed explorers Burke and
Wills.

The first settlers needed feet-in-the-mud practicality to survive on a
continent that is not everywhere the paradise it appears on first sight.
Yet the Australian imagination soars untrammeled in wonderful motion
pictures. Not only first-class entertainment, movies like *Breaker Morant* and *Gallipoli* leave a thoughtful resonance in the mind. *Breaker
Morant* depicts the moral issues faced by Australians fighting for the
British against the Boers in South Africa. *Gallipoli* depicts Australians
fighting for the British against the Turks in Asia Minor—and meeting
defeat so gallantly that the battle became their national pride. The most
popular recent movie, *"Crocodile" Dundee*, depicted the Land of Oz
fitted up for the tourist trade.

The best Australian movies are old-fashioned stories that start at the beginning, proceed steadily through the middle, and stop at the end. They are like listening to an old itinerant sheepshearer telling fairy tales in a voice gritty with whiskey and cigarettes. Even *"Crocodile" Dundee* sparkles a little with that tough magic.

Most Australians, some 95 percent, are city people, but all like to think of themselves as horny-handed outdoorsmen. That frontier spirit makes them feel still unfettered. Whatever the reality, they believe passionately in their freedom and their opportunities.

That buoyant mentality has also created novels that are as fresh and evocative as the smell of newly baked bread. A favorite of mine is *The Year of Living Dangerously,* in which Australian candor and naïveté confront the guile, the sadism, and the primitive witchcraft that darkened Sukarno's latter years. The optimistic Australian temperament was first incredulous and then revolted by the sexual, political, and social obscenities it encountered.

American preoccupations are more somber and more complex than Australian preoccupations. Since Viet Nam, Americans have been haunted by awareness of their limitations and failures in great affairs and small. Australians are still sunny; they feel they are only at the beginning.

Yet the surface of Australia is constantly growing more like the United States. Superficial Americanization is obviously advanced when Sydneysiders talk of elevators, *not* lifts; trucks, *not* lorries; and pants, *not* trousers. Yet speech and behavior originally American have been spread so widely by television, movies, and videos that they constitute a new *international* style and are no longer uniquely American. Australians are becoming internationalized, not Americanized.

Australia is, I believe, still more British than American, if only by a whisker. British means not only English, but a population that is Scottish, Welsh, and more than a quarter Irish by ancestry. The former Moira Brady, herself an admixture of England and Ireland, once mused on a rainy day, "So many things about Australia I used to think were home-grown. After living in Ireland, I see those traits are pure Irish: the panache and the eloquence, the laziness and the envy!"

The final judgment, at least for the moment, must be that Australia is, above all, *itself.* Having displaced the nomadic aboriginals, a small group that is still overwhelmingly European in descent clusters on the edges of the largest island in the world. That island lies just two hundred miles from New Guinea, the southern tip of Asia, the continent where live the largest non-European groups in the world.

Primarily British in origin despite increasing Asian immigration, superficially Americanized in habits, brightened by the quicksilver slyness and wit of the Irish, those people are quintessentially Australian. A new breed that has evolved in only two hundred years, they still behave as if the world will always leave them alone to do as they please.

The Lucky Country, Donald Horne called his book about Australia. Although he insistently reaffirms his ironic intent, he was right the first time. Australia has been very lucky, so lucky that it could afford to go its own way. No full battle has ever been fought on Australian soil, although Japanese bombers hit Darwin hard and Japanese submarines shelled Sydney glancingly. So lucky was Australia that it could, until 1941, when the Japanese attacked throughout Asia, send its sons abroad to fight for the British Empire.

Australia was shielded from direct attack—and, perhaps, occupation—by American might. Grateful Australia sent its sons to fight alongside American forces in Korea in the 1950s and in Viet Nam in the 1960s. Vocal opinion-makers, who are not necessarily representative, are now determined that Australia will never again assist America—certainly not by force of arms, and preferably not at all. Those new isolationists also appear determined to make Australia pull away from Asia.

On ANZAC day, 1987, which marked the seventy-second anniversary of the Australia New Zealand Army Corps going into action at Gallipoli, a talk show host named Ray Martin invited two American veterans of Viet Nam to appear on his program. One was a master sergeant wearing the Congressional Medal of Honor; the other was a former Marine lieutenant. Each had seen the recently released film *Platoon* alone because he did not know what to expect of it—or himself.

"Wasn't *Platoon*," Ray Martin put it to them, "a moving and accurate portrayal of the Viet Nam War?"

"Moving, yes!" both replied. "Accurate, no!"

"No unit," the sergeant said, "ever saw a quarter as much action in such a short time as that platoon. And the way the movie soldiers felt about each other and the enemy was nothing like the way real soldiers felt."

"You couldn't run a platoon like that," the lieutenant said. "If you did, everyone would've been dead in a couple of days."

By the end of his hour, Ray Martin had maneuvered both veterans into affirming that *Platoon* was not merely poignant, but a wholly accurate picture of Viet Nam. He had manipulated his guests by playing on their innate courtesy. To contradict him, they would have had to call him an outright liar—on television.

The moral Martin drew was clear: Australia must never again engage in military action abroad, certainly not as an ally of America or Britain—and not even on its own behalf. *Since Australia need fear no military threat from abroad, Australia required no armed forces, except, perhaps, for ceremonial purposes.*

In 1986 a report commissioned by Paul Dibb, minister of defense in the capable Labor government of Bob Hawke, amended that thesis. It foresaw a possible need to secure coastal supply routes in the unlikely event of any major war involving Australia. For that task, a handful of destroyers and a few naval helicopters were judged adequate.

The only real threat appeared to come from Indonesia. That fear is in part a legacy of the days when Sukarno rattled his divisions, his MiGs, and his missile boats before taking over western New Guinea. Moreover, the relationship with Jakarta is still embittered by the five audacious and feckless Australian war correspondents also killed by Indonesian troops in Timor in 1975. Despite its own quirks, the present government of Indonesia hardly poses an armed threat to its neighbor Australia. Yet Suharto is seen as a right-wing totalitarian dictator with designs on Australia.

Australia would be hard-pressed to finance and man a significant fighting fleet. Its resources are limited. A country of not quite 17 million with a coastline nearly nine thousand miles long can do only so much to defend itself. Australia was dependent for its defense upon Britain until Winston Churchill renounced that responsibility in 1941. Since then, Australia has been dependent upon America. The psychological legacy persists. Even the neo-isolationists, who are highly suspicious of the United States, feel instinctively that Australia can depend on the United States for its defense.

Dependence and the new isolationism have reduced Australia's capacity to influence events in Asia and the Pacific—even those events that bear upon its security and its interests. When ethnic Fijians mounted an implicitly right-wing—and undeniably racist—coup against the Indian majority, the Hawke government was anxious for a return to constitutional government. But it possessed no real power either to intimidate the miscreants or to compel them when the Fijians refused to listen to reasoned pleas.

The new isolationism is doing Australia no good culturally. Fewer students study Chinese, to take one major language, than did so twenty years ago, despite affirmations of Australian fellowship with Asians and boasts of secondary-school courses in Asian languages. The greatest effort is devoted to Indonesian, which is easy to learn superficially, but very hard to learn well. Statistics showing increased study of Asian languages are therefore misleading. Yet, more Australians are studying Japanese than did so twenty years ago. They want the business of the

Japanese, who buy Australia's raw materials and make much of Australia's finished goods.

The new isolationism is doing no good economically, either. Having committed its future to exploiting its cornucopia of natural resources, rather than to developing its manufacturing industry, Australia is in trouble with its Asian customers. Japan above all, but Taiwan and South Korea, too, are its mainstays. Those customers complain that they cannot depend either on the prompt delivery or uniform quality of its ores.

Despite Australia's excellent diplomatic representation, Asians sense its withdrawal—and it loses influence. Some Australians are shocked by new Asian assertiveness. Diplomats were flabbergasted when senior officials of the Japanese Ministry of Foreign Affairs told them pithily and candidly in the new Japanese style exactly what was wrong with Australian foreign *and* domestic policies. Still talking as if they had everything to teach Asians, Australians find it hard to recognize that Asians now have much more to teach them regarding success in the late twentieth century.

When customers abroad, which means primarily Asia, cut their orders, Australians suffer. A little of the sheen rubs off the quality of their lives, which is, nonetheless, probably still the best in the world. Since leisure is abundant, stress is low, and striving is not encouraged, almost all Australians live very agreeably. Their environment does not, however, necessarily breed toughness or endurance. Dissatisfaction abroad is causing difficulties at home, but the instinctive response is to retreat further toward isolation.

The Anglo-Saxon and Celtic majority still feels a certain contempt for pigmented Asians. Even today, most white Australians consider themselves superior to Japanese, Chinese, and Malaysians—even if they are demonstrably inferior in education, ability, and wealth. For years, the Australian labor unions, including the left wing, insisted on racist restrictions on immigration. The White Australia Policy, which has now lapsed, is still resented by Asians. Yet Asia is critical to Australians. Britain has rejected Australia twice, first in 1941, when Winston Churchill renounced all responsibility for its defense, and again in 1972 when it entered the Common Market—thus choosing Europe over the Commonwealth. America is far away. Besides, many vocal Australians consider that day ill spent in which they have not attacked, or, as they say, "rubbished" the United States. Yet Australians are not comfortable with their Asian neighbors.

That attitude was summed up brilliantly by Frank Mount, an Australian with great knowledge of Southeast Asia, in a political novel built around the mysterious disappearance of Prime Minister Harold Holt in 1967. Mount wrote at white heat in a fiercely apocalyptic vein:

[Intelligence] reports, usually British or American, revealed to Holt an Asian world of convoluted intrigue, of political murders and assassinations, of both endemic and spectacular corruption, of military organisations financed by drug running . . . of secret funds laundered through apparently reputable financial institutions. . . . All this was played out in a world of spies and counter-spies, agents and double agents, information and disinformation, and cast against a backdrop of poverty, social injustices and human degradation. . . .

. . . it came as quite a culture shock to this essentially straight and decent man. He now believed that if Australia was to play the role [in Asia] of his vision, it would have to come to terms not only with Asian cultures and patterns of thought, but with a kind of intrigue, corruption, rapaciousness, and lack of institutional restraint most Australians would find disorientating at best and probably distasteful in the extreme.

Given the orderliness of Australian politics, even in its most vicious and divisive times; the timidness of a bureaucracy steeped in legalism and inflexible procedures; the ultra-conservatism and Euro-centricity of the nation's managerial elite; and the country's general insularity and arrogant indifference towards Asia, Holt feared that if ever Australians were to [find] a place in Asia, it would take a long time.

Thirty years ago, as I have observed, Sydney and its suburbs were very British, although they were on the brink of change. Pubs stood hospitable sentry on almost every streetcorner; restaurant menus were stodgily British; no one ever said a word against the Royal Family; and England was *the* place to go—even for the sons and daughters of Irish-Australian fathers who talked sedition against the Crown in private.

Not everything has changed. London is still awash with young Aussies, but they also flock to nearby Asian countries. A visit by the Queen or the Prince and Princess of Wales ("The Chuck and Di Show" to the irreverent, who are the majority today) still evokes spasms of jealousy and back stabbing among social climbers determined to meet them. But royal visits also produce public demonstrations in a nation toying with the notion of becoming a republic, an idea it will probably toy with for a long time. Moreover, restaurant menus are adventurous, and wine, once considered a sissy drink, is now sold in cardboard boxes or cans for the two-fisted Australian drinker. Better indeed, superb wines are available in bottles. Exports to Europe and America have increased enormously in the past five years, and are still growing.

The new face of Australia has also been shaped by the second wave of refos. No longer are the bluff, fair men and women from the British Isles the *beau ideal,* although social prejudices erode slowly. Over a generation, the ways Australians live has been altered by immigrants from Greece, Turkey, and Italy—in fact, from the entire Mediterranean basin and Eastern Europe. Many were originally displaced persons, and others were driven out by tragedies like the abortive Hungarian Revolt of 1956. Not only the art of living, but music, painting, writing, and architecture have been transformed by the talents of immigrants since World War II.

Thirty years ago, most Sydneysiders were psychologically incapable of eating a meal that was not based solidly on meat and potatoes. They then learned about quiche, omelettes, hummus, and even salads. Today they devour sushi and squid—and a bottle shop at Newport Beach advertises SASHIMI TUNA, $18.90 A KILO (U.S.$6 a pound). Sometimes the influence works the other way: two streets away on a busy Sunday, a notice in the window of Yoko's Japanese Café read, GONE SAILING. Driving through the long ribbon of Sydney's northern suburbs to the Blue Mountains, I found the roadscape radically altered. The number of pubs had decreased markedly; French and Italian restaurants were numerous, although no more so than a decade earlier; Chinese, Vietnamese, Indonesian, Thai, and Japanese restaurants were sprouting everywhere.

Those New Australian cooks work with superb material. To my taste, the Granny Smith apples that cost $2.10 for twenty by the roadside in the Blue Mountains are the best in the world. The oysters of the Sydney area, the crustaceans called Moreton Bay bugs, the scallops, the crabs, and the Townsville lobsters may not be totally beyond challenge, but they are at least equal to the best of the United States or Europe. And there are the wines. A Cabernet Sauvignon/Shiraz blending from South Australia is not a Lafitte-Rothschild. It is spectacularly itself.

In general, I believe change for the better during the past twenty-five years has been several times greater than all change during the preceding century. The catalysts have been the new migrants, most from southern Europe and, more recently, an influx of Asians—Vietnamese refugees chief among them. The originally staid and soberly clad society has taken on Mediterranean vivacity and Oriental brilliance.

Australia almost missed that glorious transformation. Finally convinced the country had to "populate or perish," postwar governments set out to lure immigrants. Like calling to like, they first advertised in the British Isles "assisted passages" for £10 a person. When Britain did not provide enough immigrants, they went to the Nordic countries—Holland, Germany, and Scandinavia—to find congenial and preferably fair-haired new Australians. At length, they opened their gates to the southern and eastern Europeans who were to make a greater contribution precisely because they were so different.

All those New Australians were members of the white race, even if some had swarthy complexions. After all, sponsored immigration had arisen in good part from fear that a small Australian population would be swamped by its Asian neighbors. Therefore, the White Australia Policy. In the late 1940s, only a few Asians were already settled, most having arrived originally during the Gold Rush of the 1840s and 1850s. Emulating the American Exclusion Laws, which had once inflamed the Japanese, Australia committed itself to keeping out all Asians.

Said one politician definitively, "Two Wongs don't make a White."

The speaker was Arthur Caldwell, the leader of the Labor Party, not its conservative opposition. The most savagely racist remarks I have ever heard were in Sydney in 1959 from the president of the Steel Workers' Union. As it had in the United States, organized labor led the campaign to restrict immigration. Labor had most to lose: union leaders their positions; union members their leisurely ways; and Labor Party politicians their assured majorities.

In 1975 Labor Prime Minister Gough Whitlam, avowedly a great friend of Asia, echoed the same fears. Reluctantly consenting to allow Royal Australian Air Force transports to bring out refugees as Saigon was falling, he instructed Sir Nicholas Parkinson, secretary of the Department of Foreign Affairs: "Don't bring me any more DLP voters!" He meant Catholics, for the Democratic Labor Party, largely Catholic in membership, was fiercely opposed to Whitlam.

Ironically, many manufacturing jobs are now gone—*not* because of a flood of low-priced labor. Dogged by union strikes that were often political rather than economic, the industries were frittered away by shortsighted management.

Yet, as early as April 26, 1939, when Robert Menzies began his two-decade reign as prime minister, immigration policy was fixed. The conservatives of his Liberal Party and their allies, the Country Party, were not as pathologically opposed to Asian immigration as was Labor. After all, they had less to lose. But Menzies was an Empire loyalist, fervently devoted to the Throne, the British way of life, and the homogeneity of the white race. His ideal of Australia emphatically did *not* include hundreds of thousands of newcomers with dark skins and slanted eyes filling the country lanes and the city streets with their runny-nosed offspring.

I must confess to a prejudice. When I met Menzies at a garden party in Bangkok, he looked me up and down suspiciously and then demanded, "Are you a pressman?" When I nodded, he declared, "In that case, I won't shake hands." I still do not know for whose sins I was being punished.

In the 1960s attitudes toward Asians finally began to change. Australians were stung by international condemnation of their racism. They also realized that skilled and/or wealthy Asians could stimulate their economy. Restrictions on Asian immigration were, therefore, gradually relaxed. In the end, Australia took more than 130,000 refugees from Indo-China, a greater number than any other country except the United States and France. The Asians, in turn, began to change Australia—as the new Australians from Europe had before them.

Superficial change is widespread today. But not that many Asians yet live in Australia. Concentrated in four cities, they are highly visible, but they are no more than 3 percent of the population. Moreover, two linked matters should not be confused. The first is the rapid adaptation of old Australians to new ways, particularly new kinds of food and drink. The second is the extent to which increasing immigration will alter fundamental attitudes and behavior. So far, that alteration has been perceptible, but not dramatic.

Certain Australian attitudes will take a good deal of changing. Except in the smart restaurants and splendid hotels like the Sydney Regent, service is still grudging. The Australian attitude toward personal service, the fastest-growing sector of their economy, reveals a great deal. Assertive egalitarianism and ill-concealed insecurity lead to behavior summed up by the old wisecrack: "The well-balanced Australian has chips on both shoulders."

Moira and I were dramatically reminded of the attitude locally called bloody-minded or bolshy (from Bolshevik, meaning "rebellious") when we last flew from Sydney to Melbourne. We had been warned that Trans-Australia Airlines was neither particularly gracious nor outstandingly efficient. But on that Easter weekend, all Australia seemed on the move. We could not get berths on a train, but we could get seats on Trans-Australia.

Since we had left for the distant airport in midafternoon, we were ready for whatever food Trans-Australia could give us after take-off at 8:00 P.M. We settled into our seats; the aircraft took off into the blackness; and, shortly afterward, a stewardess offered: "Coffee or tea?" I asked for wine, a normal request in the new wine-loving Australia.

We sipped our wine, waiting for the meal. When I saw that all behind us were chomping away, I pushed the call bell. After waiting for five minutes, I pushed it again. In time, the senior stewardess drifted in from first class and promised to send us something to eat.

About five minutes later, our original stewardess appeared empty-handed to upbraid us: "But you didn't ask for anything." I explained that I had assumed the wine was a pre-dinner drink. Unmollified, she continued to upbraid us.

I finally said: "Let's not debate. May we please have some food?"

"It's not food. It's supper!" she retorted and darted off.

A third stewardess finally brought us small plastic trays. Our original stewardess had retired, presumably to gloat on having had the last word.

She was right. It wasn't food, not really.

The return trip by railroad proved more comfortable—and even more complex sociologically. The evening train from Melbourne to Sydney was quiet, spotless, and manned by courteous porters. Ingeniously, each single sleeping compartment had its own folding washbasin and toilet. On long hauls, there is also an individual shower. At A$120 (U.S.$84) a person, it was also more reasonable than the A$160 (U.S.$112) Trans-Australia charged for the six-hundred-mile journey. Moreover, a taxi took us directly to our own carriage by the public road that runs alongside the tracks.

There was only one snag. Since ours was an additional train put on for the holiday traffic, it carried no dining car. Going to bed hungry, we were cheered by the porter's promise that a buffet car would be open for breakfast.

After sleeping well, I shaved, dressed, and set off for the buffet car just before 9:00 A.M. No, the redheaded chief stewardess told me, I certainly could not have breakfast at the counter. In fact, I could not have anything at all to eat. Breakfast time was over.

As a concession, she would let me buy two paper cups of tea to carry away. When I pleaded for food, she replied with hauteur, "I shall explain my position first—and then you can have your say."

I was not foolish enough to remind her that she presided over a buffet car, not a debating society. Instead, I slunk away clutching my containers of tea.

The porter explained. I had appeared at a minute or two past nine, and the buffet car had been open since two that morning. Union rules require catering staff to spend no more than seven hours on duty—regardless of whether they are actually working. Having been on duty, albeit sleeping, for the statutory seven-hour shift, the staff had to close down operations.

Sipping cardboard-flavored tea, I realized that I was so cowed I had not asked the obvious question: "Whom did you serve between 2:00 A.M and 5:00 A.M?" Nor did I ask who ordered the buffet car to open at two, when no patrons were about. I asked no further questions, but was silent—as Australians are if they know what's good for them.

*   *   *

In a country still more than 50 percent unionized, the unions are still the major force they originally became by enabling exploited workers to assert their rights. Sadly, they are often also a retrogressive force. Many union leaders are reactionaries who are still fighting the ideological battles of the past. Like any group long entrenched in power, they are determined to preserve their prerogatives, regardless of the cost to their members and their country. Yet they are not immovable. The unions are slowly—glacially, it appears to exasperated sympathizers—changing their imperious ways.

Nearly disabling burdens are, however, still imposed on the economy by featherbedding, slowdowns, wildcat strikes, and, above all, by irrational, antiquated, petrified rules. Such constraints tightly hobble both the manufacturing industry and the export of the raw materials by which Australia lives. Within living memory, mills in China would import wheat from Canada because they could not depend on either the uniform quality or regular delivery of wheat grown nearby. Today Asians buy less from Australian coal because of uncertain delivery owing to strikes and slowdowns.

Reactionary unions are only one problem of what is—second, perhaps, only to Sweden—the world's most comprehensive welfare state. Having lived in those fully fledged welfare societies, Britain and Germany, I am still bemused by the scope of Australian paternalism. As in *"Crocodile" Dundee*, the typical Australian is seen as a rugged individualist, almost pathologically independent and self-reliant. In reality, he is a bit of a wimp.

Aussies have been systematically mollycoddled by their officious nanny state. Their independence is largely rhetorical, since their initiative, their ingenuity, and their enterprise are largely smothered. They are the victims of a benevolently intrusive, consciously self-serving, insidiously compassionate, and smugly all-knowing bureaucracy, which is allied with a quasi-private welfare industry.

The inside cover of the Sydney telephone directory is a catalogue of services available at the other end of a wire: BROKEN CHAIN CARE LINE (24 HRS); CHILD PROTECTION SERVICE; CRIME STOP HOT LINE 24 HOUR SERVICE; CRISIS CALL; CRISIS CENTRE; DRUG INTELLIGENCE REPORTING CENTRE—Canberra (FREE CALL); INTERPRETER SERVICE FOR MIGRANTS; LIFELINE (5 LOCATIONS); MISSION-BEAT; POISONS INFORMATION CENTRE; RAPE CRISIS CENTRE; SALVO CARE LINE; SALVO SUICIDE PREVENTION AND CRISIS CENTRE; STARTOVER; TELEFRIEND; YOUTH LINE.

Everyone needs a friend in the wilderness of a modern metropolis. Sydney is perhaps a little less desperate a place than most metropolises because of the benevolent climate, both atmospheric and economic. Anyway, that's just the beginning. The highlights of the "Help Reference Page" give the flavor.

Under the heading ADVICE AND TELEPHONE COUNSELLING, the following entries appear: ASSN. OF RELINQUISHING MOTHERS (24 HR); ASSN. OF SELF HELP ORGANISATIONS & GROUPS; GRIEF LINE; KARITANE MOTHERCRAFT (UP TO 3 YRS OF AGE, PARENT-INFANT COUNSELLING—24 HRS); LIFELINE (24 HRS); PEOPLE TO PEOPLE; PEOPLE WHO CARE (24 HRS); TELEFRIEND (24 HRS); TENANTS UNION HOTLINE.

My first reaction to that cornucopia of assistance was satisfaction. God knows, we all need all the help we can get in an automated and dehumanized world.

Afterward, I began to wonder at the profusion. Ninety-five separate entries seemed a shade excessive. Checking, I found that my own telephone directory for Slough, in England, which is not deficient in such services, has seventeen such listings.

How is it possible, I wondered, to find hundreds of qualified people, many of them presumably volunteers, to man all those posts? The community called Sydney must verge on earthly perfection if it is so replete with men and women possessed of Solomonic wisdom and blessed with Christian compassion.

Whether so endowed or not, Australia is bountifully endowed with rules and regulations. Sometimes they are gloriously self-defeating. Often they simply go too far. Only after a long struggle were the wowsers (bluenoses) defeated—and was the 6:00 P.M closing hour for pubs canceled. In the old days, fear of being deprived of beer resulted in a stampede called "the six-o'clock swill." Buxom barmaids frantically handed white-foamed schooners to drinkers six deep in front of long bars in cathedral-sized saloons with walls white-tiled like public lavatories.

I cannot argue with savage penalties for drunken driving. In Sydney, however, the police can stop any car for a random test and toss erring drivers into jail overnight. Meek acquiescence to arrest for taking a drink or two is more characteristic of Australians than stubborn independence.

In 1983 we asked a couple of dozen friends to a small cocktail party at the Sydney Regent. We remembered them as convivial, indeed bibulous, newspapermen, diplomats, and politicians. But all ordered "light ale," a virtually alcohol-free drink concocted to replace the powerful Australian beers for those in peril on the roads. No bad thing that, but how different from the stereotype of the hard-drinking Aussie.

That boozing, footloose, devil-may-care frontiersman still exists, but his numbers, already small, are dwindling rapidly. Anyway, he has not been typical since the early days. If the sky were a jot less blue or the climate a little less benign, gray conformity might cloud Australian life.

As long as Australians can sport in the wonderful playground that is the habitable rim of their vast but largely uninhabitable island, they will put up with almost anything. If their cherished picture of themselves as rugged, tanned, independent outdoorsmen and outdoorswomen is not threatened, they will tolerate severe infringements of their actual freedom.

They are not so much lazy as disinclined to make too much effort. A young Australian advertising man who spent six months working in England shook his head in astonishment as he left. "They work so hard," he said, "the English!" Noted for its tolerance and its traditions, England has lately received very few compliments on its diligence. It is in truth often censured by its fellow Europeans for its slothfulness. But he was thinking of the four-week holiday Australians get at Christmas and of hospitals' closing for all but emergency cases through January.

"Sydneysiders," it has been mischievously observed, "are so laid back, so lazy they make Southern Californians look energetic."

That slur on two great groups of human beings should not be taken *too* seriously. Yet the sloth encouraged by idyllic nature is reinforced by human actions. Eleanor Roosevelt once observed that Southern California was not a good place to bring up children. Because the environment offered few challenges, she wrote, many children would grow up too soft to meet the challenges of life elsewhere.

That observation also applies to Australia. If Australians still did not have to compete with the outside world—as they long did not—they could continue to revel in their complacent, narcissistic hedonism. Human beings are, however, not as kind as nature. External threats like Asia's rapidly growing population, Japan's illimitable ambitions, and Soviet expansion will in time force Australians to adapt or to decline further.

But not yet. A generation ago, Robert Neville wrote an article on Australia for *Life*, perceptively titled "The Theory of the Leisurely Working Class." That still holds true. The workingman who would rather be on the beach than in the money has given the world words like *sickies*, the sick leave he always takes because it is his due, even if he is not ill; and *smoko*, the obligatory break that seems to come every fifteen minutes.

On my last visit I learned two new terms: RSI and RDO. Also known as the Dread Kangaroo's Paw when it was unique to Australia, its birthplace, RSI stands for Repetitive Strain Injury. It arises from such repetitious tasks as typing or working at a supermarket checkout or on a production line in, say, a clothing factory, although that work is now done by Asian migrants. Dreaded RSI can, however, be warded off by a statutory fifteen-minute break every hour for remedial exercises. Reporters and editors on some publications have demanded the same therapeutic breaks because using a word processor also occasions RSI. But how to meet deadlines?

For those already afflicted by RSI, retraining at state expense is available. A bank teller who was found to be suffering from the syndrome has recently been retrained to be a baby-sitter. I am not making this up.

An RDO is a Rostered Day Off. Elsewhere it would be called compensatory time off, but the Australian term has a fine bureaucratic resonance. Awards for working overtime or on holidays, RDOs are normally preferred to cash—particularly since they can be stacked together almost without limit to yield months-long additional vacations.

Another right is remarkable, although also practiced in Europe. An Australian is paid an additional 17 percent of his salary when on regular vacation. After all, playing costs more than working.

Some workers can, however, be lured by overtime that can run to 350 percent of regular pay. Only in Australia have I seen on the restaurant check on a Sunday the cryptic legend HOL CHG. That stands for "holiday charge," and helps proprietors pay inflated overtime. Otherwise restaurants would have to close—even though some employees would work weekends for much less. Fixed by the unions and enforced by the official Australian Arbitration Commission, overtime is standard everywhere in the country, regardless of local conditions: three and a half times normal pay on Sundays, and two and a half times on Saturdays.

Not surprisingly, the free-lance taxi service is dominated by recently arrived New Australians. Hard times, however, alter cases. A driver from the Middle East told Moira, "Things are getting so bad even some natives are beginning to work harder. They took out big mortgages in the good times—and they'll lose their houses if they don't work."

Another immigrant's tale is illuminating. Finding a job in the post office, the newcomer saw that every group of standing immigrant workers was supervised by a native Australian seated on a chair. He resented the evident distrust. Why was an overseer required to ensure that the newcomers worked diligently? He soon realized that the native Australian was making sure the newcomers did *not* work hard. Too much diligence would spoil things for everyone.

Discussing the welfare state with its intrusive social services, its petrified union power, and its consequent languor, I have, I fear, neglected the extraordinarily attractive aspects of Australia. Since the well-balanced Australian with chips on both shoulders is quick to anger and slow to forgive, I hate to leave the impression that I can only criticize the fair country. Life could be unpleasant the next time we go back. And go back we will. Despite my carping, Australia is one of the most pleasant places on this earth.

Aside from an endearing reluctance to prostrate itself before the Golden Calf, Australia has one great fault. It is too far from everywhere except New Zealand and the South Pole, which rank about the same for spontaneous gaiety and intellectual stimulation. Coming from the U.S. or Europe, one usually arrives exhausted by the long flight—only to be totally exhausted by the compulsive hospitality.

The benign climate and the subtropical vegetation of the inhabited coastal fringe are perhaps its greatest attraction. On a mid-autumn afternoon in Sydney I realized that I was wearing the same clothing I had worn for a midsummer garden party in England. Although that may say more about English weather, Australian weather is generally close to ideal: Southern California without smog, Bali without typhoons.

New sophistication has, moreover, not destroyed the charms of a simpler society. There is very little poverty, and elaborate mechanisms are in place to alleviate suffering. There are no large pockets of urban, rural, or regional poverty such as endure in both Europe and America. And there are virtually no class divisions.

The aboriginal people, who have been crushed by the juggernaut of Western civilization, are a particular case. The aboriginal problem is almost as complex as the problem of the American Indian—and even more pitiful. No white Australian boasts of having aboriginal blood.

The appearance of complete egalitarianism is, of course, illusory. Never has there been a truly classless society, and, there may never be. Australia, nonetheless, has a good start. The divisions are drawn between the privileged and the less privileged, not between upper, middle, and lower classes. Distinction is defined by degrees of wealth rather than by tastes, manners, and bloodlines, as in Europe and even America.

Whether very wealthy or just comfortable, Australians play side-by-side on the seas that surround them: British-born Alan Bond, the billionaire super-tycoon, with his America's Cup twelve-meter sailing yachts and, say, Bruce Trevor, the fifteen-year-old son of a railway worker, with his twelve-foot dinghy. They are very differently situated, but their enthusiasm—and their optimism—are much the same. Neither feels himself better than the other, although Bond is tougher and luckier. But Bruce knows he is younger and potentially even more successful.

None of that has anything to do with class. Life in Australia is neither tense with class antagonism, as it is in Britain, nor chilled by class hauteur, as it is in France. Australians also shy away from the frenzied, envy-powered pursuit of status and gimcracks that obsesses so many elsewhere. They would rather have leisure than the aggro of work. Besides, they already enjoy a materially abundant existence sustained with minimal effort—and substantial borrowing. In 1990 the foreign-trade deficit was close to $10 billion annually, and the foreign debt was more than $100 billion, which made it among the highest in the world, absolutely as well as per head.

Australians, however, are beginning to chase the gilded rabbits of consumerism and social pretense like conditioned greyhounds. The species yuppie is breeding rapidly, chiefly in the warrens of high finance. Lack of imagination and implacable optimism fit young Australians for the financial markets of London and New York, where money is traded as a commodity. The insensitivity of those who are antipathetic to the life of the mind is perhaps the ultimate qualification for the money traders. But even those hearty, hard-drinking lads and lasses are burned out by thirty-five.

Not only the young are infected. A corporation lawyer I know bought matched MGs for his twin son and daughter on their twenty-first birthday—to go with the matched Mercedeses he and his wife drive. In Hong Kong, of course, it would have been Ferraris and Rolls-Royces, so all is not yet lost. Australian contempt for pretense, however, limits the grosser excesses. Most professionals live well, but not ostentatiously.

Few dare defy the egalitarian pressure applied by the Ocker. Assertively crude, beer-swilling, macho, and sexist, the Ocker embodies some Australian traits—and personifies one aspect of Australia. He hates pretension, as he defines it, and he derides most courtesy as snobbish and sissified. In public he belches aggressively, scratches his private parts, and makes raucous jokes—even before he gets drunk. The Ocker is the last long, loud gasp of the tradition of mateship, which values above women, even above wives, the mate with whom a man goes into the dangerous bush—and the no-nonsense manners of such rugged individualists. It does not matter that very few Australians ever go into the bush, or that even fewer are individualists, rugged or otherwise. A country that creates excellent ballet, painting, and literature is still symbolized as much by the Ocker as by the soaring white wings of the Sydney Opera House.

Ockerism is an obstacle not only to social and artistic grace, but to education. A survey in the mid-1980s found that only 36 percent of Australian students completed twelve years of schooling, against 85 percent in the U.S. Although 15 percent of Japanese of the appropriate age were attending universities and 27 percent of Americans, no more than 7 percent of Australians were. Both figures rose a little when the threshold for unemployment benefits was raised from sixteen to eighteen. But Australia is falling farther and farther behind in a knowledge-powered world.

The Australian language, which has only a tenuous connection to Cockney, has, however, benefited greatly from the curiously matter-of-fact imaginativeness of the Ocker. American English, once the richest in colorful slang, has, I believe, been surpassed by Australian. *Whingers* (pronounced "winjers"), *wowsers*, and *ratbags* are, respectively, constant complainers, puritanical killjoys, and obsessed eccentrics. A Jimmy Woodser is a solitary drunk because Jimmy Woods ran a pub to which no one came, and he drank up the stock to keep his spirits high.

Australia is itself often called Oz with affectionate self-derision, for Aussies are inveterate abbreviators. Students put their *tinnies* or *tubes* (beer) into an *Esky* (Eskimo cooler) in a *ute* (utility truck), hang a *yewie* (make a U-turn) and get away from the *uni* (university).

One of the gaudier sights of Canberra, the custom-made capital, is formally known as the United States War Memorial. But it is usually called the Bugs Bunny Memorial because the wings of the golden eagle atop a column rear up like a rabbit's ears. It commemorates, above all else, the Battle of the Coral Sea in 1942, when the U.S. Navy turned back a Japanese invasion fleet apparently bound for Australia. Yet I once found myself in the shadow of the Bugs Bunny Memorial explaining to a U.S. assistant secretary of state for East Asia and the Pacific the significance that battle holds for Australians. That conversation took place in 1968, during the Viet Nam War, when Australia was one of America's few allies. Regardless of the nature of the Viet Nam War, that participation delineated the attitude of most Australians toward the U.S.

Although a recent poll showed 95 percent of the citizens of Western Australia still welcomed the visits of American warships, most university-educated Australians believe the U.S. is a malignant force. When the USS *Missouri* came calling, press and television bombarded their audience for two weeks with advice on what to do if her nuclear weapons exploded by accident. Nonetheless, a quarter of a million Australians visited the ship.

Andrew Bleasel, an intelligent neurologist in his early thirties, believes there is virtually nothing to choose between the United States and the Soviet Union. Both superpowers are aggressive, he contends, and both are implacably determined to expand their evil influence, even at the risk of war. If anything, the U.S. is more to be blamed because it is more powerful. If the Americans only left the Russians alone, he believes, the Russians would not be aggressive. Besides, he says, "Americanization" is ruining the world, even remote Fiji.

Viet Nam catalyzed the formation of such beliefs, which are almost universally held by young educated Australians and their university teachers. It is very disturbing to find the younger Australian professors, journalists, and professionals almost unanimous in their conviction that the U.S. is the font of most of the evil in the world.

Bleasel, who has been grilling me for years, pondered after I pointed out that Viet Nam and the American role in Asia were both much more complicated and much less black-and-white than he thought.

"Maybe they are," he finally said. "I'm not convinced, but I'll think about what you said. . . . You know, it's been years since I heard another viewpoint. My friends, my teachers, and my colleagues all say exactly the same thing—and it's certainly not that international politics is complicated. To them it's all simple and clear-cut."

No more than Andrew does his brother Nick, a copywriter in his late twenties, quarrel with his contemporaries' views. He does, however, feel that instruction at Sydney University rather relentlessly pounds home one way of thinking.

"Every examination in every subject," he says, "demands the same line. Even in fine arts. Dealing with a painting or a sculpture, they'll ask, 'Relate this to the political, social, and economic conditions at the time.' Social means feminist—and you'd better not forget it."

Robert Beveridge, a China specialist at Monash University, observes: "Most of the students I meet who know about the Berlin Wall—and there aren't many—believe it was built to prevent an invasion of East Berlin by the West. . . . Isolationism is growing. Despite all the ballyhoo about Asia, interest is declining."

As Rudyard Kipling pointed out in *Kim*, it is quite a feat for an individual to hold two contradictory ideas at the same time. But not for a nation. It is unusual for a nation *not* to hold at least a half-dozen mutually contradictory ideas at any one time.

Attitudes toward that ever-central issue, the economy, are particularly rich in paradox. Although most Australians know why their recession has lingered for years, their natural inclination is to make matters worse. Their difficulties have largely been created by the reluctance of their customers abroad to buy more of their raw materials. The instinctive response has been withdrawal into further isolation—as if they could solve their problems by turning their backs.

Australians dislike taking pains. Rather than develop native industry, they have chosen to sell their abundant natural resources unprocessed. How much easier to ship out oil, coal, copper, lead, tin, zinc, iron ore, bauxite, and uranium ore than to work those raw materials. Other major exports are unprocessed meat and grain.

An Australian production engineer I met on a ship argued, as early as 1967, against the bother of adapting household appliances to Asian standards. The home market, he insisted, would always take all that could be produced. As a result of failing to adapt, Australia has lost both markets. The home market is now virtually monopolized by Asian products ranging from automobiles and dishwashers to shoes and shirts. Even the People's Republic of China, hardly an industrial powerhouse, sells knitted sweaters in Australia made from Australian raw wool. Australian industry has clearly been in decline since the 1970s.

Unperturbed by warnings that they were becoming dangerously dependent, Australians happily created a colonial economy, selling raw materials for cash to buy foreign manufactured goods. Those less abundantly endowed with natural resources, such as Singapore, Hong Kong, and Japan, might be obsessed with "adding value" by making raw materials into goods. But lucky Australians only had to scoop ore out of the ground and ship it abroad.

The vision of glorious ease amid unending abundance has been dispelled. Australians should now appreciate that, at the very least, they must work hard to sell their raw materials. Yet their response has been to withdraw further. During the last two decades, Australian economic, political, and defense activity in Asia have all actually decreased. They still talk about Austral*asia*; they still talk about being Asian geographically, even if not ethnically; and they still talk about learning Asia's languages. But talk is not reality.

Australia lies on the edge of the greatest explosion of human energy in half a century. Yet Australian investment in Asia is flagging. And much of it is bandit money—that is, bids to take over existing concerns. Australian entrepreneurs are not so much enterprising as daring. Major international financiers like Alan Bond, Robert Holmes à Court, and John Elliott are all billionaires, even if a billion isn't what it used to be. Sadly, they do not always create wealth by their activities. They acquire wealth—as Bond did with a HK$1.5 billion (U.S.$200 million) deal to acquire a new skyscraper office building in conjunction with EIE, a Japanese corporation that has also bought heavily in Australia.

Some tycoons, a shrewd Australian consultant pointed out, don't know the difference between inflation and the creation of wealth. One boasted that the shares of a major company had gone up 10 percent since he took over. He had actually done no more than sit and let rising prices take their course.

In the recent past, Australians generously shared their expertise with Asians. They contributed generously to the Colombo Plan, which gave technical knowledge to Asia, and they have educated many Asian students at Australian schools and universities. Asians can now teach them a few things. Australia graduates 46 engineers for every million of its people—about 750 a year. Japan graduates 629 for every million—

about 75,000 a year. Not remarkably, the Japanese have taken over Australian markets.

The great diplomatic influence Australia once exerted in Southeast Asia is now diminished. For the past decade, Canberra has been withdrawing its forward defense units, the warplanes and ground units that once helped guard Malaysia and Singapore. The recession from diplomatic activism is justified by Asians' wanting to make their own choices, as is the recession from military commitment. Yet many statesmen in Southeast Asia have stressed the need for a continuing Australian presence.

Soviet fishing fleets are trolling for influence as well as tuna in the Southwest Pacific. But Australia can do little about it. Australia's depreciated military capability and isolationist sentiment are graphically revealed by one major deficiency. The Royal Australian Navy, the first line of defense of the vast island, possesses not a single aircraft carrier. Quite starkly, that means Australia has *no* effective naval capability in the broad oceans that link it to its neighbors in Southeast Asia and the Southwest Pacific. Lacking air cover, Australian ships cannot venture against any enemy who can put planes into the air over the vast, open seas. The Soviet naval presence in the Pacific is growing. Australia, which cannot quite defend its own shores, certainly cannot project its power elsewhere.

The same misgivings about the exercise of Western military and economic power, prevalent elsewhere, have been compounded by Australian hedonism. The result has been to deprive Australia of both significant military power and effective economic power. A young country that should be dynamic is falling into lassitude even before attaining full vigor All that Australians want is a quiet, pleasant life. But, one wonders, will they be allowed to enjoy that life indefinitely?

Withal, the sheer ebullience of Australia compels belief in its future. Radio and television, which shape nations today, are more American than British in tone. But, above all, they are Australian. Where else would the weather map characterize different places as FINE: 20 . . . SUNNY: 21 . . . TERRIFIC: 22 . . . BEAUT: 23?

As Australia entered its third century of colonization by outsiders, originally Europeans, but now more and more Asians, it still appeared buoyant and confident. But it was not as assertively optimistic as it had been, say, two decades earlier. Australians were slowly realizing that economic growth could not be infinite—and that even limited growth required hard work. Behind the sunny façade a crisis of confidence was breaking. Independent, yet longing for friends, Australia was no longer quite so smug.

Crime was worrying men and women who glorified road agents like

Ned Kelly and admired the rogues portrayed in Cyril Pearl's wonderful book *Wild Men of Sydney*. A country entirely middle class, by its own estimation at least, had long thought criminals were swarthy men with Italian or Greek accents, nasty refos who dumped each other into Sydney Harbor wearing cement overshoes. But at the beginning of the 1990s, clean-cut Anglo-Saxon/Celtic types, women as well as men, were being arrested for drug-running and murder—not only in Australia, but in Southeast Asia, where their white skin no longer saved them from long jail terms or the mandatory death sentences that Malaysia imposes on drug traffickers.

Some crime was a by-product of prosperity. From automobiles to video recorders, more goods than ever before were available not only to purchasers, but to thieves. During the decade that began in 1980, the incidence of serious assault, rape, fraud, and robbery more than doubled, while car theft and burglary increased 60 percent.

A senior commissioner of the Australian Federal Police was murdered in Canberra at the beginning of 1989. He had been directing the investigation of two mass shootouts by narcotics traffickers in Melbourne. Organized crime was growing strong and reaching into many lives.

Previously immune upper-middle-class communities like once-secluded Greenwich Point on the North Shore felt menaced. A friend who once lived across the street from Moira, but now lives in New Jersey, reported after her first return visit in twenty years: "All the houses have metal 'Neighborhood Watch' signs on them. People are terribly afraid of burglars, apparently for good reason. Much drug-pushing and drug abuse and all sorts of murder and mayhem in the Sydney area!"

Her reaction was, I believe, a little strong. Although inured to crime in the U.S., she was shocked to discover that the tranquil Sydney she remembered no longer existed. Time had not stood still in Greenwich Point.

The external threat is also disturbing. Some believe the swarming island of Java will dump its surplus population into the great Australian emptiness, presumably at bayonet point. That fear, however, ignores two facts. First, Jakarta has difficulty in moving Javanese even to neighboring islands like Sumatra and the Celebes. Second, Australia could offer them only a dry welcome, because most of the vast interior, the outback, is arid and presently uninhabitable.

Water is the great issue of tomorrow. Nowadays, ranchers run anywhere from one to ten sheep an acre, depending on the limited supply of water. Some cattle ranches are measured in thousands of acres, but many are measured in square miles. Again the differences from well-watered to arid land are great—anywhere from one head to two acres all the way to one head to four hundred acres. New sources of water and more efficient use of existing supplies could, however, open vast areas to development. Australia is an underdeveloped and undervalued asset with enormous potential.

Clearly, the Japanese do not undervalue the great empty continent five thousand miles south of their own crowded islands. Their intense interest naturally gives Australians further cause for worry. Japanese firms have not only taken over domestic automobile manufacturing and a number of mines, as well as hotels and factories, but are moving on an imperial scale into real estate in Queensland and Northern Australia. In conjunction with entrepreneur Alan Bond, the very large but little-known Japanese investment company EIE has opened a big private university in Queensland. Golf courses and exclusive Japanese vacation communities are expanding, often over local opposition. Entrepreneurs are also planning enormous retirement communities where older Japanese can get much greater space and many more goods for their overvalued yen than they can at home. The northern and north-eastern coasts are well on the way to becoming a vast Club Med *à la Japonaise*.

Australians tell horror stories about the new Japanese invasion. A lawyer cousin of Moira divided his relations with Japanese clients during two decades into three stages: "First, they humbly inquired when they might see me and benefit from my wisdom. A few years later they would ring up and tell me when they'd come to my office to get my advice. Lately, though, they ring and order me to report to them at a specified time, once at two in the morning, so they can tell me what to do."

Looking north at more than two billion people in East Asia and another billion in the Indian subcontinent, Australians feel isolated, vulnerable, and curiously lonely. Whatever the future changes in their own racial makeup, they are today the only white country in the region except for New Zealand, whose 3.3 million are no great comfort to anyone.

New Zealand has excluded American warships carrying nuclear weapons and thus crippled ANZUS, the Australia-New Zealand–United States alliance. Labor Prime Minister Bob Hawke in Canberra has no wish to emulate his neighbor 1,500 miles away across the Tasman Strait, no matter what his left wing says. It would, incidentally, be intelligent if some American administration should someday send Australia a real ambassador instead of political cronies and contributors. The last such was Ambassador Marshall Green, from 1973 to 1975. In any event, Bob Hawke does not believe that American bases in Australia only make Australia a nuclear target. Unlike his eccentric predecessor

Gough Whitlam, he believes the alliance with the U.S. serves Australia's interests.

Australians do not generally go in for moralizing. New Zealanders do. Impelled by smug self-interest and naïve idealism, they appear to believe that they are uniquely virtuous in an immoral world. Australians are neither as complacent nor as self-righteous.

But Australia, too, is nervous about the umbrella that has sheltered it for so long: the American military presence in Asia. Although they are not the most voluble, most Australians appear to believe it is a bit early to fold that umbrella. Besides, they know that the American forces help maintain stability in the Asian and Pacific region.

Since Britain no longer plays a significant role in the Pacific, Australian relations with Britain are now largely sentimental. Australians still go to Britain to work for a time, in part because the qualifications for lawyers, doctors, accountants, and the like are similar. Many also feel more at home in Britain than they do in America. Yet, ties with Britain are fraying, and republican sentiments are not entirely confined to the left.

Britain's entry into the European Economic Community undermined the British Commonwealth and hurt Australia economically. Remembering that their fathers fought for Britain against the Nazis, some Australians flare into resentment in their first ten minutes on British soil. They are herded into a line for passport inspection that is designated "Commonwealth and Others." Germans go through the much faster line designated "UK and EEC Passports."

A mutually beneficial enlargement of relations with Asia is the obvious answer to Australia's isolation. Unfortunately, it is not a very practical answer.

"Why not Asia? What's gone so wrong?" I asked Sir Nicholas Parkinson, former ambassador to the United States and former secretary of the Department of Foreign Affairs—after he got out his tractor to pull our borrowed car out of the mud in the Blue Mountains, where he now raises walnuts. We discussed the matter for hours without arriving at an answer that satisfied him. The day before Moira and I left Australia, he called and briskly gave me his considered analysis.

"Nobody knows just where we're going now," Nick Parkinson said. "Ten or fifteen years ago, I could have answered with great confidence. We all saw an integrated defense, economic, and political role for Australia in Southeast Asia in particular—and in Asia in general. What's changed . . . and cast us adrift?

"First, regarding defense, the time has passed. We once mounted a forward defense in Southeast Asia, but our role isn't so necessary in an era of new alliances, an era when the obvious threats from China and the Soviet Union have decreased.

"Second, trade was supposed to grow. But that didn't come off. Largely because of internal changes, our economy and the economies of Southeast Asia were no longer as complementary as we'd thought . . . as they might have been. They didn't fit together as neatly. And there were internal stresses in Australia as our manufacturing wasted away. We simply stopped making aircraft and ships, for one thing. Also, the Asians began protecting their industries—shoes, textiles, and so on.

"Finally, the political and diplomatic aspect. ASEAN, the Association of Southeast Asian Nations,[1] was in part a political riposte to us. It became clear they wouldn't have us as a full member—and they felt they didn't need our guidance anymore. When Rajaratnam was foreign minister of Singapore, he told me, 'We won't touch you people because you're Europeans, not Asians.'

"Once we could have been with ASEAN, practically part of it, maybe a full member. But we couldn't finally because of culture, religion, race, even color.

"So we've receded from Asia. And it's hard to find another role."

Australians are nonplussed by the explosion of energy and talent among their Asian neighbors. As Nick Parkinson said, they don't know quite where to go. It's no good for them to repeat doggedly that they are really an Asian country. They are doubly disqualified: First, there are the obvious racial and cultural differences. Second, they have not only failed to progress like their neighbors, but their industry has actually declined.

Above all, however, I believe Australians undervalue themselves and their country. They think small, in good part because they cannot grasp the potential of their vast territory. They prefer to act small and to do—or to dare—as little as possible. They underestimate both their opportunities and their perils.

If Australians do not bestir themselves, they could face the reality of the fear that inspired the White Australia Policy; they could be swamped by Asians. Alternatively, Asian immigrants could help pull them out of the slough of stagnation. Not only tastes like food and manners could be decisively affected by the New Australians who are coming from Asia at the rate of about 55,000 a year among a total intake of about 150,000. In time, the talent and drive of those Asians could revitalize Australia. Depth in people as well as in territory is needed to deal with the strongest challenge and the gravest danger Australia has faced in two centuries.

---

[1] ASEAN, the home-grown virtual successor of the American-sponsored Southeast Asia Treaty Organization, is composed of Singapore, Malaysia, Indonesia, Thailand, Brunei, and the Philippines.

On the last day of my most recent visit, I discussed the prospects with Trevor Kennedy, chairman of the publishing group Consolidated Press. He was a little somber, not quite as ebulliently optimistic as I had known him to be over a number of years.

"We were working class," he said. "My father worked on the railways. But I was brought up to believe that everything was getting better all the time. We were always optimistic, looking forward to tomorrow . . . always a better tomorrow. It's hard for me to adjust now . . . hard to concede that the best days may be over. Yet, underneath, I still have the great Australian optimism. I *know* things will work out very well!"

Somehow, I share that visceral optimism.

13

China: The Long, Long Past That Shapes the Present—and the Future

THE OLDEST LIVING CIVILIZATION IS UNIQUE NOT ONLY IN ITS ENDURING CULTURE AND ITS LANGUAGE, THE MOST HIGHLY DEVELOPED AND MOST WIDELY USED IN THE WORLD, BUT IN ITS TENACIOUS ATTACHMENT TO ITS ANCIENT TRADITIONS, JUST OR UNJUST; ITS ENORMOUS, ALMOST OBSESSIVE, PRIDE; AND ITS PREDILECTION FOR VIOLENCE.

Mark Pratt, consul general of the United States of America in Canton,[1] often takes a hard look at the flat-roofed building opposite as he leaves his office in the red-pillared Dongfang Hotel. The four-story façade of glass panes backed by pistachio curtains bears big silver ideograms reading: CHINA EXPORT GOODS FAIR. Since June 4, 1989, Pratt has wondered bleakly just how far China will recede into the isolationism that building epitomizes before resuming her progress toward equal participation in the modern world. The semiannual trade fair in Canton was, only a decade ago, the *only* place many Chinese and foreign merchants could meet, and the Dongfang Hotel was the only place in Canton foreigners could stay. The two monumental structures are, therefore, potent symbols in a nation attuned to symbolism because direct expression of views has so often been suppressed. They do not, however, symbolize international friendship, but the reverse. The flat-roofed hall and the hotel were not built to bring Chinese and foreigners together, but to keep them as far apart as possible.

[1] Canton has for centuries been the English name for the metropolis of South China, just as Moscow is English for Moskva. Guangzhou, which sounds like *gwong-joe*, is the northern Chinese pronunciation of the Chinese name in the spelling adopted two decades ago by the Chinese authorities. Since no particular political or other significance attaches to the divergent spellings, I shall use the two forms interchangeably.

Only ninety miles from Hong Kong, Canton has, since the seventeenth century, been the chief meeting place for the people of China and the outsiders they called "Western barbarians." For most of the intervening three centuries, the Chinese authorities approached those meetings with two divergent, almost irreconcilable, purposes. The first was to promote trade, which required communication; the second was to prevent close communication. It was more important to keep outsiders out and Chinese in than to encourage trade. China wished, above all, to remain aloof, rather than to profit through the exchange of goods and ideas.

Mark Pratt's career was curtailed by the chasm that so long divided China from the world—particularly from the United States. He studied Chinese at the Foreign Service Language School in Taichung, Taiwan, and today speaks and reads the language well. He is a connoisseur of both Chinese art, especially calligraphy, and of Chinese food, which is an art in itself. After 1960, he served in Hong Kong, Taiwan, Laos, and France. Finally, in 1987, at the age of fifty-nine, he was assigned to Canton in the People's Republic.

Both the United States and China have suffered because highly qualified individuals on both sides were so long kept from direct contact with each other. Both countries are to blame. But, as George Orwell might have put it, the blame rests a little more equally on China, which was pursuing her traditional policy of excluding outsiders and isolating her people. The United States spent several decades withdrawn in horror from the wicked Communists' People's Republic of China. The U.S. then resumed its traditional policy of bounding into others' lands and lives like a friendly Great Dane in a cluttered Victorian parlor, careless of the havoc it might wreak.

In 1989, that havoc proved catastrophic, at least in the view of hard-line Communists. The orthodox had for several years been campaigning against the "moral pollution" by the "liberal bourgeois" ideas that had been admitted to China with American diplomats and American popular culture. The orthodox had campaigned in vain.

The pro-democracy movement, which was launched in 1986 by students and intellectuals, owed more to American inspiration than any other source except normal human longing for freedom. That movement demanded freedom of speech and the press; a regime more responsive to the popular will; a crackdown on universal official corruption; and effective economic management. Its symbol was a replica of the Statue of Liberty gripping her torch with both hands, like Chris Evert making a backhand pass.

On June 4, 1989, the old guard struck at the students and workers who had occupied the *Tienanmen Guangchang*, the "Square of the Gate of Heavenly Peace," at the center of Beijing, and barricaded the capital against the People's Liberation Army. The heavy-handed autocrats who ruled the Communist Party were forced to use troops to regain control of their own capital. The soldiers fired automatic weapons at the unarmed demonstrators, then crushed those they had missed under their tanks' tracks. Thus was order enforced and social discipline preserved.

The world recoiled when it saw the massacre on its television screens. But the clique of octogenarians that had usurped power was apparently unconcerned with outsiders' reactions. That clique ordered a savage new campaign of revenge and repression.

Some leaders of the pro-democracy movement escaped. Others were captured, displayed in abject humiliation on television, and then shot. Freedom was trampled underfoot, as was Western intellectual influence. Dissenters were converted by force; books were burned; liberal research institutes were gutted; universities were purged; political indoctrination was intensified; and intellectuals' cafés were padlocked. Abhorring liberty, the autocrats hunted down that evil as fervently as ever an inquisitor hunted down heresy. Although the leadership said it would retain its economic ties with the outside world, the shutters were going down all over China.

It all seemed to be happening again, as it had repeatedly happened during forty years of Communist rule—indeed, as it had happened over and over again during more than three thousand years of recorded Chinese history. Orthodox doctrine was clashing with practical idealism—and orthodoxy, which had the guns, was, for the moment, prevailing.

All countries are shaped by their history, but none quite as decisively as China. Moreover, no other country is quite so self-consciously aware of its long and glorious past.

Some feeling for the Chinese past is, therefore, essential to any understanding of present-day China. Since I can hardly attempt a full account here, I shall in this chapter discuss four aspects of the multifarious past that I believe are highly pertinent today and relate them to present events. They are China's exclusivity; the enormous influence of her unique language; the structure of Chinese society as seen particularly through the status of women; and China's pride, which is so great as to be self-deluding.

Since China is now unsettled, most of my examples derive from the time before the June 4 atrocity. This is the way it was shortly before the autocrats turned again to widescale suppression—when China appeared to be moving into the modern age.

It all seemed to be happening again: repression and exclusion. By 1955 the Communists had expelled almost all foreigners, but a few diplomats and very few journalists were permitted to reside in Peking.[2] Their activities were strictly circumscribed. They could discuss matters of substance with no non-official Chinese—and rarely with officials. However, a thin stream of foreign traders flowed through Hong Kong twice each year to the Canton Trade Fair. They were almost the only foreigners who could talk with non-official Chinese who did not always utter *only* the official line.

In Zürich the other day I talked with David Zaidner, who made his hundreds of millions trading in basic commodities, chiefly metals. He recalled that all travelers walked across the covered bridge at Lowu from British Hong Kong into the People's Republic because the Chinese authorities would permit no passenger trains to cross the frontier.

"When you carried your luggage across the bridge, you entered another world," Zaidner said. "You disappeared into China. For a week or two, you heard nothing whatsoever about the outside world. Anything could have happened to you—and no one would have known. It was eerie, stepping over the brink of civilization."

The Chinese authorities permitted some trade with the West during those years of voluntary isolation. But they exposed only a few of their people to corruption by the decadent culture of the West. They exposed rarely any of their own thoughts to the guests they thus just tolerated. That pattern of behavior was hallowed by the experience of past centuries.

The mandarins who ruled China had been particularly wary of the Western barbarians since the late sixteenth century, when the Jesuits were pushing against the gates of the great Ming Empire. Only in 1598 was Father Matteo Ricci of the Society of Jesus allowed to settle in Peking. Since the Jesuits were scientists and engineers as well as priests, they could be useful. But the mandarins saw no benefit in admitting ambassadors or merchants, who were otherwise useless.

The West kept pushing against the gates, its bronze cannon more effective than battering rams. In the seventeenth century, a few foreign merchants were permitted to trade with a few designated Chinese merchants at Canton. The foreigners were restricted to a narrow strip on the bank of the Pearl River. After the trading season, they had to return to Macao, where the Portuguese had, by an oversight, been permitted to plant a colony. No foreigner was permitted to study the Chinese language, lest he pry into sacred mysteries.

No more than the prohibition on Chinese leaving the country could

[2] My previous observations regarding Canton/Gwangzhou apply equally to Peking/Beijing. The latter spelling, which represents *no* change of the name that means "northern capital," conveys the pronunciation more closely, with *j* pronounced as in plain English *Jane*, not as in French *jour*. I shall use either as seems appropriate. Certain events, like the intrigues and amours of the Empress Dowager Tzu Hsi (or Cixi), obviously occurred in Peking, not Beijing.

those restrictions be enforced. In the nineteenth century, the poor fled South China for the opportunities of Southeast Asia and America, although their crime was punishable by death. The Western powers continued to batter at the gates of China, penetrating farther each decade. Some Westerners even learned the Chinese language.

Mark Pratt reflected on the arduous task of learning Chinese when Moira and I stayed in his apartment in the tower of the new Garden Hotel. Acquiring proficiency, we agreed, required persistence and a good memory more than intelligence.

At least the Communists had succeeded in teaching all Chinese to speak the language of the north, which Westerners call Mandarin because it was once the common tongue of the mandarinate. Just fifteen years earlier, Mandarin had been spoken little among the Cantonese, who are commercially the most progressive Chinese but culturally the most conservative. Yet in Canton today, young men and women speak Mandarin to each other, although they speak to their elders in Cantonese.

Rough Mandarin is even spoken by the older hawkers at Canton's Chingping Street Free Market, where Mark Pratt sent Moira and me to look for bargains in porcelains. We did not buy any of the Sung Dynasty (A.D. 960–1254) bowls that were extraordinary bargains at fifteen to fifty dollars, though a little rough and a little chipped. We were too depressed by the subtropical rain and the viruses we had acquired in Beijing weeks earlier. We had last seen the free market in 1983, just a few years after farmers, artisans, and collectors were permitted to sell their own goods at their own prices to any customer who came along. Before 1978, they could sell legally only to the state or through the state.

As always in China, food was still the most important commodity. Once the Chinese had to eat whatever nature offered in order to avoid starvation; today in Hong Kong and Canton, they consume rare animals to display their affluence. The flesh and skins of scaly anteaters, tigers, and eagles were on sale; domestic cats and dogs waited disconsolately in cages for the slaughter.

The Chingping Market makes London's Portobello Road appear staid and disciplined. The heavy fragrance of herbal medicines evokes tropical islands; the clutter of old teapots, enameled clocks, and statuettes recalls the bourgeois past. Shoppers flit eagerly from stall to stall, and the lucky ones discover the hidden treasure of ancient porcelain bowls. Over this triumph of free, almost anarchic, enterprise rears a black billboard exhorting in red ideograms: ABOVE ALL, PRESERVE SOCIALIST COMMERCIAL MORALITY!

Before June 4, 1989, such slogans had become hardly more than pious invocations. The remaining true believers might still hold that China was following the Marxist-Leninist road—despite landslides, fallen bridges, and dead ends. But true believers were very few in China then, and they are even fewer since the debacle.

Chingping Free Market is a block from the strip along the Pearl River where English, Dutch, French, and American merchants were confined until the mid-nineteenth century. The hawkers of Chingping Street are moved by the same acquisitive spirit as those mercantile adventurers—not by socialism, which they believe has brought deprivation and suffering to China.

At the end of the nineteenth century, there was an independent enclave nearby, on Shameen Island. It was called a concession rather than a colony, but foreigners ruled absolutely—and they could stay as long as they wished. Some foreigners had even studied Chinese, as well as China's history and culture.

They had learned that in China the name by which something is called is usually more important than its real character. Repeatedly saying that a concept is true can make it true—even call it into existence. As the film *The Last Emperor* showed, China could proclaim a republic and still maintain the boy emperor in imperial state. The Chinese excel in higher mathematics and theoretical physics, in good part, I believe, because of the nature of their language. Chinese is so concrete that it makes airy abstractions seem real and immediate.

Chinese normally creates new words for new things or ideas by combining ideograms that describe specific natural phenomena. Thus, telephone is *dienhua*, "electric words," and proletarian is *wuchan jyeji*, "the class with no property." Abstractions therefore acquire hard reality. Chairman Mao Tse-tung of the Communist Party was thus misled into believing that Karl Marx's speculations on the future of human society were concrete goals that could actually be attained.

Because of that constant reference to the past, the continuity of concepts is almost uncanny. About 500 B.C., Confucius taught that all things should be known by exact names, so that reality would accord with language. After such "rectification of terms," men would think clearly—and both public and private affairs would proceed properly. In 1942 Mao Tse-tung imposed his control on the Communist Party through a "rectification campaign" that sought to assure that all party members thought the same way, in the same terms.

Language and literature have for thousands of years been of primary importance to China's people. Today they call their standard language by many names: *guanhua*, the "officials' tongue," called Mandarin in the West; *putunghua*, the "common or ordinary tongue"; *gwoyü*, the "national language"; and *baihua*, the "white," meaning "simple," tongue.

All but the last of those terms refer to the spoken language. *Baihua* is, however, the simplified style, approximating speech, in which official documents and literature have been written since the 1920s. *Baihua* replaced the codelike official style that had required decades of intense study. Naturally, *baihua* is still written in the complex Chinese ideograms already discussed in connection with Korea and Japan.

China would not exist today as a single nation or civilization had it not been for the unifying effect of those ideograms. Without them, the diversity of dialects would have fragmented her into separate nations.

I recently saw an article that advised the first-time visitor to China to have lots of business cards printed. Explaining that China had many dialects, it then cautioned, "Be sure that your details are printed on the back of the card in *Mandarin,* not *Cantonese.*"

That is pure nonsense. It is impossible to write names and addresses in Cantonese rather than Mandarin. The ideograms are all the same, though pronounced differently in different dialects. The ideogram meaning "yellow" is pronounced *huang* in Mandarin and *wong* in Cantonese. But it is always written the same way.

The Chinese speak a number of dialects, although not as many as the West thinks. But they have only *one* written language, which every literate person understands.

Regional dialects are spoken by no more than 20 percent of the Chinese people; those clustered along the coast from Shanghai, south to Canton.

Yet, anyone speaking Mandarin is now understood anywhere. Differences in regional accent and idiom are not as great as differences in English as spoken in Bombay, Yorkshire, Atlanta, and Kuala Lumpur.

The stewardess, no more than twenty-two years old, was pretty in an apple-cheeked way. She was coughing heavily as the turboprop Antonov-24 bucked across the mountains of western China from Xi'an to Chengdu late on a stormy March afternoon.

Moira solicitously asked the obvious question in a nation of nicotine addicts: "Did you smoke too many cigarettes last night?"

The stewardess replied indignantly, "*Junggwo nuhaizi bu chou yan!*" "Chinese girls don't smoke!"

She had not hesitated to characterize an entire generation. Common standards of behavior and morals unite her hundreds of millions of sisters. She also spoke without self-consciousness of *Junggwo nuhaizi,* Chinese *girls,* not young women.

Feminists would say that usage reflects—and reinforces—the subjugation of women in China. They believe, with Confucius, that the name by which a thing is called shapes its character. And they would be right. The ancient attitude, hardly changed for millennia, holds women to be markedly inferior to men—and, therefore, destined to serve men.

The Communists have tried, albeit sporadically, to improve women's lot. In the early 1950s, shortly after the Land Reform Law, which consolidated their power, they enacted the Marriage Law. Designed to transform the legal and social position of women, it has made a change—but not enough of a change.

Chiding his countrymen for degrading and exploiting women, Mao Tse-tung once declared, "Women hold up half the sky."

That was an understatement. Chinese women hold up two-thirds of the sky. Doing a disproportionate amount of the nation's work, they maintain social stability and advance the general welfare. Now ostentatiously welcomed to some jobs formerly reserved for men, women still do all the work they traditionally did. Naturally, men do not object.

Few Chinese men help with the dishes or bathe the children. Household chores are for women, even though nowadays most wives work just as hard outside as husbands do. In the city, they earn the essential second salaries; in the country, they tend the cash crops. The Chinese man nonetheless says that a wife is supposed to help her husband in every way, while being modest and unassertive. Those are the paramount feminine virtues.

Among the oppressed the Communists promised to "liberate," women fought hard for the revolution. Yet they are today grievously underrepresented in government, from the supreme authority, the Political Bureau of the Communist party, to the lowest level, the Management Council of Marco Polo Bridge Township, outside Beijing. There has not for years been a single woman in the Politburo; there is only one woman among the nine members of the Management Council.

More than three-quarters of Chinese women work a "double day." Beside their outside jobs, they spend three and a half hours a day on housework, some assisted by the basic domestic appliances now on the market. Almost half also look after aging parents-in-law, as well, but usually not their own parents, who were the responsibility of their brothers' wives. Traditionally, a wife has left her own family to become a member of her husband's family.

The *China Women's Journal*, which naturally champions its readers, once cited with dismay a survey taken in a medium-sized city in Hunan, Chairman Mao Tse-tung's home province. Women employed by private manufacturers were working fifteen hours a day—and were beaten for their mistakes. Yet the Communists came to power—with women's fervent support—to end such capitalist exploitation.

In the deep countryside, one can still see groups of teenage farm girls driven along dirt roads like sheep. They are destined for sale to the highest bidder as concubines and maidservants—or for service in clandestine brothels. Many female infants are still left to die on hillsides. Sons are traditionally China's social security; they look after their parents in old age. Daughters are liabilities; they require dowries, and they look after their husbands' parents.

The director of the Women's Federation of Beijing pointed out in an interview with Daniel Southerland of the *Washington Post:* "The belief that women are inferior in the professions is not only established in the minds of men, but also in the minds of women. Some women feel they should sacrifice themselves [to the service of men]."

Chinese women have been admitted to universities since the 1920s. But they have a hard time finding employment and pay to match their education. Yet in some fields their right to work alongside men as equals is not questioned. Women regularly build, repair, and sweep roads; they tow laden carts and carry heavy burdens up steep hills; they pull plows and dig ditches; they chip stones, haul away refuse, and climb scaffolding carrying bricks and cement.

Such tasks, hallowed by tradition, actually weigh heavier on women's shoulders today. Deng Xiaoping, the paramount leader, has been pragmatist, happily reviving old practices that work. Many women are, therefore, relegated again to the subjection that Confucius believed was their proper state.

In traditional China, a woman was subject to her father before she married and then to her husband. As a widow, she obeyed the new head of the family, usually her own son. A divorcée lost her standing in society. If she went back to her own family, she would be treated as an underling by her sisters-in-law and would often suffer material deprivation.

For obvious reasons, women did not initiate divorce. Social pressure kept families intact. A well-to-do husband would take a second wife—as well as quasi-wives known as concubines. His pretext was often his first wife's inability to bear a male heir or additional male children. But she remained his wife, and *all* the children called her "mother." No matter how it hurt, wives would put up with other wives and with concubines, rather than become unpersons through divorce.

Moreover, Chinese puritanism still considers women unclean temptresses, since all sexual matters are shameful. In the modern metropolis of Canton, in 1987, a university senior called Mei became pregnant. A canny American woman believes Mei told the truth when she said she had not known she was pregnant—with all such ignorance implies. When her pregnancy was discovered, Mei was summarily aborted, sterilized, and expelled from the university. No one would marry her, and no one could employ her. She had lost her standing in society. She was an unperson.

In that prudish milieu, divorce is still a stigma. Canton is more tolerant because it is subject to much outside influence through neighboring Hong Kong. Yet in Canton Moira and I encountered two divorcées who were shamefaced in this new age when women's right to divorce is enshrined in the Marriage Law.

The first was a clever, humorous twenty-six-year-old whom I shall call Wang Ying, which is not her name. We had lunch with Ying and a friend who wore a UCLA sweatshirt and spoke excellent German. The friend confided that she was going to Europe to study—and would "never come back." Not quite as defiant, Ying said she was thinking seriously about leaving China if she could, perhaps for good.

Her story was simple—and typical. Born in Nanking, she had studied English at the Foreign Languages Institute in Canton and married a fellow student. Within a year they were divorced. A modern woman with a modern education, Ying, like all Chinese women, hates to discuss sexual matters. But she whispered to Moira that the marriage had never been consummated.

Her divorce was easy, but the consequences hard—as is the constant shame. Doing a dull job with an export firm, Ying would like to return to Nanking. That is impossible. Her parents say they have no room for her because her mother does not *want* her to return. Her divorce has brought shame on the entire family, although it was due to no fault of hers, but to her bridegroom's homosexuality.

Ying's disposition is sunny, but there is another complication: she is in Canton illicitly. Although employed by a state-owned trading company, she has no *hukou*, "resident's permit," for the metropolis. Quite illegally, she rents a corner of a female friend's small apartment.

She is lucky to have found a place at all. Desperately overcrowded, China is chronically short of accommodations, in part because legal rents are negligible. The authorities have tried allowing rent to rise to more realistic levels, in the hope that private entrepreneurs would create more housing. But that experiment fueled soaring inflation.

Ying hates the impermanence and the insecurity of her nomadic life. Her only possessions are her books and a huge ginger tomcat called Wu, after the hero of a fairy tale. She would like a home and a family, but she feels she will never marry.

"We're all very enlightened nowadays," she says without discernible bitterness. "But no respectable Chinese boy will marry a divorcée—even if his parents would let him. I just want to go abroad to graduate school—and, maybe, not come back."

Hu Suya, a successful career woman, is virtually Ying's opposite. She holds a key senior position in a highly successful pharmaceutical corporation. Smart, even soignée, she wears a black suit with a red silk lining, a silver brooch, and a silk blouse in an abstract white and brown pattern. Her slender legs are set off by gunmetal-gray stockings and neat high-heeled pumps. Even in this new China, one hardly expects such chic or such aplomb. Turned out like a Hong Kong career woman, self-assured, she epitomizes the new Chinese woman: an equal partner in the great enterprise of bringing the motherland into the modern world.

Yet, close up, the woolen fabric of her suit is a little shoddy, and the cut is a little clumsy. Canton today is like Hong Kong a quarter of a century ago, but its products are not as sophisticated as Hong Kong's were even then. The metropolis of South China is a little seedy and bedraggled, its newly constructed buildings already tarnished by neglect.

Walking along a walled path past a grimy swimming pool, I ask Ms. Hu when the pharmaceutical plant was built. She replies, "In 1984." Not hiding my surprise, I ask, "Then why is it so . . ."

"Dirty," she fills in. "I know."

Hu Suya smiles wryly. She shrugs, saying without words that she is helpless to affect her countrymen's lack of concern for their surroundings, much less the environment.

Hu Suya hails Moira and me as journalism colleagues. She is a correspondent for the *Journal of Chinese Medicine and Pharmacology*, concerned primarily with herbal medicine, whose roots go deep into China's long history. But, as her business card informs us, she earns her living as director of the Strategy Department of the Baiyunshan Pharmaceutical Factory. It is her responsibility to search out new finance, new markets, and new products for a company that has, in fifteen years, expanded from thirty employees to 5,500 and become China's third-largest pharmaceutical manufacturer. That rate of growth is unique, even though drugs are a prime growth industry. All Chinese believe passionately in taking medicine to get well, to keep well—and to become more virile.

Ms. Hu runs a vital department with six employees, four male and all university graduates. She earns the Y3,600 plus generous bonuses she receives each year. Some $1,000 to $1,500 does not seem much, considering her responsibilities. But it is the salary of a director of a large factory or a chief scientist in a country where most workers earn no more than eighty dollars a month.

She also enjoys certain perquisites: chauffeured automobiles, an expense account, and travel by sleeping car or airplane. Since all transportation is chronically overcrowded, high position or generous bribes are essential for getting a seat on an airplane or a berth on a train.

Ms. Hu made it on her own. Born just after the war, in the grubby commercial metropolis of Wuhan, at the center of China in Hubei Province, she won admission to Wuhan University. She graduated,

with a degree in economics, in 1967, into the chaos of the Great
Proletarian Cultural Revolution. Assigned to the foreign affairs section
of the Provincial Government, she had hardly time to find her desk and
the ladies' room before she was "sent down," that is, banished, to work
on a remote farm. She had made the grave error of openly criticizing
Chairman Mao Tse-tung's termagant fourth wife, Jiang Ching, who was
the evil genius of the Cultural Revolution.

Hu Suya refused to yield to despair. Besides, she was lucky. Others
even less independent suffered not merely banishment, but imprisonment, torture, and death. Yet she was allowed to return to Wuhan in
1971, after only four years in exile. She was assigned to the production
line of an automobile factory. But her intelligence and her determination saved her from a life of drudgery. In 1975 she was admitted to the
Institute of Traditional Chinese Medicine and Pharmacology, where
she studied for five years.

"Not enough time to qualify as an herbal doctor," she points out.
"That could take twenty years . . . or more."

Assigned to the Hubei Province Pharmaceutical Control Bureau on
graduation, she also became a correspondent for the *Journal of Chinese
Medicine and Pharmacology*. She doesn't say so, but she obviously did
not take on that additional work only because she was energetic and
curious. It gave her opportunities for further advancement. She had,
after all, not come that far by being shy or passive.

Hu Suya knocked on opportunity's door in 1986, when she came
to Canton to write an article on the Baiyunshan Pharmaceutical Factory. The founder-president hired her on the spot to head the newly
established strategy department. Her brief tenure in office, a period of
great growth for Baiyunshan, has crowned her spectacular personal
career.

Epitomizing China's new women, Hu Suya is not typical, but extraordinary. She should be vibrant, indeed triumphant.

Yet Moira and I find her restrained, her expression almost melancholy in repose. Perhaps foreigners depress her. Yet she meets many
foreigners, and received a delegation from Yugoslavia earlier the same
day.

We begin to understand her despondency when we touch on her
personal life. She smiles and looks away when I ask her age. She will
not say, although she must be in her middle forties.

When I ask if she is married, she hangs her head. I am astonished to
see that the tough, high-flying lady executive is shamefaced. I do not
press her. But after a long pause, she says, almost inaudibly, "I *was*
married. But I . . . I was divorced . . . a long time ago."

She responds eagerly when I ask about children. Her sixteen-year-old son is studying music at the Canton Fine Arts Academy. Her own taste, she adds, runs to Beethoven and Bach.

"How about Mozart?" I ask.

"Oh, Mozart's all right, but he's not as deep."

Hu Suya has recovered her aplomb. Except for the lingering sadness in her eyes, the painful matter might never have arisen.

She has allowed us to glimpse the shame and guilt that even a strong, successful modern Chinese woman still feels after a divorce a decade earlier. Hers is not simply the remorse and self-reproach any woman or any man must feel at the failure of a marriage. It is self-castigation, almost self-loathing.

Yet, because Hu Suya has prospered by her own efforts, she has not lost her place in society as a result of her divorce.

Each time I visit the new China, I am struck anew by how much it is like the old China. Social attitudes that are current not only among the farming and working masses, but also among professionals, intellectuals, and managers, do not differ markedly from the attitudes of their remote ancestors. Aside from a few who are enlightened—or, at least, Westernized—Chinese react not only to divorce, but to many other experiences much as did Chinese in the first century A.D.

The nation's moral consensus is founded on pride in being Chinese. Actually, pride is too mild, and arrogance not too strong to describe their conviction of cultural and racial superiority. The Chinese consider their country the center of the world. *Junggwo*, the "Central Country," is an old name still in daily use. *Tien Hsia*, "All That Is Under Heaven," is another traditional term.

The overwhelming pride that has made for China's survival as a nation is today the single greatest obstacle to China's modernization. If you are already superior to all others, why change? Why imperil your self-esteem by acknowledging that you need to learn from outsiders?

A few years ago, a penetrating and independent thinker discussed with alarm what he called "the center-of-the-world complex." Yen Jyaqi was until June 4, 1989, director of the Institute of Social Sciences at the Academy of Science, China's premier intellectual institution. In exile, he is now the intellectual mentor of the burgeoning resistance movement. In 1986, he presaged the present violent clash of values when he asserted that the Chinese conviction of absolute superiority was the greatest single obstacle to China's learning from the outside world. But, he pointed out, if China did *not* learn from others, she could *never* attain the industrial and agricultural modernization that remains today the expressed purpose of even the reactionary autocrats. Yet, Yen Jyaqi wrote, his compatriots still believed China was the center of the world because of her uniquely superior culture.

Supreme for millennia in East Asia, which knew little of Europe, China was greatly superior intellectually and materially to Europe in the fifteenth and sixteenth centuries. The Jesuits discovered that superiority when they gained admission to the secretive Ming Empire. China's previous superiority and her present illusions both derive from Confucianism, the state ideology that was dominant until the twentieth century. If China were not supreme, why should her neighbors have adopted her Confucian morality, literature, social system, and government?

In Taiwan, Korea, and Japan, as well as Hong Kong and Singapore, children are trained to study hard, to respect authority, and to strive for society's approbation. Such neo-Confucian behavior has promoted modernization. Those states are adept at producing and selling more goods than anyone else.

China is far from creating a self-sustaining modern economy. Her primary trouble is neither her material backwardness nor her unwieldy size. It is in her soul: the moral consensus so powerful it inhibits change and encourages complacency. China's institutions rest on foundations too massive, too fixed, and too deep for easy alteration.

Unlike the flexible Japanese, the Chinese cannot build a centralized modern state on the foundation of a quasi-medieval social order. They cannot operate an ultramodern economy alongside a quasi-feudal distribution system. The Japanese can exist happily amid fundamental contradictions, but not the Chinese.

More logical than the Japanese, the Chinese are less adaptable. More individual, they are far less disciplined. Seeking social harmony, they lack mass creative tension. Besides, the straightforward Chinese language is hostile to the tortuous evasions and deceptions of many-layered Japanese.

Chinese is rich in euphemisms: "flower house" for brothel, "plum quarter" for red-light district, and "plum disease" for syphilis; "jade stalk" for penis, and "jade terrace" for vulva. Such elaborations preserve from brusqueness and brutality a language that has been rubbed down by continuous use over four millennia.

Refined over those tens of centuries, Chinese has the simplest grammatical structure of any modern language. As in English, word order is most important, running subject-verb-object, as in *Wo kan ni:* "I see you." As in English, auxiliary verbs are extremely important, as in *Wo yao dzou:* "I will leave." But most of the grammatical infrastructure of English, which is itself much simplified, is absent from Chinese. A word never changes its form to change its meaning in Chinese as *run* does to *ran* or *have* to *has* and *had*. Nor does a word ever acquire a suffix to indicate the past or the plural, as in visit(ed) or auto(s). Simplicity is all.

Yet Chinese is neither inexpressive nor rudimentary. Quite supple, it can say anything English can and almost as cogently or subtly. Nonetheless, the stiff backbone of the Chinese language lies in the ancient ideograms.

Normally the spoken form shapes the character of a language, for writing alters in response to changes in speech. However, the reverence paid to the ideograms made written Chinese dominant. That dominance was deliberately fostered. The men in power hallowed the ideograms—and the literature written in those ideograms that was the source of their power.

In the sixth century B.C., Confucius had given China his wisdom— and had sanctified nine works of history, poetry, ritual, and administration. All wisdom, human or divine, was contained in those works. Understanding their mysteries, however, required rigorous study.

Decades of such study produced the mandarins, who ruled China for more than two thousand years under twenty-six successive dynasties. Their sacred written language was called *wenyen*, literally "civilized words," for it preserved the classical style of the books canonized by Confucius. No more than Latin in the modern West was *wenyen* used in conversation. Indeed, it made little sense when one heard it read aloud unless one already knew the passage being read. Deliberately dense and impenetrable, *wenyen* was a private language for the scholar-officials.

Upon the foundation of *wenyen*, those mandarins built the system of government, economics, etiquette, morals, ritual, and relationships that dominated China for millennia. With the emperor at its center, the ideal Confucian state sought not merely authoritarian, but totalitarian control. Most dynasties did not, however, attempt to regulate every aspect of the behavior of every subject. By and large, such control was unnecessary. Almost all Chinese were already conditioned by Confucian indoctrination to behave as required.

Dynasties might fall to rebels, to invaders, or to their own decay. But the doctrine was immortal. Conquerors, Chinese or foreign, invariably adopted Confucianism. It was the only way to rule China.

Normally, emperors ruled benignly—and distantly. The county chief, the lowest-ranking mandarin, was normally instructed to collect the taxes and to maintain public order. He was to avoid excessive levies and intrusions into daily life, lest he provoke discontent, disorder, and rebellion. The system worked very well. Even the Ming (1368–1644), the most totalitarian of all major dynasties, did not originally go much beyond exhorting its subjects to behave properly—and to pay their taxes. Yet no more than other dynasties could the Ming escape the curse that afflicted all in time.

Corruption, as I noted earlier, was the evil of the Confucian system. Most mandarins interpreted Confucius as charging them to look after the interests of their own families above all else, even the public interest. Most mandarins were, moreover, badly paid by a stingy Imperial Court. They were therefore forced to support their scores of kinfolk with the spoils of office. Since the Confucian system relied upon the virtue of men rather than the force of law, corrupt mandarins usually went unpunished by their corrupt superiors.

When the exactions of the mandarinate and the decadent Imperial Court fanned popular discontent, the Ming levied higher taxes and used greater force to make the people pay up. The court needed more and more money to maintain its extravagant state—and to pay the armies that put down the sporadic rebellions provoked by its oppressive rule. Rebellion therefore spread, and taxes became more extortionate.

Growing weaker and more corrupt, the Ming Dynasty also grew more bureaucratic. Even the mandarinate, the bureaucracy itself, was increasingly regimented. In official brothels the standard of furnishings, food, and drink, as well as the skills of the courtesans, were determined by the patron's rank in the nine grades of the mandarinate, just as the spaciousness of offices, the size of rugs, and the number of telephones are today determined by civil-service rank in Washington, London, Paris—or Beijing.

Bureaucracy has actually expanded in the interim, particularly under the People's Republic. Present-day reformers obviously face an immense task. A Communist bureaucracy divided into twenty-six grades, each with its fixed privileges, cannot permit, much less stimulate, the initiative necessary for economic development.

Dr. Sun Yat-sen's revolution of 1911 overthrew the Ching Dynasty—and with it the millennia-old Confucian state. But the Confucian mentality still dominated China, blocking political and economic progress—and Confucianism rested upon *wenyen*, the classical written language. Young idealists therefore urged reform of the written language in order to free China from intellectual and political bondage.

Political reform had already failed tragically. After the revolution of 1911, Dr. Sun Yat-sen had become president of the newly proclaimed Republic of China and had shortly thereafter resigned in the hope of reconciling contending factions. He actually made way for scores of rapacious warlords, whose armies fought to seize power—and loot the nation. Those independent generals made much of China a battlefield;

they killed hundreds of thousands, and they reduced most of the survivors to misery.

In 1916 a student of philosophy at Cornell University named Hu Shih argued that political reform was impossible until the Confucian mentality had been broken. He believed that the only hope lay in language reform: *wenyen* had to be replaced by a more easily understood style.

Returning to teach at Peking University, he found his platform in a new magazine called *The New Youth*. It was edited by Dean Chen Tu-hsiu, who advocated, as the cure for China's ills, *sai-yin-ssu*, "science," and *de-maw-keh-law-see*, "democracy." In 1917, *The New Youth* published an article by Hu Shih entitled "A Proposal for the Reform of Chinese Literature." He argued that *wenyen* should be replaced by *baihua*, a "white," that is, simple, written style based upon the spoken language of Peking. *Baihua* was to supplant *wenyen* in all official and legal documents; popular writing in that readily understandable style was to rally patriots to action.

Thus China, in the early twentieth century, began to make the transition from the classical to the spoken language that Europe had made during the Renaissance, half a millennium earlier. Learned and governmental papers, as well as fiction, essays, biography, and history, were thenceforth largely to be written in the vernacular, *baihua*, rather than the classical language, *wenyen*. In China that transition was to be not merely a reform, but a revolution.

Professor Hu Shih's proposal rallied idealistic young men and women—and university students realized that they could decisively influence the future of the nation. Students enjoyed great respect because they were learned scholars—and the Confucian system venerated learning. They deployed their enormous influence in the campaign to replace Confucian authoritarianism, which was based upon *wenyen*, with democracy, which was to be based upon *baihua*.

In Peking, on May 4, 1919, a new era began. The students who were fighting for *baihua* against *wenyen* took on a more formidable enemy. A thousand students demonstrated against the warlord government's decision to cede Chinese territory and Chinese rights to Japan. Meeting violence with violence when the police tried to disperse them, they set fire to the residence of the minister of communications and beat up the Chinese minister to Japan. Inspired by the Russian Revolution of 1917, the May Fourth Movement was to become a nationwide left-wing crusade for not only a new literature, but a new China.

Dean Chen Tu-hsiu and Professor Hu Shih were among those arrested by the warlord president's police for instigating that violence. Years later, Dr. Hu Shih told me that neither Chen Tu-hsiu nor he had been anywhere near the demonstration they were credited with inspiring and leading.

After May 4, 1919, such distinctions hardly mattered. The intelligentsia had thrown its great moral power into the struggle to remake China. The power of the student demonstrations on political developments was to be demonstrated repeatedly over the decades.

Professor Hu Shih was for a time to become China's most distinguished philosopher and for a time her ambassador to the United States. Dean Chen Tu-hsiu was, in 1921, to become the founding secretary general of the Chinese Communist party, whose membership was all young intellectuals. The Communist party was, in 1949, to take power and proclaim the People's Republic of China.

14

China: Everlasting Chaos

POWER GROWS OUT OF THE BARREL OF THE GUN!

MAO TSE-TUNG

VAST BLOODLETTINGS BY CIVIL WAR AND INVASION IN THE FIRST HALF OF THE TWENTIETH CENTURY WERE FOLLOWED IN THE SECOND HALF BY THE CATACLYSMIC UPHEAVALS, THE DEATH OF TENS OF MILLIONS, AND THE TOTAL DISRUPTION WROUGHT UPON INDIVIDUAL LIVES BY CHAIRMAN MAO TSE-TUNG. KILLING HAS INVARIABLY BEEN THE CHINESE COMMUNISTS' LAST RESORT——AND OFTEN THEIR FIRST. THE MASSACRE IN TIENANMEN SQUARE ON JUNE 4, 1989, WAS UNIQUE ONLY IN BEING MOUNTED BEFORE WITNESSES FROM ALL OVER THE WORLD——AND THEIR CAMERAS.

Civil violence has been endemic in China for millennia, largely because the Confucian system did not provide effectively for the orderly transfer of power. An emperor was succeeded not by his eldest son, but by his strongest son, and decadent dynasties were displaced by force. Knowing the horrors of civil strife so well, the Chinese people fear it above all else.

"At least the country is at peace," the bald man said slowly. "There is no turmoil."

He reiterated in the furry accent of Beijing, "*Junggwo bu luan!*" "China is not in turmoil!"

The word *luan*, "turmoil," was the key to that assessment of the People's Republic of China on the eve of the seventh session of the National People's Congress, in the spring of 1988.[1] *Luan* recalls the primeval chaos that existed before humanity organized to restrain its destructive passions. *Luan* also recalls the hundreds of millions of

[1] The National People's Congress, China's nominal legislature, had previously met just six times—since 1949. Intended to lend credence and a gloss of popular support to the rule of the Communist party, the NPC at its seventh session became a more open forum. The party's decisions were, by and large, enacted as drafted, but some were questioned, and a few were actually altered—slightly. The eighth session of the NPC in the spring of 1989 was, however, to be stagnant, indeed somewhat retrogressive.

Chinese who have died during recurrent periods of near anarchy over some four millennia. The last outbreak of mass violence ended only a decade ago.

The first person with whom we talked after landing in Beijing was a street hawker. But call him Everyman. He spoke for more than 1.1 billion compatriots when he rejoiced: *"May yo luan!"* "There is no turmoil!"

"We can now discuss *almost* everything," a middle-aged woman told us shortly afterward. "Everything except the senior leaders, the fundamental merits of socialism, the party's paramount role in society, and . . . and . . . certain other things."

Call her Everywoman. A distinguished liberal philosopher and author, she, too, spoke for all the common people.

After a reflective pause, she added, "Really, though, certain things should *not* be discussed—or society will be thrown into disorder."

Luan, "disorder," again. The hawker and the philosopher used the same word, which means disorder, turmoil, anarchy, even chaos. *Luan* cannot be translated by a single word; it is too heavily laden with sorrow—and with terror.

After the aged autocrats massacred the students on June 4, 1989, they tried to justify their crime by arousing the people's terror of *luan.* Only prompt and severe action, the party's leaders declared, had checked *fan'goming dungluan,* "counter-revolutionary upheavals," and prevented *baoluan,* "utter turmoil."

The people did not believe that the pro-democracy movement was a vast plot to overthrow the government by violence, although they prudently kept their doubts to themselves. They were horrified by the mass atrocity, but they were not surprised. They had learned never to rely on their rulers' word.

Distrust of authority is in particular the legacy of the terrible middle decades of the People's Republic. From 1958 to 1978, first the Great Leap Forward and afterward the Great Proletarian Revolution struck China like tidal waves. The Chinese people have often seen policy alter radically, leaving broken lives, shattered families, and corpses in its twisting wake. Their universal distrust is today the greatest obstacle to progress. It leads to evasion of responsibility—and fosters inaction to avoid punishment for mistakes.

"The Great Helmsman," Chairman Mao Tse-tung of the Communist Party of China, created the catastrophes that alienated the people from the Communist Party and the regime. Seeking to create an earthly paradise, he cast China into anarchy—*luan.*

The disasters Mao made have been denounced by the Communist Party he dominated for forty years. Paramount Leader Deng

Xiaoping[2] first acknowledged that even Chairman Mao had "made mistakes." Then the extraordinarily precise formula: Chairman Mao had been right 70 percent of the time and wrong 30 percent of the time. Later, the Secretary General of the Communist Party Zhao Ziyang told the journalist Harrison Salisbury that Mao Tse-tung had lost contact with reality in his later years and had edged China close to destruction. Only by systematically lying to the chairman, Zhao said, had conscientious officials ameliorated the havoc wrought by Mao, who, "until his last breath . . . was convinced that his view . . . was correct."

The Tai Ping Rebellion during the middle years of the nineteenth century cost forty million lives, almost overthrew the Ching Dynasty, and established on earth the kingdom of its derivatively Christian God. Mao Tse-tung's determination to create the paradise of perfect communism envisioned by his prophet, Karl Marx, may have killed even more Chinese. No one knows how many lives or how much productive wealth were destroyed when he ordered the old society razed so that a perfect new society could be built upon its ruins. Yet Mao Tse-tung was not unique, but the spiritual descendant of other Chinese zealots and tyrants.

The unbroken sweep of the history of the Chinese people from the remotest past, which is their pride and strength, also makes them emotionally vulnerable. They may have suffered no more than other peoples, but they are more aware of past suffering because it is better recorded. The Chinese may not have invented history, but they virtually invented historians. All the horrors, as well as the glories of the past are always in their thoughts.

Guanxian is half a day's drive from Chengdu, the ancient city where the factory that formerly produced parts for MiG fighters is now turning out twin-tub washing machines. The great water-control works built of stone, gravel, and straw matting by the Kingdom of Shu in about 250 B.C. are still operating. For more than 2,200 years those barrages and canals have irrigated the bountiful crops of Sichuan, China's most populous province. Pilgrims come to Guanxian to reaffirm the mystical continuity of their own lives with the ancient past of their race.

A thousand miles to the east at Wuhan stands the many-arched bridge flung across the Yangtze River in the 1960s. In its shadow stands a temple with flaring black-tiled roofs supported by faded vermilion pillars. That shrine is dedicated to the Great Yü, who, more than four

---

[2] So called for want of a better term, he dominated policy from 1980 to 1989. Although he never took a governmental title higher than vice-premier, he always held the chair of the Communist Party's Military Affairs Commission in November 1989.

thousand years ago, built barrages, dams, and canals to harness the primeval floods for an agricultural nation.

The Great Yü was once considered a myth like the Jade Emperor and his host of celestial bureaucrats, who rule the Western Heaven. But recent excavations have yielded archeological evidence that the apparent myths of China's prehistory are based on reality. Scholars no longer dismiss as legend the tale of the god-emperor, China's Noah, who did not ride the flood, but tamed it.

Legend and reality are inextricably intermixed in Shaanxi Province, whose capital, Xi'an, lies 375 miles northeast of Chengdu and 375 miles northwest of Wuhan. The equilateral triangle formed by lines connecting those three ancient cities encloses the heartland of immemorial China—and Xi'an is, quite properly, at its apex.

The yellow loess soil of Shaanxi, which means "west of the passes," was the seedbed of the Chinese race and culture. The passes led to the coast, for China began on an inland plateau that was tight against the northern steppes where lived the nomads who preyed on the settled realm. When Moira and I last visited Xi'an, the raw landscape of early spring strengthened our feeling that we stood on the edge of civilization. A short distance to the north, the Great Wall of China marks the line between the sown and the wild.

Xi'an means "western peace." That is a prayer, not a description. During three millennia of recorded history, Xi'an has rarely known peace. But it has known glory. Nearby stood the capital of the feudal state of Chin, whose king, in the third century B.C., brought six rival kingdoms under his sway and made himself the first emperor of a unified China.

Xi'an was at intervals thereafter the capital of eleven dynasties over 1,100 years, half the span of Imperial China. Near the present city lay the capital of the latter part of the Han Dynasty (207 B.C.–A.D. 221), which institutionalized Confucianism and created the bureaucratic Confucian state. Where Xi'an now stands once stood Changan, which means "prolonged peace." Changan was the capital of the splendid Tang Dynasty (A.D. 619–906), which nurtured China's most vigorous and subtle poetry, sculpture, and painting. Despite the clangor and the debris of new tourist hotels under construction, in Xi'an the past is everywhere a vital presence that awes and inspires.

The spirit of one great and ruthless man dominates the history-drenched city. The First Emperor could not have known that his dynasty would collapse a few years after his death, nor that the unified state he had made would endure for more than two millennia. He was, however, possessed by a passion for immortality.

When his alchemists failed to find the elixir of eternal life, he resolved to perpetuate his fame by structures that could never perish. He built a mortuary city so immense and so complex that only the pyramids of ancient Egypt rival its grandeur. But no single pyramid-tomb of any single pharaoh is the equal of the metropolis of death the First Emperor built as his personal monument.

Within its double city walls, a replica of the First Emperor's actual capital, Xianyang, covers twenty-two square miles, with his tomb at its center. His immense monument extends beyond those walls to sites that symbolize imperial parks, vast imperial stables, and the imperial dungeons with their instruments of torture still intact.

Not symbolic are the tombs of lesser members of the imperial clan. Harshly real even after twenty-two centuries are the mass graves filled with the bones of the tens of thousands of conscripts, convicts, and prisoners of war who built the mortuary city and were slaughtered so that they could not reveal the city's secret treasures.

The Emperor's tomb, which lies under a man-made hill, has not yet been laid open.

The half-paved path that leads up to that hill-tomb is lined by stalls selling furs, wooden toys, plastic replicas of weapons, and patchwork garments in the bold primary colors traditional in Shaanxi Province. We bought an impromptu mobile made of felt with cotton stuffing: a kelly-green cat with chrome yellow eyes and an orange-tufted tail dangling a scarlet crab and a cerise fish.

A mile away, a big country fair swirled around the corrugated-aluminum roof of a building that covers the area of three football fields. Greatly outnumbering foreigners, Chinese tourists posed for each other's chrome-striped 35-millimeter cameras, which looked clumsy and old-fashioned beside the foreigners' plastic self-focusing and self-setting marvels. Hawkers cried the virtues of their dates, walnuts, pomegranates, pears, and apples. Others touted embroideries, dolls, paintings, and clay statuettes.

I heard the accent of every region of China when the holidaymakers bargained for aromatic herbal medicines, crude fur garments, whirling paper toys, and old silk coats. Making the pilgrimage of a lifetime, the Chinese were alternately joking and reverent. The foreigners were grimly pursuing culture. All flowed into the fifty-foot entrance of the vast silver-roofed building beneath a sign displaying the curled, archaic ideograms written by a field marshal of the People's Liberation Army: THE HORSES AND SOLDIERS OF THE FIRST EMPEROR OF THE HOUSE OF CHIN.

Even the voluble Chinese fell silent as they entered the great hall. Craning over the heads of chattering Japanese, Norwegians, Germans, and Canadians, I felt as I had years earlier when Moira and I stood in the moonlight and looked for the first time on the Taj Mahal.

I could reach out and touch the past. Through the long, twisting corridors of the centuries, I could hear the voices of the remote age: the commands, the grumbling, the moans of pain, and the shouts of triumph. The ranks of life-sized clay figures imperturbably returned the stares of the crowd across the chasm of twenty-two centuries.

Thousands of soldiers stood firm with their officers, their horses, and their chariots, as they had in the final decades of the third century B.C., when their formation was called to attention. Their clothing and armor were alike, but their faces were all different. Every clay soldier in the bodyguard of the Father of China was unmistakably an individual whose face had been modeled from life.

From life, not death. Unlike earlier Chinese monarchs, the First Emperor was not attended in his splendid tomb by an entourage of corpses. His reign had, however, been marked by daring and ruthlessness, not by mercy and restraint. He did not destroy his enemies, establish his absolute rule, drive back the northern barbarians, and lay the foundations of the enduring empire by restraint and persuasion. He did so by violence, by logic, and by lavish gifts.

He was the first Chinese monarch to base his government on a systematic doctrine. In his day, two chief schools of political science contended: the Confucianists, who believed in rule by virtuous men, and the Legalists, who believed that fixed laws must rule.

Rewards and punishments sustained the state, the Legalists taught, not the Confucianists' ethical principles. Generous rewards encouraged nobles and commoners alike to obedience. But severe penalties were meted out for every transgression, even for passivity. Hundreds of Confucian scholars were buried alive, and their sacred books were burned. Tens of thousands were imprisoned, maimed, or executed. Hundreds of thousands died building the Great Wall, which linked the walls that lesser rulers had already built against the marauding nomads of the steppes.

All men and women suffered to ensure one man's absolute rule. The ideal state was totalitarian. All matters were decided by the sovereign, and all subjects obeyed in fear.

During the succeeding two millennia dynasties rose and fell. Confucianism succeeded legalism as the state ideology under the Han Dynasty; barbarians invaded, prevailed, and receded. But the basic pattern remained unaltered: exploitation and slaughter.

So, at least, believed the young intellectuals who rode the crest of the May Fourth Movement, which swept over all China in the early 1920s. The Confucian state had actually evolved—politically, culturally, and economically. But that reality did not intrude upon the simplistic view of history held by the young zealots who founded the Communist Party of China in July 1921.

A half-educated man of twenty-six was among those who dedicated themselves to the Communist revolution. His name was Mao Tse-tung.

His passion was to end forever the evils that endured: the cruelty, exploitation, and slaughter that had stained the annals of the imperial dynasties.

Mao Tse-tung was, in the end, to embrace all that he had loathed in the beginning. The romantic revolutionary was to use totalitarian methods as severe as the First Emperor's. He was to exalt the First Emperor and the Legalists in his own campaigns against Confucianism. Like the First Emperor, he was to seek to destroy traditional values, customs, literature, even traditional buildings, paintings, and sculptures—the moral bases and the chief artifacts of Chinese civilization.

Mao Tse-tung boasted that he drew back from no deception and spared no violence necessary to sustain his power. The First Emperor had killed hosts of aliens, both barbarian invaders and the subjects of rival monarchs. Equipped with machine guns rather than crossbows, Mao was to kill many more, mostly his own countrymen and countrywomen, and their children.

Not a student, but a library assistant at Peking University on May 4, 1919, Mao Tse-tung was a junior delegate to the inaugural congress of the Communist Party in Shanghai in July 1921. The secretary general was Dean Chen Tu-hsiu of Peking University, the editor of the magazine *New Youth*, which had fired the first shots of the literary revolution that became a political revolution.

The sons of the rich, who were the founders of the Communist movement, did not like Mao. Although his father was a prosperous farmer and a minor landlord, his country-bumpkin manners irritated his comrades. He was pushy, and he knew nothing about Marxism. Neither, in truth, did they. Yet he talked as if he knew everything about China's past—and possessed a sure cure for all of her ills. Worse, he talked incessantly.

The Communist Party was to endure many setbacks, some almost fatal, before Mao Tse-tung seized control and led it to victory. The three decades from 1921 to 1949 were spent in the wilderness, politically and literally.

Obeying the Soviet Union's orders, the Chinese Communists had joined with the Nationalist Party led by Generalissimo Chiang Kai-shek. But the Communists broke away in 1927. The Nationalists took power in 1928, and Chiang Kai-shek mounted massive "extermination campaigns" against the scattered rural strongholds held by Communist troops. He failed to destroy the guerrilla army, but he forced it to flee from its vulnerable bases in eastern China. At the end of that Long March in 1935, Mao Tse-tung established a firm base at Yenan, which means "extended peace," not far from Xi'an, "western peace," in remote Shaanxi.

While Nationalists and Communists fought, Japan fell under the control of aggressive officers of the Imperial Army. Those militarists set out to conquer Asia. Their first objective was China, the vast neighbor the Japanese revered as the source of culture and despised for its backwardness.

The campaign against China began in 1931 in Manchuria, which lay outside the Great Wall. In 1937 Japan struck at Peking, where resistance collapsed, and at Shanghai, where the Nationalists fought bravely. Generalissimo Chiang Kai-shek could no longer withdraw prudently before the might of the Japanese. He had to fight or lose power—and, probably, China as well.

The Japanese were, however, decisively superior in the number and the quality of their warplanes, tanks, artillery, and even small arms. Avoiding set-piece battles after Shanghai, the Generalissimo withdrew into the primitive interior, where, he hoped, the invaders' regiments would bog down. At the end of 1937, he moved his capital from Nanking westward to Wuhan. Pausing briefly, he journeyed farther west to Chungking, on the headwaters of the Yangtze River, which was to be the wartime capital from 1938 to 1945.

Chiang Kai-shek was forced to ally himself with Mao Tse-tung against the Japanese. Since they had a multitude of reasons to distrust each other, they united very warily to fight the Japanese. And they continued to fight each other as much as the invaders.

In 1945 the Chinese resumed total civil war. World War II had been to them no more than a sideshow once American involvement ensured Japan's defeat. Their common pretense of all-out war against the Japanese had, however, given both Nationalists and Communists time to build up their armies for the real shootout against each other.

After four years of battle, subversion, and propaganda, the Communists won. They were fervently supported by the all-important intellectuals, ardent young men and women who were very much like the Communist leaders thirty years earlier. University students had, since 1924, mounted demonstrations in support of the left; from 1945 to 1949, those demonstrations were crucial in turning public opinion in China and abroad against the Nationalists. The People's Liberation Army entered Peking in January 1949, victorious over Nationalist disunity, inefficiency, and corruption.

On October 1, 1949, Mao Tse-tung reviewed his victorious troops from a captured American jeep. He grasped its high handrail, as the wheels jolted over the potholes of *Tienanmen Guangchang*, the Square of the Gate of Heavenly Peace. The chairman then mounted the balcony of the massive gate, which is actually a five-story fortress guarding the Imperial City of the Ming and Ching dynasties, and looked south on his subjects as had the emperors.

On October 1, 1949, Mao Tse-tung proclaimed the establishment of the People's Republic of China. The age-old quest for social justice had at last ended in triumph, as had his personal mission. No longer would the Chinese people be brutalized, exploited, and butchered by a cruel ruling class.

On October 1, 1949, his voice shrill in triumph, Mao Tse-tung told the ecstatically cheering throng: "Today, the Chinese people stand erect!"

The killing started again in 1950 with the Land Reform Movement. It was organized, purposeful, and effective. Millions had died in the struggle for China—in battle, in purges, or because they got in the way. Both sides had ritually slain the other's civilian adherents, real or presumed. The Nationalists had generally shot their victims. Grudging the bullets, the Communists had preferred *huomai*, "live burial." Only their heads protruding from the ground, landlords, rich peasants, and counter-revolutionaries had died very slowly while their families looked on.

Those massacres, which aimed to terrorize the populace, were tactical. The slaughter that accompanied land reform was strategic. Its purpose was to change China fundamentally, by destroying the men and women who were the foundation of the old society. The Communists then planned to build a new society under their own absolute rule. No one knows exactly how many died. Landlords and rich peasants, Peking declared, made up 10 percent of the rural population, which was about 300 million, and 10 percent were executed. Deaths attributable to land reform thus total at least three million. But that again is probably low.

Landlords and rich peasants were condemned in public trials, when hundreds, under the direction of Communist cadres, screamed the obligatory verdicts. By forcing the "rural masses" to act in ways that many among them felt was wrong, the Communists bound the farmers to themselves by the ties of common guilt. The land was then distributed to those who tilled it.

Those new owners were left in possession as long as the Communists' attention was engaged elsewhere. In 1958 they were to be deprived not only of land, but of their personal belongings, their homes, and their families.

That change, too, was violent and bloody. Mao Tse-tung was accustomed to controlling the Communist Party through periodic upheavals called campaigns. He believed that orderly government through a regular administrative structure bred complacency and sloth. He preferred guerrilla government: surprise attacks to keep both cadres and the masses from digging themselves into the comfort that led to corruption.

Mao Tse-tung believed in violence as some believe in compassion. Temperamentally incapable of presiding over a routine, peaceful administration, he periodically took up a nation of more than half a billion by the scruff of its neck and shook it as a terrier shakes a rat.

After the controlled disorder of land reform, the cities were given similar treatment. Having purified the countryside, Mao Tse-tung strove to purge the evil and corruption in the Communist party and private business. The *Sanfan* and *Wufan* campaigns rose in 1951 and 1952.

The *Sanfan Yundung*, literally "Three Antis Campaign," attacked "three evil practices" that had sprung up among Communist cadres seduced by the "easy life" of conquerors: waste, corruption, and bureaucracy. Among those who fell were two major figures who had challenged Mao's absolutist rule: the rulers of China's two heavy industrial complexes, Manchuria and Shanghai. The lower ranks of the party were also purged, and Mao's control appeared beyond challenge.

Inherently corrupt, private entrepreneurs had corrupted the good Communists with bribes. The *Wufan Yundung*, or "Five Antis Campaign," was to stamp out "five evil practices" prevalent among businessmen, such as bribery, stealing state property, and evading taxes. Everyone who ran a business of any kind—from rice merchants to bankers, from ship owners to factory managers—was humiliated by public interrogation. Not only capitalists got that treatment. So did their "lackeys," which meant any loyal employee. Mao Tse-tung had two years earlier promised that private business would not be touched.

Some "corrupt capitalist elements" were hectored to death, and others committed suicide. Probably no more than a few thousand died. Mao did not necessarily want to kill the capitalists, as he had the landlords. He only wanted to destroy private enterprise and the power of the commercial, professional, financial, and manufacturing middle class. Then he would truly be unchallengeable.

A brief respite followed. Mao Tse-tung was restrained by practical men like Premier Chou En-lai and Vice-Premier Deng Xiaoping, both moderate, practical men. United for the first time in a century under a single government, China was not *luan*. Granted peace, she moved forward. Farmers working their own land brought in bigger crops. Major projects, like railways, highways, and dams, begun by the Nationalists, were rapidly completed. No longer impoverished by war, almost all Chinese were better fed and better clothed.

The mid-1950s are remembered as a halcyon time. In Beijing, Canton, Chengdu, and Wuhan, I heard essentially the same observation from academics, businessmen, and engineers: "We were at our most efficient from 1953 to 1957. And everybody's spirit was high."

*   *   *

What happened in 1957? What ended that period of relative content-
ment, unique during the lifetime of Chairman Mao? Overconfidence
happened, disastrous overconfidence followed by severe retribution.

Chairman Mao's advisers, Premier Chou En-lai chief among them,
feared that continuing repression would stifle the initiative essential for
material progress. Even dictatorships must allow men and women to
talk with some freedom if they are to move forward economically.
Knowing that his people loved him and his policies, Chairman Mao
decreed that the Chinese people might finally say exactly what they
thought. He commanded, "Let a hundred flowers bloom! Let all schools
of thought contend!"

Hundreds, indeed thousands, responded vehemently. Managers
and teachers, apprentices and students, writers, technicians, and even
non-party cabinet ministers spoke aloud of their dissatisfaction—and
the press reported their statements. All opinions were remarkably
alike, for Mao Tse-tung had made almost all Chinese think the same
way.

But they were not thinking or saying what he expected. Instead of
praising, hundreds attacked the Communists for their unrealistic economic policies; for suppressing the masses; and for unthinking adulation
of the Soviet Union.

"Pork is unavailable," a courageous student declared, "and the price
of vegetables has increased 600 percent in the last year. How can anyone
say living standards have improved? . . . In some respects the situation
is worse than it was under the Nationalists. . . . To say the Communist
Party has divorced itself from the masses is only half true. The masses
have divorced themselves from the Party."

Infuriated, Chairman Mao returned to the policies he liked best:
dictatorial repression enforced by the periodic shock treatment of a
mass movement. He proclaimed the Anti-Rightist Campaign to suppress his many critics, much as Deng Xiaoping was, three decades later,
to shoot his critics and suppress their ideas.

Even Premier Chou En-lai was caught on the wrong foot. Heralding
further relaxation one day, he had to retract the next. The intellectuals had spoken out because they believed their words would count.
None anticipated brutal reprisals, not even those who said they
were ready to suffer for their beliefs. They were courageous, but not
suicidal.

The Anti-Rightist Campaign shattered such credulity and induced
sour skepticism. The jackals of the Party's Propaganda Department,
which ruled the press and the radio, howled when Chairman Mao
roared. All intellectuals were denounced, and large numbers were
fired, deprived of civil rights, or imprisoned.

The Chairman was hailed as infallible, as a demigod who was always right. His personality cult outdid Joseph Stalin's, and the Thought of Mao Tse-tung was exalted as the greatest wisdom ever known.

Mao Tse-tung next declared that to be expert in a craft, a profession, or a science was virtually valueless. Technical expertise was useless without devotion to the Thought of Mao Tse-tung. It was far more important to be red than to be expert. Armed with the Thought of Mao Tse-tung, ordinary men and women could accomplish miracles impossible for experts who did not believe.

Know-nothingism was thus enshrined as China's guiding intellectual principle. Stalin had hailed biologists who believed that one could lop the top off a plant and expect its seeds to produce lopped-top plants. Mao Tse-tung hailed biologists who advised that swallowing tadpoles was an infallible means of birth control.

The Anti-Rightist Campaign was the first great watershed of the People's Republic of China. Crossing that divide shattered faith in the wisdom and the goodwill of the Communist Party—and cracked the image of a benevolent Chairman Mao.

Like the myth of King Arthur, the myth of Mao Tse-tung has generated a substantial industry. Diplomats, journalists, and scholars made their reputations by public intimacy with the chairman, if only for five minutes. So much personal prestige was invested in his profound theories there could be no suspicion that the red emperor might have no ideological clothes on.

Yet something was seriously wrong. What was wrong was megalomania, aggravated by Parkinson's disease. The enormity of Mao's delusions was revealed in 1958 when his ideological journal *Red Flag* declared, "Men and women in their sixties and seventies will live to see the coming of true communism."

By Karl Marx's definition, true communism is the paradise that will appear on this earth when private property no longer exists and all things are owned in common by all. No man will then argue or fight with another, nor will any woman. Since all human conflict, including war, arises from the exploitation inherent in private property, all conflict will cease with the end of exploitation by the abolition of private property.

Karl Marx had predicted that true communism would arrive spontaneously only *after* socialism had created material abundance. But Chairman Mao believed he could create that Utopia by decree. He decided to make men and women perfect by depriving them of the personal possessions and the family ties that made them imperfect— that is, envious, quarrelsome, and lazy. Get rid of all private property, and perfect communism would automatically appear.

The Great People's Communes were created throughout the countryside during the three months from August through October 1958.

When the rapid metamorphosis to "an entirely new society" was complete, hundreds of millions of peasants were to have entered an epoch of common ownership of everything except their clothing, the notebooks into which they copied political maxims, and, for a lucky few, their toothbrushes.

Organized like military units "to live collective lives," they were to possess neither garden plots nor domestic animals, neither houses nor cooking pots, not even their own hearth fires. Drawing laundered clothing from communal supply depots, eating in communal mess halls, bathing in gigantic bathhouses, and sleeping in gender-segregated dormitories, they were to become perfect "producing units."

After the unavoidably personal acts of conception and birth, parents were to be allowed neither responsibility nor control over their children, who would be brought up by the commune. Both parents and children were to slough off the bonds of "narrow, selfish family love" and direct all their love to the Motherland, the Communist Party, and Chairman Mao Tse-tung.

No Chinese was to sit in corrupting idleness for an instant. Grandmothers were to weave baskets and tie brooms in Halls of Happiness for the Aged, while mothers and daughters worked in the fields or in communal factories. Perhaps one woman in five was to occupy herself with domestic tasks, caring for children, mending clothing, sweeping floors, and preparing food for all. Those were still female tasks. With the disappearance of family ties, other distinctions between the sexes were to melt in the crucible of perfect equality.

The physical world, too, was to be altered radically by human will. By a Great Leap Forward, China was to overtake Britain's industrial production in ten years and America's in twenty. Tens of millions of unskilled workers were to make steel in miniature blast furnaces, and agricultural production was to double or triple through new techniques: deep plowing, with explosives if necessary; close planting, so that two or three stalks of wheat grew where only one had grown before; and bountiful irrigation with new dams built by a hundred million hands.

Old farmers warned that those "entirely new" methods would produce not more crops, but fewer. They warned that the result would be eroded and wasted fields—and that millions would die of famine. But the Chairman's "brilliant new conception" prevailed.

Many did die—millions. The actual figure may be hidden in the archives; but that is unlikely. It was all too chaotic for counting. Probably no one knows just how many Chinese were sacrificed to Mao Tse-tung's messianic frenzy. We do know that China was scourged by famine. As the old farmers had warned, the soil was leached and eroded by deep plowing, close planting, and amateur irrigation. Moreover, the crops failed and China's birthrate dropped steeply when severely malnourished women either stopped menstruating or aborted.

The leap into nowhere also led to a public quarrel with the Soviet Union, China's only ally in 1958. Nikita Khrushchev, first secretary of the Soviet Communist Party, said Mao's promise to attain perfect communism in a historical instant was an "opium dream." Mao retorted that Khrushchev's was "goulash communism," concerned only with immediate material advantage. Seeing danger in China's attempt to conquer the Nationalist-held island called Quemoy, Khrushchev declared publicly that the Sino-Soviet Treaty obliged Moscow to come to China's aid *only* if she were attacked first. Already angry at Soviet refusal to assist him in developing atomic weapons, Mao was infuriated by that public humiliation.

A year later, the Central Committee of the Communist Party of China convened at the summer resort called Mount Lu to discuss the domestic and international crises created by the Great Leap Forward and the People's Communes. Led by Minister of Defense Peng Teh-huai, China's most senior field marshal, a few courageous men protested against Mao Tse-tung's disastrous policies.

Although forced to postpone further development of his vision of the perfect future, the Chairman soon took his revenge. Field Marshal Peng Teh-huai was expelled with ignominy from his offices and from the Politburo, accused, among other crimes, of plotting with the hateful Soviet Union.

In 1960 Peking publicly attacked Soviet policies; Soviet economic aid ceased; and all Soviet experts were withdrawn from China. In 1962 Vice-Premier Deng Xiaoping walked out of a conference in Moscow and abruptly returned to Peking. Relations between the two "fraternal Communist parties" were severed.

Although happy to score off the Soviets, Deng Xiaoping was already in conflict with Mao Tse-tung over domestic policy. He was then secretary of the Chinese Communist Party, that is, chief of the Secretariat, which administers the Party, a position of great but not paramount power. Deng Xiaoping had stood cautiously with his mentor, Chief of State Liu Shao-chi, at the Mount Lu Conference. He had not criticized Mao Tse-tung, but neither had he endorsed the Great Leap Forward. The Chairman had complained with curious pathos, "Sometimes I feel as if I'm attending at my own funeral! Deng Xiaoping doesn't even speak to me."

An impromptu triumvirate ran China from 1960 to 1965, warding off Chairman Mao's attempts to hurl the nation into the cleansing whirlpool of chaos. Chief of State Liu Shao-chi brought his great personal authority to the task of stabilization; Secretary Deng Xiaoping controlled the apparatus of the Communist Party; and Premier Chou En-lai held the reins of the government.

Only Chou En-lai weathered the monstrous gales that rose suddenly in 1965, when the skies appeared clear. In 1966 Secretary Deng Xiaoping disappeared, as did Chief of State Liu Shao-chi, who had been Mao Tse-tung's closest associate and heir apparent for years. The two were excoriated by newspapers, broadcasts, pamphlets, and speeches as "traitors, spies, and criminals . . . the men in power following the capitalist road." The mass insanity called the Great Proletarian Cultural Revolution had broken upon China.

Liu Shao-chi was deposed, disgraced, degraded, tortured, and finally allowed to die in his own excrement on a concrete floor. Deng Xiaoping, sixty-one when his ordeal began, somehow evaded death—and subsequently returned to power to chart a new course for China.

Liu Shao-chi and Deng Xiaoping were the most prominent among millions of victims. The decade of horrors left few officials untouched—and none untouched who was in any way outstanding. Not only university presidents and elementary school principals were harrowed, but even kindergarten teachers. A generation was lost; tens of millions were cast aside, never to realize their potential. The gargantuan waste of talent was paralleled by titanic destruction of wealth from paintings to motorcars, from silk fans to drill presses, from encyclopedias to locomotives.

The decade of terror from 1966 to 1976 indelibly scarred every Chinese who is now over the age of thirty—and many younger. Everyone from party chieftains and cabinet ministers to clerks, farmers, and truckdrivers will always remember that period as the decisive years of his life. The decade when Mao Tse-tung's lunatic invention surpassed itself was also a catharsis, a cleansing of the spirit. It irretrievably altered China.

A great civilization for the first time made a radical self-assessment. The Chinese people looked into the abyss of *luan,* the primeval chaos they feared above all else, and realized that they must, above all else, ensure that they never came to the verge again. As with Western civilization after the Renaissance and the Reformation, everything thereafter has been different.

The Great Proletarian Cultural Revolution overleaped politics. It was not great, but transcendent; not proletarian, but universal; not cultural, but nihilistic; and, finally, not a revolution, but a mass uprising that soon escaped all control.

Like Samson, Mao Tse-tung was determined to pull down the pillars. Unlike Samson, he was determined to pull down not one temple, but *all* the temples he had himself built: the Communist Party and the

People's Government, even the People's Republic itself. Grotesquely consistent, the lifelong rebel against all authority closed his life's work by striving to destroy the new social order he had given all his life to erecting.

While I was reporting the Cultural Revolution from Hong Kong, I kept a list of superlatives on my desk. Upheaval, cataclysm, maelstrom, eruption, even *Götterdämmerung* and Armageddon—all began to sound commonplace. I now know that even those superlatives were inadequate.

In the calm after the gales, I spoke with many men and women about their experiences during the Cultural Revolution. It was far worse than anything I reported at the time. No outsider could report its enormity because no outsider could comprehend it. If I had, I would have been criticized for being sensational. But the Cultural Revolution surpassed all possible sensationalism.

Mao Tse-tung had striven for much of his life for absolute power over China. Virtually worshipped toward the end, he nonetheless realized that he had attained the trappings, but not the reality of power. He could not determine the future of China.

He had failed in his first attempt to create a perfect Communist society through the Great People's Communes and the Great Leap Forward. He had not been able to make all equal by wiping out all distinctions: between rich and poor, between men and women, between capital and labor, between brain-workers and hand-workers, or between city and countryside. In 1965, he determined again to create perfect equality. If they could not be *raised* to equal glory, all men and all women would be hurled down to the same level amid the rubble of the old society.

His enemies, Chairman Mao concluded, were his comrades. Once heroes and heroines, they had been mortally corrupted by peace. Men like Chief of State Liu Shao-chi and Secretary Deng Xiaoping were no different from officeholders in bourgeois governments; and the Communist bureaucracy was as conservative, obstructionist, and self-serving as any bourgeois bureaucracy. Even the People's Liberation Army was infected. Why else had its senior Field Marshal Peng Teh-huai sabotaged the Great Leap Forward in 1959?

Mao Tse-tung knew a second revolution was necessary to assert his absolute authority over the Communist Party, the Central People's Government, and the People's Republic of China. The first revolution had destroyed the corrupt Nationalist regime and brought the Communists to power. Now a second revolution was required to destroy the Communist regime—and bring a flawless new society into existence.

The Chairman found his new revolutionary soldiers among the young people. Uncorrupted youths and maidens,[3] even primary-school boys and girls, were still hotly idealistic. Most worshipped the Chairman—and resented the repressive authority of the state. They drew a sharp distinction between Chairman Mao and institutions like the party and the government; they believed all injustice would be remedied if only evil bureaucrats did not keep the chairman in the dark. The Chairman, therefore, made an alliance with youth over the heads of his officials, as medieval kings had allied themselves with the bourgeoisie over the heads of the nobility.

A few nobles were on Mao's side, a few thousand among tens of thousands of senior officials. For some, personal loyalty to the Chairman transcended all other loyalties. Others were driven by ambition, determined to "topple officeholders" and take those offices for themselves. Personal ambition, which Mao Tse-tung excoriated, certainly impelled his two most fervent lieutenants: Field Marshal Lin Piao, whom he was to anoint as his successor, and his own termagant fourth wife, Jiang Ching, who had been a minor starlet in Shanghai's left-wing cinema.

Youth was, however, the shock troops of the Cultural Revolution. The Chairman assembled, in rallies of more than a million, fervid young men and women, adolescents, and even children in Tienanmen Square. Standing on the great balcony of the Tienanmen, the Gate of Heavenly Peace, he inspired them by his presence. But he did not speak. Parkinson's disease had made his tongue too clumsy for public speeches. His loyal nobles, led by Field Marshal Lin Piao, delivered the speeches that inflamed the young in his name.

Little Generals of Disorder, those men and women called the new guerrillas, Chairman Mao's Red Guards, and they exhorted: "Dare to revolt! Destroy the entire society . . . Destroy the men in authority following the capitalist road . . . Learn revolution by making revolution . . . Disorder is good!"

Luan, primeval chaos, was thus exalted. Mao Tse-tung had declared war not only on the Communist Party and the government of the Republic of China, but on the Chinese people themselves. Those he could not reform, he would destroy.

The painter Wu Guanjong, his wife Biqin, and their children suffered much, but not as grievously as many others. He was not driven to

---

[3] The word *maiden* may sound old-fashioned, even quaint. Yet almost all were maidens. Chinese puritanism and Communist puritanism had seen to that. Only when China became somewhat more free economically and intellectually did the number of maidens decline sharply.

suicide by despair, as were thousands of writers, teachers, artists, musicians, and managers. She was neither beaten to death nor so badly mistreated that she died of exposure and neglect, as did hundreds of thousands of ordinary women and men. Nor was even one of their three children permanently maimed in body or spirit, as were millions, including the son of Deng Xiaoping.

The Wus were lucky. They only lost seven years of their lives. The Wus were still lucky when Moira and I called on them in 1988. In Beijing, where many families are crammed into a single room, they had two adjoining apartments on the third floor of a utilitarian new housing complex near the sapphire-blue roofs of the Temple of Heaven. They were thus rewarded for Guanjong's talents—and his salability abroad. His prices are phenomenal for a painter of the People's Republic: fifteen to twenty thousand dollars a painting.

Their quarters were, however, stark. Although it takes 90 percent of his earnings, the People's Republic does not coddle its artists as does the Soviet Union. But he could paint as he pleased. Although his work had always been apolitical, he was no longer attacked for that lack of commitment. He served his art as a professor at the Central Academy of Arts and Design, and he served his country as a member of the Governing Committee of the Chinese Association of Artists.

The two living rooms of the Wus' two apartments were no larger than eight by eleven feet. Still they also had two minute bedrooms, two tiny kitchens, two minuscule bathrooms—and a very small green refrigerator. They entertained in one living room, which is half filled by the table Guanjong uses for his small paintings. The other living room was without furniture because he uses the entire floor space for his larger paintings.

The Wus did not complain, although they knew what life is like elsewhere. He remembered Paris, where he studied before 1950; exhibitions in San Francisco, London, and Tokyo still took him abroad. The Wus were very well off for Beijing. They also had brand-new housing, but we were warned, "Don't take the elevator or you'll end up on the sixth floor—if it moves at all." Still, half of the elevators in a nation that cannot grasp the concept of maintenance are out of order or, as they say in China, "under repair."

Guanjong was sixty-nine years old in the spring of 1988, and his wife Biqin was a few years younger. They looked their age. His gray hair receded from a high, creased forehead, and his lean face was incised with sharp lines. His nose was slightly arched, and his eyes flashed occasionally, as they must have constantly when he was younger. He looked fierce, almost predatory. He would be a hard fighter if his art or his family were threatened.

Her hair was darker, though streaks of white showed that she did not dye it. Her face was round, and her small round nose rose from her plump cheeks with hardly a bridge to it. Her strength and endurance were tempered by a sweetness the years of suffering had not soured.

Wu Guanjong lamented the waste when he talked of his life during the Cultural Revolution. The Central Academy of Art, at which he taught, was closed down in 1966 when the Red Guards broke into museums, galleries, and schools to "destroy all bourgeois and feudal art, whether Chinese or Western." They hacked up statues, tore up paintings, burned scrolls, and broke the fingers of pianists and violinists.

All schools, from kindergartens to universities, closed their doors. For almost ten years, China's educational system was idle; if it taught at all, it taught Red Guard slogans. Thus was a generation lost. The energy that should have been directed to education and creativity, to discovering the magic of friendship and the mysteries of love, was devoted to violence.

Luckily, Wu Guanjong was not harmed physically. But he thought it wise to hide his paintings—and to give up painting. He was particularly vulnerable. He was not just a corrupt intellectual tainted by foreign culture. He had painted nudes and had even taught a life class, paying young Chinese women to expose themselves naked to the defiling gaze of men. Almost as much as they hated feudal bourgeois culture, the Red Guards hated sexual license—at least in others.

In 1968, while the Red Guards campaigned to destroy "all old culture," the entire staff of the Central Academy of Art, from president to janitor, was "sent down to the countryside to learn from the peasants." Biqin had already been sent down with the school at which she taught.

"That put the family in six places," Wu Guanjong recalled wryly. "Biqin and I in different places. Each of the children sent down to a different place. And the apartment in Beijing locked up."

He was lucky in exile. The farming village to which he was sent was near the city of Shizhiajuang, some 170 miles south of Peking. The district was controlled by the Liberation Army, which held aloof from the mass lunacy.

"In the beginning I couldn't paint at all," he recalled. "But, fortunately, the troops wanted diversion. So we put on plays. We had all kinds of specialists to help. We had professors of painting, dance, music, and theater. We taught them, and we performed for them.

"I began painting again, making scenery and backdrops. I used local materials like bamboo to stretch cloth on, and I made my own brushes."

He paused, smiled ruefully, and said, "Of course, it was all a big waste of time. But I did learn how hard the peasants work. Backbreaking! It was funny, though. They were very sorry for us intellectuals for being sent down and having to do manual labor. . . . Also, I acquired some new subjects to paint: millet and rice and the country villages and the country people."

Knowing the answer I must receive, I asked Wu Guanjong if I might buy a big watercolor depicting the city of Chungking, its soaring white buildings climbing its steep hills under curved black slabs of roofs. His oils would be too expensive.

No, he said in effect, I could not buy the painting that is so Chinese, yet so evocative of Utrillo and his Paris. Wu Guanjong has been a pioneer in combining Western and Chinese techniques in harmonious creation. He could only sell his paintings through the state, which takes its glutton's cut.

As we left, I asked again about the seven lost years. He only smiled. He had no more to say, although I suspected that he had glossed over his worst experiences—as much to spare his audience as to spare himself.

Besides, the Wus were lucky. They only lost seven years, while China ceased to exist as a coherent society. Others lost so much more. But all will remember that decade of chaos every day of their lives.

15

China: A Glimpse of the Promised Land

IT DOES NOT MATTER WHAT COLOR A CAT IS AS LONG AS IT CATCHES
MICE.

DENG XIAOPING: MOTTO FOR THE 1970S

FOR EVERYONE TO GET RICH, SOME MUST GET RICH FIRST.

DENG XIAOPING: MOTTO FOR THE 1980S

HAIL THE LIBERATION ARMY FOR CRUSHING THE COUNTER-
REVOLUTIONARY PLOT AND RESTORING SOCIALISM.

DENG XIAOPING: MOTTO FOR THE 1990S?

The pro-democracy movement that culminated in the massacre of June 4, 1989, was a response not only to the opportunities offered by *gaigo* and *kaifang*, "reform" and "openness," but to the problems the new policy had created—above all, soaring inflation and pervasive corruption. The promised land so briefly glimpsed might someday flow with wine and honey, but it also had its thorns and its serpents.

Until June 4, 1989, one could reasonably hope for the success of China's great experiment in repudiating the totalitarian bureaucratic Marxist-Leninist state. After June 4th, one could only pray desperately that *all* China's progress would not be jettisoned.

Although enthusiasm for the great experiment had been high, the Communists' extraordinary talent for contriving disasters compelled caution even before the debacle. The Chinese people knew how precarious their new happiness was. I knew that I had erred most when I was most optimistic about China. Although I drafted this chapter before the catastrophe, it was prefaced by a warning:

Not stagnation nor, certainly, stability (I had written), but rapid change attended by hopes and opportunities, shadowed by the risks and hazards inherent in allowing a relatively unrestricted free market economy, though by no means free political or intellectual debate—

unless the leadership wholly loses its nerve and attempts, disastrously, to revert to the totalitarian past.

In 1988 Moira and I were granted not just a glimpse, but a long look at a rapidly evolving society. This chapter records what we saw and learned during two months of extensive travel in China—and the insights we gained. We were fortunate in speaking Chinese at a time when so many Chinese wanted to talk, particularly to foreigners. It will, I fear, be years before they can talk so openly again. We were also fortunate in being able to range wide because we were not tied to daily events or regular duties, as were Chinese-speaking diplomats and journalists.

This account may prove valuable chiefly for showing why the confrontation between reactionary bureaucrats and progressive intellectuals occurred. Although wary of optimism, I like to believe it describes not just an era past, but a significant stage in China's continuing progress toward well-being and, perhaps, even some freedom.

My own experience of *kaifang,* "openness," was gradual. I began studying Chinese in 1945. I was finally allowed to enter China proper in 1975.

In 1975, a year before the death of Mao Tse-tung, only those specifically authorized to speak with outsiders did so—and never candidly. In 1988 almost everyone except officials did so quite candidly.

But the old ways persisted virtually unchanged in the bureaucracy, which was worried about its future. The Information Department of the Foreign Ministry had for many years disliked my reporting of Maoist excesses that were later to be denounced by the Communist Party itself. I could not obtain a visa to visit China as a journalist until Secretary of State Henry Kissinger took an interest and practically compelled the Foreign Ministry to admit me as a member of the press party covering his visit in the autumn of 1975.

From 1981 onward, it was not difficult to obtain a tourist visa. China was eager for the money it could earn by admitting foreigners and the technical knowledge it could acquire.

But, even in 1988, the Information Department was not helpful. Since I had entered on a tourist visa, the spokesman said he could not assist me. Days later, he told me I had to have a sponsor, perhaps the Writers' Union. By then, it was not only almost time to go, but I was managing quite well on my own among citizens who were practicing *kaifang,* "openness."

Later I concluded that the Foreign Ministry's attitude was due as much to bureaucratic inertia as to any dislike for me. Like every citizen of the People's Republic, every foreigner had to be neatly classified— and had to behave as was appropriate for his or her category. I had written to the Information Department months earlier. It had, with bureaucratic inefficiency, failed to tell me I needed a special visa. Nonetheless, it would not assist me. Bureaucracy was triumphantly obstructionist, although China was eager for outside approbation.

My experience in the era of *kaifang* reflects conditions throughout China. Deng Xiaoping's protégé, Secretary General Zhao Ziyang of the Communist Party, saw the bureaucracy as a major obstacle to progress. At the National People's Congress in March 1988, the authorities announced an immediate 20-percent cut in the nation's administrative staff as the first step. More drastic measures were scheduled to follow—until Zhao Ziyang lost his job because of his liberal policies.

Roman generals would decimate their legions as punishment, executing one out of every ten men. Yet the bureaucratic death for one out of every five was initially ordered by China, the country that invented bureaucracy. Zhao Ziyang obviously believed he had no choice.

In 1988, as in 1688 or 688, China was the same. Two separate nations existed: the nation of ordinary citizens on the bottom, and the nation of their rulers on the top.

In the lower nation, life was tense, cramped, and insecure. Yet the vitality of that lower realm offered the best hope of transforming China. Ordinary citizens were not bound to the past by privileges; and the future beckoned to them with its opportunities. Aware of that vast potential, Deng Xiaoping had set out in 1978 to release it.

The greatest obstacle was the bureaucrats of the upper world, who enjoyed power, security, and comfort. The higher-ranking bureaucrats enjoyed great luxury. They lived in mansions with many servants, flew in their private jets, and stayed in splendid government guest houses. Shades of the Ming Dynasty's graded brothels! Lower bureaucrats enjoyed, among other perquisites, air travel at low rates on scheduled flights effectively closed to ordinary citizens. The doors of the best hotels were open to bureaucrats, but closed to ordinary citizens.

Like the mandarins of the imperial dynasties, the *ganpu*, the Communist cadres, were a caste apart that was committed, above all, to perpetuating itself and enlarging its privileges. By and large, the past was less onerous.

The Mandarinate had been relatively small, no more than fifty thousand in a nation of some 200 million. The total number of cadres was hard to estimate, since every petty jack in office was rewarded with privileges. There were, however, in 1988, forty million members of the Communist party and additional tens of millions of "responsible cadres," in a nation of 1.1 billion. Where mandarins were instructed not to intrude, cadres had, until recently, been *required* to regulate the intimate details of daily life. Pernicious in principle, although hard to condemn in practice, the attempt to limit couples to one child was typical of such intrusions.

Shifting the dead weight of the Chinese bureaucracy made the labors of Hercules look like a job for a chambermaid with a dustpan and brush. Yet the entire upper realm had to be radically altered if China were to have a chance. The bureaucrats paralyzed thought and manacled initiative.

"I feel more *about* China than *with* China," a senior ambassador who has devoted his life to the study of China wrote me in 1988. "Even when I see somebody from the very top, I get Deng Xiaoping quotations on inflation! No new or original insight. Will they ever learn to be easy with free conversation and open thinking? I am so bored with hearing only Xinhua [the official New China News Agency] clichés."

The dragon of bureaucracy was virtually indestructible. State-run enterprises had actually increased in number and in power under the reforms designed to transfer economic responsibilities to localities and to private ownership.

Liberalization had created feudal baronies. The People's Liberation Army controlled hundreds of companies making everything from aircraft and rockets to plastic buckets and electric switches. In provincial capitals, signboards proclaimed enterprises run by other provinces— from automobile repairs and bus lines to timber, foodstuffs, and restaurants.

The Baiyunshan Pharmaceutical Factory, whose future Ms. Hu Suya plotted, was one of a half-dozen pharmaceutical companies owned by the same state corporation. The National Land Organization had been created to oversee cooperative and collective farms, all of which were swept away by the People's Communes in 1958. By 1988, the new agricultural policy had sharply increased output by effectively returning ownership of the land to farming families. The National Land Organization had nonetheless endured and operated the 160-odd companies under the umbrella of state ownership.

The appearance of companies called Southwest Airlines, Shanghai Airlines, and Manchurian Airlines had recently been given an impression of strong competition. But all were part of the airline called the Civil Aviation Administration of China, which took more income from those regional subsidiaries than it had when they were regional divisions.

A billboard overlooking Wangfujing, Beijing's chief shopping street, advertised *Lianhe Hangkong Gongsi,* "the United Airline," with a picture of a pilot wearing four gold rings on his jacket cuffs. That smartly uniformed captain looked like nothing seen in People's China, where proletarian slovenliness was still the mode for men. His idealized figure contrasted sharply with the CAAC pilots who flocked the duty-free shop at Hong Kong's Kaitak Airport. Beside the crisply uniformed captains of Cathay Pacific, Northwest, and Taiwan's China Airlines, their mismatched shoes, rumpled trousers, and stained jackets with dirty yellow braid made them look like soldiers of fortune in a time of unrelenting peace.

The billboard captain was, however, really air force. United Airline of Beijing was a child of the same Chinese ingenuity that was making the People's Liberation Army a major commercial power. The joint chiefs of the ground forces, the air force, and the navy were becoming big businessmen.

A group of senior air force officers had set up the United Airline using the seven Trident jets assigned to the commanding generals of China's military regions. They replaced the Tridents with smaller, faster Canadair executive jets. United Airline of Beijing was making so much money flying out of air force fields that base commanders were demanding a larger cut. Thus was privilege reinforced by economic reform: virtual private enterprise behind the façade of state ownership.

Some Chinese lived in luxury in walled compounds. But the luxury gap was greater than it is in the Soviet Union, where artists, musicians, and writers enjoy great privileges. When Moira and I visited painters and writers, we saw living conditions that would be considered uncomfortable, almost squalid, not only by Westerners but by Soviet artists. Like the painter Wu Guanjong, all, however, lived comfortably by Chinese standards, which are still very low.

A very small, highly privileged class was walled off from general deprivation. Such senior officials were not anxious to turn their world upside down—no more than the local Communist Party secretary, who owed his house, his servants, his rice, his telephone, his children's schooling, and his chauffeured car to his position.

Mao Tse-tung, of course, wanted to destroy the bureaucracy and its privileges. The victory over Maoist fundamentalism was celebrated by the twelfth congress of the Communist party in 1978. So was the second rehabilitation of Deng Xiaoping and his emergence as China's guiding spirit.

The new leadership virtually repudiated Marxism-Leninism, as well as the Thought of Mao Tse-tung. A brief editorial in the Communist party's organ, the *Peking People's Daily*, declared on July 7, 1984, the sacred anniversary of the outbreak of the Second Sino-Japanese War: "We cannot expect the works of Marx and Engels written then [a century and a half ago] to solve the problems of today."

Deng Xiaoping continued to speak of "socialism with Chinese characteristics." That was, however, a bow to the gods of ideology, not a definition of policy. Besides, what else could he say? He knew no other doctrine, and he could hardly come out for capitalism. Besides, socialism meant maintaining the Communist Party's monopoly on power, to which his authoritarian soul was devoted.

By 1988 most Chinese regarded both Marxism-Leninism and the Thought of Mao Tse-tung as antiquated—and irrelevant. A professor in Chengdu remarked casually that the country was "testing new ideologies and new principles." All kinds of theories were in the crucible, except discredited Marxism-Leninism and Mao Thought.

Clearing the decks, jettisoning the dogma, and placating senior officers by bribery occupied the decade from the party's Twelfth Congress in 1978 to its Thirteenth Congress in 1987. Then the new captain set course toward the twenty-first century—*his* own course, not necessarily the course wanted by the passengers or the crew.

That course was routinely confirmed by the National People's Congress in the spring of 1988. For the first time, however, some decisions of the leadership were sharply questioned from the floor. That first fluttering of free debate was reported by Chinese and foreign correspondents, who were for the first time allowed to attend the NPC sessions.

Although authoritarian by temperament and antidemocratic by conviction, the leadership had been compelled to tolerate minimal freedom of discussion; it tightly policed freedom for the press. Neither Deng Xiaoping nor Zhao Ziyang prized freedom for its own sake. But both knew that rapid economic progress required a more lively intellectual atmosphere, as well as openness to the outside world. Both were distrustful of freedom, as they had demonstrated by jailing some dissidents and expelling others from academic and party positions. They had also, from 1979 onward, suppressed both student demonstrations demanding greater democracy and the wall-posters on the Democracy Wall in Beijing that briefly stimulated free discussion. Rather ironically, Zhao Ziyang, who was himself to fall to repression in June 1989, had sternly told President George Bush in February not to interfere in China's internal affairs by inviting a dissident to a formal reception—and instructed the police to keep that dissident away.

Since even limited freedom of expression is an alien and uncongenial concept, both the Chinese and the foreign press had annoyed the authorities. The press had also lived up to its great capacity for good. Watchman, ombudsman, and chronicler, it helped restrain bureaucratic excesses, and it bolstered public morale. The Chinese press pointed to abuses of power and expressed inconvenient popular aspirations, as well as revealing widespread skepticism and distrust of authority. On behalf of the government, the Chinese press explained to the public why inflation had to be tolerated for the sake of development. On behalf of the public, the press cautioned the government by reporting present dissatisfaction—and the danger of disorder if prices were allowed to rise too high. Finally, the government had yielded to public apprehension and restored price controls, which did not work.

The foreign press was for a time even more powerful. Correspondents' reports on rough treatment of dissidents in China and Tibet impelled the authorities to go a little easier. The People's Republic prized its good name abroad after the decades in which it had been portrayed as a rogue among nations; it wanted to polish, not tarnish its image. China was availing itself of foreign loans as well as foreign trade—and owed more than $7 billion to the World Bank and the International Monetary Fund in a total foreign debt of more than $30 billion. Although those were not great sums, China wanted the goodwill of her creditors.

No more than any living organism could China survive without two-way communication between the brain and the extremities. Newspapers, radio, and television were the links between the center and the provinces, between individuals and institutions, between China and the world. They were the nerves of the body politic.

The higher leadership knew that those functions were essential. But the bureaucracy was shocked and frightened. Like the Information Department of the Foreign Ministry, its response was foot-dragging, legalism, and deception.

Zhao Ziyang therefore concluded that radical surgery, even amputation, was necessary. The National People's Congress was told to abolish and/or merge fourteen ministries and commissions in order to "reduce government interference in the economy." The authorities pledged "to change the function of government . . . [and] to separate government enterprises from economic enterprises   ." They promised: "The government will completely give up direct control over such [economic] enterprises. . . ."

Sadly, those measures were later to be reversed, as were political and social tolerance. Only six years earlier, a Chinese had been a nonperson if he did not possess a *hukou*, a "residence permit." He was bereft of food, shelter, and medical care if he did not belong to a *danwei*, his "organization unit." The respect of his fellows, his housing, his food, his medical care, even his recreations—all depended on his *danwei*. That unit was an official entity that could be anything from a ministry to a locomotive repair shop or a state-run restaurant.

The authorities in 1988 no longer pursued the millions whose actual residence was not that cited on their *hukou*, if, indeed, they possessed residence permits at all. The *danwei* was bypassed when both new university graduates and veteran engineers were briefly encouraged to work independently on contract.

Most enterprises were, of course, still state-owned. That elastic term covered the United Airline of Beijing and the Baiyunshan Pharmaceutical Factory, both of which operated quite independently. Most state-owned firms were responsible for their own fate. They could even go bankrupt, and they had to seek funds for expansion from banks or corporations, rather than the government. After paying taxes, state enterprises could keep much of their profits to reinvest or to pay higher salaries and bonuses that would encourage their employees to greater efforts.

Margaret Thatcher was then a heroine in People's China. Even party members expressed enthusiasm for Thatcher-style privatization of state-owned corporations, and age-old private charities were being revived. In that climate, state companies were encouraged to raise funds by issuing stock or by floating bonds.

Change was to be rapid, until early 1989, when the authorities were frightened into a tactical retreat by rocketing inflation and consequent public unhappiness. That was before the June 4 massacre and consequent wave of reaction.

In 1978, when the new era began, more than 80 percent of China's industrial and agricultural production had flowed from state-owned enterprises.[1] Ten years later, less than 60 percent of total production came from state-owned enterprises, many as anomalous as United Airline of Beijing and Baiyunshan Pharmaceuticals.

Industrial private ownership had been blessed by the Thirteenth Congress of the Communist Party in the autumn of 1987. Before that time, regulations permitted an individual entrepreneur to employ no more than five workers. Getting rich from others' labor was anathema. Karl Marx taught that private entrepreneurs lived in luxury on others' sweat because the "surplus value" labor put into a product provided the capitalist's profit. But the Thirteenth Congress permitted private companies to employ many workers *because the risks entrepreneurs took justified their profits.*

Private firms were usually one-man or one-woman enterprises. Run by the proprietor, assisted in the good old Chinese way by family, such firms could, after the 1987 Party Congress, legally employ hundreds of workers. Some had already been doing so while the authorities looked the other way.

Collective enterprises in China were not collectives in the old Marxist-Leninist sense. They were very much like cooperatives, or even joint stock companies, in the West. They were nothing like the old

[1]Such limited private enterprise as was then permitted already contributed a disproportionate share of production. Pigs and chickens reared on the 10 percent of the land allotted to private plots contributed much more than half of China's pork, chickens, and eggs. Private light industry, particularly repair shops, was already more productive than state enterprises, even though much of its activity was technically illegal.

authoritarian collectives managed—or, more often, mismanaged—by Communist cadres. A collective was formed when several individuals pooled their resources to start a company, or to take over a company.

China was experiencing linguistic growing pains. As social and economic institutions altered radically, it was comforting to keep the old rhetoric. Deng Xiaoping and Zhao Ziyang insisted that they were practicing socialism while they were actually dismantling the old collective enterprises to make way for the private initiative that was modified capitalism.

In 1988 capitalism wore a smiling face for most Chinese, except the diehard bureaucrats and the frightened ideologues. Despite increasing inflation, corruption, prostitution, and juvenile crime, most Chinese were enthusiastic about the attempt to transform a semifeudal society overlaid with Marxist-Leninist totalitarianism into a late-twentieth-century industrial nation.

Socialism and capitalism, corporations and collectives, state corporations and private enterprises—all are bloodless abstractions. The flesh-and-blood reality of China was exemplified by the scores of men and women with whom Moira and I talked. They varied widely in age, occupation, and places of origin; almost none were officials.

The quintessential private entrepreneur, Gu Yusheng, proprietor of the Huaqiao Electrical Appliance and Hardware Factory, I met through Daniel Southerland of the *Washington Post*. We talked at the Great Wall Sheraton Hotel, one of the "joint ventures" that allowed the Chinese to use foreign expertise and foreign funds to build their country.

Where else in People's China could you sip champagne and crunch golden Amur River caviar at Sunday brunch while a string quartet glissaded from Haydn to "Greensleeves" to the arias of Peking Opera? Where else did the ceiling lights of an indoor swimming pool look like sparkling teeth with a few missing because burnt-out bulbs were not always quickly replaced? What better place to chat with a man who personified China's aspirations, as they were then?

Gu Yusheng, who was born in 1937, was twelve years old when the Communists took control of China. From his formative years, he resisted great pressures to make him "a faithful son of the motherland and a loyal disciple of Chairman Mao."

His maverick spirit had now brought him to Beijing, which is a minor industrial center, from Shanghai, which is a major industrial center, to buy secondhand machinery. When I asked if more secondhand machinery were not available in Shanghai, he nodded. When I asked why, then, he had come to Beijing, he answered without sarcasm, "Because everyone thinks like you. Everybody goes to Shanghai to buy used machines—and nobody to Beijing. So the machines I want are much cheaper here."

The more the economy changed, the more important became *guanxi*, "connections," and the more entrepreneurs *jin houmen*, went "through the back door," which means taking semilegal shortcuts. I suspected that Mr. Gu had come to Beijing to deal with the compliant cadres of a ministry that has access to secondhand machine tools.

If I'd asked him about it, he might have replied, "And why not? I'm constantly told to be productive and to make money for China. If I can't get the tools, how can I do the job?"

Such impeccable commercial logic had always guided Gu Yusheng. Sidestepping Maoist repression was as heroic a feat as Ulysses's evading a myriad of perils. Gu Yusheng did not have to put wax into his ears. He was deaf to the songs of political sirens. Intent on his own purposes, little else was real for him.

His chief purpose was to work hard to make money—in *his* own way. He instinctively threaded the maze of a state determined that no one should make money in any way—and that everyone should behave in *its* way. His "bourgeois individualism" was inborn. The Maoists would classify his family as petit bourgeois, but almost everyone else as proletarian. His father ran a watch-repair stall in Shanghai, while his mother and his sisters worked in a stocking factory all their lives.

The self-made Gu Yusheng was still making the most of himself and his fortunes. His chief self-indulgence was Kent cigarettes at a dollar and twenty cents a pack. Reasonable elsewhere, but very expensive when Chinese cigarettes cost fifteen cents a pack. He explained defensively that he only smoked or drank when entertaining customers or suppliers—and, presumably, curious foreigners.

That plea of frugality was automatic. But he later acknowledged with pride that his enterprises took in Y110,000 (U.S.$30,000) in three months. That was affluence in a nation where Y10,000-a-year ($2,700) household was the byword for wealth.

Gu Yusheng's conservative blue-and-red-striped tie was badly wrinkled; his shirt collar was curled upward; and embossed white-on-white shirts like his had not been seen in their native New York for decades. In the warmth of the Great Wall Hotel he wore three sweaters: a blue pullover under a tan pullover topped by a beige cardigan. Yet he was by Beijing standards what used to be called a snappy dresser.

Gu Yusheng had made it big producing parts for the refrigerator factory in Huaqiao—Flower Bridge—a small town near Suchow, the wonderful city of canals and gardens about sixty miles inland from Shanghai. When that factory ceased production, he had switched to making parts for sewing machines and enameled pots for export to the United States and Japan.

Wiry and short, he was high strung, almost apprehensive, like a city sparrow, perhaps because he had spent most of his life *not* doing as he was told. Although his hair was two to three inches long, it stood up. From that dark, spiky crown his face tapered to a pointed chin in a triangle, rather like the jack of spades. The tip of a single incisor showing between his narrow lips gave him a furtive, foxy air. He was from time to time ingratiating. Mostly, though, he was self-assertive, even self-confident, in a muted, almost stealthy way. Otherwise, he could not have swum so long against the tide—until it finally turned his way for a time.

Sitting with foreigners in a splendid foreign hotel intensified his natural nervousness. Still, it takes courage to submit to an interview anywhere—and much more courage in China. Although he was now one of the elite who "get rich so that others will follow," the dire years had stamped their memory upon his nerve cells.

"Are you going to write a book about me?" he asked hopefully. Looking like a benevolent Reynard the Fox, he grinned with pleasure when I answered, "Not a whole book, but you'll be important in the part about China."

Although he asked me not to use a few embarrassing facts, Gu Yusheng was remarkably open. Like any image-conscious entrepreneur, however, he claimed that high costs leave little over for high living.

"My life is still lean," he added earnestly. "I have to put most of my earnings back into equipment. And I have to pay from twenty-five to sixty workers. They get good wages, some as much as Y500 a month [about $135 against an average industrial wage of Y80, about $22] plus food, accommodation, and transportation."

"Why so lavish?"

"I have to pay well to get the best workers. There's a lot of competition for skilled labor. They work on contract, three to six months, so their number varies. I guess I put half my earnings back into the business. But I've got enough. How can anyone spend more than Y2,000 [about $540] a month?"

Private enterprises like Gu Yusheng's, as well as collectives and state firms, paid taxes on profits. The expense-account life had, therefore, come to China. He spent Y30 (about $8) a night on hotels, but stressed, "I don't even drink coffee except when I'm with contacts."

Primarily interested in Gu Yusheng's career, I was briefly diverted by his sidelights on Chinese life. His parents, already burdened with four children, had adopted a sickly orphan girl and slowly nursed her back to health. He was expected to marry that adopted sister in the time-honored way, but had refused. She then went to work in the stocking factory beside his mother and his elder sister, who had recently retired at fifty-two with a pension of Y72 ($20), 80 percent of her respectable monthly wage of Y90 ($25).

Gu Yusheng later married an energetic young woman who was a zealous Maoist. But his luck held. She now managed the factory, not only during his protracted business trips, but when he was in Huaqiao. He was the idea man and the negotiator; she was the practical executive.

Gu Yusheng did not marry until he had made his mark, however. He was still insecure, for he remembered two conquering armies. The Japanese came when he was three years old, and the Communists came when he was twelve. He received a patchy education, and in 1956, when he was nineteen, he went off to Foochow, 270 miles south of Shanghai, to his first job.

Guanxi, "connections," in this case literal nepotism, got it for him. His uncle was the foreman for the ventilating system of the Foochow People's Broadcasting Station. Nonetheless, young Gu Yusheng worked hard seven days a week. Practicing his new craft by day, he studied it by night. After a year, he went to work for an air force unit that had a ventilation problem in its cave complex.

"Work wasn't hard to find if you had the skills," he recalls. "Anyway, my uncle was an old foreman. He had *guanxi* everywhere . . . lots of old friends in important jobs."

The first great paroxysm of Maoism, the Great Leap Forward, left him not only unscathed, but better off.

"For forty *fen* [ten cents today, twenty cents then]," he recalled, "I could eat three big meals a day in the communal mess hall. The air force always had ample supplies, and prices in the PX were very low. A pound of tangerines cost only twelve *fen* [say three to six cents, against seventy-five cents on the free market today]."

Untouched by the turmoil of the Great Leap Forward, he returned in 1959 to Shanghai, which offered greater opportunities than Foochow. Already a master of ventilation systems, he formed a private construction company with other skilled workmen, which was illegal. They contracted with state-owned textile factories to do jobs the factories' own workers could not finish on time. Working odd shifts, he was soon making a minimum of Y8 ($2.10 now, $4.20 then) a day, about Y300 ($80 now, $160 then) most months. That was splendid pay when the average wage was Y50 ($14 now, $28 then).

But the long hours and the split shifts were too much even for the compulsive worker. He contracted with the Yamei Textile Factory to build and maintain a ventilating system for a regular monthly salary of Y120 ($33 now, $66 then). Much less than he had been making, that was still more than the salary of the Communist Party secretary who ran the factory—and had hired Gu in desperation. Ten months later, the embryo capitalist quit because he wasn't making enough.

Returning to private contracting, he prospered. His only major setback came in 1967, when the Cultural Revolution paralyzed industry.

"The Red Guards never bothered me," he says. "I just kept on working hard. But work disappeared, and I lived on my savings. I also got married in 1967."

His bride had been so "progressive" that she had volunteered in 1962, when she was sixteen, to join other "educated youths" in developing China's wild west, the enormous frontier province called Xinjiang. A little disillusioned, she returned to Shanghai several times, usually without permission. Although the couple had two sons, whom his parents looked after in Shanghai, she had not been able to return to stay until 1979.

"She was still progressive," her husband insisted. "But this was a practical matter. Her father fell on the stairs and hurt his leg. So she had to look after him. Besides, her own health wasn't too good. . . . All those separations? Not good, especially the four years when we didn't see each other at all."

In 1983 Mrs. Gu was finally given official permission to leave Xinjiang. Her *hukou*, or "residence passport," was, however, not stamped for Shanghai, but for the village of Huaqiao.

"That was very good for us," Gu continued. "In fact, we arranged it. Things had changed, and private factories were legal. I couldn't get a permit to start a factory in Shanghai, but it was easy to get a permit for Huaqiao. Officially my wife was working for a state-owned factory that made refrigerators, the Fragrant Snow brand. Actually, it was a deal with the cadres. She and I were really setting up our own factory."

"Mrs. Gu is vivacious and very tough," Dan Southerland interjects in English. "She's just as impressive as he is."

The factory was completed in 1983 after machinations, disappointments, and triumphs like those of new projects anywhere. Local farmers invested their land and their savings. Gu Yusheng raised Y100,000 (about $27,000) from his savings, his wife's jewelry, and a loan against his workshop in Shanghai.

"It was hard going," he recalls. "But I'd learned to work hard as a child. . . . I can now turn my hand to anything from ducts or pots and pans to bicycle racks or machine tools. . . . Besides, I knew what I wanted: a site near Shanghai, on a main road close to the Grand Canal, in a reasonably developed area with existing factories and a good labor supply. I actually found it in 1981. That's why we finagled my wife the permit for Huaqiao."

Although many Chinese women are gifted in business, few women or men are as competent, persuasive, and tough as Gu Yusheng's wife. The company was in her name, as it might be in the West. Given their

equal partnership, that formal ownership was really an echo of the
stubborn bureaucracy's interfering ways. Only she had a residence
permit for Huaqiao. But his residence permit for Shanghai enabled
them to maintain an office there.

The Gus' enterprise suffered from the authorities' erratic swings between laissez-faire and interference. It also suffered because a growing
economy could not progress consistently. For a period in late 1988, they
could operate only half-time because Suchow got electricity only fifteen
days a month. Supplies of raw materials were erratic; the transportation
system was shaky; and business administration was, to put it gently,
often chaotic.

Called "collective township enterprise," private endeavor like Gu
Yusheng's was hailed as the model for all China. Next to the enormous
increase in agricultural production when farmers were, in effect, given
title to their land and its yield, the rapid rate of growth (28 percent a
year) of such light industry was the second great triumph of the economic liberalization. More than 17 million township enterprises employed 88 million workers and produced $16 billion worth of goods a
year, making more than 5 percent of China's Gross Domestic Product.

Great success bred great problems. Frightened by inflation at more
than 30 percent, the conservatives adopted a policy of "control and
rectification," which progressives felt was just treading water. The
alarming disruption was in part due to the vitality of township enterprises. Success, as one authority put it, had not come too little and too
late, but too much and too soon. Managing growth was proving even
more difficult than creating wealth.

Skilled workers were increasingly difficult to find, although unskilled
farmers were leaving the land, which no longer offered great rewards,
for the new Cinderella sector. Workers' illiteracy and incompetence
handicapped the enterprises, edging some toward bankruptcy. Many
were turning to exports, as had Gu Yusheng, although they were
intended to serve the domestic market.

In Xi'an, a Township Enterprise University was established in late
1988 to train entrepreneurs in management techniques and workers in
basic skills. In the Beijing area, flying squads of experts went out to
assess their efficiency and to recommend improvements. Thus the
home-grown business consultant came to People's China, although they
called it the Spark Plan after the old guerrilla slogan, "A single spark can
start a prairie fire."

The authorities had even acknowledged realistically that a long-term
nationwide strategy for township industry was not feasible. Provinces
and counties became the basic units of commercial and industrial
activity and planning. Beijing was presented with effective decentral-

ization. Millions of entrepreneurs like Gu Yusheng were leading the way, perhaps paradoxically since most only wanted to make a good profit—in their own way.

It has been a lifetime's journey for Gu Yusheng from the slums of Shanghai to the tower of the Great Wall Hotel. Beneath us spread the flat expanse of Beijing, as usual hazed by dust. Dozens of buildings were rising, the long orange arms of cranes dipping and bobbing above them like immense seesaws. No longer did coolies clamber on bamboo scaffolding with bricks or haul up buckets of mortar with crude rope-and-pulley hoists. Now numbered among the elite, skilled construction workers could earn as much as Y800 ($215) a month with overtime.

Practical entrepreneurs had made a true revolution for China's workers: not promises of paradise someday, but lighter work for more pay right now. They had also transformed Peking into Beijing. The ideograms, which mean "northern capital," are, of course, unchanged, but the spelling altered for the benefit of outsiders symbolizes enormous changes.

"A gray city, seas of gray-tiled roofs around the infrequent island of a modern building," my notes of 1975 read.

> The factories that ring the city emit great clouds of smoke, and a dark pall cuts out the daylight. Obscured by the dust in the air, the sun disappears in the west like a clouded red lollipop. The people are incurious and their garments are old, though an occasional woman or child wears a bright sweater. Old men wear traditional Chinese trousers tied at the ankles.
>
> Many, many bicycles and very, very few automobiles. Some orange-and-white buses in two sections linked by a rubberoid accordion. Chief transport is foot and bicycle.
>
> Not a vital city. The same air of detachment from the world, the same sense of unreal ease that enchanted expatriates in the 1930s. The people are slow, courteous—and as hard to move as seventeen granite mountains. They could never have been lotus eaters; they don't have the energy to chew that hard. A drab city, Peking makes even Moscow seem a center of gaiety and intellectual ferment.
>
> Slogans on billboards: OUR GUIDING SPIRIT IS LENINISM! OUR GUIDING SOUL IS THE COMMUNIST PARTY OF CHINA! . . . REVOLUTIONARY AND OPPRESSED PEOPLES OF THE WORLD UNITE! And everywhere: STRENGTH THROUGH SELF-RELIANCE!"

Not only that last cry of the isolationist Maoists, but *all* ideological slogans were gone in 1988, although they are, sadly, now coming back.

But the emphasis was clearly on remaking China, not on ideology. Beijing was outward looking, energetic, better dressed, and optimistic. It was even marginally less polluted than it had been in 1975, although grit and smog still induced tears and bronchitis.

The *big* slogans are for the traffic safety campaign [my notes of 1988 read]. It is badly needed in a capital where there are somewhat fewer bicycles and many more cars—a few, very few privately owned. The equivalent of Fiat 850s from Poland cost Y9,000 to Y12,000 [$2,420 to $3,225]. There's a two-to-three-year wait—or you "go through the back door," use connections and bribes. One catchy slogan reads: GLADLY, GLADLY GO TO WORK, SAFELY, SAFELY RETURN HOME!

The grim, anonymous façades of unadorned Maoist Peking laid a heavy weight on the spirit. Restaurants and buildings now display giant red lanterns and brightly colored signs, many of them neon. Beijing's Madison Avenue, Wangfujing, just off Tienanmen Square, is thronged with shoppers gawking at the shop signs and billboards, as many as half a million on weekends. They comment excitedly on the movie theater and the tower of the Palace, the newest and plushest of Beijing's hotels. The outside world is coming to China.

Everywhere little restaurants and stalls keep their lights on late. Taxis cruise for passengers on streets lit by their glow. One shop proclaims itself in big black letters on a crimson background: CALIFORNIA BEEF NOODLE KING. BEIJING BRANCH.

A housewife who works in a bank recalls complaints heard in New York, London, and Paris, saying, "Of course wives must work. No family with even one child can get along on a single salary nowadays."

Peking in 1975 not only looked like a different city from present-day Beijing. It was.

Physically, psychologically, in almost everything but location, China's capital was another realm then, when George Bush was chief of the U.S. Liaison Mission, which did not become a full embassy until 1979. He strolled nonchalantly through the Forbidden City in the entourage of Henry Kissinger, chatting casually with visiting correspondents.

Bush saw out the last full year of the old China, 1975. The next year broke the living chain that extended back to the last imperial dynasty. Mao Tse-tung, who had been eighteen when the Ching Dynasty was overthrown in 1911, died on September 9, 1976. His faithful lieutenant, counselor, and, some said, good angel, Chou En-lai, had gone before him on January 8, 1976. The paladins of the old guard having passed, the road was open to the reforms that began two years later, in 1978.

Ten years later, the Chinese leadership, keenly aware of their country's backwardness, was trying hard to catch up with the rest of Asia. Inspired by their desire for the new goods on the market, the people too were trying harder. But were they trying hard enough? Were they overcoming the torpor induced by three decades of numbing totalitarian rule?

An indicator I used in China, as elsewhere, was the number of young people I saw studying at odd moments: elevator operators, watchmen, receptionists, desk clerks, even salesmen and saleswomen between customers. Korea was foremost, but in Japan, Hong Kong, Taiwan, Singapore, and even Indonesia, I saw many young men and women, as well as some who were not so young, using every spare moment for self-improvement. In China they had abundant spare time, normally gained by not working too hard. But that spare time was generally spent gossiping, sipping tea, ignoring customers, and reading pulp novels. The Chinese were very efficient—at relaxing.

Moira and I deliberately traveled by train and boat, transportation not used by tourists, in order to see the China few foreigners do. We were lucky in the men and women we talked with: we met graduate students through a teacher; we met a factory manager and a senior scientist on a train.

I was prepared to feel sorry for the graduate students we met. I had been told by young foreigners who were studying the Chinese language that their Chinese fellow students at the university led a hard life.

Most got state grants of Y15 ($12) a month, perhaps receiving a few yüan more from their parents. Eight lived in a small room, sleeping in double-decker bunks. Stifling in bake-oven summer, such crowding was almost welcome in the bitter, damp winter, since their dormitories had no central heating. Communal bathrooms provided showers— thirty for 7,000 students. Even the nearly universal bicycle was, at Y200 to Y300 ($55 to $80), too expensive for many students. They had to wait for the occasional bus or walk long distances, squandering their scant leisure and their insufficient study time.

When they graduated, their chief hope of getting a good job was once *guanxi*, "connections." But change was afoot. The better students could, in 1988, choose "contract work," upon graduation, rather than submit to assignment by the state, perhaps to the wastes of Tibet. Those short-term contracts, however, offered no security. Lifetime guaranteed employment, the "iron rice bowl," was being phased out because it bred complacency, laziness, and inefficiency.

In the spring of 1989, even before June 4, the frightened government was to revert to compulsory assignment. Motivated primarily by youthful idealism, the pro-democracy movement was also motivated by resentment at the reimposition on university graduates of the semi-serfdom of compulsory assignment for life.

I did not feel sorry for the students when I met them. Despite their Spartan lives, I could not feel sorry for eight young men who were so intelligent, so well informed, and so dedicated. Ranging from twenty-two to twenty-six, they were in an advanced English class. Although we spoke Chinese for complex matters, their English was very good for a secondary subject. All were taking master's degrees in the sciences, and most would work for the Liberation Army on graduation.

I have here suppressed further details that would identify them—and make them vulnerable to the veritable inquisition mounted by the authorities in 1989 to ferret out all dissidents. From the orthodox point of view, *all* were dangerous dissidents, typical of the students who led the pro-democracy movement.

To me the most remarkable thing about that meeting in 1988 was that it took place. Their English teacher had on impulse invited me to speak to his class. Five years earlier, no one would have dared suggest such a meeting.

The students were typical of graduate students anywhere, only more eager. They expressed the strong, clear, uncomplicated views of youth, and they exuded distaste, indeed scorn, for their rulers.

All believed that the chief obstacle to China's progress was tradition, above all the Confucian tradition. As scientists, they were not concerned with social or semantic abstractions. Instead, they stressed the evil effect of *da jindai guanxi*, "the connections between those who wear sashes," that is, the ruling gentry. They referred, they said, to the favoritism and corruption of the Communists' old-boy network.

"The collusion of men in power, the government and party functionaries," they agreed, "is the root of the country's problems. *All* China's problems."

The solutions they suggested were simple, perhaps simplistic. But they revealed the way the new generation was thinking. That mentality was the next year to so terrify the old autocrats in Beijing that they warned of "counter-revolutionary upheaval" and called out the Liberation Army to suppress it.

Education and competition, the students said, must clear out the dead wood: education through the media to inspire public opinion to throw out the corrupt old guard; competition to force individuals and organizations to work better.

The students insisted that competition was the *only* way, even when I pointed out that a totally free market economy could cause much suffering. Compassion for all, they said, must wait until competition had greatly improved efficiency. They had, they said emphatically, already seen egalitarian and paternalistic policies produce not only widespread corruption, but mass suffering.

Fearful of Japan, the graduate students were even more fearful of Soviet expansionism. Those attitudes were hardly spontaneous. The students had, as their teacher said, "been brainwashed since birth." But such attitudes will continue to affect China's foreign policy, whatever rapprochements are struck with Tokyo and Moscow.

They wondered which was the better model for China's development, the United States or Yugoslavia. Aware of Yugoslavia's internal tensions, they were, nonetheless, deeply interested in it as a model.

I assumed that was because Yugoslavia was a Socialist country. But I learned that it was the opposite. They were interested because Yugoslavia was reformist, the first so-called Socialist country to break away from Moscow's domination and, implicitly at least, from Marxism-Leninism.

The graduate students were hardly committed to the Communists' goals. Impatient and critical of socialism, they grimaced wryly at the mention of Mao Tse-tung and Maoism. Rather than attacking Western capitalism, they coolly discussed its possibilities for China—neither for nor against it as yet.

Clearly, ideology played no significant role in their thinking, despite decades of compulsory "political study." Like a seventy-four-year-old Communist Party member in Beijing and a fifty-three-year-old professor in Chengdu, those young men were interested in results, not theories.

Total pragmatists, they were passionately realistic. Not only the clash in Tienanmen Square, but the ultimate fate of the Communist regime was, I believe, foreshadowed by their attitudes. They undoubtedly felt hatred of the regime and its works. Yet I sensed an even stronger and more dangerous feeling: contempt for their rulers. The graduate students, the elite of the younger generation, were contemptuous of the Communists' ignorance, ineptitude, inefficiency, and their inability to check their greed, which had led to universal corruption.

Trains encapsulate passengers in a steel shell, cutting them off from the world. Mutual isolation fostered trust when a sleeping compartment on the Chengdu-Chungking Overnight Express became our entire world for eleven hours. With Messers Wang Shuren and Li Jyaming we crossed China's most populous and most fertile province, Sichuan in the southwest.

Moira was taken aback at the prospect of spending the night with three men, even though one was her husband. Her reserve began to melt when Wang Shuren courteously stepped into the corridor to smoke his cigarette. Nor would he allow me to occupy the upper bunk to which I was assigned, but insisted that I take his lower bunk, opposite Moira. But we didn't get much sleep. The train jolted and swayed, and at odd moments the loudspeaker burst into edifying lectures.

Anyway, our compartment had become a seminar room. At fifty-six, Wang Shuren was general manager of a big factory producing pumps in Chengdu, the capital of Sichuan. At forty-seven, Li Jyaming was the chief scientist of a plant in Manchuria that made electronic equipment for the People's Liberation Army. After initial shyness, which broke down rapidly, both had a great deal to say and a great many questions to ask.

We were the first foreigners with whom either had spoken freely in many years, although both had been abroad. Wang had visited France, Italy, and Japan on business the preceding year. As he said, "We don't get much money, but we do have some perks like going abroad or traveling by sleeping car." Li had done graduate work at the University of Illinois before returning to China in the 1960s.

"I wanted to do my part in rebuilding the motherland," he said. "I bet if I'd stayed, I'd be making $20,000 a year now."

His plump face registered shock when I told him he would be making at least $50,000 a year.

The rough ride shook the lower bunks on which we were perched. An officious conductor repeatedly stuck her head through the doorway to demand tickets; to check her countrymen's identity documents, but not the foreigners'; and just to make sure we were behaving ourselves. Like all the train crew, she was sour and peremptory.

The rumpled blankets were strewn with the debris of the boxed dinners we had all brought along, for there was no dining car. Although the compartment was stuffy and smelly, the grime-smeared window was better left closed than opened to the soot and grit from the steam locomotive. Fortunately, I had extracted a bottle of Scotch before my suitcase became inaccessible under the berth.

Our conversation was not, as they say, structured, but discursive. I did not ask Li Jyaming what his plant made for the Liberation Army. Otherwise, no subject was barred, and no punches were pulled. They readily accepted us, and we rapidly learned their backgrounds.

Wang Shuren, the general manager, was fighting the first secretary of the factory's Communist Party unit for control of the state-owned factory. Such struggles, he said, were going on throughout the nation in the spring of 1988. The National People's Congress had just given sweeping authority to managers, but party secretaries were struggling·to retain the power on which their privileges rested.

Wang Shuren, the industrialist, was slender and about five foot six. He had earlier lost one such struggle—not against the Communist

Party, but against the Red Guards. During the Cultural Revolution he had been "sent down to the countryside to learn from the farmers" for three years. "It was only a short time," he said. "I worked as a mechanic."

Li Jyaming, the scientist, younger by nine years, was plump and slightly better dressed. He confessed ruefully that he had forgotten most of his English. He had spent only two years in the countryside during the Cultural Revolution, his exile shortened because he worked for the military. He now earned Y150 a month, as did his wife, who was a research scientist in the same plant. Their total income was officially the same as $82 a month, but the dollar equivalent is misleading. Three hundred yüan is about ten times $82 in purchasing power when one still gets a good restaurant meal for Y4 ($1.08). However, $82 a month had to support not only Li and his wife, but two children and two surviving parents.

"That's Y50 a month a head," Li said. "The younger generation has it much better. A young couple can make Y200 a month. But they'll only have one child, and their parents will be still young enough to look after themselves. So that's almost Y70 a head. . . . Besides, my oldest is starting university next year. I'm afraid they'll want us to pay tuition—for the first time."

Pointing to the window, I asked my stock question: "Why must it be so filthy we can hardly see out of it? The last time I traveled by train in China was seven years ago. But the compartments were clean, and the lavatories didn't stink. Nor were their floors covered with water, urine, and feces. And this is soft [first] class! How can you progress when you can't even keep railway carriages clean and well maintained?"

I expected a sharp response. But Wang Shuren, the factory manager, who was the more thoughtful of the two, smiled sadly and replied: "Sometimes I'm afraid we'll never change. But the train crew is a special case. They're sullen because they're asked to do much more work than they used to—at no more pay. In general, people won't do any more than they're forced to do. Partly that's the backlash of the Cultural Revolution. Partly it's the grip of the bureaucracy, which certainly hasn't loosened. And there are still no real incentives either. . . . Maybe we'll change. In fact, I'm fairly sure we'll change. But slowly . . . very, very slowly."

"I used to feel the same way about Taiwan, that it was hopeless," Moira interjected. "But look what they've done."

"Taiwan is a different case, a completely different case," said Li Jyaming. "We can't be compared to Taiwan. Not with our system . . . and our isolation. Our leaders are appealing to Taiwan to return to the Motherland. The Nationalists would be fools even to think of joining us."

Wang and Li repeatedly compared notes, for they, too, had met for the first time that evening. Both felt that traditional attitudes were the greatest obstacle to China's progress—not only the bureaucracy and its pervasive corruption, but the selfishness ingrained in the Chinese character over many centuries by family-centered Confucianism.

"Above everything else," Wang observed, "the Cultural Revolution ruined us. Not just one or two generations, but at least four generations. The generation of the Cultural Revolution has no culture, no manners, no breeding. They have no knowledge and certainly no learning. How can they teach their children? And who else will?"

The generation that came of age in the 1950s, the two agreed, was now carrying China on its shoulders. They were, of course, speaking of their own generation.

"We are working hard, very hard, now," Li Jyaming said. "But our generation is not getting the rewards—and we never will. . . . Yes, we do get to ride on trains and planes. But anyone can if he's got enough cash for bribes. Like everything else, railways and airlines are shot through with corruption."

Both part of the intellectual-managerial class, they both resented the revolution in agriculture that had made farmers wealthy. The prices of rice, pork, and eggs had, they said, once been roughly the same. Now pork and eggs cost four times as much as rice, which was still controlled.

"Well, we're still better off than we were, even in 1957," Wang Shuren conceded—and then repeated the plaint we had already heard: "But the spirit of the people was much better in 1957."

Neither wasted time mourning for the lost zeal of their youth. Both are practical men who faced up to practical problems.

"Running a factory is hell nowadays, worse than before the reforms," commented Wang Shuren. "I'm now *personally* responsible for profit or loss. But the state's demands haven't changed, and the paperwork is even more mountainous. I only get 20 to 30 percent of the support I used to: capital and machine tools and supplies. I'm supposed to find the rest myself. Just tell me where! And I'm expected to be *more* efficient than before."

Li Jyaming, the chief scientist, pointed out that "private owners and collectives," that is, individual proprietors and joint companies, were much better off than state employees like him, no matter how senior. They paid taxes, but they did not have to hand over a fixed proportion of their output to the state, and they did not have to give the state a big share of their profits. He grimaced when I suggested that those constraints might be a deliberate strategy to force greater private ownership.

"They're not that clever, our leaders," Li said. "Yes, in theory, it's smart to use competition to bring down prices and drive up quality. But how long do you think those tactics will take?"

Wang Shuren commented, "When everything is in short supply, competition can't accomplish much. Why sell cheap if you can sell dear? Why improve quality—at increased expense—if you can sell the same old stuff just as easily? People have to buy something."[2]

An exploding population was the root cause of most of China's problems, the practical men contended. China was growing by some 20 million annually—almost ten times what Singapore's population added every year. How, they asked, could there ever be enough goods?

They conveyed their disdain for the more pragmatic present leadership as much by gestures and facial expressions as by words. Their dislike for the Communist Party and its apparatchiks verged upon hatred. Nor were they happy with Secretary General Zhao Ziyang, who was, with Deng Xiaoping, the architect of reform. Prudent this once, they did not speak against Deng or against Zhao, who had made his reputation in Sichuan. But they would grant neither man a single word of praise.

One of the subjects better left *un*discussed, as the woman author had said in Beijing, was obviously "the leadership of our Communist Party." That was, however, the only reservation they displayed during our protracted conversation.

Wang Shuren and Li Jyaming were not malcontents. They were highly successful men, who were well integrated in the present system. They simply discussed their country's problems seriously—and honestly. Surprisingly, for practical men, both were impatient with gradual progress. I argued that China must move toward material abundance step by step. They wanted faster movement. Extreme in their hopes, they condemned the timidity and fear that were to lead the government to jam on the brakes a year later—even before it totally lost its nerve and massacred the students.

The grease-filmed windowpanes had only dimmed a little the scenes that unrolled behind as we talked. First the deep Yangtze River and then the fields of fertile Sichuan glowed in the early evening. My notes describe the scene as "resplendent," a word to which I am by no means addicted.

Slender saplings rose against the shining foliage of mature trees, and clear water sparkled in the well-kept irrigation ditches. Little tricycle tractors made in China chugged to and fro, hauling loads or plowing.

[2] That logic did not always prevail. Finding that a private taxi driver in Wuhan had doubled the normal fare, I told him that those drivers who offered lower prices would, in time, drive profiteers out of business. Thereafter, his fares were reasonable. Finally, he took us to the airport for two-thirds the fare to which I had already agreed—and refused a tip.

New houses clustered at the junctions of well-maintained roads, their roofs tiled rather than thatched. And the water buffaloes were fat.

At seven in the evening, men, women, and children in bright orange, red, and green clothing were still working in the fields. Patches of yellow rapeseed glowed around plots of jade-green vegetables. The scene was almost too pretty, like a model landscape in a real-estate agent's office.

Thus might a romantic film director depict the ideal South China: abundant and industrious, yet relaxed and happy. Thus had South China *not* been during the war, rebellion, and disorder that marked the first eight decades of the twentieth century. But the rural landscape had altered radically in the early 1980s. The People's Communes were formally abolished, and individual farmers were encouraged to till their own land for their own profit. They had soon increased the crop yield by an average of 20 to 30 percent—and by 50 to 100 percent in some cases.

At the beginning of 1988, the law had for almost a decade not only permitted farm families to till their own land for their own benefit, but to pass their land down to their heirs.[3] In April 1988 the People's Congress, obedient to the party's instructions, gave farmers the right to *sell* their land as they wished.

Well, not quite—at least not technically. "Socialism with Chinese characteristics" was preserved by an ingenious qualification that means virtually nothing in practice.

The farmers do not formally *own* their land; they only own the *right to use* the land. Yet, unlike land leases in Hawaii or Britain, the entitlements do not expire after a fixed period. Since farmers can now sell their right to use the land, as well as pass it onto their children, the distinction between owning land and using land is very fuzzy. Not entirely by accident.

Having seen many Chinese farms, Moira and I saw a most unusual farm in 1988. Unlike 98 percent of China's arable land, the fields of the Marco Polo Bridge Township were *not* individually owned and worked. Having in theory been owned by all when it was the Marco Polo Bridge Great People's Commune, those fields were still in theory owned by the Chinese people through the state, as is all land ultimately. But families have been given long-term, that is, trans-generational, rights to till their land in return for contracting to be responsible for delivering a fixed share of the crop to the state. That "contract and responsibility" system was the basis for formal abolition of People's Communes in 1981 and

---

[3] The hereditary principle has been well established in certain areas of the industrial sector for decades. Like members of particularly well-entrenched unions elsewhere, craftsmen in factories have long been able to hand their jobs on to their sons or nephews.

their transformation into townships. Most of China's land is now worked by the owners' families. But the land of Marco Polo Bridge Township is worked cooperatively.

The farmers reckon they can make more money by pooling their resources. They do. The income of the average family is around the Y10,000 ($2,700) threshold that means riches in China today.

We did not go to Marco Polo Bridge Township *because* it was unrepresentative. We went because I had visited the Marco Polo Bridge Great People's Commune in 1975, and I wanted to see what it looked like now.

The fundamental shape of the land had, of course, not changed. Nor had the long bridge with the small guardian lions perched on its parapets, which is named after the great Venetian traveler who came from the West to Cathay in the thirteenth century, when China was ruled by the Mongol Emperor Kublai Khan. The bridge has hardly changed since July 7, 1937, when the Second Sino-Japanese War—the China Incident, as they called it in Tokyo—was ignited by a confrontation between Chinese and Japanese troops on the approaches to the bridge.

Much else had changed.

In 1975 a housewife had told me triumphantly, *"Mingnyan wawmen yu dzlaishui!"* "Next year we're getting running water!"

They did. In 1976 taps were installed outside the single-story houses. Capped with red rubber nozzles, the pipes now stand solitary in the middle of tiny courtyards against the houses' pale red bricks and yellow-shellacked woodwork. Standpipes were too precious to hide against a wall.

The people of Marco Polo Bridge Township still speak reverently of the miracle of running water, although outsiders might wonder why after a decade it has not been led inside. But running water is already a great labor-saving device, requiring only a few steps across the courtyard. In some five thousand years of habitation of the Peking plain, this was the first generation not to trudge to streams or common wells carrying heavy buckets.

Aside from the standpipes, the houses were outwardly the same as those I had visited in 1975. Reading my notes of October 1975 renewed their memory:

> Mrs. Chen, forty-two with five children, made an arranged marriage in 1949, when she was fifteen. Both her husband and she previously worked the land for a landlord. He now works in a brick factory, while she works the land. She's very proud of her little house, which was built in 1955. Chrysanthemums and asters bloom in the courtyard. She keeps rabbits, pigs, and chickens.

The eggs go to market when there are more than the family needs; the pigs must be sold to the state.

No free markets. Only the state buys. But farmers have private plots. They can sell the produce of private plots to the state [at prices fixed by the state] and keep the cash. They can*not* sell anything to private individuals at mutually agreeable prices.

Next door Mrs. Chang has draped an old carpet over her *kang*, the large brick platform on which the family sleeps in the middle of their single room. Everything is spotlessly clean. [They were expecting us in 1975, as they were not necessarily in 1988.] Big thermos bottles that keep water hot for tea cost Y5.25 [$1.41 then, seventy cents now], which isn't bad. Different people, says Mrs. Chang, do different jobs and get paid differently. Women work more in the fields than men, who do brickmaking, carpentry, and the like.

The commune's general store has short opening hours. Goods are obviously low quality—and they are not abundant. But there is an obvious attempt to give the people something. Outside, customers' bicycles are all chained and padlocked. I ask if there are still thieves in China. The embarrassed manageress cannot answer. The commune's party secretary explains in good Marxist terms that class struggle persists at the present stage of society's development. Crime, he says, will persist until class struggle ends and a new social era begins.

No one talked quite such unmitigated nonsense in 1988, although officialdom still talked a lot of mitigated nonsense. Everyone *had* to talk nonsense in 1975, which now seemed so distant.

My notes on the Marco Polo Bridge Commune concluded:

In places, a fairly modern irrigation system with working sluices. But the fields creeping to the edge of the houses are sprinkled with big watering cans on yokes across shoulders—as they were three millennia ago. On the roads are a few hand tractors—i.e., not ridable, but guided like wheelbarrows—and an occasional car or truck. Many, many carts drawn by a mule and horses or a horse and two donkeys. Little question that these people are better off than they were before the Communists. But they have a long, long way to go . . . a very, very long way.

Aside from the presence of running water, I was, in 1988, struck by one absence. For a score of centuries, dwellings in North China had been dominated by the *kang*, the broad, chest-high sleeping platform heated by an internal fire. I saw no *kang* on my last visit.

I did see cast-iron radiators served by a primitive furnace in another room. Central heating had come to the Marco Polo Bridge Township before indoor plumbing, kitchen ranges, or mechanical refrigeration. Women still cooked on charcoal braziers, although many had separate kitchens, and perishable food was kept outside in the winter.

A midlevel official grinned complacently and pointed out: "No more *kang*—and no more movements. The only movements nowadays are calisthenics."

Her mild pun encapsulated the single most significant change from the Maoist days. *Yündung* means "calisthenics," or "exercise" and thus "movement" or "campaign." Because Mao Tse-tung's catastrophic campaigns, which periodically scourged China, were called *yündung*, people hate the word. In 1988 they boasted political progress had abolished the campaign, just as material progress had replaced the *kang* with central heating.

I learned of the passing of the *kang* in the house of Gwo Xiangchen, a fifty-nine-year-old factory worker and part-time farmer, now retired because of crippling arthritis, and his wife Sulan, who is forty-seven. Built in 1980, their house was outwardly identical to Mrs. Chen's and Mrs. Chang's houses. The Gwos' eldest daughter lived in one tiny room with her husband and two small children; the one-child-a-family limit cannot be enforced on farms, not even so close to Beijing. Two of her sisters worked in a storage-battery plant, the other two on the land beside their husbands.

His wooden crutches beside him, Gwo Xiangchen sat in the nine-by-fifteen living and dining room amid the appliances rural prosperity has brought to Marco Polo Bridge during the past decade. A big Chinese-made color television set that cost Y1,100 ($375) was lovingly protected by a red velvet cover; a smaller Japanese black-and-white set that cost Y500 ($135) stood undraped. Mrs. Chang, I recall, prized her old-fashioned radio in a wooden cabinet; it had been purchased in 1961 for Y177 ($24 now, $48 then), then an immense sum.

A kettle sat on the little potbellied stove that supplemented the Gwos' central heating, and a big wood-cased clock stood on a dressing table beside a white plastic cassette radio. The glass-fronted sideboard displayed wines and liquors. On the walls hung family snapshots, color plates from magazines, and a big calendar showing a sultry model in a pale mink coat.

The Gwos' was obviously a show-house. Still, it was a long way from the days of the *kang*, campaigns, workpoints, and obligatory portraits of Chairman Mao. It was also a very long way from the rural prosperity of Europe, America, or Japan. Nonetheless, the Gwos had prospered with their community.

Marco Polo Bridge Township supplied 10 percent of the vegetables consumed in Beijing. In the winter, its heated plastic greenhouses grew cucumbers, Swiss chard, tomatoes, green peppers, and leeks. The factories, which employed two-thirds of the township's work force of 27,000, produced conveyor belts, automotive parts, hot-water tanks, wooden furniture, and rubber goods, as well as processed foods such as confectionery, chicken parts, and preserved duck eggs. The 10 percent of the firms of the township that were privately owned concentrated on machinery, transportation, and, again, foodstuffs.

Marco Polo Bridge had also, since 1978, been turning out fur coats for export. Not to your taste or mine, those rather ratty furs. But good enough for sale in countries where a fur coat is a new luxury. Certainly good enough for sale within China.

For families who never had central heating, the primitive hand-fired version at Marco Polo Bridge was a wonder. For women who had never had an overcoat, much less a fur coat, Manchurian weasel cobbled together in a Marco Polo workshop would be a delight. It all depends on what one has been accustomed to.

One trend was, however, far less satisfactory: crime.

In 1975 the Information Department of the Foreign Ministry acknowledged that crime was not unknown in the People's Republic. Nor was crime unknown at Marco Polo Bridge Commune, as the commune secretary had acknowledged.

But crime had in 1988 increased significantly throughout China, keeping pace with reform. At Marco Polo Bridge, a member of the township council argued that government cadres (officials) like her husband should be better paid.

"Otherwise, they become corrupt," she said. "Corruption is already a big problem here."

She did not hesitate when I asked for examples. The worst recent case, she said, was the contractor who had skimmed Y30,000 ($8,100, a very large sum), off a construction job for the township. He was sentenced to eight years' imprisonment. Bribing cadres to secure official favors was, after all, a full-scale industry. So were minor defalcations, such as a cadre's buying a table for Y10 and charging the township Y12. The possibilities were endless in a society where officialdom remained all-dominant.

Minor cases were so common they did not normally go to court, but were dealt with by the township's own disciplinary committees. Most malefactors were not imprisoned, but were fined and/or demoted.

Crimes of violence and burglary had also increased. In Beijing, the natives blamed foreigners for ostentatiously displaying their wealth—and inviting robbery or assault. In Canton, so close to Hong Kong and the richest city in China, crimes of violence were particularly numerous, but still strikingly lower than London—and even further below New York.

White-collar crime had increased sharply, rising almost 40 percent over 1986. Most of that spectacular increase was official crime, that is, embezzlement and graft.

Reform had fostered crime as well as inflation. In order to extract every last cent from foreign visitors, Beijing issued a separate currency called foreign exchange certificates. Because only those certificates could buy imported goods in state stores, they were, in 1988, worth 100 percent more than their face value. The black market in foreign exchange certificates thrived beside the black market in foreign currency, preferably dollars.

The narrow sidewalk before the shabby Friendship Store in Chungking was jammed with black-market traders—and their eager clients. Friendship Stores selling imported goods attract outsiders bearing foreign currency. They are a favorite haunt of illegal traders, who often display the sharp features and embroidered skull caps of the Uighur, an enterprising Moslem minority from Xinjiang.

Foreign exchange certificates fostered new crimes. Every Friday, the manager of one foreign firm in Beijing would turn over Y500 ($153) in foreign exchange certificates to pay the weekly postal bill. Every Friday, the clerks would exchange those certificates for Y1,000 ($306) on the black market. After the first week, it was all profit.

Normally notable for their keen interest in each other's hairdos and manicures, the lackadaisical saleswomen at Friendship Stores were attentive when customers paid foreign exchange certificates for Chinese-made goods. They would volunteer to save the patrons' steps by taking the money to the cashier themselves. Metamorphosis into People's Dollars occurred on the way—and who could blame them?

The mass corruption that blighted the last century of the Ching Dynasty had never been completely uprooted by the People's Republic. After the Cultural Revolution, corruption became as rampant as it had been during the last days of the Nationalist regime. Unabashed corruption was, in 1988, highly visible among senior officials.

The son of the governor of Guangdong Province, a notorious playboy, drove a Mercedes sports car around Canton in the abundant leisure left him by the sinecure he occupied in a state-owned corporation. He had been persuaded by the corporation to settle for the Mercedes, which cost $100,000 to import; the Maserati he really wanted would have cost twice as much.

His father was governor of Guangdong because of a deal made by *his* father, Field Marshal Yeh Chien-ying. The field marshal, who led the conservative element in the Politburo, had agreed to go along with

Deng Xiaoping's reforms in return for secure jobs for his children. Another son was deputy director of China's foreign intelligence service, and a daughter was vice-chairwoman of the All-China Women's Association.

Yet the courts were, in 1988, already hypersensitive about the gross corruption bred by economic reform and the opening to the outside world. There was, almost for the first time, a lot worth stealing. Only a few cases could be brought to trial, but those unlucky culprits were given punitive sentences. An executive of a state jewelry house who defrauded Customs of Y30,000 ($8,100) was sentenced to eighteen years in prison. He was charged not with theft or embezzlement, but with corruption because his official position had validated the false declarations he signed. Some malefactors had been shot, but fear did not notably inhibit the new greed.

A few months before the pro-democracy movement made official corruption a critical political issue, then-Secretary General Zhao Ziyang had warned that corruption was a major obstacle to progress. He had then ordered all state economic organs to reduce their spending by at least 20 percent. That decree, which had had little discernible effect, was intended as a blow at corruption. Commodities like cars, TV sets, silks, woolens, refrigerators, and appliances were being bought by "state economic organs" at controlled prices—to be subsequently resold by individuals "for enormous profits."

Several months after the protests were crushed in June 1989, the newly purged Politburo issued a decree that aimed to curtail official theft. Many of the provisions appeared as much cosmetic as punitive. Chinese intellectuals, now skeptics to the last man or woman, were hardly convinced that it would work at all. They doubted that it would be enforced; were it actually to be enforced, they doubted its effect.

Officials were told they must use Chinese-made automobiles, instead of the Mercedes and Nissan limousines that had become the prime status symbol. Neither cadres nor their children might engage in private business, a prohibition that would, if applied rigorously, reduce economic activity in China by at least half. Were the joint chiefs of staff, for one, to give up their extensive holdings, including their share in the Palace Hotel? Of course not, since those were not private, but public— i.e., state—enterprises. Nonetheless, the Kanghua Development Corporation, in which Deng Bufang, the son of Deng Xiaoping, had a major interest, was formally abolished. Similar measures had in the recent past palliated, rather than expunged, scandals.

Inevitable evasion would assuredly make corruption worse. Simultaneously hunting down dissidents who protested against corruption and ostensibly fighting corruption, the party was floundering like a harpooned whale. Its flailing flukes would do great damage.

*   *   *

The councilwoman was unhappy when we asked to see the Marco Polo Bridge Township Hospital. Greatly expanded from the clinic I had seen thirteen years earlier, it was just moving to a new building. When we promised to make allowances, she reluctantly took us to see the hospital, now a center of traditional medicine, primarily acupuncture and herbal therapy.

I have made allowances. The Marco Polo Bridge Township Hospital nonetheless remains in my memory as one of the least inspiring sights of Asia. After herself making allowances, Moira observed, "If I had the choice of having a baby here or in the palm-shack hospital of the Cambodian refugee camp in Thailand, I'd take the refugee camp."

The chief problem was not staff or supplies. It was filth.

The concrete floors were wet, greasy, and gritty. Doctors and nurses wore once-white coats that were dark gray with ingrained grime; the walls were stained and discolored; and the antiquated X-ray machine was festooned with dust. The latrines, porcelain troughs in the floor, as is usual in Asia, were filthy and splattered, as is not usual in Asia. The women's was strewn with used sanitary napkins.

Despite all possible allowances for the disruption of moving, conditions were much worse than 1975—and they had not been good then. I congratulated Dr. Shi Jingshui, the director, on his new premises. I did not ask why he had allowed a sharp decline in simple cleanliness, which is *not* next to survival, but *is* survival in a hospital. The state of his own once-white coat was sufficient answer.

China is a big country that has rarely been too clean. Yet we had never seen such dirtiness as we did in 1988. Hospitals and restaurants, trains, airplanes, and boats were all filthy.

We took a river steamer from Chungking to Wuhan to see China at close hand and to talk to Chinese travelers at their leisure. The talk was good. But we hardly saw the great gorges of the Yangtze River for the mist and the filthy windows, which would have fallen out of their frames if the grime that cemented their putty were removed. Descending to the mess hall in the third-class saloon, each level was more Dante-esque than the last. Men and women slept in triple-decker bunks twelve to a room half the size of the cells for twelve in Beijing's Number One Prison, which were designed for no more than six. Others slept on straw mats spread on littered and stained floors. In the space occupied by one hundred passengers on the river boats for foreign tourists we had eleven hundred.

Despite some newly planted trees on its banks, the Yangtze itself was an immense sewage canal. Everywhere pipelines dumped raw industrial wastes into the river. At Yichang, a long hose, like a fat black sea snake, twisted on the water, belching effluvia. Great bubbles rose from the depths to burst on the surface, spewing noxious gases.

When we tied up at Wuhan, the desperately overworked steward-esses swept into the scuppers all the debris of three days, during which the cabins had never been cleaned. When they hosed that rubbish overboard, they were almost ready for the next passengers, who were pressing on the gates. It only remained to pull the old sheets taut and shake out the used towels.

Downriver lay Shanghai, the great metropolis that has the highest incidence of hepatitis B and consequent liver cancer in the world. A senior biologist warned us not to drink the water, even if it were boiled for tea. Drawn from the spectacularly polluted Whangpoo River, Shanghai water is pestilential. The municipal authorities were trying to raise large sums to transfer the intake to the slightly less polluted Yangtze.

The plump and amiable technical director of a cannery, who was returning to Shanghai on our boat, agreed heartily that cleanliness—the first requisite of good health and good maintenance—should have a high priority. So did everyone with whom we talked, from Beijing to Xi'an and Chengdu to Canton. The Shanghailander finally shrugged his shoulders and said, "It's the universal *cha bu duo* attitude. 'It's a little off—so what?' As long as anything goes, little will go right."

16

China: The Problematic Future

WILL THE MOST POPULOUS NATION IN THE WORLD, WHICH IS WELL PROVIDED WITH NATURAL RESOURCES, BECOME A FORCE IN INTERNATIONAL AFFAIRS? WILL SHE MOVE FORWARD CULTURALLY, ECONOMICALLY, AND POLITICALLY BY USING HER GREATEST RESOURCE: THE INTELLIGENCE AND INDUSTRY OF A PEOPLE PRESENTLY SCANDALOUSLY UNDERWORKED AND UNDERPRODUCTIVE? OR WILL SHE REMAIN A FLACCID MASS, IMPORTANT ONLY BECAUSE OF HER GEOGRAPHICAL POSITION AND HER GREAT SIZE, HER ENORMOUS POTENTIAL DESTINED TO REMAIN FOREVER UNFULFILLED?

The riverboat *Yangtze Fourteen* was letting go the hawsers that bound her to the wharf at Yichang on a cold, windy March afternoon in 1988. Six women wearing drab scarves, baggy trousers, and shabby jackets started up the iron gangplank. They were waved back by two men in uniform: a policeman and a dock official. When the women persisted, not understanding what was happening to them, the two men pushed them off the gangplank back onto the wharf.

The women waved their tickets and protested. The boat was still at the wharf and the gangplank was still out. The purser pushed the gangplank onto the wharf and beckoned. But the dock official lifted his electric megaphone and instructed the purser not to allow those last passengers aboard.

The women stood numbly on the wharf as *Yangtze Fourteen* drew into the stream. They had paid full price for their passage, probably a small bribe as well, and now their tickets were useless. Two wept quietly, still balancing on their shoulders the bamboo carrying poles hung with luggage and gifts for the families they would now not see. Duty done—or whims satisfied—the two men in uniform ostentatiously ignored that small scene of grief. High above their heads a boldly painted slogan directed: IMPROVED SERVICE, BETTER CIVIC ORDER, AND A BEAUTIFUL ENVIRONMENT.

Such abuse of authority is the bane of authoritarian China. Injustice and indignities are constantly inflicted on the common people by the often mindless and usually arbitrary exercise of the great power possessed by every official from neo-Stalinist Premier Li Ping to the lowliest policemen and clerk. The vast bureaucracy is capricious and rapacious; individual bureaucrats are even more insensitive and officious than their counterparts elsewhere. Like the corrupt mandarins of the imperial dynasties, they are virtually unrestrained. No one calls them to account. China is still ruled by men rather than by laws.

Until the total reform—or the replacement—of the sclerotic Communist regime, the Chinese people can expect little surcease from such routine oppression. In the latter half of 1989, oppression became more onerous, as a witch hunt pursued every last minor dissident. Having tasted even limited freedom and having been allowed a glimmer of hope, the volatile Chinese people were even more depressed than they had been before the decade from 1978 to 1988, when *gaigo* and *kaifang*, "reform" and "openness," had briefly flickered.

Their depression was accentuated by the pressure of human beings upon each other. The population, already more than 1.1 billion, was out of control; authoritarian measures had proved incapable of limiting its growth.

A mass of human beings, individuals hardly distinguishable in the crush, had clambered up the iron gangplank of the riverboat at Yichang. They had spread their mats in every passageway, setting out bowls, chopsticks, teapots, and radios. Overflowing the passageways, they had staked out positions on the narrow staircases. On both banks of the Yangtze River, villages, towns, farms, and factories succeeded each other, forming a continuous ribbon of habitation a thousand miles long. In China, one is hardly ever out of sight of other human beings—and never out of earshot.

The unceasing friction of great numbers wears away sensibility. Chinese *must* suppress their normal emotional responses. It is not that they inherently do not care about other human beings. It is simply that they cannot allow themselves to care too much, and so they appear callous.

The average Chinese is, however, hardly the stolid, unfeeling stock figure outsiders believe him or her to be. The average Chinese is high strung and hot tempered. If Chinese were stolid, the pressure of people and politics would not turn so many into hypochondriacs. In China traditional medicine shops are outnumbered only by food stalls and restaurants.

The characteristic Chinese response to acute strain, discomfort, and insecurity is neither the bland smile nor the impassive expression. It is the knee-jiggle. One leg tightly crossed over the other, most men—and many women—vent their tension in minute, barely perceptible spasms, often involuntarily. The chief factor creating tension is just too many people. It is not only rats that become irritable, neurotic, and aggressive when their number grows too large.

Her immense population is China's greatest problem. Her future will be determined by her success in limiting population. Her past record is not encouraging.

At once the most hopeful and the most discouraging aspects of the population problem are that 63 percent of China's population is under the age of thirty, and 29 percent is under fifteen. A young, vigorous population can work harder, more effectively, and more innovatively to build a new China than could a middle-aged and elderly population. Yet a young, vigorous population will produce many more babies to consume the fruits of economic progress—and, perhaps, negate that progress.

After the victorious Communists established the People's Republic in 1949, relative stability and new public-health measures stimulated births and reduced deaths.

In the mid-1950s, the president of Peking University warned that "the spiral of population" would prevent economic progress. Productivity would always lag behind the demands of the new consumers in an endless upward spiral, leaving little or nothing for investment to expand the means of production.

Mao Tse-tung denounced that thesis as Malthusian nonsense, for Marxism held that all things were possible to Socialist labor, including producing abundant food and goods for an ever-expanding population. China's people, the Chairman declared, were China's strength. The bigger China's population, the more powerful she would be industrially and militarily.

Yet, twenty years after Mao's Great Proletarian Cultural Revolution, China suffered from a condition the demographers rather coarsely described as a bulge of fertile women. The Red Guards, the Little Generals of Disorder, had appeared unisex as they stormed across the land. Males and females were indistinguishable either by their garb or their ferocity. They were not unisex after the lights went out. From 1962 to 1976, 25 million babies were born each year. Today, those babies are making their own babies.

In sixty-two Chinese cities the metropolitan population exceeds one million, against thirty-nine cities in the United States, which is far more urbanized. In twenty-three cities, the population of the core city exceeds one million, against six such cities in the U.S.

Beijing has finally acknowledged that population control is faltering badly. Officially, the population was increasing by 1.1 percent annually, roughly by 15 million a year from 1986 to 1990. Even by that reckoning, in the year 2000 there would have been 1.29 billion Chinese, 84 million more than had been anticipated by official pessimists in 1986. Then, in April 1989, the authorities announced that the population had just reached 1.1 billion.

At the beginning of the 1980s, they had predicted confidently that the population would not exceed 1.1 billion by the year 2000. At the end of the 1980s, they were hoping against hope that the population would be "more or less" 1.2 billion in 2000.

That hope was vain. A semiofficial Chinese estimate in early 1989 projected 1.32 billion by the end of the century. Unfortunately, even that revised estimate is low. When I put the figures through my pocket calculator, I was astonished—and a little frightened.

The official figure of 1.08 billion Chinese in 1987, who were increasing at an annual rate of 1.1 percent, gives 1.25 billion by 2000. A more realistic estimate is an increase of at least 1.4 percent annually. Projecting from the generally accepted figure of 1.02 billion in 1980 gives 1.3 billion Chinese living in 1990—and increasing at 16 to 20 million a year. There will thus be slightly more than 1.35 billion Chinese at the turn of the century.

Even before the grim revelation of Population Day in April 1989, Chinese demographers had themselves predicted 1.4 billion in the year 2040—whatever was done. They saw no hope of a decreasing population until the latter half of the twenty-first century.

Natural factors could prevent such wild growth. The upward spiral could slow as the new generation, locustlike, consumed whatever surplus the previous generation had produced—and the means of production, too. The resulting social and economic disruption would lead to *luan*, "chaos." Births would fall and deaths would rise amid famine, epidemics, and strife. But that is not exactly what the leadership wants.

Meanwhile the shrill sound of officialdom whistling as it passes the maternity ward is heard throughout the land. In Chengdu, the capital of Sichuan Province, Moira and I saw a woman in her middle fifties called Jiang Yi, who was vice-chairwoman of the Provincial Family Planning Commission. No whistler, she drew us a disturbing demographic profile of China's most populous province.

Jiang Yi introduced two male experts, both in their late thirties. Each had two children, not the single child that is the ideal—and the legal limit.

Jiang Yi showed us a foursquare countenance, but a shy smile. Both she and her twenty-six-year-old unmarried female assistant were visibly embarrassed when discussing the intrauterine coil. Yet they were professionals engaged in a professional discussion. Chinese women do not like talking about personal matters, and especially not sexual matters. If they won't even talk about it, how many will appreciate the danger, understand the contraceptive devices, and use those devices intelligently?

Moira asked most of the questions. She has studied the population issue and has worked with birth-control organizations in India and Hong Kong.

Jiang Yi candidly acknowledged the magnitude of her problem. Sichuan is home to roughly 10 percent of the Chinese peoples, with 105 million inhabitants at the beginning of 1987 and 108 million at the beginning of 1989. That is an increase of 3 million, which means an annual growth rate of 2.8 percent, twice the *unofficial* figure for all China. Later she backtracked slightly, saying that only in the peak year 1986 had the increase been 3 million. Nonetheless, she added, 1.3 million women have come of childbearing age every year since 1985— and at least the same number will do so every year until 2000.

Possessing no large cities aside from Chengdu and Chungking, Sichuan is primarily agricultural, and farm families just have more children than city families. Recognizing reality, the authorities "advocate" one-child families in the cities, but only "encourage" them in the countryside. Nowadays, a staggering two-thirds of all births in the countryside are technically infractions of the one-child policy.

Before the People's Republic was established in 1949, Jiang Yi noted, most families had six or more children. In the 1950s and 1960s, the average was four to five children. Today in Sichuan the average is still two to three children to a family.

"The people," Jiang Li said, "must be taught that it is in their own interest to keep their families down." Coercion had already failed signally.

"We must teach the people that the economic situation is not very vigorous," she continued. "There isn't enough land. In Sichuan we have only one *mou* [a sixth of an acre] per head, compared to eight *mou* [1.33 acres] in the United States. There's no shortage of labor, only a shortage of land. Really, there's too much labor available. . . . Fewer children mean more land for each child. Besides, the first child gets free education. All after that must pay.

. . . too many children cut down parents' opportunities. Nowadays, people can travel. They can change their jobs, buy more things, and have a better life."

Men are not supposed to marry before twenty-five or women before twenty-three, but only 30 percent wait that long in the countryside. Throughout China, 20 percent of all country girls marry before they are twenty, many making old-fashioned arranged marriages.

In the past, only 20 percent of the women of Sichuan used contraceptives. Now 80 percent use some device: long-term or short-term pills, condoms, foam, and, above all, intrauterine devices.

The atmosphere was momentarily tense when Moira demurred. Why the continuing high growth rate, she asked, if so many actually used the devices? And where were the paramedics trained to insert all those coils? If 80 percent of Sichuan's roughly 25 million nubile women had really acquired birth-control devices, Moira said, they were certainly not using them regularly. Otherwise the birth rate would be lower.

In the long run, Jiang Yi thus implicitly conceded, the population of China will rise until the people of China decide they want fewer children. And the Chinese have been conditioned by two thousand years of Confucianism to believe that producing many children is not only advantageous, but virtuous.

In the eighteenth century, the great Kang Hsi Emperor demonstrated his loving concern for his subjects by abolishing the head tax that had been levied on every Chinese. After eight decades the population had doubled to 313 million. By 1850, when a century of war and revolution began to reduce their numbers, there were 430 million Chinese. The population had increased almost three times in fewer than 150 years.

When Mao Tse-tung won the civil war a few decades ago, stability followed—and the population began to rise. The Great Leap Forward and the Great Proletarian Cultural Revolution checked that rise until the mid-1970s. Then stability, larger incomes, and improved public-health measures encouraged growth. In 1949 there were fewer than 500 million Chinese; at the turn of the century, there are likely to be close to 1.4 billion. A threefold increase in just half a century is staggering—and very frightening.

Nonetheless, Mao Tse-tung was right. China's greatest natural resource is her people, just as the people have been the decisive resource of the neo-Confucian societies outside China that are virtually devoid of other natural resources. Highly adaptable, the Chinese people could make their motherland powerful—industrially and commercially, as well as militarily. All they need to do is work intelligently and diligently.

But they will not do so unless their efforts are rewarded by a better life. They must receive a fair share of the earnings from whatever they produce, whether rice or washing machines. And goods must be abundant so that they can buy what they need. Such needs, of course, keep getting bigger, and such rising expectations fuel economic growth. The Chinese respond to so-called material incentives as eagerly as any other people—perhaps even more eagerly than most. Getting rich is the universal dream. Deng Xiaoping knew that when he introduced his economic reforms in 1978 with the promise that everyone would have the chance to get rich.

The initial results of those reforms was spectacular. Benefiting from their own efforts, the Chinese people increased production spectacularly. Some of the results: industrial production grew at the rate of 16 percent a year from 1979 until 1989; farmers' incomes trebled from 1979 to 1987; the Gross Domestic Product, which is, of course, the sum of all goods and services a country turns out, increased by 96 percent during the same period; and family incomes rose by 56 percent from 1981 to 1987, approximately doubling from 1978 through 1988.

Economic development was based upon a three-pronged strategy: first, *decentralization* of decision making from Beijing to the provinces, from provincial capitals to local officials, and from officials to individual entrepreneurs; second, concentration upon the coastal provinces, which enjoy easy access to the trade and the technology of the outside world; and the third, township enterprises, which have already been discussed.

Decentralization was clearly essential. China would be far too big and too diverse to be run as a unit from a single switchboard, even if she did possess good transportation and communications, which she emphatically does not. Yet relaxation of control led not only to regionalism, but to crime and severe inflation. Further, the bureaucrats of Beijing were reluctant to surrender authority to the provinces; provincial officials hesitated to give much authority to the counties; and *all* government and/or party officials hated giving up their economic power to private individuals. Economic power meant political power and privilege.

The controversial coastal policy blatantly discriminated against the interior, even though it made good sense to concentrate on the areas with the greatest potential for rapid growth. The coastal population is more adaptable and more skilled; long-distance road transport in the interior is vestigial, and air transport is totally inadequate. It was far better for exporters, as well as importers, to ship by sea, rather than by overburdened railways or inadequate river barges to and from the interior.

The interior naturally felt itself condemned to second-class citizenship. The proud Sichuanese, who had never been conquered by Japanese armies or colonized by alien merchants, compared the lopsided development to the bad old days when foreigners virtually ruled the seaboard. Foreigners lived in the Treaty Ports under their own laws, administered by their own people, having won at the cannon's mouth the privilege of ignoring the laws of China. That analogy stung Beijing.

The Sichuanese further pointed out that the coastal provinces were reestablishing the monopolies once exercised by the foreigners. True, the coastal provinces did not welcome inlanders participating in their foreign trade, or setting up factories to make goods for export. The aggrieved inlanders charged that China was again dominated and exploited by a foreign-oriented seaboard.

Semiautonomous commercial and industrial baronies were particularly strong in the coastal provinces: some of them what the Chinese call *duli wanggwo*, "independent kingdoms," which controlled many export commodities, such as tea, herbal medicines, and freshwater pearls. Those kingdoms clashed with the central government, but the balance of power was shifting in their favor. Power was also shifting from party and government functionaries to men and women like Wang Shuren, the factory manager whom we met on the train to Chungking. Power was also passing from the old political warriors to the new economic technocrats within both party and government—at the provincial and local level, as well as at the center.

In 1989, even before the tragic pro-democracy demonstrations of May and June, the old guard and the bureaucracy were fighting back hard. The Communist party's seventy-one-year-old secretary general, Zhao Ziyang, was already under attack; even the durability of the eighty-four-year-old paramount leader, Deng Xiaoping, was naturally in question. The man who had led China out of the slough of Maoism might live a good deal longer, but he might not. Ironically, Deng was under attack by progressives for slowing down reform and by the old guard for forcing the pace.

When inflation had exceeded 40 percent, the old guard forced a slowdown under the slogan "Control and Rectify." Basic projects were decelerated, suspended, or abandoned—and unemployment rose acutely among those highly paid aristocrats of Chinese labor, the construction workers. Joint ventures with foreign capital and foreign knowhow were delayed, and many enterprises were relieved of the right to deal directly with foreigners. Borrowing from abroad was curtailed, as was privatization of state-owned companies.

Above all, prices were controlled. Because there could not be free development without a reasonably free market, the authorities had originally freed some prices from state regulation. They had been planning to free most prices for commodities, services, and housing. Fixed prices enforced by the state, they had originally calculated, would amount to continuing control from the center—and, therefore, continuing inefficiency. Frightened by inflation, Beijing postponed that ultimate test.

Prime Minister Li Peng, Chou En-lai's adopted son, who was soon to become the most hated man in China, declared at the Eighth National People's Congress in March 1989, "We shall never return to the old economic mode characterized by overcentralized, excessive, and rigid control. Nor shall we adopt private ownership, negating the Socialist system."

Following that retrogressive warning, university graduates were told they would again be assigned to jobs, rather than be allowed to choose their own work. The free market in housing, planned to encourage new construction, was "postponed." Attempts were made to reinstate total price control, and the fledgling share markets were sharply restricted. The progressive secretary general, Zhao Ziyang, was thus overruled publicly—and his mentor, Deng Xiaoping, said nothing.

Influential groups were unhappy with that retrogressive policy. Both practical managers and theoretical economists knew that China could not tread water but must either move forward or backward. Intellectuals and university students were outraged—not only by their renewed relegation to serfdom, but by the portents for the country. Themselves appalled by inflation, students and their mentors knew that simply clamping on controls would not solve the problem. Besides, they had savored the unprecedented, albeit unlimited, freedom to teach openly and to discuss candidly among themselves and with foreigners; to read foreign books and see films; even to speak out and to publish. All they had won was now threatened.

The death of the former secretary general of the Communist Party, Hu Yaobang, gave the students an opening. Hu had originally been designated by Paramount Leader Deng Xiaoping to lead the reform movement. But he had become too progressive. Attacked by the old guard, he had been removed from power with Deng Xiaoping's approval after nationwide student demonstrations demanded greater democracy in late 1986.

In the spring of 1989 students in all China's big cities dedicated memorial wreaths to Hu Yaobang and praised his accomplishments. They also demanded more effective economic reform and greater governmental responsiveness to the popular will—that is, an increase in democracy.

By late April 1989, the upsurge of popular indignation was the highest since 1976, when demonstrators in Tienanmen Square had forced the reactionaries to bring Deng Xiaoping back to power.

Demonstrations in the capital, often centered on Tienanmen Square, had been a significant political force since 1919, when student militants initiated the May Fourth Movement, which led directly to the establishment of the Communist   Party of China. Demonstrations throughout China, usually starting in Peking, had over the decades vitally helped to end the era of the warlords; to bring the Nationalists to power; to rally the nation against the Japanese invaders; and, finally, to turn domestic and international public opinion against the Nationalists so that the Communists could seize power.

In the late spring of 1989, the students, inspired by the new climate of limited freedom, believed they could change the nation. By the biggest demonstrations ever mounted in Tienanmen Square, they confidently planned to compel the Communist Party to grant greater freedom and to move toward democracy.

They were, of course, wrong. Expecting China under the Communists—or, perhaps, under any government presently conceivable—to become a liberal democracy with freedom of speech, assembly, and the press was like expecting oysters to dance. Neither was built for the role.

The West equates progress with human rights and representative government. Authoritarian by temperament and training, the old guard of the Chinese Communist Party distrusts liberal democracy as debilitating, indeed as decadent and even evil. They were determined to grant the people as little freedom as they could. True, the reform leadership had recognized that economic progress required a reasonably free exchange of ideas, as did acquiring Western skills. They thought, however, that they could limit those exchanges to technical and commercial concepts.

It was the centuries-old delusion again. Western liberalism was to provide the material basis—that is, the technology and capital. Chinese authoritarianism, in this case Marxist rather than Confucian, was, however, to run the state, direct economic activity, and control the people.

The old master Deng Xiaoping said, "Inflation and crime are like the flies that come in when you open the windows after they've been closed for a long time. We can put up with the flies, since we can't do without the fresh air."

Even for most of Deng Xiaoping's supporters—and, of course, for his enemies—liberal democracy, civil rights, and free expression were also flies. But those flies, they felt, they need *not* put up with.

The Seventh National People's Congress, in the spring of 1988, had been allowed to express a wide range of opinion on political as well as economic subjects. The Eighth National People's Congress a year later was told to confine its comments to the economy—and to be circumspect in those comments.

Secretary General Zhao Ziyang had already made it blatantly clear that he would not—or could not—go as far as had Mikhail Gorbachev. The Soviet leader had not only released from internal exile Andrei Sakharov, the great theoretical physicist and profound critic of the regime, but had publicly consulted him. Zhao Ziyang had ordered that China's Sakharov, the theoretical physicist and profound critic of the regime, Fang Lizhi, be kept from attending a reception in Beijing to which President George Bush had asked him—and had lectured Bush on keeping America's nose out of China's internal affairs. That decision probably reflected Zhao's own inclination, as well as the will of his mentor, Deng Xiaoping. Both were, however, soon to be toppled by the old guard they had deposed to clear the way for the reform movement. Zhao Ziyang was to lose his position. Deng Xiaoping was to become the virtual prisoner of the reactionaries—and their mouthpiece.

Brave men and women had been demonstrating for the release of dissidents held prisoner, for civil rights, for democratic reform, and for effective economic measures. Students marched and chanted, supported by the workers. Posters denouncing Deng Xiaoping's children for corruption, and even Deng himself, warned: "Waves support a boat, but they can also overturn it!"

The regime issued repeated warnings. Dissidents would not be released, and restrictions on free expression would not be relaxed. But the student-worker alliance, inspired by older intellectuals, would not yield. A million men and women marched through the streets of Beijing—and additional millions marched in more than twenty other cities. The Communist Party felt it was under siege.

At the eleventh hour, its nominal leaders sallied forth to parley with the enemy. Both Secretary General Zhao Ziyang and Premier Li Peng went into Tienanmen Square and into hospitals to talk with dissidents who were on hunger strikes and urge them to desist.

Having been an archenemy, Zhao Ziyang became a hero to the students, who believed with some truth that he was their champion in the councils of the mighty. Premier Li Peng they did not trust, seeing in him a heartless Soviet-trained autocrat. Deng Xiaoping they mocked because he was obviously enfeebled, unable to read a speech without losing the thread. They called him "idiot" and worse. Beijing was strewn with symbolically broken bottles because Xiaoping, his given name, sounds like "little bottle." Demonstrations spread across the country, and more discontented workers joined the students in those vehement expressions of popular disgust with Communist rule.

To Deng Xiaoping it looked like a nationwide revolt in embryo. He turned to the old guard, the men he had moved from positions of power to the powerless Consultative Committee. Those half-dozen octogenarians did not believe in liberal reform, but in a rigidly planned, stringently directed economy and a strictly regimented populace. They certainly did not believe in shilly-shallying with a movement they saw as nothing less than a counter-revolutionary conspiracy, a concerted plot to overthrow socialism by violence and replace it with decadent liberal democracy. That plot, they convinced themselves, was supported by sinister external forces, primarily Taiwan and the United States.

Inspired by those diehards, ruthless Premier Li Peng proclaimed martial law. The terrible climax of the drama was played out before the world press and their cameras. Three times troops of the People's

Liberation Army sought to persuade the increasingly confident dissidents to end their occupation of Tienanmen Square. Three times those troops were humiliated and turned back, for they were either unarmed or had been ordered not to use their weapons.

Tens of thousands of students from other cities poured into Beijing to join the demonstration, which now demanded immediate reforms. The campuses of the capital became the command posts of the resistance. Supported by the workers of Beijing and lauded by the normally controlled press, television, and radio, the dissidents smelled victory. They barricaded the city with trucks, buses, and cement barriers, convinced that they could keep the Liberation Army from entering. They burned the armored personnel carriers, army trucks, and buses that attempted to breach those barriers. They were confident, as was the watching world, that the regime would not dare suppress their demonstrations by brute force, but would have to make concessions.

They were, as the world saw, very wrong. Power had passed into the hands of the reactionary gerontocracy, headed by eighty-two-year-old Field Marshal Yang Shangkun, chief of staff of the Red Army in the 1930s. He had been designated president of the People's Republic in one of those deals of ten-layered intricacy in which Deng Xiaoping specialized. Yang Shangkun had at his disposal the Twenty-seventh Army, stationed in Manchuria, which was commanded by a member of his family. In the early morning of June 4, the Twenty-seventh Army cleared Tienanmen Square.

Suppression of the popular will by force was nothing new in so-called People's China. Never before, however, had the bloodletting occurred in full view of the domestic and international media. Careless of the effect abroad, the soldiers had been ordered to shoot the demonstrators. They not only opened fire with automatic weapons, but crushed under their tanks the tents the students had erected, killing the occupants. To reinforce fear, films of the massacre were shown on domestic television.

Ruling by terror, the new leadership was only later to attempt to whitewash its atrocities by declaring that the troops had been provoked and that, in any event, only a hundred-odd demonstrators, all "counterrevolutionaries," had been killed. The actual figure was probably between one and two thousand dead, but no one was to know precisely. Bodies in Tienanmen Square and hospitals were burned by the soldiers.

I see no need to recount again the scenes of horror and heroism that were broadcast to the entire world. Few who saw those days of torment will ever forget them. Somewhat macabrely watching in their comfortable living rooms, like an audience at a play, spectators were drawn into the terrible drama, which seared their consciousness as few plays have ever done.

Secretary General Zhao Ziyang and his supporters in the Political

Bureau and the Central Committee of the Communist Party had already been neutralized. The octogenarians of the formally powerless Consultative Committee, to which Deng Xiaoping appealed, had usurped authority and concluded that they must regain control of their capital by armed force. China showed once again that she was not governed by laws, not even by the internal regulations of the Communist Party, but by the will of the men who controlled the guns. The virtual coup d'etat succeeded handily in good part because the usurpers were so old. In proper Confucian fashion, venerating great age, the Communist Party bowed to the authority bestowed by their longevity—and ignored its own constitution.

Orderly transition of authority was no more possible within the party than it was within the state structure. Having seized the levers of control, the usurpers displaced Zhao Ziyang. He was the second man Deng Xiaoping had designated to oversee reforms and the second man to whose degradation Deng Xiaoping had consented. Like Hu Yaobang before him, Zhao Ziyang had sinned by becoming too committed to reform.

He and the so-called liberal members of the hierarchy were replaced by hard-line apparatchiks. The colorless former mayor of Shanghai, Jiang Zemin, was appointed secretary general of the party. A disciplinarian, he nonetheless stood for continuing economic progress and for cooperation with foreign entrepreneurs. But he was without any inclination toward decadent "bourgeois liberalism." The old guard believed it could resume internal economic progress bolstered by foreign techniques and capital as if nothing untoward had happened. On television Deng Xiaoping, hardly capable of completing his remarks, praised the Liberation Army as heroes who had saved the nation by putting down the counter-revolutionary violence.

Thus was stability apparently restored. The new secretary general of the party was not precisely a figurehead, but neither was he even unchallengeably first among equals. The office had itself been degraded. The power of decision lay in the hands of Yang Shangkun, the president of the People's Republic and the only one of the Communists' original ten field marshals still alive and active. He controlled the troops, and power grew out of the barrel of the gun.

A new high tide of repression rolled over China. The relentless pursuit of dissidents and the systematic terrorization of the Chinese people were pressed on television, which had suddenly assumed a central role in the affairs of the nation. Apprehended student leaders were shown in humiliating postures before they were shot. The sister of one fugitive was honored for betraying his whereabouts, lest the entire family suffer.

Only two months later was the government to realize that constant reports of executions were angering the Chinese people and horrifying outsiders. The reports were thereupon halted, but the executions continued in private. Infuriated because leaders of the pro-democracy movement had succeeded in fleeing China by bribing train conductors and border guards, the authorities attempted to seal the borders. Land frontiers and seaports were heavily patrolled. Flights from Beijing and Shanghai were delayed for hours while police searched baggage containers and aircraft to ensure that no dissident had stowed away.

Those who had escaped, however, proclaimed a virtual alternative government in exile. Supported by the conscience of the world, they revealed the atrocities committed by the Communists and swore to overthrow the tyrannical regime. Beijing warned foreign governments against assisting those dissidents in their purposes, even by giving them asylum. The Communists remembered too well that Dr. Sun Yat-sen, the moving spirit in the Revolution of 1911, which overthrew the Ching Dynasty, had found safety outside China's borders and had been supported chiefly by the overseas Chinese of the Americas and Southeast Asia. Remembering how greatly the endorsement of world public opinion had helped them win their own victory, the Communists were far more frightened by the feeble dissident movement than its feebleness warranted.

A year earlier Beijing had been clamorous with the din of construction and the roar of traffic. But the yellow cranes that had bobbed on the dust-smudged horizon were still in the early autumn of 1989. Foreign tourists and foreign businessmen had virtually disappeared, and economic activity was sluggish. Stallkeepers who had been harried by customers a year earlier now had plenty of time to play cards and read. The continual patrols of soldiers did not interfere with those pastimes, not yet. But the slightest disturbance was met with a show of great force, and potential troublemakers were immediately arrested.

University campuses were funereally quiet, for the students remaining would not jeopardize their lives by overt opposition to the harsh regime. Secret police raids had harrowed the student bodies and the faculties. The number of entrants for the next academic year had been cut back. Peking University, at the center of the political storm, as it had been for almost a century, was penalized by having its freshman class reduced from 1,900 to 800. Liberal think tanks were closed or purged, and even the director of the Institute of Mao Tse-tung Thought had fled abroad. The latent anti-intellectualism of the old guard flared destructively.

Taxis no longer plied the streets at night, and the little eating places were closing down. Bursts of gunfire were heard during the hours of darkness. The Liberation Army was cleansing the capital of counter-revolutionaries. So the authorities said. But the people knew that stray soldiers were also being picked off by armed dissidents. The stability reestablished by the "heroic Liberation Army" was, to say the least, not wholly secure.

The immediate economic cost of the upheaval was just calculable. Lost production cost Y3 billion ($806 million), and lost revenues from tourism in May alone were Y40 million (almost $11 million). With no recovery in prospect, tourism losses could run as high as $100 million a year. The Gross Domestic Product, which had been rising sharply, fell back sharply in May and hardly recovered in June. Beijing showed an actual decrease in production in May, for a total loss in "missing growth" of Y800 million ($215 million).

Not remarkably, damage control was the chief priority. Despite the leadership's demonstration of contempt for foreign public opinion, foreign-related enterprises were given the highest priority. Joint ventures were promised less bureaucratic interference and were offered special assistance. The hard-line leadership continued to believe it could do business with foreigners, while, somehow, limiting foreign cultural influence.

Such contradictions beset China. Intent on economic development, the regime was dependent upon the military to maintain order. Intent upon decentralization to improve economic performance, the regime was seeking to reimpose central control on a wide range of enterprises in order to reclaim the political power that had flowed outward to the localities with the dispersal of economic power. Proclaiming itself a modernizer, the regime was determined to restore a political and ideological order based upon authoritarian control. Mounting a crusade against official corruption, the regime could depend for support only upon the cadres it was thus depriving of their perquisites. Above all, the elite of the younger generation and the intellectuals needed to guide economic development were totally disaffected.

How long, some wondered, could the dissidents hold out against overwhelming pressure? Others wondered how long the regime could rest on the maze of contradictions that were cracking its foundations.

Regardless, the orthodox believed their earlier warnings had been vindicated. Liberal ideas and luxury goods from the outside world had undeniably corrupted the youth of China. Why else should they have risen against the worthy proletarian Communist Party?

A conversation sometime before the "counter-revolutionary upheaval" encapsulated the puritan attitude, which is not entirely invalid. An elderly Chinese lady who had been educated in the United States said to me: "You're staying at the Great Wall? That hotel is *everything* that's wrong with China today. It's corrupting our youth with its sybaritic luxury. . . . A little while ago I wanted something special for a family gathering. I sent my daughter, who was visiting from England, to the baked goods shop at the Great Wall. She came back with a wonderful pink cake. She'd paid Y96, more than a month's wages for a worker. . . . No wonder our young people are acquiring false values. No wonder they're only interested in flashy things and luxury."

Of course, idealism is by no means dead, and courage is at its apogee among the youth of China. From the point of view of that elderly lady, however, it is the wrong kind of idealism, and the courage is misdirected.

She was, of course, implicitly criticizing the United States, which epitomizes the outside world for Chinese. By far the world's leading purveyor of popular culture, the United States has, since Richard Nixon and Henry Kissinger restored communications in 1972, enjoyed special access to Chinese minds. Moreover, China still respects the U.S. as a great power, indeed *the* great power that balances the Soviet threat. The Chinese also display respect not seen everywhere for the U.S. as an industrial power and a technical innovator. That is why more Chinese are studying in the U.S. than in any other foreign country.

Even more after the June 4 massacre, which has totally altered the Communists' relations with their own people and with the rest of the world, China represents a challenge, as well as an opportunity, for the U.S. Briefly stated it is this: *How best to help the Chinese people without propping up an odious regime?*

A total boycott on trade, technical assistance, and investment would, it appears to me, be counterproductive. The Chinese people, rather than their rulers, would be hurt badly. The regime has repeatedly said that it wanted to continue its economic development much as before, despite the new totalitarianism and the retreat from reform. Economic activity has, of course, suffered greatly—and will not recover readily. Nonetheless, I believe it is in the interest of both the American and the Chinese people for the United States to continue to trade and invest— with strictly military items embargoed. Certainly some militarily useful items will slip by, but that cannot be helped; and they could be purchased elsewhere, anyway.

America's imports and exports have for the past several years amounted to 10 percent of China's total trade, third in volume after Japan and Hong Kong/Macao. Although total Sino-American trade of $8.8 billion in 1988 was less than half Japan's $17.6 billion, it was a respectable figure. The U.S. was, moreover, China's second biggest investor after Hong Kong/Macao, with some $2.7 billion either in place or allocated.

The United States was, in the winter of 1989, holding slightly aloof. Others, most notably the Japanese and the Germans, were rushing back to China in renewed search of profits, having reluctantly joined the exodus after June 4. There was good reason for the U.S., too, to return, albeit cautiously. Assisting China's economic growth would not necessarily mean bolstering the regime. Indeed, it could mean quite the reverse, for the strains introduced into Chinese society by economic development had already proved inimical to totalitarian rule. That was, of course, the chief reason for the grisly confrontation in Tienanmen Square.

At the same time, the U.S. should continue to do all it can to encourage the expansion of pro-democratic sentiments and actions in China—overtly and, if necessary, covertly. Thus could Americans participate directly in China's intellectual rebirth and political transformation. As we have seen, ideas are more powerful than commodities—and could in the long run prove more powerful than guns. The U.S. is clearly the chief mentor of the pro-democracy movement. Continuing to assist that movement by whatever means are possible would assure the U.S. a continuing place in the largest and most populous nation of East Asia, the region that is certain to be immensely important, if not dominant, in the twenty-first century.

America's special place in the regard—and even the affection—of the Chinese people was demonstrated by Jang Loxi, production manager of the Shanghai cannery, when he and I stood in the darkness on the foredeck of the *Yangtze Fourteen*, running down to Wuhan. We were watching the long beams of the boat's twin searchlights play on the banks like blind men's canes.

Musing on national characteristics, Jang said, "The Japanese are very difficult to deal with. Very stiff, very hard, and very grasping. They're only interested in money—always more and more money, but nothing else. They want you to carry the whole burden while they get all the profits. . . . We want our customers and our suppliers to be satisfied. That makes for a lasting relationship. . . . The Japanese really want to control China economically. . . . They want to make us a commercial colony—as they tried to do with guns last time."

His cigarette sketched a fiery arch in the night. He flipped it away and continued. "The Koreans are good to deal with. The best, though, are the Americans. They've got the British straightforwardness, and they're a big, powerful country with a big, powerful economy. China and America should work together. Leaving out Japan, only America is big enough to really help us get going. And the Americans are happy to split the profits down the middle."

This is, of course, anecdotal evidence. But how else is one to measure attitudes? Jang Loxi's detestation of the Japanese certainly reflects the feelings of most of his compatriots. So too, I believe, from much additional evidence, does his attitude toward Americans.

Great satisfaction was felt on both sides of the Taiwan Straits during the eight-year war between Iran and Iraq. One of Iran's chief weapons was the Silkworm missile, made in the People's Republic; a number of the big tankers that were its potential targets had been built by the China Shipbuilding Corporation in southern Taiwan. More interested today in trade than in political influence, Beijing has been selling arms to virtually all comers. Taipei is, of course, a major industrial power, a leading manufacturer of locomotives, plastics, and electronics, among many other products.

On either side of the Taiwan Straits all Chinese are proud that China is overcoming her previous military and industrial inferiority. Moreover, traffic between Beijing and Taiwan was increasing daily until June 4. The political division between the two had not notably narrowed, but it was becoming less important than common feelings and common interests.

Even more now, Taiwan is determined to maintain its separate identity. Taiwanese goods enter the mainland free of duty because the island is "an integral part of China." Mainland goods are, in theory at least, still prohibited imports to Taiwan because the Beijing regime is "illegally occupying the territory of the Republic of China." Taipei is not likely to accept Beijing's invitation to become a self-governing province of the People's Republic. Little or nothing recommends such reunification to Taipei.

Although the atrocity has put the clock back, the two Chinese states will, in time, grow closer. Perhaps they will even integrate, although I have little idea when or under what conditions. Alternately, the division will be maintained for pride's sake, but will no longer be as heavily stressed. The two regimes already share much the same attitudes toward the Japanese, the Soviets, and the Americans—the other major players in the great arena of East Asia.

Older Taiwanese, remembering the Japanese era, feel not only respect but fondness for their former overlords. Young Taiwanese neither speak Japanese nor remember the Japanese era. Although their primary loyalty is given to Taiwan rather than the vast abstraction called China, they speak the common language of China and consider themselves Chinese. They therefore look at the Japanese through Chinese eyes, and they are unhappy with ruthless Japanese competition and with Japanese takeovers of their industries.

The Chinese of Taiwan also share a sense of inevitability with the Chinese of the mainland. Although they do not like it, the Japanese are their chief customers and their chief suppliers. The Chinese of Taiwan also wish the Japanese were as chary of investment in Taiwan as they are in the mainland, where most Japanese profits come from trade, loans, and royalties, rather than joint ventures.

The Americans, too, evoke roughly similar responses on both sides of the Taiwan Straits. The attitude on Taiwan is, however, more complex—and not only because American trade and investment there are much greater than in the People's Republic. Both the mainlanders and the Taiwanese on the island feel greater resentment toward the Americans than do the Chinese of the People's Republic. The mainlanders on Taiwan resent having danced to America's tune for so many years when they could do nothing else. The Taiwanese resent the Americans' expressed sympathy toward their aspirations for greater freedom because the Americans have done little to help. They also resent the American rapprochement with the People's Republic, which has hastened the day when the two parts of China come together—and the Taiwanese become the third wheel on the tandem bicycle.

Relations with the Soviet Union are the most complex of the three chief foreign engagements of the People's Republic. Beijing has for decades looked upon the Soviets with fear. Although now abating, that fear is still a dominant emotion, based as it is upon centuries of friction.

From 1949 to 1959, the People's Republic and the Soviet Union were, in territory and population, the largest bilateral alliance in human history—and potentially the most powerful. Had they not feared that an enlarged conflict could become nuclear, the two could have handily defeated the American, British Commonwealth, European, Asian, and Latin American forces that opposed the North Korean invasion of South Korea. Yet the Sino-Soviet alliance collapsed amid public recrimination less than a decade later.

The bitter invective that was normal between the pair for the next two decades has altered. Relations are not intimate, but they are closer in the era of the reformers Deng Xiaoping and Mikhail Gorbachev than they have been since 1950. In an atmosphere of rapprochement, a major question arises: *Will the two nominally Socialist colossi make up their differences and again present a formidable united front to the world?*

The answer is no. China and the Soviet Union are unlikely to reunite as close allies seeking common purposes. Too many forces divide them. The summit meeting between Deng Xiaoping and Mikhail Gorbachev was overshadowed by the pro-democracy movement. Nonetheless, China rejected a renewal of "Socialist solidarity" and clearly remained unconvinced that its neighbor's intentions were wholly peaceful.

China will remain closer to the West and Japan than to the Soviet Union—if only because material progress remains her avowed national purpose. She cannot obtain from the Soviets what they do not possess: the industrial, scientific, and technological resources available in the United States, Europe, and Japan.

Americans may congratulate themselves on their skill in playing the China card, but the Chinese have very astutely played both the America card and the Soviet card.

No magic wand has waved away the centuries-old conflicts between the Chinese Empire and the Russian Empire that were at the root of their ideological quarrel. A common border more than 4,500 miles long bred contention, and in the seventeenth century the two empires fought their first war. China lost and was forced to grant trading concessions and to cede territory in Siberia to Russia in the Treaty of Nerchinsk, which was signed in 1689. In the nineteenth century, coercion forced the Ching emperors to grant vast stretches in Siberia to the Tsars.

China does not today fear direct attack. She would not otherwise have reduced the People's Liberation Army by a quarter of its strength, about one million men, during the past few years. Seeking to increase military efficiency and to lighten the economic burden, that demobilization would, nonetheless, not have occurred if Beijing thought the Russians would march across their common border.

Beijing does fear encirclement. Soviet territory lying to the north, the northeast, and the northwest effectively commands China's land communications to Europe. To the south lies Indo-China, which is dominated by Viet Nam, a Soviet client state. Chinese and Vietnamese armies have clashed repeatedly in recent years. Moreover, the Soviet Far East Fleet menaces China's ocean-borne communications, its two major bases, like pincers: Vladivostok in Siberia to the northeast, and Cam Ranh Bay in Viet Nam to the southeast. The circle is almost closed.

Deng Xiaoping laid down specific preconditions for the summit meeting. Mikhail Gorbachev, for his own reasons, met those demands. The Soviets withdrew from Afghanistan, and the Vietnamese were withdrawing from Cambodia. Gorbachev also pledged to withdraw almost 200,000 men from the Chinese border, but will leave an equal number.

The Russians, too, have their fears. The Yellow Peril lives in the race memory of a people who were for centuries terrorized and enslaved by the Mongol hordes.

Fundamental conflicts of interest are exacerbated by such centuries-old hatreds and fears, which have been reinforced by the clashes of recent decades. Mutual Sino-Soviet tolerance is possible, though it will be clouded by suspicion. Warm friendship is virtually impossible.

The fundamental relationships with the United States, Japan, and the Soviet Union will shape China's foreign policy almost as much as do internal imperatives. China will, further, play a far more active role in the affairs of the Pacific-Asian region, particularly Southeast Asia and Northeast Asia, her old areas of primary influence.

The People's Republic is potentially a great power in the twenty-first century. If she combined with Japan, they could form a new center of world power. But old hatreds and mutual distrust make such a combination unlikely. China is more likely to make common cause with the Republic of Kore , whose skills could vivify her reserves of human and natural raw mate.:ial. That combination would prove formidable diplomatically and militarily as well as economically.

Equally, China could remain a flaccid mass, enervated by her internal difficulties. She is beset not only by inertia, bureaucracy, and mass disaffection, but by restive minority peoples like the Tibetans. Moreover, her sheer size makes efficient centralized administration impossible.

Nonetheless, China's great weight is likely to tell in the community of nations. Unlike her neighbor, the Soviet Union, China possesses a talented, largely homogeneous population with a common language, as well as national cohesion against the outside world. She is, moreover, the heiress of an extremely long tradition of cultural, economic, and political influence—often domination—over her neighbors.

17

Hong Kong: The Floating Island

A MINUTE ENTITY TOSSED BETWEEN THE BRITISH LION AND THE CHINESE DRAGON, THE CROWN COLONY OF HONG KONG WAS SIRED UPON GREED BY IMPERIALIST FORCE. PROSPERING UNDER UNBRIDLED FREE ENTERPRISE, IT BECAME A WORLD MANUFACTURING AND TRADING CENTER. IT ALSO PROVIDED HAVEN AND OPPORTUNITY FOR THE DISPOSSESSED OF CHINA. A PLACE OF PASSAGE, HONG KONG IS SOON TO PASS ITSELF. IN 1997, AFTER 155 YEARS OF SEPARATE EXISTENCE, IT IS TO BE ENGORGED BY CHINA. WITH WHAT CURIOUS RESULTS FOR BOTH?

I could not write objectively about Hong Kong even if I wanted to. It is too much part of me, the peninsula that, with its garland of islets, covers four hundred square miles at the southeastern extremity of China. I have lived amid its unremitting change over a period of twenty-five years, longer than anywhere else.

Hong Kong is home, the small place on earth I care most about. After hundreds of arrivals and departures, my throat still tightens when the airliner starts its descent toward the concrete runway thrust into the bay and I see again the brash and gorgeous pyrotechnics of its lights. Then I remember again how a subtropical backwater became a dynamic city-state in a historical instant, in not quite two decades.

Before World War II, Hong Kong was a second-rate place. Inferior to Shanghai in finance and in enterprise, it was inferior to Singapore commercially as well as strategically. Not much more than a convenient steppingstone between those two great British bastions in Asia, Hong Kong was largely by kindness included in "interport" cricket, rugby, and yacht matches—and hardly ever won. After the war it reverted to comfortable insignificance, doing just enough business to satisfy its simple tastes.

But the Communist victory in China, the Korean and Vietnam wars, and the British recession from Asia coming in succession changed all that. Hong Kong had to assert itself to survive. It is today the world's busiest container port; the thirteenth largest exporter of manufactured goods; an international financial center second only to New York, Tokyo, or London; and the hub of communications for East Asia.

Hong Kong is the biggest, gaudiest, and busiest Oriental bazaar of all time—a vast chrome, glass, and marble emporium that lures buyers from the entire world. Inventories and transactions are managed electronically on ultramodern computers served by self-switching satellite links, but individual sales are reckoned on the wooden beads of ancient abacuses. It is mile after mile of shops, department stores, boutiques, ateliers, galleries, hawkers, and stalls supplied by a million skilled workers toiling in backstreet sweatshops or supervising automated, climate-controlled, steel-faced factories where lighting is constantly adjusted by self-servo chips.

Employing an additional two million contract workers in South China, Hong Kong provides countless opportunities for exporters, importers, investors, entrepreneurs, and manufacturers—also for the accountants, lawyers, and consultants who are their pilot fish. Athwart the sea routes of East Asia, it is even more strategically situated in the air age. Most China trade and investment pays its tribute to the incomparable financial, insurance, shipping, and information services the territory offers. It possesses more Rolls-Royces per capita than anywhere else—and, more to the commercial point, more portable telephones.

For a price that is always reasonable, you can buy a single plastic doll or a thousand gross of videocassette recorders; a two-thousand-year-old Han Dynasty statuette or a mass-produced oil painting of a junk under full sail, perspicacious financial advice from a Wharton School MBA or a horoscope from a blind fortune-teller; a first-class ballet performance; a symphony orchestra concert; or an orgy—also cobra gall, rhinoceros horn, bear's paw, powdered pearls, and ginseng for vigor, vitality, and virility. Even a twelve-year-old virgin, if your taste runs that way, although prosperity has made virgins scarcer and more expensive.

When I first saw the face of Hong Kong in 1951, it was little altered from the Hong Kong of 1900, where I set the opening scenes of my novel *Dynasty*. I could, therefore, quite easily envision my heroine and hero, Mary Osgood and Charles Sekloong, crossing the harbor by ferry, jolting over cobblestones in rickshaws, and being carried in sedan chairs up to the Peak, where Chinese were originally not allowed to live.

Every day I saw the same scenes they would have seen. Low white buildings with colonnaded façades still lined the waterfront; hired rickshaws and sedan chairs still plied the roadways; and I posted my dispatches under the green copper cupolas of the Edwardian General Post Office. The foursquare, four-story Hong Kong Club still excluded Chinese, as it had in 1900. The rough board and sheet-iron shacks of refugees from the Communist revolution in China festooning the hillsides were hardly distinguishable from the shacks thrown up half a century earlier by other refugees from other upheavals in China.

In 1951 a flatiron-shaped building called Alexandra House had just risen twelve stories behind the waterfront, striking a discordant modern note. As the growth of Hong Kong quickened, two new Alexandra Houses were to be built. Three different buildings with the same name have occupied the same site since 1951, one for each decade, as land values and office rents rocketed. Nearby, the new Central Building, which displaced the old Central Building, which had displaced the old Hong Kong Hotel in the 1950s, was itself almost displaced in the late 1970s. Its neighbors, the Gloucester Hotel and Lane Crawford's department store, were displaced by a great complex of shops and offices called the Landmark. Instead of tearing the new Central Building down, however, the owner spent $3 million for a glittering glass-curtain wall, thus keeping up with the trend.

Through it all, the airline called the Civil Aviation Administration of China hung on. During the decades when no airlines flew between Hong Kong and China, CAAC mounted propaganda displays in its disused booking office in the Gloucester Hotel Building on the corner of Pedder Street and Des Voeux Road—and the faithful came to cluck over photographs showing the glories of the New China. Today the CAAC offices on the same corner in the new Landmark are booking passages to China—and explaining why most flights are late.

Today, not only in the Central District, but on the hillsides where the refugees once squatted, glass, aluminum, or steel-clad skyscrapers thrust into the clouds. The old General Post Office held out for a long time, but its red brick walls finally toppled before the high-rises. So did the Hong Kong Club, that whitewashed redoubt of leisurely colonial privilege. The slender, shining spires of Hong Kong are now a visual cliché, a widely recognized symbol of the territory's hypermodern character.

Across the narrow bay, now traversed by subway and vehicular tunnels, Kowloon coruscates with the gaudiest neon lights in gaudy Asia. Although hard pressed by Itaewon in Seoul, Akihabara in Tokyo, and Hsimending in Taipei, Kowloon, the original tourists' shopping paradise, maintains its supremacy—largely because the Hong Kong dollar is cheaper than the won, the yen, or the new Taiwan dollar. In theory contravening the nearly total freedom that Hong Kong grants private enterprise, the Hong Kong dollar is controlled to keep it low against foreign currencies—and keep Hong Kong products cheap in world markets.

In theory! Actually, Hong Kong is committed to *no* political or economic doctrine, only to what works. Such hyperpragmatism has allowed entrepreneurs to do almost anything except shoot the competition. But the government puts down any threat to business, even if it must curtail freedom—in this case the freedom to speculate on the fluctuation of the Hong Kong dollar. Anyone else's dollar, yen, deutsch mark, pound, or franc is, however, fair game for speculators.

Entrepreneurs have thrived in such virtually unlimited freedom— under the protection of British law. Three decades ago, those entrepreneurs were chiefly British. Now largely Chinese, they are remarkable for their imagination, energy, industriousness, and readiness to take risks. Although utterly different, British and Chinese have together created a spectacular marketplace that throbs with the same urgency as New York. Hong Kong embodies the spirit of our frenetic age: grasping and lavish, self-indulgent and hardworking, crass, ostentatious, and tireless. Above all, it is productive, toiling night and day to fill the world's demands for shirts and personal computers, for plastic buckets and carved jade, for steel cables and silk dresses. And Hong Kong is so successful that not only bosses but workers enjoy living standards and opportunities beyond imagining a quarter of a century ago.

Geographically a remote part of China and legally soon to be China again, Hong Kong is essentially no more China than it is Britain. Nor are its people really either British or Chinese. A place of passage and a place of meeting, Hong Kong has attracted its own kind of people, Asian and Western.

When I first came to the Colony, the non-Asian population was no more than a few thousand, and the biggest single group was the British. In 1990 the non-Asian population is more than sixty thousand, and the biggest single group is American. But citizens of almost every nation on earth are all just as much Hong Kong belongers as the great majority who are Chinese by race.

Because of its character and its location, Hong Kong has become the center of gravity of the new East Asia. Not only major multinational corporations, but publishers, broadcasters, financial traders, lawyers, engineers, and accountants have found it the ideal base.

In 1951 Hong Kong had three feeble English-language dailies competing for no more than six thousand potential readers, and a struggling weekly called the *Far Eastern Economic Review*. Today, the surviving two of the original three dailies sell 125,000 copies and two other dailies published in Hong Kong are distributed throughout the region: the *Asian Wall Street Journal* and the *International Herald Tribune.* The prosperous *Far Eastern Economic Review* is the bellwether of a flock of dozens of English-language magazines ranging from newsweeklies through travel and social chitchat monthlies to financial journals and fashion magazines, which sell throughout Asia.

At the center of gravity, Hong Kong is the base for one of the world's best airlines. Cathay Pacific Airways, which started in Shanghai with a single war-surplus two-engined DC-3 flown alternately by the American and the Australian pilots who were its founders, now has thirty-four aircraft, among them seventeen Boeing 747s. The ten Airbus A330-330s ordered in April 1989 were the single largest order ever placed by an Asian airline. Cathay had also ordered six 747-400s, the longest-range airliner flying.

Cathay's first four-engined aircraft, a venerable Skymaster, flew from Calcutta to Hong Kong, stopping leisurely at Rangoon, Bangkok, and Saigon on the way. Now Cathay flies west from Hong Kong to London, having pioneered nonstop service, and east to San Francisco. Only the Atlantic remains unconquered. Cathay leads what is no longer a remote regional market, but soon to be the biggest single aviation market in the world. A spectacular increase from the Asia-Pacific area is projected—from 18.9 percent of the world total in 1975 to 32.8 percent in 1995.

Hotels play a much greater role in Asia, particularly in Hong Kong, than elsewhere. A major hotel in an Asian city is a center of social, cultural, and even intellectual life. Foreign hoteliers have for a century and a half been intermediaries between civilizations; their hotels have been embassies more congenial than official embassies. On that neutral ground, natives and outsiders meet without awkwardness—and grow accustomed to each others' curious ways. Redoubts, outposts, universities, salons, and refuges, the hotels of Asia play a role unparalleled since the caravanserai and the inns of the Middle Ages were the focal points of secular civilization. That role is epitomized by the Regent Hotels, which are relatively new and closely attuned to the new Asia. Their flagship is the Regent of Hong Kong. The empire was once entirely Asian but has now reached to Düsseldorf, New York, and Beverly Hills. Robert H. Burns, president and major stockholder, set up the company in Hong Kong in 1970—and sees no reason to move away.

The Regent of Hong Kong is regularly listed as second only to the Oriental in Bangkok among the world's best hotels, a list that Asian hotels regularly dominate. In a recent survey by *Institutional Investor* of its well-to-do readers, six Regents were listed in the top fifty, the largest single number from one group. Burns ascribes their extraordinary service to their Hong Kong roots. At that Regent a separate fan carries away the steam of the shower enclosure. At the Regent of Sydney tea leaves are kept in airtight boxes—and thrown away if unused after a month. At any Regent, the ice is constantly renewed in the wine cooler in the room. Employees know they are being constantly assessed for promotion in an expanding organization.

A tall, thin man with white hair and a softened New York accent, Burns was sixty in 1989. Looking at his career, I am inclined to ascribe the expansion of his small but sumptuous empire first to his thorough training, which included a long period with Hilton and a time lecturing at the East West Center in Hawaii on hotelkeeping; and second to his having made a connection with Japanese financiers at the right time.

Not all his experience with the Japanese has been happy. He built the Halekulani in Hawaii from scratch, and saw it taken over by Mitsui shortly before the opening.

"We went through a five-month break-in period—rave reviews," he says. "And we were summarily dismissed at the end of the fifth month."

Nonetheless, he is now working smoothly with Japanese partners in the kind of relationship that could be a model for the future. The Japanese have the money, but they do not have the expertise to deal with foreigners—and Burns is a partner, not an employee. He also stresses the contribution made by Hong Kong's tradition of service.

"I built on the foundations laid by the three men who created Hong Kong service—which always knows in advance what the guest wants," he says. "They were Peter Stafford of the Mandarin, Hugh Moss of the Hilton, and Peter Gautschi of the Peninsula. It's a great tradition. Other places don't have it, not even in Asia."

Hong Kong also has something else: the best food in the world. The Chinese restaurants are equaled by those of Taipei, while the French, naturally, do better with their own cuisine—but only first-class restaurants. Only New York offers such an extraordinary variety, but Hong Kong also offers two dozen regional variations of Chinese cuisine—and a range from Korean to Swedish, as well as American, Mexican, and South Seas.

"The song says if you can do it in New York, you can do it anywhere," Burns recalls. "That's doubly true of Asia. I can't think of any place that tests one's business skills like Hong Kong. . . . But our senior partner here, Cheng Yu Tung, says our success has nothing to do with management. It's all because of the angle at which the plane of the entry drive intersects the plume of the fountain. That's what the *fungsui* man, the geomancer and astrologer, says. And who am I to disagree?"

*   *   *

Amid its frenetic growth, Hong Kong somehow became a community with a soul of its own. Unique in place, in time, and in spirit, it has produced its own unique breed and its own unique culture. It is home for millions who would otherwise be without homes and without hope.

Basic education and basic housing have been provided by a government that has often been denounced as callous. Government and grant-assisted primary and secondary schools have educated millions to a good standard. Two universities and a dozen-odd colleges provide higher education, although many students go abroad, largely to America. Foreign money has sustained education, much of it from American churches, for Hong Kong has many Christians.

The public housing program was the first in Asia—and remains the biggest. It has provided accommodations for more than two million, even replacing rather basic apartment houses built in the 1950s with modern structures. Private investment has housed the middle class and made substantial—sometimes spectacular—profits. After all, this is Hong Kong.

Housing was essential to avoid chaos, for the population problem is acute. At the end of the war, the population, which had been depleted by refugees to China, was about half a million. In 1990 it was closer to 7 million than the 5.5 million that had been the official figure for years. That is a fourteenfold increase in forty-odd years.

Most of that spectacular increase is refugees and their offspring. Despite restrictions, Chinese refugees were admitted quite freely until 1962. In that year of terrible famines in China, more than 200,000 poured *en masse* over the border, knocking down fences and overwhelming patrols that had been ordered not to shoot. Some 100,000 were sent back. However, the tacit understanding that illegal immigrants would be allowed to stay if they made it to the safe base of the urban areas before they were caught was not abrogated until 1979.

Marred by corruption on a Confucian scale and by periodic riots, the territory's record is nonetheless admirable. It is indeed superb for a very small place virtually devoid of natural resources and where only a quarter of the land area is fit for agriculture or building.

Although I am tempted, I shall not simply offer my own explanation of the Colony's fantastic growth. I was an observer, not really a participant, and, quite shamefully, I made no money out of the Hong Kong boom, which almost disqualifies me. I shall, therefore, let two participants tell their own stories, which will show how Hong Kong got where it is and where it may be going.

Both Jack Cater and Francis Cheung were present at the birth of modern Hong Kong, having arrived shortly after the war in the Pacific ended in August 1945. Neither spoke Cantonese, the Colony's lan-

guage, though of course both do now. Just twenty-three years old, Jack
Cater was a squadron leader in the Royal Air Force, assigned to the
temporary military government of Hong Kong. Francis Cheung, who
was three when his parents brought him to the Colony, spoke only the
dialect of the Hakkas of Waizhou, a village on the East River between
Hong Kong and Canton.

Sir Jack Cater had a brilliant career among some two thousand British
civil servants at the top of the pyramid of power. Like some other
colonial service officers, he soon gave his primary loyalty to Hong
Kong's interests, even above Britain's. Although he was several times
acting governor, that priority probably impeded his career.

Over the years, entrepreneur Francis Cheung developed strong ties
with the United States, which was from the very beginning the second
most important Western country to Hong Kong. He worked for Trans
World Airlines and for Civil Air Transport, which was American-run,
although it carried the Nationalist Chinese flag. He has high regard for
Americans, and he is profoundly grateful to TWA for the management
training that underpins his achievements. He has, nonetheless, chosen
Canada, rather than the U.S., as his refuge should he decide to leave.
A true son of Hong Kong, he is, above all, practical.

Both Jack Cater and Francis Cheung are now deeply involved in
business with China, which ultimately determines Hong Kong's destiny. British and Chinese influence have intertwined from the beginning, the lion either vying with the dragon or lying down with it.
Without the myth of "the illimitable China market," the British would
not have come to Hong Kong. Without Britain, Hong Kong would have
remained, as Queen Victoria's Prime Minister Lord Palmerston described it in the early 1840s, "a barren rock with hardly a house on it."

Anglo-Chinese relations were originally straightforward: Britain took
by force, and China yielded unwillingly. That was the story of Hong
Kong before the Japanese started the war in the Pacific—and over-
turned all existing relationships. A quick glance at the past may, however, help illuminate the present, before Jack Cater and Francis
Cheung speak for themselves—and for Hong Kong.

Lord Palmerston was quite right. The island was barren. Though the
rainy season was torrential, there was not even a reservoir to store water
for a settled population in the dry season.

It was called Hong Kong, which means "Fragrant Harbor," for the
Chinese are fond of grandiloquent names. The peninsula to the north
is called Kowloon, which means "Nine Dragons," because a legendary
beast slumbers under each of Kowloon's nine chief hills. Both the island
and the peninsula were, in the 1840s, as insignificant in China's eyes as
in Lord Palmerston's.

The small harbor on the south of the island, called *Heunggong-dzai*, "Little Hong Kong," was an occasional base for fishermen and pirates, no more. The harbor that lay between the peninsula and the island was a magnificent natural anchorage. But China, no maritime nation, ignored its potential.

Hong Kong's only distinction was an ill omen. A naval battle fought in the harbor in the thirteenth century had ended with the defeat and death of the juvenile emperor of the Sung Dynasty. Therewith, dominion over China passed to the Mongol Dynasty of Kublai Khan.

Not many outsiders came to that distant and ill-starred place. The lives of its few inhabitants were undistinguished, but not quiet. Their villages were surrounded by walls for protection against the pirates and bandits who flourished far from the emperor's law. The Portuguese, the first Europeans to arrive, called the territory's scattered islands *Os Ladrones*, "The Thieves."

Yet in 1840 British merchant-adventurers, themselves thieves by our modern standards, desperately wanted barren Hong Kong Island. Portuguese Macao, established three centuries earlier, was no longer an adequate base for their commercial ambitions. They were primarily buyers, not sellers. Chinese porcelains, teas, and silks were treasured in Europe and America, but China did not want Western goods. Unhappy at paying much silver for Chinese exports, the merchants finally found a solution to their predicament. Hong Kong was the key.

China's upper classes had for centuries smoked opium, but they did not want their servants, laborers, and artisans debauched. Native opium was too expensive for the lower classes, and its import was prohibited. But opium was plentiful and cheap in India.

In the late 1830s, British merchants were turning many a dishonest penny from the illicit opium traffic. Naturally, they wanted even higher profits, legally if possible. Legal or not, the opium trade needed the secure base that Hong Kong Island could provide. If Britain had to take the island by force, all the better. A sharp defeat would teach the Chinese that they must now trade on the foreigners' terms—surrendering not only their seclusion but their territory.

Britain got the island and major concessions elsewhere in China through the First Opium War. Through the Treaty of Nanking, signed in 1842, China bought peace at great cost. In 1860 the Second Opium War gave Britain title to the three-and-a-quarter square miles of the Kowloon Peninsula. By 1898 British exactions were a little less blatant. Through intimidation just short of war, Peking was forced to lease Britain 370 square miles of the upper peninsula. They called that expanse the New Territories, and the lease ran for ninety-nine years.

The Chinese Empire was not pleased by that last exaction. But it could have been worse. After all, who except the British wanted the New Territories? Who, for that matter, would want them after ninety-nine years?

The People's Republic of China now wants not only the leased New Territories, but Kowloon and Hong Kong Island, which were ceded to Britain in perpetuity. The Conservative government of Margaret Thatcher almost offhandedly agreed, feeling it could do nothing else. Nationalism undoubtedly moved Beijing to demand the return of all the territories in 1997, when the lease on the New Territories expires. So did practical economic interest. Hong Kong's extraordinary development under laissez-faire capitalism has made it a very rich prize.

Hong Kong's people were hardly elated at rejoining the mother country, even before the barbaric massacre of June 4, 1989, in Tienanmen Square and the repression that followed. Although 98 percent Chinese by race, they were deeply apprehensive—and already regretted the British overlords they had so often ridiculed.

When things are going smoothly, the people of Hong Kong indulge their inherent scorn for all outsiders, calling them *gwailo,* "old devils," and *gwaitau,* "devil heads," as well as "barbarians" and other terms of endearment. The British, being closest, are most heartily abused.

With British rule being supplanted, the people of Hong Kong have discovered deep affection for their rulers. Better the foreign devil we know, they say, than the Chinese devil we know too well. The people are now very angry at the British, precisely because they are going. The coming Chinese rulers have demonstrated that they are intrusive, brutal—and inept.

How can Beijing, Hong Kong wonders fearfully, possibly acquire the economic sophistication to rule intelligently? Life or death for the complex organism depends on the Chinese appreciating its intricacy, its volatility, and its vulnerability. Yet the men of Beijing clearly do not understand what made the Hong Kong miracle.

Hong Kong's modern epic began in the autumn of 1945, when the Japanese surrender left in possession the few survivors of battles, air raids, and military occupation. Reversing the normal direction, refugees had fled from Hong Kong to China, where food was not quite as scarce. Having taken refuge first in Macao and then in China, Francis Cheung's parents returned to Hong Kong when the war ended. The city they saw was uncannily empty.

"For report purposes, we came up with 460,000 inhabitants," Jack Cater recalls. "Somebody reversed it, and 640,000 became the official figure. Let's say it was half a million. The natural level was about 1.3

million, but that had swelled to 1.8, maybe 2 million, after Canton fell
to the Japanese in 1937."

"And war damage?" I ask.

"Not a great deal," Cater says. "There'd been Japanese shelling, and
the Americans had bombed sporadically. But the damage was nothing
to what I'd seen in London and the Continent. The place wasn't so much
damaged as rundown. Municipal services had to be started again:
electricity, water, garbage disposal, that sort of thing. Looting had to be
brought under control. . . . Whatever the problems, it was a wonderful
feeling. . . heady. . . . In six months, we probably achieved more than
has been achieved in any six years since. We were all young, and we
were rebuilding without old men to tell us different."

Some of Cater's contemporaries have from time to time wished he
would act his age. He has retained the enthusiasm of his youth, despite
the weight of the knighthood he received in 1979. The year before he
had been appointed chief secretary, becoming the governor's chief of
staff, the man who runs Hong Kong on a day-to-day basis. If he had not
been zealous on behalf of the people of Hong Kong, he would probably
have gotten the job and the knighthood earlier. If he had not believed
his duty was to further Hong Kong's interests above all else, he might
have been appointed governor a little later.

In 1982, however, London wanted another governor from the Foreign Service, rather than the Hong Kong Colonial Service, to follow the
long and brilliant reign of Sir Murray MacLehose. Soon created Lord
MacLehose, he had been the first governor drawn from the Foreign
Service. London knew that Jack Cater could not vigorously promote a
policy that sought, above all else, a smooth transition to Chinese rule,
regardless of the damage to Hong Kong. Since Britain now has virtually
no interests in Asia except business interests, Hong Kong's interests
have been subordinated to Britain's future trade with China. Besides,
Jack Cater had offended too many wealthy and therefore powerful
people by his vigorous performance as director of the Independent
Commission Against Corruption.

Some ICAC methods, like arresting suspects at six in the morning to
prevent destruction of evidence, may have gone too far. Cater inspired
the commission with his own crusading zeal. He hates corruption as an
absolute evil, not just for its injustice and the obstacles it interposes to
normal economic activity. He felt that corruption could destroy Hong
Kong. Yet he was reluctant in 1973, when Sir Murray MacLehose
pressed him to become Hong Kong's first commissioner against corruption.

We discussed his dilemma over lunch at the Hong Kong Club, which
by that time admitted Chinese members, though not many. Then
secretary for home affairs and information, Cater saw little prospect of

further advancement. He had already accepted the useful—and lucrative—managing directorship of the Hong Kong Telephone Company. It was, he said, time to make some money for his family and for himself. But the governor was pressing him to lead a campaign against the acute official corruption, particularly in the Royal Hong Kong Police Force.

Over tripe and onions, Jack Cater firmly decided he would not take on that assignment. He'd done all he could for Hong Kong. Besides, he really wasn't up to creating a new organization and leading it into battle against some of the most powerful forces in the Colony. By the time a dark waiter wearing a fanciful Nubian costume with a crimson fez, a scarlet bolero, and baggy scarlet pantaloons poured coffee from a gleaming copper pot, he was saying he might not be able to avoid it.

Of course, he took the job. His sense of duty would not let him do otherwise. Besides, he could never resist the adrenaline in a challenge.

Fifteen years later, in his study in Kowloon, we are talking about his experiences. Jack Cater looks all his sixty-six years. His hair is white, and his cheeks are ravined with lines. Yet, thirty-odd years before, he looked much the same. The hair was not white, nor were the lines as deep. But he has always been lean and intense—and time has depleted neither his enthusiasm nor his dedication.

Jack Cater left the Hong Kong government in 1984, after three years as its representative in London. He now directs British and Hong Kong participation in the nuclear generating station being built as a joint venture with French and Chinese interests at Daya Bay, about twenty miles inside Guangdong Province.

He is determined to ensure that all possible safety precautions are taken. When reinforcing pilings for a massive concrete foundation were omitted in error, that was not easy. Negotiating with Chinese officials has never been easy. "All Chinese are arrogant," an American executive with much negotiating experience says. "And Communist Chinese are twice as arrogant as other Chinese." The political, economic, and ecological tensions that surround Daya Bay do not make Cater's task easier.

But the job is fascinating—and it is good for Hong Kong, which will use much of that electricity. Besides, Jack Cater is now getting some of the financial rewards he assured others by helping to make Hong Kong a better place to do business. I did not ask his earnings, but they are undoubtedly substantial.

About time, too, he might say. His origins were, as is said, humble; they taught him concern for workers and hatred of unfairness. His father was a police sergeant, and Jack attended Sir George Monoux Grammar School in Walthamstow in the poor East End of London. Founded in

1557, it was a free school, but not just another primary/secondary school. Like the Boston Latin School or Townsend Harris Hall, English grammar schools offer rigorous education to a select body of students. Despite his academic promise, he left school at the age of sixteen in 1938 to work for the Port of London Authority on the docks. Because his education was advanced for a son of the lower middle class, his work was clerical.

Keeping time sheets and employment rolls on the docks, he says, "I saw grade C [casual] labor being taken on. What absolutely shattered me, I saw men virtually begging for work. It was still the 1930s, remember, the tail end of the Great Depression. Worse, I saw a lot of what we then called favoritism, but I now call corruption. Some got jobs by knowing the foreman and doing favors . . . that is bribing . . . him."

World War II abruptly ended that first phase of his life. In 1940, at the age of eighteen, he joined the Royal Air Force. After serving in night fighters, he was sent to Asia in 1945. Having seen on the mess bulletin board a circular soliciting applications for the Colonial Service, he had put his name down, asking to serve in Asia—and then forgotten about it. At the end of 1944 he was assigned to Southeast Asia Command, which was preparing to drive the Japanese out of Malaya. Officers like Cater were trained for civil affairs, which meant military government.

"After the atomic bombs fell," he recalls, "there was a big rush and I was assigned to Hong Kong. The air was full of talk of returning Hong Kong to the Chinese Nationalists. Churchill had said under no circumstances would Hong Kong be returned. But Roosevelt was insisting. The worry was that the Nationalists would get there first—or the Americans. In either case, Hong Kong would be Chinese."[1]

The British got there first, although it took the senior admiral of the Royal Navy in the Pacific three and a half weeks after the Japanese surrender. Thus was Hong Kong saved to become one of the economic wonders of the world and, eventually, a living sacrifice to Anglo-Chinese amity. But before the international rivalries and international ironies to come, Squadron Leader Cater was, at twenty-three, given a job it would normally have taken twenty years to work up to.

"Since I was an air force officer, they put me in charge of fisheries and then agriculture." He says, "London had made all sorts of plans for reviving fishing, but they were no good on the scene. . . . Boats were rundown, and sails were tattered. . . . We had to get things going by pumping in money. So we issued HK$100,000 [then a *very* large sum,

---

[1] The United States was at the time certainly talking loudly about rolling back colonialism. But the intent—as opposed to the wish—to turn Hong Kong over to the Nationalists is not proved. Roosevelt's malign design has, however, passed into British folklore as the absolute truth.

now $13,000] to a fishing population of about thirty thousand. The very first thing they asked for was not food and clothing, as we'd expected, not even nets and tackle for their boats. *It was education for their children.*

"There I was, very young—and I had two thousand people working in my department. . . . Young people don't get opportunities like that nowadays. If I wanted lorries, this, that, or the other thing, I just phoned and got them. . . . And there was no question of not working on Sundays. You bloody well did."

Those glorious days soon ended. By June 1946 the Colonial Service officers who had been interned by the Japanese were back from their long recuperative leaves, and the military government folded its tents. Jack Cater had, however, become convinced that his future lay in Hong Kong. He had also absorbed the Colony's basic philosophy, which Sir Keith Joseph, Margaret Thatcher's ideological mentor, was to hail as the "secret of Hong Kong's success."

Keith Joseph much later asked Jack Cater the origin of Hong Kong's policy of nonintervention in the marketplace. That attitude, Jack Cater told him, had been dominant even before the war. "Our policy," he said, "was simply that the businessman in the mass would know more about making the right commercial decisions than the civil servant with nothing at risk."

It was not quite that simple. Noninterference had worked well for a small enclave with a small population and small ambitions. It would not work in the second half of the twentieth century in an already over-populated Colony that had to feed and house its people by its own endeavors. The government had to assume greater responsibility. Total laissez faire could not create the optimum climate for economic growth.

"It was Christmas Eve of 1953," Cater recalls. "A tremendous fire at Shek Kip Mei in Kowloon had made fifty thousand people homeless. Until then—and it seems a bit stupid now—we assumed what would happen was what always happened with the Chinese. If there were problems in China, people would come to Hong Kong. If there were problems in Hong Kong, they'd go back to China."

This time, the people did not go back to China. More refugees were actually coming out as the grip of Maoism tightened. Hong Kong's population was already more than two million—and rising.

"We couldn't go on like that," Cater resumes, "leaving all those people in shacks on the hillsides. We had to house the Shek Kip Mei lot. So government built 'Bowring Bungalows,' which were really two-story or three-story buildings. A year or so later, we were building H-blocks, eight stories high. . . . Then came town planning for the New Towns [in the New Territories]. . . . In 1956 I was in the Department of Commerce and Industry when it planned Kwun Tong New Town. And what a mess it was! Kwun Tong is great for industry, but ghastly for living."

"After the Korean War, Hong Kong clearly couldn't live just by handling exports and imports to China, which was pretty closely sealed. Was it known by 1956, when you planned Kwun Tong, that Hong Kong had a tremendous potential for industry . . . had to industrialize to survive?"

Jack Cater ponders an instant before replying: "We knew we were approaching lift-off. All the big textile people had been coming down from Shanghai. Most came in 1948 and 1949, but some as early as 1947. They brought their foremen with them and their equipment. The machinery they'd ordered from Cincinnati and Manchester was on the high seas. So they diverted it to Hong Kong. By 1956 they were in a very advanced stage.

"And what did we have before the war or between 1945 and 1948? Rubber footwear, Good Morning [hand] towels, and enamelware. Not even plastics, yet. By 1958 we'd made such inroads we were under great pressure to restrict our textile exports to Britain. Well, you know what happened."

I do. Exports of textiles and garments grew so large that both the United Kingdom and the United States had to bargain for "voluntary quotas." After the shock of those restrictions, Hong Kong began to diversify.

"The textile industry had that tremendous boost from the Shang-hainese," Jack Cater resumes. "My Cantonese friends would hate me for saying so, but Hong Kong's real prosperity is 95 percent due to the Shanghainese. They are still very important today. Sadly, I have not heard of *one* Shanghainese who intends to stay in Hong Kong after 1997."

The vexed future of Hong Kong is, of course, on our agenda, but not just yet. First is graft and its far-reaching consequences, as well as the prolonged internal crisis of 1967. Jack Cater is best known for succeeding in the apparently hopeless task of curtailing corruption in Hong Kong's Confucian society.

It is virtually unknown that he was largely responsible for keeping Hong Kong from being engulfed in the chaos of Chairman Mao Tsetung's Great Proletarian Cultural Revolution. When the Colony was threatened by mass demonstrations, riots, and urban terrorism, Cater did more than anyone else to save Hong Kong from anarchy—or being taken over by China "to restore order."

"By 1971 everybody was talking about police corruption," he recalls, "instead of thinking back to 1967 and saying how extraordinarily well the police had done. . . . They were magnificent. Still, it has been said that many, including those in control, were safeguarding their own investments. They knew they would be the first to lose their heads if the Communists did take over—as happened in Canton when the Japanese came in. The people then got their own back against the cops, who'd been squeezing them dry."

Peggy, to whom he has been married since 1950, interjects, "You do tend to get cynical."

"Not at all," he rejoins. "Fear and self-interest were easily major reasons why the police were so heroic."

The struggle in 1967 was an extension of the Cultural Revolution in China. Local zealots sought to topple the colonial government. Although ultimately failing, terrorism and mass assaults came close to demolishing British prestige and, thus, British power.

Having become secretary for defence at the beginning of 1967, Jack Cater was at the center of the storm. His title was first changed to special assistant to the governor so that he could negotiate with the Communists, and later to deputy colonial secretary (special duties) to give him greater authority. Since his nominal superiors lacked his experience of Hong Kong, and the governor was on sick leave, he was effectively in command.

It started with labor troubles, the most virulent disputes between workers and employers for years. Postwar Hong Kong had already been shaken by two waves of riots protesting specific injustices. But they were soon over. In 1967 labor problems were lost to sight after the Maoists deployed their shock troops: the members of Communist-dominated labor unions and the students at Communist-controlled middle schools.

Sallying from Communist-owned department stores, offices, schools, and union headquarters, the Colony's home-grown Red Guards first taunted, then assailed the police. They blocked roads, turned over automobiles, and hurled missiles. Most terrorist bombs exploded in poor neighborhoods, killing thirty-nine workers and one British bomb-disposal officer. That intimidation failed. Angered by terrorism the working people saw no British weakness. They remained staunch even while wealthy Chinese and foreigners fled the Colony.

"In the beginning," Jack Cater recalls, "the hardest thing was to do nothing. We did everything possible not to provoke them."

Discipline kept immobile not only the Gurkha sentries on duty before the Government House, but even the emotionally volatile Cantonese constables. They barely flinched when scores of wild-eyed young men and women shouted, spat, and poked fingers at them. The walls and trees surrounding the governor's residence were festooned with protests in black ideograms on purple, pink, and red paper.

The fat cats of the left arrived in Mercedeses and Rolls-Royces to register their presence: trading millionaires, stage and screen stars, other "cultural personages" who wanted to stay on the Communists' good side, and the managers of Communist-owned enterprises. Most vehement was the publisher of a Communist daily who was to later become the managing director of a firm owned by the newly mercantile People's Republic: the Amur Caviar Company.

"As the demonstration came back down to Queen's Road [the main thoroughfare], they got out of hand," Cater says. "They were not only screaming, but breaking windows. . . . It was the moment the police had been waiting for. They now had cause. Good old Sam Jaffe of ABC was just outside with his camera when they broke through the windows of the Hilton Hotel Coffee Shop. . . . Directly the police moved in, all those kids were lying down . . . putting on bandages smeared with mercurochrome, though uninjured. That night the film was shown on local television news. They were shown up as ridiculous.

"Nonetheless, the struggle continued. Police descended in helicopters onto the roofs of Communist stores, unions, and schools, while others attacked from below. It was the only way to bottle up the Red Guards and prevent their escaping to spread turmoil elsewhere. At the end of June, the Communists called a 'food strike' to starve the Colony and the Motor Workers' Union refused to unload food trains from China. Live pigs were shipped back, and at the height of summer many died. When carcasses littered the tracks, Guangdong Province instructed the workers to offload pigs in Hong Kong.

"Beijing was finally telling them through Canton to cool it. Also that it was down to the account of the Communists, who would be blamed by the people of Hong Kong for their suffering."

One of the worst moments came on July 8: an apparent mass attack was mounted from China in a town called Shataukok, where only a milestone marks the border, which runs through the main street. All regular Chinese troops were withdrawn, and a torrent of human beings surged across the frontier to surround the police station in the Hong Kong side. Their assault was supported by machine-gun fire from China. In London, the *Sunday Express* reported an invasion by thousands of Chinese troops.

Not quite that bad, it was bad enough. After five policemen were killed, the border police were relieved by the Gurkhas, the coldly ferocious hillmen from Nepal. When they came up behind their British officers, whoever had sanctioned the incursion called it off. The incident had evidently frightened those military officers who still held some power on the other side of the border during the Cultural Revolution. The incident had also frightened some men who were high in the Hong Kong establishment.

"The rot was there," Jack Cater remembers.

"You can't imagine what it was like," Peggy interjects. "It seemed everyone was falling apart."

Many leading citizens—British, Chinese, and others—discovered urgent family, health, or business reasons to remove themselves from danger. Those who stayed had moments of black fantasy, and a young taipan asked me in dead earnest: "What can we possibly do when half a million Red Guards march across the border?"

The Maoist campaign of terrorism, however, petered out when the government in Beijing, recovering somewhat from its disarray, reprimanded the militants—and told them to end the struggle.

The men who had saved the Colony were honored, becoming the *Royal* Hong Kong Police Force. For a few halcyon years, there seemed to be no major differences, much less irreconcilable divisions, between the foreigners and the Chinese. All were equally, as the official terminology puts it, "Hong Kong belongers."

After its victory over Maoist terrorism, a self-assured Hong Kong moved forward even more rapidly. That turbulent year, 1967, was the great divide. Before it, the old Hong Kong of small goals, limited courage, and low, mildewed buildings; after it, the new Hong Kong of overwhelming ambition, brash self-confidence, and assertive, slab-sided high-rises.

But the seeds of the next threat to its existence were already germinating. Corruption was impeding economic growth, distorting justice, handicapping administrations—and costing the Colony at least half a billion dollars a year. The officer who had commanded the police force during the emergency made a curious condition when offered regular appointment as police commissioner. He told Cater he would take the promotion, but stipulated, "The absolute maximum I'll serve is a year and a half." Jack Cater now believes the canny officer foresaw the scandal brewing within the force—and wanted to avoid it.

"I saw the return of the criminal classes between October '45 and the spring of '46," Cater remembers. "They, too, had been away for the war. Criminals are just people, washing in and out of Hong Kong like everyone else. By the late forties and early fifties, they had Hong Kong sewn up. If I lost my wallet, I'd get it back next day, delivered to the local police station—minus the money. . . . In those days, there was very little serious crime reported. When there was anything serious, a culprit was *always* produced to take the rap."

Cater had encountered official graft as soon as he came to the Colony, not only in its natural breeding ground, the Customs and Excise Department, but even in Fisheries. The major wave of corruption that almost broke Hong Kong rose from brief rioting in 1956.

Triad gangs were then prominent in right-wing demonstrations against increased fares on the Star Ferry, which carried hundreds of thousands between Hong Kong and Kowloon every day. The Triads take their name from a secret society called the Three Harmonies. Secret societies were already ancient in the seventeenth century when they were revitalized for mutual protection to resist the alien Manchus. Because they were outside the law, they became criminals in Hong Kong. The Triads' power was broken in 1956 when two thousand of their leaders were arrested to end the Star Ferry riots.

"The removal of the Triads produced a vacuum into which the police went," Cater recounts. "Seven sergeants major were the ranking noncommissioned officers. They really ran the police force—and ran it damned well. Most crime was victimless—gambling, prostitution, and the like.

"Sometimes they had to handle problems inside the force. Again, they did it well. At one point the seven sergeants major called on a ranking British officer to say, 'Sir, you are bad joss for the force. You must leave.' When that happens, you know those people hold the real power in the police force."

The officer was retired, as his British superiors had already decided he must be. That encounter illuminated the curious role of the British in the Royal Hong Kong Police Force, in the Hong Kong government, and in Hong Kong itself. From the beginning, British firms employed local men called *compradors*, literally "buyers," to deal with the natives because they knew the language and the customs. Although some British officials in time learned Cantonese, the government inevitably became a comprador government, and the police became a comprador force.

There were no British noncommissioned officers in the Hong Kong police; expatriates started as inspectors. No British policemen ever drew routine traffic or beat assignments, as did Portuguese in Macao and Frenchmen in Saigon. British officers often did hazardous duty. But most were dependent on their Cantonese subordinates for detailed information on both the community and their own force.

"Some British officers had their own connections with the underworld," Jack Cater recalls. "But most were used. I could give dozens of examples. One returned from looking around his new patch to find in his desk drawer a brown envelope crammed with money. The next day, the station sergeant said, 'Sir, maybe you think we are doing dirty things like drugs. You have our word. All we are asking is for you to do nothing. Sometimes we may ask you to transfer people.'

"Certain lower jobs were worth a lot. A barracks sergeant at one station was running a gambling syndicate, so the job was worth HK$240,000 [U.S.$42,000 at the time]. A sergeant who wanted the job would cheerfully pay that much, knowing he'd be getting about

HK$100,000 [U.S. $20,000] a month from the system. Not a bad return.

"But they needed the occasional *gwailo* ["foreigner"] to smooth the way and make things work. And to tip them off to raids by the special anti-corruption unit. . . . Corruption was already very high. It became very noticeable to the public in a very high and very ripe curve in 1970 and 1971."

Two years later, when corruption had become a public scandal, Sir Murray MacLehose, the governor, asked Jack Cater to organize the Independent Commission Against Corruption. Cater was to break many lances against that dragon—and to inflict many wounds. Some wounds were almost disabling—for a time. None was fatal.

Yet Jack Cater was successful, not only in the light of his own limited expectations, but in the cold light of realism in a Crown Colony where almost everything had been for sale. He harried the thieves, exposed many, and broke their system—for a long time. When he left the assignment, corruption was no longer taken for granted. It was, quite remarkably, no longer respectable.

During a visit to Shanghai in 1986, Moira and I lunched at the crowded Apricot Restaurant, which Francis Cheung had recommended. We were seated at a big round table where two men in their thirties were already scanning the menu. They were remarkably well dressed for Chinese, and they spoke to the waiter in peculiar Mandarin. They spoke to us in English with the accent of Hong Kong.

An architect and an interior decorator, they were planning a new hotel. Shanghai, once the industrial and commercial center of East Asia, no longer possessed the skill to build a modern hotel on its own. They were needed, but they were not happy.

They talked of their problems with *Chinese* bureaucracy, *Chinese* stubbornness, and *Chinese* backwardness. Their presumed motherland called them *tungbao,* "blood brothers," for they were Chinese by race and largely by culture. Yet they were not really Chinese, but men of Hong Kong. Both said "them," meaning the Chinese of China; both said "us," meaning Hong Kong people, foreigners as well as Chinese.

In 1986 those two knew that China would soon control Hong Kong, and they were not happy. By the spring of 1989, tension between China and the people of Hong Kong had risen high. Hong Kong wanted insurance from Britain: "right of abode" in the United Kingdom to give some 3.2 million Hong Kong-born citizens a bolthole; and a representative government to give them leverage against the totalitarian rulers of China.

Even before the atrocity in Tienanmen Square on June 4, 1989, the people of Hong Kong were very nervous. Since then, they have been frightened—and voluble. Beijing has fulminated against Hong Kong for

encouraging the "counter-revolutionary upheavals," and Hong Kong
has denounced the Beijing regime as murderers. Even the British
government, which had been complacently congratulating itself on the
Hong Kong settlement, was forced to reconsider the rights of abode and
democracy under pressure from Hong Kong and world opinion.

Even before June 4, the people knew that Beijing had a veto on all
major decisions in Hong Kong. Anxious to please China, Britain was
virtually groveling. The Basic Law that will be the constitution for a
"semiautonomous" Hong Kong after 1997 was in theory shaped by
consultation with the Chinese authorities, but it reflected Beijing's
wishes alone. There would be no way to curb Chinese behavior after the
takeover, certainly not with the Liberation Army in the wings. Concern
for world opinion had not deterred the old men of Beijing from the
Tienanmen Square massacre.

Even before that butchery, most people talked of the future in two
ways: candidly pessimistic in private and guardedly optimistic in
public.

One man who talked much the same way in private as in public was
Gordon Wu, the ebullient founder and managing director of the
Hopewell Holdings. A graduate of Princeton in engineering, he bub-
bled with un-Princetonian fervor extolling the prospects of cooperation
with China, when we had dinner together in 1983. He talked with
immense enthusiasm of building a superhighway from Hong Kong to
Canton. (Work on the billion-dollar project began in April 1987, about
the time he completed construction of a power station in China.) The
superhighway seemed visionary to me in 1983. Further travel in the
Pearl River Delta convinced me that it was not only needed, but
practicable. Almost in spite of myself I became a fan.

Because China depends on Hong Kong, Gordon Wu contends, China
must preserve Hong Kong intact. Moreover, Hong Kong's influence
will in time fundamentally alter China. The territory's future will then
be secure under a Beijing government that experience has taught the
realities of modern production, commerce, and finance. David will not
slay Goliath, but convert him.

That thesis, always attractive, is less convincing in the days after the
great climacteric of June 4, 1989. Obviously neither logic nor compassion deters the old men of Beijing from brutal or stupid actions when
their power is at stake.

Somewhat paradoxically, the aftermath of the massacre tends to
support Gordon Wu's thesis. Naïvely or not, the same leadership has
made clear its intention of continuing to pursue economic progress
while continuing to suppress dissent. Whether the Communists will be
able to ride two horses pulling in opposite directions, Hong Kong
boosters would say, is not really the point. The point is that China will

leave Hong Kong alone because she is still striving for the industrial and commercial goals toward whose attainment Hong Kong can make a unique contribution.

Gordon Wu's verve almost makes that scenario believable. A plump, smooth man who speaks softly but very fast, he further points out that there is no alternative. Neither Britain nor certainly China wants to reopen negotiations on the fate of Hong Kong or the conditions under which it will live after 1997.

He has much at stake, but he will never lack for money. His father started as a taxi driver and ended with Hong Kong's largest fleet of taxis. Unlike the middle class, Gordon Wu need not choose between Hong Kong and exile *before* he sees which way Chinese rule is taking him. He can always get out, and he will always have somewhere to go.

He argued just as persuasively in *Asia Magazine* before June 4, 1989, that everything is going to be not just fine, but wonderful: "There is a lot of talk about emigration. . . . It's conceivable that 5 percent or a maximum of 10 percent will leave. But what will happen to the remaining five million? The show must go on. . . . Carry on the prosperity and the stability."

Emigration is already undermining stability and threatening prosperity. Institutions like the venerable Hong Kong and Shanghai Banking Corporation are looking for foreigners to fill the midlevel and lower-level clerical jobs vacated by Chinese employees who have gone to live abroad. Those were the men and women who had made Hong Kong's miracle work day by day. Many firms were experiencing labor shortages that reached, as one managing director put it, "down to the office boy and the lathe hand."

Five years earlier Catholic schools had been besieged by applicants for their superior education. Priests and nuns were then instructed *never* to discuss admissions, no matter how devout the parents might be, or how close their friendship.

In 1986 Francis Cheung's wife, Monica, met a foreign priest saying goodbye to a family of parishioners at the airport.

"Is there any promising child you know?" he asked. "We have vacancies now."

Twenty-seven thousand are reliably estimated to have left in 1987. The exodus swelled to forty thousand in 1988, and the curve was rising toward seventy thousand in 1989. That was about 130,000, almost 1.9 percent of Hong Kong's seven million people—and the exodus was swelling.

By and large, that figure did *not* include the senior executives and professionals who have already staked out their refuges abroad but continue to operate in Hong Kong. Like the working class, who have little choice, they will stay on. Unlike the working class, they will stay only as long as they like what is happening—before as well as after the Chinese takeover.

Hong Kong is a place of passage. People come and go as their interests dictate—and as opportunities arise. Above all, the managerial and professional classes were leaving—the better educated, the more able, and the more venturesome. Yet they are absolutely essential, not only to Hong Kong's economic future, but to its very existence as an integrated community.

The exodus and the crisis of confidence disturbs Chinese officials. After June 4, Beijing hastened to assure Hong Kong that all would be well after 1997. But a senior Chinese ambassador could suggest to me no way to restore confidence beyond the standard pledges of noninterference in the "self-governing territory" of the People's Republic that Hong Kong is to become. Those promises rang flat in Hong Kong ears, even before Tienanmen Square.

If it takes over a hollowed-out shell, the People's Republic will gain little except additional responsibility and some machinery it might have acquired more easily elsewhere. Although Beijing is buying into existing companies, it could also lose much of the foreign exchange it now earns through Hong Kong. The fit would be perfect if economies alone mattered.

"A lot of labor-intensive manufacturing has moved from Hong Kong into the Pearl River Delta," Gordon Wu observed in *Asia Magazine*. "Hong Kong would never have been able to fulfill all the orders for Cabbage Patch Dolls because you need someone to paint the eyes and put the wig on and comb it. And there's no way you will get two hundred girls in Kwun Tong to do that. . . . The only way Hong Kong can ever survive is to utilize and work hand in hand with the inside [i.e., China]. . . . They have water, they have land, agricultural products, and other resources. And the labor market is fantastic. But they don't have the excellent legal and financial infrastructure, the port and the airport, the road systems and telephone systems, the business acumen and the management skills. . . . Hong Kong can act as the shopfront and China as the factory."

A wonderful spiel, and Gordon Wu merits a respectful hearing. But I fear it has little connection with reality. Should Hong Kong actually succeed in raising the technical and commercial skills of "the inside," as Gordon Wu revealingly calls China, will the Chinese not just make Hong Kong over in their image?

Father Lazlo Ladany, S.J., the most acute and diligent of the China Watchers, summed it up, "I am sure of only one thing. After 1997 Hong Kong will be *very* different from today."

*   *   *

The future has been foreshadowed by the complex relationship between Hong Kong and China since they both crossed the great divide of the Cultural Revolution. One of my best guides through that maze has been Francis Cheung, who came to the Colony in the autumn of 1946, at the same time as Jack Cater.

Francis was then three years old. Having fled wartime Hong Kong for neutral Macao, forty-five miles away, his parents had later moved to the Chinese countryside to farm his mother's ancestral acre—and produce just enough to feed themselves. Francis remembers lolling on the water buffaloes, "like big, leather-upholstered sofas" plodding through the pine trees to the river, as had Chinese boys for thousands of years. Nevertheless, he is Portuguese by birth. Like his father and grandfather, he was born in Macao, legally an overseas province of Portugal.

The Portuguese passport that entitles him to live anywhere in the European Economic Community is now an ace in the hole. Most of his cards have been played developing tourism in China. Having begun as a clerk with an airline, he acquired interests in travel agencies, hotels, tours, operators, and antiques. After Tienanmen Square business fell off sharply, and he feared it could take years to rebuild.

His alternative residence is Vancouver, which has a large and growing Chinese population. He chose Vancouver in conjunction with his four partners, for they coordinate all their important moves. Two are his younger brothers; the other two are not related by blood, but by their common devout Catholicism. A confident businessman who has made his own way upward, Francis Cheung is no rugged individualist.

Francis's methods illuminate the fundamental difference in the way Westerners and Chinese function. I depend upon my friends, as I hope they do on me; no one can function alone. I can call upon close friends like Francis for help, and would be disturbed if they did not come to me when they needed help. But I make crucial decisions only in conjunction with Moira. I function primarily as an individual. Francis does not. Symbolically, he and his partners have bought five adjacent flats on two floors in Vancouver. They completely share common assumptions, common goals—and common financial interests.

United by that community of interests, Francis's group embodies the old Confucian ideal of linking family and friends for greater strength. Chinese "inside," to use Gordon Wu's term, are reverting to such useful groupings because the collective entities the Communists call *danwei*, "units," have proved unwieldy, unproductive—and emotionally daunting.

The Communists' units are cold. They are based upon coercion rather than consent, upon common fears more than common interests. Neo-Confucian groups like Francis Cheung's are warm. In Hong Kong and throughout East Asia today, such groups function very practically—and also provide emotional security.

The Chinese "inside" have much to learn, perhaps to relearn—and they say they want to learn from outsiders. Francis could serve as a classic example of the rise from humble beginnings through hard work under laissez-faire capitalism. He is a Horatio Alger hero reborn in modern Asia. He made good in a frontier society not unlike the vanished America in which Alger set his homilies of success through diligence and virtue. Like such heroes, he is deeply religious, but never namby-pamby.

In his late forties, Francis Cheung now bears little resemblance to the hell-raising youth he once was. He wears thick glasses, and at five foot seven, he is a little plump. Attacking his present sedentary work with the same determination he once brought to sports, he has inevitably put on weight. He is also soft-spoken, even a touch didactic.

I suspect that he cultivates that bland appearance. Still, he cannot entirely conceal his acute intelligence. When he is intent, his words come faster and his dark eyes flash. Although his manner is deliberately unthreatening, he can be extremely stubborn. Usually he is right.

Now afflicted with food allergies and, I suspect, an incipient ulcer, he can no longer enjoy the smelly saltfish he loved as a youngster. He eats sparingly—and that little is bland. Yet, like all Chinese, he considers himself a gourmet by right of birth. A nonplaying captain on the fields of gastronomy, he delights in ordering for his friends subtle and complex meals in Hong Kong's most sophisticated restaurants.

His mother, he recalls, came to Hong Kong and attended the primary school of the nuns of the Sacred Heart before finding work as a maid at the Peninsula Hotel on the Kowloon waterfront. There she met his father, who had started as a pageboy and risen to a captain of waiters. A second-generation hotel man, Francis remembers the "immense lobby" of the Peninsula, with "great big pillars, an enormous staircase, and two very big elevators." Since he has lived and worked within ten blocks of the hotel most of his life, the past and the present sometimes run together. He has been determined to redeem by his triumphs his father's business disasters.

The elder Cheung left the Peninsula to become chief of the room staff at the Leyton Hotel, which put up the flight crews of the China National Aviation Corporation, a predecessor of CAAC. He later opened his own restaurants, which slowly failed. Francis believes they failed because his father brought to working-class eating houses the standards of service and cuisine he had learned at the Peninsula.

His father's ineptitude was decisive in Francis's own life. Stranded in Washington, D.C., in 1966 by an aviation mechanics' strike, he could see no future in the Colony. He had just decided to stay on, attending Catholic University and working for a classmate in Chinatown. But his father cabled: "I am really broke this time. I need your help for the family."

Since that summons could not be disobeyed, he managed to hop and skip back to Hong Kong on those airlines still flying. Even if filial obedience and the welfare of the family were not absolute imperatives, Francis would have returned. He was very fond of his father—and he owed a debt to parental patience.

He had tried that patience by running through six schools— Buddhist, Catholic, and government. He wanted only to play soccer and watch the air shows at Kaitak Airport.

In 1961 his father had no more educational strings to pull—and he was close to bankruptcy after the failure of his second venture, a coffee shop in a factory district. He finally said, "Maybe you don't want to study anymore. Maybe you want to work."

That *maybe* had the force of law. The only question was, "What kind of work?" The network Francis calls the Catholic Mafia helped.

"My father knew somebody, a Catholic, high up in Civil Air Transport," Francis recalls. "That's how I got into the airline business in 1962. I worked in the Peninsula, right on the corner of Nathan and Salisbury Road. They gave me two weeks' training and they called me a traffic agent. It wasn't easy. I was the only Cantonese among all those Shanghainese.

"That's how I picked up Mandarin—and Shanghainese. I had to learn or I couldn't communicate. I worked very hard because I knew I had to if I wanted to survive and make good the way my father wanted. I went through all the manuals. After a while, I could practically recite them by heart. But I couldn't understand them."

The driven young man was competing in a society where hard work and devotion were the norm. Impelled by deprivation and ambition, the young people of Hong Kong, like the entrepreneurs of South Korea, had little to lose—and everything to gain. To excel required not only talent, but compulsive application.

"After two months, I was transferred from reservations to ticketing," Francis says. "I was glad of the contact with passengers, the chance to write tickets and to study between passengers. . . . I used to open the ticket office at eight and work a full day. Most CAT flights came in late in the day. So I volunteered to work at the airport from, say, six P.M. until the last flight left, maybe at eleven. . . . It was a twelve- or thirteen-hour day. But I wanted to learn the trade.

"Up to 1966, everything was fine. They'd made me a supervisor, and in four years my salary doubled, going up to HK$980 [U.S.$196] a month. Then I clashed with another supervisor. . . . I didn't know about corporate politics in those days. I thought if I worked hard and was honest, then I'd be all right."

CAT's corporate politics were remarkably complex. Founded by Major General Claire Chennault to carry relief supplies in China, the airline was later controlled by the CIA, which used CAT subsidiaries for its own purposes. Carrying the white-sun flag of the Chinese Nationalists on its tail, CAT was administered by Chinese, all enthusiastic intriguers.

Francis was ready to leave CAT, and he had already found his future partner. Francis Chan was also a devout Catholic. In rootless Hong Kong, a common religion, like kinship or the same native place in China, cements *guanxi*, literally "relationships," otherwise "connections." Since Catholics are a small minority, the bond is very close. Hence, the "Catholic Mafia."

"I was lucky," he resumes. "Francis Chan asked me to work for TWA. I was taking a salary cut and a demotion. But TWA would be very good for training. It was very big, not like little CAT. I knew I needed more education—and I couldn't pay for it myself."

Two years later, the budding tycoon of twenty-six, who was already the chief support of his family, got a room of his own. Before the Cheung family moved to distant Meifoosunchun in the New Territories, the three brothers had shared one room. Meifoo was cheap because it was so distant and lacked public transport. Francis organized a motorized junk to take himself and a hundred others to work every morning.

"In 1970," he adds, "I was made reservations manager with a big increase to HK$2,900 [U.S.$500] a month. . . . That was very good, because I'd met Monica at TWA. We got married the same year."

Monica moved into Francis's room in the apartment at Meifoo, having already left TWA. In 1971 their first daughter, Michelle, was born. Francis's mother looked after her, and Monica came to work for me, recommended by the Catholic Mafia. That is how Moira and I became involved in the success story of Francis Cheung.

"Management training was the best part," Francis recalls. "I only had technical skills before. And the kind of people I dealt with were different. . . . I was very happy. I was a manager with responsibility for several departments, an expense account, and a good salary."

The idyll of modern Hong Kong lasted a little over two years. In July 1974 his father died, loved and respected, although consistent only in failure. Just before Christmas, TWA told Francis Chan, station manager for Hong Kong, and Francis Cheung, reservations manager, that service would be suspended in the new year. The rising cost of fuel had forced TWA to turn its entire Asian operation over to Pan American, in exchange for routes elsewhere.

The two Francises told TWA, "We'll charter your planes and run them on your Asian routes, retaining the entire staff."

"TWA was losing money in the U.S., not in Asia, since *every* eastbound plane out of Hong Kong was more heavily loaded than *any* westbound plane into Hong Kong," Francis Cheung explains.

"We were doing a much better job than our counterparts in America."

TWA's answer was *no*. The deal with Pan American was indivisible.

"First my father . . . and then this," Francis Cheung remembers. "It was the darkest Christmas of my life." Francis Chan, his boss, was fired, and he was offered the job. But he turned it down. In mid-1974, his loyalty, which was in the tradition of the upright Confucian mandarin, was rewarded. In May, Francis Chan became Hong Kong district manager for Philippine Air Lines.

"In June, Chan asked me to come and talk," Francis Cheung says. "I needed HK$6,000 [U.S.$1,000] a month to keep the family going. He said, 'I can manage that. But you'll have to go to Manila. The senior vice-president wants to see the future sales manager, Hong Kong.'"

Francis smiles like a cat that has found the cream and resumes, "That man was a mad dog. He barked at me. He said Francis Chan had promised U.S.$5 million in sales annually, but I'd caused him more expenses and would have to deliver another U.S.$2 million. Francis Chan and I had already done a market survey. We knew we could easily do U.S.$6 million or U.S.$7 million, although PAL's sales were then only U.S.$2 million. He thought he'd got me, but he hadn't because we'd already made a full study."

A great time was beginning. The two Francises created their own system—and Hong Kong's sales soon exceeded the $7 million a year they had promised. The great break came in November 1979, a year after Ramon Cruz had become chairman of the board of PAL. The two Francises gave Cruz a dinner that ended with a cake bearing a single candle for the first anniversary of his chairmanship. Then they told him of the enormous opportunities they saw in China, which was just beginning her reform and opening. Since joining PAL five years earlier, they had been commuting to China to keep up the relationships formed from 1972 on, when they were still working for TWA.

After President Richard Nixon's first visit to China in 1972, the two Francises had been encouraged by TWA's admirable regional manager, Joseph Brumert, to get to know the Communists' China Travel Service and CAAC. It had been hard work, but they were by 1979 on good terms with the key men. The two offices had long been isolated from the capitalist travel agencies and airlines with whom they should have been dealing. All the executives were terrified of making a political misstep that could bring severe punishment.

"We cultivated the CAAC relationship, and we got them many things," recalls Francis Cheung. "All sorts of information about reservations, tariffs, routes, and so on. They couldn't get even basic information.

"Soon the Philippines became the first ASEAN country to establish diplomatic relations with China. We said to CAAC, which, of course, meant the Chinese government, 'You have good relations with the Philippines, so you can use Manila as a gateway to ASEAN. Maybe Manila can do something to persuade the other ASEAN countries.' "

The Chinese finally said, "What a good idea!" Characteristically, they then demanded: "Cancel your flights to Taiwan, and you can fly to the People's Republic."

Francis replied, "PAL cannot operate on traffic to China alone. We cannot justify the service economically, only politically. Two friendly countries do need a good air bridge."

There the matter rested, officially at least, while the two Francises continued talking to the Chinese privately. As a result of those patient explorations, a Chinese air transport delegation came to Manila in May 1979.

"All the details for the bilateral talks had already been ironed out," Francis Cheung says. "The air treaty was signed in a record three days. In August 1979 we began regular service to Beijing and Guangzhou. It was the first time a major carrier could fly to China without changing colors or changing names—and to two cities. PAL's Taiwan service was maintained without interruption. . . . After the inaugural flights, there were other agreements on tourism, building hotels, and so on. Both sides were very happy."

Considering what that triumph meant to him personally, he expounds, "CAT taught me the technical details, and TWA taught me about management. But PAL gave me the opportunity to learn how to negotiate . . . how to convince people in government."

"And how do you—or anyone—deal with the Chinese?" I ask. "Are there any general rules?"

Ten years earlier he could have replied, "Just get hold of the son or daughter of a very senior cadre and make them your agents. Also make sure you've got plenty of money for bribes." Reviewing his extensive experience since then, he now answers, "The Chinese are more political than economic. No matter what your objectives, don't consider the economic aspect primary, but always justify it politically. . . . They've changed a little now, and the political side isn't all-important. They used to worry about losing their heads if they made a political mistake. Now they must also worry about the economic effects, because their own future is tied up with it. So you must strike a balance.

"Therefore, it's now harder to deal with them. Before, you only had to know a man's political purpose—and justify it for him. Dead easy! Now you have to justify it economically too—so he can justify it to his department. Negotiating with a Chinese, the most important thing is *you* have to solve his problems.

"By finding out his problems beforehand, you avoid embarrassing him at the conference table. You talk to him in private, and then, when you come to the conference table, you give him all the face he needs. Even let him abuse you a little first. Then it'll go smoothly, *after* he shows he's in control.

"But you must be firm . . . not lose your own dignity. Make sure everybody is given face. But always be firm—and not *too* nice."

Shortly after the treaty was signed, the two Francises told PAL Chairman Ramon Cruz, "It's high time we retired."

When he expressed surprise, they explained, "We've accomplished a lot in a short time, more than most people could. There's bound to be jealousy. So, before we get PAL into trouble, we should call it quits."

They soon reached the compromise they wanted. They would become general sales agents for Philippine Air Lines in Hong Kong, but would also be free to pursue their own burgeoning business, Hillmotta Tours. Francis Cheung was ready to cut loose from salaried employment and set up on his own—as had his father. Unlike his father, he had built a strong foundation for his private enterprise.

In 1982–83 the two Francises, as PAL's general sales agents, sold passenger and cargo space worth more than $24 million. Ten years earlier, sales had been $2 million. They also ran the first cruise ships to China, working first with Greeks and later with Scandinavian shipowners. They got into antiques after a friendly CAAC executive asked how much PAL had paid them for playing midwife to the route agreements. Astonished that they had not received large bonuses, he arranged access to warehouses in China so that they could choose their own stock of antiques.

One of the Manila agreements provided for Filipino investment in Chinese hotels, but the grand theft perpetrated by President Ferdinand Marcos had left no money to spare. Ramon Cruz told Francis Cheung to find a way for PAL to run two hotels in China in conjunction with the Manila Hotel, one of the world's best. He knew that the Japanese construction company building the Palace Hotel on Wangfujing, Beijing's Madison Avenue, was looking for management from a third country, and it was to be neutral between the Japanese and Chinese partners. The joint chiefs of staff of the People's Liberation Army, who were the Chinese partner, wanted a superb showcase hotel.

Francis made his pitch to a schoolmate who represented the Japanese partner in Hong Kong. A tour de force of special pleading, it reveals what Asians, even American-oriented Asians, in these, their years of

triumph, think of Americans and Europeans. It also reveals some
reasons for their success.

"Normally, nobody would think of a Filipino firm for the job," Francis
conceded. "Frankly, their record is *not* good. I also know that seven
big hotel chains are after the contract, including Hilton, Sheraton,
Meridien, and Intercon. But just think about this: *A parent with a
hundred children or a parent with one child. Which is better for the
child?* As you know, American chains have had big problems in China
at the same time New World Hotels from Hong Kong was succeeding
brilliantly in Guangzhou. Now what's the lesson?

"The first lesson is service. How can Americans possibly teach Chinese about service? It must be Asians, a Third World country, because
they're more service-oriented, more humble. . . . Also, Americans and
Europeans are very rigid. The Americans are good at control and the
Europeans at practical work. They know how to do the cooking, but they
don't know how to serve. And what costs more, training staff in America
or in the Philippines?

"Working with a chain, you have to call New York, Frankfurt, or
London when you've got a problem. They'll say, 'My itinerary for Asia
is three months from now. I'll have my man in Hong Kong talk to you.'
The Philippines is close to China. It's a poor country, but it runs one
of the best hotels in the world.

"Maintenance is the big problem—and the big expense. Look what
happened to hotels run by Westerners. Less than a year after opening, they looked fifty years old because the expatriate management
didn't know how to maintain them. But look at the Manila Hotel. There
was no money to lavish on maintenance, but they maintained it
beautifully."

Relishing every word, Francis recalls, "I also said, 'No matter what
hotel you go to in China, you find a lot of Filipinos. They speak English,
and they're cheap, and they don't make problems. . . . The Filipino
who gets a job overseas is very happy.'

"They get lots of tips. In China very soon, tips won't be a problem.
When you tip a doorman for opening a taxi door, he says very loud,
'Thank you, sir.' He speaks in a high-pitched voice so others can know
he gets tips—just like waiters used to in old-fashioned North China
restaurants."

Francis Cheung's own role also altered, although more subtly, with
the growth of travel to China. He recently introduced one Chinese
official or investor to another, for he has a wide acquaintance among the
men—and the few women—who make the big commercial decisions.
As an outsider he can cross the high walls that separate Chinese units
and companies from each other. He thus became an innovator and a

teacher, introducing China to the ways of the world—and the world to the ways of China.

Francis was performing the function that could conceivably save Hong Kong. As I observed earlier, Hong Kong must either alter China substantially or itself be radically altered, perhaps be so distorted that it can no longer function. Francis Cheung and others like him could help China change sufficiently so that she would not change Hong Kong excessively.

After Tienanmen the crucial question was even more urgent: Can a fearful David convert an enraged Goliath in the short time remaining to him?

Before Tienanmen Square forced some reconsideration, Britain had virtually washed its hands of Hong Kong. And Britain had been rewarded for that compliance. In the bad old days of imperialism, trade followed the flag, which usually flew on gunboats. In these brave new days, increased trade can reward the hauling down of the flag. Britain confidently expects the graceful surrender of Hong Kong to prove almost as profitable as had its forcible seizure.

"The French were given the main contract for the Daya Bay Atomic Power Station because of their political record," the president of an American corporation who has much experience of doing business in China pointed out to me. "A number of countries could have handled the technical side, including the U.S. But I've heard a half-dozen times from senior Chinese that the French got the plum 'because France has been extremely helpful.' France was one of the first Western countries to recognize the People's Republic, and the Chinese have long memories. The French have also been particularly helpful in technology transfer."

"And Britain?" I asked. "Why did the British also get a piece of Daya Bay?"

"The answer is one word: Hong Kong," he replied. "Of course it's nearby and a convenient base of operations. But anybody can operate out of Hong Kong, not only the British. That, too, was a politically based decision. I've heard repeatedly from Chinese officials that Britain was rewarded for being 'very helpful and accommodating over Hong Kong.' Other contracts, too, have carried that stamp of government approval. I'm not saying those deals are the price of Hong Kong. I can't believe a deal was made in advance. But the Brits are certainly being rewarded for being nice about Hong Kong."

Deng Xiaoping himself repeatedly congratulated the British government on its cooperative attitude. London has not been embarrassed by those testimonials to the facility with which it is disencumbering itself of its last major Crown Colony—nor by the obvious rewards for not fighting for better terms for the millions who live there. It is, however, too late to wonder whether Britain could have defied Beijing's pressure—and kept the Colony.

The Falkland Islands, worth not a six-millionth of Hong Kong in human or economic terms, were retaken from Argentina—with a lot of luck. With all the luck in the world, Hong Kong is not defensible against China, short of using atomic weapons, which is not a very good idea. Besides, not only water, but cheap food and cheap labor from China are essential to Hong Kong. Although the threat of the Liberation Army was only implicit, London believed it had no choice but to give in gracefully after Deng Xiaoping made his wishes clear to Sir Murray MacLehose in 1979. The Paramount Leader told the governor of the Crown Colony that China wanted the entire territory in 1997, when the lease on the New Territories expired—not only the New Territories, but the Kowloon Peninsula and Hong Kong Island, as well.

Yet Hong Kong still wonders: First: did London have to give in quite so gracefully? Could it not have got a better deal initially? And, second: has Britain pursued subsequent negotiations on the nature of the coming Chinese administration with vigor and resolve? The answer to the first question is *probably*. London probably had no choice. But London did not look closely at the alternative.

Lord MacLehose later told me that he was surprised at being given that audience—and equally surprised when Deng Xiaoping informed him that China wanted the entire territory back in 1997. MacLehose's critics, some quite well informed, contend that he raised the issue himself because he hoped to be told that Hong Kong could go on as it was.

The issue of who spoke first is not absolutely crucial. It may be no more than a question of emphasis. Yet Britain's bargaining position would have been stronger if the Chinese had raised the issue first. If MacLehose introduced it by seeking permission to extend the expiration date of land leases in the New Territories, Britain's position was weakened from the beginning.

Still, Murray MacLehose had no reason to think that Deng Xiaoping would demand the entire territory. The conventional wisdom of that time, to which I must confess I subscribed, held that China wanted Hong Kong to remain totally unchanged because it was critical to China economically. There is, perhaps, an unpleasant parallel with the optimists' present argument that China will keep her promises because she wants to run Hong Kong as an asset, not a liability.

In 1982, however, Prime Minister Margaret Thatcher asserted in Beijing that China was bound by the treaties that gave Britain possession of Hong Kong Island and the Kowloon Peninsula in perpetuity. Granted the industrial and commercial center could not function without the New Territories, what good was the New Territories detached from the center? It looked like a standoff.

Yet, powerful advocates in the Foreign and Commonwealth Office were lobbying for a graceful surrender. A crucial luncheon party was given in London by one eminent advocate while Mrs. Thatcher was still committed to keeping Hong Kong Island and Kowloon. Several senior men presented the Chinese ambassador with a detailed proposal for a peaceful turnover of the entire territory. They felt that resisting China's demands would not only be futile, but would damage British interests.

Accordingly, the bargaining position was betrayed before the bargaining began—and the British were outflanked. Since the Chinese would thereafter never accept less, all Hong Kong had to go. The prime minister finally agreed.

Most of Hong Kong's people feel that Britain has not paid much attention to their interests. Despite Deng Xiaoping's spontaneous promise not to alter its fundamental institutions until 2047 (if then), Hong Kong did not feel secure before June 4, 1989. Since that atrocity, Hong Kong has been riven by fear.

The Basic Law was drafted by Sino-British negotiations as the constitution under which Beijing will run Hong Kong as an "autonomous region" of the People's Republic of China. The final interpretation of both the Basic Law and the decisions of local officials and courts will, however, be made by the National People's Congress in Beijing. The People's Liberation Army will be at hand to enforce that interpretation—and any alteration of the Basic Law Beijing wishes. That is not autonomy, not even close to autonomy.

An articulate group in Hong Kong contended that only an elected government could provide the foundation for the stability Deng Xiaoping promised—and, further, serve as a stronghold from which to resist Chinese impositions. That group wanted representative democracy, not a largely appointed legislature and a chief executive chosen solely by Beijing.

China said: *no!* Democracy was not on the agenda. And that was that—until June 4, 1989.

The seventy-one-story Bank of China Building, just completed on land sold cheap to Beijing, was then the tallest and most conspicuous building in Hong Kong. The triangular tower was shaped like a gigantic blade; the external decoration looked like crossed chopsticks, which are an evil omen. The superstitious Cantonese were horrified. They called Beijing's Bank "the big knife buried in the heart of Hong Kong."

Yet, after the massacre, the outcry in Hong Kong and elsewhere forced reconsideration of the two critical matters that lay within London's power: internal democracy and right of abode in the United Kingdom.

Extended democracy would undoubtedly offend Beijing, but Britain could no longer sacrifice *all* else for commercial advantage. True, democracy was not only abhorrent to the reactionary leadership in Beijing, but irrelevant. The gerontocracy would undoubtedly sweep aside all elements of democracy on taking over Hong Kong—regardless of legal technicalities. But how long, Hong Kong's leaders asked, could the gerontocracy last? The old men had to die, and younger leaders with some appreciation of the link between production and morale were in the wings.

Besides, London could no longer maintain that extending the right of abode would undermine confidence in the territory by demonstrating Britain's distrust of Hong Kong's future masters, as former Foreign Secretary Sir Geoffrey Howe had long contended. British public opinion was deeply moved by Tienanmen Square, and Portugal had granted citizenship to everyone resident in Macao in 1981. Some 200,000 new Portuguese would be entitled to live anywhere in the European Community, *including Britain*, but 3.2 million British subjects in Hong Kong had been deprived of that right in 1962 by an act of the British Parliament.

At the least, it appeared, more of Hong Kong's people would be given the right of abode in the U.K. Most of the 3.2 million had no desire to live in Britain, but wanted the *right* to live in Britain solely as insurance. Hundreds of thousands, perhaps millions, who would otherwise flee Hong Kong before 1997, would remain if they knew they could go to Britain as a last resort. That concession would actually restore confidence, not undermine it.

If the people of Hong Kong lost all confidence in the future, many would flee—and the territory would wither. China might thus inherit a shell, indeed was likely to inherit a shell, unless the trend altered sharply. An extreme proposal called for Britain to declare Hong Kong an independent city-state—and threaten that all movable assets, mechanical and human, would be withdrawn if Beijing did not accept it. That was one of those brilliant ideas that are everything except feasible.

Even moderates believed Britain must strive to convince the Chinese that they would hurt themselves severely by undermining the value of the territory soon to be theirs. At the least, a strong stand could impress on the Chinese leadership the immense difficulty of keeping Hong Kong alive to produce wealth for China unless fundamental changes in the present agreement kept its people in place and in production.

The American corporation president with great experience of business with China whom I cited earlier offered a reasonably objective final analysis.

"We're handling the Communists with kid gloves at the wrong time," he said. "So they're getting used to kicking us around. They feel they know it all already. I just can't see Hong Kong's being allowed to function on its own . . . to make its own mistakes without the Chinese intervening to fix things up. They won't be able to keep their hands off—and they're very heavy-handed."

He smiled self-deprecatingly and asked: "How can you negotiate when you've already conceded almost everything? Still, it's worth pointing out certain truths to the Chinese. After all, they do listen sometimes. They may not—probably won't—do as you wish, but they will occasionally take in what you say. . . .

"We *must* try hard, knowing full well that, whatever agreements are reached beforehand, the Chinese will, after 1997, do exactly as they please. Yet we cannot let go. We would never forgive ourselves if in 1998 we look back and have to say, 'If only we had . . .' "

18

The Philippines: America's Flawed Legacy in Asia

IF YOU CAN IGNORE THE CHORUS OF THE IMPOVERISHED, THE REPUBLIC OF THE PHILIPPINES IS A LIGHTHEARTED POLITICAL AND ECONOMIC EXTRAVAGANZA. THE MUSIC IS FANDANGO AND ROCK; THE WORDS ARE SPANISH, ENGLISH, AND PILIPINO. THE CAST IS LIVELY—A LARGELY MALAY PEOPLE DIRECTED BY A FRIVOLOUS AND PARASITICAL RULING CLASS AND BESET BY REBELLION, CORRUPTION, AND SLOTH.

On Sunday, April 20, 1988, flocks of Filipinas in bright dresses flitted like humming birds around the Cathedral of the Good Shepherd in Singapore. After mass, they sipped coffee at tables set in the open as the soft warmth of early morning dissolved into muggy heat. Some trailed the Caucasian or Chinese children who were their changes. All had come 1,400 miles from their homes to earn $150 to $200 a month—and send most of it back to their homes.

Eleven o'clock mass at St. Joseph's in Hong Kong was also thronged with Filipinas. Afterward, they clattered downhill to the Central District to squat with hundreds of others in the glassed corridors of the Landmark or settle like starlings on Statue Square. They gnawed on sandwiches and sipped cheap soft drinks until the day passed and they could return to the servants' cubicles of apartment blocks climbing the Peak.

They, too, had been forced from their home islands by grinding poverty, as had more than a million other men and women. All were happy to toil anywhere in the world for low wages.

In Manila that same Sunday morning, an American priest preached in nasal Pilipino in the Malate Church. Erected in 1634 by the Spaniards, the church is just off Roxas Boulevard, which was formerly called Dewey Boulevard, after the American admiral who drove the Spaniards out. Inquisitive children rushed to the big wooden doors when automatic rifle fire rattled just outside the fortress-thick walls.

They goggled at the platoon of the Marxist New People's Army that was charging a machine gun spitting red tracer bullets. Police and soldiers were defending a small park where a traveling circus was camped. As they exchanged fire with the rebels, a gigantic blue bus packed with Japanese men rolled past unscathed.

Self-consciously impassive, the tourists glanced at the gory scene. Advised not to be surprised by anything they saw in Manila, they were nonetheless relieved when they saw the motion-picture cameras, the imperious director, and the brilliantined pop star who was playing the anti-Communist hero as a super-Rambo.

Their thoughts then returned to the big sign they had just seen, which cajoled in crimson Japanese characters: GREATLY HONORED GUESTS! THIS CABARET OFFERS EXOTIC ENTERTAINMENT AND SKILLED SERVICES PERFORMED BY BEAUTIFUL, FRIENDLY YOUNG LADIES. COME AND ENJOY YOURSELF UTTERLY.

On Sunday evening, a fairy-tale pageant unfolded on the bowling-green lawns fringed by hibiscus and oleander behind the old Manila Hotel. Gleaming white, it rose like an enchanted ice palace above the squatter shacks fringing the blood-warm bay. From the penthouse beneath the green copper roof, General Douglas MacArthur, field marshal of the Commonwealth of the Philippines, had directed the defense against the Japanese invasion in 1941–42. Ordered to abandon that hopeless task to lesser generals, he had returned to the Manila Hotel after his forces retook the Philippines in 1944.

When I first stayed at the Manila Hotel in 1951, prominent signs directed gentlemen to check their guns before entering the dining room. That Sunday evening in 1988, I looked down from my balcony on a scene from a Hollywood spectacular of the Fred Astaire–Ginger Rogers era. Tulle and organdy transformed flower girls and bridesmaids into pink, turquoise, and scarlet cloudlets. At the long head table the mothers of the bridal couple and their contemporaries wore the traditional *terno*, with sleeves flaring like butterfly wings. The men wore the traditional *barong Tagalog*, a self-embroidered overshirt of fine piña cloth. Wine glowed in carafes at twenty dollars a bottle, and an eight-foot-high wedding cake stood under a gazebo like those that shelter Balinese altars. A wooden dance floor was laid over the adjoining lawn, and a band alternated rock and sentimental ballads. The high intensity lights of a strolling television team glared.

The daughter of the Shiotsuguos was celebrating her marriage to the son of the Rodes with a party for 150. Other receptions filled the Manila Restaurant, the Champagne Room, and other lawns. Some 1,100 guests feasted, drank, and danced at wedding parties in the Manila Hotel that Sunday night. The cost of food was $9,000—at $8.50 a head, which would have been very reasonable elsewhere. But this was a nation where a good waiter could earn at most $95 a month, a primary-school teacher $85, and a professional economist with an advanced degree no more than $357.[1]

Those diverse scenes on one unremarkable Sunday delineate the sad state of the Republic of the Philippines—and the plight of its 67 million people, whose number is increasing at 2.7 percent annually. The poorest nation of East Asia, the Republic of the Philippines is also the only nation of the region tormented by a Marxist insurgency,[2] which could seize power if present conditions do not alter radically.

The Philippines is also the only nation of East Asia that exports its daughters and sons wholesale. More than two million work abroad at jobs they cannot find at home.[3] Registered unemployment, which is only part of actual unemployment, was in October 1987 2,173,000, 9.5 percent of a labor force of 22,985,000. In the Manila region, 18.6 percent were unemployed. The workers abroad send home about $1.6 billion a year, which helps to pay the interest on their country's foreign debts of more than $30 billion. Without those remittances—and the hope of a better life they exemplify—their country would be much worse off.

Indignant at that new traffic in indentured servants, the government in 1988 orated about prohibiting the exportation and exploitation of its people. A particular humiliation was the thousands of Filipinas who have become prostitutes in Japan, Hong Kong, and even Bangkok, which is already well provided with native talent. The storm of indignation lasted just the few days it took responsible officials to teach the politicians that the country needed the money—and did not need additional millions of unemployed.

Manila was once beautiful. Today, large parts of the capital are slums. Some 2.3 million squatters, roughly a quarter of its inhabitants, are crammed into shantytowns. They are called *kapus-palad,* "the unlucky." The most degraded live—and scavenge—on the great garbage dump called Smokey Mountain because of the toxic fumes it exhales. Shantytowns have spread across Manila like a tropical fungus. Shacks of cardboard, scrap wood, and rusty sheet metal lean against the brick walls crowned with barbed wire that surround the enclave, called Forbes Park, where the rich in their mansions are attended by platoons of servants.

---

[1] The legal minimum wage in the Manila area in 1988 was 63 pesos ($3) a day, a raise of 11 percent over the previous year. Cigarettes sold individually by streetcorner peddlers cost one peso each.

[2] Except Burma, which is not only more miserable, but is threatened by several insurgencies. I have excluded Burma from this book because it has nothing whatsoever to do with the Asian Renaissance.

[3] In January 1988, 49,881 workers found jobs abroad, according to the Department of Labor and Employment, 29 percent more than had done so in January 1987.

A glacially insensitive plutocracy savagely exploits the Philippines. Ignoring the suffering of the bone-poor masses, the plutocracy also ignores the clear threat to its own privileges—and perhaps its existence—inherent in that suffering.

The growing Marxist insurgency has its roots in popular discontent. But the attitudes of the plutocracy have altered little since the regime of Ferdinand and Imelda Marcos, who stole billions from the nation. Too complacent, perhaps too dense, to realize that it is directly threatened, the small ruling class does very little to counter the menace. And it is devastating the country's natural wealth, leveling the rain forests, and wrecking the coral reefs to enrich itself.

In a decade or two, the exploiters will probably have destroyed the exquisite natural beauty of their 7,100 islands. No one will stop them, for everyone is paid off. Nearly universal among capitalists, bureaucrats, and the military, corruption is today almost as virulent as it was under the deposed Marcoses—a primary industry.

And the people, thirty million of whom live below the official poverty line, support the few thousand rich. What of the people? The lucky ones work abroad, as would millions more if they could. Tens of thousands of Filipinas are eager to marry foreigners, regardless of age, temperament, appearance, or comparative penury. They are desperate to leave a country where their best prospects are unpaid drudgery as rural or slum wives—or the evanescent glitter of the red-light districts. The most expensive bar girls, hostesses, and dance partners, generically called "hospitality girls," cater to American servicemen, Japanese tourists, and other foreigners.

The Filipinos are an attractive people. They are also extremely volatile, given to outbursts of violence, latent in Malay blood. I once saw thirteen bodies with raw gunshot wounds stacked on the floor of a provincial police station during a humdrum election—and thirty-six candidates were slaughtered in a recent election.

The Filipinos have created their own vibrant form of Catholicism, which is colored by ancient animism. They are kind and gentle, devout and generous. They are also fanatical, superstitious, and turbulent. And 10 percent of their priests and nuns militantly support the Marxist insurgency.

As Francis Cheung pointed out, Filipinos rarely make problems for their employers, whether in Saudi Arabia or China, because they are so eager for work. They are first-class craftsmen, cooks, waiters, and secretaries, in part because they are not weighted with false pride. The educated are capable administrators—if relieved of the pressure of families whose coddling spoils them and whose demands lead them to corruption. Both the Manila Hotel and the overseas services of Philippine Air Lines are among the best in Asia, which means the best in the world.

*   *   *

The Japanese tourists bemused by the film company had come to Manila for its rampant sexual opportunities. Japanese businessmen and diplomats come in the name of friendship, bearing generous loans, grants, and contracts. Their slush funds are so lavish a Japanese consul said to a Filipino friend: Tell me, whom shall I bribe?

Japanese now own a third of the bars and nightclubs, essentially retail businesses. Despite lingering Filipino antagonism, the Japanese also are taking control of large companies, as the pace of their advance is relentless. Filipinos, like other Asians, say dolefully: "The Japanese are winning in peace what they failed to win in war."

The chief buffer against the Japanese is still the Americans, who were dominant for so long. An American ambassador who has suffered Filipino-American friction remarked to Moira, "Only the American and the Japanese ambassadors really count. The American ambassador is a major public figure here, a celebrity like a movie star. It's an intense relationship with love and loathing on both sides—and great demands for affection."

As the Japanese sun rises and Filipino nationalists thunder, the American eagle is finding the atmosphere less hospitable. Having been touted as America's showcase in East Asia, the Philippines are becoming America's shame. Anti-Americanism is now highly fashionable among both intellectuals and politicians. Anti-Americanism is nearly universal among the educated younger generation, fostered by the many universities that are an American legacy. Emotional antagonism is fueled by objections to American cultural influence, as well as American political and economic actions.

Anti-Americanism comes in waves, rising and receding with the political weather. But I have never known it more widespread—and still rising. Intellectuals rail at the nation that almost to the end supported the Marcos regime, which was capriciously murderous but consistently rapacious. Moreover, the Americans denied Filipino intellectuals the right to struggle for independence like intellectuals in French, Dutch, and British colonies. Independence came too easily.

The United States had, before World War II, promised to set the islands free. Independence was formally granted on July 4, 1946, hardly a year after the war. Filipinos were then happy to show their affection for their former colonial overlord by sharing the same Independence Day. That affection declined, chiefly among the best educated, who remembered their earlier struggle against America.

Having driven out the Spanish with the assistance of Filipino insurgents, the United States in 1898 repudiated its promise to grant the Philippines independence. Led by their folk hero, Emilio Aguinaldo,

Filipinos rose against the new American overlords. Although too few to prevail against the American army of occupation commanded by Lieutenant General Arthur MacArthur, they fought hard and well. During the so-called Moro Revolt, the U.S. Army adopted the .45-caliber automatic pistol because it was the only hand weapon that fired a slug heavy enough to stop the brave Filipinos' charges.

Between 1900 and 1941 there was more cooperation than antagonism. After Pearl Harbor, Filipinos fought side by side with Americans against the Japanese, displaying a fervor matched by no other Southeast Asian people. During the Japanese occupation, there were relatively few collaborators. After the Americans returned and granted independence, however, Filipinos began to feel themselves badly done by.

"Filipinos were cruelly let down by the Americans after World War II ended," commented a prominent editor who is hardly anti-American. "They had worn their hearts on their sleeves, fought the Japanese as guerrillas—and Japanese anger had led to the massacre of 150,000 civilians in Manila. Sixty percent of the country's industrial capacity was destroyed, as well as many crucial roads, bridges, and railroad trackage. Manila was 80 percent devastated. Without repairing the damage wrought when the Philippines were still an American colony, the U.S. 'gave' them independence, went off to occupy Japan—and subsequently rebuilt the Japanese economy to the tune of $4 billion."

Nonetheless, American influence remains overwhelming—and the mass of the people still look to the U.S. for succor. But intellectuals like Foreign Secretary Raul Manglapus maintain that the Philippines can only attain maturity and forge a strong national identity by "slaying the father-figure," who is, of course, the United States.

Maximo Soliven and his family epitomize the past now shaping the future. My old friend and sometime junior correspondent is an iridescent gadfly, the most popular and noisiest columnist in the Philippines. He now stings well-meaning, irresolute President Corazon Aquino almost as hard as he formerly stung greedy, cruel President Ferdinand Marcos. The dictator finally sent Max to jail, where he shared a cell with his schoolmate and colleague, Corazon Aquino's husband Benigno. In time, both were released. When Marcos ordered Benigno Aquino assassinated, the "people's power" revolt of 1986 became inevitable.

Max now criticizes the administration that then came to power for betraying its initial promise. He maintains, however, that his country's plight is due to its unfortunate history, which has made so many of his compatriots frivolous, indeed light-minded. That history is encapsulated in the rhetorical question, *What can you expect after 350 years in a Spanish convent followed by fifty years in Hollywood?*

That, Max points out, has been the recent history of the Philippines: four centuries of domination by two utterly different foreign powers.

Before the Spaniards arrived, early in the sixteenth century, the peoples of the archipelago were ruled by petty princelings and tribal chieftains. Their lives were dependent upon the whims of nature and the caprices of their rulers. Those peoples did not develop a culture sufficiently complex to be considered significant by Western scholars, who tend to define civilization in their own image.

When the Spaniards colonized the Philippines, they took away as much wealth as they could without undue effort. They brought to the Philippines their language, which was not widely adopted, and also their religion, which was. Elitists, the Spaniards were not interested in educating their new subjects. They were concerned about saving the immortal souls of their new subjects by converting them to Catholicism. The Pope had given them the islands on the understanding that they must untiringly propagate the Faith.

Thus, "350 years in a Spanish convent."

During those centuries, the Spaniards built a separate realm on top of the existing Filipino culture. Like the garrison of an alien fortress on the crest of a hill, they were interested in the native villages on the slopes chiefly as sources of cheap provisions and forced labor.

The center of the Spanish realm in the Philippines was the Catholic Church, as it was the center of Spain itself. The Church reached out to the native peoples—to instruct them in the true faith. The Spaniards taught Catholicism to save the people's souls and simple skills to make them better workers, but hardly more. They strove with success to make the Filipinos good Catholics, but not to make them good Spaniards. The Americans were to strive to make the Filipinos good Americans.

In 1898 the United States displaced the enfeebled Spaniards. Perhaps indolent, superstitious, and greedy, the Spaniards had followed fixed principles and adhered to fixed priorities. The Americans could never quite decide whether they were primarily interested in ports, profits, proselytizing, or betterment.

That confusion shaped the absentminded imperialism the United States practiced in the Philippines. Some Americans gloried in their "manifest destiny," which, they believed, was to hold dominion over lesser races. Many Americans felt sheepish, even guilty, at ruling another people.

Consequently, the United States never worked with a single will in the Philippines. Americans sometimes strove toward several divergent goals at the same time—and did not get very far. Or they strove for one goal and then dropped it for another—and did not get very far either.

Ports for naval and merchant vessels were the original American goal. Having come late to the carve-up, the U.S. held no territory in China that was considered the great prize in Asia. Washington therefore looked upon the Philippines, its first territorial possession in Asia, as a base from which to trade and to make additional territorial gains.

Profit-seeking American businessmen also came to the Philippines. Some put down roots, made a lot of money, and contributed to the development of the islands. But the Philippines were never to be as important economically to the U.S. as India was to Britain, or Indonesia to the Netherlands. Because much of North America was still to be developed, the home market was lucrative and opportunities at home were too profuse. Therefore, few Americans were interested in investing and trading in a subsidiary territory, even if it was a wholly owned subsidiary.

Proselytizing Protestant missionaries were generally disappointed. The Spanish priests had done their work too well for Filipinos to change their colors. The U.S. did not officially sponsor Protestantism as Spain had sponsored Catholicism.

Betterment was the single purpose on which almost all Americans agreed, even those who had opposed the annexation of the Philippines. Indeed, those idealists felt very strongly that the United States must atone for seizing the islands by educating its people and making them good citizens, which meant little brown-skinned Americans.

Americans believed in education for its own sake. The schoolmarms began arriving even before Filipino patriots stopped shooting Americans. So many came on the troopship USS *Thomas* that the pioneers are still remembered with gratitude as the Thomasites. Their labors were quickly rewarded: Filipinos enthusiastically learned American English and American values. All children were offered education, regardless of their parents' social position or wealth. English became the great leveler, elevating those who had been mired in poverty.

Hollywood came to America two decades after America came to the Philippines. But the breezy moral and aesthetic standards, epitomized by Hollywood, as well as its belief in instant gratification, were immediately adopted by Filipinos. So were its casual manners, its ballyhoo, and its razzmatazz. Behavior that was, to say the least, unusual in Boston, Atlanta, or even New York became the norm in Manila, where it was regarded as typically American. The great love affair between the Philippines and the United States had begun.

Thus, "fifty years in Hollywood."

Max Soliven is like a mountain torrent racing through rapids and tumbling over cataracts. He produces six thousand words a day for his two columns: in English for *The Philippine Star*, where he is co-publisher and chairman of the editorial board; in Tagalog, now officially called Pilipino, for *Ang Pilipino Naeyan.*

He produces tens of thousands of words a day in nonstop conversation. When he is in full flow, his black eyes flash, his broad face darkens a shade, and his pipe becomes a saber slashing the unoffending air. Max is almost never outtalked, even in a nation of great talkers. He usually knows what he is talking about, and he possesses an extraordinary store of knowledge. Although Max is hardly typical, his character and his life epitomize his nation. Short and muscular, he *is* the Philippines—writ large.

Like most of the best people in a society almost devoid of racial prejudice, his ancestry is mixed. Soliven, he explains, is a Filipinization of the Sullivans, of West Cork. His paternal ancestors were among the "wild geese" who fled Ireland for Spain in the seventeenth century and later came to the Philippines with the Spanish forces.

They intermarried with Ilocano women, and the Solivens' home became Ilocos Sur, a province near the northwest tip of the island of Luzon. The Irish-Spanish-Malay admixture was further enhanced by the Chinese genes of one Li Mahong, a pioneer whom the Spaniards called a pirate because he intruded into their domain.

The Chinese have been coming to the Philippines, indeed to all Southeast Asia, for millennia as traders, explorers, and most recently as settlers. Like the British, the Dutch, and the Thais, the Spanish invited Chinese immigration because they needed skilled craftsmen and good laborers. The Malays were either too lazy or too smart to work hard when bananas and fish were to be taken by stretching out a hand. Habituated to hard work, the Chinese took up the Spanish invitation— and soon mounted bloody risings against Spanish exploitation.

In Indonesia and Malaysia, where there has been little intermarriage, anti-Chinese feeling is very strong among the native Malays, who are largely Moslem. Yet in those countries, as in the Philippines, the overseas Chinese are the cutting edge of progress. Chinese money, Chinese brains, and Chinese vitality are largely responsible for the intellectual and economic renaissance—not only in Singapore, which is three-quarters Chinese, but in Indonesia and Malaysia. Thailand, whose royal family is at least half Chinese by blood, harbors little racial prejudice. Still, one past king, ignoring his own Chinese blood, called the overseas Chinese "the Jews of Southeast Asia." He did not mean to be complimentary. It is, nonetheless, difficult to distinguish between Thais and Chinese, while their common Buddhism teaches tolerance.

The Philippines are, however, unique. There is *no* anti-Chinese feeling among the elite, largely because everyone except the peasant in the fields has at least a dash of Chinese blood. In 1988 President Corazon C. Aquino made a much-touted pilgrimage to Fukien Province to trace her roots. Her middle initial stands for Cojuangco, her maiden name, which is her Chinese immigrant great-great-grandfather's full name made into a surname. A devotee of the Confucian work ethic, he became very rich and founded a dynasty. His part-Malay descendants have become even richer—their Chinese genes clearly dominant.

"Native Filipinos are just not entrepreneurs," observes Reynaldo A. Bautista, who runs a chain of restaurants in Manila and the U.S. "That's why there are so few Filipino restaurants, even in Manila. I'm sending my children to Chinese schools."

Many descendants of Chinese have not bothered to Filipinize their names. Jaimé Cardinal Sin bears the simple surname of his immigrant father. *The* premier national hero, Dr. José Rizal, was one-quarter Chinese. In varying proportions, Chinese genes have shaped other heroes only a shade less revered, including former Foreign Minister Carlos Romolo and former president Ramon Magsaysay—as well as the villain Ferdinand Marcos. The Tans, Lims, and Gos are prominent *Filipino* families, since the separate overseas Chinese community has virtually ceased to exist. Most of the particular talents that set the people of the Philippines off from other peoples of Malay stock come from their Chinese heritage. Yet Chinese compulsiveness is constantly at odds with Malay insouciance—and Max Soliven is no exception.

He fears that Corazon Aquino's lethargy (or hyper-caution) with regard to the armed forces and reform—social as well as economic—could give victory by default to the Marxist New People's Army. Plagued by military coups, the president has, as a European military attaché puts it, "virtually chained the troops to the barracks by denying them the weapons and the freedom they need to fight effectively." She is, further, a daughter of privilege, who is reluctant to alter the society that has given her so much. Shrinking from attacking the ruling class, which is her own class, she is in many ways a conservative Chinese lady.

The Malay streak is dominant in Max Soliven as it was in his grandfather, Isabelo, who fought first the Spaniards and later the Americans for the freedom of the Philippines. Afterward, he was elected mayor of his native Santo Domingo in the province of Ilocos Sur.

"My grandfather," Max laughs, "is the only mayor of any Filipino city who one can say categorically had an absolutely clean record—no graft and no corruption. On the night of the election, he was carried off by the *bangungot*, a mysterious malady that affects only Filipino men. He was just thirty-three."

Max's father, Benito, was taken in by a distant cousin. He studied the three R's under American schoolmarms from McGuffey's Readers, which preached the then cardinal American virtues: thrift, study, work, and enterprise. When Benito came to Manila in the early 1920s, he spoke four languages: English, Spanish, Tagalog, and his native Ilococo.

His favorite language was, however, English. The Americans, whom his father fought, had given him opportunities he could never have enjoyed under the Spanish, including the opportunity to study law at the University of the Philippines. Modeled after American universities, UP was directed by an American president and largely staffed by American professors.

"UP was *the* university," Max observes. "UP students still consider themselves *the* elite. But there's one big difference. The chief American-founded university is now the most anti-American university. Of course, all our universities are now anti-American."

Born in September 1929, "in the middle of a typhoon," he says dramatically, Max was the oldest of six boys and four girls. His parents were devout Catholics, and he remembers serving mass every day in his hometown, Santo Domingo. But the family moved to Manila when his lawyer father became a congressman.

Life was pleasant in the gleaming capital, although they lived entirely on the father's earnings, and Max attended the Ateneo de Manila, the country's premier Jesuit college. That easy existence ended on December 8, 1941, when Japanese warplanes dropped out of the undefended skies over Luzon to bomb and strafe. His father volunteered for the Philippine Scouts, was promoted to major in the field, and became a prisoner when all Filipino and American forces surrendered in March 1942.

"It was the Feast of the Immaculate Conception," Max remembers. "I had just come from mass at the Ateneo when I heard the news. But I didn't really understand it. I couldn't take it in."

Max would not like to be called pro-American. Condescending anywhere, in the Philippines that description now implies a lickspittle. But he is definitely not anti-American; he is too realistic. Nonetheless, he is bitter when he talks of the Battle of Bataan.

"The Filipinos," he says, "fought harder and better than the Americans, who were only four thousand among 78,000 soldiers opposing the Japanese." He has written: "The Americans, the British and the Japanese have written their versions. . . . All three have managed to emerge heroic. . . . The hapless Filipinos, who bore the brunt of the early weeks of the Pacific War, have been depicted—even in the eyes of their own young—as dupes and fools who fought for America and were repaid in the coin of contempt and postwar neglect."

Filipinos had confidently expected the Americans to be brave—and to be victorious. Yet the Americans were defeated in that first campaign. After Douglas MacArthur, field marshal of the Philippines and general of the U.S. Army, allowed Japanese bombers to catch his warplanes on the ground and his warships at their moorings, the Americans retreated. Many fought bravely, but they lost.

Filipinos were ecstatic in 1944, when Douglas MacArthur finally returned, as he had promised. But the myth had been destroyed. Filipinos might be short, but the Americans were no longer ten feet tall.

His father, Max recalls, survived the Bataan Death March. Driven by brutal Japanese guards, the defeated soldiers went eighty hours without water—and were shot or bayoneted if they fell out of formation. In Camp McLaughlin, where Benito Soliven was held, five hundred men died of starvation, disease, and ill treatment every day.

Max's voice sinks, and his accustomed bravura is dimmed for a moment. His father, he recalls, refused to buy freedom by joining the Assembly, the puppet legislature of the New Society the Japanese had promised to create. He was, nonetheless, released after four months of treating his men's dysentery with guava leaves and their other maladies with small quantities of smuggled medicines. He was released because he was dying of malaria.

Benito Soliven left no money and no property. Relatives could give little help to the widow, for they had their own problems. At thirteen, Max peddled black-market cigarettes on the streets of Manila to feed the family. Somehow, all survived, except the smallest brother, who died of cholera when he was ten months old. Max attended the Paco Catholic School and the Greater East Asia School, where he studied Japanese. He also learned the war songs of the Japanese: "The Battleship March," "Patriots' Flowers," and, foremost, "China Nights," a sentimental ballad about Chinese girls.

His pensiveness dissipating, Max bawls out the choruses. He wonders aloud why he chose to attend the Japanese school, which was training leaders for the New Society and the Greater East Asia Co-Prosperity Sphere. Between puzzlement and self-justification, he says, "Maybe I had the idea of being a spy . . . working for the underground." Some boys of his age were couriers and informants for the resistance, and his romantic visions helped temper hard reality.

"When leftists attack me for being bourgeois," he declares, "I tell them how I came up from poverty. I'm proud to be bourgeois. I worked damned hard to come up from the masses."

I put it to Max that he is no more a child of the masses than I, whose father was also a gifted, quixotic, and penurious lawyer. "My father was a servant, an orphan," he replies hotly. "In 1943, after my father died, things got very tough in Manila. So we decided to go back home to my mother's father, a retired customs officer in his late fifties. We packed ourselves into an open truck that ran on the fumes of burning charcoal. A journey that takes eight hours today took us eight days. . . .

"One day the Japanese broke into our house, looking for guerrillas. They beat my mother and my grandfather with rifle butts. The next day my grandfather died of a cerebral hemorrhage, more from anger than

from the beating. He was very dignified, with his Spanish blood. And
I vowed . . . I kissed his cold hands in the coffin and vowed I would get
back at the Japanese."

That vow sounds melodramatic, indeed unlikely, to those brought up
in the Anglo-Saxon tradition. For a Celt or a Latin it was, however,
hardly more than a normal reaction. And Max is both Celt and Latin,
as well as hot-blooded Malay and vengeful Chinese.

"The day after the funeral," he continues, "I went to the guerrillas in
the hills. . . . They wanted to make me a courier. I said I wanted to kill
Japs, but I had no weapon. Finally I got myself a rifle by killing a
Japanese. I was on horseback, and he was all alone, and he did a funny
thing. Instead of standing and shooting me, he ran. So I got him with
my bolo, my long machete. He was foolish, a straggler. But a whole
Japanese battalion was nearby, just around the corner. . . . Later the
guerrillas told me how stupid I'd been. . . . When the Americans
landed, they gave me an honorable discharge because I was only
fourteen."

The Soliven family suffered no further casualties after the father, the
baby, and the grandfather. All nine children survived the war, but cash
was very short.

"My mother," says Max, "only knew how to sew. She became a
dressmaker—and put us all through college. . . . When we went back
to Manila in 1944, we found our house had been destroyed. You could
see for miles in all directions where Manila used to be."

The Knights of Columbus gave him a scholarship to the Jesuit Ateneo
de Manila. Graduating in 1951 at twenty-two, with a bachelor's degree
in communication arts, he won a Fulbright Fellowship. At Fordham
College in New York City, still under Jesuit tutelage, he took a master's
degree in political philosophy and communication arts. But Max's heart
was in newspapers, not in academia.

"When I got back to Manila in 1954," he confesses, "I was angry
because of the wars I'd missed. . . . And I had a massive inferiority
complex about Ninoy Aquino. He'd gone to Korea to cover the war
when he was only seventeen—and I was the guy who fired him from the
school paper."

Manila was a great newspaper town in the early 1950s, as it is today
with twenty-odd dailies, and jobs were not hard to find. Max was
successively a reporter, a business editor, and a columnist on various
papers. As a jet-borne foreign correspondent, he was later to visit Viet
Nam, Japan, Southeast Asia, and Western Europe. I met him in the
early 1960s, when I was looking for a part-time correspondent in the
Philippines for *Newsweek*.

By 1972 Max was the most widely read columnist in a nation with
nearly a hundred columnists. Every newspaper ran a half-dozen col-

umns, as they do today. His column, "By the Way," in the *Manila Times*, got under the skin of Ferdinand Marcos, who had been elected president of the Republic of the Philippines in 1965.

Marcos liked the job so much he decided to keep it for life. He was encouraged by his wife, Imelda, who was very beautiful—and insatiably ambitious. The small group of army officers, government officials, and enterprising capitalists who staunchly supported him he later rewarded by giving them entire corporations, private or government, to run as monopolies—and to loot. Imelda fell into the habit of commandeering airliners from Philippine Air Lines to fly to Europe, America, or other ports in Asia, accompanied by entourages of sixty or more. Brushing aside the regular foreign service, she designated herself the Philippines' senior ambassador to popes and potentates.

Imelda ordered very expensive gowns by the gross, and hundreds of pairs of shoes. She spent hundreds of millions, perhaps billions, on real estate, *objets d'art*, and jewelry. Determined to make Manila a center of the arts, she sponsored a glittering film festival, but found herself short of funds. Quite practically, she then imported pornographic films to make up the shortfall.

Not to be outdone, her husband fabricated a heroic war record for himself. He also bribed and threatened, jailed and tortured, abducted and murdered. But irrepressible journalists, legislators, labor leaders, and students still attacked his regime.

Prominent among those critics were Max Soliven and his old friend Benigno "Ninoy" Aquino, who had given up journalism for politics. Sheltered by inherited wealth—his own as well as his wife's—Ninoy Aquino was for a time the only opposition senator in a legislature dominated by Marcos. He became the living symbol of resistance to a regime that was daily growing in brutality, licentiousness, and rapacity.

Then, as now, it was virtually impossible to keep a secret in Manila. Although increasingly authoritarian, the government was porous.

In September 1972, Ninoy Aquino asked for an invitation to appear on "Impact," Max Soliven's weekly television talk show. He had learned that Marcos did not plan to relinquish the presidency in 1973, although the constitution limited a president to two four-year terms. Ninoy hoped to thwart Marcos by exposing his intention of making himself president for life.

Despite the public indignation ignited by Ninoy Aquino's revelation, on September 22, 1972, the dictator carried out Operation Sagittarius. Ferdinand Marcos declared a state of emergency to meet the threat posed by the Marxist New People's Army—and proclaimed martial law, which would enable him to rule indefinitely without an election.

Ninoy Aquino and Max Soliven were among the first thousand political and intellectual leaders the army immediately arrested. They were to share a cell. Initially held without formal charge in Camp Crame in northern Manila with four hundred others, they were among the fourteen who were not released within a few days. Ferdinand Marcos was clearly out of control, but they did not know how far he would go. Yet they knew that dozens of his opponents had died mysteriously, and they were frightened.

"We were treated well," Max recalls. "The jailers knew that, things being what they were, tomorrow we might be their bosses. If they started treating you badly, it meant they were going to shoot you. . . . But we didn't know that at the time."

Max was released conditionally after four months of imprisonment without trial. For seven years he was forbidden to write or publish. For three years he was not permitted to leave metropolitan Manila without written permission—and an armed guard. He could find no work, and old friends prudently crossed the street when they saw him coming. The Montessori school his wife, Preciosa, had earlier opened could just support the family. For a time, however, he managed to make a living as a management consultant.

In 1975 he was allowed to publish *Sunburst*, a glossy tourism and lifestyle magazine. An influential publisher thrice asked Marcos to allow Soliven to travel. But the dictator invariably replied, "Not yet!"

"I was very frustrated at not being able to really write," Max recalls. "Not about politics. The press was well controlled then. All you had to do was read one paper—and you got everything. They were all singing the same song.

"The day Ninoy Aquino was shot, the story was a small item at the foot of the page. The day he was buried, when four million Filipinos walked behind his cortege, the main headline in one paper dealt with another death. It read, 'Man Killed, Struck by Lightning.' The victim was actually up a tree watching the funeral, but that fact was ignored until the last paragraph."

Laughing at the stupidities of the dictatorship, Max adds, "Marcos wasn't primarily after money or gold. His orgasms came from power."

"Then why did he have to steal so much?" I ask. "Why couldn't he be content with five or ten billion?"

Max replies, "He had to keep on demonstrating his power, power to amass money and wealth. . . . They say he was loyal to his friends. But he wasn't loyal to anybody. He told his cronies, 'I have the power of life and death over you. I can make you or I can finish you off.' So they started stealing, too."

Max is still not sure why he was put in a cell with Ninoy Aquino.

"Ninoy was to be in jail for seven years and seven months," he says. "My heart sank to my knees when I was assigned to be his cellmate. I thought, 'Jesus Christ, this guy Marcos hates Ninoy worst of all. And I'm his cellmate, so Marcos hates me, too!' But I think now he only wanted to punish me. So he put me in the same room with a guy who talks faster and more than I do. Ninoy was a real talker—in two dialects, as well as Tagalog and English. He was a spellbinder, a demagogue in a way.

"But jail developed his character. Before that, he was a smartass politician. He was glib and sassy, a young man in a hurry. And he was shallow. Afterward, it was the ascent of a soul to maturity in prison. He was good when he went in, but prison made him a great man. He himself said he had to thank Marcos. He was always thanking Marcos. He said Marcos gave him time to read books and think and form a philosophy of life. . . .

"After seven years, he was allowed to go home for Christmas, surrounded by guards, of course. His first words to me were, 'I've been rotting in prison for years, and nobody has stood up to demand my freedom. But I still have faith in our people. . . . Someday soon, they'll stand up and fight.'

"But Marcos was the smartest crook, the best con man, this country ever produced . . . a malign genius. . . . He really knew how to manipulate the Filipino people."

Max was meanwhile working his way back toward the journalistic eminence he had known before his arrest. *Sunburst* was succeeded by other magazines. But he was still prohibited from writing about politics.

Benigno Aquino was condemned to death. On November 27, 1977, a military commission handed down the sentence: *Death by musketry.* Yet Ninoy was in 1978 allowed to "take part" in an election for an "interim" parliament. From his cell he organized a political party called *Lakas ng Bayan*, "People's Power." He was even allowed to give one television interview, so that for the first time in six years the people of the Philippines saw their champion again.

Ferdinand Marcos was evidently determined to prove his magnanimity—and his omnipotence. But he suppressed the party called People's Power when he realized that its candidates could win in Manila.

Then Ninoy Aquino fell ill, a hunger strike having exacerbated the effects of solitary imprisonment and almost no exercise. After his first seizure, army doctors assured him that he had suffered "a muscle spasm, not a heart attack." After his second seizure, he was taken to a civilian hospital called the Heart Center. The diagnosis was unequivocal: he urgently required a triple bypass.

Ferdinand Marcos and Ninoy Aquino were then in complete agreement. Neither wanted the operation to take place in the Philippines. On May 8, 1980, Aquino was put aboard a flight to the United States, accompanied by his wife Corazon and their children. After his operation, he talked of returning home, presumably to imprisonment. Ferdinand Marcos told him to extend his medical furlough.

That exchange, Aquino felt, canceled his tacit agreement with the dictator to refrain from political activity while abroad. By granting him fellowships, Harvard and the Massachusetts Institute of Technology gave him standing. Working from Newton, Massachusetts, he attacked the Marcos regime in lectures, broadcasts, and articles. He wrote:

> I have asked myself many times: Is the Filipino worth suffering or even dying for? Is he not a coward, who would yield to any colonizer, be he foreign or homegrown? Is a Filipino more comfortable under an authoritarian government because he does not want to be burdened with freedom of choice? Is he unprepared or, worse, ill-suited for presidential or parliamentary democracy?

Ninoy Aquino answered his rhetorical questions with a ringing affirmative. The Filipino, he declared, was well worth dying for.

And he longed for home. In telephone conversations he repeatedly talked of returning to the Philippines. Now, he said, was the moment to strike—while his reputation was high, and the Marcos regime was growing greedier and shoddier.

Imelda Marcos came to see him—and urgently counseled him against returning. He would be assassinated, she warned, if he set foot in the Philippines. Max Soliven repeated that warning and advised: "Wait for Marcos to change or die. He's seriously ill. They'll kill you if you come back. I can smell blood."

Ninoy Aquino could not wait. He told Max, "If I should die, so be it. I hope it will awaken our people to fight for their rights." He stepped off an airliner from Taiwan at Manila International Airport on August 21, 1983—and was shot within the minute.

That shot ended Ferdinand Marcos's political life as well as Ninoy Aquino's earthly life. But the closing act of the drama, when Marcos was poll dead, but did not know it, was several years of intense excitement. New political groupings appeared—to be harassed but not crushed by the dictator. Battered by rising winds of domestic and foreign disapproval, Marcos backed and filled, tacked and ran, but never held to one course. He permitted somewhat greater freedom of expression, and then he attempted to quash all opposition, and then he loosened his restrictions again.

A curious feebleness had overcome the man Max Soliven calls the "smartest crook the Philippines ever produced." Perhaps he was, as Max suggests, "staggered by the immense public reaction to Ninoy's murder," after so many other murders had gone virtually unnoticed. For whatever reason, Marcos's political touch deserted him. He could no longer trim his sails to the prevailing wind, for the storm of indignation was too strong.

The dictator made his greatest tactical error when he told an American television interviewer that he would give Filipinos the opportunity to pass judgment on his rule. He promised a snap election, confident that the people would return him to power in triumph. In the isolation high office imposes, he was not fully aware of the suffering his greed had inflicted on the people—and he was deaf to their anger.

Election day was February 7, 1986, with Corazon Cojuangco Aquino running against Ferdinand Marcos under the yellow banners of People's Power. Ronald Reagan said in the aftermath that both sides had cheated. If this was true, Marcos cheated more widely and more effectively. Nonetheless, his margin of victory was very thin.

Corazon Aquino then came to power through a virtual coup d'etat. The millions who marched through Manila to protest the fraud that had stolen the election from her, reinforced by highly visible groups of nuns and by many priests. Jaimé Cardinal Sin had thrown his enormous moral weight onto the side of the opposition. When Ferdinand Marcos could no longer depend on the armed forces to keep him in power, he fled to Hawaii in a transport provided by the United States Air Force. At the eleventh hour, the Reagan Administration had nudged him out of Malacañang Palace, the White House of the Philippines.

"Whoever follows Marcos as president is doomed to fail," Ninoy Aquino had told Max Soliven. "Marcos has destroyed the moral values of our people. He's taught the Filipinos that crime not only pays, but pays very well."

The men and women in the paddy fields had been brutally disillusioned by the public theft committed by their rulers. Devout Catholics, despite a pagan underlay, they could no longer follow the Christian injunction to turn the other cheek and meekly endure the suffering God had put upon them. Quite clearly, it was not God who afflicted them, but the dictator and his henchmen.

The clergy themselves were no longer preaching humble submission. From the cardinal archbishop of Manila to the priests of remote parishes, all had urged action. Originally nonviolent, they preached forceful political action. The attitudes and behavior of nuns and priests toward the insurgency mounted by the National Democratic Front and the New People's Army was soon to become critical to the state as well as to the Church.

19

The Philippines: The Future?

LAZY, NERVOUS DAYS IN THE SUN
WAITING FOR THE SECOND MIRACLE TO DROP

Jaimé Cardinal Sin, archbishop of Manila and effectively primate of the Philippines, is very far from the cold cardinals of the Renaissance who lusted after power. Almost against his will, he became the kingmaker. His intervention assured the popular triumph that toppled the Marcos dictatorship and brought Corazon Aquino to power.

The cardinal is now facing severe moral and political challenges raised by his own clergy. Some of the most idealistic and effective of his subordinates regularly give the Marxist rebels of the New People's Army aid, comfort, counsel—and even covering fire. His ordeal is as daunting as the Church's ordeal in Latin America, which the Philippines resemble, socially, economically, and temperamentally. Like Filipinos, Latin Americans spent centuries in the Spanish convent.

I approached Cardinal Sin in a puzzled—and skeptical—frame of mind. His public image was just too jolly. Yet a gift for laughter is good for a public man, and I could sympathize with the execrable jokes on his name he must endure, since I have the same problem.

Turning the other cheek, he greets visitors to the imposing Archepiscopal Palace, "Welcome to the House of Sin." Once, after visiting his parents' grave, he spoke of leaving behind him "the original sins." When he was young, he said he was only "a venial sin." But Ferdinand Marcos for a time dreamed of assassination to prove that he was "a mortal sin."

Yet the cardinal appeared close to Imelda and Ferdinand Marcos in their days of glory. Prudent for a prince of the church dealing with a capricious secular power, that approach did not make him look like an inspiring spiritual leader.

Sixty-two in 1990, Jaimé Cardinal Sin is not impressive physically—in fact, he is not impressive at all until he begins to speak. In a nation of self-dramatists, he is almost ostentatiously undramatic. A bit pudgy, he looks undistinguished, as if he were just another intelligent Chinese who made a fortune in trade.

Yet he is today probably the most important figure in the Philippines—more important, I believe, than Corazon Aquino. Her power depends upon the winds of politics and upon her performance in an office in which she does not appear comfortable. His power as cardinal archbishop of Manila will endure as long as he lives, unless he errs grievously or is elevated to the papacy. The Filipinos are an intensely spiritual people, and he embodies the soul of the Philippines, its faults as well as its virtues.

His fair skin and his features are the legacy of his Chinese father. Sin Puat-co, who later called himself Juan, came to the Philippines from Amoy at the age of thirty and set up as a dealer in secondhand clothing, old bottles, and used pots and pans. When he opened a general store in the town called New Washington, on the island of Panay in the middle of the long archipelago, he prospered, but not inordinately. Embracing Catholicism to please his pious bride, Maxima Lachica, he fathered nine children. All had to work their way up in the world. One became a cardinal, another a doctor, and a third a history professor in Shanghai.

The eldest brother, José, was studying in China, as his father wished, in 1949, when the Communists' triumph cut him off from the outside world. For a decade, no word of the missing brother came back to the Philippines. Although José Sin reestablished communication in the early 1960s, the chaos of the Cultural Revolution soon engulfed him again. When he finally reappeared, he was still not permitted to visit the Philippines—and his brother Jaimé was not permitted to visit China.

The cardinal finally secured an invitation to China in 1984. He was assisted by Eric Hotung of Hong Kong, the financier and philanthropist, who had encouraged me to write the novel *Dynasty*, which that extraordinary family inspired. Jaimé Sin's brother José had died three months before his visit, but he met his sister-in-law and a nephew. The cardinal also met a score of his father's children, grandchildren, and great-grandchildren by his first wife, who had remained in Amoy.

The Chinese bond is close. Jaimé Sin's office could belong to a forward-looking overseas Chinese businessman, even to the brisk efficiency with which secretaries produce documents or facts. Prudently numerous in a country that only *appears* to possess a modern telephone system, four telephones stand on the table behind his desk, under a big color photograph of Pope John Paul II bestowing a cardinal's red hat upon Jaimé Sin.

"Marcos," the cardinal declares, "destroyed the system, which had worked well in the past."

I am not convinced that the system functioned particularly well before 1965. Yet, whatever the faults of their predecessors, Ferdinand and Imelda Marcos were unique in their rapacity and megalomania.

"The generals who kept Marcos in power under martial law," the cardinal says, "were all promoted for one thing—their loyalty. No matter how stupid, they were given big corporations to run. Really, they should have been kept in the barracks."

He pauses, looks up, and says matter-of-factly, "Of course, Providence moved Marcos to call the snap election. He really believed he would win handsomely—and he didn't make the decision under pressure. He wanted to give the people a chance to show that they still loved him."

I have heard such diverse politicians as Nikita Khrushchev, Jawaharlal Nehru, and Sukarno talk like His intimates about God's intervention on their behalf. Although my instinctive skepticism abates before the cardinal's manifest faith, I still have some questions about his actions during the Marcos years.

Some say he hewed to his own line, placing the interests of the Church above all else—and the interests of the people next. To that end, he got along with Ferdinand Marcos for a long time. But he repeatedly clashed with Imelda Marcos, who once announced to an astonished press conference, "Cardinal Sin is a Communist homosexual."

She was furious because he had just denounced the carnival of pornographic cinema she was staging to finance the film festival that had brought second-rank movie stars to Manila to pay her homage. But Cardinal Sin affirms that Ferdinand Marcos and he understood each other, at least in the beginning. He did not initially oppose Marcos's plan to remake the Philippines into the New Society—for the Church was not harassed.

In January 1973, shortly before his elevation to the archdiocese of Manila, Jaimé Sin reminded the assembled bishops of the Philippines that the Catholic Church had thrived under different political systems in different eras. The Church should therefore remain above politics in the Philippines. The bishops adopted a policy of "critical collaboration." They would support the government's actions that advanced the general welfare, but would criticize actions that were detrimental to it.

That policy left the Church free to maneuver. But it was hardly a clarion call in the night. Critics pointed out that the regime had already gone beyond all decent limits. Martial law had been proclaimed; presidential elections had been postponed indefinitely; newspapers had been closed or transformed into organs of the regime; midnight arrests by soldiers were regularly followed by torture; Marcos's enemies "disappeared"; and the nation's wealth was being systematically looted.

As archbishop of Manila, Jaimé Sin did not move away from his rather uncritical collaboration with the Marcos regime until 1974. In that year the Church itself was wounded. On August 25, 1974, the army raided a Jesuit retreat house in Quezon City, searching for leaders of the New People's Army. Although none were found, twenty-one nuns and priests were held for a time. And the secretary of defense issued a public statement thanking the Catholic hierarchy for its "full support."

In reply, Cardinal Sin wrote a pastoral letter that all parish priests were instructed to read "without addition, subtraction, or comment." He protested the assault upon the Church, and repudiated the suggestion that he had approved of the raid. When the controlled press would not report the content of the letter, he called on his nuns to distribute copies in the streets.

The reign of Ferdinand Marcos was capricious and changeable, extraordinarily cruel one day and blandly tolerant the next. In 1974 the authoritarian hand still lay rather lightly on the mass of the people, particularly outside Manila. Only those who stood in direct confrontation with the dictator knew the full extent of the reign of terror: teachers, writers, lawyers, politicians, some capitalists, and, as time went by, increasingly the clergy.

The dictator was stealing billions—and putting almost nothing back. When his unrestrained avarice sapped the economy, even more Filipinos protested against his misrule. The country's scant wealth was depleted, and the people suffered greatly.

A spiritual and intellectual pilgrimage took Cardinal Sin from cautious collaboration with the dictatorship to the barricades. Appalled by Marcos, many of the younger clergy supported the liberal democratic opposition personified by Ninoy Aquino. Many were attracted to the New People's Army and the National Democratic Front, which was the legal ventriloquist's dummy of the outlawed Communist Party of the Philippines. A conservative man who had risen to the heights of a conservative profession, the cardinal remained aloof. But in the waning days of February 1986, he joined Corazon Aquino to drive Ferdinand and Imelda Marcos from power.

The popular rising that followed the snap election was regarded with suspicion by Ronald Reagan in the White House. He hated to turn his back on his old pal Ferdinand Marcos, whom he had hailed as a paladin of anticommunism. Even when the people of Manila took to the streets against the army, Reagan wanted to remain neutral.

Jaimé Sin telephoned to tell Ronald Reagan that the United States *must* support Corazon Aquino, who stood for the future. When the president expressed concern for Marcos's fate, the cardinal recalls, "I told him the Philippines had never assassinated a president—unlike the United States."

They call it "the miracle of EDSA,"[1] the virtually bloodless coup that pitted a few hundred soldiers armed only with pistols and rifles against thousands of soldiers with artillery, tanks, and air power. But Cardinal Sin is not the kind to expect God to do all the work. When he realized that a miracle was needed, he called out his legions: priests, nuns, schoolgirls, schoolboys—and the people of Manila. Marcos had the big divisions, but God helped those who helped themselves.

The crucial decision came on February 22. The puppet congress had declared Ferdinand Marcos the victor in the closely fought snap election. Riposting with a mass rally in Rizal Park, opposite the Manila Hotel, Corazon Aquino had declared herself the victor and proclaimed a mass boycott of the Marcos government—effectively a general strike. Moreover, eight bishops had concelebrated a mass at that rally.

Yet it looked as if the Marcoses could carry the day. The army was still doing Marcos's bidding, although Juan Ponce Enrile, secretary of defense, and General Fidel Ramos, deputy chief of staff, had defected when he decided to crush the mass protest by armed force. Besieged in Camp Aguinaldo, Enrile made three telephone calls. The first summoned a press conference to focus the world's attention on his predicament. The second asked a Jesuit bishop to come and hear his confession. The third advised Jaimé Cardinal Sin that Johnny Enrile and Fidel Ramos would both be dead within the hour if he took no action.

"Consider the situation," the cardinal later asked in a speech at Georgetown University. "Enrile had 103 men in all, Ramos had 198, a total of 301. Moving against them were at least twenty-five tanks and at least six thousand men in combat gear. And the dictatorship had the air force and the artillery. How could the tiny rebel force hold out?

"So I called three congregations of contemplative nuns. I told them: 'Sisters, go into the chapel now and pray. Pray with arms extended . . . until I tell you to end it!'

"Then I called Radio Veritas [the archdiocesan broadcasting station]

---

[1] The acronym EDSA stands for the eight-lane highway in northern Manila where the confrontation occurred. It is named after Epifanio de los Santos, an obscure librarian whose name, to the delight of the faithful, means the epiphany of the saints. EDSA, a canyon of honking traffic filled with gasoline fumes, runs past the military camps where the issue was decided.

and went on the air. I told the people, 'Go into the streets. Get between the forces of Enrile and Ramos and the advancing tanks!'

"The people came out at once. They filled the streets, and they met the tanks. They put flowers into the muzzles of the soldiers' rifles. The nuns knelt in front of the tanks and prayed [sic] the rosary. Schoolchildren linked arms and stood in front of the armored personnel carriers.

"It was wonderful."

Thus ends the Cardinal's Tale.

Much of the world saw the climax of the drama on its television. Soldiers would not advance over the bodies of nuns and schoolchildren, and unit after unit turned against the dictator. Marcos made a television soap opera out of his talks with his advisers, melodramatically ordering his generals not to fire on the massed civilians. Finally he took the oath for another term as president of the Philippines at almost the same moment Corazon Aquino was taking the same oath of office on another television station.

That was the last episode of the Ferdinand and Imelda Show. Advised by Ronald Reagan, he agreed to board a helicopter to the American Air Force Base at Clark Field, despite Imelda's objections. She could not believe the party was over, after two decades. But the Marcoses tarried just long enough to pack up a few million dollars' worth of jewelry; to crate other valuables; and to pack several large cartons with U.S. banknotes before flying from Clark Field to Hawaii with a party of fifty-eight.

A conservative man in a conservative profession, Jaimé Cardinal Sin professes himself well pleased with the administration of Corazon Aquino. I wonder whether this man, who was so incisive at the critical instant, is committed to reforming secular society. Or is he happy with any status quo that does not interfere with the Church? Will he tolerate indefinitely the baroque intrigue that Manila's politicians practice as ardently today as they did before the miracle of EDSA?

Yet the cardinal cannot avoid secular politics—and not only because the lower clergy are so deeply involved. I am concerned about his commitment to social reform because he is a key figure—over the long run, perhaps *the* key figure—in the Philippines.

I remind the cardinal that many Filipinos are now saying a new miracle is desperately needed. The man who was the catalyst of the first miracle counsels patience.

"Mrs. Aquino has done an enormous job in less than two years," he says. "We now have a functioning constitution instead of a dictatorship. Also, the three branches of government are firmly established again: executive, legislative, and judicial."

"Yes, but what now?" I persist. "We've seen weeks of squabbling over confirmation of a new chief of staff by the Senate—all hinging on a technicality. And this in a country that is fighting for its life against an insurrection."

"We've restored the system of checks and balances," he replies. "Democracy takes time—and democracy must show that it is acting democratically." His eyes glinting mischievously behind his gold-rimmed glasses, he adds, "But there's been no civil war. We are forty years old—and there has been no civil war. Not like the United States!"

That second comparison of Filipino virtues with American failings is self-evidently compulsive. Filipinos resent the United States but want American approval. No more than most of his compatriots is the cardinal proof of those primal emotions. Defensively, indeed rather irrelevantly, he has twice cited American disasters to make light of Filipino faults: presidential assassination and the Civil War.

Yet he deals very practically with the Filipino habit of wooing powerful men with lavish presents. That practice springs from the Malay custom of offering tribute to sultans in order to secure justice, as well as the Chinese custom of bribing underpaid Confucian mandarins. Nourished by Spanish venality, those are the deep cultural roots of the corruption that is today universal in the Philippines.

Cardinal Sin does not disdain gifts. In fact, he solicits presents for his birthday—and he prefers cash. The large sums he collects go to his personal charities, primarily the housing colonies that now shelter thousands of families. Practical as he may be, I cannot quite accept his confident declaration: "Real economic recovery will start very soon. We are very rich in natural resources."

Jaimé Sin is an optimist by profession and by temperament. But I am skeptical. Too much treasure and too much energy have already been expended on "recovery," with far too little result. Besides, the natural resources on which he bases his faith are already being looted wholesale. Tropical rain forests, fisheries, and mines are being destroyed by ruthless exploitation. The chief island, Luzon, once heavily wooded, is now heavily populated and almost bare. One stand of timber that had endured because it was inside Clark Field was reduced to naked soil within a year of being turned back to the Philippines.

Poor farmers chop down trees and uproot shrubs to feed the fires under their cooking pots, and the nets of fishermen in small boats sometimes scrape away the coral reefs. Hard-pressed human beings are naturally more concerned with their own existence and their minimal comforts than with the abstraction called the environment. Semiliterate peasants cannot know that their depredations imperil their children's lives.

The continuing gang rape of the Philippines' natural resources, however, is impossible to justify. It is not individual farmers or family enterprises that are denuding the islands. It is mass logging that threatens famine by driving out game animals, inviting erosion, depriving the remaining soil of essential nutrients, creating alternate droughts and floods. Nor is it subsistence fishermen who systematically destroy the marine habitat.

On Palawan Island, which is not heavily populated, protected nature reserves are being indiscriminately lumbered under "special permits" issued to big corporations. Timber-hungry Japan pays handsomely for tropical hardwoods. Off Palawan, the coral reefs are being killed by cyanide released by commercial exporters to stun tropical fish. Collectors pay well for those bright-hued exotic species—and minute coral organisms are destroyed. Dynamite fishing, which also devastates the coral reefs and slaughters marine creatures, is overlooked by the coast guard. The dictatorship has been overthrown, but big commercial malefactors continue to loot nature—at the expense of the poor.

"I am very happy that the president is a woman," the cardinal observes. "A man would be too strong . . . too forceful. At this time, we need the compassion of a woman."

He is clearly thinking of Corazon Aquino's reluctance to move forcefully against her enemies on the left or the right. But the manifold problems of the Philippines require a strong hand, regardless of gender. They cannot be ameliorated, much less solved, by a president of whom a former supporter says with intimate knowledge, "Cory takes forever to make up her mind, delaying decisions while she wavers to and fro. Once she's announced a policy, she digs her feet in like a donkey—even if the policy proves disastrous."

Even patient Jaimé Sin acknowledges that Corazon Aquino's compassion has not always worked for the good of the country—or the good of his church. Foreigners were the most virulent among the priests who collaborated with the Marxist New People's Army during the Marcos years. They were finally expelled, but he says: "They all came back when Mrs. Aquino became president."

Corazon Aquino has sincerely tried to make peace with the National Democratic Front and its New People's Army. Social Democrats by inclination, the new men and new women of her administration believed that they could reach an understanding with the Marxist rebels. But all attempts at reconciliation have failed. The enemy was not interested in the broad concessions she offered, and she could not offer broader ones without turning the government over to them. Their aim is a regimented society that would make Marcos's dictatorship look benevolent.

During sixty days of negotiations in 1986, the NDF/NPA were treated like any law-abiding political organization. Immune from attack under a cease-fire, they won respectability and prestige by negotiating as equals with the national government. No longer underground, as hunted criminals, they moved through society with total freedom. Naturally they replenished their arsenals, reorganized their forces, filled their coffers, and recruited new troops. The truce intended to win over the enemy instead strengthened him. The insurrection is now much stronger than it was when Corazon Aquino came to office.

The cardinal is concerned with the role of priests and nuns, foreign as well as native, in that insurrection. He has a lot to worry about. Above all, the clergy make the Marxist NPA acceptable, indeed heroic, in the eyes of the common people by preaching that the rebels' cause is wholly just. Nuns and priests also provide food, funds, intelligence, weapons, and guidance to the rebellion.

They run and/or sponsor many of the scores of "cause-oriented organizations" that have appeared since the miracle on EDSA. A few are made up of wholly sincere social reformers, untainted by Communist control. Most are, however, fronts for the rebellion. Moreover, the faculties of Catholic high schools and universities are stiff with instructors who teach that only a revolution can bring justice and prosperity to the nation.

Foreign priests and nuns are particularly useful. They have easy access to the funds raised by the well-meaning abroad, largely in Europe, for social reform in the Third World. Those funds supplement the taxes collected by the NDF and help buy the guns of the NPA.

Without the clergy, the insurrection would not pose a major threat to the present system. With the clergy, the NPA has moved far beyond the Stalinist Hukbalahap, who were crushed in the 1950s by President Ramon Magsaysay with guns and social reforms. The Huks never got much beyond Luzon, but the NPA is a nationwide movement that effectively controls a sixth of the population.

"Priests began falling away under the Marcos regime," the cardinal explains. "They were assigned to remote districts where there is no government. They therefore acted like Red Cross agents rather than priests. They were constantly exposed to one point of view . . . and some became Communists. In the southern islands, there are now some priests who are members of the hard core [the Communist Party of the Philippines].

Having earlier thrown his clergy into the struggle to depose the dictator, the cardinal now forbids them to run for office or even to express political opinions. Some of the most intelligent, eloquent, and effective fellow travelers of the NDF/NPA are nuns and priests. He wants to keep them from using the new political authority of the Church, which was won at EDSA, against the democratic government.

"Liberation theology [which justifies the insurgent clergy] is really godless," the cardinal says. "It accepts violence as a legitimate means—

and violence always begets more violence. . . . The church must work for justice . . . and the road is economic and social development. But liberation theology nurtures great evils: pride, selfishness, egotism, and materialism."

In 1988 Jaimé Sin marked the second anniversary of that miracle by calling for an "immediate, genuine, far-reaching, effective land reform." Too long, he declared at an open-air mass on EDSA, had Filipinos been afraid to attack their *fundamental* problem.

The archepiscopal master of public relations closes with a reflective— if ambivalent—plea to journalists, particularly Americans: "We Filipinos must learn to fish for ourselves . . . and end our dependence on America. . . . We are very sentimental [meaning, presumably, emotional and volatile]. We are Asians, but we have been educated to be Americans. . . . So don't ring the bell every time we do something wrong, but try to help. . . . If the Americans support us, everything will be all right. . . . I know America will not abandon us. But if America plays politics, that is the end."

I do not fully understand what he means about America's playing politics in the midst of a mortal struggle against a ruthless insurgency in a country where corruption is rife and the distribution of wealth is dazzlingly unfair. In any event, the cardinal has greater faith in America than I do. He believes it has both the power to hasten the second miracle and an unbreakable commitment to the Philippines.

The clergy's perplexing role and great influence in the insurrection are explained by Father Bienvenido Nebres, who is the director of the Jesuits in the Philippines.

"Because Marcos had infiltrated—or destroyed—most of the Marxist front organizations, church-related groups were the best umbrella for the Marxists. And Marcos's oppression made the young clergy even more susceptible to their message.

"Many are weak in their knowledge of history, culture, and society. Those who've gone over hold two contradictory ideas, confusing Marxism and the transcendent [the spiritual]. . . . Most can't distinguish between social reformers and the hard left. . . . The marriage between the Church and the left has moved the left along. The clergy are used as a stalking horse every time the NPA infiltrates a new *barrio.*

"The hard core is small, only 10 percent of the clergy, native and foreign [more than fifteen thousand in 1988; more than half of that number being nuns]. *But they work twenty-four hours a day.*"

Even more than the Filipino clergy, the militant foreign clergy project the struggle onto a global screen.

"The left network is very strong internationally," the Jesuit Provincial says. "The other week, foreign missionaries met in Cebu. Their line was thus: *All the government's actions are part of American ambitions. Ultimately the struggle is against American imperialism."*

When I first landed in the Far East, coming ashore from a freighter at Manila in August 1951, the American response to threats was robust. The American commitment to Asia and the Philippines was unquestioned, and no Asian talked of being abandoned, as Cardinal Sin does today.

It was only a year since the United States had reaffirmed its commitment to Asia by sending its armed forces to the defense of South Korea. In the Philippines, the Hukbalahap insurgency was already in its fourth year, having begun in 1948 with the string of Communist risings that crackled across Asia like firecrackers. After those "spontaneous uprisings," few doubted that an international conspiracy was being directed from Moscow.

That simple analysis was not wholly wrong the day I opened my suitcase for Philippine Customs on the broken rubble of war that still strewed the wharf. Tables, much less sheds, were beyond the means of the war-ravaged nation, and the women passengers were embarrassed by having their undergarments minutely examined before gawking porters, taxi drivers, and touts. Things were simpler in those days, and women were more easily embarrassed.

I was too delighted at landing in a foreign port as a full-fledged foreign correspondent, complete with trench coat and portable typewriter. I was just twenty-three, a young man in a great hurry to penetrate the mysteries of the East. I had never before held a proper job, but I knew I would write incisive copy for the Overseas News Agency, the struggling feature service run by Landrum Bolling, who had promised to pay me sixty dollars a week—or seventy-five when he had it. Robert Martin, ONA's Far Eastern correspondent, who was a brilliant and meticulous reporter, had created the opening by accepting a Nieman Fellowship at Harvard.

My glamorous self-image was slightly marred by the discovery that I had paid twice the amount on the taxi meter for the ride to the Manila Hotel. High on excitement, I had given the driver dollars instead of pesos. A dollar was then worth two pesos at the legal exchange rate—and four pesos on the black-market rate, which I was too prissy to use.

In 1988 one dollar was to be worth twenty-one pesos, and it was to be virtually impossible to overpay a taxi driver. In 1988 all taxi meters were to be so far behind inflation that it was to be customary to pay *at least* twice the registered fare—three or four times if you kept him waiting.

The Manila Hotel was then also quite different. The annex, all I could afford, was a number of long wooden buildings like barracks. I called first on Ford Wilkins, the American editor of the *Manila Bulletin*, which subscribed to ONA. American influence was apparent everywhere, not only in the style of newspapers and broadcasts, but in the few cars on the streets, the general run of products, and in popular attitudes. Another American, Dave Bogulsav, edited the *Manila Chronicle*.

Although puffed up with my own glamour, I was just smart enough to ask for their advice. A day later I found myself in a battered jeep driving north on the MacArthur Highway. My destination was Angeles, the city on the perimeter of Clark Field, the biggest U.S. Air Force base in Asia. I was with a woman called Iay Marking, a celebrated political commentator and activist. From her I heard about Ramon Magsaysay, who was in 1953 to become president of the Philippines with American backing—a liberal, militant president wholly different from the tyrant Ferdinand Marcos, whom the U.S. was later to support.

It was my first day in the countryside of Asia, the great hinterland that has shaped the fate of peoples and nations. Some of the memories of that day have become intertwined with the memories of a thousand other days in that rural hinterland, but some are still very sharp. I remember vividly my shock when I saw the chickens.

They were not like the leghorns and Rhode Island Reds with which I was casually familiar. Long, scaly, sickly yellow legs sprouted from meager thighs joined to emaciated torsos surmounted by bony heads with flat, staring eyes. Their feathers were like soiled straw, and the crests of the undersized roosters were dull. They darted around our feet, ceaselessly pecking for food in the dust—and raced away in terror on their stilt legs at a casual gesture.

Seeing those pauper fowl, I realized how desperately poor were the people of a land that could not find chicken food to fatten them. Later, I gnawed unhappily, and a little guiltily, at the fried chicken we had brought from Manila. Meager, stringy, and dry, it offered little nourishment. Yet it was the peasants' chief meat, eaten perhaps twice a month.

I was overwhelmed by the universal languor, the knotted, inert blanket of heat, the dry cracked earth in the sun-seared landscape, and the sweat prickling on my shoulders. I felt as if I had been transported to the poverty and the misery of Mexico, rather than to fabled Asia. Yet I was in Luzon, the richest island of the Philippines, and only ninety miles from Manila.

The capital had not disappointed a susceptible tyro correspondent. Beneath its fringed palm trees on the edge of the South China Sea, Manila was the quintessential tropical city of Joseph Conrad. Behind their pillared verandas, the low white buildings on the seafront were a little dingy. The old Spanish buildings in the Intramuros, the citadel "within the walls," had been blasted by both the Japanese and the

Filipino-American forces. The half-moon of the bay, with the fortress island of Corregidor in the distance, was spiky with rusted masts.

The jeep bounced northward on the MacArthur Highway, springs creaking and body groaning as its bald tires skittered between potholes. The highway was no more than a blacktop road that twisted between dusty sugar cane fields. Drawing away from Manila, the villages grew more meager; jerry-built shacks and huts with rusty corrugated-iron roofs clustered around dilapidated churches. When we approached Angeles after five hours, the road got rougher and the dogs got thinner.

In 1988 Moira and I bowled over the same distance in an hour and a half in an air-conditioned Toyota on a four-lane toll road, passing occasional billboards. We were to spend a crowded day in Pampanga Province and to see the heartland of the New People's Army, the garrison city of Angeles, the present state of rural Luzon, as well as two mayors, a general, and a colonel.

Above all, what we saw was that the balance had tilted in the other direction. The capital was miserable, and the countryside was in comparison well off. Manila was jammed with old vehicles and tired people—and the paint was peeling from its grimy buildings. Blotched with mildew and stinking with decay, the city was a weary old hag, scratching her scabs and sores.

The countryside was, however, fresher, greener, and more abundant than it had been decades earlier. When we left the little-traveled toll road, I saw that the improved MacArthur Highway, formally now a secondary artery, carried much heavy traffic. The chickens scratching by the roadside were marked by their shape and color as descendants of those I had seen decades earlier. But they were bigger, fatter, and bolder, although still scrawny compared to leghorns or Rhode Island Reds.

Rising sheer from the green-and-silver rice paddies, Mount Arayat suddenly filled the windshield of the Toyota. A perfect cone with a jagged top, the 3,700-foot mountain dominates flat Pampanga Province. Black smoke no longer drifts from the crater, nor does lava flow down its symmetrical flanks. The old volcano is extinct geologically, but not politically.

Pampanga drew me in 1951 because Mount Arayat was the center of the Hukbalahap insurrection. From that fortress the guerrillas dominated the surrounding districts. Today, the New People's Army controls large areas around Mount Arayat.

A ghostly community stood in the loom of the volcano. Precisely spaced streetlights arched eerily over bare earth where there should have been neatly intersecting roads and smart little houses. Most of the hundred-acre site was given over to rows of green-roofed factories and warehouses. All were empty and deserted, never having been occupied for an instant. Too expensive to complete and too valuable to raze, the spectral industrial town was a monument to the megalomania of Imelda Marcos. She had decreed its construction, presumably to lure the people away from the Communists with regular jobs and comfortable housing. But she had abandoned it as arbitrarily as a child tosses aside a toy.

At the end of the road lay Angeles, which they pronounce *Ahn-huk-lace* in the Spanish fashion. It is now a prosperous city of a quarter of a million—by day. At night, musicians, barkeeps, bouncers, pimps, touts, and "hospitality girls" pour in to entertain the warriors and the paper pushers of Clark Field. The main street is lined with two- and three-story clapboard buildings painted dusty pastel shades: the pale green of pistachio ice cream and the pink of tomato soup. Behind those façades, businesses cater to the Americans: travel, employment, and real-estate agencies and furniture, food, and sports stores. Most of the best houses, as well as many less choice, are rented to Americans. Clark Field is the chief industry of Angeles, although the surrounding districts produce marble, furniture, sugar, and rice.

Angeles is also the educational center of southern Luzon, with two universities, three colleges, and numerous technical institutes where a hundred thousand study. The big private hospital rising alongside the university is, like the university itself, the property of a former congressman who was a crony of Ferdinand Marcos. That coincidence of public office and private wealth the Filipinos, with masterly euphemism, call an "anomaly." Angeles is a substantial and reasonably prosperous city. Although no contender for a "tidy town" award, it is conspicuously well kept after the squalor of Manila.

The living heart, the reason for Angeles's being, is the concrete arch that stands before Clark Field. The legend REPUBLIKA NG PILIPINAS proclaims Filipino sovereignty over territory presently leased to the United States. Around the gates, clustered like blowflies on a wound, are the bars, nightclubs, and massage parlors that entertain more than fifteen thousand bored servicemen. McDonald's, Pizza Hut, and Kentucky Fried Chicken are a few blocks away. All are guarded by blue-uniformed private security men with shotguns, pistols, or even automatic rifles. The snappy, gold-braided private guards seen everywhere epitomize universal insecurity in a country of violent people virtually unrestrained by venal police forces. One tycoon keeps six personal bodyguards in Manila and a dozen uniformed guards surround his mansion. On his plantation on Mindanao he maintains a private army four hundred strong.

A big placard in the window of the Bali-Hai Seafood House helps explain that insecurity. Educational levels, if not necessarily standards, are high, and unemployment is far higher.

WANTED *Six Waiters and Busboys, 6 Waitresses, 6 Dishwashers &*
Maintenance Boys. Requirements: At least high school graduate,
preferably two years college; Can communicate in English; With
agility and pleasing personality. Beautiful smile; Police clearance;
Diploma & transcript of record.

    Applicants must be at least 5′2″ in height; if female, between 18
and 22 years old; if male, between 19 and 25.

No wages are stated, since any job offer will attract many applicants.
Those paragons can expect to receive P1,000 ($48) a month, which
could, with luck, be doubled by tips.

    The heart of Angeles is the bar district. Every afternoon, small lithe
females lounge in the sun. Most are tragically young: fifteen, sixteen,
or seventeen. Their stick-thin brown legs and arms are left bare by
shorts and halter tops. Their shoulders are frail, their protruding col-
larbones and shoulder bones the legacy of malnutrition.

    Two hospitality girls look incuriously at us over a wrought-iron
balcony. Just beneath their feet, an unlit neon sign reads: SWEET CHAR-
ITY'S BAR *Booze, Broads, Booze.* A hand-lettered placard on a closed door
advertises: DANCERS WANTED—P1,500 A MONTH. That is $72. But dancers
can make more in fees for personal services.

    Part of the red-light district has recently been leveled. The reason is
practical, not moral: to make way for a new road. But trade is healthy
at Mr. Johnson's Playboy Club, at Love Birds, and at Queen of Hearts.
The Good Shepherd Medical Clinic nearby specializes in venereal
complaints—and prospers.

    No one likes talking about AIDS, which even the Good Shepherd
cannot cure. Besides, Angeles is not quite as high, wide, obstreperous,
and diseased as Olangapo City, on the edge of the immense U.S. Navy
base at Subic Bay, which is known even in the Philippines as Sin City.
When the ships come in, the streets are a blare of noise, color, and
unarmed combat.

    About thirty hospitality girls of Olangapo were known to carry the
AIDS virus in 1988. Summoned to a private meeting by Mayor Dick
Gordon, whose father was American, only one agreed when he suggested that the bar owners pay the afflicted girls a reduced allowance
for *not* working. To a woman, the others protested that they felt quite
well, which they did. All asked roughly the same question: "Who will
look after me, my children, and my parents if I can't work?"

    The unkind daylight blanches the glitter of Day-Glo and neon, the
raw and tawdry good-time quarter of Angeles. Markedly altered since
the Korean War, it is bigger, brassier, brighter—and even more pestilential.

    But Mayor Antonio Abad Santos loves his town. In much of Angeles the American presence is beneficent, rather than malignant. American needs have encouraged construction of spacious villas for officers, given much custom to merchants, and provided large-scale employment, both direct and indirect. The mayor would be desolate if the Americans left.

"I personally believe the Americans are here to stay and give protection to Southeast Asia, to the Philippines, and the U.S.A.," he tells us. "But the U.S. should make the best of it and pay more for our bases—about $1 billion a year, like Turkey."

Angeles already enjoys an income of tens of millions of dollars a year through consumer spending and direct assistance. But the mayor explains earnestly, "We need more projects to make the city better. I am asking the U.S. government to help us with 40 to 50 million pesos [$1.9–$2.4 million] for the perimeter road I'm building. I'm sure the Americans will also help with P50–P60 million [$2.4–$2.8 million] for the new public market."

Abad Santos is an engaging and energetic figure with slightly receding, heavily oiled black hair and a smile that shows slightly crooked eyeteeth. But there is nothing slight about the heavy gold watch on his left wrist or its heavy gold watchband. The multicolored seal of the City of Angeles is embroidered on the left breast of his white shirt, which is nipped at the waist like a short-sleeved Eisenhower jacket. Beneath the seal is embroidered, A. ABAD SANTOS, MAYOR.

The office is his almost by right of descent. The mayor, fifty-one years old in 1988, is the scion of a dynasty. His cousin José was minister of justice for Ferdinand Marcos, with all that implies. His great-uncle José, who stands in heroic bronze effigy before the clapboard City Hall, was chief justice of the Supreme Court of the Philippines before he was killed fighting the Japanese in 1942. His father, who was mayor when I came to Angeles in 1951, served until 1959.

Antonio Abad Santos affirms repeatedly that he is a *reform* mayor. He has, he says, fired more than fifty corrupt bureaucrats and is fighting the remnants of the Marcos faction. Yet coming into his presence is like being received by a medieval princeling.

Moira and I climb a broad wooden staircase on which lounge thirty to forty men and women. A long queue is waiting in an anteroom where two female secretaries contend with constantly ringing telephones. Squeezing through the throng of kibitzers, applicants, supplicants, and idlers, we are received by His Honor the Mayor in a spacious office paneled in dark plywood. A dozen-odd courtiers depart when he jerks his head, leaving only the mayor, his counselor, and his police chief. Instinctively gallant like so many Filipinos, he addresses himself to Moira, virtually ignoring me.

Chatting affably in a husky voice, he disregards the intermittent shrilling of the three telephones behind him. Nor does he react when the roar of jet engines shakes the room each time an airplane takes off from Clark Field.

His two chief problems, he confides, are "first, peace and order and, second, the economy and the people's livelihood." The chief elements in both of those problems are the U.S. Air Force and the New People's Army.

Quite simply, widespread agitation in Congress in Manila demands that the air force base should revert to the Philippines. If it ever does, the people of Angeles will lose almost half their income. Meanwhile, Antonio Abad Santos is striving to maintain law and order so that American money will keep flowing into Angeles. The base, he points out, draws criminals.

"American servicemen," he adds delicately, "have so much more to offer [to thieves] than do Filipinos."

Ironically, the constant burglaries the American presence generates are driving the Americans back behind the base's wire fences. More than five thousand American families live off base, but the Americans are putting up five hundred houses inside Clark Field. Any further moves will hurt Angeles, which derives 40 percent of its income from American sources. The mayor tosses out an estimate of $150 million a year.

Violence is also costly. When things get too rough, young airmen are frightened away or confined to base. The mayor's Special Squad therefore harries muggers, thieves, and pickpockets. Police patrol in two conspicuously painted jeeps donated by Clark Field's civic-action program. Joint Filipino-U.S. patrols operating under the aegis of the Peace and Order Council, itself a joint committee that meets on the base, are made up of a U.S. Air Force policeman, a Philippines Air Force policeman, a soldier of the Philippine Constabulary, and a municipal policeman. When disorder rises, those units mount a counteroffensive.

"For two nights," Abad Santos says, "we'll pick up fifty-six or sixty a night. Then all's quiet on the third."

So does the precious balance between American and Filipino aspirations, nationalism, and interests look to the practical man on the spot. The mayor is not as realistic when he talks of marked progress in the battle against the Marxist insurgents of the New People's Army.

Then he yields the floor to the captain who heads the Intelligence Division of the Angeles Police Force. The captain is more specific—and more candid. Since October 1987, when three Americans were killed in Angeles, he says, the government has been more aggressive. Raids have captured arms caches and driven the NPA out of Angeles itself.

"Of course, we don't know who they all are," he confesses.

When I tell him that in the last years of the Emergency in Malaya,

British intelligence had a biography and a picture of every last "Communist terrorist," he blinks in astonishment. The Philippines has evidently not learned from the experience of either Malaya or Viet Nam. Nor has the Philippines learned much from the experience of the Philippines itself. Not if the approach of a police captain in a major center like Angeles is a valid indicator.

"The difference between insurgents and common criminals is their tactics and methods," he says. "Otherwise, they're just the same. The only distinction is their political motivation."

The captain has demonstrated that the Intelligence Division of the Angeles Police Force does not understand the basic principles of Communist guerrilla warfare. Without such understanding it is, even in the happy-go-lucky Philippines, impossible to fight an ideologically directed revolt. If the police continue to approach disciplined Marxist-Leninist troops as if they were common criminals with a political gloss, the insurgents will soon be sitting in police headquarters, arresting culprits for political crimes.

"We can identify some of the leaders in Angeles," the captain says defensively. "We even have pictures. But they are heroes to some people, and we can't arrest them except for a specific crime. Otherwise, the civil-rights people will be after us."

The Aquino administration keeps the security forces on a tight rein. Hypersensitive to charges that it acts as repressively as the dictatorship it supplanted, it is uneasy with the military and the police, who sustained the dictator. Moreover, "cause-oriented" and civil-liberties organizations monitor every move the security forces make. Some are Filipino, and some foreign; some are honest watchdogs against official excesses, and some are puppets of the insurgents.

Nonetheless, the captain agrees with the mayor that things have improved since the Aquino administration came to power in February 1986—and even more since Antonio Abad Santos was elected mayor in February 1988.

"The people now cooperate and tell us about men with guns," the captain says. "We mount saturation raids like military operations after sightings of armed men. We surround a *barangay* [ward or village] and then check to find any outsiders. . . . Still, the civil-rights people object. And 130 policemen just aren't enough for all our jobs. We need three or four times as many."

"The mayor says the NPA are still in the first phase: organizing, recruiting, and collecting taxes in Angeles, harrying only the big companies in nearby San Fernando.

It would, however, be extraordinary if the NPA were actually still in the first phase in an area that was a Marxist stronghold even before the present revolt began in 1969. The NPA appears to me to be conducting normal political operations because it is so strong it need not mount offensive operations. Organizing, recruiting, and collecting taxes are, after all, normal governmental functions. Still, I believe both men have been honest. I wonder when Antonio Abad Santos talks about corruption.

"The former administration, which I defeated by a landslide—I, a poor man—it was corrupt," he says. "I listen to public complaints. I call on all departments and inspect them regularly. And I throw out anybody who I find is corrupt—or discourteous to the public. Above all, I keep my people from being corrupt by my example."

Antonio Abad Santos still runs an automobile business. He was, moreover, a city counselor for thirteen years under Marcos, and his family has been well established for a long time. Nonetheless, I was startled when, at dinner with Max Soliven and his wife, Preciosa, at the Inter-Continental Hotel in Manila that evening, I saw the mayor waving animatedly across the room. With a party of five, he was consuming air-freighted Australian oysters, which are rather expensive.

"By my example, I keep my subordinates from being corrupt!" declares the mayor of Mexico, Javier Hizon, a robust man of forty-two with a stainless-steel wristwatch and a genuine smile whose gleam is accentuated by a blackened upper incisor.

The legend on his yellow T-shirt reads CREATION CONFERENCE, LUZON MUNICIPAL MAYORS. At that conference, held in 1986 in Baguio, the resort city in northern Luzon, shortly after Corazon Aquino came to power, the newly appointed mayors were, I believe, told *exactly* how to answer questions about corruption.

Javier Hizon looks honest, and he lives honest—in a small stuccoed bungalow with a very small front garden. As a mayor, he earns a total of P5,310 ($253) a month.[2] His wife, Anita, who is forty-one years old and the mother of four boys ages eleven to eighteen, earns P2,000 ($95) a month teaching the third grade. She gets no overtime for tutoring in remedial reading.

The Hizons thus have a grand total of P7,310 ($348) a month to cover *all* expenses, including official expenses. He does have an official car, which is an old jeep, and food prices are low. Nonetheless, that is a ridiculously low income for a man in his position, with his obligations. The mayor explains that he still earns some income as a travel consultant and also draws on his savings.

His eldest son, Joey, who attends Far Eastern University in Manila, lives with Anita's sister, who is well off. Joey gets an allowance of P10

---

[2] Salary: P3,700, up from P2,300 in 1986. Cost of living allowance: P350. Representation and entertainment: P500. Travel: P1,260.

(fifty cents) a day for incidentals. Since Jeffrey, the sixteen-year-old, will enter college next year, the Hizons are worried about the P3,000 ($143) matriculation fee.

Antonio Abad Santos's urbanity arouses suspicion, probably unjustly. The Hizons' rustic simplicity encourages trust. So do their candid smiles and the frizzy black coiffures both wear. Obviously they don't spend much on their appearance or on their simple furniture. Javier wears his T-shirt outside cotton trousers, and Anita wears a mauve cotton pullover with a big-flowered cotton skirt.

I want to believe the Hizons are as good as they appear to be: the hardworking, clean-cut, public-spirited citizens the Aquino administration needs. Both hold bachelor of science degrees from Manila universities, his in business administration and hers in education. To get ahead, he worked for American post exchanges in Viet Nam from 1967 to 1971.

But he denies that he was in any way interested in the war in Viet Nam. An American or European mayor, anxious to enhance his image as a statesman, would probably claim great knowledge. Yet Javier Hizon disclaims not only knowledge, but any interest in the greatest political confrontation of his time in Asia.

"I just went to earn money," he says.

Yet he is now deeply interested in politics. After two years as an appointee, he ran for mayor against a large field, including one candidate generally regarded as the Communists' man. Javier Hizon's territory is more like a township than a city, for it includes many small villages. Mexico has a population of eighty thousand, served by forty civil servants and sixteen policemen. There should be eighty policemen, one for every thousand people, Hizon says, but money is short.

Five or ten times that number would not be too many policemen. Lying in the shadow of Mount Arayat, a few miles from Angeles in the heart of the old Huk country, Mexico is a major stronghold and recruiting area for the NPA. Marxism is as prevalent as Catholicism.

Guerrilla warfare is for many the family business, handed down from father to son. Yet rural villages do not nowadays provide the quality of recruits the increasingly sophisticated insurgents want. Like the Bali-Hai Seafood House, they prefer college men. Still, Mexico is very useful to them.

The mayor has one of the toughest jobs in the Philippines. His chief priority, I imagine, is to avoid assassination. He is no good to anyone dead. I balk when he assures me again that he takes no interest in politics. But what other answer can he give—and stay alive?

He discusses corruption freely, however. His assumption and mine are almost identical: *The Philippines became known throughout the world for blatant public theft on an enormous scale during the Marcos dictatorship. Virulent then, corruption remains heinous today. Vast sums are made by violating laws with impunity. Only by reducing corruption radically can the Philippines survive as a nontotalitarian society.*

After the obligatory incantation about his own example's inspiring honesty, he adds: "Officials are also scared of being caught. I terminated some and reorganized others when I came to office. Now, if I suspect anyone, I transfer him or her to a department where there's no temptation, like the Population Commission. . . . Also, we've rebuilt all the broken-down bridges and newly repainted the Municipal Hall [which is a modest structure]. I've raised money from the rich and by holding fiestas: P100,000 [$4,760].

"I don't make the people come to me," he says. "I go to them in the *barangays*. . . . Before I became mayor, there were many killings. Many more were unreported, but those reported came to thirty or forty over five years. There's been only one since I came into office. . . . I believe the people are fed up. . . . No, I can't say why the Communists have slowed down. All I can do is give good government to my constituents."

The final judgment on that engaging enigma Javier Hizon is pragmatic. It comes from Reynaldo Mandalang, one of his constituents, who works in Manila but returns regularly to his family in St. Joseph's Village. Commenting on the mayor's survival, Rey says, "The NPA only shoot bad mayors, not good mayors."

Time is short. It is already afternoon, and we have an appointment with the general commanding the military forces of the district. There is just time for a quick sandwich and, evocatively, fried chicken, which is better than it was in 1951, but still pretty scrawny.

In his concrete-block and nipa-palm-mat house in St. Joseph's Village, Rey introduces us to his family. For an instant he has an ambassadorial air, this very short, very lean, shock-haired man of thirty-nine, who can, like most Filipinos, read English and Tagalog, but not well.

Not quite as large as a two-car garage, Rey's house has an attic-like second floor with two minute bedrooms, one for Rey and his wife, Elena, the other for their sixteen-year-old daughter, Jocelyn. He is building a bathroom at the foot of the stairs to replace the outhouse and the water buckets they now use. The kitchen, which is outside under a tattered palm tree, may someday be brought under the same roof. But there is no money for that luxury now.

Besides, the Mandalangs lead an indoor-outdoor life. There is no glass in their windows. Even though wooden shutters serve just as well most of the time, since it never gets really cold, Elena feels it would be nice to have glass windows.

Rey makes about P2,000 ($95) a month as a driver. He says very precisely the house has so far cost him P52,000 (about $2,500), about half what it would have cost if he did not do all the work himself.

Elena is momentarily embarrassed at being able to offer her guests no more than a soft drink, and she is happy to share the sweet crackers we have brought. We are knee-to-knee in the cramped sitting area and the furniture is meager. Yet St. Joseph's Village, deep in the country-side, got electricity in 1954.

Prosperity is, of course, relative. Pampanga Province, in densely populated Luzon, is reasonably well off by comparison with more remote islands. Rice and sugar are still good crops, although sugar is in oversupply throughout the world. Nonetheless, Rey has been forced to find work in Manila, or, I should say, has been *lucky* enough to find work in Manila. Others from St. Joseph's have gone much farther afield. As we leave, Rey points to a white and green three-story stucco house with a roof garden, which stands apart behind a stone wall. "The man who owns it is a telephone technician," Rey says. "He's been working in Saudi Arabia."

I had a day earlier spoken to a lieutenant who was the aide of the general commanding the regional Philippine Constabulary,[3] the chief force fighting the insurgents. The lieutenant had genially assured me that his general would be happy to receive me at two-thirty in the afternoon. When we arrived at two that Friday, we found not a single officer on the post. A helpful sergeant told us that the lieutenant to whom I had spoken had left for the weekend and the general was at lunch.

A colonel appeared after an hour. When I told him my story, he shrugged and said: "So Lieutenant———is at it again. He never told me—and nobody gave him permission to leave the base."

When the general arrived, he showed neither surprise nor anger at his aide's dereliction. Obviously, the lieutenant knew he could get away with it. His failure to make the appointment and his casual departure were characteristic of the negligence of so many privileged Filipinos, civilian or military. Such self-indulgence is a hell of a way to run a business or a country—and a nearly incredible way to run an army.

The military and the civilian appraisal of the insurgency, I find are different, almost opposite. Both mayors had assured me that everything was much better since Corazon Aquino came to office. Antonio Abad Santos had added, "President Aquino is a God-given gift to the Filipino people. Being guided by God, she cannot make mistakes."

[3] Offered by regular soldiers, most of them graduates of the Philippine Military Academy, the Constabulary derives its name from the force established by the Americans before the war. Related to the army in the Philippines as the U.S. Marines are to the U.S. Navy, the Constabulary is intended to live among the people in one place for a long time. It thus has sterling opportunities to gather intelligence—and bribes.

The general and the colonel flatly disagree. They believe security has deteriorated under the Aquino administration—and that the initiative has shifted to the New People's Army. But it is a seesaw battle in central Luzon.

Here the Constabulary score a victory that is prominently reported in the press and television; there the NPA score a victory that is given almost equal publicity. Now, the government wins a propaganda advantage, and a few fainthearted guerrillas leave the jungle to hide in Manila; then, the NPA's tax collectors make their regular visits, taking less from the people than do the government and the landlords. At one point, the Constabulary finds an arms cache; at another point, the insurgents capture a few rifles and a machine gun to add to their ample stock of purchased weapons. A guerrilla defects, but finds his life in danger because the parish priest is an informer for the Communists. The NPA makes a videocassette for propaganda purposes, but it falls into the hands of military intelligence, which identifies a half-dozen rebels.

The epitaph of the insouciant Philippines may be the same as that of the carefree Austro-Hungarian Empire: *The situation is hopeless, but not serious.* The ferocious killing when clashes occur is also characteristic. This is no comic opera. Perhaps a farce, but a tragic farce.

The strength of the NPA has increased in central Luzon since the miracle on EDSA in February 1986. There are now more than 1,500 armed effectives, three hundred in Mexico alone. The Constabulary claim two guerrillas killed for every soldier killed. That mildly encouraging ratio does not give hope of victory, soon or late. The guerrillas' progress is measured by their numbers, and their numbers are increasing.

A highly politicized population gives the NPA not only recruits, supplies, and intelligence, but also obedience. The Marxists run their own revolutionary governments in a number of *barangays*. They have achieved partial territorial control, although they cannot keep the Constabulary out, not even by night. But the Constabulary cannot be everywhere and, above all, cannot control the civilian population. Bayonets are good for stabbing and for opening cans, not for governing.

Again I heard the plaint: "We expected so much, but there's been no second miracle. We need it. We need to mobilize and take the fight to the enemy. . . . But the steam generated by the People's Power revolt has leaked away."

The troops have, however, been getting better material support since EDSA. "Soldier items," like boots, radios, uniforms, and tents, are getting down to the man in the field as they did not in the days of Marcos's universal corruption. Confidence, trust, and moral support, however, remain in short supply.

The military are cast as villains—not only by the intelligentsia, but by the government. They are suspect to the administration, as well as to the democratic left, although officers contend that the armed forces have proved their loyalty by suppressing several coups mounted by disaffected officers against President Aquino.

"I'm putting my life in hock," the veteran colonel told me. "I've been risking my neck for my country since I fought the Huks. And what do I get? A slap in the face."

Antipathy between civilian officials and the military touches all levels. The worst effect is lack of cooperation; civilian efforts are not coordinated with military efforts. Generally, the civilian response to the insurgency is inadequate; the NPA/NDF, not the government, is winning the hearts and minds of the people.

The New People's Army musters 30,000 to 40,000 throughout the Philippines, with some 20,000-odd in armed units. The *total* strength of the armed forces of the Philippines is no more than 150,000. Yet a *minimum* of ten government soldiers to each insurgent is normally necessary to put down a guerrilla rising. The enemy is, however, *not* trying to defeat the armed forces in direct combat. The NPA fights to further the political purposes of the Communist Party by guaranteeing Political cadres access to the people and by tying up the armed forces. That strategy had, in 1988, already won predominant influence in almost a quarter of the *barangays* in the entire country—and in a much higher proportion of rural *barangays*.

The New People's Army and the political cadres of the Communist party, who work so well together, are also well provided with sophisticated equipment. The NPA is adept at call C^3I, which stands for command, communications, control, and intelligence—the functions vital to victory. In addition to machine guns, rocket launchers, and automatic rifles, it possesses computers with modems for telephone communication, radios for long- or short-range work, and access to private companies' single sideband radio networks—as well as the radio networks of church organizations.

Such progress makes the Hukbalahap look amateurish. But there remains the element that foreign diplomats delicately call "the Filipino factor." They mean the slapdash approach, the lack of application, and the failure of persistence that often mar brilliant endeavors in the islands. The NPA are not supermen, but children of their environment. They, too, can be excessively casual; they, too, can be directed by emotion rather than logic.

Yet many cadres are tough, determined, and self-sacrificing men and women whose militant stand owes as much to idealism as to personal discontent. If dedication and willpower were all, the NPA would be the certain winners.

The government's superiority in numbers, equipment, and organization has, however, produced a shifting equilibrium. Every day the advantage moves minutely in different localities. Nationally the purely *military* situation has settled into a stalemate like the Mexican standoff in central Luzon. Neither side can hurt the other badly. Behind that military stalemate, the Marxists are making strong political progress.

Yet the NPA has not been able to resist the use of terror. It is one thing to close down sawmills that refuse to pay the tribute called tax, whose total is estimated at P1 billion ($48 million) a year. Though such peremptory action will cause unemployment and perhaps provoke popular resentment, the Communists must show who is boss. When it murdered thirty-six candidates in the mayoral elections of 1988, the NPA displayed its power to kill with surgical precision. An assassination campaign by so-called Sparrow Squads in the metropolis of Manila is another matter, a descent into "left-wing adventurism," as the Marxist-Leninist terminology puts it.

It looks like a slow decline in the government's position and, perhaps, an eventual Communist victory by default. To reverse the trend, the government must make major changes. Above all, it must use the military in a political role in the countryside. Failure to involve the armed forces in nation-building will cripple the administration's efforts to create a popular foundation for democratic government.

American military attaché Colonel Stephen Perry sums it up in a brisk sentence: "The armed forces can't win against the insurgents, but they could lose."

The rift between military and civilians so visible in Pampanga extends from Malacañang Palace to the most remote villages. Democracy is seeking to preserve itself by largely military measures while hobbling the military—and virtually disregarding the political, psychological, and economic fronts.

One good reason for the government's reluctance to use the armed forces politically is the corruption of the Philippine Constabulary. I am not talking about the general and the colonel I saw. Typically, however, the Constabulary has exploited its long stay in one locality and its power in local communities for its own benefit.

"PC commanders are like Chinese warlords," says Max Soliven. "They control their territory, and they take their due—on gambling, on perishables, on transport. Under Marcos, rival PC factions fought for control of the black market that spewed out of the PXs of Clark Field. Now the numbers racket and the lottery are preyed on by *both* the PC and the NPA."

Father Bienvenido Nebres, the Jesuits' director, observes, "If the military are good and the commanding officers are good, then the people go with them. But the PC are undisciplined and corrupt. In

Zamboanga del Sur, when the Marines moved in, the tide turned. But the NPA went south with the PC. . . . Bishops keep telling the government that bad commanding officers are a major element in defeats. But they can't discharge those officers. Instead, they are transferred. Often the people would prefer to cooperate with the government, but the military drive them into the arms of the NPA. The Communists get recruits not just because of poverty, but because of abuse."

Systematic corruption within the government structure has been reduced since the dictator's time—a little. No longer ostentatious, it remains strong, indeed blatant. Corruption is simply *the* way of life in a corrupt society. Like a fish, that society rots from the head down, starting with the small and highly privileged ruling class.

"In Taiwan," a diplomat comments, "even if they can't stop corruption, they don't allow it to interfere with progress. The Chinese New Year custom of clearing accounts by paying debts and making gifts is a great help. They get a big chunk of their bribery over with at one go.

"Businessmen from Taiwan are shocked when they come here to buy, say mangoes. People don't stay bribed. Customs expects constant bribes, refreshers every day, while the mangoes rot on the docks. The Taiwan people say in disgust, 'Chinese New Year comes every day in Manila.' "

Wholesale corruption severely hinders economic development. Taiwanese merchants will pay bribes to get their mangoes onto the ships. They will not pay for mangoes that rot on the docks. Multiply that case by a thousand: the Philippines, with a very large foreign debt, lose desperately needed foreign exchange—and businesses go to the wall.

Even the poor peasants, who love cockfighting, are systematically cheated. They bet passionately when the spurs flash in the torchlight in coconut-mat arenas. Yet the contenders are often ringers. Sometimes, better fighters are substituted. Sometimes, their plumage clipped and dyed, local bantams are substituted for out-of-town champions. Either way, the poor punters lose their stakes.

Constant rumors of corruption and double-dealing are demoralizing, whether always true or not. Riven by cynicism, the people cannot credit honest, much less altruistic motives. Nor can they realistically hope to advance through hard work or by normal entrepreneurial risks.

A single column by the respected journalist Luis Beltran is a sample of the charges that are always current—and, therefore, not worthy of the front-page coverage they would get elsewhere.

"Suspicion remains that the current administration has become a haven for members and sympathizers of the CPP-NPA," Beltran began. Military intelligence reports of such agents working in Malacañang Palace, he asserted, had been ignored. In the Department of the Environment and Natural Resources, printouts listing all holders of logging concessions, many obtained corruptly, had been handed over to the NPA, which duly sent tax demands to the Manila offices of those companies. After CPP-NPA agents had reached high positions in the Bureau of Customs, two-thirds of the vast bribes taken at the International Airport and the Port of Manila went to the Communists—and one-third to the Customs staff.

Reporting that a syndicate in the Department of Foreign Affairs was selling Filipino passports to illegal aliens, Beltran declared, "What Foreign Secretary Raul Manglapus should investigate is the background of some of the people he brought with him [when he took office]. . . . At least two were senior officers of the Communist Party of the Philippines—and could still be."

Quite a crop of indictments for one column! All the charges are unlikely to be true. Indeed, all could be false. Yet none can automatically be disbelieved, and few Filipinos disbelieve such constant rumors. If not these, other "anomalies" are real. So, they ask, what's the difference?

Floating somewhere between rumor and demonstrable fact, one report fascinated everyone—and chilled some. Tarlac Province Congressman José Cojuangco, known as Peping, is Corazon Aquino's younger brother. A while ago, an Australian businessman appeared waving a receipt for the $1 million he said he had paid Peping's wife, Tingting, to obtain a license to run a gambling casino. He didn't mind paying the bribe, but he did mind not getting the license.

The National Bureau of Investigation made an inquiry—and did not conclude that the charge was fabricated. The Australian, it found, had been duped by a woman who was a double for Tingting Cojuangco. The Australian did not sue, as he had threatened.

"Perhaps," mused a lawyer, "she paid him back."

Close relatives of presidents are, of course, fair game. Whatever the truth, Filipinos believe such reports—because so many are true. Although her elder brother Pete is notoriously honest, President Aquino is thus tarred by association.

Projected into office by the miraculous events that followed her husband's murder, Corazon Aquino now appears overwhelmed. True, she was virtually compelled to become president. But she did campaign for the office—and she did assume it. Her initial great achievements were reorganizing the government; restoring public confidence in the government; and releasing the energies of thousands of competent lower-level officials who had been manacled by Marcos. But she has been drifting since then, and time is growing short. The people are losing confidence in Corazon Aquino—and, thus, in the democratic process.

Disturbed by President Aquino's apparent isolation, I raised the issue with an Asian ambassador who is her great supporter. "She doesn't appear to be growing in office," I said. "From whom does she draw counsel and support?"

"She has grown," he replied, and after some thought added, "She gets advice from her family . . . she learns from her family."

Since the Cojuangco family is at the center of the privileged class that is wrecking the Philippines, she is clearly not getting the radical advice that alone might save the situation. Land reform, as Cardinal Sin has pointed out, is essential—even if it cannot be wholly fair and will not necessarily produce immediate increases in crops. Land reform has, therefore, become the touchstone of the administration's will to reform. A watered-down version of the original bill was finally passed in mid-1988. A year later, all redistribution of land was suspended because of wholesale corruption; landowners were getting richer, but poor farmers were getting no land.

Most of the Cojuangco family holdings had previously been sheltered from many of the bill's provisions. In central Luzon, other landowners had subdivided large tracts into housing developments, giving them names like Rainbow Heights. Since residential land was not to be distributed, those phantom developments would remain in the original hands.

You can't blame them for trying. Or can you? You certainly cannot commend an entire class for committing suicide through its own greed. That class was embodied for me by a glamorous young lady at Tito Rey's Restaurant. She plays at being a society reporter, coddled by the wealth of her father, who is a politician, landowner, and industrialist. Reflexively anti-American, she is not very bright, but then neither are many of her peers.

The Filipino working class, she declared, without perceptible irony, has no need of the luxuries that Westerners consider necessities. Bathrooms would only spoil them. Anyway they did not even notice the squalor that appalls visitors to Manila. Poor Filipinos, she said, were completely different from Westerners.

"Those who peel garlic for market are happiest," she said earnestly. "They have no cares and no responsibilities. A whole family works together, and can make a dollar a day. So they sing as they work."

I wondered whether she was pulling my leg. But I concluded that she was too naïve to sustain the jape as she swished out of the restaurant in her beautifully cut green silk sheath dress with matching stilt-heeled shoes and handbag, to step into her chauffeur-driven car.

Not all are that bad. Otherwise, the country would already have disintegrated. But many are just as silly and just as callous.

If the Philippines fall into totalitarianism—or, as is almost as likely, anarchy—it will be the fault of the ruling class, which cannot adjust because they see no need to adjust. The insurgency and the economic crisis are almost unreal to them. Their behavior is determined by catchy slogans, shallow emotions, obvious self-interest, and the desire for immediate gratification.

I have deliberately avoided detailed discussions of economics in this book, even though it was inspired by the greatest economic upsurge of the twentieth century. I am interested in major economic phenomena, not fine detail—as are, I believe, most readers. Besides, many other sources are available that discuss the Asian economic Renaissance in detail. I have chosen to concentrate on the cultural and psychological factors, the human element, behind the material phenomena.

Still, a brief excursion into the economic life of the Philippines may be enlightening. I shall distill all my conversations on the subject to a single short account, as if I had talked to only one expert.

In good part, the expert said, economic chaos springs from the same roots as social turmoil: unrestrained privilege in the old Spanish manner, as in Latin America. Manila has a model zoning law, which should make it a beautiful city. But every property owner flouts that law—and many other laws. The privileged class believes it is above the law, as it largely is.

Moreover, fundamental policy has, since the 1950s, resulted in further concentration of wealth and power. According to the "trickle-down theory," accumulation of wealth at the top results in benefits for the lower levels. But not much has trickled down. Instead, high tariff walls designed to protect weak industry have produced stagnation, unemployment, and high prices.

It sounds sensible to encourage development of domestic industry to serve the domestic market. Yet cosseting domestic manufacturers with tax rebates and high tariffs has proved anything but sensible. After an initial spurt of growth, that policy halted growth in the longer run. Like a shot of adrenaline, "import substitution" produced a flurry of hyperactivity—and then a letdown.

Competition was thus muted in a domestic market for light manufactured goods already limited by poverty. Consequently, local industry now produces inferior products at high cost, and great unemployment has followed saturation of the market. Surprisingly, imports also increased. Philippine industry could not produce every part of, say, an electric motor, largely because production runs were too small. Manufacturers therefore became dependent on imported parts.

"The result," said the expert, "has been near stagnation. Only 12 percent of present employment, for instance, is attributable to growth. And that is a *very* low figure in modern Asia. But the business community was content with its protected earnings—and it prevailed upon

Congress to maintain protectionism. Thus there are no significant Philippine exports except raw materials: timber, agricultural products, and ores—all sold on volatile world markets."

The World Bank and the International Monetary Fund offered help—if certain conditions were met. The ruling class, angry at proposed austerity, attacked the Bank and the IMF as "tools of Yankee imperialism." Yet a senior cabinet minister, who made his fortune in protected industry, still pleads, "Give industry a chance!" And Corazon Aquino says, "The private sector will be the engine of growth!"

"But she will not allow proper competition," the expert pointed out. "As a result, unemployment increases. And there are no safety nets here, no alternative employment and no social security."

Government policy also depresses agriculture. In Taiwan and South Korea higher prices for farm products, even food, put more money into the hands of consumers and thus primed the economy. That policy is tricky and dangerous, as China's struggle with inflation shows. Understandably reluctant to squeeze the poor urban masses for the benefit of the rural population, Manila has settled for no movement at all.

"Land reform and agriculture are a long story," the expert sighed. "So I'll make it short. I do not believe redistributing the land would do much good. Except for Dole, Del Monte, and the like, there are no huge plantations—and theirs is leased land. Otherwise, the average holding is no more than fifty acres."

Where holdings are already small or infertile, I agreed, land reform can produce no great benefit. Nonetheless, the Philippines badly needed the popular inspiration land reform could provide.

The expert shrugged and said: "Cory is on the back of the tiger. Expectations of the democratic left *cannot* be realized—and she could make the right very angry. . . . She has learned that it's dangerous to talk of revolution if you don't have the heart of a revolutionary. So she's more moderate now. . . . Besides, she often cannot make her policies operate in reality. Privatization, for one. She's tried to get the government out of the private marketplace, where Marcos put it. She's talked about selling off many government-owned companies, Philippine Air Lines and the Manila Hotel among them. But the bureaucracy—and her friends—are very good at slowing things down . . . making implementation so gradual it never happens."

"Miracle rice," the short-stalked, heavy-headed varieties that produce high yields, is now commonplace throughout Asia. In the Philippines, where it was developed, the government holds down agricultural prices for the benefit of the urban consumer. Consequently, farmers don't have the cash to buy the fertilizers that miracle rice requires—and the fertile Philippines are actually importing rice.

"The next couple of years," the expert summed up, "are going to be very taxing for the Philippines. They will also be a very complex time for the United States."

Most discussion of the Philippines gets back to the United States, and not only because the United States ruled the islands for almost fifty years. The United States also contributed greatly to the Philippines' present plight by its almost unswerving support of Ferdinand Marcos.

The dictator created the political and economic chaos amid which the people have suffered and the insurgents have thrived. He was not very good at fighting the Communists, but he was very good at ringing anti-Communist statements. Washington liked that—and did not like meddling with the status quo, however baleful. Washington therefore supported him, although not always uncritically. In his goodhearted, bumbling way, Jimmy Carter tried to force Marcos to restore civil liberties. But Carter got nowhere. On balance, he made matters worse, for Marcos learned that he could resist American pressure without incurring serious penalties.

Under Ronald Reagan, American support was not merely uncritical, but enthusiastic. Even at the end, when Cardinal Sin, the people of Manila, and Marcos's own secretary of defense and deputy chief of staff turned against the dictator, President Reagan refused to believe that his good friend, his companion-in-arms in the crusade against communism, was actually a discredited villain. Nor did Reagan realize that the Marcos dictatorship actually aided the Communists.[4]

The disasters still flowing from the twenty-one-year reign of Ferdinand and Imelda Marcos also cast into question the Kirkpatrick doctrine, which was a major prop of Reagan's foreign policy. To ensure that we are starting from the same point, to synchronize our mental watches, so to speak, I will summarize—and, I fear, thus inevitably over-simplify—my understanding of the proposition put forward by Jeane

---

[4] Reagan had been warned, not only by the State Department and the Central Intelligence Agency, but by the press, including a periodical he found ideologically compatible. In December 1985 *Commentary* ran a long, thoughtful, and exhaustively backgrounded article by Ross H. Munro. Munro disagreed with the journal's editor, Norman Podhoretz, who believed Marcos was indispensable. To his credit, Podhoretz ran the article. Munro wrote: "In news reports from the Philippines, nearly all the responsibility for the Communist upsurge is being given to Ferdinand Marcos. And indeed he has played an essential role. During his twenty years in power, the country has suffered from colossal mismanagement of its economy, corruption akin to looting, and the near destruction of the nation's basic political institutions. Without all this help from Marcos, it seems, the Communists would have remained about as inconsequential as they are today in, say, Indonesia or Thailand."

Given the self-indulgent, self-destructive character of the ruling class, the Communists might not have remained quite so inconsequential as Munro implies. But nonetheless, in reality it was Marcos who made them so powerful and so threatening.

Kirkpatrick. It was based largely on conditions in Latin America, which is so like the Philippines.

Professor Kirkpatrick contended that the United States should draw a sharp distinction between totalitarian regimes and authoritarian regimes. As she used it, *totalitarian* was a code word for leftist regimes in league with Soviet imperialism. Authoritarian regimes could be almost anything else that was unmistakably *not* democratic, indeed repressive—from Pinochet in Chile to Marcos in the Philippines. Totalitarian regimes, she declared, were implacable enemies of the United States. Authoritarian regimes might be deplorable, but they were not necessarily antagonistic to the United States. Since they neither sought to overthrow democratic regimes nor opposed the United States, authoritarians should be treated as friends—and as allies against Soviet imperialism.

The case of Ferdinand and Imelda Marcos reveals the limitations of that doctrine. Tenacious American support of Marcos not only made the situation in the Philippines disastrous; it severely damaged the American image elsewhere by associating the United States with his reprehensible deeds.

My view differs from Jeane Kirkpatrick's. Sometimes, I believe, the tactical situation may force the U.S. into temporary alliance with authoritarians. Sometimes, overwhelming immediate advantage may make such an alliance worthwhile, even essential. Such were the alliances with the murderous Khmer Rouge and with the most reactionary theocratic elements in Afghanistan. But such alliances must be temporary—and the United States must not delude itself regarding the nature of its temporary allies. In the long run, I believe, it is disastrous to cling to dictators who repress, loot, torture, and murder their citizens. It is also wrong—not only morally, but also practically.

Foreign policy is based upon interests rather than upon moral fervor, John Foster Dulles and Jimmy Carter to the contrary notwithstanding. Nonetheless, the U.S. cannot pursue national interests in a moral vacuum, as can, perhaps, more mature and less idealistic nations like Britain, France, and Japan.

Washington is debarred from such Machiavellian tactics because the people always find out, and Americans have little capacity for protracted cynicism. Besides, Americans are not very good at intrigue and deception, however adept they may be at fooling themselves. A retired American diplomat who was at the storm center during the critical later years of the dictatorship summed up: "Marcos must have read Jeane Kirkpatrick with great satisfaction. So must the Communists."

Having succeeded brilliantly by supporting and counseling crusading President Ramon Magsaysay—until he died in an airplane crash, perhaps through sabotage—the United States failed ignominiously by supporting predatory President Ferdinand Marcos, who was deaf to all counsel. Supporting Corazon Aquino appears the only course today—and 30 percent of $3 billion in total American aid to the Philippines has been granted since she came to power. But Washington cannot indefinitely prop up the emotional, goodhearted, self-indulgent, and self-deluding circle that is now making the Philippines's domestic and foreign policy.

Raul S. Manglapus, who was seventy in 1989, was the second foreign secretary of the Philippines sworn in since Corazon Aquino was sworn in as president. Late in 1988 he and American Ambassador Nicholas Platt reached an impasse. They had originally been unable to agree on terms for extending the leases on the U.S. air and naval bases at Clark Field and Subic Bay until 1992, when entirely new leases would have to be negotiated.

Late in 1988 a musical called *Yankee Panky* opened for a short run off Broadway in New York. The author-composer was Raul Manglapus, who is a talented jazz musician. The theme was the misdeeds committed by the Americans when they took over the Philippines in 1898. Those misdeeds were undeniable. Nonetheless, did it not seem odd for the foreign secretary to be lampooning the foreign country that is most important to his country—particularly when he was engaged in negotiations that required American goodwill?

Behind his righteous talk about independence, Manglapus had already declared that he would bury his principles if the U.S. agreed to pay a high rental for the bases. He wanted the money badly, yet he was alienating those he wanted to pay him the money. Moreover, he knew his best chance lay with outgoing President Ronald Reagan. Unlimited American military expenditures would soon be one with unstinting American support for Ferdinand Marcos.

Raul Manglapus finally went to Washington and got his money: about half a billion dollars a year, plumped out with deals for bonds and redemption of a portion of the Philippines' foreign debt. But he did it the hard way, in part, to please his anti-American constituency in the Philippine Congress and among the intelligentsia.

Raul Manglapus is a good and a versatile liberal. He is also, not surprisingly in the Philippines, a good Catholic, who is the leader of the Christian Socialist party. Thoughtful and courteous, he is also talented and intelligent—if not an original thinker.

America has been good to Raul Manglapus. During the thirteen years he spent in the U.S. as a fugitive from Marcos, he was feted by the foreign-policy establishment, liberal and conservative alike. Like Ninoy Aquino, he lectured at Harvard and at Georgetown. Subsidized by

Freedom House, he published a little book on the roots of democracy in the Third World. Although the research was a little loose and the conclusions a little forced, he was praised for his scholarship and his insight.

Returning in triumph, he declared that Filipinos had to "kill the father figure." They had to break loose from the U.S. before they could become mature and self-reliant. That thesis is self-evidently true, although it is unlikely that even killing the father figure, whatever that emotive slogan really means, would make the privileged class grow up.

Having met Manglapus first during the presidential campaign of 1957, when he supported a reforming liberal candidate who did not win, I was very pleased to see again this striver after justice and democracy. Our brief talk covered a lot of ground.

Having once been a strong proponent of the Southeast Asia Treaty Organization as a barrier to Sino-Soviet expansionism, Manglapus today feels that neither China nor the Soviet Union is a threat to his country or the region. The Soviet base at Cam Ranh Bay in Viet Nam and the American bases in the Philippines, he stresses, are "part of a super-power confrontation" that has nothing to do with the Philippines.

In a sense, he is right. American allies are quite understandably becoming recalcitrant because American policy has, over several decades, reduced outside threats to Southeast Asia. Nor does Manglapus care if he looks churlish in repudiating the American protection he formerly sought, while demanding large sums to allow that protection to continue. He says it is no longer necessary, and he may be right. He may also be wrong, but he is, for the time being, having it both ways.

I do not believe that Raul Manglapus ever doubted that the United States would come through with the cash—and continue to provide the protection he says he no longer wants. No more than the cardinal, the mayor of Angeles, the hypothetical average man behind the water buffalo, or the hypothetical average woman peeling garlic did he believe the United States would abandon the Philippines.

A student of the American record in the Philippines, he knows much to resent, including systematic economic exploitation. In *Yankee Panky* he impaled the father figure. He has, however, not been quite so quick to kill the sugar daddy.

Manglapus resented the United States paying more to other countries for base rights than to its favorite child. Yet he also contended that retaining the bases was "a polarizing issue" that splintered and weakened Filipino society. Without the bases, he said, the Aquino administration would be less vulnerable to left-wing charges that it was an American puppet—and, thus, better placed to face down its right-wing opponents.

As the issue of the bases swells toward a new denouement in 1991, that argument is advanced by vocal intellectuals and politicians. As far as I can tell, it does not represent the thinking of most Filipinos. A lawyer friend put it succinctly: "If the bases go, the Communists will win. It's that simple. The consequent collapse of public confidence in the United States will bring down democratic government."

Perhaps alarmist, that proposition is not unfounded. Without visible American support and a visible American presence, Corazon Aquino could lose her remaining popular appeal. So, I fear, could any democratic government in a country that is a long way from dispensing with the father figure.

If Raul Manglapus had driven the Americans out of their bases, he could soon have found himself in a new predicament that has nothing to do with superpower rivalry. The power vacuum created by the American withdrawal would be filled not only by the Soviets, but by the Japanese, the Chinese, even by the Indonesians, who now provide discreet aid to Muslim separatists in the south.

Independence and self-reliance are noble, indeed essential, goals for the Philippines—and stability is vital. But self-sufficiency requires psychological and economic maturity, as well as social justice. Stability requires a balance of power in the region.

When those conditions appear attainable, there will be no need to kill the father figure. He will, as the Filipinos' most redoubtable father figure of modern times, General Douglas MacArthur, once declaimed, like an old soldier, "just fade away."

Unfortunately, that will not happen for some time yet.

20

Thailand: The Pivot of Southeast Asia and
Indo-China: The Graveyard of Empire

IF IT PULLS THIS ONE OFF AND DEFEATS THE UNITED STATES, HANOI
WILL DESERVE TO RULE THE WORLD. IT HAS ALREADY DEFEATED
THE FRENCH, DEFIED THE CHINESE, AND MANIPULATED THE
SOVIETS.

> PROF. MILTON SACHS,
> BRANDEIS UNIVERSITY, IN 1966

THE LAND OF THE FREE IS THE FULCRUM OF SOUTHEAST ASIA,
WHERE RIVAL FORCES CONVERGE AND CLASH. INDO-CHINA, ABOVE
ALL VIET NAM, IS THE BLOODY GROUND WHERE ILLUSIONS WITHER
AND EMPIRES PERISH.

They're always cutting my wire," Colonel Poo said petulantly.

"What about the geese?" I asked not wholly irrelevantly, though I felt like Alice in Wonderland. "Do you raise them to eat?"

Emotions marched in procession across his dark features, indignation, affection, and anger close upon each other. Gazing fondly at the seven statuesque white fowl with egg-yolk yellow feet and beaks, he snapped: "Certainly not! They're not for eating, but for guarding. They're supposed to warn me of robbers and snakes. Someone's always cutting my wire, but they don't warn me."

I might have been talking with an old centurion sent out from Rome to watch a remote frontier with inadequate auxiliary forces. He, too, would have depended for early warning of incursions on the hisses and squawks of a flock of sacred geese.

Poo Pengchan, in his mid-sixties, was a retired colonel of the army of the Kingdom of Thailand. He had cause for annoyance. He could not adequately carry out his mission on the Cambodian frontier with his ragtag force of 160 half-trained Rangers in baggy black uniforms.

Barbed wire surrounded the 1,300-acre refugee camp called Site Two, which lay a mile and a quarter west of the Thai-Cambodian border. The wire was meant to deter robbers or other predators from entering—

and to keep the inmates from wandering out, although they were not prisoners. But both outsiders and insiders kept snipping Colonel Poo's wire.

Site Two housed about 160,000 Cambodians and 4,000 Vietnamese, all refugees from fighting that has not ceased since the 1920s. They were a living reproach to man's inhumanity, the embodiment of the suffering of Indo-China. They were also a major weight in the balance of power—for Thailand, China, and the United States, an important instrument of national policy.

In the spring of 1988, the retired officer with the gentle manner was custodian of those refugees—and the flexible foreign policy that has for centuries kept his country from foreign domination. In the nineteenth century, while all the surrounding lands fell under British or French rule, Siam remained independent.[1] Diverse and subtle stratagems kept the Siamese free—despite Burmese invaders, European colonizers, and Japanese imperialists. Using yellow-billed geese and hundreds of thousands of refugees to that end is, therefore, perhaps unusual, but nothing to raise eyebrows.

Like Britain, Thailand has been compelled by geographical position and relative weakness to preserve itself by maintaining a balance among its enemies. Unlike Britain, Thailand is not protected by a sea moat. Its coasts on the Gulf of Thailand, which is part of the South China Sea, and the Andaman Sea, which is an arm of the Indian Ocean, are as vulnerable as its land frontiers, which abut four countries. Since they could not defend those frontiers, the Thais have for centuries alternately placated and defied their enemies, adroitly changing allies as necessary.

The Thais themselves say that they, like the bamboo, have always bent before the wind of superior power. Like the flexible bamboo, they have never been broken. But the bamboo is passive, and the Thais have actively manipulated others. Like the British, the clever Thais have been called perfidious.

Glance at a big wall map or even the minuscule world map in a pocket diary, and it jumps out at you: Thailand is the center, the pivot of Southeast Asia. Anyone who aspires to dominate the region must control Thailand. It is a spearhead pointed at the underbelly of China; it is also a rich prize with long, soft borders. That geographical position has shaped the character and the actions of the Thais, as well as their institutions and their policies.

In the west, the border with Burma extends southward from Chiang Rai almost 1,000 miles to the Andaman Sea. The narrow Kra Isthmus, between the Andaman Sea and the Gulf of Siam, reaches from Burma

---

[1] Thailand, which means "Land of the Free," became the official name in 1939, but Siam is still used. The divergent names have no strong political significance.

350 miles south to Malaysia. In the east, the border runs north from the Gulf of Thailand, abutting Cambodia for 400 miles and Laos for 850 miles, to meet the western border near Chiang Rai. There Laos, Burma, and Thailand come together in the Golden Triangle, which is notorious for its opium production. Only 150 miles north of Chiang Rai lies the vastness of China.

Much of that long frontier is ill-defined and virtually impossible to patrol. Across the porous borders move guns, gold, drugs, smugglers, refugees, and guerrillas. The traffic is usually two-way, often guns for opium. The movement of refugees has been overwhelmingly one way: away from the Marxist regimes of Laos, Cambodia, and Viet Nam. During the past decade, more than half a million have fled to Thailand—and a few thousand have chosen to return home.

In the spring of 1988, more than 400,000 men and women were living with their children in refugee camps strung along the Laotian and Cambodian borders. The largest concentration was about thirty miles northeast of the city of Aranyaprathet: Site Two, where Colonel Poo Pengchan was responsible for security to the Thai Army, which ran the sensitive border area. His job was to keep an eye on the Thais' deterrent: the guerrilla war staged out of camps like Site Two, which were deliberately placed very close to the border.

Sustained largely by American money funneled through the United Nations, the refugee camps were the rear bases of some 45,000 to 60,000 Cambodian guerrillas. Their arms and equipment were provided openly by China and covertly by the U.S., the increasingly reluctant peace officer of Asia. Both China and the U.S. worked through the Thais to equip and inspire those irregulars to harry the hold of the Vietnamese-nominated government in the Cambodian capital, Phnom Penh.

The limited guerrilla offensive in Cambodia had for a decade restrained whatever desire the Vietnamese may have felt for further expansion—and thus kept the peace of Asia. The low-level conflict, which neither side could win, was a prophylactic against a bigger conflict that might have pitted Thailand, with its new ally, the People's Republic of China, on one side, against Vietnam, with its sponsor, the Soviet Union, on the other. Constant pressure on Hanoi through Phnom Penh maintained the classic balance of power—and kept Thailand free.

Only twenty years earlier, China had frightened the Thais by providing revolutionary propaganda, organizational counsel, military training, and material support for the Thai Communist Party. That party is now virtually defunct; the insurgency has vanished; and China is keen to maintain the vital balance of power in the region.

Once again, the supple Thais have formed a new alliance at the right moment. They can be bellicose. In 1988 they fought a long inconclusive battle with the Laotian Army, which is not the world's most formidable force. Above all, however, they have been intelligently flexible, appearing to yield, but never quite yielding.

Early in the Pacific war, Bangkok was forced to invite the Japanese to use its territory as a base. Unlike Indo-China, which was also occupied by agreement rather than by *force majeur,* Thailand was not crushed. The Thais preserved their monarchy and their institutions. Unlike the Philippines, Malaya, and the Dutch East Indies, which were occupied by force, Thailand was not scourged by massacres and mass looting.

The unheroic Thais survived virtually unscathed. Under Japanese pressure, Bangkok had declared war on the United States. But the Thai ambassador in Washington is reported to have locked the explosive document in his safe, rather than deliver it. Apparently sensible at the time, that could have been a grave mistake—for America is always most generous to its former enemies. Yet, later, when America needed help in the war in Indo-China, the Thais were extremely cooperative—and Thailand was treated very generously. The balance of power was preserved, and Thailand prospered.

A balance is never static. The pointer hovers, but never quite settles. The balance in Southeast Asia—political, economic, and military—is today being tested by transformed ideologies, shifting friendships, and altered perceptions.

The single greatest weight in the coming decade is likely to be China. Between them, China and India have exercised primary political and cultural influence over the region for two millennia. But China has usually been dominant. She was closer; she was activist; and she was usually united, while India was often passive and divided. Chinese predominance has evoked respect—and fear.

Japan, too, has returned to the scene of her great military triumphs. The great Japanese trade offensive that was to conquer the world began in Southeast Asia. The region is now a Japanese economic stronghold, and strongholds must in time be garrisoned.

The United States appears to be receding from its interests and commitments in the region. But the U.S. is still there in strength. Finally, the Soviet Union, a Pacific power with legitimate interests in Asia, is determined to extend its influence. General Secretary and later President Mikhail Gorbachev proclaimed that intention in his Siberian speeches—at Vladivostok in 1986 and at Krasnoyarsk in 1988. Factor into that complex equation the military power and strategic positions of Viet Nam and Indonesia—and the interplay of forces becomes very complex.

*   *   *

The major pieces in the great world power game range from armies and steel mills to spies and forced laborers, from satellites and newspapers to murderers and smugglers. The pawns are ordinary human beings arbitrarily moved by the rival players—and by fate. The most pitiable pawns are refugees: men, women, and children driven from their homes by terror, oppression, and deprivation.

Some politicians want to divide refugees into two groups: those who fled in fear of their lives or because they could no longer endure repression; and those who fled because they could no longer scratch out a living or because they yearned for greater opportunities. The former would be classified as "political," that is, genuine, refugees; the latter would not be considered refugees at all. True refugees would be admitted to sanctuary. The others would be turned away to wander forever; or would be forcibly repatriated, as Hong Kong hoped to treat some 70,000 Vietnamese refugees in 1990; or would simply be left to die.

I am glad I do not face the politicians' choice of either condemning suffering human beings to misery, and perhaps death, or allowing them to enter in numbers that could overwhelm the host people. Yet I believe that a refugee is anyone who has been driven by unbearable pressures to leave homeland, family, friends, and a place in society, however lowly, to make a new life in a strange land among strangers speaking a strange language. The decision to dislocate one's life is so horrendous that I feel anyone who does so is entitled to the status of refugee—for whatever good it may do.

In September 1951, when I first landed in Taiwan, I found an entire Chinese government in exile. With their followers, the Nationalists numbered almost two million men, women, and children. All longed to return to the mainland from the beautiful but strange island whose residents did not even speak intelligible Chinese. All were refugees.

In Hong Kong, my next port of call, the hillsides sprouted refugee shacks, and I hiked over a mountain to Rennie's Mill, where lay the camps of other refugees from the Chinese mainland. Another day, I saw a young man swim the river that separates Gwangdong Province from the New Territories and walk straight into the hands of a British police inspector who was obligated to send him back, but, I suspect, did not.

A month or two later I found the people of South Korea displaced by war. All Asia seemed one vast encampment of refugees. By 1955 I thought I was hardened to their plight, but in March of that year I had my most moving encounter with refugees.

Joseph Fromm of *U.S. News & World Report* and I had flown from Saigon in non-Communist South Viet Nam to Haiphong in Communist North Viet Nam in a DC-6 used primarily by the International Control Commission. The ICC was policing the truce accords signed in 1954 at

Geneva that had divided Viet Nam into northern and southern regimes. The airliner refueled at a town called Tourane, where a clapboard terminal no bigger than a three-car garage offered splendid little French sausages. The rough landing strip was to be the nucleus of one of the world's largest airports when the French Tourane became the Vietnamese Danang—and the Americans came to Viet Nam.

Haiphong, the chief port of North Viet Nam, was foreboding under low, weeping clouds—more like Gary, Indiana, than the sunny tropics. Military convoys pounded toward the docks past buildings gray with grime on streets gritty with coal dust. Artillery pieces, tanks, jeeps, trucks, even motor scooters—all were being loaded on ships for the long voyage to France. The French were leaving Viet Nam, and they were leaving little behind for the Vietnamese. It was a miserable time in a miserable place.

My spirits were not lifted when General René Cogny, commander of the French forces, told Joe Fromm and me why the French had lost their war against the Viet Minh led by Ho Chi Minh. It was, he said, because they chose to fight at Dien Bien Phu.

And who, Cogny asked rhetorically, chose Dien Bien Phu? Only Raul Salan, he answered dramatically, the former commander-in-chief. And why, Cogny asked passionately, had General Salan chosen to fight at that remote crossroads in the mountains, which had no strategic importance? He answered himself indignantly: Because, *Messieurs*, Dien Bien Phu was the junction of the opium routes from Laos to Viet Nam—and Raul Salan was making a fortune in the opium traffic until the day he left.

Dien Bien Phu was also vital according to conventional strategic thinking. Beyond the opium trade, General Raul Salan had been convinced that he could destroy the Viet Minh if he could only draw them into a set-piece battle. He finally got his battle, but he did not destroy the Viet Minh. Instead, the Viet Minh forced the garrison of Dien Bien Phu to surrender. That spectacular defeat forced the French government to agree at Geneva to the ignominious withdrawal from Viet Nam.

Fourteen years later, American General William Westmoreland, commanding in Viet Nam, was to hold tenaciously to the same faith in positional warfare. He therefore lured—as he believed—the regular People's Army of (North) Viet Nam into besieging his troops in another mountain valley. Khe Sanh was in the south, Dien Bien Phu in the north not being available. Far better supported by airlift and air bombardment, Westmoreland did much better than Salan. He was not forced to surrender his beleaguered garrison, who killed thousands of PAVN soldiers.

Yet the battle of Khe Sanh made no impression on Hanoi. The Communist high command would quite happily have taken much heavier losses to demonstrate that its resolution was not affected by superior American arms. That implacable resolution, Hanoi's most powerful weapon, was to defeat the Americans, as it had the French.

In 1955, the year after their humiliation at Dien Bien Phu and Geneva, the French naturally did not blame themselves for their defeat. Aside from Cogny, who blamed Salan, all the French officers and officials with whom Joe Fromm and I talked blamed the Americans.

Although hard-pressed in Indo-China, they said, France had sent a battalion to fight beside the Americans in Korea. But the Americans had not sent a single soldier or a single warplane to fight beside them in Indo-China. After the truce in Korea, President Dwight Eisenhower and Secretary of State John Foster Dulles had rejected all French pleas for additional aid. The U.S. would not send its own forces—and it would not provide atomic weapons.

I pointed to the liberal supply of conventional American equipment and munitions shipped south from quiescent Korea. Moreover, the air drops for Dien Bien Phu had been made by C-119 Flying Boxcars flown by the American pilots of Civil Air Transport, the Central Intelligence Agency's private airline.

That was not enough, said the French in Haiphong. It was obvious that the Americans wanted to take for themselves the rich territory of Indo-China, which was all the more beautiful after the infusion of French culture. Beyond doubt, the Frenchmen concluded darkly, their withdrawal was entirely due to the ungrateful and deceitful Americans!

The antagonism embraced American correspondents. The emotional temperature was subzero on the bridge of the American-made LST (landing ship, tank) outbound from Haiphong on a warm April morning in 1955. The captain, a young lieutenant of the French Navy, had been ordered to transport me. But he would on no account talk to me. Fortunately, the petty officers did not feel as strongly. They asked me to lunch in their mess and poured rough red wine from cans to accompany the best meal I have ever eaten on a naval vessel.

The LST was carrying several hundred refugees through the Baie d'Along to the deeper water where the *Marine Adder* of the U.S. Naval Transport Services lay at anchor. I have sailed through the Inland Sea of Japan and into the beautiful harbors of Sydney, San Francisco, Hong Kong, and Naples. But I have never been more deeply moved than I was by the Baie d'Along.

Gray cliffs rose sheer from the dark green water like the furrowed flanks of enormous mammoths. Folklore related that enormous dragons had left their bones in that fastness of immemorial Asia—and their bones had petrified. The tricolor on the stern staff barely stirring, the LST steamed among the scores of granite hillocks that jutted vertically from the unruffled surface.

The LST tied up to the USNT *Marine Adder* in a world where dragons were long extinct. The transport was to carry several thousand refugees from the Democratic Republic of (North) Viet Nam to the Republic of (South) Viet Nam. The new Communist rulers of the north had agreed in the Geneva Accord to permit the departure of all those who wished to leave. The accord also provided for the French withdrawal and, within two years, for elections throughout Viet Nam, to choose a single government for the entire country.[2]

Ho Chi Minh's men evidently believed they would lose only a few thousand of their citizens, defectors they were glad to be rid of. They had agreed not only to permit but to assist the departure of anyone who preferred the bourgeois south. They kept that promise—until it became clear how many were going. Between 900,000 and a million finally left their homes in the north for an uncertain welcome in the south. An exact count could not be taken amid the haste of the mass evacuation.

Unquestionably, more wanted to leave—perhaps many more. The refugees with whom I talked during the two-day voyage to Saigon all said that at least as many more wanted to leave as had been permitted to leave. But Hanoi abruptly cut off the flow. The Communists had realized that this was no medicinal bloodletting, but a hemorrhage of people—a tremendous loss of labor, knowledge, and talent.

Not all or even most were rich, as the Communists claimed. That first great wave, like later waves of people fleeing Hanoi's rule, have been described as greedy bourgeoisie who were constitutionally averse to hard work. They were characterized as prostitutes, black marketeers, gangsters, and exploiters, all carrying hoards of gold and jewels looted from the common people. But they did not look it on the *Marine Adder*.

If those people were wealthy, they had worked a rather long time to get out and chosen remarkably uncomfortable transportation. Not much in the way of worldly goods would go into the small straw valises, canvas suitcases, and bandanna-wrapped bundles I saw. This was no luxury cruise—and there was no baggage in the holds, which were full of human beings. I did see a few gold ornaments, which, in the prudent, bank-shy Asian manner, represented the modest savings of entire families. I also saw entire families crammed into corridors and holds, even into corners between deckhouses and under lifeboats. The un-mistakable stench of poverty filled my nostrils—raw, rank, and rotten.

Not all were very poor, and they had different reasons for exiling themselves. Some were petit bourgeoisie, that is, small shopkeepers and craftsmen. A good many were overseas Chinese, who should,

---

[2] Those elections did not take place. Ngo Dinh Diem, who had been elected president of the republic in the south, refused to participate because, he said, there could be no guarantee of freedom of choice in the north. The Communists were indignant. They felt they had been cheated of their due.

perhaps, have welcomed a new government that was closely allied with the People's Republic of China. Having already experienced the reality of Ho Chi Minh's rule, they wanted no more. A substantial number were Catholics, whose priests had urged them to leave. Some 300,000 were Buddhists, neither Chinese nor Catholic, just ordinary Vietnamese.

The first great wave of refugees from Communist-ruled Viet Nam should have sounded the alarm. The United States should have been concerned to provide against future crises in Viet Nam. But times were good; Eisenhower was in the White House; and everyone knew there would be no more American wars in Asia.

The exodus of 1955 was the most dramatic until the "boat people" began leaving Viet Nam in 1975, after the regime in the south collapsed under the hammer blows of the north's tank columns and massed artillery. With the help of bribed officials, at least 1.5 million were to escape in leaky, underpowered, underprovisioned skiffs, boats, and junks, setting out even in the typhoon season. Again, no exact estimate is possible. More than 700,000 arrived safely in harbors throughout Asia, some to be resettled in countries outside the region, others to sit year after year penned in refugee camps. At least an equal number, probably more, died at sea by drowning, starvation, disease, and pirate attacks. No one knows how many have been lost. In 1989 the exodus was continuing despite threats to send the refugees back forcibly.

The war in Indo-China was the second most critical political and/or military event in Asia in the decades after the Korean War, second, I believe, only to the Great Proletarian Cultural Revolution and the bankruptcy of Maoism in China. Just consider: the American commitment of troops; the American war; the American withdrawal; and the final conquest of not only South Viet Nam, but Cambodia and Laos by Hanoi or forces controlled by Hanoi. They were epoch making.

It is, however, virtually impossible to discuss those events without exploring a mine field of value judgments whose detonation precludes a reasoned exchange of views. Although the last American official scurried out of Saigon half a generation ago, the American role in Viet Nam still arouses passionate controversy. The arguments concern not only the justice or wisdom of the commitment and the morality of American actions, but also both political and military tactics and strategy. There is still no wide agreement as to what really happened—or whether it should have happened.

Naturally, I have my own views. They are based on the experience of Indo-China extending over twenty years. I was first in Viet Nam in the spring of 1955. My last visit was in the spring of 1975, shortly before the Communists took Saigon. Nor am I dispassionate. Although I feel strongly, I still wonder just how sure I, or anyone, can be in making an overall judgment.

This book is intended as an examination of the present state of East Asia against its historical background—not as another postmortem on the Viet Nam War. Analyzing the controversial American record in Indo-China would distract from that purpose. However, since the war cannot be disregarded in an account of modern East Asia, I shall look instead at its effects.

The experience was disastrous for the United States domestically, and it was devastating for the American image throughout the world. Although America's 1960s might have happened in much the same way without the Viet Nam factor, the 1960s *did* happen as they did *with* Viet Nam in the foreground of the popular consciousness.

The fiscal and economic effects on the United States have been as deleterious as the wounds to morale. While losing the political war, which was all that counted in Indo-China, the U.S. was also losing the trade war, which counted even more in the world at large. Trying to finance the war without raising taxes was the first step toward disastrous inflation and the devaluation of the dollar, a process accelerated by the withholding of oil by the Organization of Petroleum Exporting Countries. To a large extent, the world as it presently exists owes both its prosperity and its insecurity to Viet Nam.

The U.S. engagement was also disastrous for Indo-China, as witness the tide of refugees and the present condition of Viet Nam, Laos, and Cambodia. South Viet Nam, for one, lost a government that, however corrupt or ineffectual, was committed to economic progress and to some degree of personal freedom. With American advice and American support, that government had built an economy that was remarkably prosperous for wartime. Afterward, Viet Nam gained a narrow-tracked regime that clung with totalitarian rigor to economic and administrative models discarded by both Beijing and Moscow. The result has been an economic catastrophe.

U.S. intervention in Indo-China was, however, highly beneficial to a number of other countries. That effect does not, of course, justify a conflict the U.S. entered with no clear idea of its strategic objectives. Above all, the U.S. could not win because it never knew exactly what it was fighting for. The benign consequences elsewhere were happy accidents, rather than the outcome of reasoned policy. Yet the American engagement, however misjudged and mishandled, did stop the clock for at least a decade.

During that time stolen from eternity, a number of things happened. Freed of fear of external threats, the other countries of Asia, particularly Southeast Asia, could (1) build up their economies, (2) create more stable political structures, and (3) develop the Association of Southeast Asian Nations as a buffer against external threats to replace the Southeast Asia Treaty Organization, which was sustained by outsiders, notably the U.S.

During that same decade, other things happened. Above all, the People's Republic of China turned its back on crusading Maoism. Not guerrillas, but conventional forces, won the war in Viet Nam. The failure of the guerrilla campaign punctured Chairman Mao Tse-tung's doctrine of the "inevitable victory of people's wars of liberation fought by guerrillas." Disillusionment went with the chairman's vision encouraged China to reject his vicious excesses at home and his grandiose ambitions abroad.

Even the vicious aberration of Tienanmen Square has not vitiated that true liberation, for even the gerontocracy does not wish to return to People's Communes or exporting revolution. China's repudiation of dogmatic Marxism-Leninism in turn encouraged the Soviet Union to remake its own ramshackle economic and administrative structures. Eastern Europe followed when Soviet controls relaxed somewhat.

During the same stolen fragment of time, Japan went into orbit. East Asia became the most dynamic part of the world, and with Japan in the lead, began, perhaps, to make the West obsolete. Both of those developments arose directly from the great economic opportunities created by events in Indo-China.

The American engagement shaped not only Southeast Asia, not only Asia, but the entire world—for better and for worse. The United States clearly lost the war and suffered greatly thereby. Almost in spite of itself, the United States won the peace and attained its objectives: stability and prosperity in Asia. Certainly Asia won the peace—except for Viet Nam, Laos, and Cambodia.

The tides of refugees flowing out of Cambodia and Laos never rose as high as those from Viet Nam. Fighting was never as intense, and populations were much smaller. Only after Hanoi and Washington signed a truce in January 1973 could the Khmer Rouge, literally the Red Cambodians, stage a major offensive against the government in Phnom Penh. Even then, very large stretches of Cambodia were free of the devastation of war, as I found when I drove unaccompanied to the southerly market town called Kampong Cham in the spring of 1973. There was no pressing, much less overwhelming, reason for Cambodians to flee.

The Khmer Rouge came to power in 1975 on the wave created by the blitzkrieg of the People's Army of (North) Viet Nam that took Saigon and destroyed the Republic of (South) Viet Nam. The Khmer Rouge immediately mounted a reign of terror: mass relocation of the populace was enforced with mass murder just as ferocious as the Nazis' extermination campaigns—and more frenzied. In less than four years, the Khmer Rouge slaughtered more than a million, perhaps twice that number, among a population of about seven million—and they did it without benefit of modern technology. Led by the maniacal Pol Pot, a French-educated bourgeois intellectual, the Khmer Rouge virtually wiped out the bourgeoisie and the intelligentsia. The shadowy leadership, which called itself Angka, "the Organization," also set out to destroy the cities, presumably so that Cambodia would revert to an idyllic pastoral society unmarred by modern complexity and corruption.

A macabre, indeed eerie, precedent existed. The greatest of all Khmer cities, Angkor Wat, had been abruptly abandoned by the entire population in the fifteenth century. But this was primitive communism with a vengeance.

Tens of thousands of men and women were killed because the palms of their hands were soft like idlers', not calloused like peasants'. The children who clung to their parents' soft hands or wept on their bloodied bodies were also killed; they came of bad stock. Everyone who survived was put to forced labor. Many were executed because they laughed or smiled, others because they did not. Almost all city dwellers were moved into the countryside, where, under the muzzles of Khmer Rouge guns, they toiled unremittingly on the land, which now belonged to Angka.

Cambodia became a vast concentration camp devoted to slave labor and mass slaughter. Pol Pot had evidently resolved to expunge not only all foreign influence, but all culture down to the simple skills of reading and writing. Even primary-school teachers were slain as corrupt intellectuals, as were pharmacists, auto mechanics, and veterinarians. Literacy was apparently to be reserved for the men of Angka, who presided over the shambles.

Refugees began moving into Thailand—when they could escape. The high tide began in 1978, when the People's Army of Viet Nam marched into Cambodia to overthrow its former ally, Pol Pot. Hanoi was outraged, but not because Pol Pot was a mass murderer. The Vietnamese could no longer abide his assertion of independence, particularly his allying himself with their new enemy, the People's Republic of China. The renewed conflict threatened the people's lives even more than had Angka, but the attendant confusion allowed them to escape in much larger numbers.

It was not that they preferred the home-grown tyrant. They hated the Vietnamese, who had made war upon the Khmer people for centuries.

*   *   *

Hundreds of thousands of refugees thus became for the Thais at once a problem and an instrument of policy.[3] When Moira and I visited Site Two with Nick B. Williams, Jr., of the *Los Angeles Times*, it housed the greatest single concentration: 160,000 Cambodians. Colonel Poo Pengchan's command post was a bamboo-frame pavilion thatched with palm fronds. Above the waist-high walls woven of split bamboo, lattices of bamboo let the occasional breeze blow through.

The colonel had little real power. Neither his geese nor his ragtag Rangers could stop the continual coming and going of black marketeers and thieves through his barbed wire. Nor could he prevent occasional cross-border forays by Vietnamese troops, who laid mines and blew up the tank trucks that carried the camp's drinking water. Even if he could, he would not have dreamed of interfering with the guerrillas who used the camps as their rear bases. The Thais insisted only that the guerrillas hide their weapons and ammunition outside; refugee compounds are not supposed to look like the military bivouacs these were in part.

Although self-governing, the communities in exile were supported by the United Nations Border Relief Organization. Most of the $40 million a year required for food, clothing, education, medical attention, and other essentials was provided by the United States. The dozen or so private agencies actually performing such services included the International Rescue Committee, Médicins Sans Frontières, the American Refugee Committee, and the Catholic Relief Services. Aside from a few professional administrators, the few dozen foreigners working for the refugees were poorly paid volunteers.

Doctors and nurses got only a subsistence wage. They also got to work with diseases and problems they would never see elsewhere. Leprosy is not often encountered in Sioux City or Liverpool. Nor do family practitioners often have to cope with the organisms of pseudo-malaria that almost instantaneously, it seems, adapt to every new antibiotic. The doctors and nurses were assisted by Cambodian paramedics, whose bible was the comprehensive yet straightforward *Medic Training Manual* compiled for refugee hospitals by the American Refugee Committee.

"The problem is not getting young doctors to work for $900 a month while living in primitive conditions. The big problem is their good-heartedness," I was told that by their director, Dr. Rudi Coninx, a youthful Belgian who has, through much experience of natural and man-made disasters, become a specialist in relief and refugee medicine. He explained, "It takes the new ones a while to learn that every refugee

[3] Some 110,000 refugees from Laos are of lesser importance politically. Most are members of the minority tribes who fought the Communist Pathet Lao with clandestine, though hardly secret, American backing. I must largely omit Laos from this discussion. It is a fascinating backwater, but a backwater nonetheless, and I lack the time and space to do it justice.

is not a saint just because he's suffered. Like any community, we've got our share of thieves, con men, prostitutes, extortionists, and strong-arm men."

Visitors, too, must guard against their surprise at good conditions leading them to excessive praise. Site Two was remarkable, particularly to us, who had seen many refugee and resettlement sites in Asia. Most remarkably, there was no stench of confinement. There was nothing like the sour, rotten smell that usually hangs over such concentrations of the displaced and the dispossessed, but only the normal scent of dusty roads and tropical vegetation, the fragrance of spices and garlic and woodsmoke. Yet the inhabitants were not coddled—not on thirty cents a head per day.

An elderly farmer asked us into his home. His dark face was ravined with vertical lines, and he looked like an attendant warrior in one of the great bas-relief stone carvings that are the glory of Cambodian art; those stone pageants depict the life of the Buddha or the Indian epics that are the two great springs of Cambodian culture. He lived in a minuscule hut with his two wives and five children, the youngest of whom were two small daughters of different mothers.

Not coercion but realism had led into the marriage his pretty younger wife, who was twenty-four. Young men are not plentiful after years of conflict, and no other career than wife, mother, and household worker is open to an illiterate peasant woman. The husband she shared was in his sixties, but he was whole. Many of the surviving young men hobbled on crude crutches or on peg legs; land mines have maimed a generation.

Home for the family of eight was a bamboo-and-palm-frond hut a little too small to garage a Hyundai Pony automobile. Along its inside walls stretched narrow bamboo platforms that served as beds, sofas, and tables. From such dark hutches, poorly lit by lattice openings, came schoolchildren, adolescents, and young people wearing immaculate shirts and freshly ironed trousers or skirts.

Every structure at Site Two was made of the same plentiful materials: palm thatch and woven or latticed bamboo. All were single-story, and all were rectangular, but their size varied with function. The substantial community had its own police, law courts, and hospitals, as well as its own street cleaners and garbage men. The red-earth roads, edged with deep ditches to draw off flash floods from tropical cloudbursts, were well swept and free of litter—much cleaner, in fact, than the streets of New York or London.

Schools were heavily attended, not only by children, but by adults studying mechanics, literature, electricity, English, French, and Chinese. The worst enemies of the people of Site Two were boredom—and stress born of idleness and hopelessness. Fortunately, the largely peasant population was seeded with enough intellectuals to offer a variety of adult courses. Other shelters from despair were Buddhist, Moslem, Catholic, and Seventh-Day Adventist chapels, all well attended.

A missing-persons bureau on a street corner attempted to reunite families. High bulletin boards protected by miniature palm-thatch roofs carried hundreds of notices, each bearing a photograph. The mimeographed forms asked for such information as *Name, Age, Birthplace, Relative or Friend Sought, Where and When Last Seen.* No computers assisted the heartbreaking search, only bursting file boxes and eager clerks. There was no electricity for computers.

Nor was there any running water, for there was no source nearby and no network of pipes. Brought fifty miles in tank trucks, water for drinking, cooking, laundering, and bathing was stored in earthenware jars made in the camp. The largest, shaped like Middle Eastern oil jars, could just hold one of Ali Baba's forty thieves, as long as he was a fairly small thief. Each held fifteen gallons, and the administration hoped in time to provide two for each family. Believe me, for eight persons, thirty gallons between indefinite refills is not much.

The camp hospital is a series of woven and latticed split-bamboo structures that are connected by walks sheltered with palm-frond thatching. The largest structure, which houses the busy maternity ward, is as big as a hangar for light aircraft. Each of its many bamboo pillars is six inches in diameter; a tracery of bamboo poles bound with grass rope braces the roof. On the patients' beds, which are bamboo platforms covered with straw mats, squatting women smoke, gossip, and nurse their children. Swaddled in bright red patchwork comforters, babies swing in woven palm-fiber hammocks. Just born, most of those scrunch-faced and black-fuzzed infants still bear the stumps of umbilical cords.

One is born every hour. Eight percent of the women between fifteen and forty-four are now using an injectable or oral contraceptive. Yet at least 15 percent must do so to have any impact on population growth. And an American nurse observes: "Just try preaching birth control and child spacing after Pol Pot and the Khmer Rouge wiped out tens of thousands of children!"

A small boy, no more than three, squalls wildly as a paramedic examines a gash in his foot. But his heart-shaped face brightens and he rubs away his tears with one grubby fist when his other fist is clutching a red gumdrop. Moira has equipped herself with several pounds of gumdrops for the visit. Unafraid, he peers playfully around the big bamboo pillar at the new foreigners. He has seen strange people with big eyes and red hair all his life, for he was born in camp.

The American nurse briskly directs patients to X-ray or surgery or maternity. Other specializations are also provided in this impressive hospital—impressive, of course, in its context. A hand-lettered sign in

English instructs paramedics in techniques, reading: RIGHT WAY TO GIVE MEDICINE: RIGHT—PATIENT? MEDICINE? ROUTE? DOSE? TIME?

Simple, but the paramedics are not Rhodes Scholars. Most have never seen the inside of a secondary school, much less a university or a medical school. Maintaining a reasonably sterile operating room with such personnel under such conditions is itself a wonder.

A greater wonder is visible. A big red, white, and blue sign hanging from the bamboo rafters exhorts in Khmer and English: NO SPITTING. Almost miraculously in an Asian hospital with peasant patients, that injunction is obeyed.

Well looked after, the refugees were definitely not coddled—and nothing was permanent. Some had been in camp six or seven years. Yet they did not want to put down roots—and thus implicitly surrender their hope of going home. Besides, the soil was too arid and too alien. They were living no more than two miles from their own country's border, only fifty or a hundred miles from the land their families had tilled for decades. But power politics and doctrinal disputes made that distance immense.

Following the tortuous border, a killing zone ten miles wide in places stretched for hundreds of miles. Eerily deforested and depopulated, that wilderness within a wilderness had been made by the Vietnamese Army to keep refugees in and guerrillas out of Cambodia. It was strewn with land mines, pocked with concealed pit-traps studded with poisoned *punji* sticks, and strung with razor wire, which cuts to the bone and makes old-fashioned barbed wire seem humane. Aside from wild animals, the only regular denizens were the bandits who preyed on refugees and the guerrillas who somehow made their way to and from Cambodia. Vietnamese troops, sometimes accompanied by their Cambodian puppet-allies, lay in ambush for both refugees and guerrillas.

Situated on the edge of man-made chaos, Site Two was divided into districts like any conventional community. Some four thousand Vietnamese refugees lived in their own neighborhood. Anti-Vietnamese feeling ran so high among the Cambodians that even Vietnamese who had also fled Communist tyranny would not otherwise have been safe. The other big division in Site Two was between north and south. The dividing line was not, however, political or ideological, but the main road.

The mayor of the South Side, where seventy thousand lived, was a forty-seven-year-old former law student and professional youth leader named Thou Thun. His title was director of administration, but the children called him *Tah*, which means Grandpa. Not Colonel Poo, but Thou Thun was the figure of authority for children and adults alike.

Thou Thun was an educated man in a largely uneducated community, but his was not a case of the one-eyed man's being king in the land of the blind. He had the personality of a leader. Strong but accommodating, he was the right man to lead a people who arrive at decisions by consensus rather than confrontation. He had, further, for two decades been close to former Premier Son Sann, who commanded a larger, though softer, following than either the Khmer Rouge or the former king, Prince Norodom Sihanouk. Besides, his people knew that Thou Thun could have left them years earlier for a far easier life if he wished.

He possessed two priceless assets, a sister and a brother living in New Zealand. Having themselves been resettled in the late 1970s, they could sponsor his entry. But he had stayed to look after his people in the camp. He said candidly that he did not know what he would do *when* he returned to Cambodia. The refugees always said *when*, not *if*, for it would be fatal to their hopes to admit to uncertainty. *When* was an invocation to assure their return.

Thou Thun represented former Premier Son Sann's Kampuchean (Cambodian) People's National Liberation Front, one of the three parties in the coalition against the Vietnamese-sponsored government in Phnom Penh. He looked like a man of authority, and that appearance enhanced his authority. A good image is no more to be disdained in a palm-and-bamboo town on the edge of Thailand's central plain than in Washington, Tokyo, or London.

Above all, his earlobes were very long, which is a sign not only of long life, but of sanctity and wisdom. The Buddha is always depicted with long earlobes. The small mole on Thou Thun's left ear and the single gold crown among his yellowed teeth, however, signaled his common mortality. His forehead was very high, fringed with thin black hair and creased by care. His square face was lightly tanned, not burnt mahogany like the peasants', and his expression was reserved. At lunch on a bamboo table under a palm-frond canopy, he confirmed the impression of intelligence and concern. But he was candid, not reserved.

His worst problem, he said, was keeping order. He had 620 uniformed policemen armed with billy clubs, as well as neighborhood-watch and ward committees. The bureaucracy of the camp included committees for investigation and justice, as well as committees for sanitation, education, security, art, and new arrivals. Brawling and assault were the most common crimes, exceeded in number only by constant domestic disputes, which were not normally a criminal offense. A new camp had just been completed, but hard cases were sent to a Thai prison. Every day at least one victim of a brawl was hospitalized, and every week thirty to sixty culprits were tried by the camp court.

Although those figures might initially appear high, they are actually low for a community with a depressed standard of living and a popu-

lation of 70,000, including 21,000 unemployed adult males. There was
a waiting list of thousands for two hundred jobs making water jars at a
weekly wage of fifteen pounds of rice and twelve cans containing two
and two-thirds pounds of mackerel or tuna.

Thou Thun considered the brawling a disgrace. Rape and murder
were, however, blessedly infrequent, which was not remarkable in a
community where there was no privacy. The Khmer are not generally
aggressive, aside from religious or ideological frenzies. Although outside gangs preyed on the inmates, the Committee of Justice was chiefly
concerned with the frustration that exploded into violent fights.

Thou Thun was sophisticated in discussing the intricate political
situation whose resolution will decide when—and if—the refugees can
go home. For the time being, three antagonistic Cambodian factions
were loosely united against the government the Vietnamese had installed in Phnom Penh. Their relationship with their sponsors—China,
the U.S., and Thailand—was tortuously complex.

"Without American help, most of my people would've gone home
already," he said. "They couldn't stay with no way to farm and no outside
help."

He did not pretend to believe the United States was primarily
altruistic. The U.S. had gained much at a low cost by providing subsistence for the refugees through the United Nations, and by direct
support of about $4 million a year for the anti-Communist supporters
of Son Sann and Norodom Sihanouk. No American funds went directly
to the Khmer Rouge, which got its guns from China. But the U.S. did
support the Khmer Rouge's claim to Cambodia's seat in the United
Nations.

As we both knew, Washington had to swallow hard to do so. When
in power from 1975 to 1978, the Khmer Rouge had committed almost
every crime known to international law, beginning with armed piracy
of the American freighter *Mayaguez* and rising to a terrible crescendo
of genocide.

The alternative would, however, have been to concede the field to
the Vietnamese and the Cambodian puppet regime they had installed
after driving out the Khmer Rouge administration. That concession
would, in turn, have badly affected American relations with China,
which backed the anti-Vietnamese Khmer Rouge in order to restrain
Hanoi and to check Soviet expansionism into Southeast Asia.

The Khmer Rouge was by far the largest and most effective guerrilla
force, although it did not, in theory, receive any direct American aid.
Thou Thun estimated that it could field more than 25,000 highly
effective guerrillas. He put the effectives of his own centrist KPNLF at
some twelve thousand and Prince Sihanouk's guerrillas at six thousand-
odd. Those estimated totals were changing every day. Yet, regardless

of numbers, the Khmer Rouge were by far the most active and most effective guerrilla force. Keeping their own counsel and excluding all outsiders from their camps, they harried the hold of the Phnom Penh government fiercely.

"A man called Nikolai from *Pravda* came to see me recently," Thou Thun recalled. "He said the Soviets were anxious to settle the Cambodian problem—and he asked what they should do. He didn't seem to like my answer. I told him, 'Simple. Just stop helping the Vietnamese.'"

Looking into a future that did not appear so far away, I asked Thou Thun how he could support the coalition that now opposes Phnom Penh: Khmer Rouge, KPNLF, and Prince Sihanouk. Did he not fear that the Khmer Rouge would dominate any restored Cambodian government—and go back to their odious old ways?

"It's a risk," he replied. "But I don't think it will happen. The Khmer Rouge can't win alone. They need us, and we can hold them back. But it's not mainly because of the safeguards we can put on them. It's mainly because of China. China won't let the Khmer Rouge take over and act again the way they did when they ruled."

That is probably the most realistic reply to the question that torments everyone concerned with the future of Cambodia. Although the Chinese did nothing to curb the excesses of the Khmer Rouge when their protégés were in power, they would face an entirely different prospect should the Cambodian coalition displace Hanoi's Cambodian puppets—or, as is more likely, come to an arrangement with the regime in Phnom Penh to form a loose coalition administration.

Having already served their chief purpose by curbing both Hanoi and Moscow, the Khmer Rouge would, under such an arrangement, be far less important to Beijing than they had been. China has already said several times that she would not tolerate a resumption of her protégés' atrocities. Yet China herself was changing after June 4, and fear of a Khmer Rouge resurgence was rising. True, external pressure, too, should restrain bloodlust. Nonetheless, fear of renewed Khmer Rouge atrocities still haunted Cambodian moderates.

The situation was greatly altered in mid-1989. Pressure on the Vietnamese and their Cambodian puppets from the Association of Southeast Asian States, the United States, and China had mounted steadily since 1979. Beijing had also applied great pressure on Moscow, which was a little weary of its needy Vietnamese ally. As a result of such pressure and mounting guerrilla attacks, Hanoi had promised to withdraw its 200,000 troops from Cambodia. By February 1989, almost half had gone, for once not replaced by new units. Hanoi then announced that it would pull out all of its troops by the end of September. Knowing that its 35,000-strong armed forces were feeble without Vietnamese backing, the government in Phnom Penh was looking for a peace settlement, but not too hard.

Nothing was said about the more than 300,000 and perhaps many more Vietnamese who had settled in Cambodia during the Vietnamese occupation. They joined the established Vietnamese colony of at least a hundred thousand, which included fishermen living around the great lake called Ton Le Sap in western Cambodia. Most of those newcomers would, however, live by farming, and farmers cling to the land. Moreover, the merchants and artisans among them would overwhelm any competition from Cambodians. Vietnamese have always overwhelmed Cambodians in war, in commerce, or in farming—with the overseas Chinese having dominated the economy.

Yet an enlarged permanent colony of Vietnamese in eastern Cambodia would only exacerbate an existing problem. Some realistic Cambodians have already tacitly ceded domination to the Vietnamese, if not outright control, of the sparsely settled areas in the east that were the rear area for the People's Army of Viet Nam during the Viet Nam War. They don't like it, but they believe it cannot be helped.

However, Vietnamese domination of Indo-China was no longer unchallengeable. Hanoi could no longer exploit the Sino-Soviet rift as it had so effectively for decades. Common Soviet and Chinese interests, which needed peace to prosper, would therefore take precedence over Vietnamese interests. Hanoi had suffered a terrible shock when it realized that Moscow's interests were running parallel with Beijing's, rather than its own. Hanoi displayed its pique at Sino-Russian rapprochement by sharply reminding Moscow that Cam Ranh Bay was a Vietnamese base, not a Russian base—a proposition that is at least half true.

The Russians wanted Vietnamese troops out of Cambodia in order to reduce international tension and to enable them to appear the peacemakers. They also wanted to reduce the constant drain that aid to Vietnam made on their weak economy, and they wanted to placate China, which was more important to them than Viet Nam. The Chinese wanted Vietnamese troops out of Cambodia to stabilize the situation, to weaken the puppet government in Phnom Penh, and to take their hereditary enemy, Viet Nam, down a few pegs.

Those troops could presumably go back if the situation of the puppet government deteriorated markedly. No troops could stop them, certainly not the Cambodian guerrilla forces. But Russian and Chinese pressure probably could—if Russia and China cared to.

Moreover, Thailand was supporting the guerrillas with one hand, while offering trade and friendship to the Phnom Penh government with the other. That sensible carrot-and-stick approach was backed by

ASEAN, which alternated pressure on Phnom Penh with inducements to make peace.

The Phnom Penh regime was already negotiating with the three opposition groups, which were also negotiating with each other. Given the volatility of those groups, particularly the Khmer Rouge and Prince Norodom Sihanouk, those negotiations were slow, dramatic, and tortuous.

But nothing important in Cambodia had ever been straightforward or speedy. How could progress toward a settlement that all would be forced to accept, though none would rejoice in, be either straightforward or speedy?

21

Indo-China, Hardly Ever Free
and
Thailand, Always Free

THE KING OF SIAM WAS ACCUSTOMED TO GIVE WHITE ELEPHANTS
TO NOBLES HE DISTRUSTED, SO THAT THEY WOULD BANKRUPT
THEMSELVES CARING FOR THE SACRED ANIMALS.

HANOI DEFEATED THE UNITED STATES BY COURAGE, GUILE,
STEALTH, AND, ABOVE ALL, PERSISTENCE. THAT GREAT VICTORY
PLUNGED VIET NAM INTO ACUTE DEPRIVATION. THE RELENTLESS
LESSER DRAGON IS NOW VERY ILL AND VERY SAD.

THE DEVIOUS AND FLEXIBLE THAIS, WHO FOUGHT ON THE LOSING
SIDE, HAVE JOINED THE ASIAN RUSH TO PROSPERITY.

I met Khang Than Nhan only once, and then only briefly in 1987. It is unlikely that I shall ever meet him again, although for me he epitomizes his unhappy country.

After decades of struggle, Hanoi had defeated all its enemies. Since they could not recognize the possibility of defeat, the Communists had attained the objective for which patriots had fought for centuries: a united Viet Nam free of foreign domination. Hanoi had also won domination over Cambodia and Laos, all the lands formerly French Indo-China. Other Asians called the Vietnamese the Prussians of Asia and wondered where they would strike next.

Supreme happiness should have flowed from those great accomplishments. But the Vietnamese Communists were not happy, and the Vietnamese people were even less so. Their glorious victory had been followed by mass poverty and administrative chaos. Acute need made Viet Nam a pawn of the Soviet Union, raising again the specter of foreign domination; and the ancient enemy, China, was again harrying its borders.

The unhappy Khang Than Nhan embodied his unhappy nation's courage, its intelligence, its militant activism—and also its humorlessness, its insensitivity, and its ill fortune. I had no high hopes when I went to see Mr. Nhan[1] in December 1987. Journalists' visas for Viet Nam were not won by brisk formal application, but by years of wooing— unless Hanoi had a show trial or a troop withdrawal it wanted to publicize.

Margot Southon, my indefatigable assistant, had telephoned Mr. Nhan repeatedly before he finally sent an application form. The completed form had been in his hands for at least two months when her genial persistence finally won a grudging invitation to come and see him. But, he warned, it would do no good.

He was right. Nonetheless, the visit was illuminating, as my notes demonstrate:

The Embassy of Viet Nam at 12–14 Victoria Road in South Kensington stands behind an iron fence with an iron-grille gate opened by a buzzer from inside. Presumably, someone carrying a hand grenade or an AK–47 assault rifle would not be buzzed in. The embassy is in a state of alert, if not a full state of siege. That defensiveness, like the meager atmosphere and the garish decoration, recall the house in Paris where the North Vietnamese received correspondents during the prolonged truce negotiations with the U.S. in the 1960s and 1970s.

A wooden-armed settee and matching easy chairs are covered in a scratchy orange-and-black wool fabric. A five-foot-high black lacquer chest bears conventional Far Eastern landscapes inlaid in mother-of-pearl and also poems in Chinese ideograms, which very few Vietnamese can now read. Atop the cabinet is a shiny porcelain statuette about four feet long and a foot high of four straining horses pulling a dray loaded with logs.

It's all good Woolworth's stuff, the sort of thing they sell to tourists in odd corners of the Orient. But these Vietnamese diplomats actually use it themselves.

Mr. Nhan is past forty, perhaps ten years older. He looks disconsolate, as if about to cry. Dark-rimmed glasses perch on his large flat nose; his hair is very black, very long, and very thick. He wears a maroon sweater zipped halfway up and a brownish woolen shirt without a tie. Over all this he wears a dark cardigan. Or is it a jacket so misshapen it looks like a cardigan?

His nondescript trousers hike up over his black half-boots, which look military, a little brutal. Yet he is somehow pathetic, ill

---

[1] Like Chinese, Vietnamese write their surnames first, then their given names. Vietnamese names, which can be written in ideograms, are essentially Chinese names pronounced differently. But there are so few surnames that men and women are known by their given names. Thus, Khang Than Nhan is addressed as Mr. Nhan, although his family name is Khang.

at ease in his own domain. He speaks in bursts and moves jerkily, constantly recrossing his legs. His trouser leg hikes up to display dark brown coarse wool socks. Above the socks, his legs are very white, indeed pallid. The shin and calf are almost impossibly thin, hardly thicker than a broomstick, as if he had suffered from polio.

He says Hanoi has not replied to my application—and asks abruptly if I have ever written anything about Viet Nam. I can now see in the file on his knee my application, which gives all such details.

"Yes, a good deal," I reply. "But not lately."

The problem, he says, is no room at the inn. In Viet Nam, he adds, there are few inns, little transport, not enough interpreters, and only a handful of press officers. He knows the problems at firsthand, having previously been a press officer at the Foreign Ministry in Hanoi. During his year in London, he says, he has received twelve hundred applications for press visas. Twelve hundred applicants—and he has managed to get twelve to Viet Nam. It is all very frustrating. He says he will ask Hanoi again. But he holds out no hope.

"People are always coming to me saying they want to present the Vietnamese point of view," he says. "They say everything has in the past been from the American point of view. Particularly those who want to make films are always talking about the Vietnamese viewpoint. They say they want to show Vietnamese heroes. But often we can't find the heroes they want to show. One hero they wanted had been dead for years."

He recrosses his legs and points out, "Besides, you can't land in Hanoi the way you could in London and just telephone the ministries and offices you want to see. Even the switchboards don't speak English or even French. Anyway, that's not the way it's done."

I say something sympathetic about the curse of bureaucracy. He does not reprove me, but nods and adds, "Everything must be arranged. Maybe two or three people a week can come as guests from everywhere. And there is East Europe and other friendly Socialist countries."

I know Hanoi is very short of hotel rooms. And I do not ask what has become of all the hotels built in the south during the war—or the many English speakers trained during the war. Such questions would only make Mr. Nhan more unhappy. An air of deep sadness hangs about him, a settled melancholy, as if he were resigned to inevitable misfortune and grief.

Everything he tells me bespeaks deprivation and inefficiency. I marvel again that his people drove the U.S. out of Indo-China—

indeed, almost out of Asia—after having driven out the French. His people, who still take on their immense neighbor, China, are magnificent warriors, tenacious, ingenious, and courageous. Yet in the arts of peace they are disastrous, as witness their present economic plight and their diplomatic isolation.

Thus my notes ended. I heard no more from Mr. Nhan, certainly nothing about a visa. After eight months, I had almost forgotten about him. Memory revived when I heard a radio report that an unnamed diplomat had threatened to shoot refugees demonstrating in front of the Vietnamese Embassy. Could it, I wondered, be Khang Than Nhan, the man behind the iron grille?

The morning newspaper confirmed my suspicion. It was indeed he who had brandished a Colt .45. The incident was front-page news. Britain takes a severe view of anyone, diplomat or not, who possesses an illegal firearm. It expelled Mr. Nhan. Displaying its extreme displeasure, the Foreign Office gave him just twenty-four hours to remove himself from Britain.

I hope Hanoi has not been too hard on Mr. Nhan because his self-control snapped. He was evidently suffering intense strain when I saw him earlier. The stress of his constant struggle against inadequate resources and public hostility apparently drove him to the pointless demonstration on the steps of his rundown embassy.

His superiors should be merciful—as they probably will not be—for he truly embodies his country's plight. Viet Nam is itself under intense strain. Its triumphs have brought it little comfort, and the euphoria of victory is long passed. Sometimes even a country badly needs to relax.

The Vietnamese are a high-strung people. Their history and culture have made them tense, assertive, abrupt, intelligent, and stealthy. A few centuries before the beginning of the Christian era, they fled before the advancing Chinese peoples, moving southward from the lower Yangtze Valley into the Red River Delta. They settled east of the mountain range called the Annamite Chain, which divides continental Southeast Asia. Although their new fastness was removed from the main currents of history, Chinese pressure never ceased entirely—and intensified intermittently.

From their base in the Red River Valley, the Vietnamese gradually pushed southward and westward. They seeped across the land, nudging the unsophisticated indigenous tribes before them. Flowing into the valleys, the Vietnamese tide drove the tribespeople up to the plateaus and the mountains. But they did not drive the more highly civilized Chams from the southern point of what is now Viet Nam until the fifteenth and sixteenth centuries.

The Vietnamese had finally come up against peoples as sophisticated as themselves. The Chams were the heirs of a civilization as advanced as Chinese civilization, but utterly different because it derived from India.

The Annamite Chain was to remain the barrier between Sinicized Southeast Asia to the east and Indianized Southeast Asia to the west. Through the deep valleys and high passes of the range flowed traders, armies, and envoys, but the mountains kept the two civilizations distinct for a long time.

To the west lay Burma, Thailand, Cambodia, and Laos. All practiced the Buddhism called Theraveda, "the True Word," which was essentially agnostic. The Buddha, himself not a god, did not direct his disciples to worship a supernatural divinity. Theraveda Buddhism was more interested in this world than in speculation about the next. It revolted against the dead weight of Hinduism, which decreed that every human being was born into a fixed social caste from which no one could escape—and was also born to a predestined fate. Buddhism rejected caste. Theraveda taught that every human being by his own deeds determined his own position in this world—and his fate in the possible next world.

Although originally a vehicle of social protest, Theraveda had carried over from its parent Hinduism a certain fatalism, an inclination to accept injustice passively. Like Hinduism, it was sometimes vague and amorphous, almost inchoate. Theraveda in time became otherworldly, no longer primarily a doctrine of social activism, but a consolation for the inequities and iniquities of this world.

Vietnamese civilization was, above all, precise—in sharp contrast to the comfortable wooliness of its neighbors. It was a sharply delineated culture with a small elite of mandarins, a Confucian culture of rigid hierarchies among both men and ideas. As in China, Viet Nam's Confucian officials believed, officially at least, in a host of gods: the spirits of the land and the water; the patrons of places, persons, and occupations; the deities of women and childbirth; the divinities of men and wealth and battle. After all, the credulous common people were more easily ruled through their superstition. As in China, mandarins were themselves agnostic—until afflicted by hard times. In China, they were then Buddhist or Taoist. In Viet Nam, they could turn to a large number of idiosyncratic sects. Although worldly, the Vietnamese had many gods and many religions, as well as many quasi-religious secret societies.

After a while it became difficult to tell a religion from a political or a criminal organization. In 1955 justice was enforced in Saigon by the Binh Xuyen, a Mafialike gang with its own theology, to whom the French had sold the police force. In that same year, two other sects turned their private armies against President Ngo Dinh Diem: the Hoa

Hao and the Cao Dai. Each had borrowed from other creeds of both East and West, and each possessed its own pantheon. The Cao Dai popes had canonized Victor Hugo and Mark Twain, among others.

Buddhism was, however, dominant. Like China and Japan, Viet Nam followed Mahayana, "the Greater Vehicle," rather than Hinayana, "the Lesser Vehicle," as its followers called Theraveda. An energetic and copious faith, Mahayana Buddhism was staffed by a full bureaucracy of gods and goddesses who worked under the Jade Emperor of Heaven— just like the temporal emperor, his mandarins, and their subordinates. Worshipers could appeal to precisely the right divinity to deal with specific problems, just as the minister of works looked after dams and the minister of justice looked after prisons. Human beings could de- cisively alter their own fate by prayer, by charity, and by good works. Mahayana was an activist religion that encouraged men and women to make their own way by their own efforts in this world, as in the next.

The Vietnamese obviously had an edge on their neighbors. If anyone were going to conquer, it would be they, who were unquestionably superior in worldly terms. Their culture was concrete, active, and immediate; they themselves were energetic, logical, and independent.

Viet Nam fought China from the moment of its creation, when a Chinese viceroy of the region declared himself an independent mon- arch in the third century B.C. Yet the culture and character of the Vietnamese were both derived largely from China. Over the centuries, the Vietnamese modified the Chinese model much less than did the Koreans and the Japanese. Long before it became fashionable to call Hong Kong, Singapore, Taiwan, and South Korea the Small Dragons of East Asia, Viet Nam was known as the Lesser Dragon.

The Vietnamese did not like that tag. Yet they were truly more like the Chinese than was any other nation. Although their language is not formally classified as derived from Chinese, it was long written with ideograms. Today, its vocabulary is at least half Chinese by origin, and its grammatical structure resembles Chinese.

Like the origins of the excellent Vietnamese cuisine, the origins of the Vietnamese language are apparent. An egg roll is still an egg roll, even if it is soft, transparent, and served with fresh mint, lettuce, and a powerful sauce called *nuoc mam*, which is made from fermented fish. A bank, *yin-hang* in Mandarin, is still a bank, even if it is called *ngan-wang* in Vietnamese,[2] for it still means, literally, "silver shop." Daily behavior, family relations, even architecture, all are largely

---

[2] Similarly, Ho Chi Minh is a Chinese name, even if not pronounced Hu Jir Min in Mandarin. Ho is a common Chinese surname, and Chi Minh, meaning "the will of the people," is an unexceptional Chinese given name. When he needed another pseudonym, Ho Chi Minh called himself Nguyen Ai Quoc, which is Ruan Ai Gwaw in Mandarin, but still means Nguyen (or Ruan), "the patriot."

Chinese in derivation. The "ancient citadel" at Hue was modeled directly on the Imperial City of Peking when it was completed by the Vietnamese Emperor Gia Long in 1802. Gia Long was formally invested as emperor of Viet Nam by the emperor of China, which made him, formally at least, a vassal of China.

Vietnamese is spoken with nine intonations to differentiate among its monosyllables, while Cantonese has eight tones and Mandarin four. The language of learning, literature, and government was, however, classical Chinese written with Chinese ideograms. The effect was even more restrictive in little Viet Nam than it was in vast China. Confucianism created a very small, virtually hereditary mandarinate. Viet Nam was a very conservative and very small China, a lesser dragon half-frozen in amber.

In the seventeenth century, when the Jesuits were redrawing the cultural map of Asia, Father Alexandre de Rhodes gave the Vietnamese a new writing system that reduced the psychological burden of dependence on China. Instead of the complex ideograms, which required feats of memorization, they would thenceforth use the Latin alphabet, slightly modified. Literature and learning became accessible to a far greater number, as did government decrees.

Alexandre de Rhodes was the best-loved Frenchman ever to live in Viet Nam. When President Ngo Dinh Diem decreed that the streets of Saigon would no longer be called after eminent Frenchmen, but after eminent Vietnamese, only two French names were retained. One was Louis Pasteur. The other was Alexandre de Rhodes.

Father de Rhodes had not only alleviated the Vietnamese inferiority complex toward China; he made the Vietnamese more susceptible to Gallicization. Although conservative Vietnamese complained that the Jesuit had cut them off from the roots of their own culture, the French were delighted to graft Vietnamese culture onto their own strong roots.

Many Vietnamese took happily to the change. It was, after all, not France but China they then hated and feared. It was the Chinese who had driven them out of their homeland and had thereafter striven to keep them vassals.

The Vietnamese had resisted the Chinese with the courage and tenacity that later defeated the French and the Americans. Daring feats against the Chinese aggressors wove a brilliant red thread of bravery into the fabric of Viet Nam's history.

Purged of French names, Saigon streets were renamed for heroes and heroines of the resistance against the Chinese—who were also glorified in monumental statuary. China was the traditional enemy to every Vietnamese.

Yet Viet Nam was vulnerable because its people were scornful of outsiders and contentious toward each other. Viet Nam fell under

French domination in the nineteenth century. European science and European organization overcame a conservative and undisciplined monarchy.

French colonial rule, unlike Dutch and British colonial rule, was not poisoned by color prejudice. Frenchwomen came later and in fewer numbers to the colonies than Dutch women and Englishwomen, so that no impenetrable line was drawn against the Vietnamese wives and mistresses of French settlers. Consequently no wholly white society evolved. The sensible French did not care what color men or women were, as long as they adopted French culture.

The goal of the French was to make Viet Nam a virtual part of France. Vietnamese cadets were trained at military academies in France, and French citizenship was extended to many Vietnamese, particularly through military service. The French convinced themselves, though not all Vietnamese, that they were not only emulated, but loved. During their sorrowful evacuation of the north in 1955, French officers asserted with total confidence that the Vietnamese attachment to French culture would ensure their quick return. It was as if they had not just been driven out by the Vietnamese.

While the French were leaving Haiphong, Vietnamese strolled home through the gloomy dusk with long baguettes of French bread under their arms. The man who drove the French from Indo-China had worked as an assistant chef in the hotels of Paris and on the great steamers of the French Line; thus acquiring the knowledge of the West he later used as a weapon against the West.

A quintessential Marxist, Ho Chi Minh was a founder of the Communist Party of Indo-China, which later, for cosmetic reasons, became the Labor Party of Viet Nam. He was a nationalist as well as a Marxist, but his dedication to Marxism was paramount early in his career. His fight for a unified and independent Viet Nam was assisted not only by the Communist International, but by the Chinese Nationalists during their pro-Soviet phase. The Communist People's Republic of China later gave Ho Chi Minh both financial and diplomatic support, as well as American artillery pieces captured in Korea. Those guns won the battle of Dien Bien Phu, and that victory broke the French will to resist.

The ultimate victory was also Ho Chi Minh's, although he died in 1969, six years before the last American ambassador left Saigon by helicopter to escape the Communist troops closing in on his fortified embassy. That humiliation dramatized the Communist victory. Having defeated the People's Army of Viet Nam in the field, American military forces withdrew by 1973. But the U.S. left the South Vietnamese armed forces to be routed by a massive conventional offensive by heavy tank columns and massed artillery. It was, nonetheless, an American defeat, the second epic defeat in the twentieth century of a major Western power in Asia, seventy years after the Russians' defeat by Japan.

Having proved itself among the foremost military nations, Viet Nam now operates a civilian economy among the most backward on earth. Yet it possesses these proven advantages: a Confucian heritage and a literate populace that rapidly acquires new skills. But it is also relentless and unswerving. The tenacity that won the war has all but lost the peace.

In 1975 Hanoi inherited by right of conquest the prosperous, functioning economy of the south. The war had destroyed most of the factories of the north, but the south had actually become richer and more productive. Ports, roads, and airports had been built to serve the Americans, who do not like to walk to war; large numbers of skilled workers had been trained to fill the many needs of Americans; and new industries had developed to meet the demands of the prosperous class created by American aid.

South Viet Nam had not been transformed into a land overflowing with limousines and private aircraft, but buses and trucks regularly plied the roads to remote corners. The buses carried capacity loads of people who for the first time had the money and the leisure to travel, and had business elsewhere. The trucks carried imported and domestic manufactured goods into the countryside, returning with rice, bananas, cattle, and pigs.

Economic life would naturally have been more abundant if young men had not been conscripted for uneconomic activities and there had been no destruction. In the paradoxical real world, however, many economic benefits had flowed to South Viet Nam as a result of war. As Nguyen Xuan Oanh, an economist who is an adviser to Hanoi, pointed out later, "in 1975 the south had laid a significant base of small- and medium-sized factories for production of consumer goods. . . . Saigon had [also] created a large service industry, including an efficient commercial banking system."

Instead of exploiting those advantages, the Communists appear to have set out to reduce the south to the level of the north. The Communists were determined to impose their will on the cocky, undisciplined southerners, even if that meant purging those who were most productive (the middle class)—those who had led the anti-Communist resistance. The Communists were also determined to "build socialism," which meant destroying the middle class. Economic institutions, competent managers, and skilled workers were, therefore, sacrificed without a thought to the future.

The muse of history, who loves irony, must have clapped her hands in delight. An early casualty was also the National Liberation Front, which had carried the banner of revolt in the south. The Communists were deterred neither by gratitude nor by the fact that it would initially be easier for them to rule through the NLF. Since the Front's largely southern membership stood in the way of absolute rule by the largely northern Communists, the Front had to go.

A purge of all officials of the former government was to be expected. Yet, remarkably, there were no mass killings like those that had marked land reform in the north in the mid-1950s, or those that had wiped out the elite when the Communists occupied Hue during the Tet Offensive of 1968. Individual and group executions occurred, but no general massacre. Yet the purge reached deep, touching not only former civilian functionaries but former officers and noncoms of the armed forces of the defunct Republic of Viet Nam, former policemen, and former auxiliary soldiers—indeed, almost everyone who had actively supported the republic.

The wasting of the south's economic potential began with the ostracism of those whose skills could contribute most to the nation. Most were middle class and therefore doubly suspect by a regime that feared infiltration and sabotage by enemy agents. During the war, they themselves had thoroughly infiltrated the government and vital institutions of the south, as well as official and private American organizations. The northerners now set out to run the south without the southerners, without even those southerners who had fought against the Saigon regime.

Following the Chinese model, Hanoi set up "Re-education Camps" to teach its enemies the error of their ways by forced study and forced labor. Hanoi also set up New Economic Zones where decadent city dwellers were to be reformed by wholesome labor in the countryside. Except for the minute contribution their manual labor might make, the skills of the inmates of those camps and zones were lost to the nation.

In the beginning, the nets were wide-meshed and only caught the bigger fish. Soon, however, the Communists were trolling with very fine nets that caught even minnows.

Lam Thau was twenty-four when the Communists came to Saigon. He had no record of "antisocial behavior," and he had managed to dodge service in the army of the south. His crimes were twofold: first, his father was an independent businessman; second, he was Chinese by race, although born in Cholon, a district of Saigon.

Essentially apolitical, he had married in 1974, when the end of the Republic of (South) Viet Nam was close, and he had expected to lead a normal life with his new wife. So he told me, when we talked in the segregated district in Site Two South called the Viet Nam Land Refugee Platform, where lived—and waited for resettlement—some two thousand inmates classified as "land refugees," to distinguish them from the boat people. Instead of embarking in ramshackle vessels, they had taken a cheaper—and even more hazardous—way from Viet Nam, through Cambodia to Thailand.

Initially the Lams had felt no need to leave. From 1975 to 1978, their life was hardly disturbed by the new order. He earned their living by "doing business," he said somewhat evasively. He was evidently involved in the black market, which defied the new government's attempt to end almost all private enterprise.

The Lams' relatively easy life ended in 1978, three years after the Communist victory with the campaign to "destroy the capitalist [bourgeois] class," much as the Chinese had in 1952, three years after their victory. His small eyes intent and his teeth very white against his tanned face, Lam Thau said he had not been particularly singled out for punishment.

"At that time," he explained, "almost all Chinese were sent to New Economic Zones. . . . We were sent to a place sixty kilometers [about thirty-eight miles] west of Saigon. It was uninhabited, only forest. . . . They gave us some tools and told us to cut down the trees to make huts. They also gave us some seed and told us to plant rice. I had never cut trees or planted rice before. They also gave us a little food. But they said we had to be self-reliant after six months . . . to depend only on ourselves and our own strength."

The Lams escaped from the New Economic Zone in October 1978. Risking punishment was preferable to spending a lifetime in the primitive countryside. Anyway, security was lax—and the guards were easily bribed. They returned to Saigon and submerged themselves in the Chinese community. Many Chinese were living in Saigon without permission, as the authorities well knew. But two thousand *dong* a month to the local policemen kept them from being arrested and sent back—or worse. That sum, perhaps a week's wages, was not very large, but neither was it small.

Lam Thau was a little vague about the period from 1978 to 1983, when his life was not only clandestine, but illegal. Since he was not allowed to live in Saigon, anything he did in Saigon was automatically a crime. Besides, he was again involved in the black market, which would have been the free market anywhere else, even in China. He was also earning some money by teaching Chinese, and he was receiving an allowance from his parents, who had left Saigon to run a restaurant in the countryside.

Saigon became intolerable in 1983, eight years after the Communist victory. Although all capitalists had been rounded up or put out of business, the Communists still faced widespread passive resistance, which they called sabotage. Determined to sever the intellectual roots of that resistance, the authorities proclaimed a "movement to purify thought." Like the Communists in China in 1957, just eight years after their victory, the Vietnamese Communists mounted a mass attack on the troublesome intellectuals. As in China, that group included everyone with the equivalent of a high school education.

"The police were ordered to arrest all 'old-style teachers,'" Lam Thau said. "I knew I was on the list because I taught Chinese classes. Most of those to be arrested were Chinese because their educational level was higher. But there were Vietnamese, too. The authorities said they were going to wipe out all 'liberal elements.'"

In October 1983 Lam Thau and his wife decided they must leave Viet Nam with their three children. They wanted to go by boat, but could not raise the four ounces of gold (roughly $2,000) for the bribes and the fare. Friends found them a guide who would take them overland for less than half that much. He was a Vietnamese who spoke both Cambodian and Chinese, a professional smuggler of human beings.

In December 1983 they left Saigon for Phnom Penh, traveling by truck through checkpoints whose guards had been liberally bribed. They were, however, forced to spend more than four months in a safe house in Phnom Penh when one of their children became too ill to travel. Once again, Lam Thau's father sent money to pay for their expensive refuge; the smugglers of people had no difficulty in smuggling money. Finally, on May 8, 1984, the Lam family arrived in Thailand.

"When we were crossing the last strip, just before Thailand, bandits attacked us," Lam Thau recalled. "They didn't want to kill us. They only took everything we had: a little money, our watches, my wife's last piece of jewelry. Then they let us go."

No country defeated by the United States has ever been in such desperate straits fourteen years after the close of hostilities as the country that defeated the United States was in 1989. Through inefficiency, corruption, maladministration, and misdirection, Viet Nam has become the most miserable of all cultured countries. Hanoi even lost all aid from well-meaning outsiders in 1979, after it invaded Cambodia. Only the Russians continued to pump in about $3 billion a year. But the Russians were becoming difficult as policies changed under President Mikhail Gorbachev.

No longer an asset, Viet Nam had become a liability to Soviet *glasnost*-style expansion in Asia and the Pacific. The Soviets provided enough aid to keep the regime from collapsing, but required better obedience to their wishes. Having waged battles for independence during most of the twentieth century, Viet Nam was again forced to bow to outsiders.

Considering the dismal state of the economy and the abysmal level of public morale, the leadership had no choice. The Vietnamese were belatedly trying their own very limited versions of *glasnost* and *pere-stroika*, "openness" and "restructuring." I should, perhaps, say *kaifang* and *gaigo*, for they had consistently followed the Chinese example since coming to power. But Hanoi drew back from the sweeping economic reforms Beijing had decreed. In China, production had risen, but so had inflation and discontent. Viet Nam did not face such problems, but it was still embroiled in the old problems—writ large. Even limited openness had revealed the stagnation of the Vietnamese economy and the breakdown of administration. As in China and the Soviet Union, a relatively progressive leader was struggling with an obdurate bureau-cracy.

Nguyen Van Linh had been elected secretary general of the Labor Party in late 1986. At seventy-two, he was a comparative stripling, and he was also an innovator. He gave economic enterprises a little inde-pendence, and he encouraged the public and the press to speak out against abuses of power. Taking the lead himself, he published in *Nhan Dan* (*The People*), which is the organ of the Labor Party, a column entitled "Things That Must Be Done Immediately."

He exposed injustices and called for vigorous remedies. To charges that he was playing with dynamite, he replied, "I believe you have to triumph over darkness and remove the weeds so that the rice can grow!"

Most weeds have not been plucked out, but the darkness has re-ceded, if only a few feet. Linh's guarded candor led to emulation. A striking example was the letter from a student called Le Vinh Nguyen of Nha Trang, in the south, which was published in the youth paper *Tuoi Tre* in July 1988:

I have a feeling of being betrayed, and I want to know why. . . . We were told at liberation that we would build a richer country ten times more beautiful and prosperous than before. Why then are people so poor? Why do they not have enough to eat? Why are those who have passed their exams unable to get into university because their parents are not of the correct political persuasion?

Innocent people in Viet Nam can only appeal to heaven. In other countries, when mistakes are made, ministers accept re-sponsibility and resign. When will Viet Nam learn to do the same?

The government gloats about beating the Americans, but is unable even to organize filling the holes in our roads.

Curiously enough, that vehement letter of protest represented progress. The people had previously been too frightened to speak out. In response to First Secretary Nguyen Van Linh's appeal, they were now expressing their deepest feelings. Naturally, the leadership did not like what it heard. Yet the new openness, although circumscribed, was a start in arousing popular enthusiasm for reform.

Some Communists warned that it would all end in tears. The bureaucracy was suspicious of Linh's policies—and charged that he was encouraging dissidents. As revelations of the government's faults multiplied, the public would see clearly how grave was the country's plight. Outspokenness, conservatives warned, would intensify discontent and lead to passive resistance—or, worse, violent opposition.

Would anything be done? *Could* anything be done? What hope could there be for a nation of approximately 65 million, which was increasing so rapidly it would number more than 100 million by the year 2000? What could be done for a nation that was mired in nearly universal corruption and had lost the goodwill of almost the entire world?

Corruption in Viet Nam was far worse than the corruption in China that former Secretary General Zhao Ziyang had warned would cripple progress if not cut back. In Viet Nam, *anything* was possible for the man who had gold or greenbacks for bribes. Virtually nothing, not even minimal legal rights, was possible for the man who did not even have dong to bribe policemen and government clerks.

The Vietnamese have given up even the pretense of honesty, official or private, when a civil servant's monthly salary will buy just a bowl of soup at a street stall. Visitors shepherded in tour groups quickly become inured to the pleas of the beggars who have flocked to Hanoi to escape famine in neighboring provinces. Those tourists are surprised by the frankness with which their guides solicit tips for performing any unusual service—or even normal service.

"Everyone has his hand out all the time," a recent visitor remarked. "Not only in hotels, but in travel agencies, at airports and banks, even in police stations. I've never seen worse in five decades in Asia and the Middle East."

That testimony is supported by the redoubtable Nguyen Van Linh, who would assuredly succeed in rehabilitating his country if candor were all that mattered. In a speech in the south on Tet, the Lunar New Year Holiday, of 1988, he charged officials with: "being haughty toward the masses, repressing democracy, performing administrative work in a bureaucratic manner, receiving salaries for very little work . . . refusing to renovate [their] thinking . . . *committing theft and practicing corruption.* . . ."

Late in 1987 a department director in the Ministry of Agriculture had been fired for extorting money from his subordinates. That is, of course, the normal route that bribes take. The lower-level officials, who are in contact with the bribe-giving public, buy toleration and protection from their superiors by sharing the loot. But Hanoi cannot fire all its universally corrupt civil servants, for it would have no one left to carry out administration.

Tongues newly loosed, the public complains that the press attacks only lower-level officials for corruption. Even a department head is not a very big fish. To that criticism, Vo Van Kiet, who is a *very* high-level economic planner, replied, "Little people are always connected to big people. If we fight the corrupt small official, the high official will be shaken."

That specious rationale came from a leader of the reform movement. Mr. Kiet had been prime minister from March to June 1987, when the National Assembly met to confirm his appointment—and his broadly reformist policies. He was unexpectedly defeated by Do Muoi, a fellow member of the Politburo of the Labor Party, who also stands for reform, but *very* cautious reform.

Violent shaking is needed to bring down the big malefactors perched at the top of the tree. It was not the little people who sold 80 percent of the Soviet publications *New Times* and *Pravda* for pulping before distribution. Nor is it only the little people who operate bogus checkpoints that extort bribes and "taxes" from merchants, although official checkpoints were abolished in 1987. Viet Nam is ruled by fear and suspicion, as well as by corruption and greed. Some changes are, however, occurring. Some may do good, but some are suspect.

Advertising has come again to Viet Nam. But why should the Import-Export Corporation of Ho Chi Minh City (which everywhere but in official documents is called Saigon again) run an advertisement costing half a million dong in the Tet edition of *Saigon Liberation*? How many foreigners who are potential importers or potential buyers of exports read that newspaper in Vietnamese? Still, advertising's return must, I suppose, be classified as a good thing, since advertising presumably stimulates economic activity.

Will the consumer goods advertised, I wonder, actually be available within the discernible future? That depends almost as much on the temper of potential foreign investors and customers as it does on revamping the ramshackle, geriatric, war-oriented structure of the Labor Party.

Foreign participation is, inevitably, attracted primarily to exploit the cheap labor Viet Nam can still provide as faster-developing countries cannot. Samsung is assembling television sets in Saigon from kits shipped from South Korea. Honda canceled an agreement to assemble motorcycles in Viet Nam only after strong protests in the United States, whose antagonism is one of Hanoi's biggest problems. But others are coming in.

The new investment law is one of the most liberal in Asia. But prodigality on paper does not make up for the difficulty foreigners encounter with the bureaucracy, even in the south, but particularly in the north. The campaign to attract tourists and their foreign exchange, as well as investors, is also hampered by the shortage of facilities—hotel rooms, guides, and transport—that Khang Than Nhan remarked upon in the London embassy.

Nonetheless, Thai, British, and Australian firms have put their toes into the water—and found the temperature agreeable, as long as they do not plunge deep. Most activity is in the south, which is not only more prosperous, but remembers how to do business with the outside world.

Viet Nam is de facto two distinct realms fifteen years after reunification. The south not only produces more manufactured goods, but more rice. Saigon also sets the style for Viet Nam's yuppies, who are identifiable by their Lacoste T-shirts, jeans, wraparound sunglasses, and ghetto-blasters. The black market is thriving in Saigon, as it has for half a century.

The new policies had, moreover, done most to accelerate inflation. The dong, officially devalued in December 1987 from 80 to 368 for one U.S. dollar, was worth about 1,000 to the dollar in February 1988, 3,000 a couple of months later, and peaked at 6,000. Released to float, it found its level around 4,800, only a few points above the official 4,500 to the dollar. In 1988 prices were rising at about 800 percent annually for the fourth year, having gone up 300 percent in three months. In 1989, however, the rate of increase slowed a good deal. Rice shortages were created by bad weather and by lack of fertilizer, but chiefly by government policy and farmers' unwillingness to labor for low returns. The result was near-famine in a large part of the north.

Hanoi complained that international enmity had cut it off from trade and aid, and that U.S. bombing had destroyed much of the north's sparse industrial plant. That was a change from the days when Hanoi reported that U.S. bombs were aimed with remarkable accuracy almost exclusively at schools, orphanages, hospitals, and old people's homes. Neither that enmity nor that damage was, however, the cause of Viet Nam's enormous problems seventeen years after American forces withdrew. The chief cause was the autocratic, ill-conceived government policies that had broken the morale and the productive capability of a tough population, as war could not.

The bonds of ideology loosened a little, the bonds of bureaucracy hardly at all. Unable to feed itself, Viet Nam was loath to let others help. Senior officials would not declare frankly that Viet Nam's need was acute or offer reasonable estimates of its needs to international agencies. They would only state "minimum needs," lest they lose face. Traditional Vietnamese independence and self-reliance were not easily put aside, even when those virtues had become liabilities—not to say offenses against the suffering people.

The rice shortage, coupled with attempts to "stimulate the circulation of commodities by flexible pricing," was disastrous. The economic insight of a Milton Friedman or a John Kenneth Galbraith was not needed to foresee the resulting hyperinflation.

If sellers can fix their own prices, but the amount of goods for sale cannot be increased, prices are bound to soar. In theory, higher prices should bring more goods onto the market—and prices should then fall. That process, however, works only in a truly free market, not the one-quarter- or one-eighth-free market permitted by Hanoi. In any event, that reaction is not invariable and usually takes a while. Meanwhile, fifty housewives want the ten saucepans that are for sale. Since there is little else on which to spend their savings, they bid up the price to five times what the saucepans would cost if fifty were available.

In Viet Nam, rice is the true measure. A kilogram cost fifty dong in Hanoi at Tet in February 1987, but 600 dong at Tet in 1988. By midsummer it was 800 dong—and rising. In 1989 a slight improvement occurred. Rice was stabilized for a time at 600–700 dong a kilogram, and the annual rate of inflation was estimated at 400 percent—*only* 400 percent.

But the professional economist and former prime minister Vo Van Kiet declared forthrightly that, in addition to stagnant food production, soaring inflation, and acute shortages of consumer goods, Viet Nam also suffered from severe unemployment. Some unemployed had been diverted to military service in Cambodia or resettled there. Tens of thousands of Vietnamese worked as laborers in Soviet Siberia, actually receiving one-tenth of the low wages they earned. The rest of the money went to the state. But Hanoi was demobilizing the troops withdrawn from Cambodia—to swell the ranks of the unemployed.

Many Americans are still bitter about Viet Nam. Some may chuckle grimly and say the present predicament of the Vietnamese serves them right.

No matter how one feels about the Communist leadership, which has in any event altered greatly since the war, it certainly does not serve the Vietnamese people right. For almost forty years the people of the north have endured the caprices, the dogmatism, the bellicosity, and the stupefying incompetence of their leaders. For a decade and a half now, the people of the south have been tormented by the same aberrations.

Whatever the United States did in Viet Nam, it believed it fought to preserve the south from the repression, the injustice, the hardships, and the executions that have now afflicted the entire country. The present plight of the people of Viet Nam should awaken the compassion both of those who supported the war and those who opposed it.

I believe it is time the United States formally recognized the regime in Hanoi, rather than play out the charade that the former enemy does not exist, as it did with China for twenty-odd years. No more than it did then, does diplomatic recognition imply approval. It merely acknowledges that the regime exercises effective control over the territory it claims to rule.

In response to diplomatic recognition and economic assistance, the Vietnamese could be prepared to implement more effective economic policies and to play a more independent role in Asia. Hanoi is not happy at the rapprochement between Moscow and Beijing, which it feels is at its expense. While maintaining the more important Chinese tie, which is a little frayed after Tienanmen Square, Washington could play Hanoi off against Beijing, as Beijing now plays Moscow off against Washington. Hanoi could also demonstrate that it wants to be a normal member of the community of nations, rather than a rogue bull.

It is very important, perhaps crucial, to the future of the United States that it reinforce and enlarge its position in Asia. A new approach to Viet Nam of a quite different kind could lead a little closer to that goal.

Don Muang Airport, about twenty miles outside Bangkok, is the hub of a dense web of air routes, the jumping-off place for Europe, the Far East, and Australia. Moira and I therefore spent many hours there during our travels for this book. We also remembered the big wooden terminal where air conditioning was unknown and where we had sweated for hours on molasses-slow immigration lines in earlier years. Its replacement was already obsolescent, a concrete barn with yellow-shellacked plywood doors and sickly mauve curtains. That makeshift terminal, always overcrowded in the jet era, was in turn superseded by a comfortable, hypermodern terminal that is distinguishable only by its Thai motifs from a dozen comfortable, hypermodern terminals elsewhere.

The new airport was a showpiece of the jubilee year 1987, when the King of Thailand attained his sixtieth birthday. The enthusiastically royalist Thais celebrated his birthday, the most significant for all Asians, with splendid contributions to the favorite charities of King Bhumipol and Queen Sirikit, who are paragons of Buddhist benevolence. The devoutly practical Thais also celebrated by proclaiming 1987 the Year of Thai Tourism—and increasing by 14 percent, to 3.2 million, the number of their visitors.

Amid the splendors of the new Don Muang appeared portents of the equally modern, but much slower rise of feminism among the docile Thai women. Moira and I saw groups of women shouting and jeering at all-male tour groups.

Chiefly Japanese or German, those stag groups were all on the same business. Strenuously objecting to that business, the women protesters waved placards bearing such slogans as NO MORE SEX TOURS! GO HOME SEX TOURS! and THAI WOMEN PROTEST!

It was more likely that those brave women would be ostracized for their immodest, un-Thai behavior than that sex tours would be halted. The protesters stood about as much chance as would Saudi Arabian women who cast off their veils and demanded an end to the oil trade.

Tourism is a major industry in Thailand. In 1986 tourists spent $1.42 billion, which more than accounted for a favorable balance of payments of $1.278 billion. In 1987, the jubilee year, that figure was $1.92 billion, very comfortably Thailand's biggest source of foreign exchange. The Thais are, therefore, hardly likely to close down their single biggest tourist attraction—Bangkok's houses of pleasure. Was it not enough that they had two decades earlier outlawed the opium trade and padlocked the opium divans to placate foreigners' notions of morality?

Long before the era of the mass tourist, Bangkok was proud of its gilded brothels. Today, half a million young women are normally at work as prostitutes in order to send money to their families and to amass dowries. Most still come from the poor countryside, but many now come from country families drawn to Bangkok in hope of riches. Most Thais consider their temporary occupation as normal as young men's becoming Buddhist monks for a few years in order to purify their souls. Well-to-do families naturally keep their daughters at home, but they do not strongly condemn those who cannot. Prejudice is social, for prostitution is patently a lower-class occupation.

It took foreigners to show the Thais that prostitution was a very valuable asset, just as it took foreigners to promote drugs, extortion, and violence in Thailand's pleasure quarters. The catalysts were World War II; the Korean and Viet Nam wars, with the consequent American military buildup in Asia; and the advent of mass tourism. Thailand's genial sexual practices made it a favorite for troop "rest and recreation," and business has been brisk ever since.

The foreigners did not need to teach the Thais about commercial sex, only about mass-producing commercial sex. Asian men have long been accustomed to taking their pleasure outside the home. As in China and Japan, male social life has centered on Bangkok's better brothels, where gastronomy, music, dancing, and poetry enhance the chief diversion.

In 1954, when I first came to Bangkok, there was already a musky sexual tang in the air. The crew of the Military Air Transport Services DC-7 on which I had flown from Calcutta raced into civilian clothes after checking into a seedy hotel on New Road. Initially contemptuous of the over-refined Thai approach, foreigners have proved highly susceptible to the gentle deceits of the young women whose existence is devoted, albeit temporarily, to commercial catering to male whims.

Few Thais would allow themselves to become besotted with someone wonderful found in a brothel. One good courtesan was much like another, and sentimentality was expensive nonsense. It was different, however, when it came to foreign women.

Western-style nightclubs were few in Bangkok in those ancient days before the network of canals called *klangs* was covered with concrete playgrounds for automobiles. A market hardly existed. But Chez Eve on New Road drew full houses of local men in those ancient days when slender sampans plied the *klangs* laden with burnished tropical fruit and enormous flowers.

The great attraction was an American redhead with milky skin who performed what in those ancient days was known as "exotic dances." In those relatively innocent times before the American soldiery landed, that meant she took off most of her clothes in time to music and then gyrated a little. Quite carefully, too, not to say tastefully. But that was all.

The stripper had a wholesome Midwestern accent, and her name was Suzy or Bobbie or Jane. I can't remember which, but I shall never forget her professional name, which was Crazy Legs and Body Beautiful. Nor, I imagine, will the Thai men who sat around a dance floor slightly larger than a poker chip and slavered over her dancing with slack lips.

Nowadays, it's the other way around. All-male parties of beefy Europeans, shy Japanese breathing *sake* fumes, and flushed overseas Chinese fall eagerly on Thai women. Young Australian, European, and American women are, however, still available to well-to-do local men. Bangkok, like Tokyo, is also noted for its transvestite male prostitutes. Venus is, as ever, an equal-opportunity employer.

Romantics and travel writers are not drawn by the assembly-line massage parlors and the meat grinder dance halls of Patpong Road or by cookie-cutter resorts like Patthya, but by the fabled lure of the East. Yet Bangkok itself is a sordid shambles, a Chicago of brick-and-concrete boxes with a few dying palm trees and a massive traffic problem—the antithesis of a magical Oriental metropolis.

The city has been cranky and crass ever since the lacework of *klangs* was concreted over—and could no longer carry away accumulated filth or evil humors. Edgy self-assertion and open greed mar the men who run the nation and its businesses. They are often irritable and abrupt, as Thais are not supposed to be. Having safeguarded their independence for more than a century, they seem constantly tensed to repel the impositions of wily Europeans and brash Americans.

The tourists' impression is, however, quite different. Most tourists are delivered in batches like packaged sausages to simmer greasily in the sun at beach resorts or to be hungrily unwrapped by dainty whores. Some tourists do come to see the great Buddhist *wats*, or "temples," and the remarkable handicrafts. Those gentle souls encounter Thais who are gentle, helpful, and courteous. Those Thais are almost invariably underlings: waiters, drivers, sales clerks, doormen, and the like. Their charm is not feigned, but instilled by generations of stern training.

In old Siam, only servants were allowed to enter the presence of the king upon their knees, so that their hands would be free to carry trays. All others crawled before royalty. In old-fashioned households, servants still enter upon their knees.

Such bone-deep humility does not pass easily. The atmosphere often crackles with tension between the upper Thais and the lower Thais, who appear to belong to separate races. Actually, they do. From the royal family to the princes, tycoons, and generals who dominate finance and commerce, few among the elite do *not* possess some Chinese blood. Their servants mostly do not. But the masters still don't like to talk about it, although China is now respectable in the salons.

Field Marshal Pibul Songgram, the most successful of Thailand's modern military rulers, told me more than thirty years ago: "China is too big for comfort. It doesn't matter who rules—Communists, Nationalists, or mandarins—a strong China is bad for my country."

It is different now. China is a big friend that keeps the balance in Southeast Asia. On the parade grounds, Chinese tanks, artillery, and small arms are replacing American weaponry. They are good and solid and easy to maintain, not like the terribly complex American arms. And the price is right—very low with nothing down, interest-free, and ten years to pay.

For thriller writers the Thais offer both hyper-Byzantine intrigue and raw violence edged with contortionists' sex. In Bangkok an author can plausibly mix a cocktail that combines the self-conscious refinement of embassy receptions and young women performing unnatural feats with cigarettes, beer-bottle caps, bananas, and Ping-Pong balls. Stirred, not shaken, Mr. Bond.

In the north Thailand meets Burma and Laos to form the Golden Triangle, the refuge of drug barons, mercenaries, and gangsters. The residue of the Viet Nam War is highly visible, and former American soldiers have settled down with Thai wives. The only American military unit remaining is, however, thirty-odd soldiers who "push papers relating to old military aid," as an American diplomat put it.

Not only thriller writers are fascinated by this assertively independent nation. Since Joseph Conrad, who did not disdain the thriller, novelists have portrayed the Thais as subtle, wise, mystical, devious, and complex—in sum, quintessential Asians.

Perhaps the Thai elite were once like that. They are no longer. Upper-class Thais are today straightforward, outspoken, volatile, gullible, and avaricious. They are also quick-tempered, impatient, irritable, and insecure.

Geographically at the center of Southeast Asia's conflicting pressures, the Thais are also poised between two antithetical cultures. On one side, Theraveda Buddhism inclines them to otherworldliness, but also from time to time incites the violence it decries—and fosters a logic that just does not work by linear Western standards. On the other side, the Thais' Chinese-related language and partially Chinese ancestry make them worldly and pragmatic. Thai painting and drama are essentially Indian, yet Thai images of the Buddha look more Chinese than Indian.

The Thais are a gentle people who invented Thai boxing, in which opponents use their feet, their heads, and their elbows everything except knives. They are violent with finesse. Criminals condemned to death by submachine-gun fire are placed behind a curtain, so that their executioners fire at silhouettes. The founder of the present dynasty, King Taksin, a Chinese who brought to Thailand many of his compatriots from Swatow, was killed by conspirators. They put him into a velvet bag and beat him to death with clubs, since it was forbidden to shed the royal blood. The Thais have also been known to put a condemned man into a big, openwork bamboo ball—and give it to the elephants to play with.

Thus was preserved the shell of the useful fiction that good Buddhists do not shed blood. The Bangkok slaughterhouse is manned by Catholic refugees from Viet Nam, who live with their families in wooden huts tied to the rafters a dozen feet above the killing pens. The Vietnamese do not necessarily like their lifestyle or their work, but Catholicism does not forbid slaughtering animals. Afterward, the Buddhist Thais do delicious things with the pork and beef the slaughterhouse provides.

The blending of violence and restraint distinguished the classic Thai coup d'etat. Agreement on the limits was instinctive, based upon the inherent moral, religious, and social beliefs held by all Thais, from the king to the street sweeper.

The coup of autumn 1957 was completely under control after a few hours. There were tanks in the street, and one soldier had been killed while cleaning his rifle. There were no other casualties. A ground hostess set the tone when she greeted me on the tarmac with the cheerful question, "Have you come to see our coup?"

The decision makers had decided it was time for Field Marshal Pibul Songgram to make his exit. The next general was ready to take the stage, applauded by the army, which was the final decision maker.

The prime minister had had his turn, a long one, and he had made his fortune, a surprisingly modest one. The slight, white-haired strongman, as foreign correspondents usually described him, did not oppose his subordinates' decision. Having already sent his family to the United States, he departed gracefully, full of years and honor.

His chief henchman, General Pow, who stood well over six feet and was appropriately bulky, spent a day or two resisting the inevitable at his big desk, which was flanked by two life-sized window-dresser's dummies in smart police uniforms. General Pow commanded the police force, which controlled Thailand's daily life—as far as anyone could control a country with poor roads and bad communications. He had, however, controlled most efficiently the opium traffic—amassing a fortune much larger than his prime minister's. General Pow finally left with his fortune intact. That was part of the deal.

Splendid public entertainment, the Thai coup d'etat was neither a manifestation of weakness nor a comic opera; it was simply the normal way to transfer power, ensuring the orderly succession of one prime minister by another. The coup d'etat remained a normal part of the political process until the young king consolidated his enormous personal authority, which today knits even closer a society already strongly knit. Prime Minister Chatichai Choonhavan, who was in office in 1989, had actually come to power through an election. But he was the first prime minister to do so since 1976.

King Bhumipol, who, like Prince Norodom Sihanouk, used to play good jazz saxophone, is a constitutional monarch with limited powers. Unassuming for a royal prince who was brought up amid servants walking on their knees, he did fire one American ambassador. The king might have excused the ambassador's lecturing him at a small dinner for the courtiers and ambassadors who were accompanying him on a tour of the northwest, but he could not excuse the ambassador's shaking an admonitory forefinger at him.

Pote Sarasin, who also possesses inherent dignity and authority, was secretary general in 1966 when the Southeast Asia Treaty Organization held its annual meeting in Bangkok. SEATO was under stress. The European allies, Britain and France, would not support American policy in Indo-China, although the Asian allies did.

When I chatted with Mr. Sarasin, he felt the United States was pushing its allies around. His dignity was offended—as a man, as a very senior official, and as a Thai.

He gave me a lift in his official car, which flew the SEATO flag. Sirens sounded, and an imperious motorcycle outrider waved us to a halt. A big American car flying a four-star flag swept by carrying Admiral Harry Felt, U.S. commander-in-chief, Pacific. Mr. Sarasin said only: "You see?"

A few years later, when Pote Sarasin was, I believe, minister for economic planning, I arrived five minutes late for an appointment.

Bangkok's traffic had grown even more chaotic. Instead of the coat and tie I normally wore to see Thai ministers, I was wearing a bush jacket to go upcountry.

Mr. Sarasin was icy. I had affronted his dignity, first by being a few minutes late and again by being informally dressed. After calling my attention to my lapses, he discussed his new responsibilities. But we were, thereafter, no longer confidants. Nowadays, many Thai ministers receive in shirts with rounded Nehru collars, a style set by a later prime minister. But their dignity is just as easily affronted.

Foreign Minister Thanat Khoman was equally dignified—and even more prickly and outspoken. He was also usually right, which is not always true of foreign ministers. In the bar of the Caravelle Hotel in Saigon he offered a tart Asian view of America, a *sympathetic* Asian view.

"You Americans think you're supermen." He was irritated with inconclusive negotiations about new weapons for the Thai military. "You think only an American can fly a Phantom fighter bomber. So you offer us little Freedom Fighters, when we need Phantoms. Sometimes it seems you think only an American can use an M-16 rifle."

He fixed me with a gleaming black eye, as if I personified the vanity against which he inveighed

"Someday . . . someday soon," he warned, "you Americans are going to wake up. You're going to learn that a Thai . . . an Asian . . . can use a rifle just as well . . . and fly a Phantom just as well as or better than an American."

That, I feel, was fair comment, particularly in the light of later events in Saigon. American assumptions of superiority and American impatience have long been major irritants to Asians. Whether ambassadors or privates first-class, Americans have too often confused technical competence with wisdom. A dash of racism has tinged their attitude, whether they swore at the "gooks" or condescendingly praised Asian virtues.

Much has changed. Amid spectacular demonstrations of Asian technical competence, no intelligent Westerner should feel technologically or culturally superior. But such prejudice dies very hard, and the Thais are very prickly.

When I was last in Thailand, the conflict no longer concerned fighter bombers, but archeological objects and rice. Thai newspapers were screaming about a lintel from an ancient temple that had been shipped to the United States. They had a point, a good nationalistic point, but they expended extraordinary righteous indignation over a minor issue.

Rice is a major issue. The Thais, who are rice exporters, feel the U.S. is competing unfairly by enacting laws that discriminate against Thai rice and promote sales of American rice.

"These things do blow over," an American with long experience in Thailand pointed out. "But one thing doesn't: the Thais feel we're only interested in the bottom line nowadays. They no longer consider us number one. Instead they look at the U.S. as a super-bookkeeper or a moneylender who is only interested in dollars."

Nonetheless, the United States is still *the* country that is most important to Thailand. Japan, of course, is second.

"Most Thais would rather go to the U.S. to study than anywhere else," the American added. "About ten thousand Thais are usually studying at American colleges and universities at any given time. Families like to maintain a link with the U.S. A son or a daughter will stay on. . . . There is still a general consciousness of America's importance. And an American accent still carries authority."

It is only natural to criticize Number One. In Thailand, as elsewhere in Asia, intellectuals attack American popular culture, but can't get enough of "Dallas" and "Dynasty." *Rambo* also plays very well. The U.S. is still foremost in the minds of the decision makers. Perhaps the time to worry will be when the U.S. is no longer the universal scapegoat. Still, it would be nice to be approved of occasionally.

Assuredly, Thai students will from time to time continue to demonstrate against the U.S.—as they did in 1975, just after the collapse in Indo-China. I chatted with those demonstrators between their choruses of anti-American slogans. They were demanding that the U.S. remove its armed forces from Thailand immediately. They were also angry because the U.S. had pulled its forces out of Indo-China three years earlier—and had thus put Thailand in the front line against Hanoi. Thais are much like anyone else, only more convoluted.

I may have seen less of the Thais than I have of the other peoples of East Asia. Still, I have been crisscrossing their country since 1954: by train from the southern border with Malaysia, where the Thai Moslem problem resides and the Malayan Communist insurgents long found refuge; from Bangkok at the center by road to Vientiane in Laos; and by road and train to Chiangmai in the northwest, where the hill tribes lovingly tended acres of their undulating opium poppies.

I find parts of Thailand hard to recognize today. Jet-propelled tourism has greatly altered even remote places like Haadyai in the extreme south on the Malaysian border and Chiangmai in the extreme north in the salient between Laos and Burma.

The area around Haadyai has always been formidably remote. In 1941 Japanese invasion troops landed on the beaches that extend across the Malay-Thai border on the east coast near Haadyai. Only several days later did the Malay states know they had been invaded.

In 1954, when I first saw Haadyai, there were two hotels: the Railway and another whose name I can't recall. I stayed at the Railway. It was supposed to be better, although it was only a row of creaky-doored, damp-splotched bedrooms with ceiling fans that had long ago given up. At last count, Haadyai had twenty-four hotels, including a totally new Railway Hotel. Gambling and girls now draw tourists from all over Asia, as well as Europe and America.

That is Thai freedom. The Thais don't care what you do, as long as you don't tread on their sensibilities and you don't hurt anyone except yourself. It is also advisable to smile while you do it.

Chiangmai, in the northwest, lures visitors with seventeen major *wats*, as well as casinos and nightclubs. Secure in its dignity, Chiangmai remembers when elephants piled teak for generation after generation of Chinese and British timber merchants.

In 1966 the Thais opened a radio station in Chiangmai to broadcast in the languages of the hill tribes, the people of the mountain range that reaches southeast from the Himalayas to the South China Sea. With Mike Brown of the U.S. Information Service, which financed the station, I stayed at the Rincome, then one of three reasonable hotels. We went into the hills to talk with the hill tribes. Their chiefs welcomed the new station—and explained why it would be impossible for their people ever to give up their opium crop.

As it was then, Chiangmai is today an imposing city. The air is fresher than it is in the plains, and great vistas lie at one's feet. It now boasts more than fifteen hotels, and the opium poppies no longer dance in the hills. They have been displaced by food crops, which do not necessarily make the tribespeople happier.

The Thai government is phasing out the hill tribes station since there is no longer any need for its broadcasts in tribal languages. The former audience is now happily watching television in Thai, which they are also learning to read and write.

Despite the march of education, Thailand is still really two countries: Bangkok and the rest. Except for Bangkok-style enclaves in tourist resorts, the capital and the countryside exist in different aspects of time.

Bangkok, with its 8.5 million inhabitants, is virtually an NIC, a Newly Industrialized Country. Almost all new industry is concentrated around the capital. Per capita income in 1989 was more than $2,200 in Bangkok—and $820 in the countryside. Allowing for the concentration of great fortunes in the capital, that disproportion is not only extraordinary, but potentially disruptive.

Driving toward Bangkok at night is an eerie transition. Your car rolls through darkened little towns on roads where you see only a dozen other motor vehicles for a hundred miles. Your headlights bore long tunnels into the night, and, when you stop to stretch your legs, the only sounds are the lowing of water buffaloes and the swishing of bicycle tires.

Bangkok is first visible as a faint glow on the horizon. That distant glimmer, like a single street light, brightens and extends across the horizon. Brilliance suddenly embraces your car, which is engulfed by traffic pouring from side roads and rushing up ramps. Gaudily lit factories and restaurants rise beside the highway, and a bass roar, lanced by petulant soprano horns, pounds on your ear drums.

Toward the center, Bangkok is high-rises crowned with bright advertising signs. Bangkok is automobiles and trucks, their engines revving impatiently, waiting at six-lane intersections for the green lights. Bangkok is a gargantuan, rhythmic aspiration, as if the city itself were sighing.

In the countryside, towns of two-story wooden buildings under rusty corrugated-iron roofs spread awnings against sun and rain over rudimentary sidewalks. Pickup trucks furred with the dust of the backroads haul manufactured goods to those towns. Farm produce is as often carried in pedal trishaws or slung over the back fenders of bicycles. Replacing the back wheel of a powerful motorcycle with a two-wheeled cart is nowadays creating a very convenient, very fast, very dangerous motor rickshaw.

The pushcart markets under temporary canvas canopies in country towns are a long way from the rhinestone glitter of Bangkok. Yet the countryside is not poor, except by the new standards of the metropolis. It has changed significantly from the recent past, although not radically. Roads are better maintained; markets are better stocked; many houses have new tile roofs; and open-fronted shops, most Chinese-run, offer good food and a range of goods. Nonetheless, the hinterland is the old countryside of familiar Southeast Asia—and Bangkok is the new Asia.

"The rest of the country is coming along very fast," Australian Ambassador Dick Smith pointed out. "And the infrastructure is in place even in the northeast, the poorest section with the biggest problems. The Thais stress the problems, and the foreigners stress the progress. A typical Thai village now means substantial houses, pickups, iron buffaloes [small tractors steered with handlebars], a paved main road, TV antennas, and a primary school, maybe a secondary school."

Nonetheless, the metropolis lures the country folk. I spoke with a taxi driver who recently came from the north, where he was earning 1,000 *baht* a month, to the capital, where he now earns 2,000 to 3,000 *baht*. Those earnings are not much better than in the Philippines. But for him the increase from forty dollars to $120 was enormous. Spending no more than 15 baht (sixty cents) for a meal at a roadside stall and sleeping in a dormitory, he sends most of his earnings home for his wife and two children. And he is happy, for prosperity is obviously relative.

Amid that prosperity, the rate of population increase has dropped sharply. The explosion that was feared has been held off, perhaps eliminated. A population of about 56 million does not overburden the resources of a country a shade smaller than France. Frank advertising for condoms—and other contraceptive devices—helped bring down the population growth from 3.2 percent to, say, 1.8 percent in just fifteen years. The advertising was placed by Michai, the Condom King, who makes a nice profit on that public service.

Under the pressure of progress, the outlawed Communist Party of Thailand, which had never been a star in the revolutionary league, perished quietly in the mid-1980s. The party used to run a brisk little insurrection in the poor northeast, which is handy to Communist-ruled Laos and China.

For decades Beijing sponsored a Thai government in exile, led by a former prime minister who made fiery statements on the Voice of Thailand, which broadcast from south China. But the Chinese withdrew their sponsorship in 1979, when the Vietnamese invasion of Cambodia coincided with Beijing's New Economic Policy. The former prime minister died in 1987, but even before his death, the Central Committee of the Communist Party of Thailand was being captured or was surrendering. Finally there were no more Communist leaders— and the show ended.

Everywhere in Asia U.S. influence is waning and Japan is next in line. Since Thailand nurtures no bitter memories of the war, it was the first country in Southeast Asia where Japanese goods and Japanese companies became highly visible. In the early 1960s, I began to see big Honda, Suzuki, and Sony billboards when riding in from the airport. Because Thailand was favorably inclined toward the Japanese and needed Japanese investment, Thai-Japanese cooperation appeared an ideal match.

So it has proved, but the road has not been smooth. The Thais were in the beginning, as always, prickly, and the Japanese had not yet learned even as much as they now know about getting on with other people. The Ugly Japanese were highly visible in Bangkok very early. Living in their own enclaves, educating their children in their own schools, the Japanese community, which was then about three thousand and is now twelve thousand, early bought its own golf courses. Such exclusivity, now common elsewhere, was just as well, since the Japanese have a tendency to drive—or walk—over other players. Still, Bangkok is not an easy post for a Japanese ambassador. There are always new irritants.

With the fanfare befitting such generosity, Japan in 1987 presented to Thailand a beautiful new Cultural Center at a cost of $45 million. Lavishly, indeed opulently equipped, it provides a separate rehearsal stage; a theater in the round with seats folding into the walls; and sophisticated machinery that can move, twist, and turn the main stage—indeed make it do everything but fly.

"The Cultural Center," an Asian businessman told me, "became the greatest white elephant in Thai history. Remember, the Thais invented the white elephant. The Thais want the Japanese to pay for running the Center. They would also like the Japanese to teach their technicians to operate the complex machinery. They would be even more grateful if the Japanese could tell them how to fill its two thousand seats for even a few performances."

The Thais bitterly resent being patronized, and the Japanese can be very clumsy as well as very arrogant. Hundreds of Thais picketed the Japanese Embassy in 1987 to protest the spectacular mishandling of their crown prince's state visit on the hundredth anniversary of diplomatic relations between Japan and Siam.

The visit was like a slapstick farce: it featured bungled invitations; the Australian-educated crown prince's insistence upon taking along his second wife as well as his first wife; the king's continuing annoyance at his son, who has not concealed his impatience to take the throne; a Japanese driver relieving himself against the prince's car; the prince's return from Japan two days before the visit's scheduled end; and a formal apology from the Japanese prime minister.

The visit also provided copious material for editorials, for demonstrations, and for gossip in Bangkok salons. It did not help relations between two Asian countries, both of which are sensitive, protocol-conscious, and proud.

More seriously, Thailand is very attractive to the Japanese because of its geographical location, its cheap labor, and its flexibility—and the Japanese must put their surplus money somewhere. The Thais are glad to have the money, although they complain, like all Asians, that Japan hardly ever parts with advanced technology. Increased investment, led by Japan, has powered an increase in growth from a respectable 7 percent in 1987, to 9 percent in 1989.

Japan's growing power, and its movement toward domination of Southeast Asia, however, set off an automatic reflex. Thais instinctively maneuver to balance Japan against other nations, although the Japanese like to manipulate others, not to be manipulated themselves. Having factored the Japanese into the power equation, the Thais will try to play them off against the Americans, the Chinese, the Russians, and their own neighbors.

Nor was Indo-China neglected. In mid-1989 the Thais were seeking much closer ties with Hanoi and the Vietnamese-sponsored government in Phnom Penh, in hope of creating a "golden peninsula" with its de facto capital at Bangkok and its currency Thai *baht*. After all, the Thai people have survived as an independent and sovereign nation by alternately allying themselves and breaking with their neighbors.

If anyone can contain the Japanese by diplomacy, it is the Thais. But I wonder whether anyone can contain the Japanese indefinitely.

22

The Twenty-First: Asia's Century?

WILL THE IMPLACABLE ASIAN DRIVE TOWARD GLOBAL ECONOMIC
HEGEMONY LED BY JAPAN REDUCE OTHER NATIONS TO TRIBUTARIES
IN THE NEXT CENTURY? CAN JAPAN BE INDUCED TO REALIZE THAT
ITS HEADLONG CHARGE, NEVER LOOKING ASIDE, WILL IN THE LONG
TERM INJURE ITSELF AS WELL AS OTHERS? CAN THE WEST, LED BY
THE UNITED STATES, RECOUP? WITH A FEW SUGGESTIONS TO AVERT
A POTENTIALLY CATASTROPHIC INBALANCE IN THE WORLD.

Racial contempt and cultural arrogance have distorted the mutual perception of the Occident and the Orient since the first encounters between those two great divisions of mankind. Occidental arrogance has generally been more apparent, although the first Jesuit visitors acknowledged that sixteenth-century China was materially and politically far in advance of Europe. Perhaps less assertive until quite recently, the Orient's conviction of superiority is ingrained and profound. Many Asians have regarded Westerners as useful, insofar as they are adept at mechanical things and ignorant of the true values of civilization and culture.

Since the West was long dominant materially, Westerners assumed that they were vastly superior. Even professional observers like diplomats and journalists were, therefore, isolated from the realities of Asia as if by plate glass that distorted what they saw and garbled what they heard. From the early nineteenth century until the last decades of the twentieth, Westerners were on the scene, but not in the scene. They might be touched by the sorrows and joys of Asians, but they could not imagine that their own lives might be vitally affected by those alien dramas.

Such condescension is no longer possible as the twenty-first century draws close. In the West, the commercial and industrial feats of East Asia are engendering a feeling of inferiority that is almost as misleading as the previous feeling of superiority. Above all, Japanese arrogance, springing from Japanese competence, makes Asia's domination appear inevitable—and destined to sweep the world in the next century.

Yet only change is inevitable, not its direction. And the nations of Asia were changing rapidly at the beginning of the 1990s.

Weaknesses behind Japan's power were revealed by the dissatisfaction its politicians encountered at home and the opprobrium its tactics aroused abroad. Korea's government, still instinctively authoritarian beneath its democratic regalia, was struggling to contain the popular discontent that had already slowed and could in time sidetrack the miracle. Although China's sheer mass made her vitally important, China was again a mess, volatile politically and unstable economically. Taiwan's attainments were great, but their social foundations were fragile. Hong Kong might well dry up as her people fled, becoming a husk even before Beijing took over in 1997. And Singapore was particularly vulnerable to the storms that periodically sweep the international marketplace because it had built high but had little depth.

In the autumn of 1989, while mergers were consolidating Japan's primacy in world banking, the political monopoly of the Liberal Democratic Party, which had endured for three and a half decades, was being challenged by feminists, consumers, and moral reformers. Although unlikely to alter the essential Japan, that improbable alliance was driving from power some of the men who had directed—and exploited—Japan's rise to international economic hegemony.

Until June 4, 1989, the People's Republic of China had appeared to be committed to at least enough intellectual and political liberalization to foster industrial and commercial growth. But the massacre in Tienanmen Square demonstrated that the aged leaders of an arthritic Communist Party valued their privileges and their preconceptions much more highly than they did economic development. Totalitarian repression was spreading—and inhibiting progress.

Nonetheless, many Chinese had learned the lesson their ancestors—and their present rulers—resisted: *Individual enterprise cannot flourish without substantial freedom to innovate and to communicate new discoveries.* And *all* Chinese were eager for the material benefits that could only be produced by individual entrepreneurs.

China was, therefore, likely to change more rapidly than anyone could imagine in early 1990. Maoism would not reappear any more than would the Confucian empire. Instead, the gerontocracy would pass— and not simply because of its great age. A few bone-stubborn old men were defying the consensus of a people who were extraordinarily patient, but not eternally patient. The massacre in Tienanmen Square and the vicious repression that followed may well have been the last gasp of traditional China. The Chinese revolution might finally be approach-

ing success—and the welfare of the people might for the first time in
centuries soon be a primary concern of their rulers. It had already come
about that, for the first time in forty years, organized opposition to
Communist rule was active in China and abroad.

That did *not* mean that China would soon—or, perhaps, ever—be a
liberal representative democracy. It did *not* mean that China would
cease to be highly bureaucratic. It *did* mean that the rulers in Beijing
would in time revert to the sensible practices of their Confucian predecessors. Strict laws might remain on the books, and intellectual
orthodoxy might be officially ordained. But whatever government ruled
would have learned not to interfere so closely with the daily life of the
people as to impede their productivity.

In different guises and degree, authoritarianism would prevail not
only in China but throughout Asia. Yet the characteristic that made
neo-Confucian states so formidable in the late-industrial twentieth
century ensured that they would in time decay as had their Confucian
predecessors. The ability to direct all human endeavors toward a single
goal made for tactical adaptability, but strategic inflexibility. Spectacular efficiency was attained—but only by sacrificing the general welfare
and retarding the evolution of social and political institutions.

Although change was inevitable, Westerners who hailed the inevitable advent of liberal bourgeois institutions in East Asia exemplified
the triumph of hope over experience—and over history. Representative
multi-party democracy was an essentially Western growth that would
not take root in Asia. Modification of Japan's plutocracy or South Korea's
oligarchy was *not* the prelude to popular rule. The decay of the bureaucratic and repressive Marxist-Leninist state in China no more
presaged liberal democracy than it did laissez-faire capitalism.

Certain aspects of Asia had altered sharply as the last decade of the
twentieth century began—as had Asia's place in the world. The fundamental conditions and the rooted attitudes that had for centuries
shaped the relations of Orient and Occident were radically different.

The Western relationship with Asia, particularly the American relationship, had from 1950 to 1980 been shaped by the crusade against
communism. The era of the dissolution of colonialism that followed
World War II had shaded into the era of the containment of communism. Yet the struggle against expansionist Marxism-Leninism had
petered out in the 1980s with a kind of victory as the great Communist
powers, China and the Soviet Union, divested themselves of much of
the trappings and the shackles of ideology. In 1990, the challenges
posed by China and the Soviet Union could no longer be characterized
as primarily ideological. The challenge of Japan had, of course, never
been ideological.

Even the Philippines, impoverished amid Asian prosperity, was in 1990 facing anarchy rather than conquest by its Marxist-Leninist insurgents. Plagued by the "Filipino factor," the Communists were losing their coherence, corrupted by the corrupt society they fought. President Corazon Aquino had, for her part, lost much support, as well as whatever resolution she had once possessed.

Clearly, the threats Asia faced and the opportunities it offered were markedly more complex than the West's. Asia was highly diverse, its individual countries markedly different in religion, culture, language, and manner of government. By comparison, the countries of Europe were in such fundamental aspects rather alike, their problems and hopes, therefore, relatively straightforward.

For policy makers the diverse problems of Asia could, however, conveniently—if somewhat arbitrarily—be divided into two major categories. The first was threats arising *within*, that is normal internal problems of a region or a country. The second was threats arising from *outside* intervention, whether by Asians or by outsiders. Those interventionist forces were primarily China, the Soviet Union, and Japan— with the United States now cast chiefly as an umpire.

The first necessity for the well-being of Asia was to provide security and to maintain stability among volatile and ambitious nations, some of which would soon possess nuclear capability. Certain regional and national problems would not be reconciled in our time. Among them were: racial tensions, particularly resentment of the overseas Chinese by other Asians; antagonism between neighbors like Viet Nam and Cambodia or Malaysia and Singapore; and economic friction as countries were transformed from primary producers of raw materials to manufacturers.

Although Asian nations were striving to diversify both their products and their markets, development was rendering many of their economies rather alike. That sameness did not encourage the growth of a harmonious Asian economic community like the European Common Market. Besides, friction among European nations has been buffered by their common Christianity, their common Graeco-Roman cultural heritage, and their common membership in the Indo-European language family. Asia possesses neither a common religion nor a common culture—but a half-dozen different language families. It has no common language except English.

At the beginning of the 1990s, China's role was the most problematical. Because of her size and her potential power she was a key factor in the equation. All other Asians were watching intently—and nervously—to see which road the Chinese would finally take. As Prime Minister Lee Kuan Yew of Singapore pointed out, a stable and forward-looking China was essential to long-term peace and prosperity in the

region. Most Asians did not primarily fear action by the bumbling
People's Liberation Army, but the incalculable changes occurring as a
consequence of the Tienanmen Square massacre. China's recently won
reputation for reasonableness had been badly compromised, and it
appeared that she might abruptly alter her foreign policy, as she had her
domestic policies.

Renewed collaboration between China and the Soviet Union was,
however, not a major fear. After all, the ideological element in Soviet
foreign policy had declined markedly. That decline did not necessarily
mean the Soviet Union was now substantially less of a threat in the
Asia-Pacific region. It could, indeed, mean the opposite. The Soviet
Union's pursuit of its national interests was, perhaps, no longer as
greatly facilitated by local Communist groups. On the other hand, the
requirements of local Communist groups no longer impeded that pursuit.

Neither *glasnost* nor *perestroika* had meant a reduction in Soviet
military power in Asia and the Pacific. The Soviet Navy had never been
stronger in that region than it was at the beginning of the 1990s, while
Soviet intelligence and diplomatic activities were constantly expanding.
The Soviets undeniably had legitimate interests in the region. But that
legitimacy did not mean that the Soviets' pursuit of their interests was
now less antagonistic to the interests of other nations.

Reacting to the Mongol challenge, Russia has been expanding eastward since the fourteenth century. Marxism-Leninism has in this century been an instrument of Soviet expansionism rather than its primary
cause. In the next century, Russia will continue to expand, albeit
nonideologically.

Yet Soviet overtures to Japan have generally proved ineffective. A
common interest in, say, developing Siberia may lead to some Russo-
Japanese cooperation. But the two powers have been rivals too long.
Mutual suspicion remains too strong to permit extensive cooperation.
After all, Japan fought the Battle of the Tsushima Straits in 1905 to block
Russian expansion, as well as to accelerate Japanese expansion. The
Soviet Union, which was only yesterday the biggest military/political
problem in the world for the West, as well as many other nations, is not
likely to make common cause with Japan, which is *now* the biggest
political/economic problem in the world for *all* other nations—and
could tomorrow be a military problem as well.

During the past five years, as much has been written abroad about
Japan as about the Soviet Union. That abundance is a remarkable
tribute to Japan's rocketlike rise to preeminence. Russia, essentially a
European power, has attracted scholars and aficionados for centuries,
while Japan, a reclusive Asian state, has attracted serious attention for

less than a century. A thriving industry has during most of this century worked the Soviet Union, giving gainful employment to economists, theoreticians, journalists, and many varieties of historians. The Japanologists, although augmented by World War II, have never approached the Kremlinologists in number.

Yet their production has been phenomenal, as has been their service in giving the West easy access to incisive knowledge of Japan. Yet their advice has often led the West, particularly the U.S., to accommodate Japan when Western interests would have benefited from a less yielding position.

The Japanese have long paid far more attention to the West, particularly the United States, than the West has paid them. They *had* to, for their fate lay in the hands of the West, particularly the United States, as it still does. Despite sharp insights, popular Japanese writing about the U.S. has generally been favorable when it was not ideologically motivated.

Yet Japanese are today bashing America even more energetically than Americans are bashing Japan. Both America-bashing and Japan-bashing are prime growth industries, catering to injured feelings and threatened interests. Americans are shocked to learn that Japan, the good little ally for which they felt condescending affection, is marching toward worldwide hegemony regardless of American interests. Japanese are equally shocked to learn that the United States, the big bumbling ally they both admire and disdain, will no longer invariably act as they wish.

Nonetheless, the interests of the two countries are tortuously intertwined—even when they are antagonistic, as they are more and more. Japan is routing out American firms as it transforms the British Isles into the offshore base for its assault on the European Common Market. Taiwan, once the island base for Japan's assault on Southeast Asia, later attracted Japanese industrialists with its cheap labor. Britain, which now attracts Japanese industrialists with cheap labor, is becoming the island base for Japan's assault on the European Common Market.

Unless other nations act decisively, Japan's search for cheap labor, new markets, and homes for its surplus capital will not stop until it has exhausted most of the world's human and natural resources. Japan is not deterred by the ecological disasters that result from its despoiling the world's oceans and forests. Nor is Japan deterred by the extremely high toll its compulsive expansion imposes on its own people, as well as outsiders. Neither principles nor premonitions of a dolorous future deter Japan. Charging head-down toward their goal, the ruthlessly pragmatic Japanese see only what lies directly ahead.

Only a tremendous shock, perhaps only a disaster like a worldwide depression, can turn them aside. Unlike the United States when it was Number One, Japan will not become a prisoner of its own success. Japan will not fling away its patrimony to assist others or to buy a life of self-indulgence for its people. A new international aid program approaching $50 billion is designed to help recipients a little in such a way as to help Japan a lot. The Japanese, as they themselves declare, are now "economic animals"—and self-interest is their lodestar.

Unless the rules of engagement are altered sharply, Japan will continue its present strategy. The resulting economic and political imbalance will be spectacular, will reach throughout the world, and will cause widespread suffering. As a consequence, most nations will either be subservient to Japan, betrayed by their own greed, or they will be overwhelmed.

I am, candidly, not sure that Japan *can* be stopped short of disaster. But, if there is to be any hope of turning Japan aside, other nations must take heroic measures now.

They should first recognize that Japan is neither invincible nor self-sufficient, but as dependent upon them as they are upon it. True, if Japanese financial houses refused to deal in American Treasury bonds, the precarious U.S. economy would totter, perhaps collapse. But any sharp reduction of American purchases of Japanese goods, not to speak of withdrawal of American military forces, would produce shocks at least as galvanic in Japan. Diversification of its markets will in time make Japan's dependence upon the U.S. less acute, but not just yet. Japan is, further, dependent upon the U.S. military for stability in Asia and elsewhere, as well as for protection from the Soviet Union. Washington may no longer view the international Communist conspiracy as a major threat. Nonetheless, Japan still looks apprehensively at the aggressive Russian bear, which still occupies islands in the north of the archipelago.

Because the Japanese are acutely aware of their weaknesses and their vulnerability they can be brought to reconsider their headlong charge— but only by nations that are themselves strong. With the exception of Britain, the European Community has recognized the inherent threat. West European nations do not bow down to free trade as to a holy icon. Even if they did, they would not grant free entry to the products of a country that practices highly restrictive import policies.

The United States, too, must recognize that free trade is not free trade unless it works both ways. The U.S. must also forego some of its enjoyment of very reasonable and very good Japanese products in order to produce for itself again. A major effort by a consortium backed by the government must regain American primacy in electronic chips and computers—or, at least, attain parity. Then the U.S. could begin to compete effectively with Japan. But this would require massive retooling every two to three years, something that is anathema to American corporations fixated on short-term returns and goals. The real profits, the real, though momentary, victory, comes in the next "generation"— and a generation in electronics is only a few years long, but requires decisions that are made in a time frame that embraces the millennium and beyond.

The United States must also recognize that its support of the Liberal Democratic Party at almost any cost is no longer useful. With the fading away of the ideological element in American foreign policy, that is, fear of the international Communist conspiracy, it is no longer necessary to sustain the conservative LDP. If other parties came to power and removed part of America's responsibility for the security of the Japanese archipelago by taking back bases, that might be all to the good. America has infrequently benefited economically from its troop dispositions abroad, but could benefit substantially by pulling back a little.

Can the U.S. alter its policies so substantially? Can it turn Japan aside?

I have briefly cited some essential measures that will, at the very least, be extremely difficult to effect. Those measures all depend upon the West, particularly the U.S., regaining its former vigor and dash. But empires are like Humpty Dumpty. Few empires have clambered back after falling, regardless of whether they were empires of self-aggrandizement or, like the American empire that endured from 1945 to 1975, they were devoted largely to discharging responsibilities.

Yet only the U.S. can bring Japan to reexamine its basic concepts— and, thus, perhaps to alter its strategy. The U.S. is still esteemed in Japan, and American views are still respected. Only the U.S. can have any hope of persuading the Japanese that they are hurting themselves and their descendants by their unceasing expansion.

A few Japanese leaders already see that destroying the environment and shredding the world economic system must in time severely injure Japan's own interests. Once a majority of Japan's leaders were so convinced, radical change would occur very rapidly, for the Japanese people remain highly flexible—and highly responsive to authority.

The United States of all nations could best undertake that task because of the strong moral and cultural authority it still exercises throughout Asia. I am not referring primarily to the great economic power the U.S. still possesses even in its apparent decline. The U.S. is also the alma mater of hundreds of thousands of Asians, having educated them as it is now educating a hundred thousand of their children. All those men and women speak the same language and hold many of the same concepts. American intellectual influence is, therefore, still powerful, perhaps predominant in East Asia.

America's real problem is at home. The decline of U.S. industry in innovation, application, and production is parallel to the decline in American morale and self-reliance.

Even the American advantage in fundamental research is slipping away, even that research which is not subject to the vagaries of the marketplace, but is liberally funded by the Defense Department. Late in 1989 the Pentagon noted with alarm that Japan was ahead in six critical areas of defense technology. A little earlier, the distinguished scholars of the Commission on Industrial Productivity formed by the Massachusetts Institute of Technology to examine America's industrial decline in 1989 had issued comprehensive recommendations for restoring American competitiveness. Many of the specific remedies were derived from Asian models, which had, rather curiously, been based originally on American practices. Just as America was still ahead in basic research, America could thus with effort recoup—if it could make the effort.

America's real problem is psychological: a rooted unwillingness to acknowledge its predicament. Perhaps self-indulgent Americans are incapable of recognizing their fundamental problems, just as a one-legged man is incapable of running a marathon. If they cannot recognize and acknowledge their problems, they obviously cannot attack them. However, I prefer to think they can.

Complacency is the greatest single obstacle to the Western—and American—revival. Yet fear of Asia could also undo us. There is every reason to respect Asian achievements, while recognizing that the Asians built on the bedrock of Western, particularly American, science and technology. To reclaim a decisive lead is, I believe, impossible. To draw even with Asia, perhaps even a little ahead, is within the West's capability.

But the nations of the West cannot act effectively toward resurgent Asia unless they know what they want. A good many more men and women should be thinking about our purposes at home and abroad, as many already are.

Above all, I believe, we lack coordination among industry, academia, government, and finance. That lack is a major, perhaps fatal, impediment when we are, in so many places, up against single-minded authoritarianism. Westerners have always concentrated their efforts and coordinated their endeavors far better in war than in peace.

We do not need authoritarianism which could cripple initiative, but a structured consensus such as normally prevails in wartime. We must, like the Japanese, agree to agree on what is vital to our survival. And we must then act in concert, recognizing that excessive competition can be destructive, rather than constructive in our era. In the long term, we must endeavor to win Asia, led by the Japanese, over to cooperation by first offering them effective competition.

A major psychological adjustment is necessary. Not only Western businessmen, but Western officials and intellectuals suffer from quarter-by-quarter vision. The immediate effect is all important to all, particularly to Anglo-American executives, who must maximize profit in every quarterly report in order to please the stock markets that provide their operating capital. Immediate gratification, corporate or personal, is in the last decade of the twentieth century no longer acceptable in individuals or nations that would survive.

Asia has taken much practical knowledge from the West—and often improved it. We must now take a profound lesson from the patient perseverance that is central to the Asian ethos: the tenacious accretion of power and virtue that lies beneath the dazzling surface of present day Asians. They think in decades, even generations, not in quarters. The Japanese, for one, save a very high proportion of their incomes, providing abundant capital for their industries; and Japanese newspapers employed special correspondents to cover only GATT, the dryer than dust General Agreement on Tariffs and Trade, as early as 1951, when few outsiders could imagine Japan's becoming a major trading country.

Moreover, as this excursion into Asia has shown, Asian societies do change, sometimes dramatically. But they change only after attaining an almost mystical consensus regarding their new course—and the old values endure.

Individualistic Westerners living in laissez-faire societies are unaccustomed to arriving at fundamental decisions by such patient and profound processes. They do not normally agree on new courses without friction and discord that often result in discarding old values. Above all, they do not look far into the future, sustained by their confidence in the past, and they do not plan for the distant future.

Westerners must change. If they cannot change of themselves, they will be changed by forces beyond their control. The world will belong to a resurgent Asia that has not yet learned to restrain its destructive ambitions for the common good.

The two most important and influential human developments of the latter half of the twentieth century both had their roots in Asia. The first was the elevation of industrial, commercial, and technological attainments to new heights by the nations of the Far East led by Japan. The second was the repudiation of the Marxist-Leninist bureaucratic state by China in 1980, which led to the dismantling of totalitarian rule in

Eastern Europe and the Soviet Union, although the Chinese had themselves reverted in part at the end of the 1980s.

The rise of the East is a magnificent achievement, a triumph of the human spirit and will that is in itself good. It is now up to the West, at least as much as the East, to ensure that it does not become injurious.

Index